Microeconomics

for Public Decisions

Anne C. Steinemann
Georgia Institute of Technology

William C. Apgar
Harvard University

H. James Brown
Lincoln Institute

THOMSON

SOUTH-WESTERN

Australia · Canada · Mexico · Singapore · Spain · United Kingdom · United States

THOMSON

SOUTH-WESTERN

Microeconomics for Public Decisions
Anne C. Steinemann, William C. Apgar, and H. James Brown

VP/Editorial Director:
Jack W. Calhoun

VP/Editor-in-Chief:
Michael P. Roche

Publisher:
Michael B. Mercier

Senior Acquisitions Editor:
Peter Adams

Senior Developmental Editor:
Susanna C. Smart

Senior Marketing Manager:
John Carey

Senior Marketing Coordinator:
Jenny Fruechtenicht

Production Editor:
Emily S. Gross

Manufacturing Coordinator:
Sandee Milewski

Technology Project Editor:
Peggy Buskey

Media Editor:
Pam Wallace

Design Project Manager:
Rik Moore

Production House:
Trejo Production

Cover Designer:
John Robb, JWR Design Interaction

Cover Image:
© PhotoDisc, Inc.

Internal Designer:
Lisa Albonetti

Printer:
Quebecor World
Kingsport, TN

For permission to use material from this text or product, submit a request online at http://www.thomsonrights.com. Any additional questions about permissions can be submitted by email to thomsonrights@thomson.com.

For more information contact South-Western, 5191 Natorp Boulevard, Mason, Ohio, 45040. Or you can visit our Internet site at: http://www.swlearning.com

DEDICATION

To my parents, John and Patricia Steinemann

BRIEF CONTENTS

Preface xiii

PART 1 MICROECONOMICS AND THE MARKET ECONOMY

1 Overview of Economics 3
2 Demand and Supply 19
3 Market Dynamics and Interventions 47
4 Choice and Demand 75
4A Appendix: Utility Maximization 101
5 Costs and Supply 105
5A Appendix: Production Functions 127

PART 2 PUBLIC SECTOR ECONOMICS AND MARKET FAILURES

6 Efficiency and Equity 139
7 Welfare Economics 157
8 Monopoly 173
9 Externalities 191
10 Public Goods 223
11 Imperfect Information 251

PART 3 COST-BENEFIT ANALYSIS AND APPLICATIONS

12 Intertemporal Costs and Benefits 301
13 Cost-Benefit Analysis 321
14 Cost-Benefit Applications 349

Epilogue 371
Appendix A 373
Appendix B 394
Glossary 413
Index 419

CONTENTS

Preface xiii

PART 1 MICROECONOMICS AND THE MARKET ECONOMY

1 OVERVIEW OF ECONOMICS 3

Private Sector and Public Sector Perspectives 3

The Foundations of Economics 5
  The Economic Premises 6
  Another Perspective of the Economic Premises 6

The Economy as a System 7

Economics and the Ecosystem 9

The Market Economics Framework 10
  The Market Economics Framework and Public
    Decisions 11
  Public Sector Involvement in the Market System 12

Using Economics Wisely 16

Overview of the Textbook 17

Review Questions 18

2 DEMAND AND SUPPLY 19

Demand 19

Supply 24

Elasticities 28

Price Elasticity of Demand 29
Elasticities and Total Revenue 31
Factors That Influence the Price Elasticity of Demand 35

Other Types of Elasticities 41
Price Elasticity of Supply 41
Factors That Influence the Price Elasticity of Supply 42
Income Elasticity of Demand 43
Cross-Price Elasticity of Demand 44

Review Questions 45

3   MARKET DYNAMICS AND INTERVENTIONS 47
Market Demand and Market Supply 47

Market Equilibrium and Competition 51

Market Dynamics 54
Changes in Demand and Supply 54
Market Dynamics 56

Market Intervention 60
Taxes and Subsidies 60
Price and Output Controls 66

Review Questions 73

4   CHOICE AND DEMAND 75
The Concept of Utility 75

Willingness to Pay 77
Willingness to Pay and Consumer Surplus 80
Consumer Surplus and Distribution of Benefits 83

Indifference Curves 84
Substitution and Income Effects 85

Budget Constraints 88

Deriving the Demand Curve 90

Review Questions 99

4A   APPENDIX: UTILITY MAXIMIZATION 101
Utility Function and the Marginal Rate of Substitution 101

Utility Maximization 103
Summary 104

5   COSTS AND SUPPLY 105

Types of Costs 105
Nonmonetary Costs 106
Opportunity Costs 106
Sunk Costs 107
Production Costs and Cost Curves 108

Marginal Analysis 109

Additional Topics in Production Decisions 114
Breakeven and Shutdown Points 114
Accounting Profit and Economic Profit 115
Short-Run Production 116
Deriving the Supply Curve 117
Long-Run Production 117
Long-Run Equilibrium 120
Producer Surplus 121
Difference Between Producer Surplus and Profits 122

Review Questions 126

5A   APPENDIX: PRODUCTION FUNCTIONS 127
Factor Substitution 130
Mathematics of Production Functions 131
Diminishing Marginal Productivity 132
Constrained Maximization or Minimization 135

PART 2   PUBLIC SECTOR ECONOMICS AND MARKET FAILURES

6   EFFICIENCY AND EQUITY 139

Efficiency and the Market Economy 139
The "Invisible Hand" Doctrine 139
Types of Efficiency 140
Efficiency Criteria and Equity Issues 143

Equity and the Economic System 143
Types of Equity 143
Equity of Endowments 144
Equity of Process 145
Equity of Outcomes 145

Market Failures: Deviations from Efficiency 146

Public Provision and Government Interventions 148

Efficiency and Equity: Concluding Thoughts 155

Review Questions 156

7   WELFARE ECONOMICS 157

Economic Welfare and Social Surplus 157

Social Surplus and Perfect Competition 158

Social Surplus and Market Interventions 160
Price Floor 160
Price Ceiling 162
Output Quotas 163
Tax 164
Subsidy 166
Considerations 167

Distributional Effects 168

Review Questions 171

8   MONOPOLY 173

Barriers to Entry 173
Economies of Scale 174
Institutional Protection 174
Product Differentiation 174
Tactics 175

Monopoly Production 175
Supply and Demand 175
Price and Output Determination 178
Effects of Monopoly 179

Regulation, Public Ownership, and Antitrust Policies 182

Public Policy Implications 185

Review Questions 189

9   EXTERNALITIES 191

Negative and Positive Externalities 191

Negative Externalities 192

Positive Externalities 194

Examples of Externality Problems 196

Challenges in the Resolution of Externality Problems 199

Determining the Optimal Level of Production 201

Determining Benefits and Costs 202

Methods for Nonmarket Valuation 203

Strategies for Dealing with Externalities 209

Voluntarism 210

Prohibition 210

Separation 211

Directive 212

Regulation 213

Taxes 214

Subsidies 216

Marketable Permits 218

Review Questions 221

10 PUBLIC GOODS 223

Theory of Public Goods 223

Public Goods: Valuation and Demand 226

Public Good Provision 230

Public Pricing 235

The Role of Prices 236

Evaluation Criteria 236

Efficiency 237

Revenue Generation and Cost Recovery 238

Equity Considerations 239

Administrative and Institutional Considerations 240

Public Pricing Options 240

Marginal Cost Pricing 240

Average Cost Pricing 241

Two-Part Tariff 242

Price Discrimination 242

Peak Pricing 243

Review Questions 250

11 IMPERFECT INFORMATION 251

Imperfect Information and Market Failures 252
  Asymmetric Information 253
  Market and Nonmarket Responses to Asymmetric
    Information 256
  Adverse Selection 257
  Cream Skimming and Cherry Picking 259
  Moral Hazard 260
  Principal-Agent Problem 261
  Public Sector Provision of Information and Insurance 264

Expected Value, Expected Utility, and Risk 268
  Expected Value 268
  Expected Value and Risk: Lotteries with Uncertain
    Outcomes 271
  Utility Theory 273
  Certainty Equivalents, Risk Premiums, and Insurance
    Premiums 274
  Risk Aversion, Risk Proneness, and Risk Neutrality 278
  Variability and Risk 282
  The Utility Function of Money 283

Decision Analysis 287
  Value of Perfect Information and Imperfect
    Information 292
  Bayes' Theorem 293
  Decision Analysis: Strengths and Limitations 295

Review Questions 296

PART 3 COST-BENEFIT ANALYSIS AND APPLICATIONS 299
12 INTERTEMPORAL COSTS AND BENEFITS 301

Time Value of Money 302

Calculating Present and Future Values 304

Discounting 305

Annuity (or Uniform Series) 306

Uniform Gradients 307

Factors for Present Values, Future Values, Annuities, and
  Gradients 308

Cash Flow Diagrams 311

Review Questions 320

13 COST-BENEFIT ANALYSIS 321

Cost-Benefit Analysis: Private versus Public Decisions 321

Cost-Benefit Analysis and Efficiency 324

Performing a Cost-Benefit Analysis 325
Develop Alternatives 326
Determine the Scope of the Decision 326
Determine the Costs of Each Alternative 328
Determine the Benefits of Each Alternative 330
Quantify the Costs and Benefits of Each Alternative 332
Evaluate the Costs versus the Benefits 335
Evaluate the Equity Impacts 342

Cost-Benefit Analysis: Strengths and Limitations 344

Review Questions 346

14 COST-BENEFIT APPLICATIONS 349

Cost-Benefit Problem: Sultan Island Bridge 349

Cost-Benefit Problem: Recreational Facility 360

Cost-Benefit Problem: Air Pollution Control 367

EPILOGUE 371
APPENDIX A 373
APPENDIX B 394
GLOSSARY 413
INDEX 419

PREFACE

Decisions that affect the public often depend on microeconomics. Yet courses in public sector economics face a chronic problem: the lack of a suitable textbook. Though many texts cover microeconomic principles, they provide scant coverage of economic techniques and societal considerations vital to public sector decisions. In addition, the analytic perspective of these texts is typically that of a private firm rather than a public agency or the public in general. Moreover, texts often require prior training in economics or mathematics, presume future study in economics, or focus on theory development rather than application to public issues.

Microeconomics for Public Decisions meets a need for a core textbook that covers the essential microeconomic principles and applies them to public decisions. Further, this text strives to analyze the societal effects of these decisions, examine the economic arguments of different public choices, and offer real-world issues that will motivate students to learn microeconomics. This text offers features that address these needs and distinguish it from other texts:

A PUBLIC SECTOR PERSPECTIVE

This text covers the key principles of microeconomics, such as supply, demand, and market processes. Plus, it provides extensive coverage of topics that concern public sector decisions, such as public goods, externalities, welfare analysis, and cost-benefit analysis, and their unique complexities.

For instance, public sector decision makers often need to consider multiple societal goals, not only profit maximization. They often need to consider the impacts of their decisions on both the private and public sector, not only their own agency. And they often need to assess many types of benefits and costs, not only those placed in monetary terms.

As examples: How can a public agency set an appropriate fare for public transit services, which may never show a monetary profit, yet can benefit the community in other ways? How can a county government evaluate a public resource, such as open space, and compare it to proposals for private housing development on that land? How can state officials choose among strategies for reducing pollution, when some may be less costly but also less effective? How would a cost-benefit analysis differ between a private sector firm and public sector agency, and what are the implications for privatizing a public service? Further, in each example, who would gain the benefits and who would bear the costs?

Public sector decision makers, of course, also need to understand the dynamics of private markets and the principles of efficient production. By relating traditional topics, such as market equilibrium and efficiency, to public sector issues, the text demonstrates the applicability of economic concepts to a wide range of decisions.

SUITABILITY

Microeconomics for Public Decisions is designed to serve as a core textbook for basic microeconomics courses that addresses public sector issues. These courses are offered, and often required, in programs such as public policy, city and regional planning, urban affairs, public administration, business, resources management, environmental studies, civil engineering, and government.

The level of the text is targeted toward master's level graduate students and upper-division undergraduate students, although it is suitable for other levels and does not require prior coursework. As a core text, additional materials are not necessary, although instructors may choose to supplement the text with current events, media reports, journal articles, and examples from their work.

ACCESSIBILITY

A feature of this text is that students do not need prior training in economics or calculus to understand the material. In fact, experience with the text has shown that students with little or no such prior training can still perform at the top of the class. Further, students who have already taken economics will find much of the material new, and even standard concepts are expanded and applied within the context of public sector decisions.

The text covers economic principles without heavy dependence on mathematics that could limit its accessibility. For those who desire calculus-based proofs, mathematical appendixes are provided on topics such as theory of consumer behavior and theory of the firm. The relative lack of calculus, however, should not be confused with a lack of rigor. A goal of this text is to explain economics with clarity and precision, so that complex topics can be relatively straightforward to learn. The text also includes topics that are often treated in more advanced microeconomics texts, such as welfare economics, public goods pricing, and cost-benefit analysis.

PRACTICALITY

Students crave relevance and often learn best in context. This text blends theory with applications so that students will understand how and why microeconomics is important to them.

Before writing this text, I asked many former public sector economics students, "How do you currently use economics in your work? What were the most useful things that you learned in your microeconomics course? What were the least useful? What economic applications have been interesting or complex? What would be most important to cover in a microeconomics text?"

Many said they learned theoretical concepts, but did not adequately learn how to apply these concepts to everyday decisions. Armed with these comments, I present principles and applications that make economics meaningful to students.

ESSENTIAL AND CONCISE TREATMENT

Writing this textbook involved difficult decisions about topic selection and extent of coverage. I decided to focus on topics that would be most important to students in their future careers, education, and lives. This text was not designed to provide an encyclopedic treatment of microeconomic theory, but rather to focus on essential principles and analytic techniques for making decisions, especially those that affect the public.

Students will learn both how to apply microeconomic principles and how to evaluate economic analyses. In their future work, students may not be doing the analyses themselves, but will need the expertise to evaluate results and recommendations based on analyses performed by others. Thus, the text will help students to develop a solid understanding of both microeconomics and its appropriate use.

EXPANDED, REORGANIZED, AND UPDATED COVERAGE

I wrote and pretested this text while teaching a graduate course in economics for planning and public policy. Many of the ideas for this text evolved from the 1987 text by Apgar and Brown, *Microeconomics for Public Policy*. My goal was to build upon the strengths the earlier text, while providing more comprehensive and detailed coverage of key topics, with updated examples and applications to current issues.

This new text offers a more systematic treatment of fundamentals such as supply, demand, equilibrium, market processes, and interventions. It also expands topics such as equity and efficiency, monopoly, externalities, and public goods. Further, it provides new material on welfare analysis, imperfect information, risk and uncertainty, investments and discounting, and cost-benefit analysis. *Microeconomics for Public Decisions* was designed for a wider audience that includes not only policy and planning, but also other disciplines that involve economics and the public sector.

OVERVIEW OF THE TEXTBOOK

The text is organized in three parts. The first part, Chapters 1 through 5, presents the fundamentals of microeconomics and the market economy, such as demand, supply, elasticities, equilibrium, market dynamics, and market interventions. These chapters also provide a public sector framework that is important to analyses throughout the text.

The second part, Chapters 6 through 11, examines topics that are central to public sector decision making, such as the economic role of government, and cases where markets and governments may fail to achieve desired outcomes. These topics include equity and efficiency, welfare economics, monopolies, externalities, public goods, risk, and imperfect information.

The third part, Chapters 12 through 14, provides the concepts and analytic techniques for assessing benefits and costs that occur over time, and for evaluating projects and policies. These chapters detail the process of conducting a cost-benefit analysis, considering both market and nonmarket effects. In addition, these chapters provide applications and evaluations of cost-benefit analyses, with attention to public sector concerns.

CHAPTER SPECIFICS

Chapter 1 provides an overview of microeconomics, a preview of future chapters, and the rationale for the importance of economics to both private and public sector decisions.

Chapter 2 lays the analytic foundation for microeconomics: demand and supply. It looks at decisions of consumers and producers, interactions in the market, and effects on market price and quantity.

Chapter 3 builds upon the study of demand and supply with more advanced analyses and applications. It examines market interventions, such as taxes, subsidies, price and output controls, and the effects of these interventions on market participants.

Chapter 4 takes a closer look at demand, covering utility theory, willingness to pay, indifference curves, and derived demand curves. It develops the concept and application of consumer surplus, and the measurement of benefits among different sectors in society. A mathematical appendix details the principles of utility maximization.

Chapter 5 takes a closer look at supply. It details various types of costs, such as monetary costs and opportunity costs, and their use in marginal analysis and production decisions. The chapter also covers profit, producer surplus, economies of scale, and short-run and long-run supply. A mathematical appendix develops the theory of the firm and production functions.

Chapter 6 leads off the second part of the book by examining the multiple goals of public sector decision making, and the concepts of efficiency and equity. It explores the roles and rationales for government intervention in the market economy, cases where both the private sector and public sector can fail to achieve societal goals, and possible remedies.

Chapter 7 extends these concepts through the study of welfare economics. It presents techniques to analyze the efficiency and distributional consequences of decisions, the trade-offs between the two, and the effects of market interventions.

Chapter 8 looks at the case of monopolies, such as public utilities, and their effects on efficiency and equity. It compares competitive and monopolistic markets, examines different types of regulation and pricing strategies, and discusses public policy implications.

Chapter 9 examines the causes and consequences of externalities in both public and private sector decisions, and the challenges of resolving externality problems. It compares strategies for managing externalities, such as regulation and marketable permits, develops evaluation criteria, and offers detailed examples that illustrate strengths and limitations of each strategy.

Chapter 10 looks at different classes of goods, public and private, with attention to goods and services that the public sector typically provides. It covers techniques for valuing public goods, setting the price of public services and resources, and evaluating approaches for public good provision.

Chapter 11 addresses issues associated with imperfect information, such as adverse selection, moral hazard, and the principal-agent problem. It provides methods for making decisions under uncertainty, covering topics of utility theory, risk, insurance, decision analysis, and the value of information.

Chapter 12 leads off the third part of the book by providing techniques to assess benefits and costs that occur over different time periods. It covers discounting, equivalencies, present values, amortization, and investment decisions.

Chapter 13 examines concepts and methods, specifically cost-benefit analysis, for evaluating projects, programs, and policies. It discusses challenges and considerations such as the valuation of nonmonetary goods, the choice of a discount rate, and the distribution of benefits and costs in the present and future generations.

Chapter 14 presents three detailed examples of cost-benefit analysis, which illustrate methods from previous chapters, and practical considerations for using economic analyses for public sector decision making.

ONLINE RESOURCES

Thomson Business and Professional Publishing provides students and instructors with a set of valuable online resources that make an effective complement to this text. Each new copy of the book comes with two registration cards. One is for Economics Applications. The other is for InfoTrac® College Edition.

Economic Applications

The purchase of this new textbook includes complimentary access to Thomson Business and Professional Publishing's Economic Applications (e-con @pps) Web site.

The e-con @pps Web site includes a suite of regularly updated Web features for economics students and instructors: EconDebate Online, EconNews Online, EconData Online, and EconLinks Online. These resources can help students to deepen their understanding of economic concepts by analyzing current news stories, policy debates, and economic data. These resources can also help instructors to develop assignments, case studies, and examples based on real-world issues.

- EconDebate Online provides current coverage of economics policy debates, including a primer on the issues, links to background information, and commentaries.
- EconNews Online summarizes recent economics news stories and offers questions for further discussion.
- EconData Online presents current and historical economic data with accompanying commentary, analysis, and exercises.
- EconLinks Online offers a navigation partner for exploring economics on the Web, with a list of key topic links.

The Thomson Business and Professional Publishing Economics Web site at **http://economics.swlearning.com** also includes free access to Newsedge, which culls and organizes the most recent news and economic information.

Students buying a used book can purchase access to the e-con @pps site at **http://econapps.swlearning.com**.

InfoTrac College Edition

The purchase of this new textbook also comes with four months of access to InfoTrac. This powerful, searchable online database provides access to full text articles from more than 1,000 different publications, from popular press to scholarly journals. Instructors can search topics and select readings for students. Students can search articles and readings for homework assignments and projects. The publications cover a variety of topics, with articles that range from current events to theoretical developments. InfoTrac College Edition offers instructors and students the ability to integrate scholarship and applications of economics into the learning process.

ACKNOWLEDGMENTS

I am grateful to many people for their help with the text. First, I thank my students at the Georgia Institute of Technology who used this text, offered suggestions, and greatly improved the final product. I am also grateful to my colleagues and friends for their contributions, insights, and support. Those who contributed in special ways include Thomas Debo, Steve French, Larry Keating, Nancy Green Leigh, Chris Nelson, David Sawicki, Bryan Norton, Dan Cayan, John Williams, Mark Duncan, Val Gaccione, Greg Lindsey, and Leonard Ortolano.

This text benefited from the professors and their students who pretested the material and offered valuable feedback: Michael Ash, University of Massachusetts, Amherst; Russell Janis, University of Massachusetts, Amherst; Marlon Boarnet, University of California, Irvine; and Arthur C. Nelson, Virginia Tech, Alexandria. Reviewers of the textbook also offered helpful comments and improvements on earlier versions.

Michael Ash, University of Massachusetts, Amherst
Sam Sherrill, University of Cincinnati
Bob Williams, Guilford College
Jonathan Levine, University of Michigan
Arthur Brooks, Syracuse University
Arley Williams, Arizona State University
Arthur C. Nelson, Virginia Tech, Alexandria
Walter Nicholson, Amherst College
A. Abigail Payne, University of Illinois at Chicago
Robert Archibald, College of William and Mary
Irving Hoch, University of Texas, Dallas

I am indebted to my talented and hard-working research assistants who dedicated themselves to the text: Carlton Basmajian, Nita Bhave, Luiz Cavalcanti, Jian Chen, Janeane Gilbreath, Hyun-Hee Kwak, Jia Li, Mary Jane Lim, and Rebekah Morrison.

Deep thanks go to my co-authors, Bill Apgar and Jim Brown, for their masterful work on their earlier text, for encouraging the development of this text, and for entrusting me to carry it forward. The work on this textbook received support, in part, from the National Science Foundation under CMS 9874391; the Walter L. and Grace Doherty Charitable Foundation, Inc., through the Department of Marine and Environmental Systems at the Florida Institute of Technology; and the National Science Foundation ADVANCE Program under SBE 0123532 through the Georgia Institute of Technology. Any opinions, findings, conclusions, or recommendations expressed in this text are those of the authors and do not necessarily reflect the views of the funding organizations.

I thank the excellent team at Thomson Business and Professional Publishing, especially my acquisitions editor, Peter Adams, my developmental editors Jeff Gilbreath and Susan Smart, editorial assistants Sarah Curtis and Steven Joos, production editor Emily Gross, Margaret Trejo, and marketing managers Janet Hennies and John Carey. Special thanks go to Thomas Gay and Laurie Runion, who guided this book with care and wisdom while at Harcourt College Publishers. I am deeply grateful to Andy Miller for his support throughout this project. Finally, I thank my parents, John and Patricia Steinemann, to whom this book is dedicated.

— Anne Steinemann

ABOUT THE AUTHORS

**Anne Steinemann** received her Ph.D. from Stanford University in Civil and Environmental Engineering, and is currently Associate Professor at the Georgia Institute of Technology. Professor Steinemann received the highest teaching awards for both her College and the Institute. She also received the National Science Foundation CAREER Award, the highest honor for junior faculty in science and engineering. Professor Steinemann specializes in environmental planning and decision-making— applying microeconomic principles to problems such as water resources and energy management, climate change, indoor air quality, and sustainability. She advises numerous federal and state agencies, including appointments as Special Adviser to the governor of Georgia and to the President's National Drought Policy Commission. Professor Steinemann serves on the editorial board of *Environmental Impact Assessment Review*, and has published numerous articles that bridge economics, the environment, and societal decisions.

William Apgar returns to Harvard's Joint Center for Housing Studies and Kennedy School of Government after a leave of absence as Assistant Secretary of Housing/ Federal Housing Commissioner at the U.S. Department of Housing and Urban Development. At HUD he administered the FHA single family and multifamily mortgage insurance funds, multifamily rental assistance programs, and grants for the construction of housing for elderly and disabled populations.

Formerly, the Joint Center Executive Director, Apgar now is a Senior Scholar at the Center and directs the Center's evaluation of the Community Reinvestment Act, national legislation to promote housing investment and economic development in low income communities. Other research interests include demographic analysis, housing finance, and housing and community economic development.

As a Lecturer in Public Policy at the Kennedy School, Apgar teaches a course titled, "Policy-Making in Urban Settings." The course examines economic development and job growth in the context of metropolitan regions and the emerging "new economy," and assesses federal, state, and local government strategies for expanding community economic development and affordable housing opportunities.

H. James Brown is the President and CEO of the Lincoln Institute of Land Policy, an educational institution dedicated to the study and teaching of land policy, land economics and taxation. From 1970 to 1996, he was a Professor at the John F. Kennedy School of Government, Harvard University. During this time he also served as Director of the Joint Center for Housing Studies, Chairman of the City and Regional Planning Program, Director of the State, Local and Intergovernmental Center at Harvard University and Director of the MIT/Harvard University Joint Center for Urban Studies. Brown received his Ph.D. in economics from Indiana University.

Brown has edited and published numerous books and articles, including *The State of the Nation's Housing*, an annual review of housing trends, *Microeconomics and Public Policy* (1988), and *Land Use and Taxation: Applying the Insights of Henry George* (1997).

Brown has worked with a variety of public and private organizations. He currently serves as a Director of BMC West Corporation and American Residential Investment Trust. He previously served as a Managing Partner of Strategic Property Investments, Inc. and as a Director of Pelican Companies, Inc.. He was a member of the Boston Mayor's Advisory Group on the Linkage Between Downtown Development and Neighborhood Change, the Governor's Task Force on Metropolitan Development, and the Boston Chamber of Commerce's Technical Committee on the Third Harbor Tunnel. He served on the Board of Directors of the Massachusetts Government Land Bank. He was a Fellow of the Urban Land Institute, Vice Chairman of the Massachusetts section of the American Institute of Planners, and he has served on the Executive Committee of the Association of Collegiate Schools of Planning.

PART 1

MICROECONOMICS AND THE MARKET ECONOMY

1 OVERVIEW OF ECONOMICS 3

2 DEMAND AND SUPPLY 19

3 MARKET DYNAMICS AND INTERVENTIONS 47

4 CHOICE AND DEMAND 75

4A UTILITY MAXIMIZATION 101

5 COSTS AND SUPPLY 105

5A PRODUCTION FUNCTIONS 127

OVERVIEW OF ECONOMICS

PRIVATE SECTOR AND PUBLIC SECTOR PERSPECTIVES

Economics is part of everyday life. A student choosing a college, a family buying a new home, a private firm expanding operations, and a city agency providing public transportation are all cases in which economics can help us to make better and more informed decisions.

Just as in the private sector, economics pervades the public sector. In a typical day, many of us drive on public roads, receive mail from a federal postal service, drink water regulated by government agencies, attend schools that receive public funding, and buy food products that are subsidized or taxed. And many of us, in our careers and our lives, will make decisions that affect the public interest.

The economic principles for private sector and public sector decisions are similar, yet the goals and analyses can differ. For instance, a private firm typically seeks to maximize profits. In determining profits, which are total benefits minus total costs, the firm would include benefits such as revenues from product sales, and costs such as expenditures on materials for production.

A public agency, however, often needs to consider goals in addition to profit maximization, such as equity, employment, environmental protection, and quality of life. Thus, a public agency might be concerned with a range of benefits and costs, even if they did not have direct monetary equivalents. A public agency might also continue to provide a service, even if the service never generated a monetary profit. For example, many cities operate public transit systems, even though revenues collected may not fully cover the costs of operations. Yet public transit can provide other benefits to society, such as reduced highway congestion, improved air quality, improved mobility, and affordable transportation for many citizens. Costs to society should also be considered, such as increased pollution near transit stations, and foregone opportunities to use city funds and resources in another way.

Another feature of public sector decision making is the scope of analysis. When analyzing a decision, a public agency generally looks at benefits and costs that affect the wider public, not just the agency itself, whereas a private firm generally considers benefits and costs that just directly affect the firm. Consider, for example, a private developer clearing land in order to build new homes. Costs to society from the development, such as the loss of trees, are usually not included in the developer's accounting. Benefits to society, such as reduced unemployment through the hiring of workers, may also have been excluded. Yet these costs and benefits would be within the scope of what a public agency would consider.

As another example, from the perspective of private firms and individual citizens, taxes imposed by a government agency are a cost. From the perspective of that government agency, however, the tax may be viewed as a transfer of resources within the public. It results in costs to some members of society, but benefits to other members of society.

Public sector decision making also requires defining "the public." This is not a straightforward task. The public could include the decision maker's community or, more broadly, other communities affected by a decision. Consider, for example, a city proposing to develop a major sports arena that could attract thousands of additional tourists each year. Opponents argue that the project would impose costs, such as additional traffic congestion and noise, on both residents of the city and residents of nearby communities. Proponents argue that the project is desirable from the city's perspective, and that costs to other communities do not need to be considered.

Which definition of "the public" is correct for the analysis: Is it just the city, or the city and its neighboring communities? This question has no single correct answer, because it depends on the criteria applied by decision makers. Some decision makers employ a narrow definition of the public; others use a much broader one. The answer can also depend on who has standing; that is, who has a right to be considered in the decision. Also note that "the public" normally refers to all constituents within the defined scope, whether they are individuals, households, organizations, public agencies, private firms, and even the resources within that scope.

The preceding distinctions between economics in the private sector and the public sector are not absolute. Some private sector firms make decisions with a solid concern for public welfare, accounting for the wider impacts of their products and practices on society. Some government agencies make decisions with a distinct focus on profitability. The point is that, regardless of the sector, economics can provide a framework for understanding choices and making better decisions.

A goal of this text is to help you learn how to use economics to evaluate decisions and their effects within society. From a public sector perspective, this evaluation often considers criteria in addition to profit maximization, such as equity, and benefits and costs in addition to those represented by monetary equivalents. This text covers the economic principles found in classic microeconomics texts, and that apply to both public and private sector decision making. Thus, this text can prepare you to work in a government agency, run a business, as well as make more informed decisions as a consumer.

THE FOUNDATIONS OF ECONOMICS

Economic analyses are important to a variety of public and private sector activities. For example, federal agencies use economics to evaluate the benefits and costs of different engineering projects. State officials use economics to design university scholarship programs. Local governments use economics to determine user fees for public facilities. Private firms use economics to determine how many workers to employ. Individuals use economics to decide whether to purchase a new computer, take a vacation, or invest that money to spend later.

Economics also helps us to understand critical issues in society. It can inform questions such as: Why did unemployment rise in our city? Who benefits and who bears the costs of agricultural subsidies? Is the proposed tax cut equitable? How should we generate revenue to cover the cost of the new water facilities? What is the appropriate price for development impact fees? How can we use economic tools to reduce pollution into the river? Should we use public funds to build a parking deck, or to purchase and preserve land as open space?

Economics is the study of how society allocates its scarce resources to produce and distribute goods that are valued. The field of economics consists of *microeconomics* and *macroeconomics*. As the names suggest, **microeconomics** studies the smaller parts of the economic system, and **macroeconomics** studies the larger system as a whole. More specifically, microeconomics examines the behavior of individual units, such as households, businesses, and governments, and their spending patterns. Macroeconomics examines aggregate measures of those units, such as gross domestic product (GDP).[1]

To compare the two, microeconomics would ask a question such as, "Why did the unemployment rate for low-wage workers rise in our city this past year?" Macroeconomics would ask, "How much did the national unemployment rate change this past year?" The two fields are not completely separate, however, because individual actions affect aggregate measures, and large-scale economic policies affect local economies and individual decisions.

It is also useful to distinguish between positive economics and normative economics, and statements concerning them. **Positive statements** are based on facts and data, such as, "Thirty percent of racial minorities had no health insurance in our city last year." These types of statements concern *what is*, and can be verified empirically. **Normative statements** are based on value judgments and opinions, such as, "Thirty percent is an unacceptably high uninsured rate, and should be lowered." These types of statements concern *what should be*, and can be debated, because they have no single objectively correct answer. Moreover, seemingly positive statements can be normative because subjectivity, values, and bias can influence data collection, analysis, and reporting.

---

[1] Gross domestic product is the total market value of all final goods and services produced domestically.

Public sector decisions often involve both positive and normative economics. For instance, an agency might analyze the benefits and costs of a proposed policy (positive economics) and then decide whether they should implement this policy, based on whether it is considered equitable (normative economics). Some believe that economics should limit itself to positive analysis, whereas others believe that economics should be concerned with normative issues as well.

THE ECONOMIC PREMISES

The study of economics is based on two premises: (1) People have unlimited wants for material goods, and (2) resources for producing those material goods are limited. Let us examine more closely these foundations of economics.

The first premise says that people always want more than what they have. Granted, over a specific period of time, a person can get more than what they want of a particular good. For instance, after the third piece of chocolate cake, a person may not want a fourth. Yet this first premise refers to the general class of material goods, not just one specific good. Material goods include various goods and services, such as ice cream, designer jeans, home furnishings, automobiles, automobile repair, health care, computer equipment, education, and even textbooks. This premise also suggests that even when basic needs (such as food, clothing, and shelter) are fulfilled, people will still want more. And those "wants" drive the economic system.

The second premise says that resources are scarce and finite. Economic resources are placed in three general categories: land, labor, and capital. **Land** includes more than just the soil; it includes all natural resources, such as forests, mineral deposits, water, and air. **Capital** refers to (nonhuman) resources used to produce and deliver other goods and services, such as buildings, machines, tools, and automobiles. (Note that capital does not mean accumulated assets or money, as it does in other contexts.) **Labor** refers broadly to all the physical and mental talents of people that are used to produce goods and services.

From these premises, economics establishes the goal of trying to satisfy people's unlimited wants for material goods with available and scarce resources.

ANOTHER PERSPECTIVE OF THE ECONOMIC PREMISES

Now consider another perspective of the economic premises, one that this textbook puts forth: People may often have *limited* wants for *limited* (material) goods, and *unlimited* wants for *unlimited* (nonmaterial) goods. The wants for material goods may be actually to satisfy wants that are ultimately nonmaterial. For example, when a schoolboy wants a tenth pair of shoes to impress his friends, he may want those shoes not for their material properties (because he already has nine pairs of shoes), but rather as means to ends that are *nonmaterial*, such as attention, acceptance, and friendship. In contrast to the limits for producing material goods, such nonmaterial goods can often be *unlimited*. For instance, it could be argued that people have an unlimited capacity to give and receive love. Ask a parent with more than one child:

Did the arrival of the second child diminish their love for the first? Even though finite resources, such as time and money, have to be apportioned among the children, the unlimited resource does not have to be. An implication is that a goal of economics could be to meet basic material needs for as many as possible, and to focus on overall improvements in quality of life, instead of quantitative increases in the production and consumption of material goods.

THE ECONOMY AS A SYSTEM

We will now look more closely at the workings of the economic system. Production and consumption activities in the United States involve the decisions of millions of households, firms, and public agencies. Broad aggregate measures of the performance of an economic system, such as GDP, are but summaries of the actions of these individual decision makers. This section looks at the various types of decision makers and economic units, and how they interact in an economic system (Figure 1-1).

Each unit in the economic system can engage in both consumption and production activities. **Consumption** means to use or derive benefits from an economic good or service. A consumption activity can be going to a park, watching a movie, buying a computer, or benefiting from a public safety program. **Production** means to create or make available an economic good or service. Production activities can include the operation of police services, the protection of open space, the construction of new homes, or the provision of labor.

A **household** is a basic unit of consumption (and production) in the economy, and consists of one or more individuals. Households make decisions about work, spending, and the use of personal property. These decisions can be based on any number of goals, but in general, economics assumes that people will try to maximize their satisfaction. (We will study this concept in Chapter 4.) Although households differ, and individuals within households differ, each must make basic decisions about how to obtain and spend income on goods and services. Income can be derived from work, returns on investments (such as real estate or stocks), gifts (such as money from parents), savings (such as pensions), and transfers programs (such as welfare programs and social security). Households are not only consumers, but also producers of goods and services. For instance, individuals in a household provide labor to firms, and households can run businesses that sell goods to other consumers.

A **firm** is a basic unit of production (and consumption), involving the conversion of inputs into outputs (goods and services). Profit maximization is a primary goal of most firms.[2] A variety of private firms operate in the U.S. economy. Large businesses, such as Ford, IBM, and General Electric, have numerous products, plants throughout the country, hundreds of employees, and billions of dollars in sales.

---

[2] Some firms may choose not to maximize profits for other reasons. For instance, a company may be content to make less profit with less risk, to pursue other social goals, to maximize the salaries of its executives or employees, or to promote research and development.

FIGURE 1-1   *The Economy as a System*

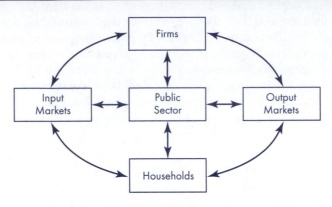

Smaller businesses, such as family-run stores, usually have a single product or single facility, fewer employees, and corresponding lower levels of sales. Firms can also act as consumer units; for instance, firms hire employees, purchase materials in order to manufacture their products, and contract for outside services.

In the United States, firms can be categorized as (1) corporations, which are legal entities in themselves, separate from the people that own them, (2) partnerships, which are owned and operated by two or more individuals, and (3) sole proprietorships, which are run by an individual. Corporations currently generate about 90% of the sales in the United States, although partnerships and sole proprietorships account for about 80% of the total number of firms.

Public sector, in Figure 1-1, includes governmental bodies (such as a city council or state government), public authorities (such as a regional transportation agency), and not-for-profit organizations (such as a university or hospital). Such public agencies often have primary goals in addition to (or other than) profit maximization. Like private firms, public agencies are often concerned with least-cost methods of operation. A large not-for-profit hospital, for example, needs to run cost-effectively to stay within its budget, and can often behave like a private firm: engaging in competition, coaxing patients to use its services, and generating millions of dollars in "surplus" (revenues in excess of costs).

Public sector agencies are both consumers and producers of goods and services. For instance, as a consumer, government purchases the labor of individuals and the products of firms. As a producer, government provides subsidies to businesses and health care coverage to elderly, disabled, and low-income citizens. Similarly, the **private sector** includes both private consumers and producers, such as firms.

A **market** is an organization or structure that brings together consumers (buyers) and producers (sellers) of particular goods and services. A market does not have to be a building with shoppers and a cash register. It can be any arrangement in which a good or service is provided, such as education, health care, long-distance telephone service, public recreations facilities, or the Internet.

It's often thought that consumers are households and producers are firms, which is not always the case. Both consumers and producers can include individuals, households, private firms, public agencies, or other entities. For instance, in the market for public transit trips, consumers are individual riders, and producers are the public transit agency. In the market for industrial labor, consumers are the firms that hire labor, and producers are the laborers themselves. The principle is that consumers are the ones demanding or purchasing a good or service, and producers are the ones supplying or selling that good or service.

Studying a market system often requires an in-depth look at the decision-making processes of consumers and producers. To do this, economics uses the two fundamental concepts of demand and supply. **Demand** represents the consumers' side of the market. **Supply** represents the producers' side of the market. Together, demand and supply influence the price and quantity of a good or service. At the equilibrium price (a concept examined in the next chapter), consumers are willing to buy the quantity that producers are willing to sell.

Economic transactions involve the decisions of these three major participants: households, firms, and the public sector. The final step is to knit together the market transactions of these participants to represent the market economy as an integrated system, as illustrated in Figure 1-1. The two major market activities include the market for outputs (goods and services) and the market for inputs (resources). An economic system transforms inputs (land, capital, and labor) into outputs (goods and services) for now or the future.

ECONOMICS AND THE ECOSYSTEM

Many economics textbooks present a circular view of the economy, as in Figure 1-1. This view may suggest that the economy is self-perpetuating; that resource inputs appear and waste outputs disappear, seemingly without limit or cost. Yet this perspective does not necessarily address the question of whether the economy is approaching the limits of what can be sustained by the ecosystem.[3]

Thus, an expanded view of the economy could include one more component—the ecosystem—that provides a source of inputs for the economy, and a sink for the waste outputs of the economy (Figure 1-2).[4] Because the ecosystem is essential to life functions, many argue that its value is theoretically infinite.

---

[3] The ecosystem, a contraction for "ecological system," includes biotic (living) organisms, such as plants, animals, and humans, and abiotic (nonliving) resources, such as water, air, and land. Interestingly, the words *ecosystem* and *economics* derive from the same Greek word—*oikos*, which means house. Ecology is the study of the house, and economics is the management of the house.

[4] See H. Daly (1996), *Beyond Growth: The Economics of Sustainable Development,* Boston, MA: Beacon Press.

FIGURE 1-2   *The Economic System Within the Ecosystem*

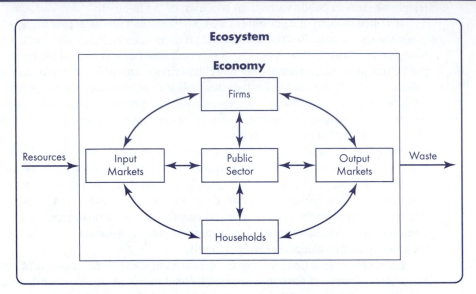

Traditionally, a measure of economic performance has been growth: The more output that can be produced, the higher the economic performance. This measure implies that growth is desirable, and that accounting measures are reasonable indicators of societal welfare. Yet some accounting measures, such as GDP, can exclude the social benefits and social costs related to ecosystem functions, such as loss of natural resources and increases in pollution that result from production and consumption activities. One recent study assessed the market value of services provided by natural resources, such as the assimilation of pollutants by wetlands, and found an average value of $33 trillion per year, which exceeds the GDPs of all nations combined.[5]

THE MARKET ECONOMICS FRAMEWORK

Three basic questions frame most economics decisions:

1 What goods should be produced?
2 How should they be produced?
3 For whom should they be produced?

---

[5] R. Costanza et al. (1997), "The Value of the World's Ecosystem Services and Natural Capital," *Nature* 387: 253–260.

The market economy works to answer these questions in the following ways:

1　Goods are produced that maximize the sum of net monetary gains for producers and net monetary value for consumers.[6]
2　Goods are produced using least-cost methods.
3　Goods are produced for and consumed by individuals who value them most, where value is determined by monetary expenditures.

Fundamentally, in the framework of the market economy, goods should be produced that yield the greatest overall net benefits (benefits minus costs). This principle gives rise to a decision-making criterion central to economics: **efficiency**. Efficiency, in economic parlance, means the absence of waste: An economy's resources are being used to produce goods that provide the greatest benefit at the least cost. A key type of efficiency is **Pareto efficiency**[7]—defined as a resource allocation where no one could be made better off without making someone else worse off. This type of efficiency characterizes the point of equilibrium in perfectly competitive markets.[8]

The criterion of Pareto efficiency may seem difficult to meet, especially for public sector decisions. For instance, government programs designed to benefit some members of society often impose costs on other members of society. This trade-off gives rise to another criterion, called **Kaldor-Hicks efficiency**[9]—defined as a resource allocation that makes some better off, and some worse off, but the net benefits are positive. This means that the gainers could, in theory, fully compensate the losers, so that at least one person is better off and no person is worse off. Yet this criterion does not explicitly address the distribution of benefits and costs (who gains and who loses), nor does it require the actual compensation of losers by gainers. (We will examine the strengths and limitations of different efficiency criteria in Chapters 6, 7, and 13.)

THE MARKET ECONOMICS FRAMEWORK AND PUBLIC DECISIONS

For public sector decisions, the market economy's answers to the three basic economic questions can raise additional questions:

---

[6] We will study these concepts later in the book, but a brief definition is provided here. Net gains for producers, or "producer surplus," is the amount that producers are paid for a good minus their costs for producing the good. Net value for consumers, or "consumer surplus," is the amount that consumers are willing to pay for a good minus their actual payments for the good.

[7] This principle is named after the Italian economist Vifredo Pareto (1848–1923).

[8] "Perfect competition" will be examined in detail in the chapters that follow. It refers to market conditions with many buyers and sellers, homogenous products, and easy market entry and market exit, so that no producer or consumer is large enough to influence the price.

[9] This concept is named after the work of the economists Nicholas Kaldor (1908–1986) and Sir John R. Hicks (1904–1989).

1 *What goods?* In this framework, goods that generate the greatest monetary expenditures from consumers, and the greatest profits for producers, are the ones that will be produced. Still, concerns arise in the use of money as a full representation of consumer value and determinant of what producers should produce. For instance, many valued goods do not have clear market prices such as walking through the woods or breathing clean air. Also, many valued goods, such as environmental preservation and protection, may not be profitable to produce.

2 *How produced?* Methods that are least-cost from a producer's perspective may not be least-cost from a public sector perspective. This can occur when private costs do not incorporate the full social costs of the production activity. For instance, using the earlier example of land development, social costs can include externalized costs (costs imposed on external parties, such as loss of trees and generation of pollution) as well as opportunity costs (costs representing a missed opportunity, or the highest value of that land and resources in another use.)

3 *For whom?* The individuals who are able to pay for the goods will obtain the goods, and the goods that receive the greatest payments are regarded as those most valued. By that standard, 100 gallons of water for someone to wash their car is more valuable than 100 gallons of water for homeless people to drink, if the car-washer were willing to pay more for the water than the homeless people. Also, consumers may "value" (want, need, appreciate) certain goods, even if they are unable to pay for them. An individual needing surgery in order to live would value that good, but may be unable to pay for it, and thus would not obtain the good.

These examples are simple, but intended to illustrate some of the challenges of using a market economy framework for public sector decisions. Many economies today, however, are generally not strict market economies, but rather mixed economies; that is, both the private sector and the public sector have economic functions. In the United States, government plays an important role. It provides public services, it engages in input and output markets, and it establishes the legal framework (such as property rights) for the market economy to exist. In the next section, and more extensively in later chapters, we examine the activities and rationale for government intervention in the economy, as well as why government intervention may have unintended or undesirable consequences.

PUBLIC SECTOR INVOLVEMENT IN THE MARKET SYSTEM

The United States and many other societies rely on the market to determine which particular goods and services to produce, how to produce them, and how to distribute them to consumers. In some cases, however, a market economy may not achieve an efficient allocation of resources, due to one or more conditions. These conditions are referred to as **market failures**.

Market failures provide one of the rationales for government intervention in the economic system. Another rationale is that societal goals, such as equity, may not be guaranteed by efficiency. On the other hand, government intervention may not necessarily correct market imperfections, and the public sector is subject to its own sources of failures, such as political pressure, lack of information, bureaucratic inefficiency, and limited control over market responses. Much of this textbook concerns market failures and public sector functions, and some examples are provided here.

A **monopoly** occurs when one supplier controls the market. Examples of monopoly power are familiar, such a water utility, a small town with a single grocery store, the U.S. Postal Service, and a pharmaceutical drug under patent protection. A concern with a monopolistic market is that it can result in higher prices, lower output, lower quality, and less freedom of choice for the consumer than what would occur in a competitive market. Many monopolies arise naturally because it can be more cost-effective for a single producer to produce the entire output, rather than for several firms to each produce part of the output. These so-called *natural monopolies* include utilities for electricity, water, gas, and telephone service. They are often publicly regulated or owned to promote fair pricing and to reduce possible misuses of monopoly power. In the last few decades, deregulation of monopolies sought to promote competition, efficiency, and innovation. Yet if controls are removed before competition is effective, the monopoly can enjoy the benefits of market power but without price restrictions. As seen in some industries, deregulation can lead to concerns about safety, service quality, and availability. Reregulation has emerged as a way to counter some of the effects of deregulation. We will study monopoly in Chapter 8.

Externalities are another example of market failure. Externalities are common, and occur when actions of producers or consumers impose additional costs or confer additional benefits upon others, without those others receiving compensation. A *negative externality* imposes costs upon others. An example is the generation of pollution. A chemical plant that discharges its waste into a river imposes external costs on society, including downstream water users, industries that rely on the river, and fish populations. Even though the plant may incur costs to discharge pollution, these costs to the plant may be less than the full costs of the pollution to society. This situation can result in an underpricing and an overproduction of the good (pollution). A *positive externality* creates benefits for others. An example is education. Children who receive education benefit not only themselves, but also the larger public, for instance, by learning skills to function in society and eventually contribute to the workforce. In this case, the direct benefits to the individuals are less than the full benefits to society, which can result in an overpricing and an underconsumption of the good (education). Several strategies are used in dealing with externalities, such as market-based approaches and government interventions, and we will illustrate and evaluate these strategies according to criteria of efficiency, equity, administration, flexibility, uncertainty, and incentives. The subject of externalities is covered in Chapter 9.

Public goods are another category of market failure. Public agencies often produce a wide range of goods and services that private firms are unable or unwilling to produce. These goods typically possess characteristics of public goods, which are nonrival and nonexclusive. (The term public goods does not mean goods provided by the public sector, even though they often are.) *Nonrival* means that one person's consumption does not reduce its benefits to others; there is not rivalry for benefits among consumers. For example, one person's enjoyment of a scenic view does not reduce another person's ability to enjoy that view, assuming one is not standing in another's way. *Nonexclusive* means that it is practically impossible to exclude people from consuming or deriving the benefits of the good. For example, in the case of radio, all residents of a community can listen to the programming, even if they don't contribute to that radio station. Examples of public goods include clean air, a lighthouse, and environmental protection. A private firm may have little incentive to provide a public good because it cannot divide the good among consumers and charge a price for its consumption. Thus, public agencies often must step forward and provide the good, or contract for its provision with a private firm. Public goods will be the focus of Chapter 10.

Imperfect information is common in life. We don't always have all the information we may want or need in order to make efficient decisions. Information failures can lead to market failures when a market participant has information or incentives that another lacks. Cases include those of adverse selection, moral hazard, and the principal-agent problem. *Adverse selection* occurs when products that are low-quality (or high-risk) are self-selected or attracted to the market. For instance, the used car market can attract low-quality cars, because consumers lack information on the true quality and value of the cars for sale. *Moral hazard* means that once insurance is obtained, the insured has a reduced incentive to avoid the insured-against event. This can help to explain why car owners, once they have automobile theft insurance, may be less cautious about locking their car, and the insurer lacks information and ability to monitor the car owner's behavior. The *principal-agent problem* refers to differing incentives between a principal (one who employs an agent) and the agent (who is employed to achieve objectives for the principal). For example, an hourly wage employee (an agent) may lack incentives to complete a task as quickly as possible, even though the employer (the principal) would like the work to be conducted as cost-effectively as possible. Information failures have motivated private and public sector actions to improve the quality and availability of information. For instance, government provides information through consumer protection laws (e.g., requirements for testing and labeling of drugs), public information services (e.g., weather and climate forecasts from the National Weather Service), and funding of research and development. Moreover, imperfect information is a motivation for government provision of social insurance, such as Medicare and Social Security, because private insurance may be unaffordable, incomplete, or unavailable for many individuals. Topics of information and uncertainty are covered in Chapter 11.

We just looked at cases of market failure, meaning a deviation from efficiency. Yet even an efficient market outcome may deviate from other societal goals, such as a more equitable distribution of resources. Such deviations provide a second set of rationales for government intervention in the economic system.

Equity is one of the most important concepts in public sector economics, yet it receives relatively little treatment in many microeconomics texts. There are many concepts and definitions of equity, based on principles such as equality, fairness, demand, responsiveness to needs, and ability to pay, among others. One common concept, distributional equity, generally refers to the distribution of benefits and costs among individuals and groups in society.

Yet equity is not an easy concept to operationalize or to measure. Questions arise: Who should benefit and who should bear the costs, and in what proportion, and by what metrics? How should benefits and costs be compared among people in the same generation and among different generations? There are no easy answers to what is an equitable allocation, because it is a normative decision, and depends on definitions, individual values, and public policy. Yet economics can guide the positive analysis, and assess the impacts of a decision and its alternatives on specific groups and individuals. (These concepts and techniques are explored in Chapters 6 and 7.)

As an example of equity issues, consider a government agency that needs to decide where to locate a new freeway within an existing city. Two potential routes are being considered: one through a predominantly low-income minority neighborhood, and the other around the periphery of an affluent neighborhood. Further assume that the route through the low-income neighborhood would not provide those residents direct access to the freeway. Because land acquisition costs may be lower in the low-income neighborhood, and because neighborhood opposition is less likely to delay the project (because, for instance, residents cannot afford the legal fees to fight the decision), the route through the low-income neighborhood may result in lower costs to the highway agency. Yet it may not seem fair that the low-income minority neighborhood should bear a disproportionate burden of the harmful impacts of the freeway, relative to benefits received, simply because of cost-effectiveness. Equity demands that something more than cost-effectiveness be considered in the location decision.

Equity also intersects with ethics. Some economists argue that if a market exists for a good or service, and if individual buyers and sellers are willing, then the transaction should be permitted. Yet this scenario raises questions about broader societal welfare. For instance, should we allow people to sell their body parts, or to sell babies that they bear for others? Should we allow the open sale of illegal drugs or prostitution? Here, market-based decisions have ethical implications.

As another example, suppose that in the next presidential election, voters were willing to sell their vote. Should we allow a candidate to buy the votes needed to be president? The market might say "yes," because buyers and sellers would both consider themselves better off because of the transaction. On the other hand, citizens may feel that democratic elections should be beyond the bounds of the economic system, and that vote selling should not be permitted on ethical grounds.

Also concerning equity, the market system may be unable to appropriately value the future. Traditional methods of project evaluation, such as cost benefit analysis (covered in Chapter 13), use discounting (covered in Chapter 12) to translate future costs and future benefits into present values. As a brief introduction, discounting is the process of taking future amounts and converting them to present amounts. It is based on the same concept as interest, but in reverse. For instance, if you invest a dollar today, at an interest rate of 10% per year, you would have $1.10 a year from today. So $1.10 in the bank, one year from now, is worth $1 today, assuming a 10% annual discount rate and no inflation.

Discounting seems appropriate when dealing with monetary investments. But how should society discount nonmarket or intangible goods, such as human lives or natural resources? At common discount rates, future costs and benefits can be reduced to insignificant amounts in present value terms. For instance, at a discount rate of 10%, saving 304 lives, 60 years from now, would be equated to only one life now. Would a grandparent say that their grandchild's life is only 1/304 as valuable as theirs? Similar problems arise when trying to discount natural resources. Is the value of 304 acres of a national park, 60 years from now, worth only the value placed on one acre today? The need to account for future societal welfare, as well as the valuation of public and nonmarket goods, are challenges that face public sector decision making, and are treated in this book.

USING ECONOMICS WISELY

This text will help you to understand microeconomics, its role in public sector decisions, and its wise use. Because money is a powerful influence in both the public and private sector, and because trade-offs must be made in choosing one project or policy over another, economics is often used in decision making. Yet economics can also be misused. Thus, it is important to be vigilant about sources of bias and inaccuracies, and to couple economic analyses with sound judgment.

- *Question numbers.* The formal mathematics of economic theories and the use of computers to analyze data provide the ability to investigate complex economic questions empirically. When faced with data and numerical results, be sure to understand what the data seek to represent, how the data were obtained, what assumptions were made in the calculations, and how the results can be influenced by changes in assumptions or methods. Also remember that economics is a social science. Even though quantitative analyses can be useful and valid, social science phenomena are not always amenable to strict numerical descriptions and manipulations. When numbers are assigned to things that are not inherently numerical, the resulting analyses may imply more accuracy than warranted. Moreover, a singular focus on numerical results may overlook other information that is important to decision making.
- *Question assumptions.* Economics, like many other disciplines, often requires the use of simplifying assumptions to study and model phenomena.

These assumptions include, for instance, "perfect competition" or "all factors other than price held constant." It is important to understand the effects of deviations from these assumptions on the end result. For example, economic analyses in textbooks typically represent demand and supply curves as precise lines. These curves, in actuality, may be fuzzy broad bands; thus, predictions of future prices and market conditions may be uncertain. This is not to say that these analyses would not provide useful information, but rather they should be accompanied by an understanding of their assumptions and limitations.

- *Question assertions.* Economic statements abound, such as "What's good for a company is good for the country," or "Everyone pursuing their own self-interest will make everyone better off." These assertions, for instance, may characterize the "fallacy of composition": What is good for an individual is not necessarily good for the whole, and gains to an individual can impose costs upon others. Also question assertions of causation, such as, "The reduction in taxes led to the growth in employment," or "The rise in minimum wage caused the simultaneous reduction in employment." Just because an event precedes another event, or just because two events are correlated, does not mean that one caused the other. Causes and effects are often difficult to isolate in economics because many factors are changing and influencing one another. As you will find, a single policy problem can generate different and strident prescriptions, each one supported by economic analyses. Remember that even seemingly objective economic analyses and assertions can often involve values and subjectivity.

- *Question context.* Economic analysis is an important part of decision making, but it is not the whole story. Social, political, and institutional factors can influence outcomes. For instance, an economic analysis may suggest that placing an emissions tax on industries will increase their production costs, and thereby increase costs to consumers. The tax may in fact spur industry innovation and result in more efficient and less costly operations by reducing resource consumption, improving internal operations, and reducing waste. The result can be lowered costs, not increased costs, to both producers and consumers. With public sector decisions, economics can be an important factor, but not the sole factor that needs to be considered.

OVERVIEW OF THE TEXTBOOK

The text is organized in three parts. The first part, Chapters 1 through 5, presents the fundamentals of microeconomics and the operations of the market economy, such as demand, supply, elasticities, market dynamics, and market interventions. These chapters also provide a public sector analytic framework that is important to understanding the rest of the text. The second part, Chapters 6 through 11, examines topics that are central to public sector decision making, such as equity and efficiency trade-offs, welfare economics, market failures, monopolies, externalities, public goods, risk, and imperfect information. The third part, Chapters 12 through 14, provides the concepts and techniques for assessing benefits and costs over time, for performing a cost-benefit analysis, and for evaluating these methods, with attention to applicability as well as limitations of economics.

REVIEW QUESTIONS

1. Why could a public agency's focus on "cash costs" perhaps lead to an inaccurate assessment of the "full costs" of an activity?

2. One can find disagreement among economists on almost any policy question. What does this lack of consensus imply about economics as a science?

3. Economists typically make two types of statements: (a) descriptions about economic conditions, and (b) statements about which policies should be adopted. Should one distinguish between these two types of statements?

4. Why do you think the traditional view of the "economy as a system" overlooks the role of the ecosystem? What are the implications for production and consumption decisions?

5. Why do you think economics uses money and monetary equivalents as a metric for analyses? Would some other metric be more appropriate for public sector decisions?

CHAPTER 2

DEMAND AND SUPPLY

This chapter lays the foundations of microeconomics: demand and supply. Demand represents the quantity of a good that consumers are willing and able to purchase at each price, and supply represents the quantity of a good that producers are willing and able to provide at each price. Together, the interaction of demand and supply in a market can determine the price and quantity provided of a good. Moreover, the concepts of demand and supply can help us to understand incentives of consumers and producers.

DEMAND

Demand focuses on the consumers' side of the market. The demand for a good or service depends on many factors: the price of that good, the number of consumers, their income levels, their preferences, their expectations about future prices, the price of related goods, and the availability of substitutes, among others.

From experience, we know that the price of a good can influence how much we would buy of that good. In order to study the effects of **price** on **quantity demanded**, economics uses the demand curve (Figure 2-1). The **demand curve** represents the relationship between the *price* of the good and the *quantity demanded* of that good during a specific time period. To study this relationship, economics assumes that all other factors that could influence quantity demanded (e.g., number of consumers, incomes, preferences, desirability of the good, quality, season of year, prices of other goods, etc.) will be held constant during that time period. This is the assumption of *ceteris paribus*, which is Latin for "the others equal": holding all other factors (other than price) at their same values, during a specific time period.

For demand, price and quantity are inversely related. This concept, called the **law of demand**, is familiar: When price goes up, the quantity demanded goes down, and vice versa. This results in a downward-sloping demand curve (Figure 2-1). In other words, consumers usually demand more of a good when the price is lower, and

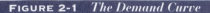

FIGURE 2-1   *The Demand Curve*

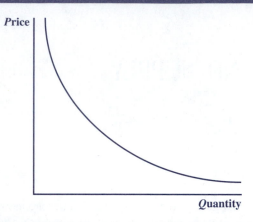

demand less of a good when the price is higher. This relationship holds true for virtually all goods, over virtually all price levels.[1]

The demand curve slopes downward for three main reasons. A first is the **income effect**: As the price of a good increases, a consumer's overall purchasing power decreases, thereby reducing their consumption of that good. Consider, for instance, a student who flies back home once a month. The roundtrip airline ticket costs $200, and the student's discretionary income, after paying for rent, tuition, and books, is $500 per month. If the price of the airline trip rises to $350, then the student's overall purchasing power will decrease, because the student would have only $150 per month to spend on items such as food and clothing, rather than the usual $300 per month. So in this case, the student may reduce the number of airline trips back home, illustrating the income effect: The price increase caused a decrease in the student's discretionary income, which decreased the consumption of the good (airline trips).

A second is the **substitution effect**: As the price of a good increases, its substitutes look more attractive, and consumers will buy less of that good and more of the substitute goods. In the previous example, assume that the student could also take a train back home for a cost of $125 roundtrip. Here the train is a substitute good. Although the train takes more time, it costs less, and it could become more appealing as the airline ticket price rises. Driving is another substitute, which would cost $50 for the roundtrip, but is also more stressful. The student would choose driving if the price of the airline ticket (and the train) became high enough. Generally, if goods are substitutes, then the price of one can affect the quantity demanded of the others.

A third and related principle is **diminishing marginal utility**. *Marginal* is a common term in economics: It means a one-unit change, either one more unit or one less unit. *Utility* is also a common term: It represents the level of satisfaction derived

---

[1] In rare cases, quantity demanded can increase as price increases over a certain range. For instance, some goods, such as designer clothing and accessories, may increase in desirability as price rises.

from the consumption of goods. (Utility will be examined in Chapter 4.) Diminishing marginal utility means that as a person consumes more and more of a good, the person will derive less and less additional satisfaction from each additional unit of a good, assuming that consumption of other goods is held constant. Note that this principle does not mean that total satisfaction ("total utility") declines; just the additional amount of satisfaction derived from each additional unit of the good ("marginal utility") declines.

To illustrate this concept, think about a day at school. You just got out of a class, the weather is warm, you crave a cold soda, so you go to the vending machines. That first soda tastes really good. A second soda might also taste good, but probably not as good as the first. A third soda might have very little value, and a fourth soda, well, you might have to be forced or paid to drink it. Thus, additional satisfaction to the consumer, or marginal utility, diminishes with each additional unit of consumption, assuming consumption of other goods remains constant.

Note that the demand curve (Figure 2-1), a particular representation between price and quantity demanded, is valid only as long as all "other" factors (other than price; i.e., those under the *ceteris paribus* condition) that affect demand do not change. Changes in any of the other factors that affect demand will alter the particular relationship between price and quantity. Then the entire demand curve will change, which is illustrated as follows.

Suppose that Figure 2-1 represents the demand for bottled water. As summer approaches and the weather becomes warmer, the demand for bottled water would likely increase. For every price along the demand curve, the quantity demanded would increase. This relationship would be represented by a shift of the demand curve to the northeast (NE) (Figure 2-2). As Figure 2-2 shows, for a certain price P^*, the quantity demanded would increase from Q_1 to Q_2.

Later, when summer ends and the weather becomes cooler, the demand for bottled water would likely decrease. The quantity demanded at each price would decrease, which would shift the demand curve to the southwest (SW) (Figure 2-3). As Figure 2-3 shows, for a certain price P^*, the quantity demanded would decrease from Q_1 to Q_3.

Figures 2-2 and 2-3 depict a **change in demand**. Demand increases from D_1 to D_2 (Figure 2-2), and demand decreases from D_1 to D_3 (Figure 2-3).

Note: Most economics textbooks refer to shifts in the demand curve and shifts in the supply curve as "up" or "down." These terms can cause confusion because it is not always clear which way is up or down. Therefore, this book adopts a convention of using compass directions to describe movements. The positive *y*-axis points north, and the positive *x*-axis points east. Thus, a demand curve shift toward the upper right corner will be toward the northeast, and so forth. Also note that a "demand curve" or a "supply curve" does not need to be curved—it can be a straight line.

FIGURE 2-2 *Increase in Demand*

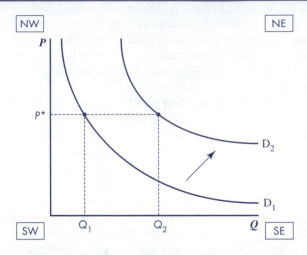

FIGURE 2-3 *Decrease in Demand*

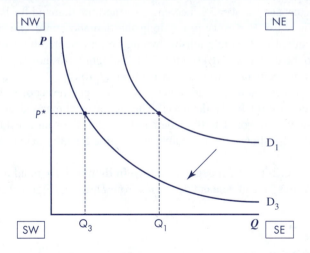

What happens if only price changes? This effect is depicted by a **change in quantity demanded**: a movement along the demand curve.

Assume, in the demand curve for bread (Figure 2-4), an initial price of $P = \$2$ per loaf and an initial quantity demanded of $Q = 3$ loaves, which is represented by point A. If the price of bread increases to $3 per loaf, and *all other factors stay*

FIGURE 2-4 *Decrease in Quantity Demanded*

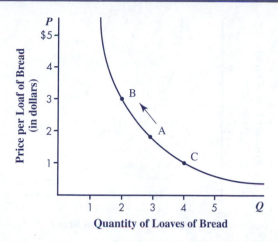

constant, then quantity demanded will decrease, moving from point A to point B. The new quantity demanded will be found by a movement along the demand curve to the northwest, ending up at $Q = 2$ loaves.

Now instead of a price increase, suppose the price decreases to $1 per loaf, with all other factors constant (Figure 2-5). This change will lead to an increase in quantity demanded, which is depicted by a movement along the demand curve to the southeast, moving from point A to point C, ending up at $Q = 4$ loaves. Thus, quantity demanded decreases when price increases (point A to point B), and quantity demanded increases when price decreases (point A to point C).

One of the most common mistakes is to confuse these two concepts: change in demand and change in the quantity demanded.

- *Demand* is the entire demand curve: the price-quantity relationship for a particular time period, all other factors held constant.
- *Quantity demanded* refers to a particular point on the demand curve that is associated with a particular price and quantity (demanded).
- *A change in demand* is a shift in the entire demand curve. It occurs when some factor other than price changes; that is, some factor under the *ceteris paribus* assumption (income, preferences, substitutes, etc.) changes. An increase in demand is shown by a shift of the curve to the northeast. A decrease in demand is shown by a shift of the curve to the southwest.
- *A change in quantity demanded* results from movement along a particular demand curve. It occurs when the price changes, and all other factors that affect demand are constant. An increase in price will generally cause a decrease in quantity demanded, which is shown by a movement along the

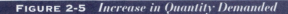

FIGURE 2-5 *Increase in Quantity Demanded*

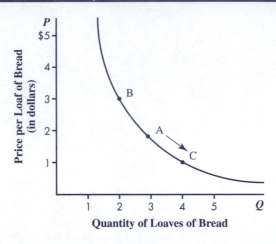

same demand curve to the northwest. A decrease in price will generally cause an increase in quantity demanded, which is shown by a movement along the same demand curve to the southeast.

SUPPLY

Supply focuses on the producers' side of the market. The supply of a good or service depends on many factors: the price that the producer can obtain for that good, the number of producers, the available technology, the price of inputs to production (such as labor and materials), prices of related goods, the number of competitors, government regulations, and other factors such as weather.

Of these factors, price is a major determinant of the quantity of a good or service that producers are willing to supply. In order to study the effects of price on quantity supplied, economics uses the supply curve.

Similar to our study of demand, the **supply curve** represents the relationship between the **price** of the good and the **quantity supplied** of that good during a specific time period. It also assumes *ceteris paribus*: all other factors (other than price) that could influence quantity supplied will be held constant during a specific time period.

For supply, price and quantity are directly (rather than inversely) related. This **law of supply** means that as price of the good rises, quantity produced also rises, and when the price drops, quantity produced drops. This relationship results in an upward-sloping supply curve (Figure 2-6).

A main reason for the upward slope relates to **diminishing marginal returns**, which means that additional units of input will result in declining increments of out-

FIGURE 2-6 *The Supply Curve*

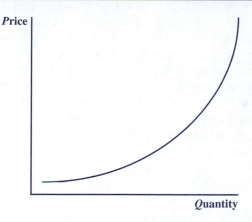

put, even though total output increases. Thus, in many cases, per-unit production costs will increase as production increases. So producers will need to get a higher price to cover their costs. (This concept is illustrated here, and then covered more extensively in Chapter 5.)

As an example of diminishing marginal returns, consider a local coffee shop where customers are always lined up in the morning. One employee is in charge of fulfilling coffee orders, and can produce drinks at a rate of 50 per hour. A second employee is hired to assist. Together, they can make drinks at a rate of 80 per hour. Eventually a third employee is hired and the three of them together can make drinks at a rate of 95 per hour.

Even though each additional unit of input (each new employee) increased total output (from 50 drinks to 80 drinks to 95 drinks per hour), it resulted in declining increments of output (from 30 additional drinks per hour per additional employee, to 15 additional drinks per hour per additional employee). This declining increment is because the employees needed to use the same coffee machine, share the same confined space, and spend time coordinating tasks. Thus, each unit of input was less effective than the one before.

As another example, suppose you are studying for an economics exam. The first hour is productive and you learn a lot. The second hour is also productive, and you learn, but not as much. The third hour is less productive, and you learn hardly anything new. By the fourth hour, you are ready to go to sleep. Thus, each additional unit of input (hours of study) results in declining incremental units of output (additional knowledge of economics), even though total output (total knowledge of economics) increases.

The supply curve illustrates that producers generally produce more of a good when the price is higher, and they produce less of a good when the price is lower. A higher price provides an incentive to increase the quantity produced and sold. It also assumes that production costs do not increase more than revenues increase, in order to increase profit. (Profit is equal to total revenues minus total costs.)

The supply curve, just like the demand curve, represents a particular relationship between price and quantity during a specific period of time. This particular curve is valid only as long as all factors other than price that affect supply do not change. Changes in any of the "other factors" will alter the particular relationship between price and quantity, and the entire supply curve will change.

For example, if the price of labor for producing the good decreases, the supply of that good is likely to increase. For every price, the quantity supplied will be larger. This effect would be represented by a shift of the supply curve to the southeast, from S_1 to S_2 (Figure 2-7). As Figure 2-7 shows, for a certain price P^*, the quantity supplied would increase from Q_1 to Q_2.

Similarly, if the price of labor for producing the good increases, the supply is likely to decrease. For every price, the quantity supplied would be less, which would shift the supply to the northwest, from S_1 to S_3 (Figure 2-8). As Figure 2-8 shows, for a certain price P^*, the quantity supplied would decrease from Q_1 to Q_3.

Both of these examples represent a **change in supply**.

What happens if only price changes? This effect is depicted by a **change in quantity supplied**: a movement along the supply curve. Consider Figure 2-9. If the price of bread increases from $2 per loaf to $3 per loaf, and all other factors stay constant, the quantity produced will increase from 3 loaves per day to 4 loaves per day. This change is depicted by movement along the supply curve to the northeast, from point A to point B. Similarly, as shown in Figure 2-10, if the price decreases from $2 per loaf to $1 per loaf, and all other factors stay constant, the quantity produced will decrease from 3 loaves per day to 2 loaves per day. This change is depicted by a

FIGURE 2-7 *Increase in Supply*

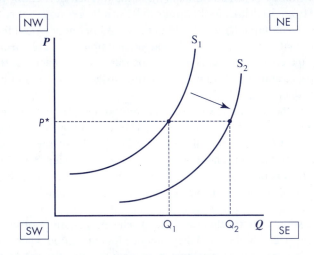

movement along the demand curve to the southwest, from point A to point C. Both of these movements represent a change in quantity supplied.

As with demand, one of the most common mistakes is to confuse these two concepts: change in supply and change in the quantity supplied.

- *Supply* is the entire supply curve: the price-quantity relationship for a particular time period, all other factors held constant.

FIGURE 2-8   *Decrease in Supply*

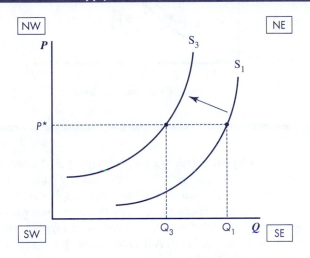

FIGURE 2-9   *Increase in Quantity Supplied*

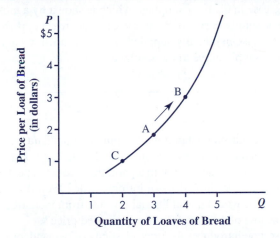

FIGURE 2-10 *Decrease in Quantity Supplied*

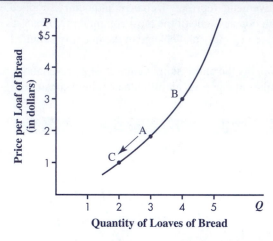

- *Quantity supplied* refers to a particular point on the supply curve that is associated with a particular price and quantity (supplied).
- *A change in supply* is a shift in the entire supply curve. It occurs when some factor (other than price) changes; that is, some factor under the *ceteris paribus* assumption changes. An increase in supply is shown by a shift of the curve to the southeast. A decrease in supply is shown by a shift of the curve to the northwest.
- *A change in quantity supplied* results from movement along a particular supply curve. It occurs when the price changes, and all other factors that affect supply are constant. An increase in price will generally cause an increase in quantity supplied, which is shown by a movement along the same supply curve to the northeast. A decrease in price will generally cause a decrease in quantity supplied, which is shown by a movement along the same supply curve to the southwest.

ELASTICITIES

We can extend our understanding of supply and demand with a new concept: elasticities. **Elasticity** measures responsiveness to change. For instance, if an agency decreases the price of admission to a park, they would expect attendance to rise. But how much more would it rise—a lot or a little? Would total revenue increase or decrease; that is, would the additional revenue from increased attendance be enough to offset the loss of revenue from the decreased price?

This section introduces the price elasticity of demand, provides applications, and discusses three other types of elasticities: price elasticity of supply, income elasticity of demand, and cross-price elasticity of demand. Although elasticity has numerous applications, it is especially useful in demand analysis.

PRICE ELASTICITY OF DEMAND

If the price changes, how much will quantity demanded change? The price elasticity of demand can help to answer that question. The **price elasticity of demand** measures the percentage change in the quantity demanded of a good, relative to the percentage change in price of that good. In other words, elasticity measures the degree of relative responsiveness.

An **elastic good** is one in which the percentage change in quantity demanded is *greater* than the percentage change in price. For instance, a percentage decrease in the price of meals at a fast-food restaurant can result in a larger percentage increase in the number of fast-food meals demanded. Thus, in this example, fast-food meals are said to be price elastic, or more responsive.

An **inelastic good** is one in which the percentage change in quantity demanded is *less* than the percentage change in price. For instance, a percentage increase in the price of water often results in a smaller percentage decrease in the amount of water demanded. Thus, in this case, water is said to be price inelastic, or less responsive.

A **unitary elastic good** is one in which the percentage change in quantity demanded is *equal* to the percentage change in price. For instance, suppose a percentage decrease in the price of bicycles results in an equal percentage increase in the number of bicycles demanded. Thus bicycles are said to be unitary elastic, or equally responsive.

The price elasticity of demand (E_D) can be calculated as follows:

$E_D = \%\Delta Q\ /\ \%\Delta P$

where

E_D	=	price elasticity of demand of a good	
$\%\Delta Q$	=	$\Delta Q / Q_i$	(percentage change in quantity demanded)
$\%\Delta P$	=	$\Delta P / P_i$	(percentage change in price)
ΔQ	=	$Q_f - Q_i$	(change in quantity demanded)
Q_f	=	final quantity demanded; after the price change	
Q_i	=	initial quantity demanded; before the price change	
ΔP	=	$P_f - P_i$	(change in price)
P_f	=	final price; after the price change	
P_i	=	initial price; before the price change	

Putting it all together, we get

$$E_D = \frac{(Q_f - Q_i) / Q_i}{(P_f - P_i) / P_i}$$

The elasticity formula, E_D, can be interpreted as follows (see Figure 2-11).

Elastic	$E_D < -1$	e.g., $-2, -3, -4.5$
Inelastic	$E_D > -1$ (but < 0)	e.g., $-0.2, -1/2, -0.63$
Unitary elastic	$E_D = -1$	
Perfectly elastic	$E_D =$ undefined (horizontal line)	A horizontal demand curve: a given price at which any quantity can be sold
Perfectly inelastic	$E_D = 0$ (vertical line)	A vertical demand curve: a given quantity that will be demanded regardless of price

Typical values of price elasticities of demand are provided in Table 2-1.

FIGURE 2-11   *Price Elasticity of Demand*

(a) Elastic

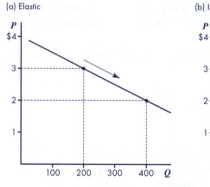

(b) Inelastic

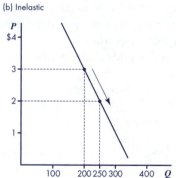

(c) Unitary Elastic

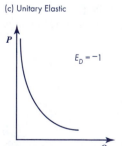

(d) Perfectly Elastic

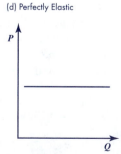

(e) Perfectly Inelastic

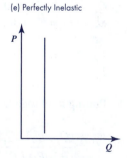

TABLE 2-1 *Estimates of the Price Elasticity of Demand*	

(Based on empirical studies and compilations of price elasticity of demand data)

Good	Price Elasticity of Demand
Housing	–0.01
Residential electricity	–0.13
Bread	–0.15
Bus travel	–0.20
Coffee	–0.25
Sugar	–0.30
Medical insurance	–0.31
Legal services	–0.37
Automobile repair	–0.40
Cigarettes	–0.51
Gasoline	–0.60
Milk	–0.63
Movies	–0.87
Automobiles	–1.2
Beer	–0.9
Tires, short run	–0.9
Tires, long run	–1.2
Beef	–1.27
Tableware	–1.54
Restaurant meals	–2.27
Airline travel	–2.4
Foreign travel	–4.0
Fresh tomatoes	–4.6

ELASTICITIES AND TOTAL REVENUE

Another interesting property of elasticities is that it can help us to understand the effects of a price change on total revenue. **Total revenue** (TR) is total sales; the price of the good (*P*) multiplied by the quantity sold of the good (*Q*).

$$TR = P * Q$$

Let's say you run an ice cream shop, and you want to increase revenues, so you think about increasing the price of your ice cream cones. As you know from your study of demand, when price increases, quantity demanded typically decreases. An increased price may seem to increase revenue, but a decreased quantity demanded may seem to decrease revenue. So will this price increase be enough to offset a quantity decrease, and thereby lead to an increase in total revenues? You are not sure.

So instead you consider decreasing the price of your ice cream cones. You know that when price decreases, quantity demanded typically increases. The decreased price may seem to decrease revenues, but an increased quantity demanded may seem to increase revenues. So will that quantity increase be enough to offset the price decrease, and thereby lead to an increase in total revenue? You are not sure about that either.

What to do: increase price or decrease price? Which effect—a price change or a quantity change—outweighs the other in the calculation of total revenue?

The answer will depend on elasticities.

- *With elastic demand, a price increase will decrease total revenue, and a price decrease will increase total revenue.* Recall that elastic means a more than proportional response. Also recall that TR = $P * Q$, and that P and Q vary inversely. In this elastic case, a percentage change in price will result in a greater percentage change in quantity demanded, in the opposite direction. Thus, the price change will be dominated by the quantity change. So total revenue will change in the opposite direction of the price change.

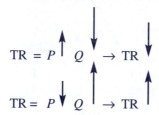

- *With inelastic demand, a price increase will increase total revenue, and a price decrease will decrease total revenue.* Recall that inelastic means a less than proportional response. So a percentage change in price will result in a lesser percentage change in quantity demanded, in the opposite direction. Thus, the price change will dominate over the quantity change, and total revenue will change in the same direction of the price change.

- *With unitary elastic demand, a change in price will not change total revenue.* The percentage change in price is matched evenly by the percentage change in quantity demanded, so total revenue will remain the same with a price change.

$$\text{TR} = P \uparrow Q \downarrow \rightarrow \text{TR (no change)}$$

$$\text{TR} = P \downarrow Q \uparrow \rightarrow \text{TR (no change)}$$

We will see how elasticities and revenues can be calculated, and the usefulness of these principles, through an example here and then others later in this chapter.

EXAMPLE   **Elasticities and Public Park Fees**

Consider a community park, where visitors pay a small fee to enter the park and enjoy the facilities for a day. The parks and recreation agency is considering a decrease in the fee in order to encourage more visitors to come to the park. Some community residents are concerned, however, that the decreased fee will also decrease overall revenues to the community.

To evaluate the economic effects, the elasticity of demand can help determine how much quantity demanded (number of visitors) will change in response to a decrease in price (the entrance fee), assuming all other factors remain constant. Then the change in quantity demanded can be used together with price information to determine effects on total revenue.

First, a definition: Total revenue (TR) is total sales; the price of the good (P) multiplied by the quantity sold of the good (Q). In this case the "good" is park visits.

$$\text{TR} = P * Q$$

Now, the analysis. Agency staff developed two possible demand curves to represent the relationship between park fees and visitors. One is depicted in Figure 2-11(a), and the other is depicted in Figure 2-11(b).

The formula for the price elasticity of demand is

$$E_D = \%\Delta Q\,/\,\%\Delta P = \frac{(Q_f - Q_i)\,/\,Q_i}{(P_f - P_i)\,/\,P_i}$$

The agency proposed a fee decrease from \$3 to \$2, so $\%\Delta P = (P_f - P_i)\,/\,P_i = (\$2 - \$3)/\$3 = -1/3$.

Using the demand curve in Figure 2-11(a), the quantity demanded for park visits would increase from 200 to 400 visitors per week, so $\%\Delta Q = (Q_f - Q_i)\,/\,Q_i = (400-200)/200 = 1.0$.

Using the demand curve in Figure 2-11(b), the quantity demanded for park visits would increase from 200 to 250 visitors per week, so $\%\Delta Q = (250-200)/200 = 0.25 = 1/4$.

continued on next page

The elasticities of demand, within the range of the price decrease ($P = \$3$ to $P = \$2$), can be calculated as follows:

$$E_D = \%\Delta Q\ /\ \%\Delta P$$

$$E_D = 1.0\ /\ (-1/3) = -3$$

so demand is elastic, as in Figure 2-11(a).

$$E_D = (1/4)\ /\ (-1/3) = -3/4$$

so demand is inelastic, as in Figure 2-11(b).

What about the effects on total revenues?

$$TR = P * Q$$

For elastic demand:

Before fee decrease: TR = ($3)(200) = $600
After fee decrease: TR = ($2)(400) = $800

For inelastic demand:

Before fee decrease: TR = ($3)(200) = $600
After fee decrease: TR = ($2)(250) = $500

So with elastic demand, a fee decrease would lead to both an increase in visitors and an increase in total revenue. With inelastic demand, a fee decrease would lead to an increase in visitors, but a decrease in total revenue. Do these results mean the fee should not be decreased? Not necessarily. Other factors may be important, such as providing benefits of the park to more community members, even with the decrease in total revenue in the inelastic demand case. (We will study techniques for evaluating such benefits and trade-offs in Chapters 4 and 7.) The park is currently uncrowded, so this option would allow more visitors to derive benefits from the park without imposing significant costs upon others. If crowding becomes an issue, however, then the agency may need to reconsider the price change or take other measures to deal with congestion at the park. (These aspects of public goods will be studied in Chapter 10.)

What is interesting is that depending on the price elasticity of demand, the same fee decrease can cause different responses in quantity demanded, and in total revenue. (Later in the chapter, we will examine relationships between elasticities and total revenue.)

Why would one demand curve be elastic and the other inelastic? Several explanations are possible, and here are two. For elastic demand, the price decrease may be sufficient incentive to attract visitors away from other activities (e.g., substitutes). For inelastic demand, the price decrease may not matter that much in decisions whether to visit the park, because the higher fee is relatively small compared to incomes of residents. We will now look at the factors that can influence the price elasticity of demand.

FACTORS THAT INFLUENCE THE PRICE ELASTICITY OF DEMAND

The price elasticity of demand depends on several factors, and generally becomes more elastic[2] with increases in each of these factors, as described next.

Availability of Substitutes

The more and better substitutes that are available for a good, the more price elastic the demand for that good can be. For instance, for many people, bread (considered price inelastic) does not have close substitutes. Therefore, if the price of bread increases, people would not decrease their consumption of bread by relatively as much. They would prefer to pay the higher price on bread than to switch to, say, crackers. On the other hand, as restaurant meals (considered price elastic) become more expensive, the consumption of restaurant meals may decrease relatively more. This is because, for many people, restaurant meals have substitutes, such as cooking at home or purchasing take-out food.

Time Period

The longer the time period that is considered, the more price elastic the demand for that good can become. This is because consumers have time to adjust their preferences and habits, and to find more substitutes, in response to price changes. Consider, for instance, the demand for train trips. If the price rises on train trips, ridership may not drop that much in the short term (inelastic), because people are set in their routines. Over time, however, ridership may drop much more, relative to the price change, as people find other modes of transportation (elastic).

---

[2] Here, "more elastic" will mean that the price elasticity of demand is a greater negative number. For instance, a good with $E_D = -2$ is considered more price elastic than a good with $E_D = -1$. Similarly "less elastic" will mean a smaller negative number. For instance, a good with $E_D = -0.8$ is considered less price elastic than a good with $E_D = -1.0$.

Expenditures Relative to Income

The larger the percentage of a consumer's income that is spent for a good, the more price elastic the demand for that good can be. Not only will a price change alter the relative prices of all goods, including substitutes, it will also reduce the purchasing power of the consumer. For instance, new cars are relatively price elastic because they represent a major portion of a consumer's discretionary income. If the price of new cars increases, then consumer purchases of new cars can be expected to decrease by a greater percentage. This is because consumers may wait to buy new cars until they become more affordable, or buy used cars instead of new cars. Yet for a wealthier consumer, new cars may be less price elastic because they represent relatively less of the consumer's income.

Optionality

The more discretionary or optional a good, the more price elastic the demand for that good may be. Water is a necessity, and hence it is usually price inelastic, but some water purposes are more elastic than others. For instance, water for washing cars tends to be more elastic than water for drinking. As another example, automobile repairs are relatively price inelastic, even though automobiles are elastic. This is because once a household has purchased an automobile and requires it for transportation, repairs become more of a necessity.

Other Factors

Factors such as the durability of the good and expectations about future prices, among others, can also influence elasticities. For instance, housing is durable, and many individuals do not continually adjust their consumption of the number of homes. Long-term leases or ownership may prevent immediate changes in quantities consumed to changes in price. Thus, this factor contributes to the relative price inelasticity of demand for housing. On expectations about future prices, if consumers believe that the price of a good will rise in the near future, they may buy more of it now in order to avoid higher prices later. Similarly, if they believe the price will drop, they may curtail their purchases now until the price is lower.

As Table 2-1 indicates, examples of goods with elastic E_D include foreign travel, restaurant meals, tableware, and automobiles. Examples of goods with inelastic E_D include housing, electricity, bread, and automobile repairs. Again, elasticities can vary, depending on the consumer and the situation.

Before continuing, we note some important points about the price elasticity of demand:

- *Elasticity is a ratio of percentage changes, not absolute changes in quantity and price.* Using percentages is important for several reasons. One is to compare among products. A 25-cent price increase on a pound of bananas will have a different effect on quantity demanded than a 25-cent price increase on a car. Another reason is to remove the influence of units. Otherwise, an absolute price change reported as 100 pennies or $1 could produce different elasticity results. Yet another reason is to compare relative changes. If the number of houses sold increases from 50 to 100, the additional 50 houses represent a 100% increase in the quantity sold. Selling another 50 houses increases sales from 100 to 150, which increases the quantity sold by only 50%.

- *Elasticity is not the same as slope.* As shown in Figure 2-12, elasticities vary along a demand curve. Even though elasticities are not the same as slope, a general observation can be made: The steeper the demand curve, the more price inelastic the demand curve; the flatter the demand curve, the more price elastic the demand curve. These are only guidelines, and an assessment of elasticity values depends on specific analyses. Note again that the "demand curve" does not need to be a curve.

- *The same good may have different elasticities.* Elasticities depend on consumers and on situations. For instance, airline flights may be elastic for some consumers (students on tight budgets who fly home when the price is affordable), and inelastic for other consumers (professionals who need to fly on weekly business trips, regardless of price). Even for one particular consumer, elasticities can change depending on context. For instance, airline flights may be elastic for a student during the academic year (when the student is considering going home to visit family), but inelastic during the summer (when the student is already living at home).

- *Conventions differ on the sign of* E_D *(negative or positive).* The price elasticity of demand will usually be a negative number because, for most goods,

---

FIGURE 2-12   *Elasticities Vary Along a Straight Line*

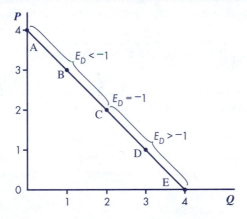

price and quantity are inversely related: An increase in price will decrease quantity demanded, and vice versa. Some conventions, however, define E_D as the absolute value of the formula provided earlier. This approach would mean that the price elasticity of demand would always be a positive number, which would miss cases (albeit, few) where the price and quantity were directly related instead of inversely related. To avoid confusion, this textbook defines the price elasticity of demand (and other elasticity measures) by using data *unaltered by an absolute value conversion.*

- *Conventions also differ on which term to use in the divisors (in the numerator and denominator of the elasticities formula) in order to calculate percentage change.* For instance, recall the formula for the price elasticity of demand:

$$E_D = \frac{(Q_f - Q_i) / Q_i}{(P_f - P_i) / P_i}$$

Three common conventions are (1) the initial values of price P_i and quantity Q_i (as used here), (2) the average of initial $(P_i + P_f)/2$ and final values $(Q_i + Q_f)/2$,[3] or (3) the final values, P_f and Q_f. This book uses option (1), the initial values of price and quantity, P_i and Q_i. In case the divisor equals zero, which is an undefined fraction, another convention can be used, but must be used for the determination of *both* %ΔP and %ΔQ, not just the term in the undefined fraction.

For small changes between initial and final values, the differences among these three conventions may not be significant. Another formula, the "point elasticity," can yield a more precise value, because it calculates the price elasticity at a specific point on the demand curve. The formula is given by $E_D = (P_a/Q_a)(b)$ where a is a point on the demand curve, with price P_a and quantity Q_a, and b is the inverse of the slope of the demand curve at that point, which is the first derivative (dQ/dP).

Other elasticity formulas will also be presented in this chapter. These same conventions for calculating percentage change will also pertain to them. This book uses the initial values in the divisors, although other conventions are also appropriate.

EXAMPLE   **Public Transit Revenues and Fare Changes**

We know that if price changes, quantity demanded will normally also change. Using what we have learned about elasticities, we can now examine the effect of a price change on total revenue.

A public transit agency increased fares on their commuter train in order to generate additional revenues. They expected a decrease in ridership, due to the fare increase. Yet they hoped that, overall, total revenue would still increase. Did it?

---

[3] This convention is known as the "arc elasticity of demand" formula.

We can arrive at the answer to this problem in two ways: (1) through direct calculation of total revenues, and (2) through our knowledge of elasticities.

Here is the problem information: The original fare was $1.00 per ride. It was increased by 25 cents, to a new fare of $1.25 per ride. The original ridership was 10,000 riders per day Three months after the price increase, the ridership dropped to 8,500 riders per day. One year after the price increase, the ridership was down to 7,000 riders per day.

P_0 = original price = $1.00
P_1 = new price = $1.25
Q_0 = original daily ridership = 10,000
Q_1 = after 3 months, daily ridership = 8,500
Q_2 = after 12 months, daily ridership = 7,000
Total Revenue Calculations

Total revenue (originally) = ($1/ride)(10,000 riders/day) = **$10,000/day**

Total revenue (after 3 months) = ($1.25/ride)(8,500 riders/day) = **$10,625/day** (an increase of $625/day)

Total revenue (after 1 year) = ($1.25/ride)(7,000 riders/day) = **$8,750/day** (a decrease of $1,250/day, compared to original ridership)

Thus, total revenue increased over the first three months, but total revenue decreased over the next nine months and for the first year overall.

Price Elasticity of Demand Calculations

Elasticities from time $T = 0$ to $T = 3$ months:

P_0 = original price = $1.00
P_1 = new price = $1.25
Q_0 = original ridership = 10,000
Q_1 = after 3 months, ridership = 8,500

$E_D = \%\Delta Q / \%\Delta P = (-1,500/10,000) / (\$0.25/\$1.00)$
$= (-0.15)/(0.25) = -0.6$ **Inelastic**

Elasticities from time $T = 0$ to $T = 12$ months:

P_0 = original price = $1.00
P_1 = new price = $1.25

continued on next page

Q_0 = original ridership = 10,000
Q_2 = after 12 months, ridership = 7,000

$E_D = \%\Delta Q / \%\Delta P = (-3,000/10,000) / (\$0.25/\$1.00)$
$= -0.30/0.25 = -1.2$ **Elastic**

As we see here, the price elasticities of demand became more elastic with time. This result is consistent with what might be expected. With greater time periods, people find other ways to get to work, change their travel patterns, or carpool.

A caveat: Elasticities assume that the change in quantity demanded is due to the change in price. Yet other factors can also affect ridership, such as changes in the level of service, or changes in employment and housing patterns.

EXAMPLE   **Setting Admission Prices to Maximize Total Revenue**

You are in charge of setting the admission fee to a park. The elasticity of demand is the same as in Figure 2-12. At which point (A = $4, B = $3, C = $2, D = $1, E = $0) would you set the admission if you wanted to increase total revenues?

Answer: You would set it at point C, equal to $2. This is because, for any price higher than C (i.e., A or B), decreasing the price would increase total revenues, because that part of the demand curve (between A and C) is elastic. For any price lower than C (i.e., D or E), increasing the price would increase total revenues, because that part of the demand curve (between C and E) is inelastic. The process of moving along the demand curve to increase total revenues will converge at point C, which is unitary elastic. Neither raising nor lowering the price would increase total revenues.

Here is another example, which is a favorite among economists: Is it possible that a bumper crop of wheat (an increase in supply) could decrease total revenues for wheat farmers as a whole? Assume that demand for wheat is highly inelastic.

Answer: Yes, it is possible. The increase in supply of wheat would likely decrease the price. For an inelastic good, such as wheat, the decreased price would decrease total revenues. This example assumes, however, that all farmers are in the same market, and that the market price decreases for everyone.

Table 2-2 summarizes what we have learned, and provides a useful reference:

TABLE 2-2	*Relationships Between Price Elasticities of Demand, Price, Quantity, and Total Revenue*		
E_D	Price	Quantity	Total Revenue
inelastic	increase	decrease	increase
inelastic	decrease	increase	decrease
elastic	increase	decrease	decrease
elastic	decrease	increase	increase
unitary	increase	decrease	no change
unitary	decrease	increase	no change

OTHER TYPES OF ELASTICITIES

The price elasticity of demand is probably the most commonly used measure of elasticity. We now examine three other elasticity measures: price elasticity of supply, income elasticity of demand, and cross-price elasticity of demand.

PRICE ELASTICITY OF SUPPLY

Similar to the concept of price elasticity of demand, the **price elasticity of supply** (E_S) measures the percentage change in the quantity supplied of a good divided by the percentage change in price of that good.

$E_S = \%\Delta Q \,/\, \%\Delta P$

where

E_S = price elasticity of supply of a good
$\%\Delta Q = \Delta Q/Q_i$
$\%\Delta P = \Delta P/P_i$
$\Delta Q = Q_f - Q_i$
Q_f = final quantity supplied; after the price change
Q_i = initial quantity supplied; before the price change
$\Delta P = P_f - P_i$
P_f = final price; after the price change
P_i = initial price; before the price change

Putting it all together, we get

$$E_S = \frac{(Q_f - Q_i) / Q_i}{(P_f - P_i) / P_i}$$

Because in most cases of supply, price and quantity are directly (rather than inversely) related, the price elasticity of supply will be positive.

The elasticity formula, E_S, can be interpreted as follows:

Elastic	$E_S > 1$	e.g., 2, 3, 4.5
Inelastic	$E_S < 1$ (but greater than 0)	e.g., 0.2, 0.6, ¾
Unitary elastic	$E_S = 1$	
Perfectly elastic	$E_S =$ undefined (horizontal line)	A horizontal supply curve: a given price a which any quantity will be produced
Perfectly inelastic	$E_S = 0$ (vertical line)	A vertical supply curve: a given quantity that will be supplied regardless of price

FACTORS THAT INFLUENCE THE PRICE ELASTICITY OF SUPPLY

The price elasticity of supply generally becomes more elastic[4] with increases in each of these factors, as described next.

Time Period

For a certain good, the more time that goes by, the greater the price elasticity of supply can be. This is because producers have more time to shift resources, change production methods and facilities, and thus change the amount supplied in response to the price. Thus, for a certain good, the price elasticity of supply is usually more elastic in the long run than in the short run.[5]

---

[4] Here, because the price elasticity of supply is a positive number, "more elastic" will mean a greater positive number, and "less elastic" will mean a smaller positive number.

[5] The meaning of the long run and the short run for production will be examined in Chapter 5.

Ease in Changing Production

The easier it is to change quantities of production, the greater the price elasticity of supply can be. Smaller businesses are often more flexible than larger capital-intensive industries, and thus their products often have a higher price elasticity of supply. Also, if an input to production is in limited supply, then it can be more costly and difficult to obtain that input in order to increase production. As a result, supply will be less elastic.

Examples of goods with *inelastic* E_S include agricultural crops (once they are in the ground, quantity supplied cannot easily be changed) and land (particular lots are fixed in location, and total amount of land cannot easily be changed). Examples of goods with *elastic* E_S are small consumer goods, such as candies, books, textiles, and other products where output can be easily increased (or decreased), relative to increases (or decreases) in price.

INCOME ELASTICITY OF DEMAND

The **income elasticity of demand** is a measure of the responsiveness of quantity demanded to changes in income. It is the percentage change in quantity demanded of a given commodity divided by the percentage change in consumer income:

$E_Y = \%\Delta Q / \%\Delta Y$

E_Y = the income elasticity of demand for the good within the income range defined by Y
$\%\Delta Q$ = the percentage change in the quantity demanded of the good
$\%\Delta Y$ = the percentage change in income
$\%\Delta Q = \Delta Q / Q_i$
$\%\Delta Y = \Delta Y / Y_i$
$\Delta Q = Q_f - Q_i$
$\Delta Y = Y_f - Y_i$
Y_f = final income
Y_i = initial income
Q_f = final quantity demanded, after the income change
Q_i = initial quantity demanded, before the income change

A good is called a **normal good** if the income elasticity of demand is positive. Most goods are normal goods. People will generally buy more of a good as their income increases. Examples of normal goods are real estate, food, new clothing, and computer equipment. A good is called an **inferior good** if the income elasticity of demand is negative. People buy less of these goods as their income increases. Examples are used clothing, generic items, canned meat, and public transit trips.

CROSS-PRICE ELASTICITY OF DEMAND

A **cross-price elasticity of demand** measures how a change in the price of one good affects the quantity demanded of another good. It is defined as the percentage of change in the quantity of demanded of good *a* divided by the percentage change in the price of good *b*:

$E_{ab} = \%\Delta Q_a / \%\Delta P_b$
E_{ab} = cross-price elasticity of demand for good *a* with respect to good *b*
$\%\Delta Q_a$ = the percentage change in the quantity of good *a* consumed when the price of good *b* changes
$\%\Delta P_b$ = the percentage change in the price of good *b*

If the cross-price elasticity of demand is positive, the two goods are **substitutes**. Substitute goods means that the consumer is relatively indifferent between the two. Examples of substitutes would be a cab ride to the airport from company A and a cab ride to the airport from company B. If the rates of company A rise, consumers will purchase more trips from company B, assuming all else equal.

If the cross-price elasticity of demand has a negative sign, the two goods are **complements**. Complementary goods mean that the two goods go together, such as gasoline and cars, or coffee and coffee filters. If the price of coffee goes up, consumers would probably buy fewer coffee filters.

If the cross-price elasticity of demand is zero, or near zero, the two goods are **independent**. That means a price change in one good results in no direct change in the consumption of another good. A change in the price of good *b* (butter) may not noticeably affect at all the consumption of good *a* (airline flights).

EXAMPLE   **Purchases of New Cars and Used Cars**

The price of new cars has risen 10%, affecting demand for used cars. The cross-price elasticity of demand for used cars with respect to the price of new cars is 0.3, suggesting that the two are substitutes. By how much does the quantity demanded for used cars increase?

Answer:

$E_{ab} = \%\Delta Q_a / \%\Delta P_b$ = cross-price elasticity of demand for good *a* with respect to good *b*

Good *a* is used cars. Good *b* is new cars. In this case, the cross-price elasticity of demand = 0.3. The percentage price change in new cars (good *b*) is +10%, which means that $0.3 = \%\Delta Q_a / .10$. So $\%\Delta Q_a = (0.3)(0.1) = 0.03$. Thus, if the price of new cars increases by 10%, the quantity demanded of used cars would increase by 3%, assuming that all other factors are constant.

This chapter equipped us with the tools to analyze changes in demand and supply and their effects on price and quantity. These tools will be among the most useful throughout your study and application of economics. We will now apply them and build upon them with more advanced analyses in the following chapters.

REVIEW QUESTIONS

1. Use supply and demand diagrams to determine the likely immediate effect on either supply or demand (increase or decrease?), on the price of fish (increase or decrease?), and on the quantity supplied/demanded of fish (increase or decrease?). Assume the following are independent events.
    a. The cost of operating fishing boats increases.
    b. Studies indicate that eating fish can reduce the risk of cancer and heart disease.
    c. Other studies indicate that pregnant women and children should reduce their consumption of fish.
    d. More fish hatcheries open up and produce more fish.
    e. The price of beef rises dramatically. (Assume beef and fish are substitutes.)
    f. Polluted waters kill thousands of fish.
    g. New laws significantly limit the amount of fish that can be caught.
2. What immediate short-term effect will each of the following have on the *demand* for good B? That is, will demand increase or decrease?
    a. Product B becomes less popular.
    b. The price of substitute product C falls.
    c. Consumers' incomes decline. (Assume B is a normal good.)
    d. Consumers anticipate that the price of B will be higher in the future.
    e. The price of complementary product D falls.
    f. Taxes are imposed on B.
    g. More consumers enter the market for B.
3. What immediate short-term effect will each of the following have on the *supply* of good B? That is, will supply increase or decrease?
    a. A technological advance makes it less costly to produce B.
    b. A ban is placed on complementary product D.
    c. The price increases for the resources required to produce B.
    d. Producers anticipate an increase in demand for product B.
    e. Taxes are imposed on the sale of B.
    f. A subsidy is given to the producers of B.
    g. More producers enter the market for B.
4. If both supply and demand increase, one can predict the direction of change of quantity, but not of price. If supply increases, but demand decreases, one can predict the direction of change of price, but not of quantity. Explain.
5. Currently, an employer pays for 90% of its workers' health care expenditures. It plans to lower that share to 80%. If the workers' elasticity of demand for health care is -0.2, by how much will the employer's expenditures decrease?

MARKET DYNAMICS AND INTERVENTIONS

Now that we have the tools to understand demand and supply, we can put them together to understand market forces. This chapter examines the dynamics of markets and government actions that create incentives and disincentives for the production or consumption of a good. We will see that market decisions can trigger a complex set of effects that influence the prices and outputs of goods, the decisions of consumers and producers, and even the larger public.

MARKET DEMAND AND MARKET SUPPLY

A market consists of all individuals, organizations, firms, and public agencies that produce or consume a good or service. In the previous chapter, we studied demand curves and supply curves. These curves can represent individual consumers or producers, or they can represent aggregations of all consumers or all producers in a market. The aggregate curves are called the *market demand* and the *market supply*.

The **market demand curve** is the sum of all the individual demand curves for consumers in a market. It shows the relationship between price and quantity demanded of a particular good or service by all consumers participating in that market.

To see the market demand curve algebraically, consider a market that has only two consumers—Consumer A and Consumer B—for a given product. Table 3-1 presents the quantities that these two consumers are willing and able to purchase at various prices. To calculate the market demand, or the total amount that all consumers are willing and able to purchase at a given price, simply sum across the table. Thus, at a price of $2, Consumer A will purchase 15 units, while Consumer B will purchase 6 units. Thus, the total quantity demanded at a price of $2 is 21 units (i.e., $15 + 6 = 21$).

To see the market demand curve graphically, refer to Figure 3-1, which illustrates the data from Table 3-1. Consumer A's demand curve is D_A, and Consumer B's demand curve is D_B. As noted, at a price of $2, the two consumers in this example

TABLE 3-1   *Derivation of the Market Demand Curve from Individual Demand Curves*

Price	Consumer A	Consumer B	Total Quantity Demanded (market demand)
(P)	(Q_A)	(Q_B)	$(Q_T = Q_A + Q_B)$
$8	0.0	0.0	0.0
7	2.5	0.0	2.5
6	5.0	0.0	5.0
5	7.5	0.0	7.5
4	10.0	2.0	12.0
3	12.5	4.0	16.5
2	15.0	6.0	21.0
1	17.5	8.0	25.5
0	20.0	10.0	30.0

demand 15 and 6 units, respectively. The market demand curve, D_M, can be determined by horizontally summing the individual demand curves. The market demand curve, then, is the sum of the quantities demanded by each individual at each price. Confirming the results from Table 3-1, at a price of $2, the total quantity demanded is 21 units (i.e., $15 + 6 = 21$). This result corresponds to the point of $P = \$2$, $Q = 21$ units on the market demand curve, D_M.

Market demand curves, like individual demand curves, generally slope downward and to the right (from northwest to southeast). Changes in any one of the individual demand curves will shift the market (aggregate) demand curve. Figure 3-2 illustrates an increase in the market demand curve, from D_M to D_{M*}, resulting from an increase in Consumer A's demand, from D_A to D_{A*}. This shift would occur, for instance, if Consumer A's real income increased, and if the market good were a normal good. At a price of $2, the quantity demanded by Consumer A increases from 15 to 20 units, the quantity demanded by Consumer B remains the same at 6 units, so the total market quantity demanded increases from 21 to 26 units. This result corresponds to the point of $P = \$2$, $Q = 26$ units on the new market demand curve, D_{M*}.

Now we apply the same techniques to supply. The **market supply curve** is the sum of all of the individual supply curves for producers in a market. It shows the relationship between the price and quantity supplied of a particular good or service by all the producers participating in the market.

The market supply will first be determined algebraically (Table 3-2) and then graphically (Figure 3-3). We will assume that only two producers—Producer A and Producer B—represent the entire market. Table 3-2 shows how the market supply can be determined by adding the quantities produced by these two producers at each possible market price. Thus, at a price of $4, Producer A would produce 4 units, and Producer B would produce 2 units, which results in a total quantity supplied of 6 units.

FIGURE 3-1 *Derivation of a Market Demand Curve*

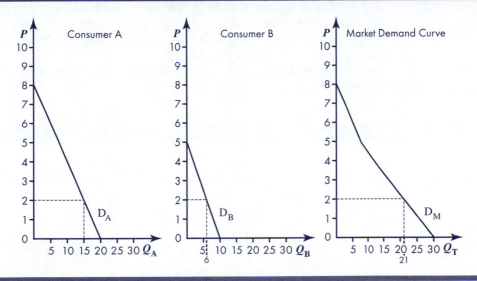

FIGURE 3-2 *Effect of an Increase in Individual Demand on Market Demand*

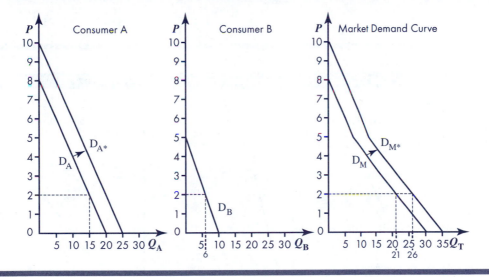

Figure 3-3 shows how the market supply curve can be determined by horizontally summing the supply curves of all the producers, just as the market demand curve was determined. The supply curve for Producer A is S_A, and the supply curve for Producer B is S_B. At a price of \$4, the quantity supplied by Producer A would be 4 units, and the quantity supplied by Producer B would be 2 units. The total quantity supplied is 6 units at a price of $4. The market supply curve, S_M, contains this point: $P = \$4$, $Q = 6$ units. The same calculation can be performed at any price. For instance, at a price of $8, Producer A would supply 8 units, and Producer B would supply 4 units, for a total quantity supplied of 12 units. The market supply curve, S_M, also contains this point: $P = \$8$, $Q = 12$ units.

We have looked at demand and supply individually; we will now put them together to study the market.

TABLE 3-2   *Derivation of the Market Supply Curve from Individual Supply Curves*

Price	Producer A	Producer B	Total Quantity Supplied (market supply)
(P)	(Q_A)	(Q_B)	$(Q_T = Q_A + Q_B)$
$8	8	4	12
7	7	3.5	10.5
6	6	3	9
5	5	2.5	7.5
4	4	2	6
3	3	1.5	4.5
2	2	1	3
1	1	0.5	1.5
0	0	0	0

FIGURE 3-3   *Derivation of a Market Supply Curve*

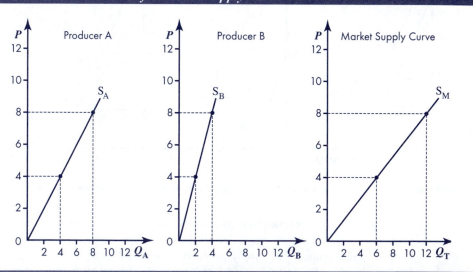

MARKET EQUILIBRIUM AND COMPETITION

In a market economy, demand and supply interact to determine the price of the good and the quantity of the good exchanged. The demand curve indicates what consumers are willing and able to purchase at each price, while the supply curve indicates what producers are willing and able to provide at each price.

Now we will put the two together. Using our previous example, we combine the market demand curve from Figure 3-1 with the market supply curve from Figure 3-3. The intersection at point E, as shown in Figure 3-4, corresponds to a price of $5 and a quantity of 7.5. This is known as the point of equilibrium.

Equilibrium, in economic analysis, is a balancing of forces between supply and demand. The **equilibrium point** (see Figure 3-5 for a general depiction) is the intersection of supply and demand, which represents the **equilibrium price** (P_E) and **equilibrium quantity** (Q_E). It is also the point at which the "market clears." In other words, equilibrium represents a situation in which consumers are willing and able to buy what producers are willing and able to sell, at a mutually acceptable price and quantity. Note, however, that equilibrium does not imply anything about equity. Rather, it simply represents a price and quantity that satisfies both producers and consumers at that time.

The behavior of consumers and producers tends to move a market toward equilibrium. In a **competitive market**, no individual consumer or producer can significantly influence the market price of the good. Further, in a **perfectly competitive market**, three conditions must hold:

FIGURE 3-4   *Market Demand and Market Supply Together*

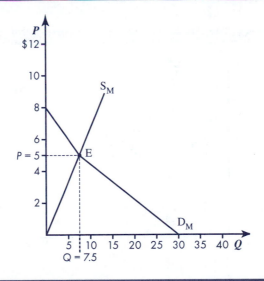

1 *Many consumers and producers.* Numerous buyers and sellers must partici-
pate independently in the market, so that no individual participant can
affect the market price. Instead, each participant in the market must accept
the prevailing market price.

2 *Homogeneous or indistinguishable products.* Consumers must view a good
as essentially the same, regardless of the producer, so they do not have
strong preferences about which producer they buy from. Thus, producers
cannot raise their price without the risk of losing consumer sales.

3 *Easy entrance into and exit from the market.* Both consumers and producers
must be able to enter or leave markets easily, and move resources, so they
can freely buy and sell goods. Consumers can switch from one producer to
another, and producers can seek profitable markets and leave unprofitable
markets.

Markets can exhibit degrees of competition, ranging from perfect competition
to pure monopoly, as we will see in Chapter 8. Even though few markets approach
perfect competition, the competitive model can nonetheless help to understand and
predict market behavior.

To see how market forces will move the price and quantity toward equilibrium,
we will look at cases of shortage and surplus. In Figure 3-5 the market demand curve
and the market supply curve intersected at price P_E, where producers wish to sell Q_E
units and consumers wish to buy Q_E units. This is the point of equilibrium: the price
at which the quantity demanded equals the quantity supplied.

If the price (P_1) is below the equilibrium price P_E (Figure 3-6), the quantity supplied by producers (Q_S) is less than the quantity demanded by consumers (Q_D). This
situation creates a **shortage**. Producers will have incentives to increase price and

---

FIGURE 3-5 *Market Equilibrium*

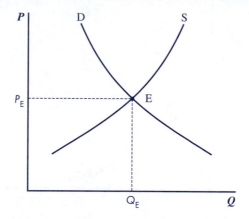

increase production because consumers are willing to pay more, thus bidding up the price. As price rises, consumers will buy less (movement along the demand curve to the northwest) while producers will supply more (movement along the supply curve to the northeast). Equilibrium is regained when, at a given price, the quantity demanded just equals the quantity supplied (point E).

If the price (P_2) is above the equilibrium price P_E (Figure 3-7), the quantity supplied by producers (Q_S) is larger than the quantity demanded by consumers (Q_D). This situation creates a **surplus**. Producers, concerned about the inventory building

FIGURE 3-6   *Shortage: Quantity Demanded Greater Than Quantity Supplied*

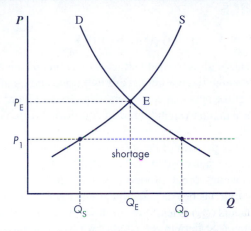

FIGURE 3-7   *Surplus: Quantity Supplied Greater Than Quantity Demanded*

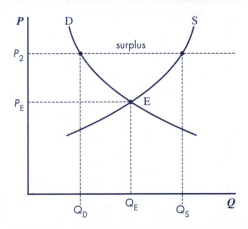

up, could cut prices and even cut production. As price falls, producers would produce less (movement along the supply curve to the southwest). The lower price would encourage consumers to buy more (movement along the demand curve to the southeast). Equilibrium is regained when, at a given price, the quantity demanded just equals the quantity supplied (again, point E).

Note that in these cases, neither the supply curve nor the demand curve shift. The only changes are in price and quantity; all other factors are held constant. Movements remain along the curves themselves. Next we will examine cases in which the curves shift, because some factor other than price changes.

MARKET DYNAMICS

CHANGES IN DEMAND AND SUPPLY

Dynamics deals with forces and effects of change. Changes in demand and supply will usually change the market equilibrium price and quantity. Consider, for example, the market for personal computers, depicted in Figure 3-8. The current equilibrium point is at A, corresponding to an equilibrium price of P_A and an equilibrium quantity of Q_A.

Now assume the cost of labor to produce computers increases, which results in a supply decrease. This is depicted by a shift in the supply curve to the northwest, from S_1 to S_2. At any price, producers will produce less because their costs of production have increased. For instance, at a market price of P_A dollars per unit, producers would supply only Q_F units instead of Q_A units, which is a reduction of $Q_A - Q_F$ units at the price P_A. Viewed another way, to continue producing Q_A units, pro-

FIGURE 3-8 *Change in Equilibrium Due to a Supply Decrease*

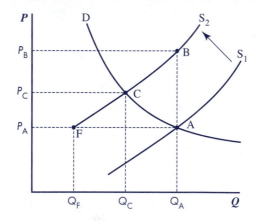

ducers would need to get P_B dollars per unit instead of P_A dollars per unit, or an increase of $P_B - P_A$ dollars per unit for the quantity Q_A.

The final equilibrium point is not at B, but rather where the supply intersects demand, at point C. The new equilibrium price is higher (P_C) and the quantity supplied is less (Q_C) than at the original equilibrium conditions, at point A. Notice that the demand curve did not change, and only the supply curve changed. Consumer purchases simply move along the existing demand curve, to the northwest, in response to a shift in the supply curve. The result is that the decrease in supply increased price and decreased quantity.

Now return to initial conditions (Figure 3-9), with equilibrium at point A. Assume that the real income of consumers increases. Also assume that personal computers are a normal good, so an increase in consumer income will increase demand, as depicted by a shift in the demand curve to the northeast, from D_1 to D_2. At any given price, consumers will now purchase a larger quantity than they did before. For instance, at a market price of P_A dollars per unit, consumers would demand Q_G units instead of Q_A units, which is an increase $Q_G - Q_A$ units at the price P_A. Viewed another way, for Q_A units, consumers would be willing to pay P_H dollars per unit instead of P_A dollars per unit, or an increase of $P_H - P_A$ dollars per unit for the quantity Q_A.

The new equilibrium point is at F, with a higher equilibrium price P_F and a higher quantity Q_F. To meet this increased demand, producers may increase production and move along the supply curve to the northeast, assuming all other factors constant. The increase in demand increased both price and quantity. Remember in this case that only demand changed.

FIGURE 3-9   *Change in Equilibrium Due to a Demand Increase*

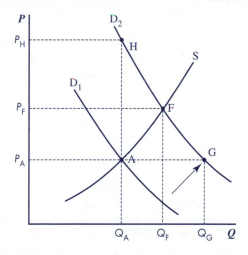

We now extend our analysis to consider cases in which both supply and demand change, and more than once.

MARKET DYNAMICS

For this example, suppose that consumers go to the grocery store to buy fresh produce, and they are faced with two choices: organically grown produce[1] or conventionally grown produce.[2] During the past decade, consumers have increasingly demanded organic over conventional produce, such that organic has become one of the fastest growing segments of U.S. agriculture.[3] What will be the effects of these trends on price and quantity? We can analyze this relationship using supply and demand.

First consider initial conditions for conventional produce.[4] Supply and demand are shown in Figure 3-10, with the equilibrium point at E_1. Assume that demand for conventional produce is decreasing (Figure 3-11), as more consumers choose organic produce. The market demand curve for conventional produce will move to the southwest, from D_1 to D_2. The new equilibrium point becomes E_2, the market price will decrease from P_1 to P_2, and the market quantity will decrease from Q_1 to Q_2.

At that price, P_2, some producers may leave the market for conventional produce, which would cause a decrease in supply (Figure 3-12), depicted by a shift in the market supply curve toward the northwest, from S_1 to S_2. This shift would then lead to a new equilibrium point of E_3, a market price increase from P_2 to P_3, and a market quantity decrease from Q_2 to Q_3.

Acting together, a demand decrease and a supply decrease will decrease the market quantity: Q_3 is less than Q_2, which is less than Q_1. Yet the overall effects on market price, as shown here, are indeterminate, because the demand decrease will decrease price (from P_1 to P_2, as shown in Figure 3-11), but the supply decrease will increase price (from P_2 to P_3, as shown in Figure 3-12). Note that P_3 and P_1 are two distinct prices, and probably not the same.

Now consider the market for organic produce. As seen in Figure 3-13, demand for organically grown produce is increasing, moving the equilibrium point from E_1 to E_2. Market price would increase, from P_1 to P_2, and market quantity would

---

[1] The definition of "organically grown" depends on the certifying organization; it usually means the prohibited use of pesticides, irradiation, sewage sludge, genetic engineering (among other restrictions) in foods marketed as organic. See, for example, the Organic Foods Production Act of 1990, as amended (7 U.S.C. 6501 et seq.), available at http://www.ams.usda.gov/nop/.

[2] "Conventionally grown" implies products that are not grown according to organic standards.

[3] Organic produce sales in the United States were estimated at $3.3 billion in 2000, a 20% increase over 1999 sales. See U.S. Department of Agriculture, Economic Research Service, based on industry sources, available at http://www.ers.usda.gov/briefing/Organic.

[4] This example uses general supply and demand curves; the shape of these curves depends on the good and on market conditions.

increase, from Q_1 to Q_2. More producers then enter this market, increasing supply of organic produce from S_1 to S_2 (Figure 3-14), with a new equilibrium point of E_3. That increased supply would cause a price decrease, from P_2 to P_3, and a market quantity increase, from Q_2 to Q_3.

Acting together, a demand increase and a supply increase will increase the market quantity: Q_3 is greater than Q_2, which is greater than Q_1. The overall effects on market price, as shown here, are indeterminate because the demand increase will increase price (from P_1 to P_2, as shown in Figure 3-13), but the supply increase will

FIGURE 3-10 *Demand for Conventionally Grown Produce*

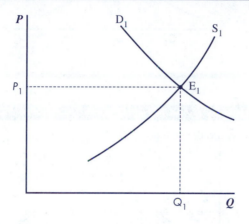

FIGURE 3-11 *Decrease in Demand for Conventionally Grown Produce*

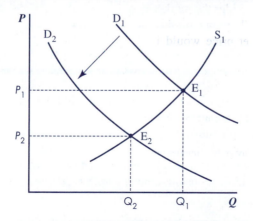

FIGURE 3-12   *Decrease in Supply for Conventionally Grown Produce*

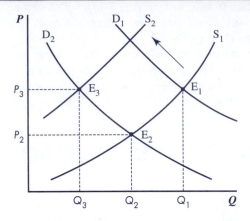

FIGURE 3-13   *Increase in Demand for Organically Grown Produce*

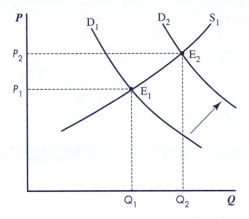

decrease price (from P_2 to P_3, as shown in Figure 3-14). Here again, P_3 and P_1 are two distinct prices, and probably not the same.

This example illustrates a key point: There is rarely just a single effect in a market, and supply and demand change and adjust to a variety of factors.[5] It also illustrates another point: An effect in one market can create effects in other markets. The analysis of interrelationships among markets and cross-price effects is called *general*

[5] We use a simplified example here to track changes in supply and demand, but many other factors can influence the market for produce, such as government subsidies to farmers.

equilibrium analysis. The analysis of a single market is called *partial equilibrium analysis*. Partial equilibrium analysis is usually acceptable in cases where changes in one market do not significantly affect other markets. Both approaches have and can be used to understand equilibrium conditions in a perfectly competitive economy.[6]

Table 3-3 summarizes what we have discussed so far about the relationships among supply, demand, price, and quantity in equilibrium analyses.

FIGURE 3-14 *Increase in Supply for Organically Grown Produce*

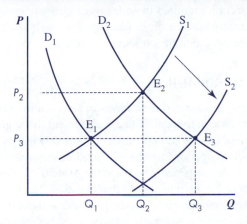

TABLE 3-3 *Effects of Changes in Supply and Demand on Equilibrium Price and Quantity*

Supply	Demand	Equilibrium Price	Equilibrium Quantity
increase	no change	decrease	increase
decrease	no change	increase	decrease
no change	increase	increase	increase
no change	decrease	decrease	decrease
increase	increase	indeterminate	increase
decrease	increase	increase	indeterminate
increase	decrease	decrease	indeterminate
decrease	decrease	indeterminate	decrease

[6] For more extensive treatment of general equilibrium analysis, see for example, K. Arrow and F. Hahn, *General Competitive Analysis* (San Francisco, CA: Holden-Day, 1971); and R. Kunne, *The Theory of General Economic Equilibrium* (Princeton, NJ: Princeton University Press, 1963).

MARKET INTERVENTION

The rationales for government intervention in the market were introduced in Chapter 1, and will be studied closely in the latter chapters of this text. Briefly, two primary reasons for such intervention are to correct market failures and to promote social goals in addition to efficiency, such as equity.

Many forms of market intervention can be classified as a tax or a subsidy on the production or consumption of a product, or a control on the market price or level of output. This section examines these forms of intervention and analyzes their impacts on market participants. Later, in Chapter 7 we will analyze, in greater detail, the effects of these interventions on societal welfare.

TAXES AND SUBSIDIES

Taxes and subsidies are common forms of intervention found at each level of government, from federal to local. A **tax** is a payment to the government on the production or consumption of a good or service. A **subsidy** is a payment by the government for the production or consumption of a good or service.

Who bears the costs and who reaps the benefits of taxes and subsidies? An analysis of incidence can help to answer that question. The **incidence** of a tax or subsidy is the ultimate economic effect on the producer and consumer. For example, a sales tax may be paid to the government by producers, but the actual burden of the tax falls on both producers and consumers. A subsidy may be provided from the government to a consumer, but the actual benefit accrues to both producers and consumers.

As we will see later in this chapter, whether the tax or subsidy is placed on the producer or the consumer, the economic incidence will be the same amount (even though societal effects may differ). Who bears what part of the tax, or who gains what part of the subsidy, depends on the relative price elasticities of supply and demand. Whoever is less elastic—producers or consumers—will have the greater incidence: a greater tax burden or a greater subsidy benefit.

The incidence is calculated as the difference between the final (actual) price and the initial (actual) price. *Actual* refers to the price actually paid out of pocket by the consumer, or the price actually received by the producer, rather than the market price. The incidence is usually given in absolute value terms, even though it can represent a net loss or a net gain.

Incidence of a Tax

Let's consider the case of an excise tax, which is a per-unit tax on a good, such as gasoline, tobacco, or food. Figure 3-15 depicts a good with an equilibrium price of $6 per unit and quantity sold of 40 units, at the initial equilibrium point E_1. Assume that the government imposes an excise tax of $2 per unit, to be paid by the producer. At any given market price, the producer will generate less output, because the pro-

FIGURE 3-15 *Before a Tax*

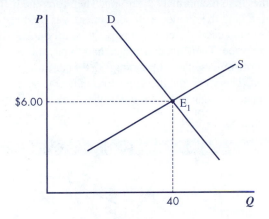

ducer's costs have been increased by $2 per unit of output. Supply will decrease because of the tax. The supply curve will shift to the northwest (Figure 3-16), from S_1 to S_2. How much does the supply curve shift? It moves by a vertical distance equal to the tax. In this case, it shifts by $2, vertically, for each quantity.

At the new equilibrium E_2, the quantity of the good sold has decreased to 25 units and the market price has risen to $7.80. Note that at this new equilibrium, the price to the consumer has risen by $1.80 and the producer's revenue per unit has fallen by $0.20. Even though the producer receives $7.80 per unit, the producer is responsible for paying the $2 per unit tax to the government, which effectively reduces the producer's revenue to $5.80 per unit.

If the $2 tax had been imposed on the consumer rather than on the producer, the economic outcome would have been the same (Figure 3-17). Consumers would demand fewer units at any given market price, because the total per-unit price they would need to pay (market price plus tax) increased. Demand would decrease, and the demand curve would shift to the southwest, from D_1 to D_2. The amount of the shift would be the vertical distance of the tax: $2.

At this new equilibrium, E_3, the quantity of the good sold has decreased to 25 units and the market price has dropped to $5.80. Consumers must pay the $5.80 per unit to the producer, plus another $2 per unit to the government, totaling $7.80 per unit as before. Producers receive as revenue the $5.80 per unit from the consumers, but do not need to pay the tax.

Compare the two cases: The market price is different in each case, but the outcome is the same in terms of costs, revenues, quantity demanded and supplied, and incidences.

In the first case, the producers collected the $7.80 per unit from the consumers, then gave the $2 per unit to the government. The producers ended up receiving only

$5.80 per unit rather than the normal $6 per unit. The consumers had to pay $7.80 per unit rather than the normal $6 per unit. Therefore, the incidence to producers was $0.20 per unit, and the incidence to consumers was $1.80 per unit.

In the second case, the consumers paid the producers $5.80 per unit, according to the market price. Then, the consumers had to pay the government $2 per unit. So, in sum, the consumers ended up paying $7.80 per unit, and the producers received $5.80 per unit. Therefore, the incidence to producers was $0.20 per unit, and the incidence to consumers was $1.80 per unit—the same as in the first case!

FIGURE 3-16   *After a $2 Tax on Producers*

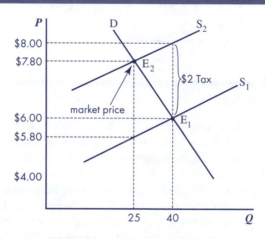

FIGURE 3-17   *After a $2 Tax on Consumers*

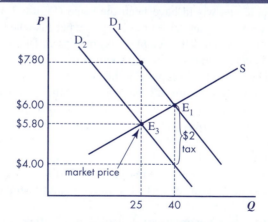

In this example, demand was more price inelastic than supply. So consumers bore more of the incidence of the tax burden ($1.80 versus $0.20). If demand had been more price elastic than supply, more of the $2 tax would have fallen on the producers.

The result: The incidence of a tax falls most heavily on whomever—producers or consumers—is less price elastic. If either the producer or consumer is perfectly inelastic, the entire burden falls on that party. If either the producer or consumer is perfectly elastic, the entire burden is shifted to the other party. The intuitive explanation is that the more elastic, the more choice and ability to change—and to avoid or reduce the tax burden.

Incidence of a Subsidy

A subsidy can be thought of as a "negative tax." Like taxes, the economic impact of a subsidy can be analyzed in terms of shifts in supply and demand. Suppose, using the preceding case, that the government would provide a per-unit subsidy for the production or consumption of the good (Figure 3-18).

First, assume the subsidy is given to the producers (Figure 3-19). Supply would increase, from S_1 to S_2, because for any quantity supplied, producers would be willing to accept a lower price if they are receiving an additional amount of money from the subsidy. The supply curve will shift to the southeast. The amount of the shift is the vertical distance of the subsidy—in this case, $2. The new equilibrium point is E_2. The new market quantity is 55 units, and the new market price is $4.20. Producers receive $4.20 plus $2, for an actual total of $6.20. Consumers pay the market price of $4.20.

Now, assume the subsidy is given to the consumers (Figure 3-20). Demand would increase, from D_1 to D_2, because for any given quantity demanded, consumers

FIGURE 3-18 *Before a Subsidy*

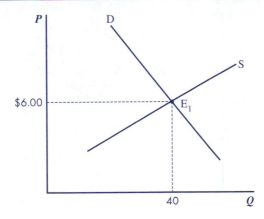

would be willing to pay more because part of their expenditures would be covered by the subsidy. The demand curve will shift to the northeast. The amount of the shift is a vertical distance of $2. The new equilibrium point is E_3. The new market quantity is 55 units, and the new market price is $6.20. Producers receive the market price of $6.20. Consumers pay $6.20, but receive $2 in a subsidy, for an actual cost of $4.20.

In the first case (Figure 3-19), when the subsidy is given to producers, they are willing to accept a lower market price. Before the subsidy, producers received $6.00

FIGURE 3-19 *After a $2 Subsidy to Producers*

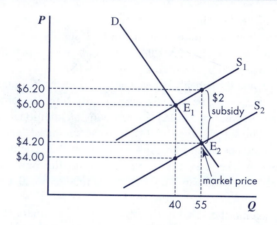

FIGURE 3-20 *After a $2 Subsidy to Consumers*

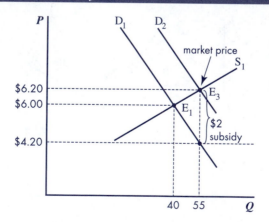

per unit. Now they receive, per unit sold, $4.20 from the consumers and $2 from the government, for a total of $6.20 per unit. Consumers pay $4.20, when they used to pay $6.00. The incidence to producers is $0.20 per unit. The incidence to consumers is $1.80 per unit.

In the second case (Figure 3-20), when the subsidy is given to consumers, they pay a higher market price, $6.20, but actually only have to pay $4.20 out of pocket because the government provides $2 per unit to consumers. The producers receive the total $6.20 from the consumers. The incidence to producers is $0.20 per unit. The incidence to consumers is $1.80 per unit—the same as in the first case!

In this example, consumers were less price elastic than producers, so the consumers received a greater incidence (benefits) of the subsidy: $1.80 versus $0.20.

Important points to note about taxes and subsidies include the following:

Whether the tax or subsidy is given to the producer or consumer, the incidence would be the same amount, according to economic analysis, yet societal implications can differ. For instance, consider the need for low-income housing, and the question of whether to provide a subsidy to low-income housing producers or provide a subsidy to low-income households (consumers). In the first case, giving it to the producers, the subsidy could encourage new additions to housing stock, if it were of sufficient size to bridge the gap between what the target population could afford and the cost of new construction. Also, this subsidy program would require careful, prolonged oversight and administration to make sure the new units serve the populations they are designed to assist.

In the second case, giving it to consumers, the subsidy (such as a voucher) would allow consumers to purchase housing that ordinarily may not have been affordable. However, a consumer subsidy program would not necessarily provide new additions to housing stock. The subsidy may not sufficiently increase the price in order to provide incentives for producers to increase the quantity or quality of housing stock. In addition, this consumer subsidy program could be eliminated, by the stroke of a political pen, after a few years, whereas the producer subsidy program could provide longer-term results (the construction of housing units). Low-income housing advocates often recommend producer subsidies, administered by third-party independents or housing authorities, to reduce the possibility of misuse of funds and to promote the construction, maintenance, accessibility, and preservation of affordable units.

Providing a subsidy or imposing a tax will affect the market price of a good, which affects all consumers and all producers. But not all consumers or producers will gain or lose equally. With any form of intervention, the affected public should be disaggregated into groups to determine the relative benefits and costs to each group. (The techniques for this type of analysis will be covered in Chapters 4 and 7.)

To illustrate, consider a government food subsidy program, targeted to producers, yet designed to assist low-income households. The producer subsidy will lower prices to consumers of all income groups. The primary beneficiaries of this program may be middle- and upper-income households, even though low-income households benefit, but proportionally not as much. This result can occur for several reasons, one of which is that low-income households, as a group, often spend less (total) on food than other income groups.

Similarly, taxes can affect different income groups differently. The terminology is that taxes can be "progressive," "regressive," or "proportional." A tax rate is progressive if it increases as income increases; that is, high-income taxpayers would pay a higher percentage of their income than low-income taxpayers. A tax rate is regressive if it decreases as income increases; that is, high-income taxpayers would pay a smaller percentage of their income than low-income taxpayers. A tax rate is proportional if it is equal for all income levels; that is, high-income and low-income people would pay the same percentage of their income. The tax rate can be the average tax rate (total tax payments divided by income) or the marginal tax rate (the incremental tax on an additional unit of income). We will study the efficiency and equity of taxes in Chapter 7.

PRICE AND OUTPUT CONTROLS

Whereas taxes and subsidies affect the market price and the quantity of a good indirectly through changes in demand and supply, other interventions affect price and quantity directly: price ceilings, price floors, and quotas.

Price floors establish a minimum price at which a good may be sold. Examples are the minimum wage and price supports for agricultural products. **Price ceilings** set a maximum price at which a good may be sold. Examples of price ceilings are rent control, credit card interest-rate ceilings, and World War II price controls on butter. **Output quotas** restrict the quantity that can be brought to market. Examples are restrictions on drugs and foreign imports. The terminology here is counterintuitive. Price ceilings are set *below* the equilibrium price, and price floors are set *above* the equilibrium price. We will examine these concepts graphically.

Price floor (Figure 3-21): Assume a market equilibrium price of P_E and a price floor of P_F is set. The new equilibrium point is E*, the new equilibrium price is P_F, and the new equilibrium quantity is Q_D. Thus, if P_F exceeds the equilibrium price, surpluses will develop because the quantity supplied (Q_S) exceeds the quantity demanded (Q_D) at the controlled price. The actual amount exchanged is the lesser of the two quantities, which would be Q_D.

Price ceiling (Figure 3-22): Now assume a market equilibrium price of P_E and a price ceiling of P_C is set. The new equilibrium point is E*, the new equilibrium price is P_C, and the new equilibrium quantity is Q_S. Thus, if P_C is less than the equilibrium price, shortages will develop because the quantity demanded (Q_D) exceeds the quantity supplied (Q_S) at the controlled price. The actual amount exchanged is the lesser of the two quantities, which would be Q_S.

Output quotas (Figure 3-23): An output quota Q_O is imposed that is less than the equilibrium output Q_E. At this lesser quantity, Q_O, the price that consumers are willing to pay, P_D, is greater than the price that producers would need P_S. Consumers will bid the price up to P_D, and producers enjoy windfall profits, which is the difference between P_D and P_S for the quantity Q_O. Thus, the actual price charged for the amount Q_O would likely be the greater of the two amounts, which would be P_D.

A few more points are important to mention. Market intervention rarely causes only one direct effect. A number of indirect effects can also result. Some examples of price and output controls illustrate these interrelationships. Also, in these cases, the new "equilibrium" prices and quantities occur because of the intervention, rather than because of entirely free market forces.

FIGURE 3-21   *Price Floor*

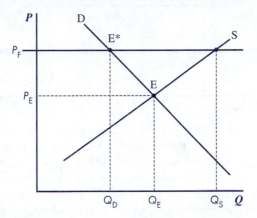

FIGURE 3-22   *Price Ceiling*

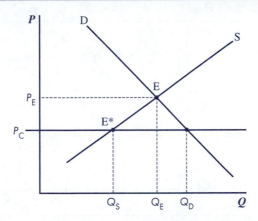

FIGURE 3-23 *Output Quota*

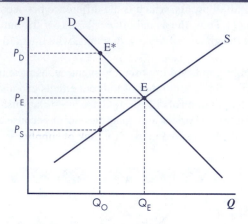

EXAMPLE

Rent Control

An example of a price ceiling is rent control, which establishes maximum prices on rental units. Refer to Figure 3-24. Assume that, for a block of apartments, the unregulated market rent is $1,000 per month. After rent control, the maximum rent is $500 per month. The analysis in Figure 3-24 shows that, at rent-controlled prices, not all consumers can find rent-controlled apartments. Shortages develop because quantity demanded (Q_D) is greater than quantity supplied (Q_S). This shortage can lead to other effects. Non-price rationing can occur, which means that people obtain units by luck, persistence, or prior arrangements. Black markets can also emerge. Units that typically go for

FIGURE 3-24 *Rent Control*

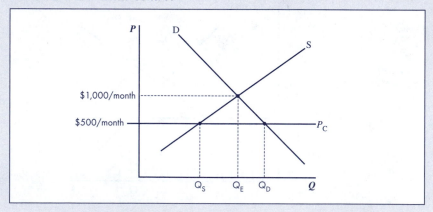

$1,000 per month are now only $500 per month under rent control. So the black market might offer that unit for $800 per month, and both seller and buyer would be money ahead. Also, because owners may have little financial incentive to maintain the units, the quality of controlled units may deteriorate. In fact, owners may try to get out from under rent control by converting them to condominiums. Rent control may also lead to a reduction in the market value of the properties, and a redistribution of property tax revenues. In the long run, rent control can lead to decreased construction of new units, thus increasing problems associated with lack of supply.

EXAMPLE   **Agricultural Price Supports**

A price floor can be exemplified by price supports for agricultural products, which establish minimum prices on products. The analysis in Figure 3-25 shows that, at controlled prices (P_F), producers can be left with surpluses: Quantity supplied is greater than quantity demanded. These surpluses can be managed in several ways. First, supply can be reduced; for instance, by limiting the number of acres that farmers can plant, and limiting other inputs to production. Second, government can purchase the surplus goods and hold them in stock, sell them abroad, donate them, or destroy them. Third, demand can be increased, for instance, by developing new uses or new markets for the product. Fourth, output can be restricted, for instance, at a level Q_D, but that approach could result in windfall profits to producers.

The effects of price supports and output quotas (import restrictions) can be illustrated by the market for sugar in the United States. Although farmers

continued on next page

FIGURE 3-25   *Agricultural Price Supports*

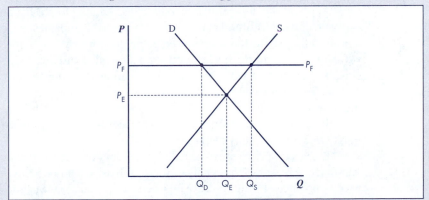

gain from price supports, U.S. consumers pay a higher price (P_F) that is almost double the world price. Further, the price effects are regressive, meaning that lower-income households spend a larger percentage of their income on sugar than higher-income households. Production can create social costs, such as water contamination from fertilizers and pesticides, and ecosystem degradation. Finally, price supports may lead to an overallocation of resources to sugar production, above what would be generated by a free market.

These examples illustrate why the use of market interventions requires a careful analysis of both direct and indirect effects of the policy. Governments often institute price and quantity controls on equity or efficiency grounds, but the initial intent needs to be justified in light of the subsequent impacts. We now look at an example of the proposed use of a government intervention to alleviate shortages, and differing perspectives on the effects. At the end of the example, you will be asked to analyze the different perspectives using supply and demand analysis.

EXAMPLE   **The Electricity Crisis in California**

"Severe shortages have led to rolling blackouts and soaring prices, with wholesale prices rising about 700 percent in a year, jolting the state's economy. . . . Gov. Davis [of California] lobbied hard for federal regulators to impose a price cap on power companies—a maximum price that wholesalers would be permitted to charge.

"The president [George W. Bush] dismissed the governor's demand, offering an economics lecture instead. 'I oppose price caps,' he explained, because, 'price caps do nothing to reduce demand and they do nothing to increase supply.' That's a pretty sound argument, based on Economics 101. If price caps don't increase supply, they cannot relieve shortages.

"Applied to a competitive market, caps threaten to reduce output—the opposite of what California needs—by driving out companies that can't make a profit selling at the lower prices set by the government.

"Yet while Mr. Bush's lecture would sit well in most introductory Econ classes, it did not sit well with some of the nation's leading authorities on regulation. Ten prominent economists have sent a letter to the president calling for the federal government to clamp down on wholesale energy prices. Nostrums suitable to the textbook world of perfect competition, they argue, do not fit the messy facts of electricity markets.

"Electricity prices skyrocketed in California in part for standard supply-and-demand reasons. The supply of power fell as rising prices for natural gas, used to produce electricity, drove up its cost of production. Supplies dwindled further as power companies in neighboring states exported less electricity to

California. And demand rose swiftly along with the increasing use of computers and other electricity-guzzling hardware.

"In truly competitive markets, attempts to withhold supply to raise prices are fruitless. If Farmer Brown withholds her 10 bushels of corn from a market of billions of bushels, corn prices would not rise one cent. But the market for electricity, California style, is different. . . . By withholding electricity at the price offered in the morning of a typical day, the power companies can count on the officials to come back later in the day and plead for power at a substantially higher price.

"If the 10 economists are right . . . price caps, they say, can indeed increase supply. Once they are in place, prices can no longer rise. So power companies would have nothing to gain by withholding supply. They would sell more electricity, easing the shortage. The economists warn against setting price caps so low that power companies quit the industry. Instead, they call for setting caps somewhat above the actual costs of production—which would allow companies to make a profit.

"The economists don't advise adopting price caps indefinitely. Left in place, the controls would discourage investors from building new power plants—which, along with fixing perverse incentives under deregulation, is the best near-term solution to California's energy crisis. Fortunately, price caps won't be needed very long because enough power plants are under construction to ease the shortage in 18 months or so. Then, the lessons of Econ 101 might start making sense again."

Source: Excerpts taken from Michael M. Weinstein, "Econ 101: It's Right and It's Wrong," *New York Times*, June 3, 2001.

Questions

Analyze the following economic arguments in this example, using supply and demand curves.

(a) As stated in the second paragraph, "price caps do nothing to reduce demand and they do nothing to increase supply." (A price cap is a price ceiling.)

(b) As stated above, supply of electricity decreased (due to increased costs of production, and then to decreased imports from neighboring states), and then demand for electricity increased (due to increased use of computers and other hardware). What happens to equilibrium prices during these changes, assuming no price caps?

(c) A price cap, combined with increased supply, can help to alleviate the electricity shortage. What else would alleviate the shortage?

continued on next page

Answers

Refer to Figure 3-26, which provides simplified diagrams.
- (a) With a price cap, neither demand nor supply changes, and the shortage persists.
- (b) Without a price cap, price continues to increase with a supply decrease and a demand increase.
- (c) With a price cap and an increase in supply, equilibrium quantity increases and the shortage is reduced. The shortage could also be reduced through a decrease in demand, such as through energy conservation.

FIGURE 3-26 *Supply and Demand with a Price Cap on Electricity*

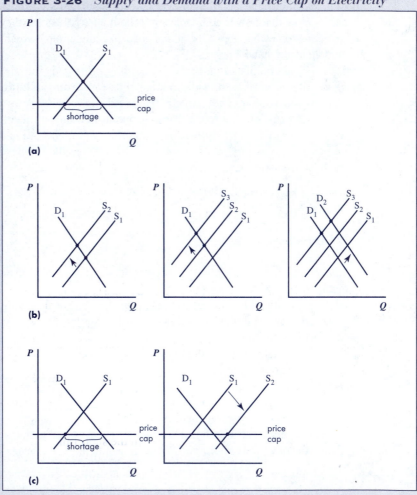

REVIEW QUESTIONS

1. You are the head of a university housing agency, and you want to determine the likely effects in the short run on the equilibrium price and quantity of apartment rentals near a university after each of the following changes. Assume that these apartment rentals are normal goods.

    To answer these questions, first draw supply and demand curves. Then determine which curve(s) change, and in which direction. Then determine the effects—on both price and quantity: Increase? Decrease? Indeterminate?
    a. A price ceiling on apartments is set at $500 per month.
    b. A price floor is placed on construction workers' wages, which raises the costs of construction, and affects apartment construction near the university.
    c. Students realize they don't like living in the university apartments because they are located right next to a freeway, so they start to look for apartments in other parts of town.
    d. The newspapers report that crime rates have decreased around the university.
    e. The university constructs more university apartments *and* the university's student enrollment increases.
    f. Students see the quality and maintenance of university apartments deteriorating *and* a new construction technique allows new university apartments to be built at less cost.
    g. Apartments around the university are being torn down and replaced by retail shops *and* tuition rises, so that fewer students are able to afford living in apartments by the university.
    h. More students want to live in apartments near the university *and* the apartments near the university are being converted into retail outlets.
2. Senator DoRight is upset with the economist testifying before the Senate committee: "You just testified that rent control lowers the equilibrium level of housing. Last week you testified that the minimum wage lowers the equilibrium level of employment. It can't be the case that a price ceiling and a price floor have the same effect on quantity. Which week were you lying?" Explain this seeming inconsistency in the economist's testimony.
3. An urban revitalization program for a downtown district recently began to show some success, as many of the older buildings in the area are being rehabilitated. Some of the structures are being converted from single-family homes into apartments and retail outlets. The redevelopment agency would like to preserve the single-family character of the area and has asked the Planning Board to rezone the district for only single-family use.
    a. What would be the likely effect, in the short run, of the proposed rezoning on the equilibrium price of existing apartments in the area?
    b. Some owners of single-family homes in the area assert that the value of their properties will fall unless the rezoning occurs. Is their assertion correct?

4. A state government proposed a 20-cent per gallon tax on milk to consumers, in order to raise revenues and maintain profitability for dairy farmers. Discuss some of the implications of the proposed tax.

5. Under what conditions will consumers bear the entire burden of an excise tax? Under what conditions will producers bear the entire burden of an excise tax?

4

CHOICE AND DEMAND

Economics studies choices. Consumers are continually faced with choices to make about purchases, given their preferences and budget constraints. Governments must also make choices about which goods and services to provide to their constituents. In any decision, the choice of one alternative over another implies that one is preferred, based on criteria of the decision maker. For instance, individuals may seek to maximize their family's well-being or satisfaction. Private firms try to produce goods in ways that will maximize their profit. Government officials may have more complicated sets of criteria, in order to reconcile multiple needs and objectives of the public. This chapter examines the basis of choice and its relationship to consumer demand.

THE CONCEPT OF UTILITY

In economics, **utility** refers to the satisfaction or pleasure derived from consumption, and it is a fundamental concept for studying demand and consumer choice. Economics assumes that consumers seek to maximize their utility. Economics also assumes consumers are **rational**, meaning that consumers will use their money to buy the collection of goods and services that will lead them to the highest possible level of satisfaction.[1]

Utility has its roots in the work of the English philosopher Jeremy Bentham (1748–1832) who defined utility as "that property in any object, whereby it tends to produce benefit, advantage, pleasure, good, or happiness" or "to prevent the happening of mischief, pain, evil, or unhappiness."[2] Bentham proposed that society should be designed to promote the "greatest happiness of the greatest number." One concern

---

[1] This assumption allows that consumers can also derive utility by not spending money or by donating it to charity, for instance.

[2] Bentham, Jeremy. 1781. *Introduction to the Principles of Morals and Legislation*.

is that, by focusing on the sum of individual utilities, it overlooks the distribution of utility among individuals. (We will explore this and other considerations of utility later in the chapter.) Utility was further developed by economists such as William Stanley Jevons (1835–1882), Léon Walras (1834–1910), and Carl Menger (1840–1921) to help explain consumer behavior, showing that consumers would make decisions based on the marginal utility of each good.

Marginal utility is the additional amount of satisfaction that an individual derives from consuming an additional unit of a good, holding consumption levels of all other goods constant. For instance, as we saw in Chapter 2, the downward sloping demand curve illustrates diminishing marginal utility, or decreasing amounts of satisfaction with each additional unit consumed. Marginal utility needs to be distinguished from total utility. **Total utility** is the total amount of satisfaction derived from consuming a certain quantity, whereas marginal utility is the incremental amount of satisfaction derived from consuming just one additional unit.

One approach to studying consumer choice is to employ the utility-maximizing rule: To maximize satisfaction, consumers should allocate their monetary expenditures so that the last dollar on each product yields the same amount of marginal utility.[3] To illustrate this principle, suppose that a consumer can choose between two goods, park visits or pool visits, and that the consumer has $6 to spend. Assume that, at this point, the park visit would yield 20 *utils* (units of utility) and cost $5, and the pool visit would yield 15 utils and cost $3. The marginal utility of the park visit is 4 utils per dollar (20 utils/$5), and the marginal utility of the pool visit is 5 utils per dollar (15/$3). Thus, the rational consumer would choose the pool visit, because it provides greater marginal utility for each dollar at this point. But what happens with increasing consumption of a good? Marginal utility declines. If the price stays the same, so would marginal utility per dollar. Suppose that the next pool visit would yield only 12 utils, which would be 4 utils per dollar (12/$3). At that point, the marginal utility of pool visits is the same as park visits, and the consumer's budget ($6) is spent. So the utility-maximizing rule says that this consumer reached an equilibrium point: The consumer would purchase levels of goods so that each one provides the same amount of marginal utility per dollar, when a consumer's income is completely allocated.

This approach, however, suggests that utility can be used as a *cardinal measure*: that consumer satisfaction can be quantified. Yet many economists argue that utility should be used as an *ordinal measure*: that consumer satisfaction can be rank-ordered but not quantified directly. In other words, economics can indicate which choices provide a consumer more utility or less utility (ordinal measures), but that economics cannot necessarily quantify *how much* more or less utility, or *how much* total utility (cardinal measures). Thus, rather than attempt to place an absolute number on utility, economists generally prefer to use utility to discuss relative preferences for goods or collections of goods.

---

[3] This principle will be proven in the appendix to Chapter 4.

Moreover, many economists argue that *interpersonal comparisons* of utility cannot be performed in a scientifically valid way; we cannot compare utility among individuals. Even if we could measure utility cardinally—for instance, that a pool visit would provide 15 utils to you and 15 utils to your friend—it would be difficult to decide whose "15 utils" provided more individual happiness. Similarly, we would have difficulties determining whether 15 utils to your friend provided more happiness than 10 utils to you. Thus, the quantification of a util is not only difficult, but also not strictly comparable or constant among all consumers.

The same challenge arises not only with goods and services, but also with the utility of income. For instance, a $100 per week raise would probably increase utility for both you and your friend. But it would be difficult to determine whose utility increased more from the $100 raise, and by how much more. In other words, individuals have different **marginal utilities of income**. For example, an additional dollar to a poor individual may provide greater utility than an additional dollar to a wealthy individual.

In addition, and related to this previous discussion, it has been argued that *social aggregations* of utility cannot be performed in a scientifically valid way; that is, we cannot add up individual utilities to obtain a measure of social utility. The aggregation would assume that individuals' utilities could be combined mathematically and according to a consistent scale. Although we could say that certain decisions would increase utility for some individuals and decrease utility for other individuals, it may not be possible to quantify the gains and the losses in utility among individuals, or to derive a single utility function that aggregates the utilities of individuals.

A numerical approach does exist, however, for studying demand and choices and is examined in the next section. This approach has been widely used in assessments of costs and benefits, and although it has limitations as well, it can nonetheless help to determine the implications of different choices.

WILLINGNESS TO PAY

Another important concept for studying demand and choice is consumers' willingness to pay. **Willingness to pay (WTP)** is a measure of how consumers evaluate the worth of various goods and services. It uses the monetary amount that an individual is willing and able to pay for a good as a measure of that good's value to the individual. The concept is straightforward: Willingness to pay assumes that if an individual is willing to pay more for good X than for good Y, then good Y provides more value to the individual.

Suppose, as in our previous example, that a city offers two main recreational opportunities: a park and a pool. If Peter likes going to the park more than the pool, he would be willing to pay more for a park visit than a pool visit, all other factors equal. (Willingness to pay, in this example, would include not only the admission fee, but also the costs of travel and other expenses related to the visit.) The WTP criterion would say that Peter places a higher value on the park visit than the pool visit.

Willingness to pay also has a direct relationship to demand. As we studied in Chapter 2, the demand curve represents the quantities that consumers would be willing to purchase at each price. The area under the demand curve would be the total WTP of consumers up to a given quantity of a good. In Figure 4-1 the total WTP for a quantity Q_1 is shown by the areas $A + B$. The total cost to consumers, or what they have to pay for quantity Q_1 at a price of P_1, is shown by the area B.

Note that a consumer's willingness to pay is not the same as what they actually have to pay. The difference between value (as measured by WTP) and cost to consumer (based on price) is the *consumer surplus*. The consumer surplus would be the area A, which is the difference between total value or WTP (areas $A + B$) minus total cost (area B).

Consumer surplus will be detailed later in this chapter, but consider a simple example for now. The entrance fee to a park is $2 per person. Peter pays that $2 fee, and so does Lars. But perhaps Peter would be willing to pay $3, and Lars would be willing to pay $4. In both cases, the value to the consumer, based on WTP, is greater than the cost to the consumer, and this difference is consumer surplus. The amount of the consumer surplus for that one park visit would be $1 for Peter and $2 for Lars. This consumer surplus does not necessarily mean, however, that the park visit provides less utility to Peter than to Lars, as we will see later.

This study of willingness to pay leads to the question: How appropriate is WTP as a measure of value? No doubt, WTP has quantitative appeal. It can provide a measure of individual value in terms of a monetary amount. Those monetary amounts could be aggregated among individuals to come up with a measure of overall societal value. This technique, however, presents theoretical and methodological challenges that have been widely discussed and debated. We examine some of them here, and some in Chapters 7 and 9.

FIGURE 4-1   *Consumer Surplus (A)*

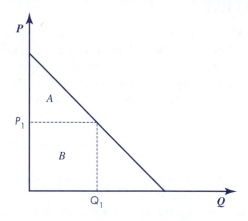

First, WTP depends on the distribution of wealth in society. Understandably, an individual's wealth can influence willingness to pay to obtain a desired good. For instance, a wealthy individual would likely be willing and able to pay more for a desired good than a poor individual. Thus, assessments of social benefits and social costs, based on WTP, can be heavily influenced by the distributions of wealth. Different distributions of income could then lead to different assessments of WTP for goods, and possibly different decisions and policy outcomes.

Second, WTP as a measure of value may obscure that individuals have different marginal utilities of income. For instance, suppose that two consumers, Sara and Elisabeth, are both willing to pay $4 for a park visit. Sara is much wealthier than Elisabeth. So the expression of WTP may correspond to different levels of utility: The $4 park visit may provide more utility to Elisabeth, who has less income and would be willing to give up relatively more in order to go to the park, than to Sara. Similarly, from the earlier example, the park visit may even provide more utility to Peter (who was willing to pay $3) than to Lars (who was willing to pay $4).

Third, from a policy perspective, the use of WTP to measure benefits and costs can create distributional concerns. Suppose that a proposed project would give $500 of benefits to a wealthy individual and impose $400 of costs on a poor individual. On the surface, it would appear that the benefits outweigh the costs, as measured by WTP. Yet total utility could decrease if the utility gain (to the wealthy person) from $500 was less than the utility loss (to the poor person) from the $400 cost. These issues of efficiency and equity will be examined further in Chapter 7.

Fourth, WTP assumes ability to pay. So expressions of WTP may be incomplete measures of how individuals evaluate the worth of a good. Suppose that both Elsa and Ann need a surgical operation. Elsa requires it to save her life, but for Ann, it is optional. Elsa is not able to pay for the full cost of the operation, but Ann is able to pay the full cost. Thus, Elsa does not obtain the surgery, but Ann does. Does that outcome mean that the operation would provide less value to Elsa than to Ann, because Elsa's WTP is less than Ann's WTP? Not necessarily. The problem illustrated here is that expressions of WTP could fail to account for the full value that individuals would derive from a good, just because they were not able to pay the full price of the good.

Fifth, methodological challenges can arise in the measurement of WTP.[4] One common method is the use of surveys. Yet surveys can be subject to bias. For instance, because the question of "how much would you be willing to pay?" is typically hypothetical, respondents may misstate the actual amount they would be willing to pay. Even if respondents were told they needed to pay the amount stated, they may understate their contribution if they believed the good would be provided regardless of their individual payment. In addition, the measurement of WTP assumes that consumer preferences are given and stable for the period of analysis. Yet consumer preferences can be variable and context-dependent. The respondent may have inadequate infor-

---

[4] Several methods exist to determine WTP, and we will examine these methods in Chapter 9.

mation about the good being valued, and new information could alter their valuation. Survey design can also affect responses: The format and order of the survey questions, the response categories, and whether the respondent has other goods to value can influence the respondent's stated value of a particular good.

WILLINGNESS TO PAY AND CONSUMER SURPLUS

The individual demand curve provides information about one consumer's willingness to pay for goods and services, and that consumer's responsiveness to price changes. To see this relationship graphically, look at Figure 4-2. A consumer would be willing to pay $5.00 for the first park visit during a year (remember that demand and supply curves are always subject to associated time periods), $4.50 for the second, $4.00 for the third, $3.50 for the fourth, $3.00 for the fifth, $2.50 for the sixth, $2.00 for the seventh, and so on. This decline in WTP illustrates diminishing marginal utility: As more of a good is consumed, its marginal utility declines. Each additional unit provides less value to the consumer, which helps to explain the downward-sloping characteristic of the demand curve.

As we saw in Figure 4-1, a difference is notable between the amount that a consumer is willing to pay and the price the consumer actually paid. This difference is the **consumer surplus**. It is the extra benefit to the consumer: the total value to the consumer minus the total cost to the consumer. It accrues because consumers often pay the same price for all units, which is the price of the last unit consumed, even though earlier units are worth more to the consumer than the last unit (assuming diminishing marginal utility). Thus, consumers enjoy a surplus of benefits on those earlier units.

FIGURE 4-2   *Willingness to Pay for Park Visits*

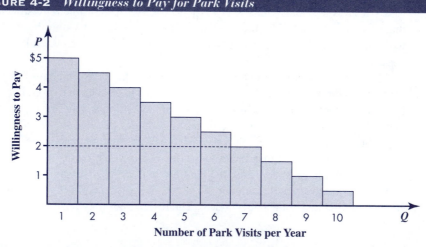

Refer again to Figure 4-2. If the entrance fee for each park visit is $2, the consumer would make seven park visits a year. The total value of the benefits received by this consumer exceeds what the consumer actually pays, $14 (7 visits times $2 each visit), because the consumer is willing to pay more than $2 for each of the first six park visits. Measured by willingness to pay, this consumer would receive $24.50 worth of benefits from seven park visits ($5.00 + $4.50 + $4.00 + $3.50 + $3.00 + $2.50 + $2.00). The consumer surplus would be the consumer's net benefits, which is the consumer's WTP minus the amount paid for each visit. For seven park visits this would be $10.50 ($3.00 + $2.50 + $2.00 + $1.50 + $1.00 + $0.50).

Now refer to Figure 4-3, which represents the demand curve for an individual consumer for park visits, based on the WTP information in Figure 4-2.[5] The area ACED under the demand curve (Figure 4-3) is the measure of the total benefits ($24.50) of seven visits per year. This amount ($24.50) also represents a consumer's willingness to pay for those seven visits. Of these total benefits, area BCED ($14) is actually paid in park entrance fees. Area BCED represents total costs to consumers, because this area equals BC (price paid) times CE (number of park visits consumed).

FIGURE 4-3 *Demand Curve for Park Visits*

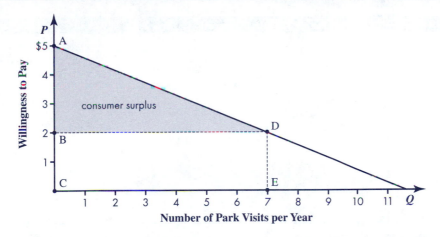

---

[5] The demand curve in Figure 4-3 results from a smoothing of the WTP information in Figure 4-2. Economics texts commonly present demand curves that are smoothed, rather than stepped. Smoothing assists in the calculation of benefits, and is assumed to provide a reasonable approximation to the stepped WTP information.

Area ABD ($10.50) is consumer surplus, or net benefits. It is the difference between total benefits ($24.50) and total costs ($14) to consumers. It is also the area between the demand curve and the price,[6] ABD, or $10.50.

Using the demand curve to assess consumer benefits is simply a reverse reading of the demand curve. Because a demand curve shows the quantity demanded for each price, it can also show the price consumers are willing to pay for each quantity.

What if the price changes? Figure 4-4 illustrates the effect of a change in price on consumer benefits and consumer surplus. At this lower price, total benefits would be area ACHG, and the amount paid in entrance fees would be area FCHG. The shaded area BFGD is the *change in consumer surplus* resulting from the change in price. This addition to consumer surplus has two components: area BFID, representing consumer surplus gained from a lower price for each of the first seven visits, and area DIG, representing the additional consumer surplus gained from the additional park visits the consumer now makes because of the lower price. The new total consumer surplus is area AFG, which is equal to area ABD (original consumer surplus) plus area BFGD (the change in consumer surplus). In general, as price decreases, total consumption and total benefits increase, as does the consumer surplus. An increase in price will generally result in less consumption, lower benefits, and a smaller consumer surplus.

FIGURE 4-4 *Effect of a Price Change*

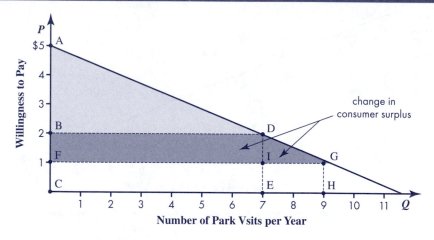

---

[6] The area between the demand curve and the price represents a *positive* consumer surplus when the demand curve is above the price, and a *negative* consumer surplus when the demand curve is below the price. Positive means net gains to consumers, and negative means net losses to consumers.

CONSUMER SURPLUS AND DISTRIBUTION OF BENEFITS

The concepts of utility, willingness to pay, and consumer surplus are useful for understanding and assessing consumer benefits. We already examined some strengths and limitations of utility and willingness to pay. Now we examine consumer surplus.

EXAMPLE

Distribution of Benefits for Health Care Visits

Consider a health clinic in a low-income area. Clinic costs are partially covered by the government so that each patient pays $5 per visit. As shown in Figure 4-5(a), at a fee of $5, neighborhood residents make 300 visits to the clinic each month. If $25 (the actual cost of a visit) were charged, only 100 visits would be made each month by neighborhood residents.

A second group of patients also uses the clinic: students living nearby. The clinic happens to border a large university. At the $5 fee, as shown in Figure 4-5(b), students make 300 visits per month. At the $25 fee, no student visits would be made. Students might not be willing to pay the higher fee because they have other options, such as visiting the university's student health clinic or visiting the family doctor when they go home on vacations.

The shaded areas in Figure 4-5 show the consumer surplus of each group using the clinic, at the $5 fee. Are these surpluses comparable in terms of the well-being they provide to each group of consumers? In this case, it could be inappropriate to make direct comparisons. The low-income group might need to forego basic necessities to receive medical care and may have no low-cost alternative to the clinic. Yet the students may not need to sacrifice those essentials and might also have a ready alternative on campus or at home.

FIGURE 4-5 *Comparison of Consumer Surplus*

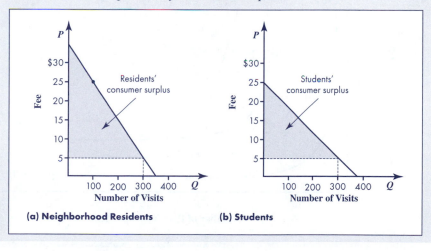

(a) Neighborhood Residents   (b) Students

Willingness to pay provides one method for evaluating the worth of a good or service. However, the willingness to pay of one group is often not strictly comparable to that of another. In such cases, disaggregating the groups based on income or other characteristics is important to assess the effects on each group. We detail that method with an example later in the chapter and in Chapter 7.

INDIFFERENCE CURVES

The concept of utility can be represented and analyzed graphically using indifference curves. An **indifference curve** represents different combinations of two goods that would provide the consumer equal satisfaction (see Figure 4-6). Stated another way, for any points along one particular indifference curve, a consumer would be indifferent among the amounts of two goods as represented by those points. Indifference curves can be thought of as *isoutils*, or curves of equal utility.

To see how indifference curves work, suppose a consumer has only two commodities from which to choose: museum visits and park visits. Figure 4-6 presents indifference curves for an individual facing a choice between some number of museum and park visits for a year. A particular indifference curve is the locus of points, or combinations of museum visits and park visits, that would yield equal levels of satisfaction, or in economic terms, equal levels of utility.

In this example (Figure 4-6), this individual would be equally satisfied with 20 museum visits and 10 park visits (point A), or with 10 museum visits and 30 park

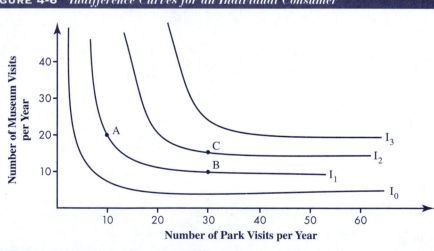

FIGURE 4-6 *Indifference Curves for an Individual Consumer*

visits (point B), which are both on indifference curve I_1. A combination of 15 museum visits and 30 park visits (Point C) would yield an even greater level of satisfaction, which is on indifference curve I_2. Any combination on I_2 is preferred to any combination on I_1, because I_2 represents combinations of museum visits and park visits that yield a higher level of satisfaction than the combinations on I_1.

Theoretically, each individual has a "family of indifference curves" for each pair of goods, which includes one indifference curve for each level of satisfaction. Economics assumes that individuals will always prefer combinations of goods that yield higher levels of satisfaction (Point C is preferred to Point B or to Point A), but will be indifferent among combinations of goods along a particular indifference curve (Point B and Point A are equally preferred).

Economists generally offer the following characteristics and conditions about indifference curves:

- Utility increases as indifference curves move away from the origin (toward the northeast). Any point on I_2 will be preferred to any point on I_1. Similarly, any point on I_3 will be preferred to any point on I_2.
- Utility is constant along any one indifference curve (by definition).
- Utilities are ordinal, and not amenable to standard mathematical operations. Although any point on I_2 provides greater satisfaction than any point on I_1, a point on I_2 does not necessarily provide, say, twice as much satisfaction as a point on I_1.
- Utilities cannot be validly compared among individuals. Each individual has their own set of indifference curves, which cannot be directly compared to others' indifference curves.
- Indifference curves are usually convex to the origin, because consumers will require larger amounts of one good to compensate for lesser amounts of the sacrificed good. The rate at which one more unit of a good can be substituted for one less of another good, while maintaining a constant level of satisfaction, is called the marginal rate of substitution.[7] Graphically, the marginal rate of substitution is the slope at any point on the indifference curve.

SUBSTITUTION AND INCOME EFFECTS

Recall from Chapter 2 that we examined the substitution effect and income effect of a price change on quantity demanded. The substitution effect says that as the price of a good increases, its substitutes look more attractive, and a consumer will buy less of that good and more of a substitute good. The income effect says that as the price of a good increases, a consumer's overall purchasing power decreases, thereby reducing that consumer's demand for that good. The obverse is also true: As the price of a good decreases, its substitutes look less attractive, a consumer's purchasing

---

[7] This concept is detailed in the appendix to Chapter 4.

power increases, and a consumer will buy more of that good. We will use indifference curve analysis to examine these effects graphically.

Let's examine what happens when the price of a good decreases. Let's take the case of park visits, which we assume to be a normal good. Refer to Figure 4-7. Suppose the consumer's optimal quantity demanded of museum visits and park visits is point A, with a budget line at L_1. Then, to reflect the price decrease in park visits, with the price of museum visits constant, the original budget line L_1 rotates outward to L_3. The consumer now chooses the amount B, which is tangent to the highest indifference curve, I_3, and tangent to the budget line, L_3. As we can see, the combination of park visits and museum visits represented by B is preferred to A, because B is on a higher indifference curve (I_3) than A (I_1). Thus, the reduction in the price of park visits allowed the consumer to increase his or her level of satisfaction derived from the combination of park visits and museum visits. The total change in quantity demanded of park visits is the difference between Q_A and Q_B. Now let's look at the components of this change due to the substitution effect and the income effect.

The substitution effect is the change in quantity demanded of a good associated with its change in price, while keeping the level of utility constant. This effect can be determined in the following way. Refer to Figure 4-7 again. Starting at original point A, move along the same indifference curve (I_1), in order to keep utility constant. Continue on that indifference curve until arriving at the point of maximum utility on budget line L_2, which is point C. L_2 is a (hypothetical) budget line drawn parallel to the new budget line (L_3) that reflects a new relationship between relative prices of museum visits and park visits, due to the change in price of park visits. The effect due to substitution is the change between points A and C, so the change in quantity demanded of park visits would be between Q_A and Q_C. It shows that when the price

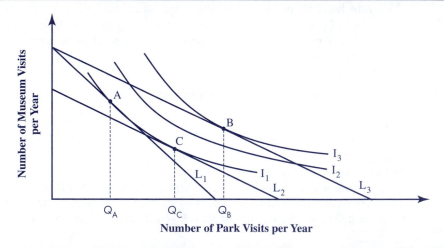

FIGURE 4-7   *Substitution and Income Effects for a Normal Good*

of park visits decreases, the substitution effect leads to an increase in quantity demanded of park visits, keeping utility the same.

The income effect is change in quantity demanded of a good associated with a change in income while keeping relative prices constant. Here the income effect can be determined by moving from point C on the hypothetical budget line (L_2) to the parallel and new budget line, L_3. The consumer chooses point B on the new budget line, because B is the point of highest utility. The budget lines are parallel because relative prices are the same. The effect due to income is the change between points C and B, so the change in quantity demanded of park visits would be between Q_C and Q_B. This shows that when the price of park visits decreases, the income effect leads to an increase in quantity demanded of park visits, keeping relative prices constant. So the overall change in quantity demanded, due to both substitution and income effects, would be from Q_A to Q_B.

The case we just examined was for a normal good. Now let's look at the case of an inferior good: When income increases, quantity demanded for that good decreases, and vice versa. Refer to Figure 4-8. Assume that park visits are an inferior good, which could be the case, for instance, if consumers go to another recreation area instead of the park if they have more income. Suppose the price of park visits decreases. The substitution effect, as before, is the change in quantity demanded from Q_A to Q_C. As the price of park visits decreases, its substitutes still become less attractive, but as income increases, quantity demanded decreases (for an inferior good) from Q_C to Q_B. So the net change in quantity demanded, due to both income and substitution effects, is the difference between Q_A and Q_B. Even with inferior goods, the income effect is usually smaller relative to the substitution effect. So when the price of an inferior good decreases, its quantity demanded still usually increases.

FIGURE 4-8   *Substitution and Income Effects for an Inferior Good*

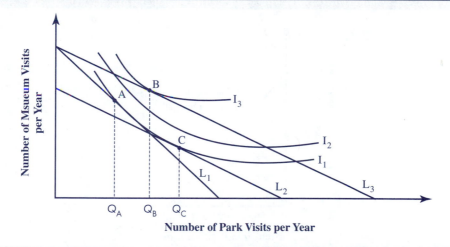

BUDGET CONSTRAINTS

Without budget constraints, a consumer could choose to purchase any amount of any good. Realistically, consumers need to make choices within budgets. To determine levels of consumption, it is necessary to know the goods' prices and the budget allocation. This information is represented by a *budget line*, which is expressed as follows:

$$Y = P_1 Q_1 + P_2 Q_2$$

or alternatively as

$$Q_1 = (Y/P_1) - (P_2 Q_2/P_1)$$

where

Y = budget allocated to the consumption of goods 1 and 2
Q_1 = units of good 1, plotted on the horizontal axis
P_1 = price of good 1
Q_2 = units of good 2, plotted on the vertical axis
P_2 = price of good 2

Figure 4-9 shows budgetary choices for a consumer who has $80 to spend on museum visits (good 2) and park visits (good 1), and these visits cost $4 and $2, respectively. The consumer may purchase several different combinations of these visits for a total of exactly $80: 0 museum visits and 40 park visits; 10 museum visits and 20 park visits; 15 museum visits and 10 park visits; 20 museum visits and 0 park

FIGURE 4-9   *Budget Line for Budget Constraint of $80*

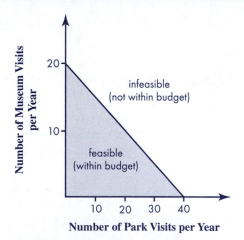

visits; and so on. Of course the consumer can purchase fewer visits and spend less than $80. In Figure 4-9, points that are on or inside the budget line are feasible. They represent combinations of the two goods that cost $80 or less.

This previous example shows a budget analysis for only two goods. Budget analysis can easily be extended to more than two goods. The budget line would be replaced by a more general budget constraint that defines, for any given set of product prices, all feasible combinations of levels of consumption for each product.

Now let's overlay information about the consumer's utility onto the budget constraint, as shown in Figure 4-10. The rational consumer would choose the mix of goods that will maximize utility, which is point D: 10 museum visits and 20 park visits. *The point of maximum utility is where the budget curve is tangent to the indifference curve.*

To confirm, look at point E and point F. Point E provides more museum visits than D, and F provides more park visits than D. Both are feasible because they are on the budget line. But both are on an indifference curve of less utility (I_0) than the indifference curve where point D lies (I_1). Point A and point B would be on the same indifference curve as D, but neither point is possible because they lie outside the budget constraint. Point C would provide more utility than point B, but again, it is not feasible because it is outside the budget constraint.

Let's suppose the consumer receives an extra $40 to spend on visits, for a new total of $120, and also assume that visits are a normal good. Refer to Figure 4-11. The new (solid) budget line intersects with the indifference curve of highest utility at point C. This point C represents 15 museum visits and 30 park visits. (The dashed line is the previous budget line.) The *income-expansion path* shows the relationship between changes in income (represented by changes in the budget line) and the different levels of consumption.

FIGURE 4-10 *Point of Maximum Utility*

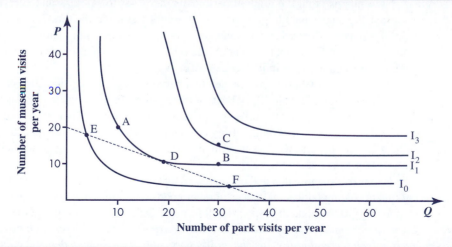

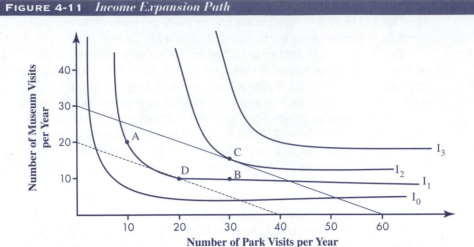

FIGURE 4-11 *Income Expansion Path*

DERIVING THE DEMAND CURVE

We can use the preceding concepts to derive the demand curve. Given a budget, the various prices of a good, and a consumer's indifference map, the utility-maximizing quantity at each price can be determined.

Refer to Figure 4-12(a). In this example, we will derive an individual consumer's demand curve for one of the goods: *park visits*. Assume a budget of $80, and museum visits are at a price of $P_M = \$4$, as before. For park visits at a price of $P_1 = \$2$, the optimal quantity consumed would be at point D, which is 20 park visits.

Now suppose that the price of park visits increases to $P_2 = \$4$, and everything else stays the same, including the price of museum visits and the total budget. At $P_2 = \$4$, the slope of the budget line changes, and the new optimal quantity consumed would be at point G, which is 10 park visits. These optimal points are where the budget lines are tangent to an indifference curve.

We now have two points on the demand curve for park visits: ($2, 20 visits) and ($4, 10 visits). See Figure 4-12(b). Each of these points corresponds to the maximum utility that the consumer can derive, given budget constraints. Why does the demand curve reflect points of maximum utility at each price? Economics assumes that consumers are rational and will use their money to buy the collections of goods that will maximize their satisfaction.

To obtain the entire demand curve, repeat that process for each possible price of a park visit, holding budget and prices of other goods constant. Then determine the corresponding quantity, and those points will form the demand curve as in Figure 4-12(b). *Even though each point represents the utility-maximizing quantity for each price, not each point has equal utility*. Instead, utility normally varies along a demand curve.

A final note: This important conceptual exercise can be difficult to use in practice. To determine demand, analysts often employ other methods, such as exam-

FIGURE 4-12 *Derivation of Demand Curve*

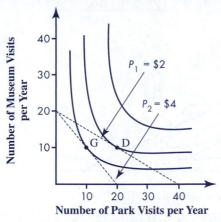

(a) Equilibrium Points for Two Prices

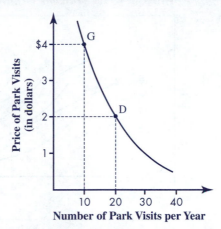

(b) Relating Prices with Quantities Demanded That Maximize Utility

ining market behavior or performing market research, rather than drawing utility curves.

EXAMPLE

Intergovernmental Grants for Water Supply Infrastructure and Housing

We now use the concepts in this chapter to evaluate how various public policies affect the choices of private individuals or public decision makers.

Intergovernmental grants are funds from one agency to another and can be provided with no conditions attached, with strict conditions, or with some arrangement in between. Organizations that award grants usually attempt to ensure that grant money is spent in ways consistent with their goals. To analyze these mechanisms more carefully, we examine three different types of funding given from the federal government to a local government: income grants, subsidies, and tied grants. For the sake of this example, we assume that the local government runs only two programs: infrastructure (water lines) and housing development.

One of the easiest ways for an organization to give money to another is a straight *income grant*, which carries no restrictions and can be used in the way the grantee chooses. As shown in Figure 4-13, the income grant increases the city's resources for its activities, shifting the budget line out from B_0 to B_1, resulting in potentially greater expenditures for both activities. The amount of infrastructure increases from W_0 to W_1 and the number of housing units increases from H_0 to H_1. With increased spending power, the city is able to move to a higher level of satisfaction, from indifference curve I_1 to I_3. Even

continued on next page

FIGURE 4-13 *Income Grant for Infrastructure*

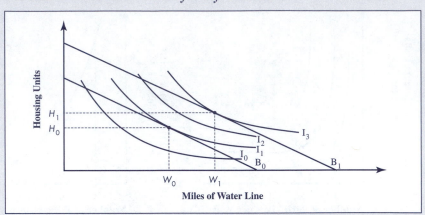

though an income grant will increase the amount of infrastructure that the city replaces, some of the money may be used for other purposes, which the federal government may or may not favor. Other types of grants place more restrictions on how the money can be used.

A *subsidy* allows the grantor, in this case the federal government, to reimburse the grantee, the city, for a predetermined percentage of the costs of a specified activity or program. In this instance (Figure 4-14), the subsidy would reimburse the city for part of the costs of every mile of water line they install or replace. For example, if the replacement costs for each mile of water line were $20,000 and the federal government agreed to pay 75% of those costs, the effective cost to the city would be only $5,000 per mile. Because of the reduced cost of water line replacement, the city would presumably increase the

FIGURE 4-14 *Subsidy for Infrastructure*

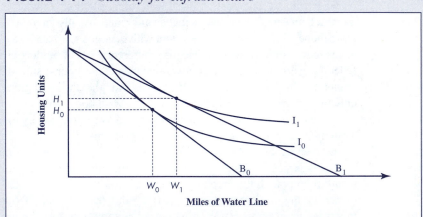

level of the subsidized activity. Exceptions to this case occur when the grantee either finds the activity too expensive even after the subsidy or would not benefit from further line replacement even at the lower price. Normally, a subsidy produces the same effect as a reduction in price of the subsidized activity, which shifts the budget line out from B_0 to B_1 (Figure 4-14). The actual level W_1 may be uncertain, but given our information, it would likely be an amount greater than before the subsidy (W_0).

A third way that the federal government could distribute funds to the city is through a *tied grant*, which is a lump sum payment that must be used for a particular purpose, in this case, infrastructure replacement. For example, if the federal government gave the city $200,000 for water lines, the grant would cover the first 10 miles of water lines, and the city would have to pay for additional lines itself. After the first 10 miles have been constructed, a tied grant is similar to an income grant, because the leftover money can be used for either activity. Notice that the budget line, B_1, shown in Figure 4-15, does not include less than 10 miles of water lines, which is what the federal government provided.

FIGURE 4-15 *Tied Grant for Infrastructure*

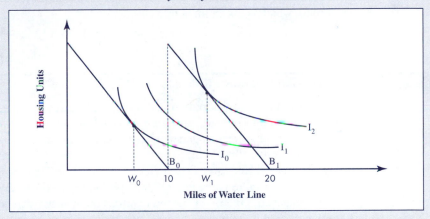

The example illustrated ways in which choice can be influenced by the grantor through the mechanisms to distribute funds. Each mechanism has advantages and disadvantages, which depend on the nature of the organizations and the activities. Income grants are appropriate when some or many activities carried out by an organization are worth encouraging. They also tend to be the most desirable from the grantee's point of view. Subsidies can result in the greatest increase in a particular activity, but predicting their impact requires much information about institutional factors. Tied grants ensure a minimum level of a program, and once an organization reaches the minimum, they become similar to income grants.

Although various grant alternatives have been discussed in general terms, each one has real-world counterparts. As an example of an income grant, a general revenue-sharing program is a federal income grant program to support the general functions of local government. Like other types of unrestricted grants, the revenue-sharing program provides local governments with the flexibility to determine how to spend the funds. As an example of subsidies, the federal government provides funds to state governments to run a health insurance program for uninsured children. The state agency develops the program, specifying the target populations, medical services covered, and other provisions. The federal government approves it, and then provides approximately 70% of the costs of running the program. As an example of a tied grant, the federal government operates a number of special revenue-sharing programs, such as the Community Development Block Grant Program. In this program, a block grant—a lump sum of money—is provided to eligible cities and towns to support specified community development activities.

The preceding example also used indifference curve analysis to examine the effects of different grants from the perspective of a government agency. Although this approach is commonly presented, it faces theoretical and methodological concerns, such as the derivation and validity of a social utility function that is intended to represent the aggregation of individual utilities. In practice, decision makers often use other techniques to determine the benefits of proposed projects, such as consumer surplus, which is exemplified next.

EXAMPLE　　**Benefits to Public Transit Riders from a Fare Decrease**

In the 1970s, a city transportation authority (CTA) initiated an experiment called Dime Time to increase ridership on rapid rail transit. On weekdays, from 10 A.M. to 3 P.M., passengers could ride all rail transit lines operated by CTA for $0.10 rather than $0.25. The CTA also operates buses and trackless trolleys, but these routes were not included in the Dime Time program, and passengers continued to pay a fare of $0.25 per ride at all times. By lowering fares, proponents of Dime Time hoped to attract many new riders to rail transit, and this could help to remedy problems associated with center city congestion and air pollution, among others. Moreover, some Dime Time proponents argued that the increased ridership would lead to an increase in the total amount of the fares collected, a feature that would help offset the costs of operating the rapid rail system.

As indicated in Table 4-1, the Dime Time program did result in an increase in rapid rail passengers during the hours of 10 A.M. to 3 P.M. Although Dime Time represented a 60% reduction of fare (down $0.15 from the initial $0.25 level), it produced just a 41% increase, overall, in Dime Time rapid rail ridership (from 22,850 riders to 32,290 riders). Low-income ridership increased 58% from 9,500 to 15,020, and moderate-income and upper-income ridership increased only 32% and 26%, respectively. Thus, all groups had price inelastic demand during this time period.

Just looking at the totals in Table 4-1, however, may be misleading, because some of the increase in rail ridership came from individuals who previously rode other modes of CTA transportation. Table 4-2 provides more details on the composition of rail ridership during Dime Time hours, after the fare reduction.

TABLE 4-1 *Weekday CTA Rapid Rail Passenger Averages Before and During Dime Time Program*

	Dime Time Program	
Income Class	Before Dime Time (Fare = $0.25)	During Dime Time (Fare = $0.10)
Low	9,500	15,020
Moderate	8,250	10,860
High	5,100	6,410
Total	22,850	32,290

TABLE 4-2 *Dime Time Weekday CTA Rapid Rail Passenger Averages by Prior Mode of Travel*

	Income Class			
Prior Mode of Travel	Low	Moderate	High	Total
CTA Rapid Rail— Dime Time Hours	9,500	8,250	5,100	22,850
CTA Rapid Rail— All Other Times	625	380	310	1,315
CTA Buses and Trackless Trolley	1,080	680	340	2,100
Private Auto Driver	895	525	400	1,820
Private Auto Passenger	220	75	80	375
Walk	850	380	90	1,320
Trip Not Previously Made	1,850	570	90	2,510
Total	15,020	10,860	6,410	32,290

continued on next page

Now we ask the question: What were the effects of reduced fares on total revenues? As expected, due to the price inelastic demand, the price decrease to the $0.10 fare resulted in a loss of revenue to the CTA. Prior to the program, the 22,850 midday riders generated $5,712.50 in revenues or total fares. Though ridership increased to 32,290, at a fare of $0.10, total fares collected dropped to $3,229. As studies suggest, transit ridership can be relatively price inelastic. As this case showed, a drop in price also reduced total revenues for the producers. Yet the fare drop resulted in benefits to consumers, as we will now analyze.

The price and quantity information for rail transit ridership presented in Table 4-1 represents points along the demand curve for each of three income groups and for the market demand curve. Figure 4-16 plots the demand curves consistent with information presented in Table 4-1, assuming that over the range of prices, each demand curve can be approximated by a straight line. Notice that the market demand curve is the horizontal summation of each demand curve for the three income groups. These demand curves for each income group, in turn, represent a summation of individual demand curves within each group.

FIGURE 4-16   *Aggregate Demand by Income Group*

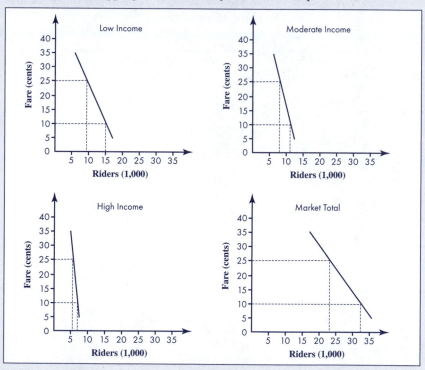

Based on the information presented in Figure 4-16 and Table 4-2, it is possible to calculate the total change in consumer surplus that results from the Dime Time program. To understand this computation, consider the change in total ridership illustrated in Figure 4-17. Before the introduction of Dime Time, total consumer benefits from midday ridership were equal to the area under the market demand curve, up to and including 22,850 riders. Total fares were equal to the area OABC, on the rectangle formed by the price line at $0.25 and the quantity line of 22,850 riders. Consumer surplus, then, is the area below the demand curve and above the $0.25 price line.

As the transit fare drops, total consumer benefits increase by an amount equal to DFBC. Notice that the increase in consumer surplus can be attributed to the reduced fare for previous riders (DEBC) and the attraction of new riders (EFB).

For 22,850 previous riders, the fare reduction represents a windfall gain. As a result of the fare reduction, the consumer surplus for these riders increases by $0.15 per ride, for a total increase in consumer surplus of $3,427.50. In Figure 4-17, this component of the change in consumer surplus is equal to area DEBC.

Consumer surplus also increases as a result of new ridership. In Figure 4-17, total benefits to new riders equals the area under the demand curve between 22,850 and 32,290 riders. Because these riders pay $0.10 per ride, their consumer surplus is equal to area EFB. Assuming that the demand curve is a straight line between the price of $0.10 and $0.25, this dollar value element of the consumer surplus can be calculated using the formula for the area of a triangle. Thus, consumer surplus for new riders equals $708, which is $(1/2 \times \$0.15) \times (9,440)$, where 9,440 is change in ridership.

FIGURE 4-17 *Total Change in Consumer Surplus*

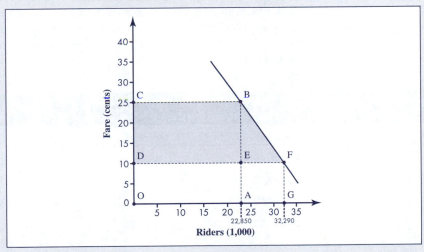

With a market demand curve of known shape, it is relatively straightforward to measure the change in consumption that results from a change in price. It is also straightforward to calculate the change in aggregate consumer surplus associated with a change in price, but interpreting the change in aggregate consumer surplus may prove somewhat more difficult.

Though a change of fare may not significantly influence the well-being of an upper-income individual who rarely rides public transit, a change in fare may be very important to a low-income individual who depends on public transportation to get to and from work. This example is yet another illustration of the difficulty of making interpersonal comparisons of well-being.

In such problems, it is often useful to disaggregate the market demand information to illustrate the effects of a policy change on various population subgroups, such as socioeconomic characteristics. Table 4-3 presents estimates of the change of consumer surplus for each of the three income groups in the preceding example. Again, the total change in consumer surplus is divided into the change in surplus going to previous riders and the change in surplus going to new riders. The calculations use the data in Tables 4-1 and 4-2 on ridership and follow the procedure employed in calculations of total consumer surplus just presented. As indicated in the table, most of the consumer surplus goes to low-income and moderate-income individuals who rode the rapid transit before the Dime Time fare reduction took effect. Of the change in surplus resulting from new riders, more than 58% ($414 out of $708) goes to low-income riders.

Though it is difficult, if not impossible, to make interpersonal comparisons of well-being, public decision makers frequently must evaluate the merits of fare reduction programs or other programs that redistribute resources. Indeed, evaluating the differential impact of programs and policies on individuals and groups is at the heart of public sector decision making.

In the preceding example, the fare reduction resulted in a loss of revenue, which it could be argued, places an additional burden on taxpayers to cover the transit system deficits. The gain in utility to riders is offset, to some extent, by the loss of utility to taxpayers. In an era of tax-cutting fervor, it may be tempting to restore the fare to $0.25 to raise revenues.

TABLE 4-3   Change in Consumer Surplus for Precious and New Riders (dollars per day)

Income Class	Previous Riders	New Riders	Change in Consumer Surplus
Low	$1,425.00	$414.00	$1,839.00
Moderate	1,237.50	195.75	1,433.25
High	765.00	$ 98.25	863.25
Total	$3,427.50	$708.00	$4,135.50

Yet several things should be considered. First, public sector decision making is generally concerned with public well-being. Profit maximization is not necessarily the primary objective, and many public services are run at a loss in order to provide a benefit to the greater society. Social benefits need to be weighed against the social costs of providing the service, however, which include the opportunity costs of taxpayer funds and other resources. Second, as we saw in the previous chapter, increasing the fare would not necessarily increase revenues, especially with a good that could become more elastic with time. Third, distributional issues arise. For instance, many of the taxpayers who would benefit from lower taxes would be the same low-income and moderate-income individuals who benefit from the reduced fares. Finally, the calculations here may underestimate the total benefits to low-income and moderate-income individuals. These individuals might be willing to pay more if they were wealthier. So their demand curves may not represent the total value that they derive from the service. Consequently, the market (aggregate) demand curve would underestimate the total value that the service provides. These challenges of assessing the benefits of a publicly provided service are explored in greater detail in Chapter 10.

REVIEW QUESTIONS

1. Your county is facing severe economic distress after a recent drought. Several members of Congress propose special funding to help the communities in the area; they disagree, however, on how to most effectively help these communities. Senator Tobin strongly believes that these communities know better than the federal government about how to restore prosperity. Senator Eckmann, on the other hand, strongly believes that the funding should be targeted for environmental purposes. Finally, Senator Kronen agrees with Senator Tobin that the decision-making process should take place at the local level. At the same time, however, Senator Kronen believes that some financial input from the communities would promote responsible decision making. What ways could the federal government provide financial support to your county in order to meet the goals of each senator?

2. A federal highway administrator spoke out against the criticism of highways: "I have heard comments from advocates of the mass transit mode that building new highways simply promotes congestion because as soon as we build them, they fill up. Well, that only proves that they were needed."

    a. Explain the effect that additional highway construction has on demand for highway trips versus demand for mass transit trips.

    b. Critique the use of the term *needed* based on the concepts of demand.

3. You just completed a study estimating the gain in consumer surplus that would be reaped by lowering the admission fee for a national park. Before the fee is reduced, the company that provides transportation for visitors to the park

announces a price cut. Should you revise your estimate of the gain in consumer surplus? If so, in what direction?

4. Studies of gift-giving have suggested that noncash gifts are inefficient because the recipient values the gift less than its actual cost. Instead, economists argue, people should give cash gifts: It would be more efficient because individual consumers know best how to maximize their satisfaction, given the resources (the cash gift). Yet people continue to give noncash gifts, and people continue to enjoy receiving noncash gifts, sometimes even more than cash gifts. Why does this type of gift-giving continue if it is allegedly inefficient?

5. Utility is a fundamental concept in economic theory. Why would utility be a difficult concept to use in practice?

CHAPTER 4 APPENDIX: UTILITY MAXIMIZATION

UTILITY FUNCTION AND THE MARGINAL RATE OF SUBSTITUTION

This appendix provides the formal mathematical proof of the concepts presented in the chapter on consumer choice and utility maximization.

The utility function, $u = U(x,y)$, shows the various levels of utility, u, that can be attained for different combinations of two goods, x and y. This function can be expressed as

Utility $= u = U(x,y)$

This relationship can be used to draw an individual's indifference curves that represent the various combinations of two goods, x and y, that generate the same level of utility (Figure A4-1).

The **marginal rate of substitution** (MRS) is defined as the number of units of y that would be needed to compensate for one unit of x and still maintain the same level of utility. Geometrically, the MRS represents the negative slope of the tangent

---

FIGURE A4-1 *Hypothetical Indifference Curves for an Individual*

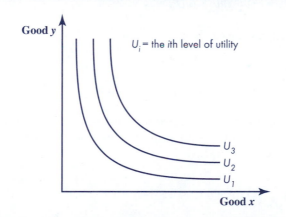

to the indifference curve at a certain point representing a combination of x and y. The slope will vary along the curve, unless the two goods, x and y, are perfect substitutes. Mathematically, the MRS can be expressed as the negative of the derivative of y with respect to x (which is the negative slope of the tangent), holding utility constant

$$\text{MRS} = -\left.\frac{dy}{dx}\right|_{u = \text{constant}}$$

We will now show that the MRS equals the ratio of the marginal utilities of x and y (MU_x/MU_y). The marginal utility of a good is the change in utility from one additional unit or one less unit of the good. We first demonstrate intuitively why this relationship between MRS and marginal utilities occurs before we move to a more formal proof using differential calculus.

Suppose that, for a particular combination of x and y, $MU_x = 2$ and $MU_y = 1$, so that $MU_x/MU_y = 2$. If we were to lose (gain) one unit of x, we would lose (gain) two units of utility. And if we were to lose (gain) one unit of y, we would lose (gain) one unit of utility. Because we wish to maintain the same level of utility (i.e., remain on the same indifference curve), we would need to acquire two units of y to compensate for a loss of one unit of x. Thus, the MRS, the number of units of y that compensate for one less unit of x, is equal to 2—which is equal to the ratio of the marginal utilities (MU_x/MU_y).

We will now show the proof of the relationship between MRS and the ratio of marginal utilities using differential calculus. We first obtain the total derivative of utility

$$du = (\partial U/\partial x)dx + (\partial U/\partial y)dy$$

Because we want to hold utility constant, we set the change equal to zero

$$du = 0 = (\partial U/\partial x)dx + (\partial U/\partial y)dy$$

This expression can now be rewritten as

$$\frac{\partial U/\partial x}{\partial U/\partial y} = -\left.\frac{dy}{dx}\right|_{u = \text{constant}}$$

But $\partial U/\partial x$ is simply the marginal utility of x, and $\partial U/\partial y$ is the marginal utility of y. We can, therefore, express our results in the following form, which proves the relationship.

$$\text{MRS} = -\frac{dy}{dx}\bigg|_{u\,=\,constant}$$

$$= \frac{\partial U/\partial x}{\partial U/\partial y}$$

$$= \frac{MU_x}{Mu_y}$$

UTILITY MAXIMIZATION

We will now determine the combination of goods x and y that will maximize the consumer's utility. This objective can be expressed as

Max $U(x,y)$ subject to $P_x x + P_y y \leq B$

where

P_x = the price of x (per unit)
P_y = the price of y (per unit)
x = number of units of good x
y = number of units of good y
B = the budget constraint

We assume that the consumer will seek the combination of x and y that will provide the maximum level of utility, yet remain within the consumer's budget. This combination will be found at the point where the budget line is just tangent to the indifference curve with the highest utility. We will show that at this optimal point (maximum utility), the ratio of the marginal utilities of goods x and y (MU_x/MU_y) will be equal to the ratio of their respective prices (P_x/P_y).

First, suppose that $P_x/P_y = 2$ and that the consumer has chosen a combination of x and y where MRS = $MU_x/MU_y = 1$. In this case, the allocation of the consumer's budget is suboptimal, because one additional unit of y can provide the same amount of utility as one additional unit of x while being half as expensive. From the price ratio, $P_x/P_y = 2$, we know that if the consumer bought one less unit of x, that would free up enough money to buy two more units of y. From the MRS = 1, we know that each of these two units of y would provide as much utility gain as two additional units of x. Therefore, to maximize utility, the consumer should change the budget allocation so that each unit of x provides twice as much utility as each unit of y, because x is twice as expensive. This allocation would be MRS = $MU_x/MU_y = 2 = P_x/P_y$. At this optimal allocation, each dollar spent, on either x or y, would provide the same increase in utility.

We are now ready to more formally prove that MRS or MU_x/MU_y must be equal to the ratio P_x/P_y in order to maximize the consumer's utility. We can rewrite the conditions that must hold if x and y are chosen to maximize utility, subject to a budget constraint, by using the Lagrange multiplier method:

$$\text{Max } L(x,y,\lambda) = U(x,y) + \lambda(B - P_x x - P_y y)$$

The first-order conditions for a maximum are found by taking the partial derivatives of L with respect to x, y, and λ, and setting the results equal to zero:

$$\partial L/\partial x = \partial U/\partial x - \lambda P_x = 0$$
$$\partial L/\partial y = \partial U/\partial y - \lambda P_y = 0$$
$$\partial L/\partial \lambda = B - P_x x - P_y y = 0$$

Note that the last equation is simply our budget constraint. Rearranging the equations yields:

$$(\partial U/\partial x)/P_x = \lambda$$
$$(\partial U/\partial y)/P_y = \lambda$$

so that

$$(\partial U/\partial x)/P_x = \lambda = (\partial U/\partial y)/P_y$$

which can be written as

$$\frac{MU_x}{P_x} = \lambda = \frac{MU_y}{P_y}$$

where, as before, $MU_x = \partial U/\partial x$ and $MU_y = \partial U/\partial y$. Thus, at the optimum, the ratio of the marginal utility of a good to its price is constant across goods. Put another way, at the optimum, an extra dollar will yield the same extra utility regardless of the good on which it is spent. The optimality condition may also be written as

$$\frac{MU_x}{MU_y} = \frac{P_x}{P_y}$$

SUMMARY

We can summarize the relationships in the appendix in the following form

$$\text{MRS} \equiv -\left.\frac{dy}{dx}\right|_{u \,=\, \text{constant}} = \frac{\partial U/\partial x}{\partial U/\partial y} \equiv \frac{MU_x}{MU_y} = \frac{P_x}{P_y}$$

where the first relationship is definitional, the second relationship is mathematical, the third relationship is definitional, and the fourth relationship holds only at an optimum.

COSTS AND SUPPLY

TYPES OF COSTS

The meaning of *costs* may seem clear, whether to a public agency, a private firm, or an individual consumer. For instance, if a community agency pays a fee to a local school in order to use a classroom after hours, the agency would view that fee as a cost. If a firm buys oil to run industrial processes, the firm would consider the cost of buying the oil in their accounting. If an individual spends the weekend painting a room, the cost of the project would be the price paid for the paint and supplies.

Yet each of these examples includes other types of costs that may not be recognized. For example, the payment by the community agency may not cover the full costs of using the classroom, such as additional maintenance, increased traffic around the neighborhood at night, or forgone alternative uses of the room. The cost of oil to the firm may not cover the full social costs of using that resource, such as impacts on the environment and public health. The individual painting a room may not account for the cost of personal time spent completing the project or the adverse effects from breathing paint fumes. In each of these cases, the costs extend beyond strict monetary costs. These types of nonmonetary costs also can be among the most significant in public sector decisions.

This chapter focuses on costs. It first describes different categories of costs, and then follows with a step-by-step analysis of production costs, which are important for both public sector and private sector decisions. It builds upon this analysis to look at cost considerations in decision making, including short-run and long-run factors, profit maximization, and economies of scale. Examples include a cost analysis for a meals-on-wheels service and for community development activities. An appendix provides the mathematical foundations of production functions.

NONMONETARY COSTS

Production activities usually involve costs in addition to direct monetary outlays. Nonmonetary costs can be incurred by private firms, public agencies, households, or the general public. They can also involve indirect expenses, the use of resources, or the imposition of intangible costs. In the previous chapter, we saw that benefits involve more than monetary revenues. Similarly, we will see that costs include more than monetary expenditures.

Public sector decisions often require a more complete accounting of costs than private sector decisions. For instance, the use of a previously acquired government asset, such as land, may represent a real program cost, even though the government is not charged for using the land. The true cost of using the land depends on other possible uses of the land or even the value of not using the land.

Government programs often require some sacrifices of community resources. Although such losses represent important costs of a program, their monetary value is often difficult to measure. At the same time, the loss of intangible resources needs to be documented. When evaluating and choosing among programs, a full accounting of every cost is important, even if those costs cannot be expressed in monetary terms. It is also necessary to determine which costs are relevant for a particular decision. The answer depends on the perspective of the decision maker. As we will see, the perspective can be quite different, depending on whether it involves the private sector or public sector.

OPPORTUNITY COSTS

The cost of a production activity also includes an **opportunity cost**: the highest value of the resource in an alternative use or uses. An opportunity cost provides a more complete accounting than monetary cost because it captures what is sacrificed by choosing to use a resource. This accounting considers the forgone benefits or uses of a resource over time. For instance, the opportunity cost of cutting down forests and developing the land should consider not only the value of those trees and undeveloped land at the present, but also the benefits to future generations. These benefits include the trees' ability to reduce pollutants, provide habitat for species, and provide aesthetic enjoyment.

Both private and public decision makers need to include opportunity costs in their decisions. For a private firm, the opportunity cost is typically the rate of return that the money could earn in an alternative investment. For a public agency, the opportunity cost should also include nonmonetary factors, such as forgone benefits from the use or allocation of resources. From the perspective of an individual citizen, these resources may appear free if citizens do not have to pay directly for them. For instance, a "free" city park (that does not charge admission) requires the commitment of land, labor, equipment, and other resources to operate—resources that could have been used for other city functions and public benefits. These are real costs from a city government perspective, even though the park may appear free to residents.

Opportunity costs are important to practically every public decision, because resources devoted to one activity could be used for other activities instead, and these forgone benefits (whether monetary or nonmonetary) need to be factored into decision making. The other activities should be those that are reasonable and possible because, interpreted at its extreme, the opportunity costs for any activity could dwarf a budget and paralyze decision making if one considers all imaginable uses of resources and what theoretically could be done instead. Also, opportunity costs include what has to be sacrificed now and in the future, rather than what has already been sacrificed and is unrecoverable, or sunk costs.

SUNK COSTS

Another cost concept is **sunk costs**. These previously incurred costs cannot be recovered, and thus are not relevant to current and future production decisions. Although it may be difficult to accept, the concept is to let bygones be bygones. As an example, consider an urban renewal agency that is redeveloping an old waterfront area. Several years ago, the agency conducted feasibility studies, determined that the proposed redevelopment would be profitable and beneficial for the community, and thus cleared the land and prepared the site for redevelopment. The costs for the studies and preparing the site were $5 million. Then, new and unanticipated problems arose at the site that would require remediation for the project to continue. The project was put on hold, pending a revised economic analysis. The analysis found that the redevelopment project would cost an additional $6 million to complete, with expected monetary benefits of $8 million. The decision now facing the agency is whether to go ahead and complete the project.

Opponents of the project claim that because the total costs ($11 million) exceed the total benefits ($8 million), the project should not be completed. Proponents point out that the $5 million already spent on the project, for conducting feasibility studies and preparing the site, cannot be recovered—it is a sunk cost. Thus, they argue that the appropriate comparison is between the costs ($6 million) and benefits ($8 million) of completing the project. Under this calculation, the project should be finished, because the net benefits would be $2 million. This calculation is consistent with the economic principle to exclude sunk costs from current decisions.

This reasoning assumes, however, that no benefits would result if the project were not completed. For instance, if the agency could sell the cleared land for $4 million, then this potential value, or opportunity cost, should be included in the calculation. The project's costs would then be $10 million: $6 million in costs to complete the project, plus $4 million in opportunity costs (the revenue if the cleared land were sold). The $5 million in sunk costs are still excluded. According to this calculation, the costs ($10 million) would be greater than the benefits ($8 million), and the project should not be completed. Both proponents and opponents agreed that the concept of sunk costs should not be used to justify or neglect cost overruns, and that better planning, monitoring, and economic analyses should be performed in the future. (Note that this preceding analysis is from a purely fiscal perspective. Other types of benefits and costs are likely to be important to the decision.)

PRODUCTION COSTS AND COST CURVES

We now examine an important category of costs from the perspective of the supplier: *production costs*. Both private firms and public agencies consider production costs. Understanding the relationship between costs and level of output (quantity produced) is important for a producer who seeks to minimize production costs or maximize profit. This section examines the specific measurement of four aspects of production costs: fixed costs, variable costs, total costs, and marginal costs.

Fixed costs are costs that do not vary with the level of output. For example, a restaurant must pay its monthly lease regardless of how many meals it serves during a month. A city's fire department must pay the weekly salaries of its permanent office staff whether the department attends to a dozen fires or no fires during a week.[1]

Total fixed costs (TFC) are the sum of all fixed costs. **Average fixed costs (AFC)** are the total fixed costs divided by the level of output (X):

$$AFC = TFC/X$$

Variable costs are the costs that *do* vary with the level of output. For instance, using the previous examples, variable costs for a restaurant would include the food for each meal, the dishwashing, and the electricity to cook each meal (above what would be required just to keep the restaurant open, even if no meals were served). For the fire department, variable costs would include the cost of fuel to run the fire trucks to attend to fires and the cost of water to put out fires.

Total variable costs (TVC) are the sum of all variable costs. **Average variable costs (AVC)** are the total variable costs divided by the level of output (X):

$$AVC = TVC/X$$

Total costs (TC) are simply the sum of total fixed costs and total variable costs. **Average total costs (ATC)** are equal to the sum of average fixed costs plus average variable costs.

$$TC = TFC + TVC$$
$$ATC = AFC + AVC$$

---

[1] Although some textbooks refer to fixed costs as sunk costs, the two can be distinguished. Fixed costs include recurring expenses that do not depend on output, such as equipment rentals and salaries of permanent employees. Sunk costs are previously incurred expenses that cannot be recovered, such as one-time nonrefundable fees and purchases, and prior expenditures on research and development.

Whether costs are classified as fixed or variable depends on the time frame. In the **short run**, a producer cannot fully adjust all factors. Some factors will remain fixed, such rental payments on equipment, insurance, salaries of long-term employees and the manufacturing plant. Other factors can be varied, such as the number of temporary employees and the materials to manufacture the product. Thus, the short run typically includes both fixed costs and variable costs.

In the **long run**, however, all factors can be adjusted. In other words, all costs (even formerly fixed costs) can become variable costs. For instance, over the long run, the producer can build additional manufacturing plants, lease more equipment, or hire more permanent employees. In fact, the definition of the *long run* is the period of time over which all factors can be adjusted fully, so all costs become variable costs. Thus, fixed costs in the long run are equal to zero.

Marginal costs (MC) are the additional costs to produce one more unit of output, or the reduction in costs to produce one less unit of output. Marginal costs are the difference between total costs for one more or one less unit of output.

$$MC_X = TC_X - TC_{X-1}$$

or

$$MC_X = TC_{X+1} - TC_X$$

MARGINAL ANALYSIS

The term *marginal* is one of most important concepts in economics. We commonly make decisions at the margin, or *marginal analysis*. We look at the costs of producing one more or one less unit, or the benefits of buying one more or one less unit. In other words, decisions are usually small incremental changes, rather than big leaps. Marginal analysis, for production decisions, can help to determine how changes in level of output will affect profits. A criterion is as follows: The profit-maximizing level is where the *marginal benefits equal marginal costs*.

This criterion leads to an important point. Private and public sector decisions use the same concepts of marginal analysis to help determine the appropriate level of production by setting marginal benefits equal to marginal costs. What gets included in that determination, however, often differs. For a private firm, the benefits are the revenues from the sale of a good, and the costs are those of production. For public production, the costs and benefits can be both monetary and nonmonetary. The objectives typically concern more than just profit maximization. In fact, the public sector may provide services at a running loss (monetarily), so one objective may be loss minimization rather than profit maximization.

The techniques of marginal analysis and the decisions of public versus private firms are illustrated through the following example.

EXAMPLE

Meals-on-Wheels Service

For years, the Crandall Cafe ran a good business serving truck drivers and tourists traveling along a busy U.S. highway. But when a new interstate highway opened, the cafe lost much of its business. Though it continued to serve local customers, the loss of the trucker and tourist trade reduced the cafe's business by nearly 50%.

In an effort to increase revenues, the cafe decided to provide a meals-on-wheels service to local residents. Customers could call in an order before 12 noon for meals that would be prepared at the cafe and delivered to their homes by 6 P.M. The service would be available to anyone, but the cafe owners expected that the majority of customers would be the elderly or disabled. Such meals-on-wheels services are often provided by public service agencies. With cutbacks in available funding for social services, however, no comparable service was currently available to local residents.

To start this service, the cafe rented a delivery van for $15 per day. Then, by charging $6 for each meal, the cafe hoped to supplement its normal business revenues while providing a useful community service.

Table 5-1 and Figure 5-1 show the costs and revenues for the cafe's meals-on-wheels service. We will go through each column in Table 5-1 to explain the terms and calculations. The *Number of Meals per Day* is, as the heading suggests, the number of meals sold during a one-day period for the meals-on-wheels service. The *Total Revenue* is how much money the cafe receives from

TABLE 5-1 *Costs and Revenues for Meals-on-Wheels*

Number of Meals per Day	Total Revenue ($)	Marginal Revenue ($)	Fixed Cost ($)	Variable Cost ($)	Average Variable Cost ($)	Total Cost ($)	Average Total Cost ($)	Marginal Cost ($)	Profit ($)
0			15.00	0		15.00			−15.00
1	6.00	6.00	15.00	3.00	3.00	18.00	18.00	3.00	−12.00
2	12.00	6.00	15.00	5.50	2.75	20.50	10.25	2.50	−8.50
3	18.00	6.00	15.00	7.50	2.50	22.50	7.50	2.00	−4.50
4	24.00	6.00	15.00	10.00	2.50	25.00	6.25	2.50	−1.00
5	30.00	6.00	15.00	13.00	2.60	28.00	5.60	3.00	2.00
6	36.00	6.00	15.00	16.50	2.75	31.50	5.25	3.50	4.50
7	42.00	6.00	15.00	20.50	2.93	35.50	5.07	4.00	6.50
8	48.00	6.00	15.00	25.00	3.13	40.00	5.00	4.50	8.00
9	54.00	6.00	15.00	30.00	3.33	45.00	5.00	5.00	9.00
10	60.00	6.00	15.00	35.50	3.55	50.50	5.05	5.50	9.50
11	66.00	6.00	15.00	41.50	3.77	56.50	5.14	6.00	9.50
12	72.00	6.00	15.00	48.00	4.00	63.00	5.25	6.50	9.00
13	78.00	6.00	15.00	55.00	4.23	70.00	5.38	7.00	8.00
14	84.00	6.00	15.00	62.50	4.46	77.50	5.54	7.50	6.50

FIGURE 5-1   *Cost Curves for Meals-on-Wheels*

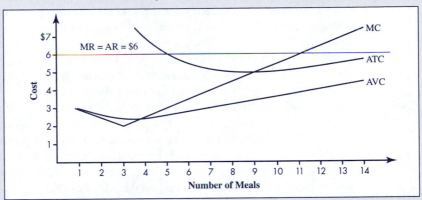

the sale of the meals. Total revenue is the number of meals sold, multiplied by $6, the price per meal. The *Marginal Revenue* would be the difference in revenue for the sale of one additional meal; which would be $6. In this case, the marginal revenue is the same as the price, which is the same for all quantities of output (meals sold). The *Fixed Cost* is $15 per day, the cost of renting the van, which must be paid even if no meals are sold. The *Variable Cost* varies with the number of meals sold, and includes the costs of gasoline for the van, the actual food for the meals, the paper plates, among others. The *Average Variable Cost* is the variable cost divided by the number of meals per day. The *Total Cost* is the sum of the fixed costs and the variable costs. The fixed costs remain constant during the period of analysis, whereas the variable costs will vary, depending on level of output. *Average Total Cost* is the total cost divided by the number of meals per day. *Marginal Cost* is the difference between the current total cost and the previous total cost, which is the additional cost from producing one additional meal. Note that marginal costs are different from variable costs because variable costs are a cumulative measure, and marginal costs are an incremental measure. *Profit* equals total revenue minus total cost.

Where is the profit-maximizing point? Is it where average total costs are lowest ($5), which is at eight or nine meals? No. The profit-maximizing point is where *marginal benefits equal marginal cost*s. In this case, marginal benefits are the marginal revenues, or the price ($6). The profit-maximizing level of output is thus at 11 meals, where marginal benefits (MB) = marginal costs (MC) = $6.

Why is the profit-maximizing point at 11 meals? At 10 or fewer meals, the marginal cost of producing an additional meal is less than the marginal revenue that would be earned, so the cafe could increase profits by selling an additional meal. At 12 or more meals, the marginal cost of producing an additional meal is greater than the marginal revenue that would be earned, so the cafe could

continued on next page

increase profits by reducing output. (Whether the cafe would actually reduce output and deny people meals for the sake of increasing profits is a topic addressed later.) For instance, producing 13 meals instead of 12 meals generates an additional $6 in revenues but also an additional $7 in costs. The last column, *Profit,* confirms this conclusion.

Note that the profit-maximizing level of production is not necessarily the point where average total costs are the lowest. Profit maximization depends on the relationship between marginal benefits and marginal costs. At the point of maximum profit, marginal costs will equal marginal benefits (marginal revenue) and either reducing or increasing output would reduce profits.

What if the cafe decided to sell the meals for $3.50 each? Refer to Figure 5-2. At this new price, the average revenue (price) is less than the average total cost, regardless of number of meals produced. Does that mean that the cafe will not ever make a profit, and should shut down and go out of business? Not necessarily. In the short run, determining whether to shut down depends on the relationship between marginal revenue and average variable costs, not between average revenue and average total cost.

The reason is that, although failure to cover the average total cost is not ideal, the cafe may continue to provide meals and eventually make a profit, even if its average revenue were less than its average total cost. To begin the meal service, the cafe had to incur some fixed costs, which included leasing a delivery van. These fixed costs do not vary with the level of output, and represent costs that in the short run must be absorbed even if the output were cut to zero. Variable costs, on the other hand, *do* vary with the number of meals produced and include items such as gasoline, paper plates, and actual food.

As long as the cafe is covering its average variable costs with its marginal revenues, it can start to pay off its fixed costs. So, to operate in the short run, a firm does not necessarily need to make a profit, but rather be able to cover its

FIGURE 5-2   *Marginal Revenue Greater Than Average Variable Cost*

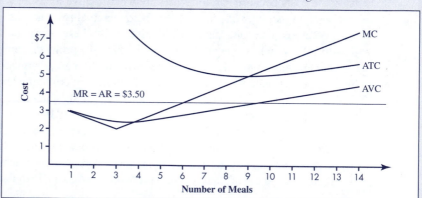

variable costs of operation, and start to pay off the fixed costs. So it may prove profitable for the cafe to continue operation, even if average revenues were less than average total costs, as long as *marginal revenues are greater than average variable costs*.

Now assume that, after a month of operation, the cafe discovered that it could only sell its meals for $2.25. In this situation, depicted in Figure 5-3, the marginal revenue is less than the average variable cost for all levels of output, so the cafe is better off shutting down the meals-on-wheels program. If it continued to operate, it would have to pay the $15 in fixed costs in addition to whatever variable costs were not covered by the sale of the meals. If it shut down, it would lose only those fixed costs involved in securing the van for its meals-on-wheels service.

The preceding scenario is the short-run result. In the long run, the situation could differ because the cafe could change its fixed costs as well. For only a few meals, it might not need the big delivery van. So the cafe might be able to cut fixed costs and find a profitable level of operation. If adjusting the fixed costs still failed to generate a profitable level of output in the long run, then the cafe might have to eliminate its service. Yet this analysis assumes that the primary objective of the cafe is profit maximization. The decision might be different if the meals-on-wheels service were run by a public agency, or if other goals were important to the cafe (such as community service), as we will see next.

FIGURE 5-3 *Marginal Revenue Less Than Average Variable Cost*

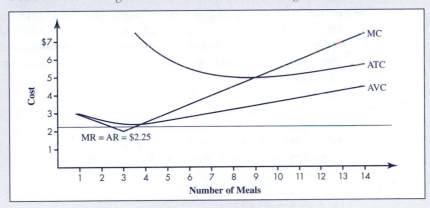

PRIVATE SECTOR AND PUBLIC SECTOR PRODUCTION DECISIONS

As we discussed, private firms typically operate to maximize profits, whereas public agencies typically consider additional objectives and a broader set of social benefits and social costs. Though the Crandall Cafe is a profit-making establishment, services such as meals-on-wheels are often provided to elderly, disabled, or special needs populations by public agencies. Providing meals-on-wheels may result in additional social benefits, beyond the revenues collected for the meals, such as improved health of the recipients.

The issue here is that the sales price of the meals may underestimate the total social benefits of providing the meals. For instance, improved health of the recipients can, in turn, provide benefits to the rest of society, which is considered a positive externality (as we will study in Chapter 9). Thus, the marginal benefits to society would be greater than just the marginal revenues to the cafe. If that were the case, a public agency should expand production beyond what a private firm would provide. It also means that a public agency would probably not be as willing to reduce output (deliver fewer meals) in order to increase profits, calculated in a strict monetary sense, because the meals provide other benefits not considered in that calculation.

Both private and public producers must determine the optimal level of production. Despite possible differences in objectives, the same principle applies: the profit-maximizing point, or the loss-minimizing point, will be where marginal costs equal the marginal benefit. We now look at additional criteria for production decisions, starting with the breakeven and shutdown points.

ADDITIONAL TOPICS IN PRODUCTION DECISIONS

BREAKEVEN AND SHUTDOWN POINTS

The **breakeven point** (Figure 5-4) is where marginal revenue (price) equals average total cost. To break even does not mean that a producer does not make a profit. Costs include opportunity costs, which is what the producer would have been earning in the highest alternative use of resources. At this point, the producer makes a normal "economic profit," which is examined in the next section.

Breakeven point: MR = ATC

The **shutdown point** (Figure 5-4) is when the marginal revenue (price) is less than or equal to average variable costs.[2] In these cases, the firm will minimize its losses by shutting down.[3]

Shutdown point: MR ≤ AVC

---

[2] In this case, MR (price) intersects with AVC at two points. The point representing the greater quantity (given the same price) would producer greater total revenues (remembering that TR = $P*Q$), and thus is the relevant point of production.

[3] A shutdown typically refers to a decision to stop production in the short run because of current conditions. In the long run, the decision becomes whether to exit the market entirely, as we will examine later in this chapter.

FIGURE 5-4 *Breakeven Point and Shutdown Point*

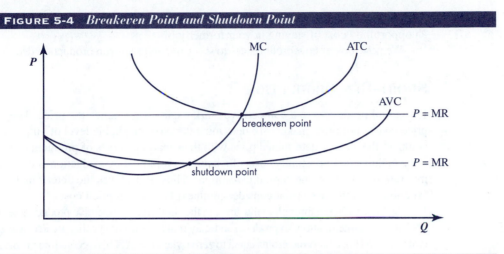

ACCOUNTING PROFIT AND ECONOMIC PROFIT

As we saw, the definition of profit is straightforward: revenues minus costs. However, a distinction can be made between *accounting profit* and *economic profit*. Accounting profit is how many people think of profit: It is the money left over after all the bills are paid. In other words, *accounting profit is equal to revenues minus explicit costs*. Explicit costs involve a direct monetary expenditure.

Economic profit, however, considers not only explicit costs (such as bills to pay) but also implicit costs such as self-employed resources, interest on capital already owned by producers, and the opportunity cost of resources. Thus, *economic profit is equal to revenues minus both explicit and implicit costs*. Implicit costs do not require a direct monetary expenditure.

To illustrate this distinction, suppose that you quit your office job to open up a coffee shop. At the end of the year, your accounting statement from the coffee shop shows $300,000 in revenues from sales, and $230,000 in operating costs, which include equipment rental fees. To rent the equipment, you placed a deposit of $10,000, which is fully refundable. You pay yourself a $40,000 salary, and have $30,000 left over. You are pleased because you have made a profit—an accounting profit—this year. But are you really profitable?

It depends. At your former job, you worked 40 hours per week. Now, to run the coffee shop, you work 80 hours per week. So the accounting costs overlooked the opportunity costs of your time, such as the money that you could have earned from the additional 40 hours per week, and the salary you would have earned from your former job. It also overlooked the interest that could have been earned on the $10,000 deposit to rent equipment. If those additional implicit costs exceeded $30,000, your coffee shop would not show an economic profit. On the other hand, the enjoyment of running the coffee shop may provide benefits that exceed those opportunity costs, so the coffee shop would provide an economic profit. Viewed another way, those benefits—the enjoyment derived from your time at the coffee shop—would be considered an opportunity cost of staying in your former job.

We now look at how profit relates to short-run and long-run production decisions.

SHORT-RUN PRODUCTION

Individual producers in a competitive market cannot influence the price. They are price takers, not price makers. To determine the most profitable level of output, they compare the market-determined price with their marginal costs of production. These costs include the opportunity costs of resources employed in production and the normal rate of return on the capital investment. Thus, it involves the determination of "economic profit" because it considers both explicit and implicit costs.

As Figures 5-5 (a through c) illustrate, in the short run, competitive producers set $P = MC$, to determine quantity to produce, and may make economic profits greater than zero (when $P >$ ATC), economic profits equal to zero (when $P =$ ATC), or economic profits less than zero (when $P <$ ATC). Profit $= (P -$ ATC$) \times Q$. At the breakeven point in Figure 5-5 (b), a competitive producer earns a normal economic profit (also known as "zero economic

FIGURE 5-5 *Short-Run Production*

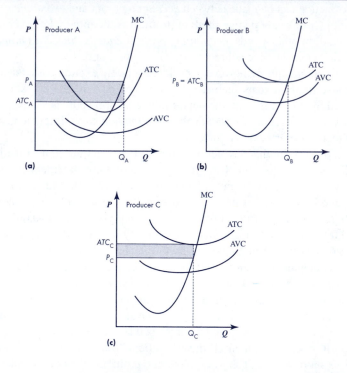

profit"), meaning that the competitive producer makes a normal rate of return on its invest-ment. Zero economic profit may seem undesirable, as if the producer is not making money. But recall that we are considering economic (not accounting) profit, which includes the amount that could have been earned in the highest alternative investment.

Producer A is earning economic profits greater than zero because the market price P_A exceeds the average total costs, ATC_A, for the profit-maximizing quantity Q_A. These profits, represented by the shaded area, are in addition to the normal profits included in the producer's cost curves. Producer B is earning economic profits equal to zero because the prevailing market price P_B just covers the average total costs, ATC_B, at the profit-maximizing quantity Q_B. It is called making a *normal return*, typical of compet-itive markets. Producer C is earning economic profits less than zero, and experiencing a loss, because the market price P_C is below the average total costs, ATC_C, for the loss-minimizing quantity Q_C. In the short run, however, Producer C may continue to pro-duce because the price, P_C, is greater than the average variable costs (AVC).

As seen in Figure 5-5, the short-run ATC curves are U-shaped. Where MC inter-sects ATC is the point of minimum ATC. When MC is less than ATC, it pulls down ATC. When MC is greater than ATC, it raises ATC. An analogy is to think of ATC as your cumulative grade point average (GPA) for all your terms in school, and MC as your grade point average for one term. When your GPA for one term is less than your cumulative GPA, that brings down your cumulative GPA. But when your GPA for one term is greater than your cumulative GPA, that raises your cumulative GPA.

DERIVING THE SUPPLY CURVE

From these concepts, we can also see how the supply curve is derived (Figure 5-6). In the short run, a profit-maximizing producer will supply the quantity for which the marginal revenue (price) equals marginal cost (MR = MC). This quantity is the profit-maximizing point at that price. Now, for each price (P_1, P_2, P_3, P_4, P_5, etc.), which represents *marginal revenue*, find its intersection with *marginal costs*. Each of these points is profit-maximizing and is noted along the marginal cost curve (Figure 5-6). The locus of profit-maximizing points, for each possible price (above the shut-down point), creates the supply curve. Thus, for a profit-maximizing producer, in the short run, *the supply curve is the marginal cost curve above the shutdown point.*

LONG-RUN PRODUCTION

As we saw, in the short run, producers cannot vary all inputs. Each additional unit of variable input, added to the fixed input, often results in diminishing marginal units of output. This effect is the law of diminishing returns, as we studied in Chapter 2. For example, at low levels of production, hiring one additional worker can increase output significantly. At higher levels of production, however, each additional worker might start to get in the way of the others, or need to wait in line to use the equip-ment. Each additional worker, thus, is not able to be as productive as the previous one. Total output still increases, but at a diminishing rate.

FIGURE 5-6 *Derivation of the Supply Curve*

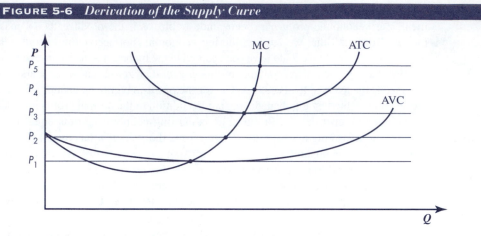

In the long run, fixed costs become variable, and the producer can change all input factors, such as adding new facilities. Each new facility would have associated with it a short-run average total cost (SRATC) curve. The long-run average total cost (LRATC) curve is formed by connecting the least-cost points (i.e., the minimum average cost for the given level of output) from each of the short-run average total cost (SRATC) curves (Figure 5-7). The long-run average total cost curve represents the lowest average cost for each level of output in the long run, when all the inputs are variable.

We will now examine the relationship between long-run costs and output. **Economies of scale** mean that long-run average total costs decrease as output increases. **Constant returns to scale** mean that long-run average total costs stay the same, regardless of level of output. **Diseconomies of scale** occur when long-run average total costs increase as output increases.[4] They explain the U-shape of the long-run average total cost curve (Figure 5-8).

In Figure 5-8, the first section (A) displays economies of scale, which typically result from labor and managerial specialization, efficient use of capital, and declining per-unit costs associated with start-up expenditures. Specialization matches people's talents with tasks. A person with years of experience at a task can be more proficient and efficient than a new employee at that task. Efficient use of capital means, for instance, that a coffee maker with 10 times the volume may

---

[4] The terms *economies/diseconomies of scale* are not to be confused with the terms *increasing/decreasing returns to scale*. Economies/diseconomies of scale are decreased/increased LRATC as output increases. Increasing/decreasing returns to scale are when increasing inputs, all in the same proportion, leads to proportionally greater/lesser output. Economies of scale can result from increasing returns to scale, but economies of scale are a more general case of decreased costs with increased output, and allows for inputs in different proportions.

require only twice as much electricity to run. Declining per-unit costs with start-up expenditures occur because as output increases, start-up costs are spread over more units.

Eventually, the potential for economies of scale are reduced and depleted. The section of the LRATC curve (B) exhibits constant returns to scale, where the slope of the LRATC curve is zero (or approximately zero). The final section of the cost curve (C) exhibits diseconomies of scale. Factors causing diseconomies of scale include the same factors that create economies of scale, but were carried too far, such as overspecialization, or growing so large as to create inefficiencies. For instance,

FIGURE 5-7 *Long-Run Average Total Cost*

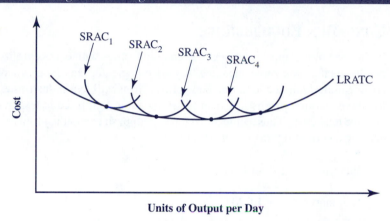

FIGURE 5-8 *Long-Run Average Total Cost and Economies of Scale*

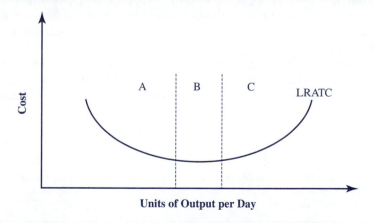

employees who perform the same task repeatedly may become tired and bored. Growing large often means more complex equipment, more bureaucracy, more layers of employees, and more inefficiencies. This result is true of many organizations, both private firms and public agencies.

Note that diseconomies of scale are different from diminishing marginal returns. Diseconomies of scale are increasing average total costs for increased output, in the long run, when all inputs are variable rather than when only some inputs are variable. Diminishing marginal returns are related to increasing marginal costs for increased output in the short run, where more of one input is added and other inputs are constant. The U-shape of the LRATC curve results from economies and diseconomies of scale, not due to the law of diminishing marginal returns (as with the short-run ATC curve).

LONG-RUN EQUILIBRIUM

In the long run, competitive firms will enter industries with excess profits (economic profits greater than zero), meaning that price is greater than long-run average total cost.[5] Similarly, in the long run, competitive firms will exit industries experiencing losses (economic profits less than zero), meaning that price is less than long-run average total cost.[6] Thus, competitive forces will push economic profits to zero (firms earning a normal return) within an industry.

Enter market if $P > $ LRATC

Exit market if $P < $ LRATC

In long-run equilibrium in a competitive industry, with firms earning economic profits equal to zero, and with free entry and exit, firms operate at the minimum point of the long-run average cost curve. This point, with zero economic profit, is the breakeven point, where $P = $ long-run MC $= $ minimum LRATC. The competitive firm's long-run supply curve is the portion of the marginal cost curve that is above the exit point ($P \geq $ LRATC), or equal to or above the breakeven point (Figure 5-9).

Before leaving our study of costs, we will examine one more important concept—producer surplus—which represents net benefits to producers, just as consumer surplus represents the net benefits to consumers. We conclude with an example of costs for a public agency development decision.

---

[5] This result follows from the earlier discussion on economic profit. An alternative way to arrive at this criterion is by examining the profit relationship, $P = $ TR $- $ TC. For profits greater than zero, TR $> $ TC. Dividing by Q, we get $P > $ ATC.

[6] Similarly, for profits less than zero, TR $< $ TC. Dividing by Q, we get $P < $ ATC.

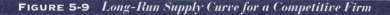

FIGURE 5-9 *Long-Run Supply Curve for a Competitive Firm*

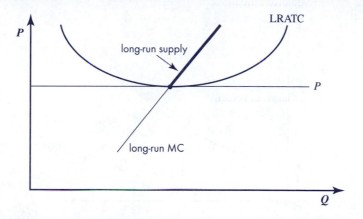

PRODUCER SURPLUS

We examined consumer surplus in Chapter 4. Its corresponding measure on the supply side is producer surplus. Both of these measures are important because they can help to assess benefits and costs resulting from decisions, and we will apply them in later chapters.

Producer surplus is the net gain to producers in a given market. The gain results because the price that producers receive is often greater than the minimum price they would need to receive to supply a certain quantity of a good. As shown in Figure 5-10, producer surplus is simply the area between the supply curve and the price.[7] In other words, it is the difference between the minimum total revenue that producers would need to receive, and the amount they actually receive, to produce a given quantity. Referring again to Figure 5-10, the area OP_1EQ_1 is the minimum total revenue that producers would need to receive in order to be willing to produce the quantity of Q_1 at the price of P_2.[8] But the total revenue they actually receive is the area of OP_2EQ_1. Thus, the difference between the two is the shaded area P_1P_2E, which is the extra benefit, or producer surplus.

A change in price or quantity can change the amount of producer surplus. Referring to Figure 5-11, note that a decrease in price, from P_2 to P^*, would reduce producer surplus. The new producer surplus is represented by the shaded area $P_1P^*E^*$. Producers would only need to receive $O\,P_1E^*Q^*$ to produce Q^*, but they

---

[7] The area between the price and the supply curve represents a *positive* producer surplus when the price is above the supply curve, and a *negative* producer surplus when the price is below the supply curve. Positive means net gains to producers and negative means net losses to producers.

[8] This area is also equal to the total variable cost, which is the integral of the marginal cost curve.

FIGURE 5-10 *Producer Surplus*

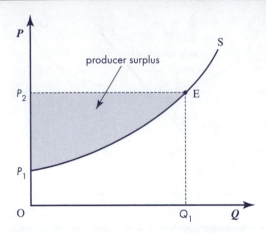

FIGURE 5-11 *Decrease in Producer Surplus Due to a Decrease in Price*

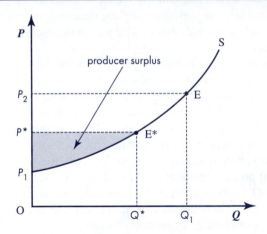

receive $OP*E*Q*$, which is an extra benefit of P_1P*E*. This area, though, represents a decrease in producer surplus from the previous price P_2, by the amount $P*P_2EE*$.

DIFFERENCE BETWEEN PRODUCER SURPLUS AND PROFITS

A common confusion is the relationship between producer surplus and profits. To examine this relationship, we first distinguish between short-run producer surplus and long-run producer surplus.

Producer surplus is total revenues minus total variable costs, or the area between price and the supply curve. Profit is total revenues minus total costs. (Recall that total costs are total variable costs plus total fixed costs.) Short-run producer surplus, then, represents short-run profits plus total fixed costs.[9] To determine short-run profits, fixed costs would need to be subtracted from producer surplus.

In the long run, however, fixed costs are zero (all costs are variable costs), and economic profit is zero (for perfectly competitive firms in an industry). So long-run producer surplus represents "economic rent" earned by factors of production. Economic rent is the return earned by an input factor that is in excess of the minimum return required to supply that factor. In other words, rent is the total payment given to a factor of production in excess of its opportunity cost.

Long-run producer surplus represents the total net gain to anyone involved in the production of the good, including suppliers of input factors, and this is the sum of long-run profits. For welfare analysis (as we will study in Chapter 7), it is common to use long-run producer surplus.[10]

EXAMPLE   **Cost of Community Development Activities**

A large northeastern state enacted an Urban Aid program to supplement federally funded Community Development Block Grants. This program provided small block grants to urban communities to permit them to expand existing community development activities or to develop new activities. Under this program, a large city was designated to receive $1 million for the next calendar year. After consulting neighborhood groups, civic leaders, and local politicians, the city decided to spend $500,000 for sidewalk repairs and street tree plantings, $300,000 for an emergency housing repair program, $100,000 for a parks and recreation program, and $100,000 for a vacant lot clearance program.

The City Council scheduled a public hearing to review the proposed plans. At the hearing, Council members and citizens voiced general approval of both the broad allocation of funds and the specifics of the four programs, but several members expressed reservations about the vacant lot clearance program. As shown in Table 5-2, the program would spend $66,000 of the $100,000 to employ high school students for 20,000 hours, with a remainder of the budget ($34,000) allocated to supervision and equipment.

continued on next page

---

[9] Producer surplus = TR – TVC = TR – (TC – TFC) = TR – TC + TFC = profits + TFC.

[10] For a more extensive treatment of producer surplus, see W. Nicholson (2001), *Microeconomic Theory: Basic Principles and Extensions* (8th ed.), Fort Worth, TX: Dryden Press.

TABLE 5-2 *Vacant Lot Clearance Program*

Brief Description: Program will hire high school students on a part-time basis to clear brush and debris from vacant lots in four target neighborhoods. Only city residents are eligible to work in the program with preference given to residents of the four target areas.

	Budget
Part-time Young Employees:	
Wage (20,000 hours @ $3)	$60,000
Fringes (10% of wage bill)	6,000
Supervisory Personnel:	
Quarter-time project manager	5,000
Two full-time crew chiefs	18,000
Materials:	
Trash bags, rakes, etc.	5,000
Truck rental and insurance	6,000
TOTAL	$100,000

Questions

a) Council Member Richardson proposed instead that 25,000 hours (compared to the original 20,000 hours) of student labor be used (raising costs by $16,500) while keeping the total allocation for vacant lot clearance at $100,000 and continuing to pay the same wage and fringe rate in force at that time. The council member maintained that this approach would further mitigate the youth unemployment problem, while costing the city nothing. Is the council member correct that this modification to the proposal is without cost to the city? Why or why not?

b) Council Member Wyatt responded by saying that Richardson's proposal would be a waste of funds if it did not provide necessary additional supervision. Instead, the additional 5,000 hours could be provided, without cost to the city, by allocating $16,500 from the housing repair program to provide the necessary funds for the increased wages and fringe benefits, and to provide efficient levels of supervision and equipment. Is the council member correct that this modification to the proposal is without cost to the city? Why or why not?

c) Council Member Harrison agreed with Richardson and Wyatt that further increasing youth employment was a worthy goal, but Harrison did not want to cut into badly needed housing repair funds. Harrison claimed that the way to provide the extra hours of employment at no cost to the city was by taking the extra funds for labor, supervision, and equipment from general city revenues. Although this approach would deplete city revenues, Harrison claimed that the revenue loss would be offset exactly by wage and benefit payments to city residents—the youth employed—and thus would only redistribute city resources while costing city residents nothing as a whole. Is the council member correct that this modification to the proposal is without cost to the city? Why or why not?

Answers

a) Not really. Assuming that the original mix of labor, supervision, and equipment satisfying the budget constraint of $100,000 is the best mix for clearing lots (i.e., clears the most lots), then the changed mix of factors (increased labor) would impose an opportunity cost. This opportunity cost would include the reduced number of lots cleared, because of insufficient supervision and materials, and the value of the highest alternative use of the increased labor. Yet the council member could be correct if the expert on lot clearance, who originally drew up the allocation of factor inputs, erred on the side of too little labor. Then increasing the proportion of youth labor would result in more lots cleared for the same money. A second possibility, assuming again that the original mix was optimal for lot clearance, is that the technology may be such that, within the range of the suggested modification, substitution is possible. Labor then may be substituted for equipment and supervision at a rate exactly equal to the rate at which their costs allow such substitutions without any loss in output. More likely, however, diminishing returns would accompany the use of more labor.

b) Not really. Although Wyatt's revised mix of factors provides for more youth labor and is likely to be more efficient for lot clearance, Wyatt does not recognize the additional opportunity cost in the form of housing repairs that would not be not made. Furthermore, in the description of the program, the City Council members agreed on the broad allocation of funds among programs. Thus, we might assume that, at least originally, the Council believed the benefits derived from an additional $16,500 spent on lot clearance was not worth the opportunity cost of fewer housing repairs. Otherwise, they would have originally allocated $116,500 (total) to lot clearance.

c) Not really. Net benefits could still be derived by using the revenues to purchase something else of use to the city. And they would need to consider the opportunity costs of using the revenues for employment rather than another activity. If used for employment, the city could have the same youths that Harrison would hire for clearance instead deliver meals to the elderly. Delivering meals to the elderly is an opportunity cost of hiring the youths to clear the lots, and in this case, the redistributive consequences that the council members desire are similar.

REVIEW QUESTIONS

1. Your city's public works commissioner has a workforce of 100 workers. All workers receive $7 per hour, but 50 are eligible for federal subsidies (of $6/hour/worker), so their net cost to the city is only $1 per hour. All 100 workers are currently employed on jobs around the city. Unfortunately, no more federal funds are available for additional workers. Your city's mayor wants the commissioner to assign some workers to fix up a neighborhood park. The job will take 100 labor hours. The mayor argues that it's worthwhile because the average cost of a worker is only $4 per hour (50 workers at $7.00 and 50 at $1.00), so costs are relatively small—only $400.
    a) Comment on the mayor's analysis, assuming that additional workers need to be hired to fix up the neighborhood park, because existing workers are needed on other projects.
    b) Suppose the commissioner's workforce is fixed at 100 workers, and no additional workers may be hired, so that in order to do the mayor's job, workers must be taken off other jobs. In this case, what cost should be ascribed to the labor used on the mayor's project?

2. City government employees occasionally use their own automobiles on official business. The current reimbursement rate is $0.25 per mile. The employees' union complained to the city manager that the cost of operating an automobile is really $0.45 per mile, so the current rate is too low. The city manager notes that at the current rate, workers seem delighted when they have a reason to use their own cars and get reimbursed at $0.25 per mile. Assuming that both the union and the city manager are justified in their comments, explain this seeming inconsistency.

3. Two years ago, a professor hurt his back. Shortly after he recovered, he went skiing. After he returned, a colleague (an economist) asked him why he had gone, because he had risked considerable pain to his back. He replied, "I wouldn't have gone, but I'd already paid for the trip long before I hurt my back, and I couldn't get any money refunded. I suppose that economists would say that was irrational, because sunk costs are sunk so the fact that I had shelled out a lot of money shouldn't have made any difference to that decision. But I went anyway, so there!" Comment on the professor's decision.

4. Suppose that you are a consultant to a firm that designs software programs. The firm is about to produce a new software package that will sell for $200 per copy. The fixed cost of publishing the software packages is $100,000. The variable cost is $100 per copy. What is the breakeven point for this software package?

5. Classify the following types of costs for the meals-on-wheels example provided in this chapter. Are they fixed costs, variable costs, or some of both?
    a) The paper plates used for each meal
    b) The gasoline used to deliver meals in the leased van
    c) The annual insurance on the leased van
    d) Real estate taxes on the restaurant
    e) Wages for permanent, full-time employees
    f) Electricity to operate the restaurant

CHAPTER 5 APPENDIX: PRODUCTION FUNCTIONS

This appendix provides an extension to the preceding chapter by examining relationships between costs of inputs and quantities of output. A **production function** shows the maximum output that can be attained for given inputs entering the production process. It can be thought of as a table, graph, or equation showing the relation between inputs and outputs.

Mathematically, a production function can be expressed as:

$$Q = f(X, Y, Z, \ldots)$$

This equation states that the level of output Q of a good is a function of the inputs X, Y, and Z, and so on. Consider, for example, the production function of a municipal sanitation department:

$$Q = f(T, N, X)$$

where

Q = the tons of trash collected per day
T = the number of trucks used each day
N = the number of labor hours devoted to trash collection
X = the number of transfer sites available each day

The production of a trash collection service uses some inputs that are easy to change, while other items are more difficult to alter. The addition of a new transfer site would require considerable planning and a large expenditure of funds. Alternatively, the number of available trucks could change more easily through modification of a lease arrangement or through the sale or acquisition of trucks. The production function thus serves as a reminder that, in the short run, production can be constrained by the fixed supply of certain factors of production.

The exact specification of a production function depends on a number of both technical and managerial factors. The amount of trash collected by a given number of trucks and workers will depend on their specific characteristics. Some trucks will require one driver and one or two additional workers or collectors. Smaller trucks may require only one worker who doubles as driver and collector. In addition to the characteristics of the trucks, assignment of crews could depend on work rules established as part of collective bargaining between city employees and city officials. Thus, even though it would be technically feasible to operate a specific piece of equipment with two workers, other concerns could result in use of three-person crews. The production function is not a substitute for this detailed evaluation of technical or management issues, but rather a simple framework for characterizing the relationship between inputs and outputs.

Assume, for example, that for the Cambridge Sanitation Department (CSD), the tons of trash collected per day is primarily a function of only three inputs: number of trucks, number of labor hours, and number of transfer sites. In the short run, the number of transfer sites is fixed, but trucks can be leased, and employees hired, fired, or transferred to or from other city departments. Table A5-1 shows how output changes in the short run in response to changes in the two variable factors of production, given the availability and use of three transfer sites. As shown in the table, with five trucks and 100 labor-hours, CSD can collect 35 tons of trash per day. Similarly, with 15 trucks and 250 labor-hours, CSD can collect 130 tons daily.

TABLE A5-1 *Tons of Trash Collected per Day as a Function of Daily Use of Trucks and Labor-Hours*

	Trucks per Day			
Labor-Hours per Day	5	10	15	20
50	20	40	50	60
100	35	60	80	100
150	50	80	100	115
200	65	90	116	128
250	75	100	130	140
300	84	110	140	151
350	93	120	147	161
400	100	125	153	170
450	104	130	159	179
500	107	134	165	187
550	109	137	170	193
600	110	139	174	199
650	110	140	177	205
700	110	140	180	210
750	110	140	182	214
800	110	140	183	217

Note: Table assumes three transfer sites available. A different table could be constructed for any fixed number of transfer sites.

Table A5-1 indicates that increases in the number of trucks and the number of employees generally lead to increases in the tons of trash collected. The relationships, however, are not linear: Adding trucks without increasing labor-hours, or increasing the labor-hours without adding trucks produces successively smaller increases in output.

For example, with 20 trucks available, expansion of the labor-hours from 150 to 200 (adding 50 hours) increases output from 115 tons to 128 tons or an increase of 13 tons. Further expansion to 250 hours (adding 50 more hours), however, increases output by only 12 tons, from 128 to 140. Similarly, with 200 hours of labor, expanding the number of trucks from 10 to 15 trucks (adding 5 trucks) increases output by 26 tons (from 90 to 116), but the move from 15 to 20 trucks (adding 5 more trucks) only adds 12 tons per day to output (from 116 to 128). These comparisons illustrate the law of diminishing returns, which means that each additional unit of input results in diminishing increments of output.

The law of diminishing returns can be formally defined in terms of the marginal productivity of a factor of production, or the marginal product. **The marginal product** is the change in the level of output that results from a one-unit change in one factor of production, holding constant the other factors or inputs. In Figure A5-1, the marginal product of labor given the availability of 10 trucks is the slope of the curve labeled "10 trucks." At low levels of labor input, additional labor sharply increases output, hence the marginal product of labor is greater. Eventually, the slope of the line reduces and output reaches a maximum level of 140 tons for 10 trucks. At this point, the slope of the line is zero and the marginal product of labor is zero because additional units of labor input result in no increase in output. Thus, the law of dimin-

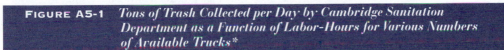

FIGURE A5-1   *Tons of Trash Collected per Day by Cambridge Sanitation Department as a Function of Labor-Hours for Various Numbers of Available Trucks**

*This figure plots data from Table A5-1.

ishing returns says that increased use of one factor of production, holding all other factors of production fixed, will eventually result in a decline in the marginal productivity of the factor. Also, notice from Figure A5-1 that the marginal product of a factor will depend on the level of the other factors used. Marginal products for one factor are almost always greater, given a larger level of other factors. Thus, as the number of trucks increases, the marginal product of adding another labor-hour will also increase.

FACTOR SUBSTITUTION

The City of Cambridge generates approximately 100 tons of trash per day and operates three transfer sites. Taking the number of transfer sites as fixed, Table A5-1 indicates that the CSD could collect this amount of trash using several different combinations of labor and trucks. For example, the CSD could use 400 labor-hours and 5 trucks, or 100 labor-hours and 20 trucks. Conceptually, it is possible to trade off the number of trucks used with the number of labor-hours employed and still collect a fixed level of trash.

Figure A5-2 expresses graphically the information on the various combinations of trucks and labor-hours that produce 100 tons of output per day. This curve is an **isoquant**, or a curve of constant quantity, showing all possible efficient combinations of inputs that are capable of producing a certain quantity of output. *Efficient* refers here to the requirement that factors of production are not wasted; that is, that the factors of production are employed to produce the maximum possible output. For example, with 400 labor-hours, the curve indicates that 5 trucks are required to produce 100 tons of trash collection. The 100 tons also could be collected using 400 labor-hours and 10 trucks, but this second combination is wasteful of resources (because

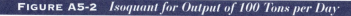

FIGURE A5-2   *Isoquant for Output of 100 Tons per Day*

FIGURE A5-3 *Isoquants for Various Daily Output Levels*

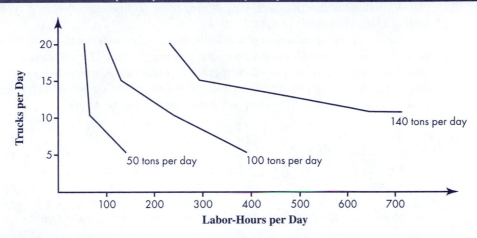

only 5 trucks are needed) and is therefore not on the isoquant for 100 units of output. Figure A5-3 displays isoquants for other levels of output, consistent with data presented in Table A5-1. Thus, for example, the 140 ton isoquant includes the point representing an input of 300 labor-hours and 15 trucks.

The shape of an isoquant depends on the possibility of substituting one input for another in the production of a given amount of the good or service. The **marginal rate of technical substitution** (MRTS) is the rate at which one input can be substituted for another input while maintaining a constant output. In the case of the CSD, the MRTS of labor for trucks is defined as

$$\text{MRTS (of } N \text{ for } T) = -dT/dN, \ Q = \text{constant}$$

Where N = number of labor-hours, T = number of trucks, and dT/dN is the derivative of T with respect to N. Thus, MRTS equals –1 times the slope of the isoquant. MRTS decreases as we move to the right along an isoquant, and so does the absolute value of the slope of the isoquant.

MATHEMATICS OF PRODUCTION FUNCTIONS

We will now examine other properties of production functions. Consider a production function of the general form $Q = f(K,L,M)$ where

Q = the quantity produced
K = the quantity of capital
L = the quantity of labor
M = the quantity of materials

All other factors are held constant.

A production function with typical properties will be classified as a type of Cobb-Douglas function[1]: $Q = AK^aL^bM^c$.

Let's assume a production process where $a = 1/2$, $b = 1/2$, and $c = 0$. We can solve for the isoquants characterized by the process $Q = 10K^{1/2}L^{1/2}$. Because an isoquant represents all points producing a given constant output, we set the quantity Q equal to the desired output. Thus, the isoquant for 60 units of output for a production process characterized by $Q = 10K^{1/2}L^{1/2}$ would be (see Figure A5-4):

$$
\begin{aligned}
60 &= 10K^{1/2}L^{1/2} \\
6 &= K^{1/2}L^{1/2} \\
36 &= KL \\
K &= 36/L
\end{aligned}
$$

More generally, if we solve for K and L in terms of any Q, we obtain:

$$
\begin{aligned}
Q &= 10K^{1/2}L^{1/2} \\
Q^2 &= 100KL \\
K &= (Q^2/100)(1/L)
\end{aligned}
$$

Inserting $Q = 60$ would give us $K = 36/L$, but by inserting any Q, we can generate the entire family of isoquants. (See Figure A5-5.)

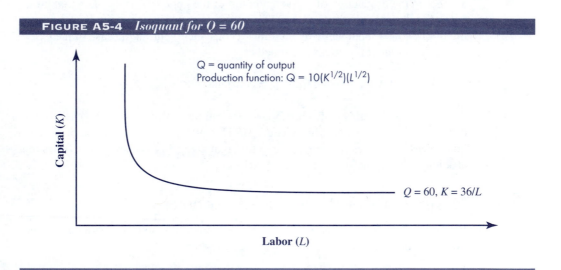

FIGURE A5-4 *Isoquant for $Q = 60$*

Q = quantity of output
Production function: $Q = 10(K^{1/2})(L^{1/2})$

Capital (K)

$Q = 60$, $K = 36/L$

Labor (L)

---

[1] When $a + b + c = 1$, the production process exhibits constant returns to scale. When $a + b + c > 1$, it exhibits increasing returns to scale. When $a + b + c < 1$, it exhibits decreasing returns to scale.

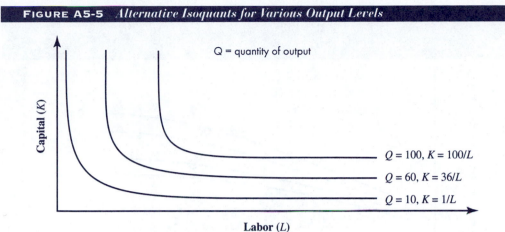

FIGURE A5-5 *Alternative Isoquants for Various Output Levels*

Q = quantity of output

Capital (K)

$Q = 100, K = 100/L$

$Q = 60, K = 36/L$

$Q = 10, K = 1/L$

Labor (L)

DIMINISHING MARGINAL PRODUCTIVITY

The marginal product of a factor, such as labor-hours, can be represented as the slope of the total product curve graphed as a function of labor-hours for given fixed amounts of other factors, such as capital (or trucks in Figure A5-1, reproduced as Figure A5-6).

If we evaluate the marginal product at a point where large inputs of labor are utilized, such as at points A, A_1, A_2, or A_3, we see that the slope of the curve diminishes (becomes flat) for any fixed amount of trucks. The slope of the curve at these points can be represented geometrically as the tangent to the curve at these points. In calculus, the marginal product of labor would be the derivative of Q with respect to L, holding capital fixed, noted as dQ/dL with K = constant. But with fixed K, we can simply define the marginal product as the partial derivative of Q with respect to L, which is $\partial Q/\partial L$.

The marginal product of labor, $\partial Q/\partial L$, for the production process characterized by $Q = 10K^{1/2}L^{1/2}$ is given by

$\partial Q/\partial L = 1/2(10)\ K^{1/2}L^{-1/2}$
$\partial Q/\partial L = 5K^{1/2}L^{-1/2}$

Figure A5-7 shows this marginal product curve ($5K^{1/2}L^{-1/2}$) for various fixed amounts of capital and variable amounts of labor-hours. At the point in the production process where $K = 100$ and $L = 25$ (Point A), MP = 10. Similarly, the marginal products for other combinations of capital and labor-hours can be determined: $K = 400$, $L = 25$, MP = 20 (Point B), and $K = 100$, $L = 9$, MP = 16 (Point C).

FIGURE A5-6   *Tons of Trash Collected per Day by Cambridge Sanitation Department as a Function of Labor-Hours for Various Numbers of Available Trucks**

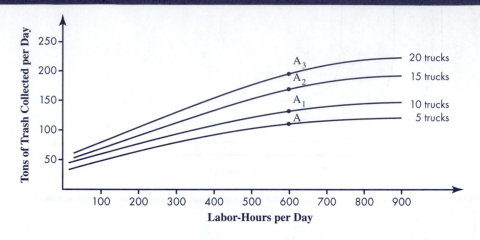

*This figure plots data from Table A5-1.

FIGURE A5-7   *Marginal Product Curve ($Q = 5K^{1/2}L^{-1/2}$) of Production for Fixed Amounts of Capital*

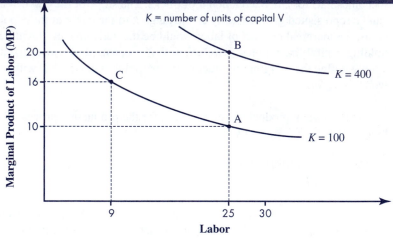

Diminishing marginal productivity (illustrated by this function) means that the marginal product of labor-hours gets smaller as more L is used with a fixed amount of K, as shown in Figure A5-7.

Using calculus, the change in the marginal product with respect to labor-hours with K constant is simply the second partial derivative, $\partial^2 Q/\partial^2 L^2$. For our example ($Q = 10K^{1/2}L^{1/2}$), the first partial derivative is

$$\partial Q/\partial L = 5K^{1/2}L^{-1/2}$$

and the second partial derivative becomes

$$\partial^2 Q/\partial^2 L^2 = -2.5K^{1/2}\,L^{-3/2}$$

Because K and L are positive, $-2.5K^{1/2}\,L^{-3/2}$ is negative. Thus, our example of the mathematical form of a typical production function exhibits diminishing marginal productivity as L increases.

CONSTRAINED MAXIMIZATION OR MINIMIZATION

In general, the production problem can be viewed as either maximizing output given a budget constraint or minimizing costs given an output to produce. Mathematically, these production decisions are called constrained maximization or minimization problems.

For example, assume a production function of the form $Q = 5LK$ and a budget constraint of $\$2L + \$1K = \$100$. We want to maximize Q subject to the constraint of the budget. Because the point will have to satisfy both relationships, we can solve for K and substitute in the production function. Because $K = 100 - 2L$,

$$Q = 5L(100 - 2L) = 500L - L^2$$

Using calculus, first-order conditions for maximization set the first derivative equal to 0. Thus,

$$
\begin{aligned}
dQ/dL &= 500 - 20L \\
0 &= 500 - 20L \\
L &= 25
\end{aligned}
$$

Because $K = 100 - 2L$, $K = 50$. Thus, if the firm uses 25 units of labor-hours and 50 units of capital, it will satisfy the budget constraint while achieving maximum output.

PART 2

Public Sector Economics and Market Failures

6 Efficiency and Equity 139

7 Welfare Economics 157

8 Monopoly 173

9 Externalities 191

10 Public Goods 223

11 Imperfect Information 251

EFFICIENCY AND EQUITY

his chapter examines two of the most important criteria in public sector decision making: efficiency and equity. Historically, economists have focused on promoting efficiency. Yet efficiency does not guarantee an equitable outcome. Even a perfectly competitive and efficient economy can produce outcomes that are unacceptable in terms of equity. On the other hand, government interventions to improve aspects of efficiency or equity can cause losses to either or to both. As we will see, issues concerning efficiency and equity, and their trade-offs, pose some of the greatest challenges in the public sector.

The first section of this chapter examines the primary definitions and criteria of efficiency, and the second section examines concepts of equity. In the third section, we examine cases in which the market may fail to produce an efficient outcome, providing one rationale for government intervention in the market. Another rationale, explored in the fourth section, is where markets may be efficient, but intervention is justified on other grounds, such as to promote a more equitable distribution of resources, even at costs to efficiency. The chapter that follows (on welfare economics) will provide the analytic and quantitative methods for examining these efficiency and equity consequences of decisions.

EFFICIENCY AND THE MARKET ECONOMY

THE "INVISIBLE HAND" DOCTRINE

Adam Smith, writing in the late eighteenth century, argued that the competitive market operates as an "invisible hand" that translates the utility-maximizing behavior of consumers and the profit-maximizing efforts of firms into market outcomes that provide the most benefit to society as a whole.[1] In other words, Smith's argument was

---

[1] A. Smith (1776), *The Wealth of Nations*, New York, The Modern Library, p. 423.

that the individual consumer or firm, seeking its own self-interest, would automatically and collectively promote the public interest.

The rationale behind Smith's tenet is straightforward: If there were some good that individual consumers valued, and if their willingness to pay exceeded the costs of production, then individual producers, seeking profit, would step forward to produce that good and in the least-cost way. In this perspective, government intervention is not necessary. Consumers' utility-maximizing behavior and producers' profit-maximizing behavior would naturally lead, by virtue of the invisible hand, to the production and distribution of goods and services that provide the greatest value at the least cost.

Several counterarguments to this perspective can be presented: (1) Not all markets are perfectly competitive and efficient; (2) even efficient markets can have undesirable equity consequences; and (3) competitive markets depend on governments to establish and enforce property rights, contracts, and regulations. We look at each of these counterarguments in turn.

First, markets achieve efficient outcomes only under idealized conditions: perfect competition, perfect information, no externalities or other market distortions. However, few markets have these ideal, or even near-ideal, conditions. Economists call a situation in which a competitive market deviates from efficiency as a **market failure**.

Second, even though the term *market failure* generally applies to issues of efficiency, both competitive and noncompetitive markets may fail to produce an equitable allocation of resources. Therefore, **equity** is also an important consideration for public decision makers, recognizing that even an efficient market could produce a socially undesirable outcome. Markets may allow both producers and consumers to benefit from an exchange, yet the extent of that benefit often depends on other factors, such as the initial distribution of wealth among individuals in society. Individuals who bring relatively little to the market may gain relatively little from the exchange. The desire to alter the market-generated distributions is a common rationale for government intervention in an economic system.

Third, for competitive markets to exist and function generally requires some sort of government intervention. Governments establish property rights, which protect the ability of individuals and firms to buy, sell, and use their resources in a market economy. Governments also enforce contracts, which ensure that transactions between consumers and producers will be carried out as agreed. Governments promulgate laws, such as antitrust regulations, to control monopoly power and promote competition (as we will see in Chapter 8). Thus, governments serve vital functions to provide a system upon which a market economy depends.

TYPES OF EFFICIENCY

Although different types and definitions exist, **efficiency** generally means obtaining the most benefit for the least cost, or producing the greatest level of satisfaction with the fewest resources. When economists refer to the efficiency of competitive markets, such as the efficiency that characterizes the equilibrium point under conditions of perfect competition, they generally mean the criterion of **Pareto efficiency**. A resource allocation is Pareto efficient if no one could be made better off without making someone else worse off. Stated another way, everyone is as well off as possible without making someone else worse off. A "Pareto improvement" is an action that makes at least one person better off and no one else worse off.

Many government programs, however, do make some people better off and some people worse off, even though the overall program shows potential net benefits (benefits minus costs). This trade-off is the basis for another criterion, **Kaldor-Hicks efficiency**,[2] also called "potential Pareto efficiency." Under this criterion, some will win, some will lose, but the net benefits are positive so that the winners could, in theory, fully compensate the losers, such that at least one person is better off and no person is worse off. A "potential Pareto improvement" is an action that generates benefits greater than costs.[3] (Again, benefits and costs are typically meant in monetary terms.) This type of efficiency is the basis of cost-benefit analysis, which is explored in Chapter 13.

We can see why Kaldor-Hicks efficiency is called potential Pareto efficiency. For instance, if a decision generates $100 in benefits to one individual and $90 in costs to another individual, then the winner could provide $90 in compensation to the loser, and the winner would still be $10 ahead. Or the winner could provide $95 in compensation to the loser, and both would be $5 ahead.

Despite the widespread application of this criterion, difficulties arise in its use as a social decision rule. One difficulty is that *a potential Pareto improvement may actually reduce overall social utility*. It can occur, for instance, when individuals have different marginal utilities of money. If a policy provides $100 of benefits to a wealthy person, and imposes $90 of costs on a poor person, then the utility gain (from the $100) of the wealthy person may not be enough to compensate the utility loss (from the $90) of the poor person. Another difficulty is that *the improvement is potential rather than actual*. The losers are not necessarily compensated fully by the winners. Only if the winners fully compensate the losers can the decision be claimed as an actual Pareto improvement.

---

[2] This criterion is named after the work of Nicholas Kaldor (1939), "Welfare Propositions of Economics and Interpersonal Comparisons of Utility," *Economic Journal* 49(195), pp. 549–552; and John R. Hicks (1940), "The Valuation of the Social Income," *Economica* 7(26), pp. 105–124.

[3] The determination of "benefits greater than costs" depends on the algorithms employed, such as "net present benefits" or the "benefit-cost ratio," and this topic will be examined in detail in Chapter 12.

Government Actions, Compensation, and Efficiency

Intrinsic to any government action is the likelihood that at least one person will be made worse off in order to make others better off. Therefore, governmental entities must constantly be asking whether the benefits from some action exceed its costs. Sometimes this weighing of costs and benefits is explicit through the use of a formal cost-benefit analysis, but it is typically undertaken in a far more informal way; for example, by holding hearings where proponents and opponents air their views, or by having officials weigh the pros and cons on their own. Even if it is as "simple" a decision as whether to put a stop sign on Main Street where it crosses High Street, the town select board will look at the costs and the benefits of such action. The costs would include the explicit costs of buying and installing a stop sign and the more implicit costs of increased inconvenience to those having to stop on Main Street. The board would then have to balance all these costs against the expected benefits of reduced accidents at that busy corner and any other positive impacts (such as an improved ability for pedestrians to cross the street). In other words, the board must make a determination of whether putting in the stop sign is Kaldor-Hicks efficient.

One might ask whether government could achieve a Pareto efficient action through the following compensation scheme: collecting payments from those who benefit and then compensating those who are hurt. The logistics of such a solution, however, are likely to be overwhelming. Imagine the select board trying to figure out the identity of every person who would be helped or hurt by the stop sign (including those potentially involved in an accident), trying to determine by how much they would be helped or hurt, and then actually collecting money from those who are helped and paying compensation to those who are hurt.

The likely result of requiring such a compensation scheme would be very few stop signs due to the time, expense, and logistics of making such determinations. Even though the full benefits of the stop sign might exceed its full costs, requiring compensation likely would keep the sign from being put in, and therefore the town could be worse off, overall, for the lack of that stop sign. Furthermore, even if an accurate compensation scheme were somehow implemented, the costs of implementation would reduce the net benefit created by the stop sign. In sum, Pareto-efficient actions by government likely would not be possible, and Kaldor-Hicks-efficient actions would be greatly deterred and any positive impact reduced. (Another approach to this compensation problem is addressed by the Coase Theorem, which is discussed in Chapter 9.) Thus, many argue that making such decisions on behalf of the people, without compensation, is the role an elected government is supposed to fill.

Source: Contribution by Russell A. Janis.

EFFICIENCY CRITERIA AND EQUITY ISSUES

Recall that an efficient economy allocates resources to maximize social surplus (the sum of consumer surplus and producer surplus), where goods are produced using least-cost methods and distributed to consumers who value them the most.[4] Yet these criteria can raise equity issues.

First, on the allocation of resources to goods that generate the greatest social surplus (measured by consumers' willingness to pay minus producers' costs): Because WTP depends on the distribution of wealth in society, individuals with greater wealth can have a greater influence in determining resource allocations.[5] Similarly, producers of goods and services that may not generate a large monetary profit but provide other societal benefits may be slighted in the market allocation of resources.

Second, on the production of goods by least-cost methods: Costs may not include the full social costs of production activities. And these externalized costs are borne by individuals in society, both in this generation and future generations, and in ways that may not be equitable. Those who gain the benefits of least-cost production methods may not be those who bear proportional costs.

Third, on the distribution of goods to consumers who value them most: The determination of value based on willingness and ability to pay can set up a system in which those with wealth may obtain more goods and services, while those without wealth may lack the ability to obtain goods and services to meet even basic needs.

Even though many economists agree that even an efficient market can be far from ideal in other social respects, they would also agree that the market provides advantages to society, such as greater choices, lower costs, and incentives for innovation. We now turn to issues of equity and the economic system, especially as they apply in public decisions, and cases in which the decision maker faces trade-offs between efficiency and equity.

EQUITY AND THE ECONOMIC SYSTEM

TYPES OF EQUITY

An economic system operates under rules that define acceptable activities. Determining the extent to which activities, decisions, or policies generate socially desir-

---

[4] More specifically, the conditions for Pareto efficiency are (1) exchange efficiency: marginal rate of substitution between any two goods is the same; (2) production efficiency: marginal rate of technical substitution between any two inputs is the same; and (3) product mix efficiency: marginal rate of transformation is equal to the marginal rate of substitution.

[5] The implication for decision making is that because benefits and costs to consumers are typically measured by changes in consumer surplus, impacts on wealthier individuals will have a greater influence in the decision because of their higher WTP. Even though a decision may generate net benefits, it could actually result in a net social loss of utility because of individuals' differing marginal utilities of money, as we saw in Chapter 4.

able market outcomes has long been a topic of concern to economists. The definition of what constitutes a desirable economic outcome depends often on values and beliefs.

Faced with the challenge of trying to determine what constitutes a socially desirable outcome, some economists have argued in favor of a nonintervention (laissez-faire) approach. In deciding not to intervene in a particular market, the laissez-faire approach implicitly endorses the distributional consequences of an unregulated economy.

Moreover, the notion of an unregulated economy is something of a myth, for as we saw previously, governments establish rules that are necessary for the functioning of markets. Thus, even in a largely laissez-faire system, the question remains: Is the market-generated distribution of resources equitable?

Determining what constitutes an "equitable distribution" depends on the concept of equity employed. Many concepts and definitions exist, based on principles such as equality, fairness, sameness, demand, responsiveness to needs, distribution of income, distribution of wealth, benefits received, and ability to pay, among others.[6]

For instance, tax systems often consider two concepts of equity: "horizontal equity," meaning that individuals who have similar abilities to pay taxes (e.g., similar income levels) should be taxed similarly, and "vertical equity," meaning that individuals that have different abilities to pay taxes (e.g., different income levels) should be taxed differently. For instance, vertical equity can imply that those with greater income should pay greater amounts of taxes. Yet these concepts lead to questions about measurement. For instance, how should different income levels and abilities to pay be defined, and corresponding tax rates be determined?

The point is that there is no single correct definition of equity, and decision makers often need to consider several concepts of equity and the possible trade-offs among them. To illustrate some of these issues, we will examine three common concepts of equity related to endowments, processes, and outcomes.

EQUITY OF ENDOWMENTS

This standard looks at the fairness of the initial distribution of wealth and resources among individuals in a society. Some would argue that each individual member of society is entitled to returns on endowments obtained through fair means such as

---

[6] The literature on equity is voluminous. See, for example, A. Sen (1997), *On Economic Inequality*, Oxford, UK: Oxford University Press; J. Rawls (1970), *A Theory of Justice*, Cambridge, MA: Harvard University Press; K. Arrow, S. Bowles, and S. Durlauf (eds.) (2000), *Meritocracy and Economic Inequality*, New Delhi, Oxford University Press; J. Metzger (1996), "The Theory and Practice of Equity Planning: An Annotated Bibliography," *Journal of Planning Literature*, 11(1): 112–126; B. G. Norton (1999), "Ecology and Opportunity: Intergenerational Equity and Sustainable Options," in A. Dobson (ed.), *Fairness and Futurity*, Oxford, UK: Oxford University Press, pp. 118–150; B. Barry (1989), *Theories of Justice: A Treatise on Social Justice*, Vol. 1, Berkeley, CA: University of California Press; E. Talen (1998), "Visualizing Fairness: Equity Maps for Planners," *Journal of the American Planning Association*, 64(1): 22–38.

inheritance, discovery, and innate skills. Thus, it would be considered fair for a parent to decide to forgo consumption and transfer accumulated wealth to their children. As the recipients of such inheritance, some individuals come to the marketplace with a larger initial stock of endowments, and hence are likely to capture a larger share of consumer benefits.

Critics of this standard argue that intergenerational transfer of wealth is inherently unfair. They allege that, although it is fair for individuals to receive the fruits of their own labor, inheritances should be taxed and redistributed for the common good. This standard poses difficult issues, because inheritance is not limited to material goods. Parents give children many things, including social skills that improve a child's ability to function in the marketplace. Moreover, certain biological characteristics, such as height, body type, and susceptibility to certain diseases are passed without a deliberate choice from parents to children.

In short, initial endowments of individuals will differ, giving some individuals an advantage or even disadvantage that may be regarded as unfair. Although eliminating all differences may not be possible, compensatory efforts have been and can be made to reduce inequalities.

EQUITY OF PROCESS

Another set of standards focuses on the process. This standard would hold that everyone is entitled to what they can earn in a competitive market, or that all people should have an equal opportunity to earn income commensurate with their abilities. The distinction between equity of endowments and equity of process can be illustrated with the example of a running race. Equity of endowment relates to the characteristics of each runner at the start of the race. Equity of process relates to the race itself: To be fair, the course needs to be the same distance, with the same conditions, for each runner.

Of course, many market situations violate both of these concepts of fairness—endowments and process. For instance, racial minority children may be born into a low-income household, in an underfunded area of a city, and receive a poorer quality of basic education than the rest of the community. Compounding the unfairness of the initial endowments, many of these same minority individuals, once leaving school, face discriminatory actions in higher education and in the workplace. On the other hand, efforts to compensate for inequities can create inequities themselves. A commonly cited example is that affirmative action programs can lead to discriminatory hiring practices. Again, there is no easy answer on what is the fairest approach to many policy problems.

EQUITY OF OUTCOMES

This set of standards recognizes that although outcomes may be unequal, they do not need to be unfair. Using the foot race analogy, a fair race will still have a winner. One standard of a fair outcome is that everyone has sufficient resources to support an adequate standard of living. Another standard is absolute equality of outcomes. Given the inability to compare one person's well-being to another, however, absolute equality of outcomes is a difficult goal to achieve. Another standard considers the concept of "from each according to their abilities, to each according to their needs." Yet the concept of need is elusive. One individual may argue that a week of vacation is a genuine need, while another individual may regard that vacation as a luxury, not a necessity.

Equality of income can be easier to measure and used as a standard. Another standard, based on utility theory, is that satisfactions should be equalized, given that the marginal utility of an extra dollar to a poor person is often greater than the marginal utility of a dollar to a rich person. This standard implies that redistribution of income from rich to poor will increase total satisfaction of all the members of society. This standard also assumes that comparisons of well-being among individuals can be made, which is not necessarily valid, as we saw in Chapter 4.

Efficiency often conflicts with equity: Not all economically efficient outcomes are equitable, and not all resource reallocations made on equity grounds are efficient. Many public policies require trade-offs between the efficiency of resource utilization and the equitable treatment of individual members and groups of society. Policies designed with an overriding concern for equity issues may lead to deviations from efficiency. Preoccupation with narrow efficiency criteria may also result in an allocation of resources that is inequitable. Even standards of equity may conflict. For instance, equality of income may be a high-priority goal, but moving to this standard may involve a process of redistribution of resources that is judged as unfair.

MARKET FAILURES: DEVIATIONS FROM EFFICIENCY

According to economic theory, under conditions of perfect competition, the market will lead to efficient outcomes. Yet few markets can be assumed to be perfectly competitive. Even if competitive conditions hold, other conditions may cause deviations from efficiency. A **market failure** is a condition under which a market does not produce an efficient outcome. This section examines some of the most common sources of market failure, each of which is addressed in more detail in Chapters 8 through 11.

Monopolies, and degrees of monopoly power, exemplify a market failure. Recall that for competitive markets to achieve efficiency, no single producer (or consumer) can be able to influence the price, among other conditions (from Chapter 3). But a monopoly is the only producer, and (if unregulated) can set its price without fear of being undercut by a competitor. As a result, a monopoly can charge a higher price and produce less output than what would occur under competitive conditions. These factors result in a deviation from efficiency, and concerns about equity, such as loss of consumer surplus and excess profits for the monopoly. Plus, because only one producer is supplying the market, consumer choice is limited, and other producers may not be able to compete in that market.

Another example of market failure is **externalities**. Negative externalities result when actions of a producer or consumer impose costs on others, without compensation. For instance, if a factory discharges its waste products into a river, downstream residents and users will incur the costs of polluted water. Positive externalities result when actions of a producer or consumer confer benefit to others. For instance, a homeowner who fixes up a dilapidated house can also benefit the neighborhood. Because full social costs and social benefits are not included in decision making, price and quantity will deviate from the most efficient level: goods with negative externalities will be underpriced and overproduced, and goods with positive externalities will be overpriced and underproduced. Equity considerations mean that those who bear the costs are not necessarily those who reap the benefits, and vice versa, and those adversely and involuntarily affected by negative externalities may lack resources to obtain recourse or remedy.

Public goods are those that provide benefits to the public, but that private producers are typically unable or unwilling to supply because of difficulties in charging for the good. Pure public goods are defined by two characteristics—nonrivalry and nonexclusivity—that permit all to enjoy the benefits of the good without limitation (nonrivalry) and even if they do not pay (nonexclusivity). Examples of public goods include a lighthouse, consumer protection laws, an uncrowded public beach, public radio, community safety programs, uncrowded public roads, and clean air, among others. In such cases, the public sector must often provide the good or service, or it would be supplied below socially efficient levels. Deciding what goods to produce, and at what levels, can involve equity issues. For instance, traditional measures of consumer value, such as monetary expenditures, may be difficult to obtain for public goods and further may be inadequate indicators of utility gains from providing public goods.

Market failures can also occur because of **imperfect information**. Efficiency requires that all relevant information be available to consumers and producers. Consumers must be aware of the characteristics, both good and bad, of goods and services, or they cannot make utility-maximizing decisions. Similarly, producers must be aware of characteristics of available inputs and methods for production, or they cannot make profit-maximizing decisions. With lack of information, outcomes can deviate from the efficient level and lead to equity implications. For instance, a consumer buying a used car may lack information about its quality and may pay more than its true value; then other sellers of used cars may not obtain their cars' true value because of consumer wariness. As another example, an automobile insurer may lack information about the risky behavior of its insured driver; then if the driver's premium is set too low, excess costs may ultimately be spread to other policyholders. When information is costly or difficult to obtain, government efforts to provide information and to require disclosure of information (such as on used cars, and on driving history) can improve overall efficiency and equity, because both producers and consumers have access to information that may influence their decisions.

The availability of information relates to *transaction costs*, which are the costs of conducting an exchange or agreement, such as obtaining information on a good or service, paying legal and administrative fees, and time spent going to a store, among many others. Transaction costs are often assumed to be negligible in market analyses. Yet most market exchanges do involve some costs, and if they are too high, efficient exchanges may not occur. For instance, if prospective homebuyers are unsure about the quality of a home, they may not purchase it, even though the purchase may make both them and the seller better off. By establishing rules governing contracts, the purchase and sale of real estate, and other transactions, the government attempts to improve the operation of an economy by reducing possible barriers and inefficiencies.

Subsequent chapters of this book will deal with various types of market failures and associated public policy responses. The next section presents a brief summary of the range of possible market interventions.

PUBLIC PROVISION AND GOVERNMENT INTERVENTIONS

Each of the conditions discussed in the previous section can lead to inefficient market outcomes. Government intervention into the market system is often based on the rationale of improving the efficiency or the equity of market outcomes. Methods of government intervention include the provision of goods or services, the use of taxes and subsidies, and the regulation of product price or methods of production.

Public provision, where the public sector is the provider of the good or service, is a direct form of government intervention. Market failures provide a class of examples for public provision. For instance, in the case of a monopoly, public entities may step in to produce or regulate the product, rather than to let a single firm control price and output. With externalities, public provision may be necessary, otherwise the good could be overproduced and overconsumed in the case of a negative externality, or underproduced and underconsumed in the case of a positive externality. Public goods are other cases; private firms could be unable or unwilling to provide the service, because it may not be profitable.

Many publicly provided goods and services could, however, be provided by the private sector, and already are. Communities across the country have privatized services such as gas, water and electric utilities, trash collection, transportation, and health care. The motivation is that private firms—facing competition, fewer restrictions, and greater incentives for innovation and efficiency—could provide the same service at a lower price and with more efficiency than public agencies. Yet that may not always be the case. Some services can be provided more cost-effectively in the public sector than in the private sector. For example, some states have run their health insurance program for uninsured children at a lower cost within the public sector, within their existing Medicaid program, than if contracted out to a private firm. Also, state-run liquor stores in the United States charge prices that, on average, are lower than those charged by privately run stores. Apart from efficiency, a larger societal question develops: Would a profit-maximizing private firm act in the public interest?

For these reasons, the public provision of goods and services is likely to continue, especially when a broader range of societal objectives is important. Public education offers an example. Suppose that primary and secondary education were provided only by private entities. Competition among schools could lead to higher performance, less waste, and higher-quality instruction. Yet the quality of education could then depend on the wealth of the student (and their family). Families with the highest willingness to pay would gain the most and best services. Without public oversight or public provision of education, private schools may find little incentive to educate children of poorer families or children with special education needs. This argument is primarily one of equity, but it brings up efficiency implications as well. One is that education provides positive externalities. Developing a child's talents and skills through education benefits not only the child but also society as a whole. Although neither argument suggests that all schools must be run by public bodies, they do point to the role of the public sector as either a direct provider or a regulator of private providers.

Government interventions can also influence the efficiency and equity of market operations. Economists identify two broad categories of government regulation: economic and social. Economic regulation, such as price and output controls, can be used to redistribute resources. Social regulation, such as labor laws and environmental policies, can be used to try to improve societal conditions.

Taxes and subsidies affect the distribution of social benefits and costs, and can create incentives and disincentives for the production or consumption of a good. Consider, for example, a policy that places a tax on the consumption of gasoline. This tax can provide incentives for industry innovation, such as alternative-fueled vehicles, and incentives for consumer behavior changes, such as walking instead of driving, as well as disincentives for driving, because of increased costs. The tax could also be seen as a way for individuals to internalize some of the externalized costs to society due to gasoline consumption. In turn, tax revenues could be used to offset some of the externalized costs.

Economic regulations on price and output include price ceilings, price floors, and output quotas, as we studied in Chapter 3. In some cases, these interventions are implemented on equity grounds, when the prevailing market equilibrium price is considered too low or too high. For instance, renter groups arguing that rents are too high and impose unfair burdens on low-income households have gained passage of rent control legislation. This approach can lead to inefficiencies, however, because individuals who are willing to pay rent-controlled prices may be unable to find suitable rent-controlled units.

Price floors, such as federal agricultural price support programs, set a minimum on the price at which certain farm products can be sold. Price support programs often guarantee that the government will purchase all of the excess goods generated at that price. These programs can lead to inefficiencies and inequities because the price is higher to consumers than it would be under competitive markets. The result is a transfer of wealth from consumers to producers, often adding to the profits of large corporations.

Output quotas, such as price controls, directly alter market outcomes. For instance, zoning regulations are a form of output quota because they limit production activities in particular locations. Other examples include limits on the number of licensed physicians or limits on the number of taxicabs permitted to operate in a city. With quotas, inefficiencies can result if some citizens are unable to obtain services because they cannot afford the cost, even though their willingness to pay is greater than the marginal cost of providing the service. Inequities can also result from the exclusion of consumers or producers from being able to obtain or provide the good or service.

Thus, price and output controls are a widely used form of market intervention, suggesting that decision makers are often willing to give up some degree of efficiency in exchange for more equitable outcomes. It is important to realize, however, that a single intervention will usually have side effects, both intended and unintended, on the entire system.

Finally, governments also can determine which goods can be sold and purchased. For instance, in the United States, individuals are not permitted to buy or sell election votes, body parts, or illegal drugs. Even though consumers and producers may judge themselves better off as a result of buying or selling these goods, broader societal reasons often determine market policies.

EXAMPLE   **Government Subsidies for Health Care**

We now examine the concepts in this chapter within the specific context of health care. In the United States, the government is involved in the provision of health care services through programs such as Medicaid and Medicare[7] . In this discussion, we examine issues of efficiency and equity, as well as rationales for public sector involvement.

Government programs such as Medicaid and Medicare subsidize the cost of medical care for low-income, disabled, and elderly individuals. These programs are supported on equity grounds because they guarantee minimally adequate medical care to those individuals. Yet economists may argue that subsidy programs such as these are undesirable because they represent an inefficient allocation of resources.

The reason for this inefficiency, as the argument goes, is that program recipients may face a lower price for medical care and, as a result, will consume more than the efficient amount, and will continue to consume additional medi-

---

[7] *Medicaid* is a federal/state funded program that provides health care for low-income individuals. Medicaid was established in 1965 under the Social Security Act (U.S.C. §§1396–1396v, subchapter XIX, chapter 7, Title 42). *Medicare* is a federal entitlement program that provides health care benefits to individuals aged 65 years or older, blind, disabled, or who have end-stage renal disease. Medicare Part A provides hospital insurance that pays for inpatient hospital stays, skilled nursing facility care, home health care, and hospice care. Medicare Part B provides medical insurance that helps pay for doctor's services, outpatient hospital care, durable medical equipment, and other medical services not covered by Part A. Medicare was established in 1965 under the Social Security Act (U.S.C. §§1395–1395ccc, subchapter XVIII, chapter 7, Title 42).

cal care as long as any benefits are received, no matter how small. Because program recipients may pay less for medical care than nonrecipients, they may value the last unit of medical care less than nonrecipients, which represents an inefficient allocation of resources. Also, subsidy programs violate consumer sovereignty because low-income households may prefer to consume goods other than the subsidized commodities. A direct unrestricted cash grant to low-income households could result in smaller efficiency losses than the subsidy.

This argument sounds logical, based on economic theory. Yet when applied to health care, in practice, the importance of understanding context becomes apparent. First, this argument assumes a market for health care with perfect competition and no market failures. Yet the market for health care violates both of these assumptions.

Competition is imperfect, for several reasons: (1) consumers may not be able to choose among many competing producers (health care providers and insurance companies), and producers do not necessarily compete for each of those consumers; (2) the products (health care services) are not homogenous, and vary widely by price, service, and quality; and (3) both producers and consumers face barriers to entering the market for health care, such as institutional restrictions (e.g., not all hospitals can obtain a "certificate of need"[8] to provide certain services, such as heart surgery, which can create monopoly effects), contracts (e.g., consumers must select from a limited number of doctors within a health maintenance organization[9]), and preexisting health conditions (which can prevent consumers from obtaining affordable health care insurance).

Market failures include the following: (1) monopoly power (e.g., a single hospital or single group of physicians can control the provision of goods and services); (2) externalities, both positive and negative (e.g., because a healthy/unhealthy individual can generate external benefits/costs to society); (3) elements of public goods (e.g., emergency rooms cannot exclude individuals needing treatment on the basis of ability to pay);[10] (4) lack of information (e.g.,

continued on next page

---

[8] In many states, a provider must obtain a "certificate of need" in order to offer a new or different health service, or to construct or modify a health facility. A certificate of need is generally required of hospitals, surgical units, nursing homes, and rehabilitation centers.

[9] A health maintenance organization (HMO) is a group that contracts with medical providers, facilities, employers, consumers, and other units to provide health care services at a fixed price.

[10] In 1986, Congress enacted the Emergency Medical Treatment and Labor Act (EMTALA) [42 U.S.C. §1395dd et seq (1985)]. Under EMTALA, hospitals are required to provide emergency care to patients, regardless of patients' ability to pay. EMTALA was designed to prevent "patient dumping": the practice of refusing to provide emergency treatment to uninsured patients, or transferring these patients to other hospitals before they are stabilized. EMTALA applies to all hospitals that receive Medicare funds. Many hospitals that don't receive Medicare funds have even voluntarily agreed to follow standards of EMTALA.

consumers are often not able to judge and compare the quality of health care services); and (5) transaction costs (e.g., administrative expenses, monitoring insurance programs, and filling out forms).

Now we look at specific points. First, consider the point that health care subsidies would encourage recipients to consume "additional medical care as long as any benefits are received, no matter how small." Recipients encounter disincentives to continue to consume additional medical care. One is that individuals do not have unlimited time to engage in activities to obtain all possible marginal benefits (which is also true of other goods). Going to the doctor's office takes time and resources. An individual may have to take the day off from work, find a way to get to and from the doctor's office, and then wait for several hours before being able to see the doctor. (These examples represent transaction costs.) Another is that marginal costs exceed those of the doctor's visit itself. For instance, the result of a doctor's visit is often a costly prescription, and many recipients under Medicare do not have adequate coverage for prescription drugs. In addition, many states charge Medicaid recipients a co-pay on doctors' visits, which creates yet another disincentive to unrestrained consumption of medical care.

Second, consider the point that "because program recipients may pay less for medical care, they may value the last unit of medical care less than nonrecipients." That a recipient pays less for medical care does not mean that they value medical care less than nonrecipients. For that point to be valid would require that all individuals have the same marginal utility of money—a strong assumption. In fact, because recipients are often low-income individuals, they may value each dollar of medical care more than nonrecipients (even though economists warn against making interpersonal comparisons of utility). Finally, price paid is not the same as benefits received, as we know from our study of consumer surplus.

Third, take the point that a "direct unrestricted cash grant to low-income households would result in smaller efficiency losses than the subsidy." Let us suppose, then, that low-income individuals would be given cash directly, rather than access to affordable health care. What would happen? Individuals would probably spend much of the grant on goods and services that are most needed at that time, such as groceries and rent, and some may even try to save for future medical expenses. These actions are still consistent with the principle of consumer sovereignty. But what happens when individuals get sick and they don't have enough money to cover the doctor's visit? They may put off seeing a doctor until the condition becomes significantly worse, or even life-threatening. Then they go to an emergency room to be treated. Currently, in the United States, hospitals cannot refuse or delay emergency treatment to patients, even if they are unable to pay. So hospitals could see many more cases of individuals arriving at emergency rooms, without health insurance, and with problems that could have been treated more cost effectively earlier in the process. Moreover, this cost of emergency room treatment for uninsured individuals is eventually passed on to other consumers (a negative externality). So the direct cost grant could create its own set of inefficiencies

Apart from efficiency considerations, government involvement in health care provision is often justified on the basis of equity. Even a perfectly efficient health care market could exclude those individuals who were unable to pay for and receive adequate health care. Many argue that access to a basic level of health care is a societal right, just as voting or even education, and that this right should not depend on ability to pay. On the other hand, economists may argue that health care should not be treated differently than other commodities—that individuals who are willing and able to pay more for health care should be able receive those services. A middle ground could entail a system whereby all individuals could receive basic health care services, regardless of ability to pay, yet individuals could also have the opportunity to purchase additional health care. We conclude this section with a last look at the health care system in the United States, and examine possible sources of market failures and remedies.

EXAMPLE   **Health Insurance: Market Imperfections and Inequities**

The health care system in the United States operates as an imperfect market. In many situations, consumers lack the information to pick medical providers or health insurers based on quality of services. And groups often shunned by health insurers—such as small businesses and chronically ill individuals—can face steep prices from carriers reluctant to assume the risk for that care.

Currently, almost 50 percent of health care bills are paid for by government programs, especially Medicare and Medicaid. And the role of government in health insurance continues to expand. During the 1990s, the Clinton administration pushed a program through Congress that extended health coverage to children who have no insurance.

Unlike private insurers, government programs do not shun members based on their health problems. Many free-market proponents, mainly from a philosophical standpoint, oppose government involvement in health care. Yet without Medicare and Medicaid, millions more Americans could fall through the cracks of the private insurance market because they would be unable to get affordable coverage. Doctors, hospitals, and others would be forced to give more care that is free, and raise their prices to offset those losses.

continued on next page

Still, many Americans are covered by insurance obtained through the workplace. Though most employers subsidize this coverage, employees generally pay a portion of the premium, often about 20% to 25%. On top of that, the worker is faced with out-of-pocket costs, such as co-pays and deductibles.

Yet this private system shows signs of fraying. Facing annual double-digit percentage increases in their health costs, many employers are dropping coverage for their retirees, raising contributions from their workers, and increasing co-pays for items such as prescriptions. In many companies, family coverage is increasingly expensive for both employers and their workers. In addition, small businesses struggling for profitability often decide not to offer coverage for dependents, or even for the employees.

For example, health insurers may battle for the business of medium- and large-sized employers—employers with hundreds and thousands of employees. But if Joe and Mary's Pizzeria, with four employees, seeks coverage, health insurers rarely compete on price to sign them up, especially if one of the four or a family member has a chronic medical condition. Some state laws may mandate insurers to offer a policy to a small firm, but may not provide regulation on the ultimate price of coverage. So even if the pizzeria obtains a policy, it may face increases of 100% or more upon renewal.

What skews the health insurance model is the fact that more than 40 million Americans have no insurance. They do get care, but it's often postponed to the point where they have more serious health problems than if they had received treatment promptly. A telling fact about the uninsured: Two-thirds of them are in families headed by a full-time worker. But that worker may work in a job where insurance isn't offered, or is so expensive that it doesn't appear affordable.

So these uninsured groups live in anxiety over medical care. If it's needed, hospitals and doctors, either by law or conscience, end up treating the uninsured, who often are unable to pay the entire bill for their care. So medical providers write it off as a loss, and ultimately raise their prices to those with health insurance.

Even those with seemingly good insurance have gaps in that coverage. The Medicare program, for example, currently doesn't provide coverage for outpatient prescription drugs. For an elderly person without private drug coverage, prescription bills can amount to hundreds of dollars a month. And many workers who have employer-based insurance lack coverage for long-term care. The cost of a prolonged stay in a nursing home isn't covered by Medicare, so either the person must spend down their assets to qualify for Medicaid, or pay the entire nursing home cost, which can run $30,000 or more a year.

The current insurance trends portend more problems ahead. Private employers have been paring benefits to workers for years as their corporate medical bills soar. An economic downturn may lead many firms to raise the price even higher to workers—or even drop coverage entirely. Under that scenario, more Americans will be dumped into the ranks of the uninsured.

The United States is currently the only Western fully industrialized country that does not offer health coverage for everyone. Many reformers have advocated a switch to a system run by the government, like the Medicare program, where every American has insurance. Free-market advocates push for more competition with Medicare and Medicaid, with private solutions where health insurers would vie for membership and, thus, profits. Medical savings accounts are also touted. These policies provide catastrophic coverage with a high deductible, and an individual can roll over unspent money in a savings account into the next year. A similar concept, called defined contribution, may give employers a way to cap their costs, and employees to control their health care spending and choose by price. Informed shopping on medical care is rare under the U.S. system currently.

In any event, the problems of lack of competition, high costs, variable medical quality, and the uninsured appear entrenched in our current health care system, with no relief in sight. The private market and government have at times provided pieces of solutions, but the underlying sources of inefficiencies and inequities remain.

———

Source: Contributed by Andy Miller.

EFFICIENCY AND EQUITY: CONCLUDING THOUGHTS

In this chapter, we looked at cases where trade-offs need to be made between the goals of efficiency and equity. A natural question may arise: Is it possible to promote both efficiency and equity simultaneously? The answer is yes. The remaining chapters highlight such approaches and examples. For instance, market-based approaches for reducing negative externalities associated with pollution may simultaneously improve efficiency (reducing costs for producers and ultimately for the public), equity (reducing adverse and involuntary impacts on others who do not directly benefit), and environmental quality (reducing amount of pollution emitted).[11]

A general approach for finding such win-win situations is to look for Pareto improvements, where decisions can make people better off and no one worse off, and then to evaluate the equity implications of the distribution of benefits (such as, who

———

[11] The ability to promote both economic efficiency and equity, along with environmental quality (often referred to as the "three Es") has led to a groundswell of interest and activity in "sustainable development" or "sustainability." The principles of sustainability have been applied from the international level to the national, regional, community, and even individual level. For examples, see P. Hawkin, A. Lovins, and L. H. Lovins (1999), *Natural Capitalism: Creating the Next Industrial Revolution*, Boston: Little, Brown and Company.

gains and by how much). In cases of potential (not actual) Pareto improvements, where some are better off and some are worse off, further identify the groups affected, assess the impacts on each group, and then evaluate the implications and trade-offs for efficiency and equity, along with other goals important to the public. The next chapter on welfare economics, which is concerned with societal well-being, will provide you the conceptual and analytic tools for making and evaluating such decisions.

REVIEW QUESTIONS

1. The philosopher John Rawls argued that economic justice will not emerge as long as people are aware of the initial inequality of endowments, that is, if they know about their wealth relative to others' wealth. Thus, if people operated behind a "veil of ignorance" concerning relative endowments, they would not agree to anything that could reduce the wealth of the least-wealthy individuals in society, because those least-wealthy individuals might in fact be themselves. Can you think of any shortcomings of this view, from the perspective of societal welfare?

2. "Virtually no sector of the market economy is described by the perfectly competitive model. Rather, each market situation is characterized by inefficiencies such as monopolies, imperfect information, high transaction costs, and spillover effects. Therefore government intervention in every part of the economy is justified." Can you think of any shortcomings of this view, from the perspective of societal welfare?

3. Some states use market mechanisms to auction off a locally undesirable land use (LULU), such as a landfill, to the community that is willing to accept the LULU at the lowest cost. Explain how such a transaction, which appears to be acceptable on efficiency grounds, and in which both parties agree to what appears to be a mutually beneficial exchange, can be unacceptable on equity grounds.

4. What are the conditions for a perfectly efficient outcome? If no market is perfect, are all markets then subject to market failures?

5. The concept of intergenerational equity is central to "sustainable development," which has been defined as "development that meets the needs of the present without compromising the ability of future generations to meet their own needs."[12] What are some of the challenges in implementing this concept of equity?

---

[12] World Commission on Environment and Development (1987). *Our Common Future*, Oxford: Oxford University Press, p. 43.

WELFARE ECONOMICS

Welfare economics is the study of how decisions affect the allocation of resources, and thus the well-being among members of society. It grapples with questions about what is "best" concerning economic functions—questions such as whether to raise the minimum wage, whether to implement rent control, whether to tax resource consumption more and tax labor less, and whether to provide educational subsidies. These types of questions pose some major political and ethical issues in society.

For example, consider a program that will tax high-income individuals in order to transfer resources to low-income individuals. Proponents argue that the program is desirable on equity grounds because it will redistribute resources more evenly. Opponents argue that the program is undesirable because the tax would cause losses in efficiency. Who is right? Both sides make valid points. An overriding point, however, is that important trade-offs often exist between equity and efficiency. For instance, a higher tax rate can have a greater efficiency loss, even though it can lead to a greater redistribution of resources. On the other hand, a tax may be more efficient than price and output controls as a way to target certain groups and to redistribute resources. The techniques in this chapter can help decision makers to analyze the distributional and efficiency consequences of different approaches to achieving social goals.

Note that the term *welfare*, as used in the expression *welfare economics*, does not refer to government welfare programs for low-income individuals. Nor does welfare necessarily refer to happiness or quality of life. Rather, welfare here is focused primarily on economic efficiency, and welfare economics examines how different alternatives affect the efficiency of resource allocations in society.

ECONOMIC WELFARE AND SOCIAL SURPLUS

The *first fundamental theorem of welfare economics* states that a perfectly competitive market will lead to outcomes that are Pareto efficient. The *second fundamental theorem of welfare economics* states that any redistribution of wealth will also lead to Pareto efficient outcomes, if left to operate under the forces of a perfectly competitive economy. Together, they mean that the perfectly competitive market will maximize "aggregate economic welfare," or what is known as "social surplus."

Social surplus is the sum of consumer surplus (willingness to pay minus amount paid), producer surplus (payments received minus costs), and third-party surplus (such as revenues and costs to government). In other words, social surplus is a measure of the total net economic benefits to society. The view that competitive markets maximize economic welfare is a primary reason why many economists advocate the model of perfect competition as a basis for decision making.

The focus on efficiency as a basis for welfare, however, can neglect distributional issues. A policy that provides benefits to the wealthy and imposes costs on the poor could nonetheless be considered efficient. It also could neglect benefits and costs that were not represented by supply and demand curves. One rationale for government intervention has been to redistribute resources and improve efficiency, but interventions themselves are not without costs to efficiency or even equity. These effects and trade-offs present some of the most complex choices for the public sector, and this chapter provides the concepts and analytic tools to examine them.

SOCIAL SURPLUS AND PERFECT COMPETITION

Let us first examine how social surplus is maximized at the perfectly competitive level. Consider market conditions under the assumption of perfect competition (Figure 7-1). The equilibrium point of E* corresponds to a price of P^* and a quantity of Q^*. For quantities less than Q^*, the value to consumers is greater than the cost to producers (the demand curve is above the supply curve). For quantities greater than Q^*, the cost to producers is greater than the value to consumers (the supply curve is above the demand curve).

Social surplus is the shaded area $P_SP_DE^*$, which is the sum of consumer surplus ($P^*P_DE^*$) and producer surplus ($P_SP^*E^*$). It means that both consumers and producers receive net benefits: Consumers pay less than the maximum amount they were willing to pay, and producers receive more than the minimum amount they needed to receive to supply the good.

Social surplus varies with changes in price and quantity, and it is maximized at the competitive market equilibrium point, E*. Refer to Figure 7-2, which depicts the same market as in Figure 7-1, but with different quantities produced than the equilibrium quantity. At the lesser quantity, Q_A, the demand curve is above the supply curve, which means that the benefits to consumers (represented by willingness to pay) is greater than the costs to producers (represented by the minimum payment required).

Total surplus, at quantity Q_A and price P^*, is represented by the area $P_{SA}P_SP_DP_{DA}$, which is the sum of consumer surplus ($P^*P_DP_{DA}A$) and producer surplus ($P_S P^*AP_{SA}$). Increasing the quantity of production from Q_A to Q_B would increase total social surplus from $P_{SA}P_SP_DP_{DA}$ to $P_{SB}P_SP_DP_{DB}$, which is a net gain of $P_{SB}P_{SA}P_{DA}P_{DB}$.

This gain occurs because the demand curve is still above the supply curve in going from Q_A to Q_B, and thus additional social surplus can be generated by increasing quantity produced (and sold). This result will hold true for quantities up to the competitive equilibrium point, E*.

FIGURE 7-1 *Social Surplus Under Competitive Equilibrium Conditions*

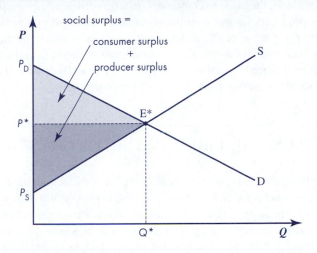

FIGURE 7-2 *Changes in Social Surplus Due to Deviations from the Competitive Equilibrium Point, E**

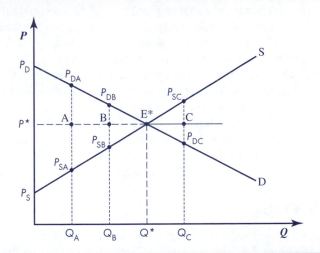

Beyond the competitive equilibrium point, however, increasing quantity produced would decrease social surplus. The demand curve would be below the supply curve, with the price in between, as seen at point Q_C. Here, social surplus would be a net loss—the negative amount represented by the area $E*P_{SC}P_{DC}$. This result occurs because social surplus is the sum of producer surplus (the negative amount of the area $E*P_{SC}C$—because the supply curve is above price) combined with consumer surplus (the negative amount of the area $E*P_{DC}C$—because the demand curve is below price). In other words, the value to consumers (in terms of willingness to pay) is less than the cost to producers (in terms of the minimum amount of payment required), for the quantity Q_C at the price $P*$, which results in a loss of social surplus.

A "loss of social surplus" is an important measure in welfare economics: It is commonly referred to as the **deadweight loss** or **welfare cost**. It is the reduction in social surplus resulting from deviations in efficiency.

SOCIAL SURPLUS AND MARKET INTERVENTIONS

To see how interventions affect social surplus, we examine the five cases from previous chapters: price floors, price ceilings, output quotas, taxes, and subsidies. In each case, we analyze how the intervention leads to changes in consumer and producer surplus, as well as changes in revenues or expenditures to third parties such as government, which collectively will result in changes in social surplus. These analyses are useful because they address questions of distribution (who gains the benefits, who bears the costs, and how much) as well as efficiency (changes in social surplus).

Before beginning, note the following points:

- The change in social surplus is equal to the social surplus "after" an intervention minus the social surplus "before" an intervention. "Change" is calculated as "final" minus "initial," or "after" minus "before."
- A loss in surplus will be indicated by a negative sign in front of a positive geometric area (represented by a Roman numeral).
- A loss (or gain) of social surplus is measured in terms of deviations from efficiency, and does not necessarily imply that the action is undesirable (or desirable) from a societal perspective.
- The effects of the interventions will be analyzed in two ways: first, by changes in surplus among participants in the market, and second, by distribution of benefits and costs to participants in the market. Tables 7-1 through 7-5 will present the results for each of the five cases that follow.

PRICE FLOOR

Consider a price floor, such as minimum wage or agricultural price supports, as illustrated in Figure 7-3. The original equilibrium point (before the price floor) is E, where the price is P_E, and the quantity is Q_E. After the price floor is implemented, the

FIGURE 7-3   *Change in Social Surplus Due to a Price Floor*

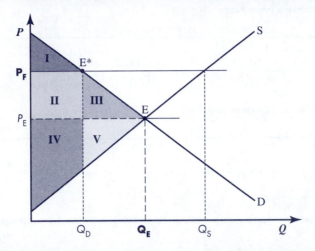

new equilibrium point is E*, where the price is P_F, and the quantity is Q_D. (Remember that at a price floor, quantity exchanged is the lesser of quantity demanded and quantity supplied.)

First consider the change in consumer surplus. Before the price floor, consumer surplus is the area I + II + III. After the price floor, consumer surplus is the area I. This change in consumer surplus is a loss, equivalent to –II – III. Consumer surplus decreases because consumers pay more per unit and have fewer units available to purchase.

Now consider the change in producer surplus. Before the price floor, producer surplus is the area IV + V. After the price floor, producer surplus is the area II + IV. Even though producers sell fewer units, they receive a higher price on the units they do sell, because consumers are willing to pay more than what producers would need to receive in order to supply the quantity Q_D. The change in producer surplus, equivalent to II – V, could be a net gain or net loss. If area II is larger than area V, it is a net gain, and if area V is larger than area II, it is a net loss. Whether it is a gain or a loss is influenced by elasticities.

We now consider how changes in elasticity can influence surplus: Producer surplus can become a net gain (area II larger than area V) if demand becomes more inelastic or supply becomes more elastic. Producer surplus can become a net loss (area V larger than area II) if supply becomes more inelastic or demand becomes more elastic. For instance, in the case of minimum wage, if demand for labor becomes more inelastic or supply of labor becomes more elastic, then surplus to producers (the laborers) would increase.

The total change in surplus (see Table 7-1) would be obtained by aggregating the changes in consumer and producer surplus. In this case, the net loss of social surplus is equivalent to –III – V. Although producers may gain because they receive a higher price on fewer units, this gain is offset by the loss to consumers.

TABLE 7-1   *Changes in Total Social Surplus Due to a Price Floor*

Changes in Surplus from a Price Floor

	Before Price Floor	After Price Floor	Change
Consumer surplus	I + II + III	I	– II – III
Producer surplus	IV + V	II + IV	II – V
Social surplus	I + II + III + IV + V	I + II + IV	– III – V

Distribution of Benefits and Costs of a Price Floor

	Benefits	Costs	Net
Consumers		– II – III	– II – III
Producers	II	– V	II – V
Society	II	– II – III – V	– III – V

PRICE CEILING

Now consider a price ceiling, such as rent control, as illustrated in Figure 7-4. The original equilibrium point (before the price ceiling) is E, where the price is P_E, and the quantity is Q_E. After the price ceiling is implemented, the new equilibrium point is E*, where the price is P_C, and the quantity is Q_S. (Like a price floor, the quantity exchanged is the lesser of quantity demanded and quantity supplied.)

First consider the change in consumer surplus. Before the price ceiling, consumer surplus is the area I + II. After the price ceiling, consumer surplus is the area I + III. This change is equivalent to the area III – II. Change in consumer surplus can be a gain or a loss. It is a gain if area III becomes larger than II, which can occur if demand becomes more elastic or supply becomes more inelastic. It is a loss if area II becomes larger than area III, which can occur if demand becomes more inelastic or supply becomes more elastic.

For instance, in the case of rent control, if the supply of rent-controlled housing becomes more elastic (which can happen in the long run), then net benefits to consumers (those seeking rent-controlled housing) would decrease. Although some consumers would gain from being able to secure a rent-controlled unit, others who could not obtain units would lose.

Now consider the change in producer surplus. Before the price ceiling, producer surplus is the area III + IV + V. After the price ceiling, producer surplus is the area V. Change in producer surplus is a loss, equal to the area –III – IV, because producers would receive a lower price on a lower quantity of goods provided.

The total change in surplus (see Table 7-2) would be a loss of –II – IV. The ones who could buy the product would receive a gain in consumer surplus. Some would be excluded from buying the product at that price, however, because shortages occur.

FIGURE 7-4   *Change in Social Surplus Due to a Price Ceiling*

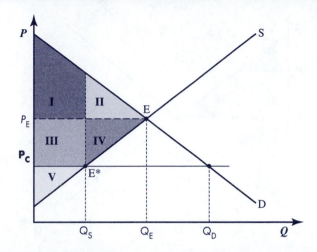

TABLE 7-2   *Changes in Total Social Surplus Due to a Price Ceiling*

Changes in surplus from a price ceiling

	Before Price Ceiling	After Price Ceiling	Change
Consumer surplus	I + II	I + III	III – II
Producer surplus	III + IV + V	V	– III – IV
Social surplus	I + II + III + IV + V	I + III + V	– II – IV

Distribution of benefits and costs of a price ceiling

	Benefits	Costs	Net
Consumers	III	– II	III – II
Producers		–III – IV	–III – IV
Society	III	–II – III – IV	–II – IV

OUTPUT QUOTAS

An **output quota** is a limit on the quantity produced or the quantity of imports into a market. Refer to Figure 7-5, which follows the same approach as in the previous examples. The original equilibrium point (before the output quota) is E, where the price is P_E, and the quantity is Q_E. The new equilibrium point (after the output quota) is E*, where the quantity (the level of the output quota) is Q_O, and the price is P_D (because producers charge what consumers are willing to pay).

FIGURE 7-5   *Change in Social Surplus Due to an Output Quota*

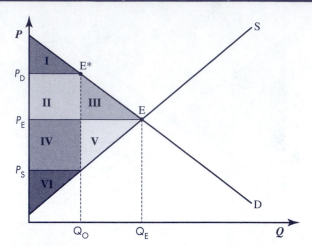

The consumer surplus before the output quota is the area I + II + III, and after the output quota is the area I. The producer surplus before the output quota is the area IV + V + VI, and after the output quota is the area II + IV + VI. Thus, the change in consumer surplus is –II – III, and the change in producer surplus is II – V.

Consumers have a loss of surplus because they pay a higher price for fewer units. Producers receive extra revenue on the units sold, Q_O, because consumers are willing to pay more than producers would need to receive for that quantity. Yet they sell less quantity, decreasing from Q_E to Q_O. Producer surplus would be a gain if area II were greater than area V, which could occur if demand becomes more inelastic or supply becomes more elastic. And producer surplus would be a loss if area V were greater than area II, which could occur if demand becomes more elastic or supply becomes more inelastic. Overall (see Table 7-3), the gains by producers are offset by losses to consumers, resulting in a net loss of social surplus of the area –III – V.

TAX

We will now look at the effects of a market intervention on not only consumers and producers, but also on third parties—in this case, the government. Consider the case of an excise tax, as depicted in Figure 7-6. The tax is placed on producers, causing a decrease in supply from S_1 to S_2 (although, as we saw in Chapter 3, the analyses could also be performed by placing the tax on consumers). The amount of the per-unit tax is $P_2 - P_3$, which is represented by the vertical distance between S_2 and S_1.

The original equilibrium price, before the tax, is P_1, corresponding to an original equilibrium quantity Q_1. The new price after the tax, from the consumer's perspective (price consumers pay) is P_2. The new price after the tax, from the producer's

TABLE 7-3 *Changes in Total Social Surplus Due to an Output Quota*

Changes in surplus from an output quota

	Before Quota	After Quota	Change
Consumer surplus	I + II + III	I	–II – III
Producer surplus	IV + V + VI	II + IV + VI	II – V
Social surplus	I + II + III + IV + V + VI	I + II + IV + VI	–III – V

Distribution of benefits and costs of an output quota

	Benefits	Costs	Net
Consumers		–II – III	–II – III
Producers	II	–V	II – V
Society	II	–II – III – V	–III –V

FIGURE 7-6 *Change in Social Surplus Due to a Tax*

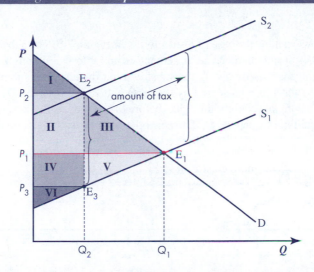

perspective (price producers receive) is P_3. The new equilibrium quantity after the tax is Q_2.

Consumer surplus before the tax is the area I + II + III. Consumer surplus after the tax is the area I. Producer surplus before the tax is the area IV + V + VI. Producer surplus after the tax is the area VI. Thus, the change in consumer surplus is the area –II – III and the change in producer surplus is the area –IV – V. Both are losses.

Now consider revenues to government. Remember that revenue is price multiplied by quantity. The tax will generate revenues equal to the amount of the tax ($P_2 - P_3$) multiplied by the quantity sold (Q_2). This would be ($P_2 - P_3$) $\times Q_2$, which is the area II + IV.

Adding them up (see Table 7-4), the benefits to the government, along with the loss in consumer and producer surplus, is the change in social surplus, which is the area –III – V. This is a net loss—a deadweight loss.

The magnitude of the loss of surplus (the deadweight loss) depends on elasticities as well as the magnitude of the tax. As supply or demand becomes more price inelastic, the deadweight loss decreases. As supply or demand becomes more price elastic, the deadweight loss increases.

In terms of the tax itself, the deadweight loss of a tax increases with the magnitude of the tax rate, all other things equal. Geometrically, the deadweight loss is an area of a triangle, and the tax rate is the base of that triangle. In Figure 7-6, the area of the triangle representing the deadweight loss V + III is equal to 1/2(base)(height). The base of the triangle is the tax rate ($P_2 - P_3$), and the height of the triangle is the difference in quantity due to the tax ($Q_1 - Q_2$).

SUBSIDY

We now examine the case of a subsidy, as in Figure 7-7. The subsidy is given to consumers, causing an increase in demand from D_1 to D_2, although we could also perform the analyses by giving the subsidy to producers. The amount of the subsidy is $P_3 - P_2$, which is represented by the vertical distance between D_2 and D_1.

The original equilibrium price, before the subsidy, is P_1, corresponding to an original equilibrium quantity, Q_1. The new price after the subsidy, from the consumer's per-

TABLE 7-4 *Changes in Total Social Surplus Due to a Tax*

Changes in surplus from a tax

	Before Tax	After Tax	Change
Consumer surplus	I + II + III	I	–II – III
Producer surplus	IV + V + VI	VI	–IV – V
Government		II + IV	II + IV
Social surplus	I + II + III + IV + V + VI	I + II + IV + VI	–III – V

Distribution of benefits and costs from a tax

	Benefits	Costs	Net
Consumers		–II – III	–II – III
Producers		–IV – V	–IV – V
Government	II + IV		II + IV
Society	II + IV	–II – III – IV – V	–III – V

FIGURE 7-7   *Change in Social Surplus Due to a Subsidy*

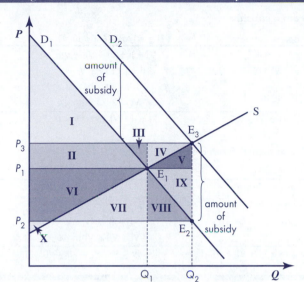

spective (price consumers pay) is P_2. The new price, from the producer's perspective (price producers receive) is P_3. The new equilibrium quantity after the subsidy is Q_2.

Consumer surplus before the subsidy is the area I + II. Consumer surplus after the subsidy is the area I + II + VI + VII + VIII, or the area between D_1 and the price P_2. Producer surplus before the subsidy is the area VI + X. Producer surplus after the subsidy is the area II + III + IV + VI + X, or the area between P_3 and S. Thus, the change in consumer surplus is the area VI + VII + VIII and the change in producer surplus is the area II + III + IV. Both are gains.

Now consider total costs to government. The subsidy will cost the amount of the subsidy $(P_3 - P_2)$ multiplied by the quantity sold, Q_2. It would be $(P_3 - P_2) \times Q_2$, which is the area –II – III – IV – V – VI – VII – VIII – IX.

After adding them up (see Table 7-5), the costs to the government, along with the gain in consumer and producer surplus, result in the loss in social surplus, which is the area –V – IX. Like a tax, the deadweight loss of the subsidy generally increases with the price elasticity of demand or supply, and with the magnitude of the subsidy, and vice versa.

CONSIDERATIONS

We have seen that, in theory, a perfectly competitive market maximizes social surplus. We have also seen that market interventions can cause a net loss in social surplus, due to losses in economic efficiency. Does it imply that the market would be better off without government intervention in order to maximize social surplus?

TABLE 7-5	*Changes in Total Social Surplus Due to a Subsidy*

Changes in surplus from a subsidy

	Before Subsidy	After Subsidy	Change
Consumer surplus	I + II	I + II + VI + VII + VIII	VI + VII + VIII
Producer surplus	VI + X	II + III + IV + VI + X	II + III + IV
Government		−II − III − IV − V	−II − III − IV − V
		−VI − VII − VIII − IX	−VI − VII − VIII − IX
Social surplus	I + II + VI + X	I + II + VI + X −V − IX	−V − IX

Distribution of benefits and costs from a subsidy

	Benefits	Costs	Net
Consumers	VI + VII + VIII		VI + VII + VIII
Producers	II + III + IV		II + III + IV
Government		−II − III − IV − V	−II − III − IV − V
		−VI − VII − VIII − IX	−VI − VII − VIII − IX
Society	II + III + IV + VI + VII + VIII	−II − III − IV − V − VI − VII − VIII − IX	− V − IX

Although it sounds like a logical conclusion, it is not necessarily the case. Other considerations are important.

First, in practice, few markets are perfectly competitive. Second, even perfectly competitive markets can be subject to market failures, which would hinder the efficient allocation of resources. Third, interventions may seek to accomplish other societal goals.

Remember that determination of social surplus is based on measures of efficiency, and that public decision makers are often concerned with goals in addition to or other than efficiency. So a focus on social surplus alone could overlook other aspects of societal well-being. For these reasons, it is important for public decision makers to consider aspects of social surplus, but with other criteria.

DISTRIBUTIONAL EFFECTS

Decisions that are clear Pareto improvements, where at least one person is better off and no one is worse off, are relatively easy to make. More difficult are those decisions that are not Pareto improvements. In these cases, decision makers need to evaluate trade-offs between efficiency and distribution. Aggregate measures of efficiency, such as social surplus, while useful, can obscure information about who benefits and who bears the costs of decisions. Thus, to evaluate trade-offs, decision makers need to examine the distribution of effects.

A common approach is to look at the impacts on different groups, such as different income categories, or different communities. Although an assessment of effects on each individual (rather than on each group) could provide more information, it is difficult to implement in practice; thus decision makers typically focus on group effects. Once distributional effects are assessed, the next step is to make judgments about trade-offs, such as how much more (or how much less) to count the benefits and costs that affect different groups.

First, let us examine the rationales for treating different groups differently. Recall that, from a distributional perspective, the analysis of social surplus treats gains and losses similarly among groups: It does not matter who receives a dollar or who pays a dollar as long as there is a net benefit (in terms of a potential Pareto improvement). Yet several economic arguments exist for treating gains and losses differently among different income groups.

The first argument is that the marginal utility of income can differ among income groups; more specifically, the marginal utility of a dollar generally decreases as total income increases. This means that an extra dollar to a low-income individual would provide more utility than an extra dollar to a high-income individual. It also means that a dollar less to a low-income individual would reduce utility more than a dollar less to a high-income individual. For this reason, it is argued, gains and losses to a high-income individual should count less in an analysis than gains and losses to a low-income individual.

A second and related point is that society may be more concerned with total utility, rather than total social surplus. As we saw in the previous chapter, increases in social surplus may not necessarily increase total utility. A potential Pareto improvement becomes an actual Pareto improvement only if compensation occurs. In addition, total utility is an aggregate measure; it does not tell us about the distribution of benefits and costs among individuals.

A third argument is that benefits and costs should consider other criteria, such as the number of individuals affected, or relative income, rather than just willingness to pay. These criteria address the concern that, because of their higher willingness to pay, wealthier individuals could have more influence than poorer individuals in decisions based on changes in consumer surplus. Thus, as the argument follows, expressions of willingness to pay, if they are used, should be adjusted according to income or other distributional criteria.

Finally, in addition to the economic arguments based on income levels, decisions are often made to provide resources to targeted groups. Examples include programs to provide public transit access to a community that previously was not served, or to provide health insurance to groups that currently lack coverage. Here the justification for differential treatment of different groups is to reflect goals of the programs.

Returning to an approach for considering trade-offs, an important activity is to detail impacts on different groups. Our analyses earlier in this chapter looked at impacts on consumers and producers, broadly. A next step would look at subgroups of consumers and producers, and could also examine a range of impacts, not just those with monetary equivalents. (Methods for assessing nonmonetary impacts are examined in Chapter 9.) This activity may provide sufficient information for decision makers to assess the relative impacts and make trade-offs.

Some analysts may choose to assign "distributional weights" to the impacts on different groups.[1] For instance, benefits and costs accruing to low-income groups can be multiplied by a number, such as 2.0, to give them more weight in the analysis. The difficulty here is determining the weights—moreover, determining who determines the weights. There are no simple answers to these questions, and they have been long debated.[2]

Nonetheless, economists have suggested some guidelines. First, the use of distributional weights could be limited to policies targeted to the disadvantaged, and either decrease social surplus but make low-income persons better off, or increase social surplus but make low-income persons worse off.[3] Second, sensitivity analyses should be conducted, using a reasonable range of weights, to determine the influence of weighting on outcomes. Some argue that weights of low-income groups should be no higher than 1.5 or 2.0 times those for high-income groups, based on estimates of efficiency losses under transfer programs.[4] Others argue for weights based on measures such as the marginal utility of income. Assuming that a doubling of income reduces the marginal utility of income by a factor of 2 to 4, weights of low-income groups would be 2 to 4 times those for middle-income groups that have twice as much income.[5] Finally, if weights are used, benefits and costs to different groups should be displayed without weights and presented to decision makers along with any weighted analyses. Remember that a primary goal of economics is to inform decisions, and that summary measures, such as a weighted aggregation of benefits and costs, can obscure critical information.

---

[1] See, for example, A. C. Harberger (1978), "On the Use of Distributional Weights in Social Cost-Benefit Analysis," *Journal of Political Economy* 86(2): S87–S120.

[2] See, for example, A. M. Freeman III (1970), "Project Design and Evaluation with Multiple Objectives," in *Public Expenditures and Policy Analysis*, R. H. Haverman and J. Margolis (eds.), Chicago: Markham; P. O. Steiner (1969), *Public Expenditure Budgeting*, Washington, DC: The Brookings Institution; E. M. Gramlich (1990), *A Guide to Benefit-Cost Analysis*, 2nd ed., Englewood Cliffs, NJ: Prentice Hall.

[3] See A. E. Boardman, D. H. Greenberg, A. R. Vining, and D. L. Weimer (2001), *Cost-Benefit Analysis: Concepts and Practice*, Upper Saddle River, NJ: Prentice Hall, pp. 461–469.

[4] E. M. Gramlich (1990), *A Guide to Benefit-Cost Analysis*, 2nd ed., Englewood Cliffs, NJ: Prentice Hall, pp. 123–127.

[5] J. E. Stiglitz (2000), *Economics of the Public Sector*, New York: W.W. Norton, p. 116.

REVIEW QUESTIONS

1. Some economists argue that decreasing the income tax rate could not only pro-
    vide more incentives to work, but could also increase tax revenues. Could a
    lower tax rate actually increase tax revenues? Why or why not?
2. The analysis of economic welfare, as seen in this chapter, focuses on changes in
    "social surplus." What types of benefits and costs can be overlooked in the mea-
    sure of social surplus?
3.   Why would a tax on milk be desirable or undesirable? Consider both efficiency
    and equity issues.
4. Consider the case in which government implements a tariff on foreign imports
    of a good, such as clothing.
       Figure Q7-1(a) shows market conditions before the tariff. The domestic
    price, with no international trade, is P_1. The domestic price, with international
    trade, is P_2. The domestic quantity demanded, with international trade, is Q_{D1}.
    The domestic quantity supplied, with international trade, is Q_{S1}. The quantity of
    imports, with international trade, is $Q_{D1} - Q_{S1}$.
       Figure Q7-1(b) shows market conditions after the tariff. The new domestic
    price, with a tariff on imports, is P_3. The amount of tariff (per unit) is $P_3 - P_2$.
    The domestic quantity demanded, with a tariff on imports, is Q_{D2}. The domestic
    quantity supplied, with a tariff on imports, is Q_{S2}. The quantity of imports with
    international trade, and subject to the tariff, is $Q_{D2} - Q_{S2}$.

    a) Analyze the effects on domestic social surplus, before and after the tariff,
       both with international trade. Fill in the following spaces using numerals for
       areas provided in Figure Q7-1(b).

    Changes in Domestic Surplus with International Trade, Subject to a Tariff

	Before Tariff	After Tariff	Change
Domestic consumer surplus			
Domestic producer surplus			
Domestic government			
Domestic social surplus			

    b) What would be some of the arguments for and against a tariff?
5. Comment on this statement: "If a policy maximizes economic welfare, then that
    policy is desirable."

FIGURE Q7-1 *Effect of a Tariff on Social Surplus*

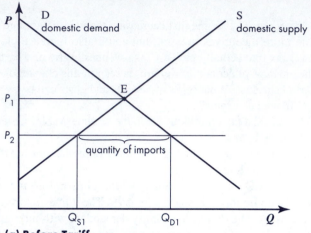

(a) Before Tariff

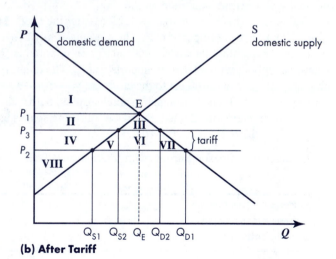

(b) After Tariff

MONOPOLY

Monopoly comes from the Greek word *monpolion*, which means "sole seller," or one producer in a market. A monopoly is considered a market failure because it violates the conditions of perfect competition, and results in an inefficient allocation of resources. Recall the conditions for perfect competition: (1) many buyers and sellers, (2) homogeneous products, and (3) easy entrance into and exit from the market. A monopolistic market has one seller, no close and readily available substitutes, and barriers to other producers wanting to enter the market.

Monopolies can affect both efficiency and equity. First, regarding efficiency: With a monopoly, the price can be higher, and output lower, than what would occur in a competitive market. Technical progress and innovation may be stifled because the monopoly faces little if any competition. Second, regarding equity: Because of the higher price and lower output, wealth can be shifted from the many (consumers) to the few (the monopoly). Plus, consumers lack the ability to choose from which producer they buy, and other producers lack the ability to compete effectively in that market.

This chapter first describes how and why monopolies form. It then provides analytic tools to determine supply and demand, price and output, and efficiency losses under monopolistic conditions, compared with competitive markets. This analysis leads to a section on government approaches to deal with monopolies. The chapter also examines the policy implications of monopolies and the regulations to control their effects, illustrated with current examples.

BARRIERS TO ENTRY

Monopolies often form because other producers cannot enter the market. In a purely competitive market, each producer supplies such a small share of the total output that changes in their production cannot influence the market price. In the long run, competitive producers will adjust their operations to produce output at the lowest possible costs; they will enter markets experiencing excess profits and leave those experiencing chronic losses.

In contrast, in a monopolistic market, a single producer is large enough to influence the market price, and profits in the industry do not ensure that new firms will enter and bid away excess profit. Other firms are not able to enter the market because of *barriers to entry*. These barriers allow the monopolist to accumulate long-term profits, keep other producers out, and maintain market control. The most common barriers—economies of scale, institutional protection, product differentiation, spatial impacts, and marketing tactics—are described in this section.

ECONOMIES OF SCALE

Economies of scale, as we studied in Chapter 5, occur when long-run average total costs of production decrease as output increases. Economies of scale are common in industries where fixed costs or initial capital costs far exceed the variable costs. Examples are industries such as transportation, telecommunications, and public utilities.

Because of economies of scale, a large firm can often supply a product or service at a lower cost than small firms. New firms trying to enter these markets often cannot build the large plants and infrastructure necessary to compete with established producers. Thus, a few large producers with lower average costs can undercut the prices of smaller producers.

A **natural monopoly** arises when a single firm, exhibiting economies of scale, can supply the entire market at a lower cost than a number of competing firms. Thus, competition would not necessarily create a lower price for consumers. Natural monopolies are often subject to public regulation or public ownership to ensure socially acceptable pricing and practice.

INSTITUTIONAL PROTECTION

Institutional arrangements, such as licensing procedures, government contracts, patents, and zoning, may also create and protect monopoly power, and prevent other producers from entering the market. Examples include licenses for taxi firms, contracts for military weapons production, franchises for professional sports teams, licenses for post offices, and patents for prescription drugs.

PRODUCT DIFFERENTIATION

By presenting their product as different or superior from that of competitors, producers can often capture a large share of the market and thereby increase their influence over market price. For example, a name-brand aspirin company captured a large part of the market by convincing consumers that their product is superior, even though it is chemically identical to generic brands. Trademarks and designer names have a similar effect, by creating consumer loyalty and conditioned purchasing.

TACTICS

A firm may also gain monopoly power through competitive tactics, such as effective management and efficient production. Innovation and efficiency may help a firm to acquire monopoly power by cutting costs and boosting productivity, thereby increasing "X-efficiency," which means producing more outputs from given inputs. On the other hand, firms may use anticompetitive tactics to acquire power, such as deceptive advertising or below-cost pricing.

MONOPOLY PRODUCTION

To compare the differences between monopolistic and competitive producers, we will look at four main economic concepts: supply (cost), demand (revenue), price, and output.

SUPPLY AND DEMAND

On the supply (cost) side, a pure monopolist is the sole producer of a good in a market. It provides the entire quantity for that market. In contrast, a competitive producer's supply curve is just one of many producers' supply curves that make up the market supply curve. (The monopolist does not have a "supply curve" as traditionally defined, as we will discuss later.)

To compare these supply curves, refer to Figure 8-1. The competitive market in Figure 8-1(a) has only three producers. At a given price, P^*, the total market quantity supplied is the sum of what the three individual producers would provide at that price, which is the quantity $Q_C = Q_1 + Q_2 + Q_3$. For the monopolistic market, however, the monopolist is sole producer, as shown Figure 8-1(b). So the quantity (Q_M) produced at P^* is the total market output at that price.

Now, on the demand (revenue) side (Figure 8-2), an individual producer in a competitive market faces a *horizontal demand curve*, implying that the competitive producer cannot influence the market price. The market determines the price of the good (P_C) at the intersection of market supply and market demand, as shown in Figure 8-2(a). Then, at that price, the individual producer can set marginal revenue equal to marginal cost to determine the profit-maximizing output, which is Q_I in Figure 8-2(b). For the competitive producer, marginal revenue (the additional revenue resulting from the sale of an additional unit) and the average revenue (the average price received per unit) are equal: They are both the market price.

In contrast, a pure monopolist faces the entire market demand curve, *a downward-sloping demand curve* shown in Figure 8-2(c). Marginal revenue in this case is not average revenue; the marginal revenue curve falls halfway between the demand curve (average revenue) and the vertical axis. To sell more output, the monopolist must reduce the price of the commodity. Assuming that the monopolist sells all units of output for the same price, the average revenue per unit sold will equal the price. The marginal revenue, however, will be less than the price: The monopolist must reduce the price not only on the last unit sold, but also on all units (see Table 8-1).

As seen in Figure 8-3 and Table 8-1, as output increases, the price (average revenue) declines. At a price of $10, in this example, the monopolist can sell only one unit of output; at a price of $9, two units, and so forth. The lower the price, the more units the monopolist will be able to sell.

The total revenue (the number of units sold multiplied by the price per unit) rises and then falls as the price is reduced. As output increases from two to three units, total revenue increases from $18 to $24 and the marginal revenue decreases from $8 to $6. Marginal revenue declines as output increases and has a negative value when seven or more units are produced.

FIGURE 8-1 *Competitive and Monopolistic Markets: Supply*

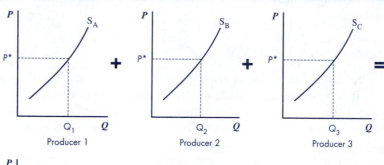

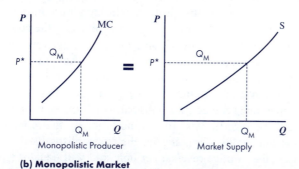

(a) Competitive Market

(b) Monopolistic Market

FIGURE 8-2 *Competitive and Monopolistic Markets: Demand*

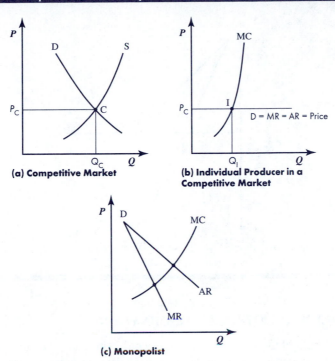

(a) Competitive Market

(b) Individual Producer in a
Competitive Market

(c) Monopolist

TABLE 8-1 *Revenue for a Monopolist*

Average Revenue (price)	Output	Total Revenue	Marginal Revenue
$10	1	$10	$10
9	2	18	8
8	3	24	6
7	4	28	4
6	5	30	2
5	6	30	0
4	7	28	−2
3	8	24	−4
2	9	18	−6
1	10	10	−8

FIGURE 8-3   *Marginal Revenue (MR) and Average Revenue (AR) for a Monopolist*

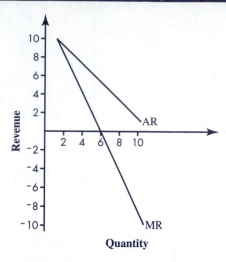

PRICE AND OUTPUT DETERMINATION

Both a competitive producer and a monopolist will follow the same profit-maximizing rule: *Set output where marginal revenue equals marginal cost*. The determination of price and output will differ, however.

In a competitive market, each producer is a *price taker*, and must accept the prevailing market price. Referring back to Figure 8-2(a), we see that the price is set in the market at the intersection of market demand and market supply, represented by point C. Then, to determine the profit-maximizing level of output, the competitive producer sets marginal revenue (market price, P_C) equal to marginal cost (the individual producer's supply curve), which is point I in Figure 8-2(b), with a level of output at Q_I.

In contrast, a monopolist is a *price taker*, and will seek a product price and level of output that will maximize profit. To do so (Figure 8-4), the monopolist compares marginal revenues with marginal costs to determine the profit-maximizing output level (point A, quantity Q_A). For quantity Q_A, the monopolist would need to receive the price of P_A, but consumers are willing to pay P_B. Thus, the monopolist will charge P_B instead of P_A, the lower price. This action leads to the monopolist's profit-maximizing point of B. Thus, at the profit-maximizing level of output Q_A the monopolist can increase the price and derive excess profits from consumers' willingness to pay. The monopolist can set both price and output, whereas an individual competitive firm must accept the market price and can only determine output. In contrast, if the market were competitive, the equilibrium price and quantity would be at point C (Figure 8-4), where marginal costs (supply) equal demand.

FIGURE 8-4 *Monopoly Price and Output Determination*

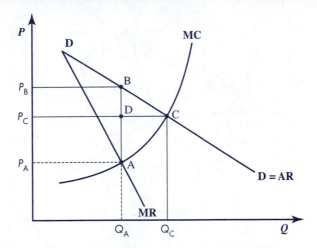

Another point is that a monopolistic market does not technically have a supply curve. Supply represents the quantity that producers in a market are willing to supply at any given price—but a monopoly, a price maker, will set the price along with setting the quantity to supply. Viewed another way, because demand can vary (it is not a horizontal line), a monopolist may supply different quantities for any given price. Therefore, a supply curve representing unique price-quantity combinations cannot be drawn for the monopolist.

To determine monopoly profits, refer to Figure 8-5. Recall that profits are equal to total revenues minus total costs. Total revenues are equal to price multiplied by quantity sold ($TR = P \times Q$). Total costs are equal to the average total cost multiplied by quantity ($TC = ATC \times Q$). The average total cost is where quantity produced, Q_A, intersects the average total cost curve at point O in Figure 8-5. Thus, total costs are equal to the average total cost of production (P_O) multiplied by the quantity produced (Q_A): $TC = P_O \times Q_A$. The total revenues are the price charged to consumers (P_B) multiplied by the quantity sold (Q_A): $TR = P_B \times Q_A$.

The difference between the total revenues ($P_B \times Q_A$) and the total costs ($P_O \times Q_A$) is the profit, which is represented in the shaded area in Figure 8-5. Profit can also be depicted as the quantity of units sold (Q_A) times the difference between the price charged (P_B) and the average cost of production (P_O). Thus profits equal $Q_A (P_B - P_O)$.

EFFECTS OF MONOPOLY

Monopolies can result in a range of effects, and economists point out both desirable and undesirable ones. A commonly noted effect is a higher price and a lower quan-

FIGURE 8-5 *Monopoly Profits*

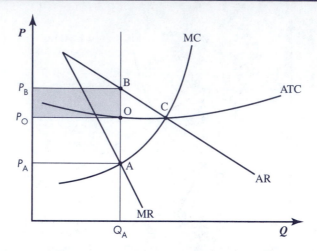

tity of output than would occur under competitive conditions. As Figure 8-4 illustrated, equilibrium in a perfectly competitive market would occur at the intersection of the supply and demands curve (point C), generating a price of P_C and an output of Q_C. If a single producer controls the market, however, the profit-maximizing output and price combination are at point B, the output produced is Q_A, and the price charged is P_B. Note that Q_A is less than Q_C, and P_B is greater than P_C.

Yet it does not mean that a monopoly will always charge a higher price than competitive firms. In fact, in the case of natural monopolies, which exhibit economies of scale (declining average total costs with increasing quantity over a range of output), a single firm can often supply the good at a lesser cost than a large number of competitive firms.

Another effect is that monopolistic markets can create an inefficient allocation of resources. As we saw in Figure 8-4, the monopolist can raise price above marginal cost and reduce output. At any output below the competitive equilibrium output, Q_C, price exceeds the marginal cost of production. The price consumers are willing to pay reflects the benefits derived from the commodity, which is higher than the marginal cost. This is a signal that more of the good should be produced. But the monopolist has cut back output from Q_C to Q_A. Unlike competitive markets, where excess profits attract new producers to the market—expanding industry output, lowering price, and ultimately eliminating excess profits—new producers cannot easily enter monopolistic markets. As a result, underproduction and overpricing of the good can persist.

Monopolies can also cause a redistribution of resources from consumers to producers. The reduction in output and increase in price leads to a loss of consumer surplus, and an increase in monopoly profits. The net loss in surplus is the welfare cost (or deadweight loss), which, as we saw in Chapter 7, represents a loss in total surplus (consumer surplus and producer surplus) because of inefficiency from market distortions.

This welfare cost can be calculated as follows. Refer again to Figure 8-4. The loss in consumer surplus between monopolistic (point B) and competitive conditions (point C) would be the area $-P_B P_C CB$. The gain in producer surplus between monopolistic and competitive conditions would be the area $(P_B P_C DB) - (DAC)$. So, combining the loss of consumer surplus with the gain in producer surplus yields a net loss, equivalent to the area $-DBC - DAC = -BAC$, which is the welfare cost.

Other monopoly effects can include reduced incentives for efficiency, innovation, and quality. Free from pressures of competition, a monopolist may tend to grow inefficient. This internal slack is termed *X-inefficiency*: an inefficient internal operation of a firm that results in higher than necessary costs. Also, a monopolist may not be under pressure to invent new method, or to apply new innovations in practice. Innovation occurs, but often at a slower pace. The monopolist may also lack incentives to provide high-quality products and services, because consumers lack the ability to purchase goods from other producers.

On the other hand, some economists maintain that it may be best to leave monopolies alone. One argument is that inefficiencies caused by monopolies are less than inefficiencies that would be caused by government intervention, regulation, or production. Another argument is that large monopolies can be the source of important advances in research and development.[1] Yet another is that a single producer offering a single standardized product, such as a computer program, could reduce inconsistencies and confusion and thereby benefit consumers.

One thing to note is that pure monopolies are rare, as are perfectly competitive markets. Most markets are somewhere in between, with some degree of market power. Close to monopolies is the case where a few sellers dominate a market, which is termed an *oligopoly*. Examples of oligopolies in the United States include airlines, breakfast cereals, automobiles, and electronics equipment industries. A collusive oligopoly can behave similar to a monopoly, and occurs when firms agree to fix prices, control output, or restrict competition. With an oligopolistic market, typically the price will be higher and output lower than in a perfectly competitive industry.

Before leaving this section on monopoly, we will mention another type of market situation—the case of a sole buyer, which is called a *monopsony*. As an example, a large industry in a small town may be the only firm hiring or demanding the services provided by workers in the town. Because this industry is the dominant purchaser of labor, it can affect the wage rates, the level of employment, and even the conditions of employment. Labor unions have organized to try to combat monopsony power, and often negotiate wage rates and employment conditions with the industry. With a monopsonist buyer, typically the price will be lower and quantity demanded will be lower than in a competitive market.

---

[1] J. A. Schumpeter (1942), *Capitalism, Socialism and Democracy*, New York: Harper.

REGULATION, PUBLIC OWNERSHIP, AND ANTITRUST POLICIES

We will look at three main government approaches for dealing with monopolies: public regulation, public ownership, and antitrust policies.

In **economic regulation**, governments can enact rules, laws, and incentives to control the price and production of goods. The regulation of monopolies seeks to curb market power, to promote competition, and to limit a monopoly's natural tendency to restrict output and charge too high of a price. In the United States, several federal agencies and commissions regulate monopolies; these agencies include the Federal Communications Commission (broadcasting), the Civil Aeronautics Board (airlines), and the Federal Power Commission (electricity and natural gas). In addition, most states have a public utility or public service commission that reviews electric, telephone, and other utility rates. At both the federal and state levels, these agencies regulate prices and control the entry and exit of producers.

Public utilities, such as electricity, gas, and water, are often natural monopolies exhibiting economies of scale. With a natural monopoly, a single utility can provide the service to an entire market at less cost than several competitive firms. Under *public regulation*, a utility is granted the exclusive right to provide the service, but is subject to oversight by a public regulatory commission. Otherwise, the utility could charge any price and generate any output it wanted. Consumers are especially vulnerable to monopoly power if the good has inelastic demand (typical of utility services), and if consumers depend on the physical system of the monopoly (such as transmission lines and pipelines, also typical of utility services). We will examine two common regulatory approaches based on price and rate of return.

In one approach, called price regulation, public regulatory commissions determine the price levels that are "fair." What exactly is a fair price is often debated among utilities, commissions, and the public. Let's examine price-based regulation for a natural monopoly (Figure 8-6).

Assume the monopolist would produce a quantity Q_M, which is the quantity associated with the intersection of the monopolist's marginal revenue (MR) and marginal cost (MC) curves, and then charge a price P_M, which is the price on the demand curve associated with that quantity, Q_M. Monopoly profits (here, excess profits) would be revenues $(Q_M \times P_M)$ minus costs $(Q_M \times P_1)$, or the area $Q_M (P_M - P_1)$.

Now assume the regulatory commission would set the price at P_C, where it equals average total costs (ATC), and require an increased output to the level of Q_C, which is the quantity associated with the intersection of P_C and demand. This regulation would help consumers by lowering the price and increasing output, but it would take away profits from the monopolist. If the regulated price is equal to ATC, then the monopolist earns a "normal profit" (zero economic profit).

Regulatory commissions typically impose average cost pricing, setting $P = $ ATC which is P_C in this case, where the maximum price the monopolist can charge is the average total cost. The question arises, though: Why isn't the price set equal to marginal costs to maximize efficiency? Although marginal cost pricing, setting $P = $

FIGURE 8-6 *Monopoly Price Regulation*

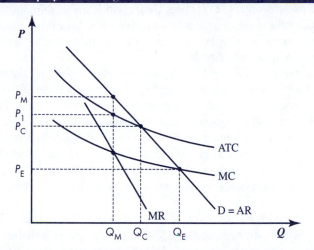

MC which is P_E in this case, would be the economically efficient ideal, it would imply a chronic loss for a monopolist that has declining average total costs, because marginal costs would be less than average total costs.

Comparing the "fair return price" ($P = \text{ATC} = P_C$) with the "socially optimal price" ($P = \text{MC} = P_E$) illustrates the *dilemma of regulation*. When the price is set at the most efficient level ($P = \text{MC}$), the regulated monopoly will suffer chronic losses and may shut down. But when the price is set at the fair return price ($P = \text{ATC}$), even though the regulated monopoly can earn a normal profit, society suffers losses of efficiency. At this fair return price, $P = \text{ATC}$, the price (P_C) is higher and the output (Q_C) is lower than they would be at the point of efficiency (P_E and Q_E). Nonetheless, the fair return price is lower and the output higher than it would be without regulation (P_M and Q_M).

In another approach, called rate-of-return regulation, the commission determines the "fair" rate of return for the utility. The rate of return is equal to utility profits divided by the rate base, which is the amount of invested capital. The valuation of the rate base is often complicated and debated. A higher rate base could permit the utility to generate higher profits for a given rate of return. The commission usually tries to hold down rates and prices to consumers, while the monopoly usually tries to maximize profits. Rates of return typically vary between 6% and 12%, and what constitutes a fair and reasonable rate is also vigorously debated.

Public ownership is one alternative to the regulation of monopolies, in which the government owns and operates the monopoly. In the United States, the post office is a prime example of public ownership, and some transit systems and electric power companies are also publicly owned and operated. A rationale for public ownership is that it would provide some social function that private ownership may not. For example, a publicly run transit system would service areas of a community that may not be otherwise profitable to service. Under public ownership, it may be easier to gain acceptance for regulating the price of monopolies. Like private monopolies, however, public monopolies may lack incentives and competitive pressures to produce efficiently and offer a high-quality service.

Antitrust policies enable the government to break up existing monopolies and prevent new monopolies from forming. *Trusts* are groups of firms, typically in the same industry, that can exhibit monopolistic behavior.

The first major piece of federal antitrust legislation was the Sherman Antitrust Act of 1890. The Sherman Act grew from public opposition to the growth of trusts, such as railroads, petroleum, tobacco, and sugar industries. Section 1 of the Sherman Act outlaws any restraint of trade. Section 2 outlaws monopolization or even attempts at monopolization. Violators of both sections are subject to criminal or civil penalties.

In September 1914, the U.S. Congress created the Federal Trade Commission (FTC), which strengthened the Sherman Act and established oversight for the Clayton Antitrust Act, which passed in October 1914. The Clayton Act, which was more specific than the Sherman Act, outlaws price discrimination not founded on cost differences, and any merger that substantially reduces competition. Specifically, it forbids tying contracts in which the purchaser of one product is bound to buy from the same seller as a condition of purchase, acquisitions of competing corporations' stock, and the formation and existence of interlocking directorates and officers, if these actions lessen competition.

Congress later passed three other pieces of antitrust legislation. The Robinson-Patman Act of 1936 outlaws quantity discounts not justified by cost differentials, and "destructive competition" (selling at unreasonably low prices to eliminate competitors). The Wheeler-Lea Act of 1938 polices "deceptive acts or practice in commerce" in order to protect the public against false or misleading advertising. The Celler-Kefauver Act of 1950, which amended Section 7 of the Clayton Act, closed a loophole by forbidding firms from acquiring the assets of another firm when the effect would be to reduce competition.

Antitrust critics argue that it may not always serve the public good to break up monopolies, especially in cases where a single large firm exhibits economies of scale and can provide a good at a lower price. As noted earlier in this chapter, natural monopolies arise when production is characterized by long-run decreasing costs. When decreasing costs are characteristic of an industry, consumers may wind up paying higher prices and getting less output if the monopoly were broken up.

This comparison is illustrated in Figure 8-7. The monopolist's marginal cost curve is MC_M, and the competitive producer's marginal cost curve is MC_C. The monopolist maximizes profits by producing output until the marginal cost (MC_M) equals the marginal revenue. The equilibrium output for the monopolist is Q_M, which corresponds to the point where the monopolist's marginal cost and marginal revenue curves intersect, point A. The monopolist charges P_M for this quantity of output, corresponding to point M on the demand curve, which is the amount that consumers are

FIGURE 8-7 *Comparison of Marginal Cost Under Perfect Competition and Monopoly*

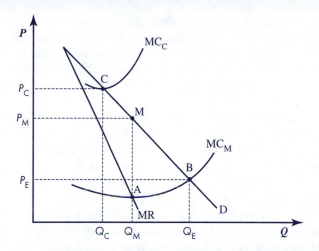

willing to pay for Q_M. If the industry were competitive, price and output would correspond to the point where the marginal cost (MC_C) and the demand curve (D) intersect, which is at point C, yielding an output of Q_C and a price of P_C. Thus, P_C is greater than P_M, and Q_C is less than Q_M.

In this situation, where the monopolist has decreasing average costs, a competitive market results in lower output and higher prices than monopolistic production. Although the monopolist produces more output than competitive producers, output is still held below the most efficient level. The efficient level of production would be where the marginal costs of the last unit of output equal the consumers' marginal willingness to pay for that last unit. That level occurs at point B, with quantity Q_E. For any output less than Q_E, consumers are willing to pay more, but the monopolist restricts output to Q_M, which is less than Q_E, the efficient level of output, but more than Q_C, the competitive level of output. Also note that P_M, the monopolist's price, is less than P_C, the competitive market price, but greater than P_E, the efficient price.

PUBLIC POLICY IMPLICATIONS

As these economic analyses suggest, monopolies create public policy issues. Although it may be tempting to criticize the inefficiency of a publicly owned firm, or the failure of a public agency to regulate a monopoly appropriately, developing an alternative and preferable solution is often difficult. In the assessment of alternatives, both economic and social factors must be considered.

The regulation of monopolies has been, historically, a primary justification for government involvement in the private market. A more recent justification has been to promote public health, safety, and societal welfare, or social regulation. **Social regulation** (as distinguished from economic regulation) includes rules, laws, and other government actions concerned with working conditions, product safety, environmental quality, and other aspects of societal well-being. The primary regulatory agencies include the Food and Drug Administration (1906), the Equal Employment Opportunity Commission (1964), the Occupational Safety and Health Administration (1971), the Environmental Protection Agency (1972), and the Consumer Product Safety Commission (1972).

As a counter to economic regulation, a trend toward *deregulation* has emerged. Since 1975, the federal government has deregulated many industries, including the Bell telephone system, airlines, and railroads. Proponents of deregulation argue that it promotes competition, thereby lowering prices, increasing output, and promoting efficiency and innovation. Opponents argue that deregulation leads to lower quality of service and to industry destabilization. The process of deregulation needs a careful balance between letting in new competition and withdrawing controls on prices. If controls are removed before the competition is effective, the monopoly enjoys the benefits of market power, but without price restrictions.

An example of deregulation concerns the airline industry.[2] In 1938, the Civil Aeronautics Board (CAB) was formed to regulate the airline industry. For 40 years, the CAB regulated the routes and protected the market positions of the original airlines. Moreover, the CAB permitted the airlines to set ticket prices and then enforced those prices against price-cutting. In 1978, Congress passed a bill to deregulate the airline industry. Airline competition quickly became intense, and created both positive and negative effects: lower prices to consumers, increased number of passengers transported, increased number of airlines in interstate service, but also declarations of bankruptcy, losses to airline workers from lower wages and layoffs in attempts to reduce labor costs, and increased fares on less-profitable routes to, for instance, smaller cities. Reregulation has been suggested as a way to deal with some of the problems stemming from deregulation, such as greater congestion at airports and concerns about airline safety.

Recently, questions have arisen about how well antitrust policies apply to high-technology and communications industries. These industries often hold a high market share (greater than 80%) and naturally evolve toward monopoly for several reasons. One reason is network externalities: the value of a product increases with the number of other people who use that product. For instance, the value of e-mail depends on other people having e-mail, so that information can be transmitted and received. A second reason is positive feedback. The value of a product, such as an operating system, increases with the number of applications written for it which, in turn, strengthens the product's market position. It then attracts more customers and more applications, which further strengthens its market position. A third reason is the

---

[2] For further discussion of the effects, see C. Winston and S. Morrison (1987), *The Economic Effects of Airline Deregulation*, Washington, DC: Brookings Institute.

first-strike advantage. Products can gain monopolistic power just by being the first to the shelf. For instance, in the market for video, Beta was considered to be a superior technology to VHS. But VHS offered more movies; the technology locked in and gained market power. Recent court cases, such as Microsoft, are redefining how to promote competition, protect innovation, and permit consumer choice in high-technology sectors.

EXAMPLE   **Professional U.S. Sports Leagues**

The National Hockey League (NHL), the National Basketball Association (NBA), the National Football League (NFL), and Major League Baseball (MLB) are the four main professional sports leagues in the United States. Studies suggest that these sports leagues have acquired, used, and maintained monopoly power in several ways. As demand for professional sports intensified, the leagues exercised institutional protection to limit the number of teams per league. In effect, the leagues responded to cities' increasing demand to host a professional athletic team by applying stringent control over the supply of teams. The leagues' power strengthened with institution-based regulations that prevented other prospective leagues from entering the market, thus restricting competition.

Because the NHL, NBA, NFL, and MLB only slowly expanded the number of sports teams in their respective leagues as demand for these teams increased, a bidding war resulted among cities. Participating cities felt that a home-based sports team would trigger economic development, satisfy residents, and enhance the city's overall image. Thus, to lure teams into calling their city "home," local governments competed for sports teams by offering appealing stadiums and attractive lease deals.

Within a matter of five decades, spending on stadiums skyrocketed from $3.8 million in the 1950s to $200 million in the 1990s (adjusted to 2000 dollars). Since 1990, approximately $14 billion in public funds and more than $7 billion in private funds have been devoted to building and refurbishing 95 stadiums and arenas for professional teams belonging to these leagues. Cities eager to host a professional sports team went so far as to fully pay for the stadium construction, charging relatively small rents to the sports franchises, and allowing the franchise to retain nearly all of the profits generated by the facility.

Professional sports leagues enjoy monopoly power because they can control where an existing team can relocate and they have the authority to grant "major league" status to any prospective franchise. Also, these leagues can purposely keep several potential cities vacant, or unoccupied by a home team. These actions can provoke dynamic bidding feuds among cities, generate increasingly attractive stadiums and profitable leasing contracts, and discourage competition from a prospective new league.

continued on next page

Professional sports leagues also enjoy monopsony power. An individual sports team acts as the single buyer who is in a position to "purchase" a stadium package offered by several different cities. Team owners can negotiate an attractive package from a current host city by threatening to pull their team out of the city, and to obstruct any other team from entering the city, unless the host city provides their team sufficient subsidies.

Public subsidies for new stadiums have often been justified on the basis of the economic developments that they confer upon the local economy, rather than on just the benefits of public consumption (consumer surplus) or the positive externalities of an enhanced community image. Yet evidence is lacking that sports facilities construction contribute significantly to economic development.

How do these subsidies continue then? Part of the explanation relates to the distribution of benefits and costs. The benefits accrue to relatively few, yet those few become strong advocates for supporting the use of public funds for procuring or retaining a team. The costs, however, are borne by many—the general public—and the public may lack the information or the incentive to oppose the subsidy.

The following strategies have been proposed as ways to reduce the monopoly power that resides in the hands of the sports leagues and to regulate the industry. One is to agree not to use public money to finance a sports facility for a privately owned team. The U.S. Conference of Mayors and the National Governors' Association have the legislative power to restrict local jurisdictions from spending public funds on stadiums and arenas for the primary use of private agencies, although this option may be politically unappealing. A second method is divestiture. This process of breaking up each individual sports league into about four separate leagues could effectively inject competition into the market. In the long run, however, an imbalance of competition might allow one league to be considered superior and even absorb the weaker, failing leagues. A third approach would be to prohibit existing leagues from exercising collective control over team relocations. Subsidies from cities to teams would diminish because leagues would not be able to prevent teams from competing to enter a city. Implementing either divestiture or a competitive market for team relocations could make team owners and players potentially worse off, even though the public would be better off. Yet increasing competition to determine the allocation of resources between the public and private sectors could improve efficiency.

So do professional sports leagues play fairly? The product they provide, entertainment to millions of Americans, is unique. Their economic situation lends itself to a monopoly, consequently yielding large profits to the leagues and reducing consumer surplus. The normative question is yours to answer!

Source: Based on J. Siegfried and A. Zimbalist (2000), "The Economics of Sports Facilities and Their Communities," *Journal of Economic Perspectives* 14(3): 95–114.

REVIEW QUESTIONS

1. Disco, Inc., has a monopoly over the production of jukeboxes, with the following cost and revenue characteristics, where Q = the number of jukeboxes produced per week:

    Marginal revenue = $1,000 - 20\,Q$
    Total revenue = $1,000Q - 10Q^2$
    Marginal cost = $100 + 10Q$

    What would be the price and quantity of jukeboxes sold under the following conditions?
    a) The firm behaved as a monopoly.
    b) The firm behaved as if the market were perfectly competitive.

2. How does a monopolist's demand curve differ from that of a perfectly competitive firm?

3. Why has it been considered socially desirable to regulate monopolies? Is it always good for society to do so?

4. Explain why some monopolies may lack incentives to innovate. Now explain why some monopolies do innovate.

5. One approach to regulating a natural monopoly is to let it determine its profit-maximizing point, then tax its profits and distribute them to consumers who purchase the good. Would this approach be preferable, from a societal perspective, to average cost pricing?

EXTERNALITIES

U ntil now, we have examined market behavior with the assumption that benefits and costs are fully reflected in the market demand and market supply curves. In many cases, however, benefits and costs accrue to other members of society, those other than the buyers or sellers in the market transaction. These spillover effects are called **externalities**, and they can be negative or positive.[1]

Negative externalities occur when actions of consumers or producers impose harm or costs upon others, without compensation to those others. For instance, an individual who drives a car degrades air quality for the rest of society. **Positive externalities** occur when actions of consumers or producers result in benefits for others, without compensation from those others. For instance, homeowners who improve their properties can also increase the value of adjacent properties. Because of the proximity of everyday activities, some type of externality arises from virtually every action, public or private.

Externalities are considered a market failure because they result in inefficient levels of consumption or production of a good. Externalities also create inequities, and although this does not constitute a market failure, it does compel decision makers to consider the effects of individual decisions on society.

This chapter first examines the problem of externalities and the ways in which externalities can create an inefficient and inequitable allocation of resources. Next, we look at common strategies for dealing with externalities, such as government intervention, and the implications of each strategy in terms of efficiency, equity, and other evaluation criteria.

NEGATIVE AND POSITIVE EXTERNALITIES

A problem resulting from externalities is that the market will often produce an inefficient level of output and consumption: The market produces too much of a good that creates negative externalities and too little of a good that creates positive externalities.

---

[1] *Negative externalities* are also called "external diseconomies," and *positive externalities* are also called "external economies."

NEGATIVE EXTERNALITIES

Negative externalities occur when the *private cost* of an activity does not fully account for the *social cost*. In this context, the term *private* refers to an individual consumer or producer, or an individual group of consumers or producers—a singular entity rather than all of society. It does not necessarily imply "private sector" as contrasted with public sector. Thus *private* can refer to public agencies, private firms, groups of people, or an individual person. Also, in the following supply and demand analyses, the subscript *p* will refer to private benefits/costs, and the subscript *s* will refer to social benefits/costs.

Both producers and consumers can engage in activities that cause negative externalities. First, we look at how *production activities* create negative externalities. Consider, for example, a large plant in a city that emits pollutants into the air. The plant may be paying a fee for the right to discharge pollutants, but that fee may not cover the entire social costs of the pollution nor compensate those who are harmed. These social costs include direct impacts, such as increased pollutants in the air, and indirect impacts, such as increased illnesses due to poor air quality, or loss of agricultural crops due to the pollution. Although the plant owners may argue that they didn't cause the air quality problems in the city, the plant did in fact contribute some portion to the overall degradation of the environment. It is those social costs that often are not considered in the firm's production costs.

Figure 9-1 shows the negative externality, using economic analysis. The demand curve D reflects consumer demand for the products of the plant. The supply curve S_p indicates the plant's private marginal costs of production. The social marginal

FIGURE 9-1 *Negative Externalities: Social Costs Greater Than Private Production Costs*

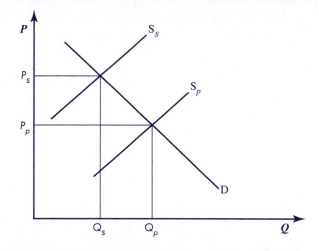

costs—the full costs to society—of the plant's production activities are represented by S_s. In this figure, the plant's private costs (S_p) do not cover the full social costs (S_s). This situation is not unusual; if producers do not have to pay for the social costs, they would probably not include them in their accounting.

From the plant's perspective, the equilibrium output would be at Q_p, where private costs (S_p) intersect with demand (D). And the equilibrium price would be at P_p. If the plant were required to "internalize" and pay for some or all of the external costs imposed on society, however, the plant's marginal costs would increase and the supply curve, S_p, would shift to the northwest. If the plant's decision incorporated *all* of the external costs that they create, the curve would shift to S_s, which represents social marginal costs. Under these conditions, the new equilibrium quantity would be Q_s, which is less than Q_p, and the new equilibrium price would be P_s, which is greater than P_p. This result implies that negative externalities result in an overproduction and an underpricing of the good.

Consumption activities also create negative externalities. Consider automobile drivers. As shown in Figure 9-2, their demand curve for gasoline is D_p, and they consume an amount Q_p. If drivers were required to compensate others for the adverse effects caused by their use of gasoline, their demand would decrease because of increased private costs. That decrease would be seen by a shift in the demand curve, D_p, toward the southwest. Now if drivers were required to internalize all the social costs that they create, the demand curve would shift from D_p to D_s. The amount of gasoline consumption, and the amount of the negative externality, would decrease, from Q_p to Q_s. Again, a negative externality implies a level of consumption that is larger than optimal.

FIGURE 9-2 *Negative Externalities: Social Costs Greater Than Private Consumption Costs*

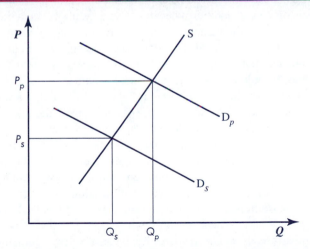

Note that in the case of the producer who creates negative externalities, P_s (price, including social costs) is greater than P_p (price, including only private costs), but in the case of the consumer who creates negative externalities, P_s is less than P_p. This difference arises because producers would need to receive more and consumers would be willing to pay less if either internalizes social costs into their production and consumption decisions.

A logical question is: Why would it be socially beneficial for producers to internalize their production costs if it would only increase price to consumers? One reason is that if costs were not internalized, then members of society who do not buy that product are forced to bear the costs, while consumers who do buy the product will benefit from the artificially low price. Another reason is that the lower price leads to a higher level of production than is efficient. Also, if the price were to reflect social costs, the higher price may provide an incentive for producers and consumers to reduce the negative externality by recognizing more of the full costs of their activities.

POSITIVE EXTERNALITIES

Positive externalities occur when the private benefits do not fully account for the social benefits from production or consumption activities. In other words, the social benefits are greater than the sum of the individual benefits to the consumers or producers of the good. Both production and consumption activities can create positive externalities.

We first examine *production activities* that create positive externalities. Consider a group of real estate developers who decide that, instead of cutting down existing trees, they will retain the natural surroundings and the mature trees, and build around them. Their decision is profit-motivated: They realize that homeowners would be willing to pay more to look at nature in their backyard than to have a clear-cut backyard with exposed dirt and some newly planted seedlings. Nonetheless, the developers' decision creates additional benefits to society, above what the developers gain in profits and above the value that the homeowners derive when they purchase their homes. These social benefits result because the native vegetation and trees improve environmental quality for the rest of the community. So in this case, the benefits to the developer underestimate the total social benefits.

This positive externality is seen in Figure 9-3, which represents the market for these homes. The equilibrium output, Q_p, comes from the intersection of the developers' (private) supply curve, S_p and consumers' demand curve D. The developers' supply curve underestimates the total social benefits S_s from preserving the natural surroundings, however. If those social benefits were included in the developers' decisions, supply would increase, and move to the southeast, from S_p to S_s. The equilibrium quantity of homes with preserved land would increase from Q_p to Q_s, and price would decrease from P_p to P_s. Thus, positive externalities lead to an underproduction of the good.

Similarly, *consumption activities* can create positive externalities. For instance, an individual's decision to preserve historic buildings can benefit not only that individual, but also society. This outcome is seen in Figure 9-4, where D_p is the individual's demand for historic building preservation, and D_s includes the benefits to society. The socially optimal level of historic building preservation is Q_s, which is more than Q_p. This positive externality implies an underconsumption of the good. Also note that P_s is greater than P_p, which implies that society would be willing to pay a higher amount for an individual to preserve historic buildings.

FIGURE 9-3   *Positive Externalities: Social Benefits Greater Than Private Production Benefits*

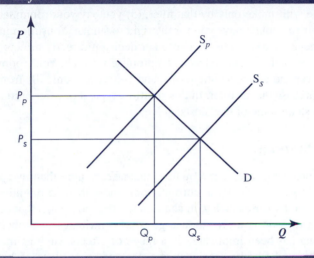

FIGURE 9-4   *Positive Externalities: Social Benefits Greater Than Private Consumption Benefits*

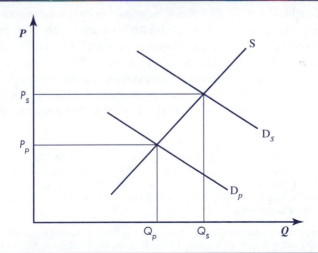

EXAMPLES OF EXTERNALITY PROBLEMS

THE SMOKER

You and your roommate have a problem: She is a cigarette smoker, and smoke makes you sick. You propose several alternatives: (1) she stops smoking altogether in the apartment; (2) she continues smoking and you have to move out; (3) she smokes only in certain rooms and when you are not home; (4) you buy an air filter and she will smoke only by that filter; (5) you pay your roommate not to smoke; or (6) your roommate pays you for the right to smoke. Your roommate's smoking is a clear negative externality because her decision directly affects your welfare. You decide on both (3) and (4) as a compromise solution. Your roommate can't smoke whenever and wherever she wants, and you suffer some ills from her smoking and also purchase the air filter. In this solution, typical of externalities resolutions, both of you share some of the "costs."

THE DRIVER

Now consider a case of externalities that affects more than two parties. An average driver in Atlanta, Georgia, currently puts more than 35 pounds of carbon dioxide (CO_2) into the air each day, in addition to other pollutants that degrade air quality.[2] Carbon dioxide is a greenhouse gas that contributes to global warming. Global warming has been implicated in a range of effects, such as increased severity of droughts and floods, sea level rise, loss of crops, loss of habitat and species, increased death and illness among humans, causing an estimated hundreds of billions of dollars of damage annually in the United States.[3] Yet the only cost that the driver recognizes is that of driving the car (and some fraction of the externalized costs that the driver bears personally). Some individual drivers may realize that they are contributing to the problem and may wish to do something about it. But if relatively few drivers reduce their emissions, they may receive little benefit other than the "feel-good" benefit of helping, because air quality and CO_2 concentrations may not noticeably improve. Furthermore, even if most drivers would make efforts to reduce their emissions, another individual can do nothing and still enjoy the benefits of cleaner air at no personal cost. Finally, in this case of global warming, the adverse effects

---

[2] Atlanta Regional Commission (2001), *Transportation Fact Book*, Mobility/Air; Georgia Department of Environmental Protection (1999), *Development of a Greenhouse Gas Emissions Inventory for the State of Georgia*, Air Protection Branch; U.S. Environmental Protection Agency (2000). *Average Annual Emissions and Fuel Consumption for Passenger Cars and Light Trucks*, Office of Transportation and Air Quality, EPA420-F-00-013.

[3] Intergovernmental Panel on Climate Change (IPCC) (2001). *Climate Change 2001: Impacts, Adaptation, and Vulnerability*, Report of Working Group II of the IPCC, Geneva, Switzerland, February 13–16. Available at http://www.ipcc.ch.

from emissions produced today are expected to have ramifications over many decades if not centuries. So the decision to drive a car creates negative externalities not only on this generation, but also on future generations. The point is that one person's driving affects millions of people, albeit some to a greater extent than others. The resolution of this externality problem is far more difficult than the smoker because it involves more than two parties, and larger temporal and spatial scales.

THE FACTORY

A factory produces chemical waste that is dumped into one of the Great Lakes. The amount of pollution is directly related to the level of production and, in turn, the total profit of the firm. Given that the firm has a major investment in the plant and its equipment, increases in output will increase profits. Figure 9-5 illustrates the relationship between the chemical discharge and the marginal profits, which both depend on the output level. As the output increases, the chemical discharges increase while the marginal profit decreases—although total profit increases. The line between points G and D illustrates this inverse relationship between the chemical discharge (output) and the marginal profit.

The chemical discharge also affects, but in a different way, the profits of a commercial fishing fleet in the lake. Greater amounts of pollution make fishing more difficult and less profitable. It also decreases demand for fish because states have issued warnings about the high levels of contaminants detected in fish from the lake, and advised people not to eat the fish regularly. The line between points O and K represents the relationship between the marginal loss in profit to the fishing fleet and the amount of chemical discharge by the polluting factory.

FIGURE 9-5 *Bargain Between Two Parties*

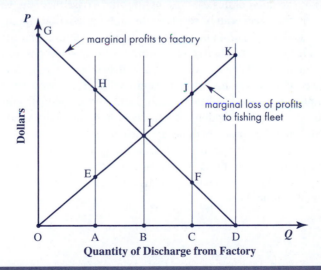

If asked, operators of the fishing fleet would probably want the factory to stop all pollution. On the other hand, the factory would like to discharge the maximum amount into the lake to maximize profits, which is the amount OD. What is the optimal level of discharge?

Assume a current level of pollution of OD—the maximum level of discharge by the factory. Reducing the level of discharge from OD to OC would increase the fishing fleet profits by DCJK while reducing the factory's profits by only DCF. Theoretically, the fishing fleet could pay the factory the amount DCF, to compensate the factory for their marginal loss in profits, and the fishing fleet would still be ahead by the amount DFJK. The factory would be no worse off with the payment from the fishing industry, and the fishing industry would be better off with this reduction in the level of discharge.

Similarly, if the factory were not discharging any waste chemicals, it could increase discharge to OA, gain benefits of OAHG, pay the fishing industry OAE for the loss in profits, and still be ahead by the amount OEHG.

If the factory and the fishing fleet were able to bargain about the level of discharge, they could come to an agreement that would make them both better off, and that would cause both to bear some costs. Again, assume a current level of discharge of OD. The fishing industry would be willing to pay up to DBIK to have the factory reduce pollution from D to B while the factory would cut back for as little as DBI.

Although the actual payment and level of pollution would depend on their bargaining, the optimal level of discharge would be at the intersection of the factory's marginal benefits (profits) curve and the fishing industry's marginal cost (reduced profits) curve. It is the amount OB on the horizontal axis of Figure 9-5. At this point, neither party can be made better off without making the other party worse off.

The resolution of this case exemplifies the Coase theorem, which proposes that externality problems can be resolved through negotiation among the affected individuals, and an efficient allocation will result, assuming that transaction costs are negligible.[4] The proposition is that government intervention is not necessary because the free market and negotiations of individuals can resolve inefficiencies. Ideally, to work well in practice, this theorem requires that property ownership is well defined, the number of people involved is small, parties have complete knowledge of benefits and costs, and the transaction costs (costs of bargaining or litigating) are negligible. Typically, however, property rights are unclear, a large number of parties are affected, some affected parties may not even know they are being harmed, and bargaining is costly and difficult. In these situations, government intervention may be needed to remedy externality problems, because private solutions could be inefficient, inequitable, or unlikely.

---

[4] R. Coase (1960), "The Problem of Social Cost," *Journal of Law and Economics* 3:1–44.

CHALLENGES IN THE RESOLUTION OF EXTERNALITY PROBLEMS

Relying on the free market and private actions to resolve externality problems may not always be effective, for several reasons. These reasons, individually and collectively, point to rationales for government intervention, and we examine these next.

- *Multiple parties.* The preceding case of lake water pollution is simplified, involving only two bargainers. Realistically, other sectors of society could be affected by the pollution, such as recreational users of the lake, homeowners around the lake, and the lake's ecosystem. Other sources could also be contributing to lake pollution, such as homeowners using lawn chemicals, which run off into the lake. Moreover, other parties and even future generations may be harmed without realizing it, and therefore may not be involved in the bargaining.

- *Transaction costs.* Negotiations and litigation take time and money. Sometimes it takes more effort and resources than it is worth to bargain or to sue, especially when the outcome may be uncertain. Transaction costs can effectively create a barrier against people's willingness to negotiate or litigate. For instance, it can be difficult for the fishing fleet to prove that the factory's discharges into the water have been responsible for reduced fish harvests.

- *Unclear property rights.* In the case of two parties and clear property rights, the resolution is relatively simple. In cases involving public goods, such as clean water, and unclear property rights, the resolution becomes more difficult. Who owns the right to clean water? Who contributes how much to the problem? Should charges be based on the amounts of effluents into the water or on the impacts of those effluents? How should effects in the future (and on future individuals' rights) be considered in present value terms?

- *Free riders.* The "free rider" problem occurs when an individual can enjoy the benefits of a good without paying the costs, because others pay the costs. Using our earlier example, let's say that the smoker is bothering not only you, but also your neighbors. Smoke gets into the building's air duct system and also seeps through the walls. Your neighbors know that you are taking action; you are buying an air filter for your smoking roommate. So your neighbors don't worry about taking action. They enjoy the benefits of your efforts without personal cost, and go along for the free ride.

- *Opportunism.* With opportunism, others will join in to take advantage of the bargaining positions. Let's say that your roommate likes to play loud music, which also bothers you. She agrees that if you pay her $5/month, she won't play her music loudly. You pay her. Your neighbors hear about this arrangement and start playing their music loudly, in hopes of also extracting payment from you.

- *Inequities.* In addition to inefficiencies, externalities also create inequities. Those who bear the costs are not necessarily those who reap the benefits, and vice versa. An example is the siting of hazardous waste sites within communities, where low-income citizens and racial minorities often bear a disproportionately greater burden of the costs, such as exposures to pollutants, but without necessarily receiving disproportionately greater benefits.[5] Also, low-income citizens often do not have the resources to bargain effectively to reduce or cease the imposition of externalities upon them.

- *Multiple jurisdictions.* Externalities are not always limited to one jurisdiction, which makes resolutions and negotiations more complex. Consider, for instance, a river that runs between two states. The downstream state complains that the upstream state is not providing them enough water and not sufficiently high-quality water. The upstream state argues that they have a right to use the river as they wish, both as a source for their growing water demands and as a sink for their wastewater discharges. The upstream state may have little incentive to internalize more of the costs—that is, to pay to treat the wastewater more than is necessary—because it saves them costs of treatment, and because it leaves their state and becomes someone else's problem. In such cases, with multiple jurisdictions and large numbers of people affected, externality problems often require government intervention to broker an agreement.

- *Resource protection.* Externalities, such as pollution, can harm not only humans, but also the ecosystem and resources upon which human life depends. How can the ecosystem enter into a bargaining agreement with those who are harming it? This is another rationale for government to protect broader social interests, such as environmental quality and natural resources.

- *Cumulative impacts.* Making decisions one at a time can overlook the cumulative impacts of decisions which, individually, may not be significant, but collectively are significant. For example, from the perspective of an individual developer, one housing project may not significantly harm the water quality of a nearby stream. And perhaps each of five developers in the city also believes that their actions create negligible impacts. However, from the perspective of the community, five large development projects will threaten the stream's water quality. Here, a broader decision-making perspective, such as a state or regional entity, may be necessary to consider the cumulative impacts on society.

- *Lack of information.* People may not know that they are being harmed by someone else's activity. Damage may take years or decades to appear. Even if people realize they have been harmed, it may be too late to reverse the damage, too costly to bring a lawsuit against the injuring party, or too diffi-

---

[5] See, for example, Environmental Protection Agency (1992). *Environmental Equity, Reducing Risk for All Communities*, Report No. EPA 230-R-92-008, Washington, DC.

cult to prove causality. Thus, government can help to protect the public by taking measures to prevent or reduce risks of the harm, rather than waiting for the harm to occur.

Because of the number and types of externality cases in which bargaining is either infeasible or too costly, the government has intervened. These types of externality problems can be more difficult for private parties to negotiate, and more complex. The following sections outline how an optimum solution can be determined, and present the various forms of government intervention that can be used to reach that solution.

DETERMINING THE OPTIMAL LEVEL OF PRODUCTION

The optimal or efficient level of a negative externality is not necessarily zero. As we saw in the earlier example of the plant and fisheries (Figure 9-5), the harm to the fisheries was simultaneously a benefit to the plant. The efficient level of discharge was the quantity OB, which was at the intersection of the marginal cost and marginal benefit curves.

To determine the efficient solution to an externality situation, the principle is to set marginal costs equal to marginal benefits. Refer to Figure 9-6. To determine the efficient level of pollution reduction, we would set the marginal cost to the private producer (MC_p) equal to the marginal benefit to society (MB_s) resulting from that reduction. The efficient level of pollution reduction is the quantity associated with point E: the intersection of the marginal cost and marginal benefit curves.

FIGURE 9-6   *The Efficient Solution: Marginal Benefits Equal Marginal Costs of Positive Externality*

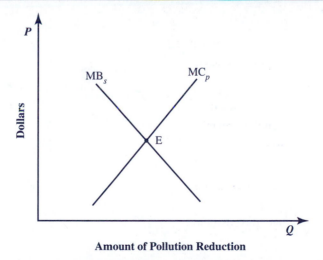

We could also find the efficient solution in terms of amounts of pollution, as shown in Figure 9-7. In that figure, MC_s is the marginal cost of pollution to society and MB_p is the marginal benefit to producers by being able to discharge pollutants. The efficient solution in this example is E, the same as in Figure 9-6: the intersection of the marginal benefit and marginal cost curves.

These analyses, however, assume that parties have full knowledge of the costs and benefits and that these effects can be placed in monetary terms. The actual task of determining the optimal level and the costs and benefits is difficult, especially in externality problems that involve nonmarket goods and intangibles. Further, as we saw in Chapter 6, an efficient outcome does not necessarily mean an equitable outcome.

DETERMINING BENEFITS AND COSTS

Benefits and costs can be placed into two general and somewhat overlapping categories: market and nonmarket. First consider *market* benefits and costs, using the previous example concerning the reduction of lake pollution. Market benefits would include, among others, the increased sales of fish caught in the lake. Market costs would include, among others, the plant's costs of pollution abatement equipment.

Many public decisions, however, typically involve benefits and costs in which markets do not exist or do not function perfectly. In such cases, we need methods to assess *nonmarket* benefits and costs. These methods can be direct or indirect. For instance, a direct method to assess the benefits of pollution reduction would be to

FIGURE 9-7   *The Efficient Solution: Marginal Benefits Equal Marginal Costs of Negative Externality*

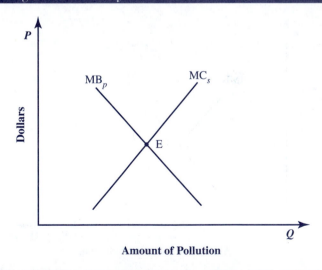

survey homeowners along the lake, asking them to state the maximum amount they would be willing to pay for improvements in lake water quality. An indirect method would be to determine the differences in real estate values between two homes that are equivalent in every respect, except one home is located upstream from the sources of pollution, and the other is downstream.

METHODS FOR NONMARKET VALUATION

We examine four commonly used methods for nonmarket valuation: contingent valuation, travel cost, hedonic pricing, and averting behavior. The first is typically considered a direct method, based on stated preferences, and the latter three are typically considered indirect methods, based on revealed preferences.

Contingent valuation (CV) is probably the most well-developed and commonly used direct method.[6] The goal of this method is to elicit from respondents their willingness to pay (WTP) for a good or their willingness to accept (WTA) the loss of a good. These monetary amounts then become estimates of benefits or costs of the good.

Contingent valuation is considered to be a direct method because it asks respondents to state their valuation of a good, rather than inferring a valuation from their behavior. For instance, a CV survey could ask respondents about the maximum amount they would be willing to pay for 50 additional acres of open space in the city. Alternatively, the survey could ask respondents about the minimum amount they would be willing to accept for the loss of 10 acres of existing open space in the city. As another example, the survey could ask waterfront homeowners the maximum amount they would be willing to pay to have an existing plant relocate downstream from them. Or the survey could ask waterfront homeowners who currently live upstream from the plant the minimum amount they would be willing to accept to have the plant relocate to a position upstream from them.

In these examples, WTP seeks to measure the benefit of improvements (increased open space or decreased pollution), and WTA seeks to measure the cost of degradation (decreased open space or increased pollution). WTA is usually greater than WTP, and one explanation is prospect theory: Individuals adopt the status quo as their reference point, and are less willing to accept possible losses than they are willing to pay for possible gains.[7] In other words, given a choice between (1) being paid to accept a loss (WTA), or (2) paying to accept a gain (WTP), the loss-averse individual would prefer to pay for a gain. Another explanation is that the amount of WTP is bounded by an individual's ability to pay, whereas the amount of WTA has no such bound.

---

[6] See R. C. Mitchell and R. T. Carson (1989), *Using Surveys to Value Public Goods: The Contingent Valuation Method*, Washington, DC: Resources for the Future; and R. T. Carson (2000), "Contingent Valuation: A User's Guide," *Environmental Science and Technology* 34(8): 1413–1418.

[7] D. Kahneman and A. Tversky (1979), "Prospect Theory," *Econometrica*, 47(2): 263–292.

Contingent valuation has been widely used and debated in decision making. Thousands of journal articles have been written about CV, discussing its appropriateness for valuing goods.[8] Some of the main issues follow.

Many argue that contingent valuation is prone to bias because it asks questions that are typically hypothetical, and respondents do not actually have to pay their stated amounts. Another concern is that responses can be highly dependent on context, such as the information provided to respondents about the good being valued, the order and wording of the questions on the survey, and the range of choices and trade-offs considered in the valuation process. Moreover, an individual's valuation of a good can change over time, but because CV studies tend to be discrete events, they may not capture that change or the reasons behind it. On the other hand, advocates of CV maintain that a carefully designed survey can address many of these concerns. Support for CV also comes from its use in practice. For instance, it was used to assess the damages in the *Exxon Valdez* oil spill, where estimates of WTP to prevent similar damage were about $31 per household, for a total of $2.8 billion.[9]

The *travel cost method* is based on revealed preferences, using market information to impute a value for a good. This method typically has been used to value recreational sites.[10] It examines the costs that people are willing to incur to travel to a site being valued, such as a park, a beach, or a lake. The travel costs include admission fees, transportation costs, hotel charges, and opportunity costs of time spent traveling, among others. The assumption is that the costs that individuals are willing to incur to visit a site can be used as a proxy for the value that individuals place on the site. From this information, a demand curve can be derived that relates the quantity of trips demanded by an individual to the total cost per trip to the individual.

This method is regarded as most appropriate for determining changes in participation: the number of trips over a given period to one given site. The method is limited, however, in its ability to model choices among competing sites or to evaluate sites that are part of multipurpose trips. One analytic challenge is determining costs, such as the opportunity cost of an individual's time spent traveling to a site. Travel time may not be entirely a cost: Individuals may derive value from the trip itself, not just the destination. Moreover, individuals may choose to pay more to live in a certain area because of proximity to a recreational site. So the travel cost method could underestimate the value of the site: Travel costs appear less, because travel time is less, even though individuals paid more to live closer to the site.

---

[8] For overviews of the issues and controversies, see *Journal of Economic Perspectives* (1994), 8(4): 3–64.

[9] R. T. Carson, R. C. Mitchell, W. M. Hanemann, R. J. Kopp, S. Presser, and P. A. Ruud (1992), *A Contingent Valuation Study of Lost Passive Use Values Resulting from the* Exxon Valdez *Oil Spill,* Report to the Attorney General of the State of Alaska, November 10.

[10] See M. Clawson and J. L. Knetsch (1966), *Economics of Outdoor Recreation*, Baltimore: Johns Hopkins University Press.

Hedonic pricing compares prices between similar goods to determine the value of an amenity.[11] For example, to assess the cost of pollution from a factory located on a river, we could measure the difference in values of two parcels of land along the river: one upstream from the polluting plant and one downstream from the plant. By assuming that the two parcels of land are identical, except for pollutant levels in the adjacent river, this method gives an estimate of the value that people place on reductions in pollutants in the river.

A strength of the hedonic pricing method is that by using a comparative approach, it can value marginal changes in nonmarket goods, such as environmental improvements, without requiring a complete specification of benefits and costs. It is useful whenever the good, such as a clean river, is capitalized in the value of an asset, such as a house. A drawback with the method is that it can be difficult to find comparable sites, and then to separate and control the numerous factors affecting the variable under comparison, e.g., land prices. The method also depends on the assumptions of competitive markets and perfect information, and that producers and consumers incorporate that information into their decisions.

The method of *averting behavior* looks at the amounts that individuals spend in order to avoid some of the consequences of environmental pollutants and to mitigate some of the effects of consequences already suffered. Consider, for example, an individual who lives in a smoggy city. This individual spends money on air filters for the home and office in an effort to reduce the adverse health effects from the air pollution. The filters, however, are imperfect substitutes for clean air, and the individual eventually develops breathing difficulties that require medical care. In this case, the averting behavior costs would include the expenditures on air filters as well as medical care. Costs associated with loss of utility from pain and suffering, however, are not directly included in the averting behavior method. Thus, averting behavior results are often viewed as a lower bound on willingness to pay and can underestimate the benefits of pollution reduction.[12]

Although this method has intuitive appeal, it faces several analytic challenges. One is that averting behaviors only partially compensate for environmental risks. As in our example, the individual nonetheless suffers adverse health effects from air pollution, despite expenditures on air filters and medical care. Another is that individuals may have incomplete knowledge about the relationships between averting behaviors and the mitigation of environmental risks. For instance, individuals may not be aware of the range of health risks caused by pollutants or of the possible behaviors to reduce those risks. Finally, an averting behavior could provide external

---

[11] For more details on the method, see R. K. Turner, D. Pearce, and I. Bateman (1993), *Environmental Economics: An Elementary Introduction*, Baltimore: Johns Hopkins University Press; N. Hanley and C. L. Spash (1993), *Cost-Benefit Analysis and the Environment*, Hants, England: Edward Elgar.

[12] For more discussion on this method, see A. M. Freeman III (1993), *The Measurement of Environmental and Resource Values: Theory and Methods*, Washington, DC: Resources for the Future; P .N. Courant and R. Porter (1981), "Averting Expenditures and the Cost of Pollution," *Journal of Environmental Economics and Management* 8(4): 321–329.

benefits. For instance, using the preceding example, the air filters could not only reduce health risks of the individual, but also others who visit the individual, as well as extend the life of the computer equipment in the office. Yet these external benefits may not be wholly considered in the individual's determination of the amount of defensive expenditures.

As we discussed in this section, attempts to measure benefits and costs can be challenging and costly. These costs must be weighed against the potential benefits that the information would provide in decision making, considering that the information may rely heavily on approximations. Moreover, distributional issues—such as who reaps the benefits and who bears the costs—may be just as important, if not more important, than precise quantifications of benefits and costs.

EXAMPLE

Determining the Value of Greenways Through Contingent Valuation

Greenways are linear open spaces of land that preserve natural areas, protect wildlife, offer scenic aesthetics, and provide environmental benefits. Privately owned, undeveloped tracts of land that could benefit the public, if maintained as greenways, evoke complex issues of property rights and public goods. Planners face challenges trying to estimate the value of these public goods.

Greenways create positive externalities that help to alleviate urban stresses, attenuate pollution, and provide economic benefits such as increased property values. As with positive externalities, an underproduction of the good occurs due to these unaccounted benefits, in part because of the absence of clear markets and information about these benefits. Proper valuation of the good can provide a basis for making decisions about expenditures on programs to preserve natural resources.

Economic evaluation of benefits supplied by greenways is similar to that of other public goods, such as open space, urban trees, and clean air. Analysts use both indirect and direct methods to estimate economic value by, for instance, computing effects on property value through hedonic price analysis, comparing the value of natural services to those of infrastructure, and querying individuals to elicit their willingness to pay (WTP) through contingent valuation (CV). The latter method provides the advantage of offering direct insight into individuals' evaluation of the total economic value of the good. Despite its popularity, the use of CV remains controversial, and one reason is the concern that individuals generally state a higher hypothetical WTP than their actual WTP.

This study addressed that concern. It used CV to elicit both hypothetical WTP and actual WTP, and compared them in the valuation of a good—urban greenways. The study took place in the city of Indianapolis, Indiana, and concerned a greenway system consisting of 11 rivers and streams, one canal, and two abandoned rail corridors. Planners for the Indianapolis Parks Department expressed uncertainty about the priority that greenways within privately owned lands should have in their Greenways Plan. To help answer this question, researchers conducted a CV experiment to assess the public's value of the Crooked Creek Greenway (CCG), an urban greenway system primarily in private ownership.

The CV experiment involved two different questionnaires, which described the greenway system, the CCG, potential projects in the CCG, and asked 33 questions. The questionnaires were mailed to CCG homeowners, CCG renters, and county residents. One half of the recipients received a questionnaire that elicited their (hypothetical) WTP for protection of the CCG. It explicitly stated, "This is not a solicitation or a request for money." (This questionnaire will be referred to as the "survey.") The other half of the recipients received a questionnaire that elicited their (actual) WTP, meaning that it was an actual solicitation for money for protection of the CCG. It stated, "The Greenways Foundation will dedicate all funds that are donated to educational and service projects that will help improve the Crooked Creek Greenway," "If you choose to make a donation, please make your check payable to the White River Greenways Foundation and enclose in the return envelope with the completed survey," and "Please complete and return the survey even if you choose not to donate funds." (This questionnaire will be referred to as the "solicitation.") Other than these sentences, the questionnaires sent to both groups were identical. A motivation for the dual approach was to assess the validity of the CV method by comparing hypothetical WTP (based on the survey) to actual WTP (based on the solicitation). Furthermore, the amounts respondents state as their WTP offer insights into their valuation of the greenway.

For a summary of the results, see Table 9.1. The percentage of respondents that expressed a positive WTP was much higher in response to the survey than the solicitation. Yet mean WTP, for those who indicated a positive willingness to pay or donate, did not differ consistently by payment vehicle. That is, mean WTP was not consistently higher among either the respondents to the survey or the respondents to the solicitation for donations. (Mean WTP included only those respondents that stated a positive WTP in their response. Those who were unwilling to contribute or did not respond to the survey are not included in this table.)

This study also revealed that the majority of the public lacked information about the existence of the greenway and the potential benefits it could offer. Respondents expressed that environmental awareness is greater for direct public health issues, such as reducing sewage in water sources, than

continued on next page

TABLE 9.1 *Results of CV Experiment for the Indianapolis Crooked Creek Greenway (CCG)*

	CCG Property Owners	CCG Renters	County Residents
Number of Respondents—Survey	197/421 (47%)	23/285 (8%)	134/519 (26%)
Number of Respondents—Solicitation	161/414 (39%)	21/288 (7%)	88/521 (17%)
Prior Awareness of CCG	18%	11%	9%
% Willing to Contribute to CCG—Survey	51%	35%	22%
% Willing to Contribute to CCG—Solicitation	36%	14%	11%
Mean WTP—Survey	$47.20	$10.71	$29.07
Mean WTP—Solicitation	$32.24	$13.33	$34.50

indirect benefits such as greenway protection. Among participants who were unwilling to contribute, the most common reasons were "government should pay," "not enough information," "no value to me," or that "greenway users pay."

Overall, these results provided evidence that CV experiments can help to understand the public's evaluation of a good, and provided credible information about the relative strength of support for public goods. Of those residents who expressed a positive WTP, the mean WTP was similar for survey and solicitation respondents.[13] Researchers noted that dealing with survey recipients who are either unresponsive or unwilling to pay is a significant aspect of the validity of CV calculations. For example, average WTP depends on the choice of the denominator — whether it is the number of respondents with a positive WTP, or the number of respondents total. In addition, but perhaps not surprisingly, mean WTP was highest on both the survey and the solicitation for CCG property owners. To the extent that an unwillingness to pay for greenways stems from a lack of understanding of their value, public education will remain an important component of public good provision.

Source: Adapted from G. Lindsey and G. Knapp (1999), "Willingness to Pay for Urban Greenway Projects," *Journal of the American Planning Association* 65(3): 297–313.

[13]The actual contributions from respondents were significantly lower than expressed WTP in the survey and solicitation, although no follow-up efforts were made to obtain funds from those who expressed WTP but did not do so. This illustrates the complexity of creating a hypothetical choice context in a CV scenario that is directly comparable to the actual solicitations used by organizations to obtain funding for these types of programs.

STRATEGIES FOR DEALING WITH EXTERNALITIES

A number of intervention strategies can help remedy and control externalities. Because of the variety of externality problems, no one method is suitable for every situation. In selecting a method, decision makers should consider the following criteria:[14]

1   *Efficiency.* Here the goal is to maximize benefits at least cost. At the socially efficient level, marginal social costs equal marginal social benefits.
2   *Equity.* Equity concerns the distribution of costs and benefits among affected groups and among the groups that contribute to the externalities. For instance, environmental regulations should seek to protect members of the public equitably and also provide fair treatment in the regulation of each polluter.
3   *Administration.* This criterion looks at the ease of implementing the strategy, the data requirements, the need for monitoring and enforcement, and the likelihood of compliance.
4   *Flexibility.* This criterion refers to the ability to adjust implementation and management practices in light of changing market conditions, new information, and improved technologies.
5   *Uncertainty.* Each of these strategies involves a level of uncertainty about the effectiveness of implementation and the impacts on both targeted groups and the rest of society. Because all impacts can rarely be predicted at the time of implementation, decision makers should expect uncertainty and be prepared to adapt accordingly.
6   *Incentives.* This criterion examines whether the strategy provides incentives to reduce the negative externality or to increase the positive externality. For instance, environmental regulations, if designed properly, can provide incentives for both innovation and compliance, even beyond required levels.

We now look at eight of the most common strategies for dealing with externalities: voluntarism, prohibition, separation, directive, regulation, taxes, subsidies, and marketable permits.

To illustrate each strategy, we consider the case of pollution reduction of two lumber plants—Knotty Pine, Inc., and the Wall Board Co.—located on a river in the northwestern United States. These plants are considered to be the only major sources of pollution on the river. Currently, Knotty Pine discharges 10 tons of pollutants per month, and Wall Board discharges 6 tons of similar pollutants. The costs in Table 9-2 represent the least-cost method for each firm to reduce its pollution.

---

[14]We illustrate these criteria and strategies through an example of a negative externality, pollution, even though they apply broadly to both positive and negative externalities.

VOLUNTARISM

Producers or consumers may voluntarily reduce pollution for a number of reasons: to be good citizens, to boost corporate public relations, to obtain a relaxation of regulations, or to avoid later and more serious restrictions. Voluntary measures tend to work best when firms can see clear financial incentives to reduce—when their actions will ultimately increase profits. Reducing pollution voluntarily may be easy to implement from the perspective of a regulatory agency, yet it may not receive uniform compliance nor reduction at the efficient level. More critically, relying on voluntary reduction of pollution often leads to unacceptable levels of ambient pollution, the costs of which are borne by society.

PROHIBITION

An activity may be forbidden, such as smoking, littering, or loitering, and can result in a complete reduction of pollution. Even though this type of strategy would be relatively easy to enforce, it would not result in the optimal level of pollution reduction unless the marginal social benefits were equal to the marginal social costs. In some cases, such as littering, the costs of complete reduction (not littering) can be relatively small. Moreover, some might argue that "not littering" is a social ethic that should be promoted, regardless of perceived benefits of being able to litter (such as not having to walk to a trash can). In many cases, however, the marginal costs of reduction increase substantially with quantity reduced, so that the last units of reduction may not be worth the marginal benefits, from an efficiency perspective.

TABLE 9-2 *Monthly Costs of Pollution Reduction*

Quantity Removed (tons)	Knotty Pine, Inc.		The Wall Board Co.	
	Total Cost	Marginal Cost	Total Cost	Marginal Cost
1	$ 200	$ 200	$ 500	$ 500
2	600	400	1,000	500
3	1,200	600	3,500	2,500
4	2,000	800	7,000	3,500
5	3,000	1,000	12,000	5,000
6	5,000	2,000	20,000	8,000
7	8,000	3,000		
8	12,000	4,000		
9	20,000	8,000		
10	36,000	16,000		

In this case, as shown in Table 9-2, the total cost of complete reduction would be $56,000 ($36,000 + $20,000) per month, and the marginal cost of reducing the last ton (Table 9-3) would be $24,000 ($16,000 + $8,000) per month. These costs contrast sharply with the marginal costs of initially reducing pollution by 1 ton for each firm, $200 and $500 per month, respectively.

SEPARATION

Separating activities that affect each other is a common way to deal with externalities. For instance, the separation of incompatible land uses is one of the main justifications for zoning. Likewise, smokers are separated from nonsmokers in restaurants. The major advantage of this mechanism is that it can be relatively easy and inexpensive to administer. But separation may not be effective for externalities that travel great distances, such as air and water pollution. Another problem is that people near the boundary of noxious land uses may experience inconvenience and reduced property values. Also, separation can create situations in which those who control scarce land zones for particular uses receive a windfall from their right to pollute. Finally, separation may not be a flexible method of control, for example, to adapt to changing technologies and land market conditions.

TABLE 9-3 *Marginal Costs of Pollution Reduction*

| Reduction (tons/month) | Monthly Marginal Costs of Reduction | | |
	Knotty Pine, Inc.	The Wall Board Co.	Total
1	$ 200	$ 500	$ 200 (KP)
2	400	500	400 (KP)
3	600	2,500	500 (WB)
4	800	3,500	500 (WB)
5	1,000	5,000	600 (KP)
6	2,000	8,000	800 (KP)
7	3,000		1,000 (KP)
8	4,000		2,000 (KP)
9	8,000		2,500 (WB)
10	16,000		3,000 (KP)
11			3,500 (WB)
12			4,000 (KP)
13			5,000 (WB)
14			8,000 (KP)
15			8,000 (WB)
16			16,000 (KP)

For the Knotty Pine and Wall Board case, we could move the firms, move those being harmed by the pollutants to another area, or move the pollutants away from those being affected by the pollutants. In each case, substantial costs could result from the relocation, although the costs could be less than for other pollution reduction methods. Note that costs include more than direct expenses of moving. For instance, some would argue that a social cost results from forcing individuals to relocate or find employment in other firms, or from moving plants to less populated areas, which may also be more pristine areas.

DIRECTIVE

A policy directive that requires producers to reduce pollution by a certain amount has appeal because it appears to require the same effort from all parties. Yet costs of pollution reduction, and the social benefits that result from each reduction, can vary widely among producers. This variation makes it difficult to establish the most efficient and equitable level of reduction. In addition, such a directive may unfairly burden those producers that have already made great strides in reducing pollution before the directive. For them, the costs of reducing, say, an extra 10% may be more difficult and costly than for those producers who had not made substantial reductions and thus have more slack and more ability to reduce. For a government to produce an efficient reduction by issuing a directive, it would need to know a great amount about the costs of reduction for all firms involved, and the corresponding marginal benefits that would accrue to society.

This kind of directive raises several questions in the Knotty Pine and Wall Board example. First, in order to determine how much reduction should occur, we would need to know the costs (shown in Table 9-2) and the benefits of reduction. If we were able to establish or arbitrarily select an amount of reduction, then the government is left with the problem of establishing the most efficient and equitable way of achieving the reduction. One method is to require equal percentage decreases by each firm. In this case, a total reduction of 8 tons could be equated to a 50% overall reduction, so each firm could be asked to reduce pollution by 50%. Knotty Pine would be required to reduce pollution from 10 tons to 5 tons at a cost of $3,000 per month, while Wall Board would be required to reduce pollution from 6 tons to 3 tons at a cost of $3,500 per month.

Regardless of whether this solution appears equitable, is does not appear to be efficient. The marginal cost of the last ton removed for the Wall Board is $2,500 per month, and the last ton removed by Knotty Pine would cost only $1,000 per month. A more efficient method would require Knotty Pine to reduce pollution by 6 tons per month and Wall Board by 2 tons per month. The total cost of the reduction would be $6,000 per month ($5,000 for Knotty Pine and $1,000 for Wall Board), versus $6,500 per month under an equal percentage reduction ($3,000 for Knotty Pine and $3,500 for Wall Board). Both the firms and society could be made better off, from an efficiency perspective, through a 60% reduction for Knotty Pine and 33% reduction for Wall Board.

With this approach, one way to determine the efficient distribution and level of reduction is to derive the combined marginal cost of reduction. As shown in Table 9-3, the least-cost way to achieve a 1-ton total reduction would be a 1-ton reduction by Knotty Pine at a monthly cost of $200. Similarly, Knotty Pine has the lowest marginal cost to achieve a second ton reduction ($400). The lowest marginal cost for securing the third ton reduction is by having Wall Board reduce its first ton ($500). This process produces the combined marginal cost shown in the last column of Table 9-3. Thus, the least-cost way to achieve an 8-ton reduction is to have Knotty Pine reduce pollution by 6 tons and Wall Board by 2 tons. All other combinations would be less efficient.

Yet this approach makes an implicit and perhaps unrealistic assumption: that a marginal reduction in pollution by either firm will result in the same marginal benefits to society. Even if the ton of pollutants from each firm were identical, the variations in the distribution and interaction of pollutants in the receiving environment would result in varying marginal benefits to society. For instance, if Knotty Pine were 10 miles away from a population center, and Wall Board were 1 mile away, pollutants from Knotty Pine might have less of an impact on human populations (although not necessarily on the ecosystem as a whole).

This approach also comes with challenges. First, the government must know a great deal about the costs of reduction for all firms involved. Second, new technologies or innovations that change the marginal cost of reduction for some firms may change not only the optimal level of the externality but also the optimal distribution of reduction among individual firms. In order to achieve the optimal combination of firm reductions through directives, the government must reevaluate the directive to every firm after every such change. Finally, because the marginal benefits from reduction must be equal to the marginal costs at the optimal level of an externality, the government must determine the social benefits from the reduction, which can impose immense analytic requirements.

REGULATION

Also referred to as "command and control," common types of regulatory programs include ambient standards, discharge standards, technology-based discharge standards, and technology standards. *Ambient standards* set goals for the quality of the surrounding environment, such as for air, water, and land. For example, the National Ambient Air Quality Standards (NAAQS) sets levels for criteria pollutants. *Discharge standards*, which are based on ambient standards, prescribe effluent standards (for water discharges) and emissions standards (for air discharges). *Technology-based discharge standards* are based on the technology available to meet ambient standards or to achieve a certain level of pollution reduction. These standards can require the use of the best practicable-control technology (BPT), and are usually prescribed for specific industries. *Technology standards* require the use of a certain pollution control device or pollution reduction processes. An example is the requirement that cars be equipped with catalytic converters.

Drawbacks with ambient and discharge standards are that they may unfairly burden some polluters over others, and may not lead to the most cost-effective outcome because marginal costs of reduction vary among polluters. Marginal benefits of reduction also vary because the effects of the discharges depend not only on the pollutant but on the receiving environment. A large amount of information is necessary to try to predict how discharges will affect ambient conditions. Technology standards can be relatively straightforward to administer and monitor, but may not provide the most cost-effective methods of reducing pollution, especially if new technologies emerge that could provide greater reductions at less cost. In addition, by using a prescribed technology, polluters may have little incentive to find additional or more cost-effective ways to reduce pollution.

TAXES

This approach places fees or taxes on the generation of pollution. Even though it is known by several names—such as Pigouvian taxes,[15] user fees,[16] emission charges or effluent charges[17]—the general concept is the same. Recall that with negative externalities, social marginal costs are greater than private marginal costs, which leads to an overproduction and underpricing of the good. The tax can try to correct for that disparity by placing a charge related to the generation of pollution, causing the private producer to internalize some or all of the external costs to society. Thus, the private marginal costs will increase, supply will decrease, the supply curve will shift to the northwest, and the amount of overproduction of the good will decrease (Figure 9-8).

Note that for a tax to fully incorporate the amount of the externality, it would need to be equal to the marginal external cost to society, or the difference between the social costs and private costs at the level of output, which is the case shown in Figure 9-8. In practice, however, it is difficult to quantify the exact amount of the marginal external cost. Yet even if a tax is not exactly equal to the external marginal cost, it can still provide incentives to internalize external costs and to reduce the overproduction of the good that creates the externality.

In terms of implementing the tax, economists generally recommend placing the tax on the externality itself (e.g., the quantity of pollution), rather than on the outputs (i.e., the quantity of a good whose production creates pollution). For example, suppose a factory produces widgets, and the production process creates hazardous air

---

[15] The term *Pigouvian taxes* derives from the English economist, A. C. Pigou, who argued for the use of corrective taxes: fines to internalize the external costs of production activities. A. C. Pigou (1918), *The Economics of Welfare*, London: Macmillan.

[16] The term *user fees* connotes a charge associated with the use of resources, such as water use fees or highway tolls.

[17] The term *emission charges* typically refers to pollutants discharged into air, and *effluent charges* to pollutants discharged into water.

FIGURE 9-8   *Tax to Correct for Negative Externality*

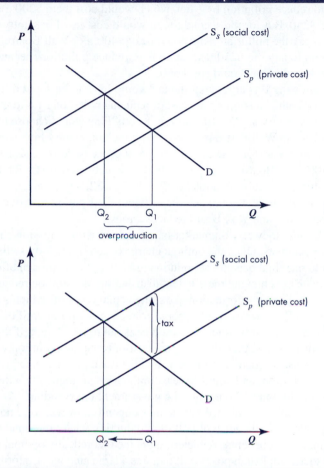

emissions. The tax could be a per-unit charge on emissions, or it could be a per-unit charge on widgets. The factory could reduce emissions by producing fewer widgets or by changing production methods so that each widget produced causes fewer emissions. Yet a per-unit tax on widgets (rather than on emissions) may not provide sufficient incentives to find the most efficient methods of producing widgets or of reducing emissions.

Taxes are conceptually attractive because they address the source of the externality. The tax represents some or all of the external costs that were not internalized in production decisions. It provides incentives to reduce pollution and raises revenues so that government may have to rely less on other types of taxes.

The lumber plant example can be used to illustrate the use of taxes or emission charges to regulate the level of an externality. Suppose the goal is to reduce pollution by 8 tons. Looking at Table 9-3, if the tax is $250 per ton, it is cheaper for Knotty Pine to reduce pollution by 1 ton, which would cost them $200, rather than pay the tax of $250. But for the second ton, it would cost less for Knotty Pine to pay $250 than to pay the pollution reduction cost of $400. For Wall Board, it would cost less for them to pay the $250 tax, rather than reduce pollution, because the first ton of pollution reduction would cost $500.

Following this argument, the tax would have to be set at or above $2,000, the total (for both plants) marginal cost of reducing pollution by 8 tons. (See last column of Table 9-3.) At, say, $2,100 per ton, Knotty Pine would choose to reduce pollution by 6 tons and Wall Board by 2 tons. With the tax, Knotty Pine would pay $5,000 in reduction costs (for 6 tons) and an $8,400 tax (4 tons × $2,100), for a total of $13,400. Wall Board would pay $1,000 in reduction costs (for 2 tons) and an $8,400 tax (4 tons × $2,100) for a total of $9,400. The $2,100 tax achieves both the optimal level of reduction (8 tons) and the efficient distribution in reduction (Knotty Pine reduces 6 tons and Wall Board reduces 2 tons).

Because they rely on market-based mechanisms, emission charges are popular with economists. Once the optimal charge is determined, by setting marginal costs equal to marginal benefits of pollution reduction, this approach offers the theoretical advantage of achieving the efficient distribution of pollution reduction among firms without requiring information about the actual costs of reducing pollution for any individual firm. Firms would choose to reduce pollution until the marginal cost of reducing pollution by one unit would be equal to the charge. If the charge were the same for all firms, then the marginal cost of reducing pollution would be the same for all firms. A second advantage is that firms would have incentives to find ways to reduce pollution, and could, at least in theory, automatically adjust to the efficient level of pollution without requiring government intervention.

These aforementioned advantages depend, however, on knowing the optimal charge, which is the level of pollution reduction where marginal social costs equal marginal social benefits. Yet determining the theoretically optimal charge can be difficult to accomplish in practice: It requires a large amount of information on the costs and benefits of reduction, and how they vary with level of output, location, and time. Another problem is that charges do not ensure a constant level of total pollution. Firms will choose to either pay the charge or reduce pollution, depending on current business conditions. Setting the charge too low could lead to levels of pollution that are unacceptably high. Finally, even though economists may consider pollution taxes to be a market-based scheme, government intervention is often necessary at each step of the process—from setting charges to monitoring performance.

SUBSIDIES

The government could also provide financial incentives, or subsidies, to producers and consumers to reduce pollution. Subsidies could be provided, for example, by distributing grants for capital equipment or by defraying costs of pollution reduction activities. For instance, for several decades, the federal government provided funds for construction of municipal waste treatment plants. As another example, home-owners can receive rebates for making energy-efficiency improvements to their homes, and also receive tax breaks for the use of an electric vehicle rather than a gasoline-powered vehicle.

Subsidies can also be used to promote the consumption and production of an activity that creates positive externalities (Figure 9-9). Examples include government-sponsored scholarships for students to attend college, or health care services offered at no cost to citizens. In the case of positive externalities, the marginal benefits to society are greater than the private marginal benefits. The subsidy will increase the demand curve, and help to correct the underconsumption of the good. A subsidy can also be used in cases of negative externalities, viewed another way. For instance, a beneficial activity that a subsidy could encourage would be pollution reduction.

FIGURE 9-9 *Subsidy to Correct for Positive Externality*

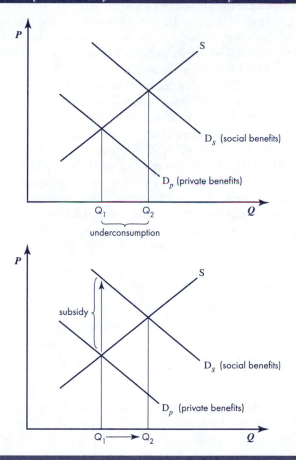

We now use the lumber plant example to illustrate the use of subsidies. Assume the government's objective is to reduce pollution by 8 tons. If the subsidy were set at $250 per ton reduced, then Knotty Pine would be willing to reduce by one ton, because it costs them $200 for the first ton, which would be a net gain of $50. But it costs Knotty Pine $400 to reduce the second ton, so they would probably not be willing to do so for a subsidy of only $250 (absent other incentives or regulations). Similarly, for a subsidy of $250, Wall Board would not be willing to reduce even one ton of pollution, because it would cost them $500 to do so.

To achieve the efficient level of pollution reduction, the subsidy must be greater than or equal to the marginal cost of reducing 8 tons, which is $2,000. With a $2,100 subsidy per ton of reduction, Knotty Pine would reduce pollution by 6 units and Wall Board by 2 units. With the subsidy, Knotty Pine would pay $5,000 in reduction costs and receive a subsidy of $12,600 (6 tons x $2,100). Wall Board would pay $1,000 in reduction costs and receive a subsidy of $4,200 (2 tons x $2,100). With the subsidy, Knotty Pine receives a net gain of $7,600 and Wall Board a net gain of $3,200.

The subsidy works much like a tax, although the financial impact on the firms and the government is quite different. First consider the impacts on the firms. With the tax, as described earlier, Knotty Pine must pay a total of $13,400 ($5,000 to reduce by 6 tons and $8,400 in taxes to discharge 4 tons) and Wall Board must pay a total of $9,400 ($1,000 to reduce by 2 tons and $8,400 in taxes to discharge 4 tons). With the subsidy, Knotty Pine receives net benefits of $7,600 ($12,600 subsidy to reduce 6 tons less $5,000 paid) and Wall Board receives net benefits of $3,200 ($4,200 subsidy to reduce 2 tons less $1,000 paid).

Now consider the impacts on the government. From the tax, the government receives revenues of $16,800 ($8,400 from Knotty Pine and $8,400 from Wall Board), and for the subsidy, the government disburses $16,800 ($12,600 to Knotty Pine and $4,200 to Wall Board). Thus, the subsidy places the burden of expense on the government, rather than on the producers and consumers of the activities that create the externalities. Also, the total marginal social costs of pollution may not include the costs of government subsidies for pollution reduction. Thus, the marginal social cost of pollution would still exceed the marginal private cost, even after the subsidy.

MARKETABLE PERMITS

This approach uses pollution permits, also known as rights to pollute, as commodities that can be bought and sold. Along with pollution taxes, this scheme is also popular with economists because it provides market-based incentives, allowing polluters to determine whether it is more cost-effective to reduce pollution or to buy a permit. It also provides the advantage of being able to maintain a certain level of pollution or ambient environmental quality.

This approach follows this general process. First, a regulatory agency determines the desired ambient environmental quality levels. Then, the agency determines the number of pollution permits to issue in order to achieve or maintain the desired ambient level. Each permit allows its owner to discharge a specific amount of pollution. Next, the permits are distributed. Finally, trading occurs within a market for the permits. In theory, firms will purchase permits until the marginal cost of pollution reduction is equal to the price of the permit. This practice would achieve an efficient distribution of pollution reduction and the least-cost approach to achieve desired levels, because each firm's marginal cost of pollution reduction would be the same and equal to the market price of the permit. As seen in Figure 9-10, as demand for discharging pollution increases from D_1 to D_2, the price of the permits will rise, but the amount of pollution will remain within the desired standards because the number of permits stays at Q_1.

Using the lumber plant example, suppose that the government sets the desired ambient levels of a pollutant at 8 tons per month and that only two firms (Knotty Pine and Wall Board) currently contribute to those pollutant levels. The government allots 8 permits, each allowing its owner to discharge 1 ton of pollutants each month. Knotty Pine receives 5 permits and Wall Board receives 3 permits. Current monthly pollutant discharges are 10 tons for Knotty Pine and 6 for Wall Board, which means that Knotty Pine would need to reduce by 5 units and Wall Board would need to reduce by 3 units.

Now introduce the possibility of buying and selling permits. Examine the marginal costs of pollution reduction, as in Table 9-3. Knotty Pine would be willing to pay up to $1,000 for a permit (the marginal cost of treating the fifth ton), allowing it to discharge rather than treat one additional ton of pollutants. And Knotty Pine would be willing to sell a permit for no less than $2,000 (the marginal cost of treating the sixth ton), requiring it to treat rather than discharge one additional ton of pollutants. Wall Board would be willing to pay up to $2,500 for a permit (the marginal cost of treating the third ton), allowing it to discharge rather than treat one additional ton of

FIGURE 9-10   *Marketable Pollution Permits*

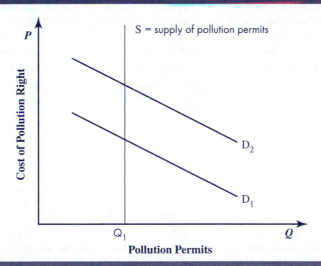

pollutants. Wall Board would be willing to sell a permit for no less than $3,500 (the marginal cost of treating the fourth ton), requiring it to treat rather than discharge one additional ton of pollutants.

Suppose the sale of one permit from Knotty Pine to Wall Board takes place. Knotty Pine would sell a permit to Wall Board at a price between $2,000 (the minimum selling price by Knotty Pine) and $2,500 (the maximum buying price by Wall Board). The exchange would not happen the other way around, because the Wall Board's minimum selling price ($3,500) is greater than Knotty Pine's maximum buying price ($1,000).

This transaction now leaves Knotty Pine with 6 tons to reduce, and Wall Board with 2 tons to reduce. Following the same logic, Knotty Pine would be willing to buy a permit for a maximum of $2,000, and sell a permit for a minimum of $3,000. Wall Board would be willing to buy a permit for a maximum of $500, and sell a permit for a minimum of $2,500. No further mutually advantageous transactions can take place unless another firm enters the market and is willing to buy or sell permits within those ranges.

This approach offers advantages of market-based incentives to reduce pollution, ensuring a standard of environmental quality. Pollutant levels can actually be lower than the standard if permits are purchased but not used. Some difficulties arise in practice, however. One is that, in setting up the market, the initial distribution of permits may be inefficient and inequitable. Although it may seem reasonable to assign permits based on current levels of pollution, this approach may unfairly penalize firms that have already made strides in reducing pollutant levels and make it more difficult to attain further cost-effective reductions. Also, as previously discussed, the social benefits of pollution reduction depend not only on the amount of pollution reduction but also on other factors such as location and timing of the discharge, interactions with other pollutants, and the receiving environment. In addition, true competitive market situations may not exist. For instance, markets may have few buyers and sellers, and markets may have barriers such that firms find it difficult to break into the trading scheme.[18]

Finally, market-based approaches, such as emission charges and marketable permits, have drawn criticism because they sanction the ability to "buy" the right to pollute. Moral issues arise: Should someone be allowed to pollute more just because they can pay for it?

---

[18] See, for example, R. Stavins (1998), "What Can We Learn from the Grand Policy Experiment? Lessons from SO$_2$ Allowances Trading," *Journal of Economic Perspectives* 12(3): 69–88.

REVIEW QUESTIONS

1. An economist testifies before a congressional committee on occupational safety and health. The testimony claims that, because workers' compensation premiums are based on average industry safety records, individual firms have insufficient incentives to improve safety. Explain why this scenario is an externality.

2. The economist's traditional prescription for regulating environmental hazards imposes an emission charge (tax) equal to the marginal damages in order to force internalization of external costs. From an equity perspective, to whom should the tax revenues be distributed?

3. Laws require that each car sold in the United States meet the same pollution emission standards. In what sense is this law an inefficient solution?

4. Europeans often comment that Americans drive too much because the price of gasoline is too low, and that gasoline should have a higher tax. Would a higher tax be socially beneficial?

5. A university just remodeled a building. Soon after, people start to become sick. The culprit is toxic chemicals from the carpets, paints, and furnishings. If the university had used less toxic materials in remodeling, or if the materials had been held to stricter health-based standards, the illnesses could have been avoided. How does this case exemplify externalities?

PUBLIC GOODS

This chapter examines the types of goods and services that are typically provided by public agencies rather than private firms. Termed **public goods**, they are defined by the characteristics of the goods, not by whether they are produced by the public sector. These characteristics are **nonrivalry** and **nonexclusivity** of consumption. *Nonrivalry* means that one individual can consume a good without reducing its availability or benefits to others. *Nonexclusivity* means that it is practically impossible to exclude anyone from consuming or deriving the benefits of the good. A classic example of a public good is a lighthouse. Everyone in the area can benefit simultaneously from the lighthouse (assuming no congestion around the lighthouse), and it is practically impossible to exclude anyone from the benefits (assuming no tolls must be paid to the lighthouse owner).

Because of these two characteristics, nonrivalry and nonexclusivity, private producers are normally unwilling or unable to provide the good. This is because more than one individual can simultaneously enjoy full benefits of consumption (nonrivalry) and their consumption cannot be limited, for instance, by charging a price (nonexclusivity). Therefore, the public sector often must step in to supply the good or service. Otherwise, it would be supplied and consumed below socially efficient levels. For this reason, public goods constitute a category of market failures.

After looking at different types of goods, this chapter details some of the important differences between public goods and private goods, such as the valuation of the good. This analysis leads to sections on public provision and public pricing: determining which goods should be supplied (partially or wholly) by the public sector, how to provide them, how much to provide, how to price them, and how to evaluate different provision strategies. As we will see, questions about public good provision are among the most prevalent and critical facing public sector decision makers.

THEORY OF PUBLIC GOODS

Most privately produced goods are *rival*. For instance, by renting an apartment, one consumer eliminates the availability of that apartment for other consumers. By going to a crowded amusement park, one consumer adds to the congestion and reduces benefits for other consumers. In contrast, pure public goods allow for nonrival consumption. For instance, one household can watch a television program without limiting the ability of another household to watch and enjoy the same program. With nonrival goods, simultaneous consumption is possible without any consumer losing benefits.

Most privately produced goods are also *exclusive*. Exclusion occurs when a producer is able to limit or exclude individuals from consuming a good, usually by requiring that the consumer pay for the good. This characteristic is vital to private producers, otherwise they could not collect payment from each consumer that uses their good. For many public goods, however, exclusion is impossible or impractical. Examples include fireworks displays, police protection, a lighthouse, and clean air. In each instance, benefits go to all consumers in a designated area, regardless of whether they helped to pay for that good.

Figure 10-1 classifies selected goods according to their degree of rivalry and exclusion. In this diagram, pure public goods appear in the lower right corner because these goods are both nonrival and nonexclusive. Pure private goods appear in the upper left corner because these goods are rival and exclusive. In addition to these two "pure" categories, many goods share characteristics of private and public goods. For goods in the lower left corner, exclusion is possible, but without rivalry in consumption. For goods in the upper right corner, exclusion is not possible or not desirable, but rivalry occurs in consumption.

These four categories, however, are not absolute. For instance, as an uncrowded toll road becomes congested, it moves from being exclusive and nonrival to being exclusive and rival. If a crowded public park starts to charge a fee, it moves from being nonexclusive and rival to being exclusive and rival. Then, as the fee leads to

---

FIGURE 10-1 *Classification of Goods*

	Exclusive	**Nonexclusive**
Rival	*Pure Private Goods* Apartments Meals Clothing Typical health services	Congested city streets Crowded public parks Crowded public beaches Fish in a lake
Nonrival	Fire protection Vacant seats at baseball game Cable TV Uncrowded toll road	*Pure Public Goods* National defense Clean streets Environmental protection laws Lighthouse

decreased demand, the park can become exclusive and less rival. Now we look at each of these four categories and their efficiency implications.

For pure private goods (in the upper left corner), private suppliers can provide them efficiently because consumption can be limited to only those individuals who pay (exclusive) and because the good is divisible among consumers (rival). The other three types of goods, however, pose problems for private suppliers, and efficient provision of these goods often requires public sector involvement.

For pure public goods (in the lower right corner), additional individuals can consume the good without imposing costs on others. As a result, it can be inefficient (and impractical) to exclude anyone who receives benefits from consuming the good. The marginal benefits would be greater than the marginal costs of allowing an individual to consume the good. Still, if private suppliers do not exclude, they may have no method of collecting payment from consumers, nor incentive for providing the good or service.

For nonrival and exclusive goods (in the lower left corner), a producer could exclude those who do not pay and accept inefficiently low levels of output. An example would be empty seats at sporting events. The marginal cost of admitting an additional individual is virtually zero, assuming that the individual does not detract from others' enjoyment, yet the ticket price may exclude individuals who would derive benefits from consuming the good. Another approach is to provide the good for free, but pay for it through some other means (other than tax collection). An example is commercial TV, which is free to those who have a television set, but is paid for, in part, by companies that advertise their products.

For nonexclusive and rival goods (in the upper right corner), one approach is to provide the good through the public sector and make no attempt to exclude. In these cases, exclusion could be possible, and revenues could be generated from entry fees or tolls. Public provision, without exclusion, is often argued on the basis of equity: that public resources should be available for all citizens, regardless of ability to pay. The lack of exclusion, however, can lead to congestion, which diminishes the benefits of consumption for everyone. Because of nonexclusivity, such goods are typically supplied through the public sector and rationed through congestion.

Goods in this category, nonexclusive and rival, include "common property resources" such as groundwater, fisheries, forests, and lakes. A common property resource, or collective good, is a finite resource to which access is not restricted. A challenge in managing common property resources is that unconstrained consumption by any individual(s) can lead to deterioration of the resource for everyone. For example, each additional well pumping from a groundwater resource can limit the availability of groundwater for others. After a certain point, if pumping continues, the groundwater resource could be depleted beyond its ability to replenish itself, and thereby be ruined for all users. Because consumers base decisions on their marginal private cost, rather than the marginal social cost, such negative externalities are created. In cases of common property resources, effective management usually requires some sort of public intervention to protect the resource from being depleted or destroyed by overconsumption.

With pure public goods (in the lower right corner), public production is the standard approach. Once the good is produced, everyone can enjoy the benefits of consumption without having to pay directly. In some cases, such as national defense, the good is supplied through the federal government. In other cases, such as a neighborhood park, the good is supplied through a local government or neighborhood association.

The nonexclusive and nonrival character of public goods provides a primary justification for a public role in the economy. Other justifications include monopoly regulation, externalities, and redistribution of resources. Still, goods that share characteristics of public goods make up a substantial part of the goods supplied through the public sector. The decision that remains is to determine the appropriate level of production of these public goods, and this decision can be aided by economic analyses.

PUBLIC GOODS: VALUATION AND DEMAND

An important difference between the analysis of private goods and public goods is the determination of total demand, which, in the case of public goods, can represent total social benefits. The derivation of individual demand curves is the same for both private goods and public goods. The difference occurs in the methods for aggregating those individual demand curves to obtain the combined demand curve.

Assume a market with only two consumers, A and B. Their demand for a good is tabulated in Table 10-1 and drawn in Figure 10-2. These data will be used to illustrate and compare private goods and public goods. The numbers will stay the same

TABLE 10-1 *Demand for Two Consumers*

Price	Quantity Demanded	
	Consumer A	Consumer B
$10	0	0
9	1	2
8	2	4
7	3	6
6	4	8
5	5	10
4	6	12
3	7	14
2	8	16
1	9	18
0	10	20

FIGURE 10-2   *Consumer Demand*

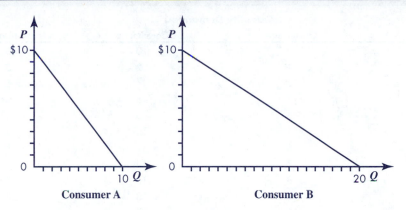

Consumer A   Consumer B

for the individual consumers, but the type of good (private or public) will change, and thus the total demand will change.

First consider *private goods*. Recall that the market demand curve is formed by the horizontal summation of individual demand curves (see Table 10-2 and Figure 10-3). The market demand curve tells us the total quantity demanded at each price. Because private goods are rival, consumption is additive; that is, at a price of $8, Consumer A will buy 2 units and Consumer B will buy 4 units, so the market demand (assuming only two consumers) is 6 units. So for a private good, the question becomes: Given a certain price, what is the total quantity demanded of the good? Given P, what is Q?

Now consider *public goods*. Unlike private goods, a public good is nonrival, which means that a certain quantity is provided for all consumers and the good is indivisible. It also means that units of consumption do not need to be added up among individuals to obtain total demand. A public good is also nonexclusive, meaning that consumers do not actually need to pay for the goods to enjoy their benefits. So, for public goods, demand represents a willingness to pay (WTP), and the aggregation of demand represents the total benefits to consumers by providing a good or service. Note the terminology: Here, the *aggregate demand curve* refers to public goods, whereas the *market demand curve* refers to private goods with well-defined markets.

To determine the aggregate demand for public goods, the individual demand curves are added vertically rather than horizontally. This is because the way to measure aggregate marginal benefits (based on WTP) is to add Consumer A's benefits to Consumer B's benefits for each level of output (Table 10-3 on page 230). As shown in Figure 10-4 on page 231, the individual demand curves are added vertically to obtain the aggregate demand curve. A level of output of 4 provides $6 of benefits to Consumer A and $8 of benefits to Consumer B, for total benefits of $14. So for a public good,

TABLE 10-2 *Market Demand: Private Production*

Quantity Demanded

Price	Consumer A	Consumer B	Market Demand
$10	0	0	0
9	1	2	3
8	2	4	6
7	3	6	9
6	4	8	12
5	5	10	15
4	6	12	18
3	7	14	21
2	8	16	24
1	9	18	27
0	10	20	30

FIGURE 10-3 *Determining Market Demand: Private Production*

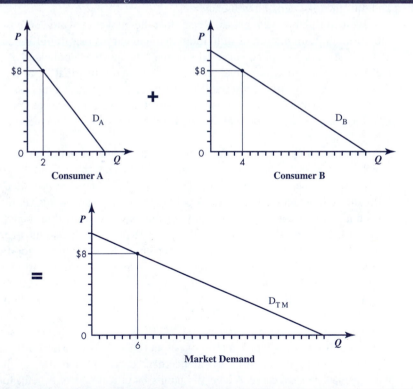

the question becomes: Given a certain level of output, what are the total benefits to consumers of that good? Given Q, what is P?

Having determined the market demand curve for the private good, and the aggregate demand curve for the public good, the next step is to determine the efficient or optimal level of production. That calculation requires bringing together information about marginal costs and marginal benefits.

First, consider a private good. Figure 10-5 on page 231 shows the marginal cost curve for producing the private good. The point of efficiency is where marginal benefits (which is the market demand curve, D_{TM}) equal marginal costs. This is point E. In this case, the efficient level of production is Q_T, which is the sum of Q_A and Q_B. For the amount of Q_T, the marginal benefit to each consumer is the same, which is P_1.

Now, consider a public good. Figure 10-6 on page 232 shows the marginal cost curve for producing the public good. The point of efficiency is where marginal benefits (which is the aggregate demand curve, D_{TA}) equal marginal costs. This is point B_E. Here, the efficient level of production is Q_E. At Q_E, benefits to consumer A are B_A, and benefits to consumer B are B_B. Benefits of providing Q_E to all consumers equals B_A plus B_B, which totals B_E.

Note another difference between public goods and private goods. At the efficient level of production, all individuals do not receive the same marginal benefits for a public good, but they do for a private good. In the example of a public good (Figure 10-6), at the efficient level of production (Q_E), consumer B receives more benefits (B_B) than consumer A (B_A). In contrast, for a private good (Figure 10-5), at the efficient level of output (Q_T), all consumers have the same marginal benefit, which is P_1.

Stated another way, for a private good, consumers value the good equally at the margin. For a public good, consumers may value the good differently at the margin. Thus, in the public sector, each consumer will judge the cost of the last unit produced as much higher than their individual view of what it's worth. This view of high costs and low benefits of public goods relative to private goods is often true even if public production were at the optimal level.

A common question is whether public goods always need to be provided by the public sector. The answer, as we will see in the following section, is not necessarily. Goods that have characteristics of both public goods and private goods could be provided by a private firm. For example, a private firm could collect payment for a nonrival, exclusionary good, such as cable television. This approach, however, would be less efficient than public production, because some individuals with a positive marginal benefit would be excluded by the required payment.

A related question is whether private goods always need to be provided by the private sector. The answer again is not necessarily. Some goods with characteristics of private goods, such as education, are nonetheless provided by government. A common rationale for publicly provided private goods is that the good provides important public benefits and that provision should not depend solely on ability to pay. For instance, education generates positive externalities, such as increased literacy, skill development, and integration among groups in society. In other words, education provides social benefits beyond what a private firm might incorporate and thus pro-

TABLE 10-3 *Aggregate Demand: Public Production*			
Quantity	Consumer A	Consumer B	Total Social Benefits
1	$9.00	$ 9.50	$ 18.50
2	8.00	9.00	17.00
3	7.00	8.50	15.50
4	6.00	8.00	14.00
5	5.00	7.50	12.50
6	4.00	7.00	11.00
7	3.00	6.50	9.50
8	2.00	6.00	8.00
9	1.00	5.50	6.50
10	0.00	5.00	5.00
11		4.50	4.50
12		4.00	4.00
13		3.50	3.50
14		3.00	3.00
15		2.50	2.50
16		2.00	2.00
17		1.50	1.50
18		1.00	1.00
19		0.50	0.50
20		0	0

duce based on pricing signals. From an equity perspective, many argue that individuals' access to education should not depend on their ability to pay, and thus the public sector should take a role in providing equality of opportunity.

PUBLIC GOOD PROVISION

We now examine issues and methods concerning public provision and pricing of goods and services. Difficult questions arise: What goods and services should be provided by the public sector? What are the optimal levels of production, and how should they be priced and financed? Even though the production and pricing of a public good can be determined theoretically, this decision is difficult in practice.

In one approach, we might select particular individuals and have them value the public goods based on their own criteria. To perform this analysis, we would need to obtain measures of individual or household benefits. We might hope that individuals

FIGURE 10-4 *Determining Aggregate Demand: Public Production*

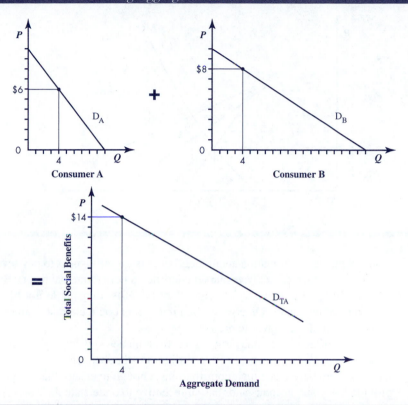

FIGURE 10-5 *Combining Demand Curves for a Private Good*

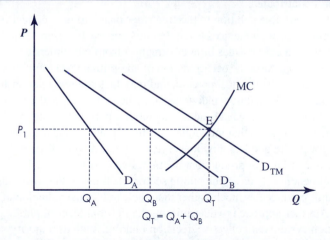

FIGURE 10-6   *Combining Demand Curves for a Public Good*

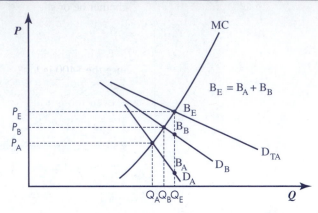

would volunteer information about their benefits or willingness to pay (even though public goods often do not have market equivalents nor require payment). But in order to discipline these voluntary statements of benefits, they could not be viewed as hypothetical payments. Otherwise, each individual could claim any amount of benefits for each of their favorite projects.

It would seem that some progress has been made—a voluntary statement of benefits accompanied by an equal cash contribution—but here enters the free rider problem. If others have made their contributions, enough to ensure that the good will be provided, any single contributor has an incentive to understate their benefits in order to obtain the good at a lower or zero cost. This individual is still free to consume the good, regardless of individual payment. An example is public radio, which is supported by listeners and other contributors, yet to which all may listen, even if they haven't contributed.

One possible solution to the free rider problem is to collect payments from all consumers through the tax system, but this approach presents problems in itself. The blanket payment provides little information from consumers about the optimal level of production. Also, the determination of an optimal level of public production can be influenced by the political process, and may lack a direct relationship to social benefits and costs. In addition, individuals may be concerned that tax revenues are wasted. Part of this concern may be valid, and another part may relate to the fundamental difference in the ways that individuals evaluate public goods and private goods. Recall that, for public goods, individuals often value the good differently at the margin. At the efficient level of production, the marginal cost is set equal to the sum of all individual benefits. Thus, in the public sector, each individual will judge the cost of the last unit produced as much higher than their individual valuation of the good.

Another approach to determining the optimal level of public good provision is through systems of collective decision making, such as majority voting. Yet majority voting has several drawbacks from both efficiency and equity perspectives.

Consider a community with three individuals, John, Claire, and Catherine (Table 10-4). Each individual needs to vote on whether he or she would be willing to pay a one-time $400 tax for an open-space preservation project. The total benefits of the project, for these three individuals, based on aggregations of their willingness to pay, would be $1,300. The total costs are $1,200 which, divided by three, would be the $400 per person tax. John votes yes because the $400 is less than his WTP ($650). Claire and Catherine each vote no because the $400 is greater than their WTP ($350 and $300). Thus, the project is defeated, even though the total benefits ($1,350) would be greater than the total costs ($1,200)—*an inefficient no vote*.

This same example can be extended to illustrate *an inefficient yes vote* (Table 10-4). Suppose now that John, Claire, and Catherine would be willing to pay $450, $450, and $0, respectively, which would be total benefits of $900. The total cost is still $1,200, which would be the $400 per-person tax. In this case, John and Claire vote yes and Catherine votes no. The majority of the community votes for the tax ($400 is less than the WTP for John and Claire), even though total costs ($1,200) exceed total benefits ($900).

Another limitation can be illustrated by the Condorcet voting paradox.[1] Consider those same three individuals and three choices for public expenditure: a bike path, a

TABLE 10-4   *Majority Voting Inefficiencies*

Inefficient No Vote

	John	Claire	Catherine	Sum
Benefits	$650	$350	$300	$1,300
Costs	400	400	400	1,200
Vote	yes	no	no	**no**

Inefficient Yes Vote

	John	Claire	Catherine	Sum
Benefits	$450	$450	$ 0	$ 900
Costs	400	400	400	1,200
Vote	yes	yes	no	**yes**

[1] This concept is named after the French philosopher, the Marquis de Condorcet (1743–1794), who noted that a majority voting equilibrium may not exist. See, for example, W. V. Gehrlein (1997), "Condorcet's Paradox and the Condorcet Efficiency of Voting Rules," *Mathematica Japonica* 45 (1): 173–199. The Nobel laureate economist Kenneth Arrow built upon this work, showing the impossibility of a social decision framework that would have the properties of transitivity, nondictatorship, independence, and unrestricted domain: K. Arrow (1963), *Social Choice and Individual Values*, 2nd ed., New York: Wiley.

TABLE 10-5 *Voting Paradox*

	John	Claire	Catherine
Path	1st choice	3rd choice	2nd choice
Park	2nd choice	1st choice	3rd choice
Pool	3rd choice	2nd choice	1st choice

Majority Voting Outcomes

Path vs. Park	⟶	Path wins
Park vs. Pool	⟶	Park wins
Path vs. Pool	⟶	Pool wins

park, and a pool. Table 10-5 provides their rank order of preferences for each choice, from 1st (highest preference) to 3rd (lowest preference). In an election of a path versus a park, the path would win (preferred by John and Catherine). In an election of a park versus a pool, the park would win (preferred by John and Claire). But in an election of a pool versus a path, the pool would win (preferred by Catherine and Claire). Majority voting, thus, yielded an inconsistent outcome: path > park, park > pool, but path < pool. The point is that different contexts can produce different preference orderings.

Public decisions may also fail to appropriately represent the public interest or to allocate resources fairly among constituents. One reason is the influence of special interest groups, which are relatively small groups of people that stand to receive disproportionately large benefits at the expense of others. Politicians may be inclined to support these groups, both to gain votes and campaign contributions. Thus, the politician may support the special interest program, even though it may not be economically efficient or socially desirable.

Another influence is rent-seeking behavior. In this case, *rent* refers not to a payment on a rental property, but to *economic rent*, which is a benefit above what would be earned in a competitive market (as we saw in Chapter 5). Industries, unions, agencies, and special interest groups can exercise political power and seek to gain rent from the government. Examples include favorable legislation and subsidies to large-scale farmers, tax loopholes that benefit primarily the wealthy, and large highways that produce social costs in excess of benefits.

Finally, short planning horizons mean that politicians are often reluctant to take hard or unpopular actions during their tenure, even if those actions could improve conditions in the future. Thus, programs are often promoted that encourage present consumption at the cost of future resources and opportunities.

PUBLIC PRICING

Pure public goods are often provided without a direct charge to the consumer. For many publicly produced goods, however, exclusion is possible and prices can be charged. The ability to charge for certain goods and services allows the public sector to encourage efficient resource use, generate revenue, and affect the well-being of different segments of society. This section identifies the kinds of goods and services for which nonzero prices can be appropriate, and discusses the factors to be considered in setting those prices.

Three major categories of publicly priced goods include (1) public utilities, which are often local natural monopolies, (2) public facilities, such as parks, and (3) public services, such as education. We examine characteristics of these goods, which will help to determine when public pricing is important and how prices should be set.

Public utilities, such as electricity, transportation, and communications companies, are characterized by large capital expenditures and declining long-run average total costs. Therefore, large producers in these industries will have lower average costs and will be able to undercut the prices of small producers. It can be more efficient to have one large producer rather than several smaller ones, which, in effect, allows a firm to operate as a monopoly in its service area. Therefore, utility services are usually provided by public agencies or regulated private firms.

Public facilities provide the possibility of nonrival consumption. Uncrowded parks, uncrowded beaches, and uncrowded highways can be used by one individual without significantly limiting the consumption benefits to others. On the other hand, more people and more consumption can limit the benefits to others. For example, when a road or a park becomes congested, consumption is no longer nonrival as additional users affect the travel time or enjoyment of others. When congestion occurs and when exclusion is possible, public pricing can help to alleviate overuse of the facility and maximize the benefits that public facilities provide.

Public services include higher education, postal services, trash collection, and state-run liquor stores. The reasons for public sector involvement in these activities include externalities, revenue generation, and historical reasons. For goods with positive externalities, consumption provides benefits to society in addition to those received by the individual. Therefore, individual consumers are willing to pay less than the value that society places on consumption. To increase consumption of these goods, society can subsidize the private producer or consumer, or provide the service directly at less than the private price. Thus, government has become involved in the provision of housing, health care, education, art museums, and many other goods and services.

Many of the goods provided by the public sector are not as easily categorized. For example, a primary purpose of public lotteries and state-run liquor stores may be revenue generation, but they are also intended to limit undesirable activities (even though they can generate additional types of negative externalities). When setting prices for these types of goods, it is important to take into account their original purpose, which may be different from the usual reasons for public involvement.

THE ROLE OF PRICES

In the private sector, prices serve two important functions. First, they allocate goods to consumers who can pay the most for them. Second, they provide signals to producers to provide more or less of particular goods. If a good's price is more than what it costs to make, producers will take advantage of this profitable opportunity. If a good's price is less than its cost, producers will reduce production of that good until the price equals marginal cost.

In the public sector, prices serve these same two purposes, in theory. First, public sector prices signal consumers to use certain amounts of a good, and therefore, ration it. A price of zero signals consumers that the amount they should or could consume is unlimited, as long as their marginal benefit is greater than or equal to zero. Therefore, prices play an important role in shaping consumption. Second, public sector prices also alert policy makers to situations where additional investments would be beneficial to society.

Prices in the public sector also serve a number of purposes in addition to allocating resources and signaling investment opportunities. For public utilities and other self-supporting public services, prices are used to generate revenue to pay for the service provided. Also, with publicly provided higher education and other merit goods, prices can be set so that consumption is greater than what would occur in the private market. Finally, prices are sometimes used to compensate for an inequitable distribution of wealth and to provide equitable access to certain goods, such as public transportation.

Public sector pricing is used to meet a number of objectives, but decision makers should not overlook its ability to influence demand and resource utilization. When prices are used for purposes such as income redistribution and revenue generation, it is important to identify explicitly how prices affect demand. High prices may generate revenue but limit the use; low prices may generate more use, but result in crowding and overuse. Different pricing mechanisms are available to raise revenue or redistribute income, and have different impacts on society's use of resources.

The next section describes ways to evaluate public pricing mechanisms and to set prices that achieve desired objectives and reduce undesirable side effects. For the purposes of this section, the size of the public facility is assumed to be fixed. In other words, the objective here is to price an existing facility (e.g., a bridge, park, recreation center), rather than to determine the appropriate size of such a facility or whether to construct the facility. These issues will be studied in Chapters 13 and 14 on cost-benefit analysis.

EVALUATION CRITERIA

The previous section showed that prices in the public sector can meet a number of goals. Yet common pricing practices may seem contradictory to public goals. For instance, in metropolitan areas grappling with sprawl, private developers are often charged far less than the marginal social costs of extending water, sewer, police, and fire services to suburban land. This section outlines ways to evaluate public pricing mechanisms.

EFFICIENCY

Primary criteria for economic efficiency are the production of the most-valued products at the minimum cost. In the private sector, under ideal conditions, competition leads to least-cost production and prices equal to marginal costs. In the public sector, efficiency is satisfied in the same way: by setting the price equal to the marginal costs. In this case, marginal costs would be full social costs.

The application of these principles would lead to efficient output and consumption. For example, the efficient price for some public goods, such as swimming in the ocean, is essentially zero, because marginal cost is essentially zero. (Technically, each person adds to the crowds in the ocean, but these costs will be assumed negligible in this example.) If a price were charged, some swimmers would not be willing to pay the fee, and society would be giving up a chance to increase benefits at no cost to society. The loss to society from charging a fee (*P*) is represented by the shaded portion in Figure 10-7.

For utilities, the same marginal cost pricing rule applies. For example, once a water company has built collection and distribution facilities, the efficient level of production is where the price equals the marginal cost of operating the facilities, shown as P_1 in Figure 10-8. Also illustrated in Figure 10-8 is the loss in consumer welfare that results when the marginal cost pricing rule is not followed. If the price is raised from P_1 to P_2 and the production decreased from Q_1 to Q_2, the loss in consumer surplus is the area ABEF. Some of the loss in consumer surplus, ACEF, becomes revenue to the producer and, therefore, is not a loss to society (although

FIGURE 10-7   *Demand for a Public Good with a Marginal Cost of Zero*

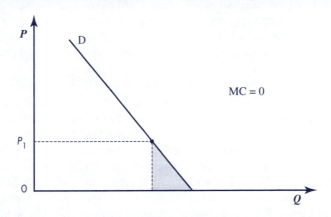

FIGURE 10-8   *Demand and Costs for a Utility Company*

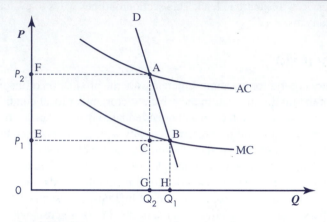

there are distributional effects). The rest of the loss, represented by the area ABC, is not compensated by a gain to anyone else and is welfare cost (deadweight loss).

REVENUE GENERATION AND COST RECOVERY

Another important role of prices is to generate revenue to support the service. This function is often at odds with the goal of efficiency, and the trade-offs between the two become important. Although the marginal costs of operating public goods can be relatively low, the initial costs of constructing bridges, parks, and other facilities are often quite large. The funds for constructing public facilities must come from one or more sources, such as user fees, general revenues, and intergovernmental transfers. If intergovernmental transfers are insufficient or unavailable and other sources of revenue (income or property taxes) are not practical or politically acceptable, public facilities then need to be self-financing. Such cost recovery pricing means that a price greater than the marginal cost must be charged, which results in an inefficient use of resources.

This pricing approach can be seen in Figure 10-8. When the price is set equal to the marginal cost (P_1), it is less than the average cost of production. Hence, decision makers must make trade-offs between cost recovery and efficient utilization of a facility. For example, in the case of municipal water facilities, because of relatively large capital costs and small operating costs, the marginal cost is often less than the average cost. Thus, for private utility companies, the socially efficient point ($P = MC$) may not be profitable because it would result in sustained losses (or below normal returns). Legal requirements of fiscal autonomy preclude some public agencies from utilizing marginal cost pricing. For a large number of public undertakings, however, construction costs and sometimes even operating costs are subsidized by outside revenue.

Subsidies and taxes can provide both incentives and disincentives, and help to achieve goals such as a reduction in negative externalities. They can also imply a welfare cost or a loss of efficiency in most cases (i.e., where demand is not perfectly inelastic). Less efficiency is sacrificed by charging user fees for public facilities that are more price inelastic with respect to demand.

As shown in Figure 10-9, the adjustment in consumption because of average cost pricing is smaller with inelastic demand D_2 (from Q_O to Q_2), than the adjustment in consumption with relatively elastic demand D_1 (from Q_O to Q_1). The loss to society (welfare cost) because of average cost pricing also differs. With relatively inelastic demand, the welfare cost is the area BCD; with elastic demand, the welfare cost is the larger area ACE.

EQUITY CONSIDERATIONS

Other major determinants of public facility pricing are the characteristics of the users, their ability to pay, and society's estimate of the value of the good or service. Many publicly provided goods and services, such as water and mass transit, are considered to be "essential" and are subsidized in order to provide minimum acceptable levels to the public. Mass transit fares are often held below operating or marginal costs to make them affordable.

Distributional effects are not always uniform, however. For example, art museums in the United States often receive public subsidies, but may be used more by higher-income groups than lower-income groups, and thus the pricing policy redistributes income toward the wealthier. Many economists argue that subsidies distort consumer choices much more than direct forms of income redistribution (e.g., cash

FIGURE 10-9   *Demand and Costs for Two Publicly-Provided Goods with Different Demand Curves*

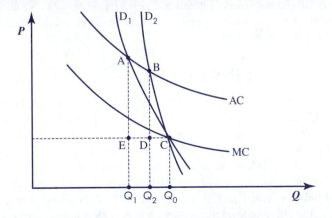

payments); however, direct income redistribution is not always feasible. In addition, it does not always result in the optimal level of provision of a good. Yet a pricing policy may be the only tool available to the government to achieve distributional objectives.

ADMINISTRATIVE AND INSTITUTIONAL CONSIDERATIONS

The criteria for choosing a pricing scheme must also take into account the costs and difficulties of collecting revenues. In some cases, such as bridge tolls, exclusion is relatively easy and collection costs are only a small percentage of total revenue. On the other hand, charging a user fee at a large park may entail building fences and staffing many entrances to make collection worthwhile. Depending on the demand, collection costs may be a large percentage of revenue. These costs and difficulties of revenue collection can influence pricing decisions.

Some public agencies have requirements to recover all expenses, including construction costs. Institutional constraints vary geographically and by level of government. Many special-purpose agencies, such as port authorities, do not have the ability to raise revenue other than through fees, while other government organizations have access to income, property, and sales taxes. Although flexibility in setting prices would help public agencies achieve their objectives, political and institutional considerations often determine the type of pricing strategy adopted. It is also important to recognize that perfect markets may not exist, especially for goods that public agencies provide, and that pricing schemes may deviate from the theoretically efficient level.

PUBLIC PRICING OPTIONS

Charging a fee or price is an important way for the public sector to raise revenue to help pay for the provision of goods and services. What price should the public sector charge? This section compares and evaluates some of the pricing options available to the public sector.

MARGINAL COST PRICING

As previously illustrated, marginal cost pricing is an important requirement of economic efficiency. For public sector decisions, marginal costs should include all known social costs, such as congestion and pollution, as well as direct monetary costs. Marginal cost pricing is used for many publicly provided goods, such as recreational facilities. Prices are often set to cover operating costs while capital costs come from general revenue. Figure 10-10 shows demand and cost curves for a typical publicly provided facility or service with decreasing average costs. In the diagram, the efficient level of production is A with price P_{MC}, where marginal costs equal marginal benefits (demand).

FIGURE 10-10 *Pricing Options for a Publicly Provided Good*

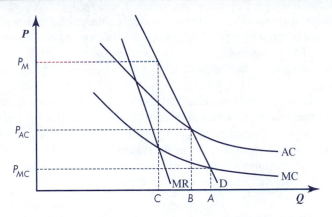

A problem arises with marginal cost pricing when average revenue is less than the average cost at the efficient price. This situation causes an operating deficit that somehow must be covered, and the source of revenue available to cover deficits can vary by level of government. Local governments rely heavily on property taxes; state governments use sales and income taxes; and the federal government utilizes an income tax for revenue.

The distributional considerations of marginal cost pricing depend on the users of the facility and the sources of revenue used to cover the deficit. As discussed earlier, important services such as public transportation are often provided at prices below the marginal cost to make the service affordable to more people. Some may argue that taxpayers should not have to subsidize users of a particular service. On the other hand, the service may generate positive externalities for society. Plus, the public sector provides many goods and services, and the distribution of total benefits may not be so uneven.

Finally, it is important to realize that perfect competition is an ideal, rather than the standard. If prices in excess of marginal costs are common, marginal cost pricing of publicly provided goods may result in excess demand for those goods. In these situations, it can be more efficient to have public sector prices that diverge from marginal costs in the same way that prices do elsewhere in the economy.

AVERAGE COST PRICING

A common alternative to marginal cost pricing is to charge the average cost of providing a good or service. This has also been called the *fair return price*, as we studied in Chapter 8. Examples of average cost pricing include rates for private and publicly owned utilities, such as water companies, where recovery of costs often depends on revenues. Although the total costs, including the initial construction and start-up costs, are covered by this pricing rule, a loss of benefits occurs from society's point of view. This relationship can also be seen in Figure 10-10. If $P = AC$, average cost pricing results in a higher price (P_{AC}) and less output (B) than with marginal cost pricing.

As an extension of the marginal and average cost pricing rules, a public agency could conceivably exercise its monopoly power, set MR = MC, produce less output (C), and charge a higher price P_M (see Figure 10-10). Such a pricing plan could result in a significant underutilization of the facility and could be justified by the desire to discourage consumption, perhaps because of negative externalities. This approach, however, is not that common in the public sector.

TWO-PART TARIFF

The debate caused by trade-offs between efficient resource utilization and cost recovery has led to a number of innovative pricing schemes. One of them is known as a two-part tariff, which involves a flat charge or membership fee for the ability to use a service, and a per-unit charge based on use or consumption. The advantages of this price mechanism is that it gives the proper price signals to the users, because each use is close to its marginal cost, and it has the potential to be self-financing. The disadvantages are that some efficiency is sacrificed for those consumers whose willingness to pay is different from the marginal cost, and some equity is sacrificed for consumers who are not able to afford the good. But it could be likely to subsidize low-income consumers, especially for the membership fee.

Two-part tariffs are common to both public and private sector pricing. Gas and electricity services often include a flat fee, with additional charges related to the level of consumption. Telephone companies charge a monthly fee for general service, and charge for calls individually. Even though two-part tariffs can be more expensive to administer and to market than other pricing schemes, they are an innovative way of generating revenue and recovering costs with less sacrifice in efficiency.

PRICE DISCRIMINATION

Another way of financing public services is price discrimination, which involves charging different groups of consumers different prices based on differential benefits. Perfect price discrimination is analogous to a tax on a consumer surplus that varies with each individual's surplus. Of course, perfect price discrimination would make each consumer pay their maximum price, which may not be possible or practical. Yet limited versions of price discrimination are in use. For example, electric utility companies charge separate rates for different classes of customers. Price discrimination can also be used to promote distributional goals such as lower mass transit fares for the elderly.

Price discrimination can be more efficient than average cost pricing, because prices are closer to marginal cost. Still, inefficiency may persist because perfect discrimination may never be possible. Although acceptable in some situations, price discrimination is often unpopular or contrary to distributional goals, with small consumers sometimes paying higher rates than larger, wealthier consumers.

PEAK PRICING

Until now, the demand for public facilities has been assumed to be relatively stable over the period in question. For many publicly provided goods, though, demand fluctuates in a periodic and predictable way. The periods can be daily, weekly, or seasonal, depending on the facility. For example, roads, bridges, and public transit facilities experience peak demand around the morning and evening rush hours, while electricity consumption often peaks in the summer when air conditioning use is highest.

With fluctuating demand, two problems arise. First, existing facilities need to be priced to result in efficient use, and second, enough capacity is needed to meet peak demand. In the simplest case of two distinct demand periods, such as rush hour (peak) and nonrush hour (nonpeak), the efficient pricing scheme is to charge the marginal social cost during each period. When facilities become crowded or congested, the marginal social cost rises as lines develop or crowding starts to reduce individual benefits or enjoyment.

In Figure 10-11, The two separate demands are represented by D_P during peak periods and D_O during off-peak times. Average demand is D_{Avg}. Efficient utilization is achieved with price P_P and consumption Q_P during the peak period, and price P_O and consumption Q_O during the off-peak period. If the average demand, however, were used to set a single price, P_A, the facility would be underused during off-peak

---

FIGURE 10-11 *Demand and Costs for a Public Facility with Variable Demand*

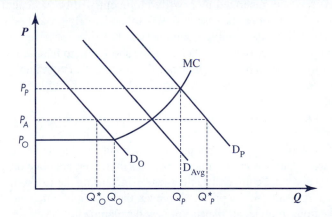

times (consumption Q^*_O) and overused during peak periods (Q^*_P), resulting in inefficient resource utilization.

Peak pricing can be difficult to administer. Not all facilities have easily identifiable peak periods. For instance, peak demand for recreational facilities may vary by the time of day and by the day of the week, making pricing difficult. If peak prices are instituted, the schedule must be known in advance so that people can change their behavior and switch to alternative facilities at off-peak times. Finally, peak pricing can lead to congestion at border times, such as overloading of telephone lines immediately following a certain time when rates change.

Peak pricing may also have an undesirable distributional impact. Peak prices may have to be high, especially if existing capacity is limited, and low-income individuals may not be able to afford them. For instance, privately owned toll roads have emerged, and many argue that tolls can unfairly limit access to low-income individuals who may have to commute during precisely those times that fares are highest. People with a low value of time favor rationing by congestion rather than by price. Others suggest that it would be better to keep prices low and ration the limited supply through a coupon or a similar system.

The point is that prices can influence consumption and behavior. They also have the capability to achieve a number of other goals and objectives, including efficient resource use, revenue generation, and income redistribution. When setting prices for an existing facility, it is important to understand that there are many ways to set prices and that no single method is right for every situation. Other factors, such as political, distributional, institutional, and historical factors are often very important.

EXAMPLE   **Development Impact Fees**

New development creates new impacts on existing public facilities and services such as transportation, education, parks and recreation, libraries, and public safety. Those impacts may impose costs on communities. Ideally, the new revenue generated by new development will be sufficient to offset the costs. This is often the case in slowly to moderately growing communities. In more rapidly developing communities, however, new revenues from new development are often insufficient in the short term to finance new or expanded facilities to accommodate demand. The result is that community quality of life can deteriorate as existing facilities and services face higher levels of use or even congestion.

One way to offset impacts of new development is to exact from it either certain public improvements or fees in lieu of improvements. Exactions are often in the form of land for parks and schools, road widenings, and extensions of water and wastewater lines. Exactions, however, are done on a case-by-case basis and can be unpredictable, thereby increasing the risk to the developer of earning a satisfactory profit. Moreover, the community may not be able to use exactions to offset all impacts of new development.

Development impact fees have emerged as one way to make the exaction process more predictable for both the community and the developer. In a sense, they are fees in lieu of making public improvements as a condition of approval. Technically, development impact fees are one-time assessments on new development to generate new revenue to help finance facilities needed to accommodate new development. They are assessed on new development to pay for only new or expanded facilities needed to serve it, including facilities with "excess" capacity, meaning that current demand is less than current supply.

Impact fees are charged for a wide range of facilities such as roads, schools, water, wastewater, drainage, fire, police, emergency medical, parks, recreation, open spaces, beaches and beach access, libraries, solid waste, and even public cemeteries. Once collected, they can only be used to finance the facility improvements on which they are based.

One of the advantages of impact fees is that they are reasonably easy to calculate. For example, if a community wishes to provide 10 acres of park land per 1,000 people, and if each acre of park costs $100,000, the impact fee for park land will be $1,000 per person ([10 acres × $100,000 per acre]/1,000 people). If the community averages 2.5 people per house, the impact fee is $2,500 per new home.

This calculation assumes that no other forms of revenue are available to finance park expansion. Yet this is often not the case. Suppose that, historically, state and federal funds were available to finance park expansion and there is every expectation that this trend will continue. Suppose further that about half the cost of park expansions in the past have been financed from such state and federal funds. The revenue needed to finance park expansion benefiting new development will thus be $50,000, not $100,000, and the impact fee will be reduced to $1,250 per new home.

More complicated is a necessary adjustment, called a credit, for new revenues (such as property taxes) generated by new development that are also used to finance the same kind of improvement as targeted by impact fees, such as park expansion in our example. Suppose local property taxes have been used in the past and will be used in the future to expand parks. Suppose further that such taxes average $10 per year per home. This is a form of credit that needs to be considered in calculating impact fees. Impact fee analysts will typically calculate the present value of this stream of annual revenues over 20 years discounted at 6% (roughly the average 30-year Treasury bond yield rate during much of the post-World War II era). In this case, the "revenue credit" is calculated to be $114.70. (We will study the methods for calculating present values in Chapter 12.)

continued on next page

If the impact fee were initially $1,250 per new home, it is now reduced by $114.70, which results in a lower impact fee of $1,135.30 because of these revenue credits. These credit adjustments are important because impact fees are supposed to be fees and not taxes. If new development generates new tax revenue that is also used to finance new park land but no credit is given for it, the impact fee will actually generate more money than needed. In our example, if the impact fee charged is $2,500, but if $1,364.70 ($1,250 + $114.70) is also generated from nonlocal sources, and if the present value of the stream of revenues for new development will contribute to park expansion, then the community will actually see $3,864.70 in total revenue for park expansion.

Where does the extra $1,364.70 go if the impact fee pays for all park expansions? Probably to the general fund. However, because more revenue was raised than needed, the excess impact fee revenue may be deemed by courts to be a form of tax and probably held void. Why? Because impact fees as "fees" can only be used to cover costs associated with the service being delivered. A tax, on the other hand, brings with it no promise that the taxpayer will actually benefit directly. So if the fee is higher than the cost, it may be considered a form of tax. Lacking legal authority to raise taxes in this manner, courts may strike down the fee finding that it, in combination with other revenue, generates more revenue than needed to cover costs.[2]

The amounts of impact fees vary widely. For an individual facility charged on new residential development, impact fees have been seen to range from a few dollars (in one New Hampshire community for only traffic signs) to tens of thousands of dollars (for roads in San Diego, California). For all facilities, impact fees range from a few hundred dollars per new detached residential unit to more than $50,000 in some parts of California. Although no federal agency collects data nationally on how much is generated annually from impact fees, estimates range from $2 billion to $6 billion.

How do impact fees compare with economic considerations? The answer is mixed. On balance, there may be better ways to finance most facilities, as will be seen shortly. General taxes, rather than impact fees, are often the preferred method of financing for such "public good" related facilities as parks, libraries, schools, and public safety (as we will see below). So why are impact fees gaining in popularity? One main reason is that taxpayers are reluctant to support efforts to raise taxes to the level needed to offset the cost of financing new facilities needed to serve new development. Impact fees are viewed in part as a politically expedient way in which to finance new

---

[2] J. C. Nicholas, A. C. Nelson, and J. C. Juergensmeyer (1991), *A Practitioner's Guide to Development Impact Fees*, Chicago: American Planning Association.

facilities needed to accommodate new development and thereby offset some of the potentially adverse impacts new development may have on community quality of life. Now we will examine impact fees in light of economic concepts.

First, consider the concept of public goods. Recall from earlier discussion that public goods are nonexclusive and nonrival, meaning in the context of public facilities that it is difficult to prevent individuals from using them and there may be a high threshold of use before the facilities become congested (such as in the case of large regional parks). As a form of pricing, impact fees can be considered appropriate where public good characteristics are not present, such as in the case of residential water and wastewater facilities. Unless a user physically connects to the water and wastewater systems and pays the fees based proportionately on consumption, water and wastewater service is normally not provided. Impact fees may be less appropriate for certain services such as parks and recreation, public safety, public libraries, and education because these services perform some measure of public good functions; that is, they have some degree of nonrivalry and nonexclusivity. Anyone can use a public park, receive fire and police service, and read books in a public library regardless of whether their taxes paid for those facilities and services. For this reason, impact fees for facilities other than water and wastewater service are often considered a second-best solution to facility financing.

Second, consider economies of scale. Often the larger a facility, the lower the cost of delivering the next unit of service. For example, water supply systems typically exhibit economies of scale (declining average total costs). Once the water distribution system is in place, each additional gallon of water costs relatively little to deliver. Other facilities have little or no economies of scale, such as fire stations distributed across a community. Economies of scale present problems for impact fees based on marginal cost pricing because marginal revenues will be less than average total costs; in other words, insufficient revenue will be generated to pay for the facility. For this reason, impact fees tend to be based on average cost pricing, even if it is less efficient than marginal cost pricing.

Third, consider equity. There are two forms of equity relevant to impact fees: vertical equity (based on ability to pay) and horizontal equity (based on equal treatment). Because impact fees are assessed on all new development as a class, impact fees typically satisfy horizontal equity principles. Vertical equity can be more difficult to address. Government provides certain goods and services when the market would otherwise price them beyond the ability of some individuals to use them despite their need for them. Government finances such goods and services mostly through general taxation. Yet, impact

continued on next page

fees for some facilities may affect disproportionately the price of housing for low-income households, and thereby run afoul of vertical equity principles. This concern may be addressed by calibrating impact fees to the size and location of housing. Some studies, for example, show that lower-income households typically impose fewer impacts on many facilities than higher-income households.[3] This is because, statistically, lower-income households typically occupy smaller homes and those homes are typically occupied by fewer people than higher-income households.[4] By calculating impact fees based on size of dwelling, they can meet vertical equity principles. Other studies show that homes located near transit facilities will be associated with fewer and shorter road trips because transit is used as a substitute for highway use. In these cases, road impact fees (usually among the highest in cost) would be reduced for homes near transit facilities, reflecting lower levels of road impact. Because lower-income households are typically found more frequently near transit facilities than higher-income households, this factor may also help meet vertical equity principles.

Fourth, consider incidence, or who actually pays impact fees. This point has been debated extensively in the literature with no clear final answer. Certain conclusions can be drawn, however. In communities with few substitute locations for housing, impact fees will tend to be shifted to the buyers, who are more price inelastic. Hence the buyer will pay impact fees in the form of higher housing prices. In communities where there are substitute locations for housing, which tends to be the normal situation, impact fees will tend to be shifted back to the seller of raw land to developers. The reason is that, to remain competitive, housing prices in the impact-fee community must remain similar to non-impact-fee communities, otherwise homes will not sell as well. It will be the seller of land who will have to discount the price of land to offset the fee. Over time, however, even in relatively competitive housing markets, impact fees will tend to raise housing prices a little and reduce land sales prices a little as all participants in the market move to a new equilibrium that accounts for the impact fee.

Also, impact fees have one distinct advantage over general taxation: They provide the very facilities needed to accommodate development. Moreover, impact fees tend to be leveraged to generate additional state or federal revenue to finance new facilities. Indeed, impact fees typically pay for only a quarter to half of the cost of facilities in part because of this leveraging. Under normal

---

[3] A. C. Nelson (1995), *Systems Development Charges for Water, Wastewater, and Stormwater Facilities*, Boca Raton, FL: CRC Press.

[4] U.S. Census Bureau (2002), Current Housing Reports, Series H150/01, *American Housing Survey for the United States: 2001*, Washington, DC: U.S. Government Printing Office, Washington, DC. 2002, from Table 2-18.

market conditions, the value of public facilities is capitalized to some extent in the property. Although prices may rise, with the "incidence" of the impact fees falling on the occupant (owner or renter), they do so in part because the benefits associated with the fee are what is being valued in the property.

A final consideration is administrative ease, and this may be a primary reason why impact fees are gaining popularity. They are relatively easy to create and administer, often costing less in personnel and legal complications than negotiating exactions on a case-by-case basis, and often doing a better job of actually delivering facilities when and where needed. In effect, impact fees reduce "transaction costs" relative to many alternatives. Impact fee methodologies are well known and courts have provided reasonably good guidance on their implementation.[5] One staff person with some clerical assistance can process tens of millions of impact fees annually. And when they are made part of the building permit process, they can become less expensive still to administer. They are also easy to enforce because it is clear who has and who has not paid impact fees; unless the impact fee is paid, a building permit or certificate of occupancy permit for new development is not issued. Compliance by developers is also assured for the same reason.

From their perspective, developers often prefer impact fees over unpredictable exaction negotiations or building moratoria adopted by local government when facilities do not have the capacity to accommodate new development. Exactions are negotiated or sometimes required after public hearings and lengthy review by local government staff and attorneys, and this delay costs money in the form of lower return on investment. In addition, just exactly what will be exacted from any given development is not known in advance, thereby instilling uncertainty in the development review process and increasing the risk of financial loss.

Impact fees, on the other hand, are based on a schedule that everyone knows. Developers know in advance what the fees will cost. Because communities using impact fees need not rely as heavily on exactions as communities without them, developers face less uncertainty and their risk of financial loss is reduced. Lower risk is normally associated with lower capitalization needs with the result that profit may increase in communities using impact fees relative to communities without them. The interesting point is that even if impact fees put upward pressure on housing prices, the reduced risk and uncertainty associated with impact fees will often make developers more efficient and their product less expensive to deliver—conceivably offsetting upward pricing pressure.

continued on next page

---

[5] A. C. Nelson (1989), *Development Impact Fees: Policy Rationale, Theory, and Practice*, Chicago: American Planning Association.

About half the states in the United States have enabled impact fees to be used by local governments. And local governments in other states without enablement, such as Florida, have sufficient legal precedent to do so.[6] To some extent, impact fees have become institutionalized as another form of revenue local governments must consider when faced with pressure to expand facilities to accommodate new development.

———

Source: Contribution by Arthur C. Nelson.

REVIEW QUESTIONS

1. Why can't the market solve the pure public good allocation problem? What makes a governmental solution for pure public goods difficult?
2. A town is faced with a serious water pollution problem. The pollution can be reduced significantly with the construction of a water treatment plant that would cost $1 million. This plant will treat all the water for the town and its residents; no one could be excluded. Yet no single family can afford to implement the project by itself, and each family makes their decision about the project independently. Why wouldn't a private firm build the water treatment plant, and then sell its services to the town's families individually?
3. Is the aggregate demand curve for a public good derived in the same way as for a private good? Explain the differences between the two, conceptually and graphically.
4. The economist Milton Friedman argued that national parks cannot be justified as public goods because exclusion is easy: We already have tollbooths at the entrances to many parks. Thus, he argues, private entrepreneurs could supply such park services if there were sufficient demand for them. Evaluate his argument in terms of the concept of a public good.
5. A small town faces severe cutbacks in public services due to statewide revenue restrictions. One source of revenues is to charge user fees for certain services that had, until this time, been provided free of charge. You are advising the city council, which is deluged with proposals for user fees for various town services such as fire, police, schools, parks, roads, and libraries. Discuss what you might consider in deciding whether and to what extent user fees would be appropriate for a particular service.

———

[6] J. C. Nicholas, A. C. Nelson, and J. C. Juergensmeyer, (1991), *A Practitioner's Guide to Development Impact Fees*, Chicago: American Planning Association.

IMPERFECT INFORMATION

To this point, the market models that we have studied, both those of perfect competition and those of market failure, have assumed that market participants have "perfect information"; that is, they have all the information they need in order to make rational and sound decisions. It does not mean that consumers and producers need to know absolutely everything about the market and the market transaction, but rather that they have sufficiently complete and accurate information for making their decisions.

In reality, however, we often do not have perfect information about current, future, or even past market variables, and we must make decisions that involve risk and uncertainty. This chapter is about those conditions, and it will provide you a set of tools and analytic frameworks for evaluating choices.

The first part of the chapter will cover cases of imperfect information that arise when a market participant has information or incentives that another lacks, leading to adverse selection, cream skimming and cherry picking, moral hazard, and the principal-agent problem. Imperfect information can help to explain the following situations: Why does a new car lose much of its value as soon as the car is purchased and driven off the car lot? Why do rising health insurance premiums lead to a rising percentage of high-risk individuals in the insurance plan? Why may car owners with theft insurance be less cautious about locking their cars than those without? Why may hourly wage employees lack incentives to complete a task as quickly as possible?

In this first part, we also examine ways that market participants, including government agencies, can reduce the inefficiencies and inequities associated with imperfect information. When obtaining information is difficult or costly, which it usually is, government efforts can improve overall efficiency. Moreover, cases of imperfect information underscore the role of the public sector in providing social insurance, such as Medicare, the Children's Health Insurance Plan, and Social Security. Without social insurance, many individuals would be unable to afford private insurance to protect against important lifetime risks, such as illness and unemployment.

The second part provides the methods and metrics for analyzing decisions under uncertainty, covering topics of certainty equivalents, risk premiums, insurance premiums, and the value of information. It presents the concepts of expected value and expected utility as ways to quantify and evaluate a decision maker's attitudes toward risk, whether risk averse, risk neutral, or risk prone. These concepts are applied to familiar examples of insurance and income, which illustrate how to assess trade-offs between expected monetary values and the uncertainty in those values.

The third part introduces decision theory and develops the framework of decision analysis to evaluate choices, given the values and probabilities of their outcomes. Decision trees are presented as a way to structure a problem, calculate the value of expected outcomes, and determine the value of perfect and imperfect information. This decision analytic approach has a range of applications, such as risk analysis and cost-benefit analysis, where outcomes may be uncertain yet nonetheless quantifiable in terms of their values and probabilities of occurrence.

As we will see in this chapter, uncertainties can be endogenous and exogenous. Endogenous uncertainty is internal to the economic system, such as information about product quality that a seller has but may not reveal to a buyer. Exogenous uncertainty is external to the economic system, such as random events of nature. For example, the amount of payment on a flood insurance policy can depend on the weather (an exogenous uncertainty) and on the actions a homeowner does or does not take to protect personal belongings (an endogenous uncertainty). Historically, the economics of uncertainty has focused on the latter, but the importance of the former has emerged in recent decades.[1] The first part of this chapter focuses on endogenous uncertainty, and the second and third parts focus on exogenous uncertainty, although the two are intertwined.

IMPERFECT INFORMATION AND MARKET FAILURES

Economic analyses often presume "perfect competition," as we studied earlier, in which these three conditions hold: (1) many producers and consumers, (2) homogenous products, and (3) easy market entry and exit. In addition to perfect competition, another assumption is frequently made: "perfect information." Although neither competition nor information may be absolutely perfect in reality, economists nonetheless assume that they are perfect enough for the purposes of making analyses and making decisions based on those analyses. Often, however, perfect information cannot be reasonably assumed. Nonetheless, expressions and quantifications of imperfect information can be incorporated into the analysis, and appropriately considered in decision making.

---

[1] For discussion of exogenous uncertainty, see, for example, K. J. Arrow and G. Debreu, G. (1954), Existence of an Equilibrium for a Competitive Economy," *Econometrica* 22:265–290; R. Radner (1979), "Rational Expectations Equilibrium: Generic Existence and the Information Revealed by Prices," *Econometrica* 47:655–678. For discussion of endogenous uncertainty, see, for example, M. Kurz, (1996), "Rational Beliefs and Endogenous Uncertainty," *Economic Theory* 8(3): 383–397; A. Sandmo (1999), "Asymmetric Information and Public Economics: The Mirrlees-Vickrey Nobel Prize," *Journal of Economic Perspectives* 13(1):165–180.

Imperfect information refers to when one or more market participants do not have the information they need for making a decision. Imperfect information can include insufficient information, inaccurate information, unobtainable information, unknown information, and hidden information. For instance, if we are buying a new house, we may not be able to assess the true quality of the house, for many reasons related to imperfect information: Problems may be difficult and expensive to detect, previous owners may not reveal known problems, future problems may emerge that could not have been predicted, and so on.

Imperfect information is a type of market failure—a deviation from a perfectly efficient outcome—because the outcome would be more efficient if market participants would have additional (necessary and accurate) information. Efficiency requires that information be provided to additional consumers as long as the marginal benefits exceed the marginal costs. The process of obtaining and providing information can be costly, however, and it may not always be efficient to spend additional resources to obtain additional information. On the other hand, when information is costly and difficult to obtain, government efforts to provide information can often improve efficiency.[2]

ASYMMETRIC INFORMATION

Asymmetric (uneven) information occurs when buyers and sellers have different information—buyers have information that sellers don't have, or sellers have information that buyers don't have, or both. (Symmetric information means that both sides have the same information.) Asymmetric information can lead to market failures, even under competitive conditions. If buyers do not have necessary information about the products they are buying, or if sellers do not have necessary information about products they are selling, then the marginal benefits and marginal costs of the market transaction can be different in actuality than believed and can deviate from the efficient outcome.

A classic case of asymmetric information is the used car market.[3] To return to our earlier example: A new car loses much of its value as soon as the new car owner drives it off the car lot even if the car doesn't lose much of its quality. The reason is that if the owner tries to sell the car, prospective buyers may not be able to assess the true quality of the car. Buyers may also wonder why the owner is trying to sell the car, especially if it's supposedly high quality, and may assume instead that the owner is trying to pawn off a low-quality car to an unsuspecting buyer.

---

[2] For discussion of market failures related to imperfect information and the role of government intervention, see B. Greenwald and J. E. Stiglitz (1986), "Externalities in Economies with Imperfect Information and Incomplete Markets," *Quarterly Journal of Economics*, May, 229–264; J. E. Stiglitz (1985), Information and Economic Analysis: A Perspective, *The Economic Journal* 95, supplement: 21–41.

[3] This discussion follows the logic of G. Akerlof (1970), "The Market for Lemons," *Quarterly Journal of Economics*, August, 488–500.

Thus is the case of asymmetric information: The seller of a used car generally knows much more about its true condition than the buyer of a used car. The buyer of a used car often has insufficient information or means to assess the true condition of the car. Consequently, a single price range generally emerges for cars that are of the same make and same year, even if the quality of those cars varies widely. We can analyze this case of asymmetric information graphically, using equilibrium analysis as shown in Figures 11-1 and 11-2.

First, let's suppose that buyers of used cars have perfect information; that is, they know whether the used car is low-quality or high-quality. This distinction is represented by the demand curves in Figure 11-1 and Figure 11-2, D_{L*} (demand for low-quality used cars) and D_{H*} (demand for high-quality used cars), where the asterisk denotes perfect information. Similarly, S_{L*} and S_{H*} represent the supply of low-quality used cars and high-quality used cars, respectively. Here the suppliers are assumed to have perfect information about the quality of the cars that they are selling. (In some cases, sellers may not know all the advantages or problems with their cars.) S_{H*} is higher than S_{L*} because sellers of high-quality cars would expect to receive more for their high-quality cars, and vice versa. D_{L*} is lower than D_{H*} because buyers would expect to pay less for low-quality cars, and vice versa.

Assume that the used car market consists of 200,000 cars total: 50% high-quality cars (100,000) and 50% low-quality used cars (100,000), and that buyers and sellers know about this proportion from market statistics. Of course the quality of cars can vary between high and low, but we will consider just these two classifications in this example.

Now suppose that perfect and symmetrical information is no longer available. Sellers know more about the quality of their cars than the buyers, and buyers learn about the full quality of the cars only after they actually purchase the cars. Thus,

FIGURE 11-1   *Market for Low-Quality Used Cars*

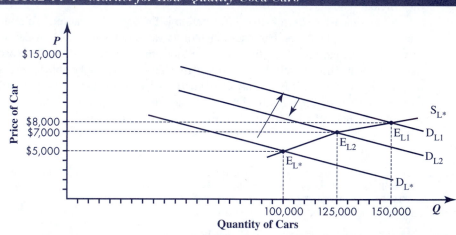

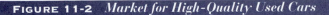

FIGURE 11-2 *Market for High-Quality Used Cars*

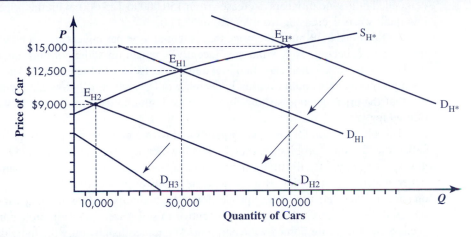

potential buyers are no longer absolutely certain that a high-quality used car is actually high quality until after they buy the car and drive it for a while. So the demand for high-quality cars will decrease because of the risk that a supposedly high-quality car will actually be a low-quality car.

As demand for high-quality used cars decreases from D_{H*} to D_{H1}, the demand for low-quality cars increases from D_{L*} to D_{L1}. These shifts occur because the market for used cars includes both high-quality and low-quality cars, and thus buyers would not know in advance that a low-quality car would actually be low quality, and they would consider the possibility that the car they purchase could be high quality.

The points of equilibrium would move from E_{H*} to E_{H1}, and from E_{L*} to E_{L1} (Figures 11-1 and 11-2, respectively). Quantity demanded of high-quality cars decreases from 100,000 to 50,000, and quantity demanded of low-quality cars increases from 100,000 to 150,000. Price of high-quality cars decreases from $15,000 to $12,500, and price of low-quality cars increases from $5,000 to $8,000.

It is not necessarily a final equilibrium, though. Buyers eventually realize that the fraction of high quality cars is now no longer 50% (100,000/200,000) but rather 25% (50,000/200,000), which drives down demand further, for both high-quality and low-quality cars. Because fewer high-quality used cars would be offered for sale, buyers would learn that a higher percentage of used cars are low quality, and thus their chances of getting a low-quality rather than high-quality car would be greater, decreasing demand for both low-quality and high-quality cars. Sellers of high-quality cars may fear buyers' supposition of low quality, thus hindering sellers' chances of getting a fair price for their high-quality cars.

As seen in Figure 11-2, demand for high-quality cars decreases from D_{H1} to D_{H2}, the price of high-quality cars decreases from $12,500 to $9,000 and quantity supplied of high-quality cars decreases from 50,000 to 10,000. Correspondingly, as seen in Figure 11-1, demand for low-quality cars decreases from D_{L1} to D_{L2}, the quantity demanded of low-quality cars decreases from 150,000 to 125,000, with the price of low-quality cars decreasing from \$8,000 to \$7,000.

As this trend continues, the price that potential used car buyers would be willing to pay can become so low that few incentives remain for sellers of high-quality used cars to try to sell their cars. In this extreme case, as seen in Figure 11-2, demand for high-quality cars could eventually decrease to D_{H3}, which is below S_{H^*}, implying that the price became so low for sellers of high-quality cars that none were offered for sale.

This phenomenon for low-quality goods to drive out high-quality goods has been called the "lemons" problem. (A lemon is a low-quality used car that is sold to an unsuspecting buyer.) It illustrates the relationship between quality and information; rather, imperfect information. Buyers judge the quality of prospective purchases based on some market statistic, such as proportion of high-quality and low-quality cars in the used car market. Sellers have an incentive to sell lower-quality merchandise, because the effects are borne by the entire market, rather than by only the individual seller. Here, the seller sells a lemon, gets a good price, and the reputation of the used car market suffers. Consequently, the market experiences a reduction in the average quality of goods sold and a reduction in its size. The proportion of low-quality used cars is higher than it would be if consumers could fully assess quality before the purchase. Thus, a seller of a high-quality used car cannot necessarily expect to receive the full value of the car, even if it were just driven off the new car lot.

MARKET AND NONMARKET RESPONSES TO ASYMMETRIC INFORMATION

Both the private sector and public sector have sought to alleviate market imperfections associated with imperfect information. These approaches range from individual actions on the part of consumers or producers, to third-party markets for providing information, to government provision of information, requirements on disclosure and minimum standards, and even outright provision of needed services. Examples of market and nonmarket responses will be examined for each type of information failure presented in each section.

In the cases of asymmetric information, such as in the used car market, we have seen the tendency for low-quality products to drive out high-quality products. But it is not always the case, because buyers have ways to distinguish quality, sellers have ways to signal quality, and third parties can also provide information.

Buyers can gather information. For instance, with used cars, a prospective buyer can hire a mechanic to check out the quality of the car (hoping the mechanic will provide an accurate and complete report), consult magazines, talk with other buyers, search on the Internet, and test drive the car.

Sellers can provide information and assurances to consumers. For instance, sellers can provide buyers with warrantees, a history of maintenance records, and a good explanation for why they are selling their car. Sellers can develop a reputation for high-quality products and customer service, so that buyers know they could return or exchange the product if it were defective. Sellers can also signal confidence that a car is reasonably high-quality by assuming some of the risk of the sale, such as offering to cover repair costs for the first year after purchase.

Third parties, both public and private, can also assist with providing information. For instance, in the used car market, some states have "lemon laws" that force auto dealers to take back defective new cars, and dealers cannot resell these cars until they make needed repairs. Government also requires disclosure of average fuel economy (miles per gallon). Private companies can enter the market for information, finding it profitable to conduct research and sell it to producers and consumers. For instance, several consumer magazines provide reviews and ratings of used cars.

So buyers can gather information and sellers can provide information and third parties can assist the efforts. A question, however, is whether the benefits of additional information are worth the costs of obtaining that information. Even if consumers and producers do not have perfect information, it does not mean that the market functions inefficiently. Information is costly, and it can be more efficient for consumers or producers to be less than fully informed if the costs of information may be greater than the potential benefits. For instance, a prospective buyer of a $5,000 used car may consider it worth $50 to hire a mechanic to check the car, but not worth $1,000 to conduct a survey of other used car buyers who purchased that particular make of car.

ADVERSE SELECTION

Adverse selection is a form of market failure that arises from imperfect information. It is the self-selection of those with higher risks; in other words, people with the highest risk are the most likely to buy insurance. Adverse selection can occur when buyers or sellers do not have enough information to accurately assess benefits and costs (quality and risk). The result is that products that are lower-quality (or higher-risk, higher-cost) than their assessment will be attracted to the market.

Consider health insurance. Suppose a health insurer is going to offer a plan to a university's employees. The insurer calculates the average cost of providing health care, based on its assessment of the average health of the university employees expected to sign up for the plan. Then the insurer uses this average cost to determine the premium when they offer their plan to the university. The employee can choose whether to buy insurance and at what level. But suppose that once the health plan is offered, the average cost to the insurer is higher than originally calculated. Many more high-cost employees (in terms of the costs that the insurer must cover) sign up for the plan than originally calculated. The insurer did not have full information about the true health care costs of employees who would select the plan, leading to adverse selection, the self-selection of the highest-cost employees who join the plan.

The adverse selection problem is not simply that higher-cost employees sign up for the plan. That expectation was included in the insurer's calculation of average costs; that is, the insurer included a range of costs in their calculations, from lower-cost employees to higher-cost employees. Rather, the adverse selection problem arose because the average cost exceeds the cost originally calculated because of lack of information about current and future health care costs of employees that would purchase the insurance. Thus, the plan led to the self-selection of higher-cost employees and that increased the expected average cost to the insurer.

Adverse selection raises costs for not only the insurer but also for the insured. If actual costs to the insurer are higher than previously expected costs, the insurer may need to raise the premiums in the next premium cycle to preserve their profitability. If the insurer raises the premium, the higher premium can cause lower-cost employees to drop out of the plan, because these employees figure that it would be less expensive to join another plan or to just pay out of pocket. When lower-cost employees leave, the average cost for covering those remaining in the plan increases again. If the insurer raises the premium again to account for the increasing average costs, it can cause even more lower-cost employees to leave the plan and higher-cost employees to stay in the plan. As this cycle continues, the premiums may become so high that employees are unable to obtain health insurance at affordable prices. This escalating problem of adverse selection in health insurance has been called the "premium death spiral" (or more generally, the "adverse selection death spiral" in other contexts).

In addition, asymmetric information affects choice for not only the insurer but also the insured. Just as insurance companies have difficulties in assessing risks among individuals they enroll, the potentially insured individuals have difficulties in assessing quality of services among providers. One reason is that individuals usually do not make repeated purchases of specific medical procedures (such as surgeries), as they do for other consumer goods and services. In addition, the success of medical procedures can depend heavily on circumstances, such as patients' health status, rather than just the provider. Information about physician quality can be difficult to obtain and assess. Here enters the role of government in seeking to remedy a market failure based on lack of information. Through requirements for testing and licensing in order to practice medicine in the United States, the public is provided a fundamental level of information and assurances about a service.

Efforts to reduce adverse selection in health insurance include the following: excluding preexisting conditions, requiring a waiting period before covering certain conditions or procedures, imposing limits on the extent of coverage, setting premiums according to expected health care costs, and offering only one insurance plan for a group of employees. Some problems are associated with these approaches. For instance, employees may be afraid to switch employers if they (or their dependents) have high-cost or preexisting conditions; but that problem is limited to some extent under HIPAA.[4] Also, the inability to obtain treatment for excluded conditions can lead to more costly and more difficult to treat conditions in the future.

---

[4] HIPAA stands for the Health Insurance Portability and Accountability Act of 1996. Under Title I of HIPAA, workers (and their families) can have their health insurance protected if they change or lose their jobs. The Centers for Medicare & Medicaid Services (CMS) implement provisions of HIPAA. Information is available at http://www.cms.gov/hipaa/.

Equity concerns also arise. Suppose premiums for individuals were set according to their expected health costs to the insurer. What if individuals were unable to afford the costs of treating their conditions? What if these higher-cost conditions were beyond the individual's control, such as being stricken by a rare disease as a child? What about the elderly, the disabled, and those with chronic illness? If people pay insurance costs in accordance with insurance benefits received, should social costs saved and social benefits generated by the individual, because of their treatment, be included in the calculation? As you might imagine, opinions differ on what constitutes an "equitable" health insurance plan.

CREAM SKIMMING AND CHERRY PICKING

As discussed, adverse selection occurs when the less desirable (higher-cost) goods are selected or attracted. On the other end, *cream skimming* and *cherry picking* are when the more desirable (lower-cost) goods are selected or attracted. With the health care example, cherry picking happens when an insurer seeks to enroll the healthier (lower-cost) individuals for their plan. For example, health insurers seeking to enroll healthy senior citizens have been known to recruit at activities such as square dances and at locations that are inaccessible to wheelchairs.

Such plans have been criticized because they often discriminate against unhealthier or higher-cost groups through exclusions and exceptionally high premiums, or because they try to increase profits by enrolling lower-cost individuals, rather than providing better and more efficient services to all individuals already in the plan. Another example is educational vouchers. Educational vouchers, in which public funds support vouchers to enroll children in private schools, have been suggested as a way to promote competition among schools, provide higher quality education, and offer greater choice to prospective students and their families. A concern is that private schools will seek to enroll students who are less expensive to educate or avoid enrolling students who have difficulties (such as learning disabilities), whereas a public school system cannot exclude and must provide education to all students, regardless of abilities or disabilities.

In the case of cream skimming and cherry picking, unlike other efforts to improve benefits and reduce costs, the gains to one group (such as an insurance company) may occur largely at the expense of other groups (other insurance companies and their insured individuals) and to the public sector. For instance, an insurance company that places strict limits on whom or what they will insure forces higher-risk or higher-cost individuals go to other companies for coverage, driving up costs for those companies and the individuals in those plans. Another issue is equity concerns about lack of affordable coverage and adequate choice for higher-risk groups, such as the elderly and disabled.

It has been argued that risk pooling, which groups many individuals into one insurance plan, can reduce the average costs of insurance. As more individuals are grouped together, the average costs to the insurer often become more stable and less risky. Thus, average costs can be reduced by spreading risk among large numbers of people, and by administrative economies of scale. Paradoxically, by restricting consumer choice through mandatory risk pooling, which requires individuals to join one insurance plan, average costs for consumers can decrease. Also, consumers often purchase an insurance plan, even if average costs of the plan are greater than their expected average costs without the plan, because of risk aversion (as we will see later in this chapter). That is, consumers are often willing to pay more for insurance than their expected average costs in order to insure against the probability, even a small probability, of a high-cost or catastrophic event occurring.

MORAL HAZARD

Another result of imperfect information is moral hazard. **Moral hazard** occurs when there is a reduced incentive to avoid the insured-against event. The insured may engage in riskier behavior, knowing that some or all of the costs will be transferred to others. The insurer may not have or be able to obtain full information about the actions of the insured. Thus, the insured can affect the probability or magnitude of a payment associated with an event. For instance, drivers, once they have car insurance, may be less cautious when driving. Athletes, once they have guaranteed contracts, may be more likely to not play when injured.

The moral hazard problem arises because the insured can influence the amount the insurer spends on their behalf, and because the costs are not entirely borne by the insured, but rather spread among all of the insured in the plan. Consider, for example, the previous example of health care for employees: Insurers set premiums based on the average costs of employees that they expect to enroll and as a result of negotiations with employers. Employers pay some part of the premium, and so do employees. Employees choose a health care plan based on factors such as expected benefits and costs, recommendations, location, and degree of choice of provider. Once employees have insurance, they then possess more information than the employer or the insurance company about the amount of health care services that they are likely to use.

Efforts to reduce the moral hazard problem include the following: restrictions and requirements such as deductibles (the insured pays a certain amount, such as the first $200, before receiving reimbursement), co-payments (the insured pays a certain percentage, such as 20%, of the costs of service), limits on services (such as number of days in the hospital), preauthorizations required, lengthy applications in order to obtain additional services (which if denied turns into a lengthy appeals process), or other managed care restrictions. Incentives include reduced premiums for patients that, for instance, enroll in health prevention programs, or are nonsmokers. Although just as with the original moral hazard problem, it may be difficult to verify individual behavior, such as nonsmoking status.

Another example of moral hazard involves credit cards. Cardholders can charge on credit cards in advance, without putting up any advance payment or even collateral, and the credit card company provides the payment to the merchant, essentially insuring against nonpayment. When the bill comes at the end of the month, cardholders who cannot make the complete payment must pay interest on the unpaid amount. Although credit card companies benefit from the interest, and in fact may prefer customers who have interest payments rather than those who pay their amounts in full at once, the credit card companies also run the risk that cardholders will not repay their amounts at all, which means costs to the credit card company. Although credit card companies investigate potential applicants beforehand and assess their credit history, applicant history doesn't necessarily predict future behavior. Potential cardholders will probably have more information about their ability to repay than the credit card company.

Here is where moral hazard enters. Once cardholders have the ability to obtain cash or merchandise in advance, they can use the charge card, default on their payments, and the costs can be borne by others. This situation can then turn into adverse selection. If the credit card company increases the interest rate to account for these costs, then cardholders who would repay with interest over a period of time may stop using their card, and new cardholders may be discouraged from signing up, because of the higher interest rates. Cardholders who did not repay would be less concerned about higher rates if they were unable to pay the amount owed anyway.

Thus, with moral hazard, the insured can influence the probability of the insured event occurring or the magnitude of the payment, the actions of the insured are largely unmonitored and unobserved by the insurer, the insurer faces greater than expected costs, and then may raise the price of their policies (leading to adverse selection).

What is the difference between adverse selection and moral hazard? Adverse selection is the result of imperfect information *before* the transaction occurs, and moral hazard is the result of imperfect information *after* the transaction occurs. The imperfect information can be hidden knowledge (in the case of adverse selection where the seller knows more than the buyer about a used car) or hidden action (in the case of moral hazard where the car driver can take actions that are unseen by the car insurer). The transaction can include a purchase, a contract signing, an insurance agreement, or an employment arrangement. These transactions also lend themselves to another type of problem—the principal-agent problem.

PRINCIPAL-AGENT PROBLEM

The **principal-agent problem** is another result of imperfect information. It refers to cases in which one party (the "principal") employs another party (the "agent") to achieve certain objectives for the principal. But then the agent pursues objectives that are contrary to those of the principal. Inefficiencies arise when those conducting the work (the agents) have different objectives and different information than those contracting the work (the principals). And this occurs because the principals have difficulties with enforcing, evaluating, or encouraging the work of the agents.

Take, for example, a contract between an employer and a particular employee. The employer (the principal) hires the employee (the agent). The employee is part of a large group of employees on a project, so it is difficult for the employer to monitor and assess individual productivity. The employer wants the employee to work hard. But the employee, once receiving the contract, realizes that the salary will be the same, largely regardless of individual effort. In addition, although the employer's profits depend on the employee's productivity, the employee does not directly receive any of the profits, so the employee may be inclined to take it easy, because the salary will be essentially the same.

The principal-agent problem has several characteristics. First, the objectives of the principal and the agent differ. In our example, the employer wants the employee to work hard, but the employee has less incentive to work hard. Second, the relationship involves asymmetric information. The agent has information that the principal does not have, or the agent can perform in a way that the principal cannot observe. For instance, an employee often knows and can control how hard they will work; yet the employee's productivity may not be able to be directly seen or assessed by the employer. Third, there is noncontractible and nonverifiable information. The principal cannot write contracts based on the information known by the agent; and the actions chosen by the agent cannot necessarily be inferred or verified from outcome. For instance, an employer may not be able to mandate that the employee engage in an exercise program every day after work in order to reduce health risks, and even if the employer could, it would be difficult to verify the employee's level of adherence to the exercise program based on the employee's overall health.

How can the principal-agent problem be reduced? In other words, how is it possible to align the goals of the agent with those of the principal? A common way is for principals to provide incentives to agents. Consider the employer-employee relationship. Monetary incentives for employees include commissions (percentage of sales), royalties (percentage of revenues for works such as books), profit sharing (percentage of firm's profits for group of employees), bonus systems (payments beyond salary), piece rates (payments related to number of units of output), efficiency wages (above-equilibrium wage rates that discourage shirking), and raises (salary increases based on productivity or other merits). In addition to incentives, employers can also use more rigorous monitoring and accountability systems to evaluate employees and their productivity.

Nonmonetary incentives can be used as well. These incentives include recognition for a job well done, appreciation from employers, and the feeling of contributing to a greater purpose. For example, teachers often find motivation for helping students through expressions of thanks, rather than monetary rewards from students. Other incentives might come from the hope for advancement in the future. For instance, undergraduate student assistants may work hard for professors in order to get favorable letters of recommendation for graduate school, and student interns may work hard for employers in order to secure employment after graduation.

Note that incentive plans need to be carefully designed because they can introduce unintended or undesirable side effects. For instance, a narrow focus on productivity can overlook other important factors, such as product quality and worker safety, which can impose long-run costs on the employer and employee. Individual productivity rewards, such as bonuses and commissions, can diminish individual willingness to be a team player. Group productivity rewards, such as profit sharing, can also set up the possibility for free riders because the less productive employees can benefit from the efforts of more productive employees.

Incentives for one principal-agent relationship can be in conflict with another within the same context. Take, for example, the principal-agent relationships among a patient, the patient's physician, and the physician's employer, a health maintenance organization (HMO). In the HMO (principal)–physician (agent) relationship, the HMO may want the physician to minimize the time and cost spent per patient. But in the patient (principal)–physician (agent) relationship, the patient wants the most effective care, which may require more time and more procedures for diagnosis than, say, a quick prescription to alleviate symptoms.

EXAMPLE   **Defined Contribution Health Plans**

"Defined contribution" is gaining interest among insurers, employers, and employees as a way to reduce health care costs. In one such plan, employees are each given $1,500 a year that they can spend as they wish on health care, without many of the constraints of managed care. Whatever they don't spend, they can roll over to the next year. If they spend more than $1,500, they must cover 100% of additional costs themselves, up to $3,000. After $3,000, the insurer covers 80% of the costs. Why has such a plan become popular? How might such a plan reduce the problems of imperfect information? What problems still exist?

This plan encourages employees to shop around for cost-effective health care and provides freedom of consumer choice. It can spark competition among health care providers, because employees now "vote with their dollars" and (in theory) seek the best care at the least cost. The employee, employer, and insurer have somewhat more aligned goals for cost-effective health care, which can reduce the principal-agent problems. Because of incentives to spend only what is necessary on health care, it can reduce moral hazard. Such a plan attracts those who predict their health care costs will be under $1,500, which can reduce adverse selection, but can lead to cherry picking. It encourages enrollment by lower-cost employees, and employees with higher costs that are not covered entirely may not find it affordable. In addition, it may not sufficiently reduce the adverse selection, moral hazard, and principal-agent problems. For instance, those who have already spent $2,900 may go ahead and spend $100 more to go over the $3,000 threshold, and have 80% of the rest covered for the year. If a plan doesn't allow the employee to roll over unspent funds, then employees have incentives to use up all the funds by the end of the year, even if they ordinarily wouldn't have made those expenditures. Some higher-risk employees who expect to spend more than $3,000 a year (where costs are covered at 80%) may also be attracted to the plan, which could lead to adverse selection after all. Finally, the plan may discourage "unnecessary" (nonemergency) but nonetheless cost-effective and important expenditures on preventive care.

Public Sector Provision of Information and Insurance

Governments have sought to reduce market failures from imperfect information by obtaining and disseminating information, by establishing protections and regulations, and by providing goods and services directly. As we have seen in this and previous chapters, government is involved in numerous activities to provide information and protections, such as requiring warning labels on consumer products, establishing consumer protections such as "lemon laws," and other social and economic regulations.[5]

Governments have also stepped in to provide goods and services directly, such as health insurance, when markets are unable to provide them because of information problems or prohibitive costs. These government programs can be viewed as social insurance programs, which are public entitlement programs that partly depend on individuals' contributions. Social insurance programs include Medicare, Social Security (Old-Age, Survivors, and Disability Insurance Program), and unemployment compensation.

Social insurance programs seek to reduce risks to individuals, just as private insurance plans do. A difference is that social insurance programs also have a function of redistributing income. With private insurance, what the individual pays for an insurance premium is closely related to what the individual will receive for benefits. With social insurance, individuals can receive benefits based on factors other than their absolute contributions.

For instance, Social Security benefits are paid as a legal right and not strictly according to need. Workers (and their employers) contribute a part of their earnings in order to provide protection for themselves and their families if certain events occur. Because each worker pays Social Security taxes, each worker earns the right to receive Social Security benefits without regard to need. Social Security has the goals of individual equity and social adequacy. *Individual equity* means that a person receives a reasonable return on their investment in Social Security. *Social adequacy* means that individuals receive a level of benefits that reflects their lesser ability to prepare for the risk. Therefore, benefits are weighted in favor of workers with low average lifetime earnings and those with families. Although higher earners receive higher benefits, lower earners receive higher benefits relative to their earnings.[6] Social Security has also helped to raise incomes above the poverty level. Without Social Security, there would be about four aged poor persons for everyone that is now classified as poor.[7]

---

[5] Recently, concepts from principal–agent theory have also been applied to incentive-based mechanisms for regulation. See, for example, J.-J. Laffont, and J. Tirole (1993), *A Theory of Incentives in Procurement and Regulation*, Cambridge, MA: MIT Press; and I. Vogelsang (2002), "Incentive Regulation and Competition in Public Utility Markets: A 20-Year Perspective," *Journal of Regulatory Economics* 22(1):5–27.

[6] Currently, earnings replacement rates are about 60% for minimum wage earners, 42% for average wage earners, and 26% for high wage earners. U.S. Department of Health and Human Services, Social Security Administration, Frequently Asked Questions, available at http://www.ssa.gov/kids/workfacts.htm (accessed September 25, 2003).

[7] Social Security Administration, Frequently Asked Questions, available at http://www.ssa.gov/kids/workfacts.htm (accessed September 25, 2003).

As another example, in 1997, the government-sponsored Children's Health Insurance Program (CHIP) was passed to provide health insurance coverage for children.[8] Before CHIP, in 1997, approximately 9.2 million children (12.2% of children younger than 18 years) lacked health insurance in the United States.[9] After CHIP, as of August 2003, more than 4.1 million children have been covered.[10] Children who enrolled were more likely to receive preventive care services and less likely to use emergency care than uninsured children.[11] This trend can lead to lowered costs in the long run; preventive treatment is usually several times less expensive than emergency room treatment for a condition. In addition, insurance for children is important both for ethical reasons and for investment in the future. Children with adequate health care can grow up and be better able to contribute to society. Here, government provision of insurance can benefit not only the insured but also the greater public.

EXAMPLE

Nobel Prizes for the Economics of Imperfect Information

In 2001, the Nobel Prize in Economic Sciences was awarded to George Akerlof, Michael Spence, and Joseph Stiglitz for their work on analyses of markets with asymmetric information.[12] In 1986, the Nobel Prize in Economic Sciences was awarded to William Vickrey and James Mirrlees for their work on the economics of information and incentives.[13] Here we examine some of the key contributions of these researchers.

Akerlof's paper on the market for lemons shows how adverse selection can cause the "bad to drive out the good," and even drive out a market altogether.[14] His first example, the market for used cars, in which sellers have more

continued on next page

---

[8] Available at http://www.insurekidsnow.gov/.

[9] R. A. Almeida and G. M. Kenney (2000), "Gaps in Insurance Coverage for Children: A Pre-CHIP Baseline." The Urban Institute, Number B-19 in Series, "New Federalism: National Survey of America's Families," May 2001. Available at http://www.urban.org/url.cfm?ID=309532.

[10] Department of Health and Human Services, State Children's Health Insurance Program, FY 2003 First Quarter Enrollment Report, available at http://cms.hhs.gov/schip/.

[11] S. Eisert and P. Gabow (2002)." Effect of Child Health Insurance Plan enrollment on the utilization of health care services by children using a public safety net system," *Pediatrics* 110(5):940–5. Also see Quarterly Newsletter about the Children's Health Insurance Plan, available at http://www.childrensdefense.org/pdf/signthemup_2001fall.pdf.

[12] Based on press release: "The 2001 Sveriges Riksbank (Bank of Sweden) Prize in Economic Sciences in Memory of Alfred Nobel," (October 10, 2001), available at http://www.nobel.se/economics/laureates/2001/press.html.

[13] Based on press release: "The 1996 Sveriges Riksbank (Bank of Sweden) Prize in Economic Sciences in Memory of Alfred Nobel," (October 8, 1996), available at http://www.nobel.se/economics/laureates/1996/press.html.

[14] G. Akerlof (1970), "The Market for Lemons: Quality Uncertainty and the Market Mechanism," *Quarterly Journal of Economics* 84, 488–500.

information than buyers regarding product quality, was examined earlier in this chapter. Other examples include health insurance for the elderly, the discrimination of minorities, and the cost of dishonesty, where dishonesty is the "lemon." Akerlof also looks at credit markets in India in the 1960s, where local lenders in the countryside charged interest rates that were several times higher than large banks in the cities. Local lenders knew about repayment abilities of borrowers and could enforce contracts. However, a nonlocal, trying to arbitrage between the rates, borrowing money at the lower bank rates and lending it at higher rates in the countryside, would likely attract the "lemons"—those who could not repay. Akerlof noted that numerous institutions have arisen to counteract the effects of quality uncertainty; these include guarantees, name brands, chain stores, licensing practices, and certifications that signify quality (and he presciently mentioned the Nobel Prize).

Spence's work investigates how individuals can credibly signal information about the value or quality of their products.[15] Spence looks at education as a signal of productivity on the labor market. To be effective, a signal must be easier for high-productivity people to give than for low-productivity people to give. For example, professional education would be a strong signal; professional clothing would be a weaker signal. Another example is why firms pay dividends to their shareholders, knowing that the dividends are subject to higher taxes than capital gains. An answer is that dividends can act as a signal: A firm with insider information about high profitability pays dividends because the market interprets this action as good news and leads to a higher share price, which can then compensate shareholders for the extra tax they pay on the dividends.

Stiglitz's work, such as his paper coauthored with Michael Rothschild, examines insurance markets where companies do not have information on the risks of individual clients.[16] The insurance company (the uninformed party) can give its prospective policyholders (the informed parties) incentives to reveal information on their risk situations through "screening." In screening, insurance companies can distinguish risk classes by offering alternative contracts where lower premiums can be exchanged for higher deductibles. Stiglitz also studied the sharecropping contract, where yields from a harvest are divided between a landowner and tenant (usually half each). Although both landowner and tenant might seemingly benefit from the landowner bearing the entire risk, because the landowner is presumably wealthier and more able to bear the risk, this type of contract would not provide strong enough incentives for the tenant to cultivate the land efficiently. Considering the landowner's

---

[15] M. Spence (1973), "Job Market Signaling," *Quarterly Journal of Economics* 87, 355–374.

[16] M. Rothschild and J. Stiglitz (1976), "Equilibrium in Competitive Insurance Markets: An Essay on the Economics of Imperfect Information," *Quarterly Journal of Economics* 90, 629–649.

imperfect information about harvest conditions and the tenant's work effort, sharecropping emerges as the preferred contract for both parties. More generally, Stiglitz and his coauthors showed that economic models can be misleading if they disregard informational asymmetries.

Vickrey examined the effects of taxation on individual work effort with respect to both the incentive problem (the effect of the tax schedule on an individual's chosen level of productivity) and the asymmetric information problem (the government's lack of knowledge about an individual's true abilities). A proper tax system, as Vickrey noted, becomes a matter of compromise between incentives and equality.[17] Following on this work, Mirrlees provided an analytic breakthrough, called single-crossing, for analyzing economic issues with asymmetric information.[18] He showed that a solution to information and incentive problems is to induce individuals to reveal their private information truthfully in a way that does not conflict with their self-interest. By applying this "revelation principle," it becomes easier to design optimal contracts and other solutions to incentive problems.

Vickrey also examined auctions, particularly the second-price auction, where an object is auctioned off in sealed bidding, and the highest bidder gets to buy the item, but pays only the next highest price offered. By bidding above one's willingness to pay, an individual runs the risk of being forced to buy the object at a loss. By bidding below one's willingness to pay, an individual runs the risk of losing the object at an amount lower than what they would pay. Therefore, it is in the individual's best interest to state a truthful bid about their willingness to pay. This work also applies to the revelation of preferences for public goods, the societal benefit of which is based on the sum of individuals' marginal willingness to pay.

Mirrlees also examined incentive schemes under imperfect information, and the trade-offs between risk protection and incentives. In designing an incentive scheme, the principal needs to consider the costs of giving the agent incentives to act in accordance with the principal's interests. The higher the agent's aversion to loss, and the higher the agent's investment in the outcome, the lower these costs to the principal. Thus, in the contract, the agent bears part of the cost of undesirable outcomes or part of the benefits from favorable outcomes. In developing a theory of incentive design and optimum taxation, Mirrlees stressed that the "central element in the theory is information."[19]

---

[17] W. Vickrey (1945), "Measuring Marginal Utility by Reactions to Risk," *Econometrica*, October 13, 319–333 (quote from p. 329).

[18] J. A. Mirrlees (1971), "An Exploration in the Theory of Optimum Income Taxation," *Review of Economic Studies*, 38, 175–208.

[19] J. A. Mirrlees (1981), "The Theory of Optimal Taxation," in *Handbook of Mathematical Economics*, Vol. III, K. J. Arrow and M. D. Intrilligator (eds.), Amsterdam: North Holland, p. 1197.

EXPECTED VALUE, EXPECTED UTILITY, AND RISK

When faced with alternatives, which may have different and random outcomes, how can we decide which one to choose? Understandably, we can't always predict the future. Still, if we have sufficient information on the possible outcomes, we can structure and account for this information in the decision.

This section provides methods by which to compare and evaluate alternatives under risk and uncertainty. We will learn the concepts and methods of expected value and expected utility, which are useful in many types of decisions, public and private, individual and organizational.

Before beginning, a distinction is often made between risk and uncertainty. With *risk*, the outcomes and their probabilities of occurrence are known (i.e., randomness is quantifiable). With *uncertainty*, all of the outcomes are known, but one or more of their probabilities of occurrence are unknown (i.e., randomness is nonquantifiable).[20] (*Ignorance* describes a situation when one or more of the outcomes and probabilities of occurrence are unknown.)

For example, when a gambler rolls two new dice, the outcome may not be known in advance, but the gambler can nonetheless assign mathematical probabilities to each of the outcomes (e.g., the probability of rolling a 7 is 6/36). After a decade of wear and tear, those two dice may still produce the same outcomes (i.e., numbers from 2 through 12), but their probabilities of occurrence may keep changing (because of imperfections in the dice). The former exemplifies risk (outcomes known and probabilities of occurrence known), and the latter uncertainty (outcomes known and probabilities of occurrence unknown). This section will maintain the conceptual distinction between *risk* and *uncertainty*, yet will follow the convention of many textbooks and use the terms *risky outcomes* and *uncertain outcomes* interchangeably to refer to situations where both the outcomes and their probabilities of occurrence are known.

EXPECTED VALUE

We will begin with a simple and perhaps familiar example: selecting classes for the next academic term. You are looking for a class to fill up an empty slot in your schedule, one that will be interesting and challenging, but that will also help you to maintain your high grade point average (GPA). You find three classes that you like—call them Class 1, Class 2, and Class 3—and each one seems equally attractive to you. So

---

[20] This classic distinction was put forth by Frank H. Knight, *Risk Uncertainty and Profit*. Some economists argue, however, that risk and uncertainty are the same thing; that uncertainty is lack of "knowledge" rather than lack of "existence" of probabilities. Other economists argue that there is no such thing as "knowledge" of probabilities anyway, because probabilities are based largely on beliefs and expectations. This text will not enter the debate, but will maintain the basic distinction put forth by Knight.

the factor that will swing your decision will be the grade that you can expect to receive.

What is the probability of receiving a certain grade in the class? Understandably, the grade will depend on several factors, including personal effort, prior knowledge, classmates with whom you study, and so on. Assuming that you feel equally confident that you can do well in each course, you decide to look at the grading history of the professors as the probability of receiving a certain grade, all else being equal. Although future grade distributions are not necessarily identical to prior grade distributions, each of these three professors has their own grading philosophy: a target grade point average, among all grades distributed in any particular class.

You do a little research and obtain information on the distribution of grades during the previous terms these classes were taught. Each class had exactly 50 students, and the grades were distributed as follows:

Class 1: 20 As, 20 Bs, 5 Cs, 5 Ds, 0 Fs
Class 2: 18 As, 30 Bs, 0 Cs, 0 Ds, 2 Fs
Class 3: 15 As, 35 Bs, 0 Cs, 0 Ds, 0 Fs,

Probabilities of Outcomes

You now need to determine the *probability* of each outcome (a specific grade), and you will base this probability on the grade distributions in the previous term.

For Class 1, the probability of receiving an A grade is 20/50 = 0.40 (40%), a B is 20/50 = 0.40 (40%), a C is 5/50 is 0.10 (10%), a D is 5/50 = 0.10 (10%), and an F is 0/50= 0.0 (0%). The same procedure is used to calculate the probabilities of grades for Class 2 and Class 3:

Class 1: 40% A, 40% B, 10% C, 10% D
Class 2: 36% A, 60% B, 4% F
Class 3: 30% A, 70% B

Again, although these calculations do not provide an exact prediction, you know that these professors typically strive for a certain average grade point in the class; distributions may vary, but the average is usually the same. In general, probabilities of occurrence can be based on frequencies, forecasts, heuristics, subjective assessments, and other methods.

Values of Outcomes

You now need to assign the *value* for each outcome. Here, the value will be the points for each grade. At your school, plus or minus grades are given the same number of points as the base grade, so units are in whole numbers (i.e., an A+ and A– are considered an A grade and each one is given 4.0 grade points).

A = 4.0, B = 3.0, C = 2.0, D = 1.0, F = 0.0

In general, the value can be measured in the metrics that are relevant to the problem; common metrics are dollars or utility, but they could be other metrics, such as grade points (here), acres of land, concentration of pollutants, or vehicle miles traveled.

Expected Value Calculation

You can now answer the question: What is the "expected value" of the grade that you could receive in each course? The **expected value (EV)** is the probability-weighted average of all outcomes. Mathematically, it is the summation of the probability of each outcome times the value of each outcome. The formula for calculating the expected value (EV) is

$$EV = \Sigma_i\, p_i\, x_i = p_1\, x_1 + p_2\, x_2 + \ldots + p_n\, x_n$$

where

Σ_i = the summation over all possible outcomes
p_i = the probability of the ith outcome
x_i = the value of the ith outcome
i = the outcome (i = 1, 2, 3, . . . n)

Using this formula, $EV = \Sigma_i\, p_i\, x_i$, we can calculate the expected values for each course.[21]

EV(Class 1) = (0.40)(4.0) + (0.40)(3.0) + (0.10)(2.0) + (0.10)(1.0) + (0.00)(0.0)
= 3.10
EV(Class 2) = (0.36)(4.0) + (0.60)(3.0) + (0.00)(2.0) + (0.00)(1.0) + (0.04)(0.0)
= 3.24
EV(Class 3) = (0.30)(4.0) + (0.70)(3.0) + (0.00)(2.0) + (0.00)(1.0) + (0.00)(0.0)
= 3.30

For Class 1, the probability of receiving an A grade is 0.40, and the value of an A grade is 4.0, so the first term in this equation is (0.40)(4.0); the probability of receiving a B grade is 0.40, and the value of a B grade is 3.0, so the second term is (0.40)(3.0), and so forth for each of the three courses.

The result is that the expected values are 3.10, 3.24, and 3.30, for classes 1, 2, and 3, respectively. Note that the "expected value" here is not an actual grade that

---

[21] If probabilities of outcomes are described by a probability density function, $f(x)$, and values of those outcomes are x, then the formula for the expected value $EV = \int x f(x) dx$.

will be given. *Expected value is a statistical measure, not necessarily the value that is expected to occur nor even the value that most frequently occurs.*

Judging only by the expected values, Class 3 appears to look the most favorable. However, information on expected values may be insufficient for making the selection. The spread and type of the grades may also be important. For example, Class 3 (with the highest expected value) has the lowest percentage of A grades, and Class 1 (with the lowest expected value) has the highest percentage of A grades. Class 2 has more A grades than Class 3, and more B grades than Class 1, but it is also the only class that had F grades. To account for these factors, we will now extend our understanding of expected value to incorporate risk and variability.

EXPECTED VALUE AND RISK: LOTTERIES WITH UNCERTAIN OUTCOMES

Suppose someone made the following offer to you:

1 You can have $100,000 for certain.

or

2 You can enter a lottery where you have a 10% chance of winning $1,000,000.

Which would you choose?
First, let's calculate the expected value of each choice.

$$EV(1) = (1.00)(\$100,000) = \$100,000$$

(The 1.00 represents 100% probability of occurrence, or certainty.)

$$EV(2) = (0.10)(\$1,000,000) + (0.90)(\$0) = \$100,000$$

(Note here that the expected value amount, $100,000, is not even one of the outcomes, $0 or $1,000,000.)

The expected monetary value of the first is the same as the second. Does that mean that each choice is equally attractive to you? Not necessarily. You may prefer the first choice over the second choice, if you wanted a sure thing. Yet you may prefer the second choice over the first choice, if you were willing to take a chance at a much larger outcome.

Now let's say you have another offer:

1 You can have $100,000 for certain.

or

3 You can enter a lottery where you have 10% chance of winning $3,000,000 but a 90% chance of having to pay $100,000.

Which would you choose?
Calculating the expected values, you find that

$$EV(1) = (1.0)(\$100,000) = \$100,000$$
$$EV(3) = (0.10)(\$3,000,000) - (0.90)(\$100,000) = \$210,000$$

The expected monetary value of (3) is now more than twice as great as (1). But (3) has the 90% probability of having to pay $100,000. So you may choose (1) rather than (3), if you did not want to take on the risk of paying $100,000.

These examples illustrate how risk can influence a decision and how expected values alone may not reveal information important to a decision. We will show ways to quantify that risk and incorporate other information later in the chapter. For now, we use these examples to introduce terms to characterize an individual's attitude toward risk.

An individual is **risk averse** if they prefer a certain outcome to a risky outcome, even if both have the same expected value. In this case, it would mean that the individual prefers (1) over (2).

An individual is **risk prone** if they prefer a risky outcome to a certain outcome, if both have the same expected value. In this case, it would mean that the individual prefers (2) over (1). (The term risk loving has also been used to mean risk prone.)

An individual is **risk neutral** if they are indifferent between a certain outcome and a risky outcome, if both have the same expected value. In this case, it would mean that the individual is indifferent between (1) and (2).

An individual can characterize any of the three types of risk, depending on the decision context. For instance, a person may be risk prone when the stakes are small, but risk averse when the stakes are high. People often tend to be risk averse toward losses and changes from the status quo; that is, they frame outcomes in terms of changes from current conditions, and they weigh losses more heavily than gains of the equal size.[22] For example, a potential gain of $100 may bring an additional 100 utils to the current level of utility, but a potential loss of $100 may cause a diminishment of 150 utils from the current level of utility. Also, these risk characterizations apply when expected values are also different among outcomes. In these examples, the same expected value was used to clearly illustrate the characterizations of risk averse, risk prone, and risk neutral.

Given that people have different preferences toward risk, and that one person can even have different preferences depending on the particular decision, how can we determine the "best" choice if we cannot fully compare outcomes based on just

---

[22] D. Kahneman and A. Tversky (1979), "Prospect Theory: An Analysis of Decision under Risk." *Econometrica*, 47, 263–291.

expected value? We will now present an approach for evaluating alternatives, accounting for risk, by relating outcomes to a specific decision criterion: expected utility.

UTILITY THEORY

Utility theory enables us to compare different alternatives that have different levels of risk. It is based on the premise that a rational decision maker will seek to maximize their expected utility, and that units of utility (utils) can be ascribed to each of the outcomes.

Expected utility (EU) is the probability-weighted average of all outcomes (in terms of utility), and is calculated in a similar way as expected value:

$$EU = \Sigma_i \, p_i \, u_i = p_1 \, u_1 + p_2 \, u_2 + \ldots + p_n \, u_n$$

where

Σ_i = the summation over all possible outcomes
p_i = the probability of the ith outcome
u_i = the utility of the ith outcome
i = the outcome ($i = 1, 2, 3, \ldots n$)

The concept of *utility* is the same as we studied in Chapter 4: Utility represents overall happiness and satisfaction. However, this type of utility function, "expected utility," is not the same as we studied earlier (which was the utility function of consumer theory). Rather, the expected utility function is a probabilistic function, based on the utility of each possible outcome multiplied by its probability of occurrence.

Also, our previous study of indifference curves and consumer choice was based on *ordinal* utility. The approach here is based on *cardinal* utility. Ordinal utility means that only the orderings are meaningful; we can rank-order the utility that we ascribe to different outcomes, but we cannot infer any other properties from them, nor perform statistical operations with them. Cardinal utility means that the actual numbers are meaningful; we can perform operations with the utilities, compare utilities, and express preferences over lotteries based on measures of utilities.

Expected utility, a measure of the ultimate value of an outcome to the decision maker, can be evaluated using a von Neumann-Morgenstern[23] utility function (developed later in this section). The scale of utility typically goes from 0 to 1 (or 0 to 100), for the worst and best outcomes, respectively. Then other outcomes are assigned utilities along that scale through a sequence of lotteries. By scaling values of utility associated with different probabilistic outcomes, the expected utility can be calculated, just as we calculated expected monetary value. Note that expected utility, $EU(x)$,

[23] J. von Neumann and O. Morgenstern (1944), *Theory of Games and Economic Behavior*, Princeton, NJ: Princeton University Press.

refers to the probabilistic outcome of utility, whereas utility, $U(x)$, refers to a certain outcome of utility.

This use of utility theory for decision making rests on three main assumptions. The first is that all possible outcomes from decisions can be ordered in terms of preferences and that these preferential rankings are transitive. By transitive, if you prefer B to A, and you prefer C to B, then you must prefer C to A. The second assumption is that you can assign preferences to lotteries involving prizes, just as you can assign preferences to the prizes themselves. It means that you can assign a utility to a lottery with a 50-50 chance of winning $100 or $300, just as you can assign a utility to either $100 or $300 independently. The third assumption is that there is no intrinsic utility in the lottery. Your preferences for certain outcomes depend only on the outcomes themselves and your attitude toward risk, not on some "fun" involved in the gamble.

CERTAINTY EQUIVALENTS, RISK PREMIUMS, AND INSURANCE PREMIUMS

We begin with an example to illustrate these three aspects of risk: certainty equivalents, risk premiums, and insurance premiums.

Your friend Jack, who just graduated from college, has the choice of two jobs. One is working as a researcher in a government agency, with a certain salary of $200 per day. The other is working in sales in the private sector where his salary would be uncertain: either $100 per day (50% probability) or $300 per day (50% probability). Which job should he choose?

First, Jack will calculate the expected monetary value of each job. The expected monetary value of the first job is:

$$EV(1) = (1.00)(\$200) = \$200/\text{day}$$

The expected monetary value of the second job is:

$$EV(2) = (0.50)(\$100) + (0.50)(\$300) = \$200/\text{day}$$

Thus, the expected values of the two jobs are the same. But that comparison overlooks risk. The first job has a certain income, and the second job has an uncertain income, which can be either higher or lower than the first job's income.

Which job should he choose, then, if the expected values of the two jobs are the same?

Here is some additional information on Jack's attitudes toward risk. Jack has five children, and his family depends on his salary as the primary source of income. So Jack prefers a certain income to an uncertain one, if the expected values of both were the same.

We will use expected utility as a way to incorporate these preferences in the analysis, with the assumption that Jack is a rational decision maker and that a rational decision maker wants to maximize utility. To do so, we calculate the expected utility of each choice, rather than strictly the expected monetary value. Jack's utility of income is depicted in Figure 11-3, which graphs utility on the y-axis, and salary ($) on the x-axis. (The method for producing this curve will be described in the following section.)

The expected utility of the first job is:

$$EU(1) = (1.00)U(\$200) = U(\$200) = 40.0$$

The expected utility of the second job is:

$$EU(2) = (0.50)U(\$100) + (0.50)U(\$300) = (0.50)(25) + (0.50)(50) = 37.5$$

Thus, the expected utility of the first job is 40, and the expected utility of the second job is 37.5. Even though both jobs have the same expected monetary value, the first one would bring Jack greater utility. The salary increase from $200 to $300 would add 10 utils, but the salary decrease from $200 to $100 would subtract 15 utils, meaning that the loss of $100 would affect Jack's utility more than the gain of $100. For Jack, who is risk averse, the marginal utility decreases as salary increases.

Based on maximizing expected utility, Jack would choose the first job. In fact, Jack may even be willing to accept a lower salary from the first job, just to be able to avoid the risk associated with the second job.

What is a certain salary, for the first job, that would make Jack indifferent between the first job (with the certain salary) and the second job (with the risky salary)?

FIGURE 11-3 *Utility of Income*

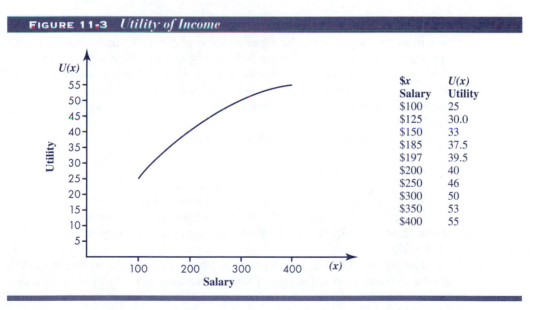

$x Salary	U(x) Utility
$100	25
$125	30.0
$150	33
$185	37.5
$197	39.5
$200	40
$250	46
$300	50
$350	53
$400	55

This certain salary would be the certainty equivalent. The **certainty equivalent (CE)** of an uncertain outcome is an amount, for certain, that would make a decision maker indifferent between the uncertain outcome and the certain amount.

To calculate the certainty equivalent, let $\tilde{x}$ denote an uncertain outcome, $\hat{x}$ denote a certain outcome, $U(x)$ represent the utility associated with a value of x, and $EU(x)$ represent the expected utility associated with a value of x.

Then $\hat{x}$, the certainty equivalent, is determined by the relationship

$$U(\hat{x}) = EU(\tilde{x})$$

where $U(\hat{x})$ is the utility of the certain outcome and $EU(\tilde{x})$ is the expected utility of the uncertain outcome. Thus,

$$CE = \hat{x} = U^{-1} EU(\tilde{x})$$

where $U^{-1}(x)$ is the inverse function of $U(x)$. Here, this means that $U(CE) = U(\hat{x}) = EU(\tilde{x})$.

In Jack's case, the CE would be the certain salary whose utility is equal to the expected utility of the uncertain salary, which is 37.5 (calculated earlier). So

$$U(\hat{x}) = EU(\tilde{x}) = 37.5$$

As shown in Figure 11-3, $\hat{x} = \$185$. This amount of $185 is the certainty equivalent.

From Jack's perspective of utility, the second (risky) job would be equivalent to a certain job that paid $185 per week. Jack would be willing to give up some of the salary from Job 1, and it would still be as attractive as the risky salary from Job 2.

We now examine what is the (maximum) amount of salary that Jack would be willing to give up, from the expected value of the uncertainty salary, in order to get a certain salary. This amount is the risk premium. The **risk premium (RP)** is the maximum amount that a risk-averse person would pay to avoid a risk (in this case, the uncertain salary) and get an amount for certain. It is the difference between the expected value of an uncertain outcome and its certainty equivalent.

The risk premium can be calculated as follows:

$$RP(\tilde{x}) = \bar{x} - \hat{x} = EV(\tilde{x}) - U^{-1} EU(\tilde{x})$$

where $\bar{x}$ is the expected value (mean) of the uncertain outcome.

In Jack's case, it would be the difference between what Jack could expect to receive from the risky salary, and the certainty equivalent salary, which is $200 - \$185 = \$15$.

This amount of $15 is the risk premium. Thus, Jack would be willing to pay $15 per day to ensure a certain income of $200 per day (the expected value of the uncertain income), which means that Jack would be willing to accept a certain salary of $185 ($15 less than $200).

The higher the risk premium, the more risk-averse the individual (all else equal, for a particular choice). For a risk-prone person, the risk premium would be negative, rather than positive, meaning that the risk-prone person would pay in order to take the risk and have a chance at the higher salary. For a risk-neutral person, the risk premium would be zero, meaning that the risk-neutral person would be indifferent between the certain and uncertain outcome, if both had the same expected value.

Suppose then that the managers from the second job really want Jack to accept their position. They are willing to make the offer more attractive, by increasing the upper possible salary (currently at $300) in order for Jack to accept. How much higher of a salary (for the upper salary) would induce Jack to take the risky job? That is, what upper salary would make the second job bring the same expected utility as the first job?

To answer this question, we need to find the value of the upper salary (along with the given lower salary of $100) that would bring an expected utility of 40, which is the expected utility of the first job with a certain salary of $200.

For the second (risky) job, set the expected utility equal to 40, and let x = upper salary.

$$EU = (0.50)U(\$100) + (0.50)U(\$x) \quad = 40$$

$$(0.50)(25) + (0.50)U(\$x) \quad\quad\quad = 40$$

$$12.5 + (0.50)U(\$x) \quad\quad\quad\quad = 40$$

$$(0.50)U(\$x) \quad\quad\quad\quad\quad = 27.5$$

$$U(\$x) \quad\quad\quad\quad\quad\quad = 55$$

$$\$x \quad\quad\quad\quad\quad\quad\quad = \$400$$

So, as shown in Figure 11-3, Jack would be indifferent between the following two options:

1 A job that paid $200 per day for certain.
2 A job that paid either $100 per day (50% chance) or $400 per day (50% chance).

The second job could also be made more attractive by increasing the lowest possible salary, in the same analytic approach as increasing the higher salary (see Figure 11-3).

$$(0.50)U(\$x) + (0.50)U(\$300) \quad\quad = 40$$

$$(0.50)U(\$x) + (0.50)(50) \quad\quad\quad = 40$$

$$(0.50)U(\$x) = 15$$

$$U(\$x) = 30$$

$$\$x = \$125$$

Jack would be indifferent between the following two options:

1 A job that paid $200 per day for certain.
2 A job that paid either $125 per day (50% chance) or $300 per day (50%) chance.

In addition, the second job could be made more (or less) attractive by altering both upper and lower salaries, or by altering the probabilities, or both, which provides many different and feasible solutions to the equation:

$$(p)U(\$\text{lower salary}) + (1 - p)U(\$\text{upper salary}) = 40$$

For instance, the second job could be made more attractive by reducing the range of possible salaries for Jack; that is, variability is reduced. Now, instead of a 50% probability of either $100 per day or $300 per day, his salary would be a 50% probability of either $150 per day or $250 per day. So the low-end salary is higher, but the high-end salary is lower.

What is the certain salary whose utility would equal the expected utility of the new (reduced range of) salaries? Here again, we determine the certainty equivalent.

$$U(\hat{x}) = EU(\tilde{x})$$

$$U(\hat{x}) = (0.50)U(\$150) + (0.50)U(\$250) = (0.5)(33) + (0.5)(46) = 39.5$$

$$U(\hat{x}) = 39.5$$

$$\hat{x} = \$197$$

The certainty equivalent is $197, and the risk premium would be only $3 ($200 – $197), which is reduced from $15 (in the previous example) because of the reduction in variability. Thus, Jack would obtain value from this additional information.

The **value of information** is the difference between the expected value of a choice with information, and the expected value of that choice without that information. In this example, the value of new information to Jack would be the change in certainty equivalents ($197 – $185) = $12 per day.

Risk Aversion, Risk Proneness, and Risk Neutrality

We now return to these three characterizations of a decision maker's attitude toward risk, using concepts we just learned to examine risk graphically and quantitatively.

Refer to Figures 11-4, 11-5, and 11-6, which represent utility curves for money under different characterizations of risk. Here utility (U) is on the y-axis and money (x) is on the x-axis. Even though each decision maker has their own relationship between utility and money, these graphs nonetheless represent general characteristics of risk aversion, risk proneness, and risk neutrality.

We will use the following notation:

$<x_1,x_2>$ = lottery with two possible outcomes, x_1 and x_2, each with probability of 50%

$\bar{x}$ = expected value for $<x_1,x_2>$

$\hat{x}$ = certainty equivalent for $<x_1,x_2>$

$\tilde{x}$ = uncertain outcome for $<x_1,x_2>$

Recall that, using formulas previously derived,

$$U[E(\tilde{x})] = U[\bar{x}]$$

$$E[U(\tilde{x})] = U(\hat{x})$$

$$RP(\tilde{x}) = \bar{x} - \hat{x} = EV(\tilde{x}) - U^{-1}\, EU(\tilde{x})$$

FIGURE 11-4 *Utility Function for Risk-Averse Individual*

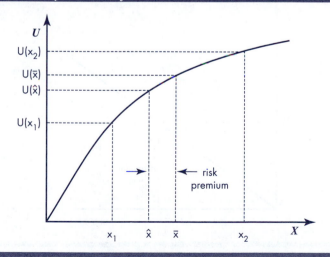

Now, the types of risk characteristics can be related to the marginal utility of income over the range of relevant values being examined, assuming a monotonically increasing function in that range.

For an individual that is risk averse (Figure 11-4), the marginal utility of income is decreasing (concave utility function). A risk-averse individual would prefer the expected value of any 50-50 lottery to the lottery itself. In other words, the utility of

---

FIGURE 11-5 *Utility Function for Risk-Prone Individual*

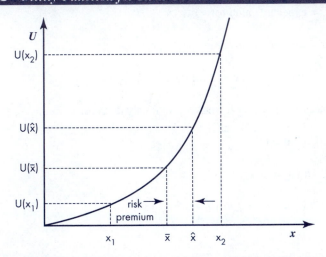

FIGURE 11-6 *Utility Function for Risk-Neutral Individual*

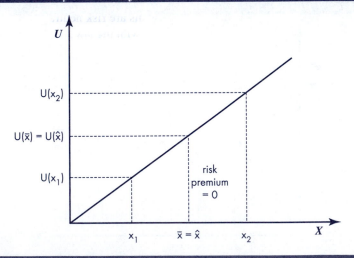

the expected value is greater than the expected utility of the lottery, $U[E(\tilde{x})] > E[U(\tilde{x})]$. In this case, the risk premium would be positive, which is the maximum amount the individual would pay to avoid the uncertain outcome and get an amount for certain.

For an individual that is risk prone (Figure 11-5), the marginal utility of income is increasing (convex utility function). A risk-prone individual would prefer any 50-50 lottery to the expected value of the lottery itself. In other words, the utility of the expected value is less than the expected utility of the lottery, $U[E(\tilde{x})] < E[U(\tilde{x})]$. In this case, the risk premium is negative, which is the maximum amount the individual would need to receive in order to give up the uncertain outcome and get an amount for certain.

For an individual that is risk neutral (Figure 11-6), the marginal utility of income is constant (straight-line utility function). A risk-neutral individual would be indifferent between the expected value of any 50-50 lottery and the 50-50 lottery itself. In other words, the utility of the expected value is the same as the expected utility of the lottery, $U[E(\tilde{x})] = E[U(\tilde{x})]$. In this case, the risk premium is zero, which means the individual is indifferent between the certain outcome and the uncertain outcome with the same expected value.

EXAMPLE

Risk of Minimum Wage Violations

A city has 10,000 businesses, and each of these businesses has exactly one employee who works 2,000 hours per year. Each business either pays the city-wide minimum wage of $6 per hour or violates the minimum wage law and pays $5 per hour. The Labor Standards Board has sufficient resources to audit 150 businesses at random at the end of the year for minimum wage violations. If the Board audits a violator, then the violation will certainly be detected. If detected, the firm will have to pay triple the unpaid wages back to the worker *and* a fine to the city. Assume that firms are risk neutral. How large must the fine be to ensure that all firms comply with the law?

Choice 1:
Pay minimum wage, pay $6/hr for 2,000 hours: $12,000

Choice 2:
Violate minimum wage, pay $5/hr for 2,000 hours: $10,000
but run risk of paying triple unpaid wages, plus fine of $x

The goal of the fine is to make the firm prefer not violating the law to violating the law.

What amount of the fine, $x, would make the firm indifferent between (a) the minimum wage salary payment ($12,000), and (b) the below-minimum

continued on next page

wage salary payment ($10,000) along with the risk of the violation (triple unpaid wages plus the fine)?

The probability of being caught at the end of the year = 150/10,000
= 1.5%
The cost of unpaid back wages (tripled) = (2,000 hours)($1/hour)(3)
= $6,000

So the problem becomes

$12,000 = 98.5% ($10,000) + 1.5% ($10,000 + $6,000 + x)

The terms in the last parentheses represent the costs if the violation were caught: $10,000 (salary, the same in both cases) + $6,000 (triple the unpaid wages) + x (amount of fine).

$12,000 = $9,850 + $150 + $90 + 1.5%x

x = $127,333

Thus, the fine must be at least this amount, $127,333, to make the firms want to comply with the minimum wage law.

_____

Source: Contribution by Michael Ash.

VARIABILITY AND RISK

Returning to our example, we can see a reason why Jack's expected utility is greater with the new information, even though the expected salary is the same, and even though the higher salary is lower: variability is reduced (and Jack is risk averse). Variability is the extent to which possible outcomes differ from the expected value. With these two jobs, the expected value is the same ($200), but the variability is different. Originally, the second job varied by ± $100, and with new information, the second job varies by ± $50. Note that new information can also increase variability. In this case it happened to reduce variability.

We can measure this variability by the **variance**: the probability-weighted summation of the squares of the deviations between the outcomes and the expected value. In simpler terms, variance measures the variability from the expected value and squares the terms so that negative and positive deviations don't cancel each other out. In mathematical terms:

$$\sigma^2 = \text{variance} = p_1\,[(x_1 - (EV(x))^2] + p_2\,[(x_2 - (EV(x))^2] + \ldots + p_n\,[(x_n - (EV(x))^2]$$

where p_i is the probability of the ith outcome, and x_i is the value of the ith outcome.

We will now calculate the variance for these jobs.

Job 2 (originally) $\sigma^2 = (0.5)(100 - 200)^2 + (0.5)(300 - 200)^2 = \$10,000$

Job 2 (new information) $\sigma^2 = (0.5)(150 - 200)^2 + (0.5)(250 - 200)^2 = \$2,500$

As we can see, the variance is reduced considerably (four times) with the new information.

The **standard deviation**, denoted as σ, is the square root of the variance and is a measure of the spread of the data from the expected value (the mean). For normally distributed data, approximately 68% of the data are within $\pm 1\sigma$ from the expected value, 95% are within $\pm 2\sigma$, and 99.7% are within $\pm 3\sigma$.

Thus, expressing the two jobs just in terms of their expected values can obscure information about risk, variability, and utility that can be important in decision making.

THE UTILITY FUNCTION OF MONEY

Before leaving this example, we will use it to construct a *utility function for money*.

We start by scaling utility from 0 to 100 and assigning the lowest possible and highest possible salaries to those amounts. For Jack's salary, these two salary endpoints happen to be $0 and $1,000 per day, denoted x_1 and x_2.

Next, we use x_1 and x_2 as the salary endpoints with known utilities, and then find intermediary points on the utility curve through a series of lotteries. To do so, we use the equation for expected utilities:

$$pU(x_1) + (1 - p)U(x_2) = U(x_3)$$

This equation finds values that make the decision maker indifferent between the lottery (the uncertain outcome with x_1 and x_2) and the certain outcome x_3 (which is the certainty equivalent of the lottery with x_1 and x_2). In other words, the expected utility of the lottery equals the utility of the certainty equivalent.

Based on the endpoints of $0 and $1,000, what salary would make Jack indifferent between that certain salary and a 50-50 chance of $0 or $1,000? Jack says it's $300.

Using the preceding formula:

$$0.50U(\$0) + 0.50U(\$1,000) = U(x_3)$$

$$0 + 0.50(100) = U(x_3) = 50$$

$$50 \qquad\qquad = U(x_3)$$

$$x_3 \qquad\qquad = \$300 \text{ (according to Jack's response)}$$

$$50 \qquad\qquad = U(\$300)$$

Thus, $300 would be the salary with a utility of 50. This value becomes a new point on the curve (already developed in Figure 11-3).

Now intermediate points can be determined. Based on two more endpoints with known utilities, such as $0 and $300, what salary would make Jack indifferent between that certain salary and a 50-50 chance of $0 or $300? Jack says it's $100.

$$0.50U(\$0) + 0.50U(\$300) \qquad = U(x_3)$$

$$0 + 0.50(50) \qquad = U(x_3)$$

$$25 \qquad = U(x_3)$$

$$x_3 \qquad = \$100 \text{ (according to Jack's response)}$$

$$25 \qquad = U(\$100)$$

So a salary of $100 has a utility of 25. This value becomes one more point on the utility curve (Figure 11-3).

Based on the newly determined point as another endpoint, what salary would make Jack indifferent between that certain salary and a 50-50 chance of $100 or $300? Jack says it's $185.

$$0.50U(\$100) + 0.50U(\$300) = U(x_3)$$

$$0.50(25) + 0.50(50) \qquad = U(x_3)$$

$$37.5 \qquad = U(x_3)$$

$$x_3 \qquad = \$185 \text{ (according to Jack's response)}$$

$$37.5 \qquad = U(\$185)$$

The salary of $185 has a utility of 37.5.

Figure 11-3 represents this relationship between utility and money for this specific decision context. Additional points on this utility curve can be calculated using the same approach. We will now bring these techniques together with concepts from the earlier section, using an example.

Automobile Insurance, Risk, and Imperfect Information

An insurance company is offering a policy for car theft, specifically for your community only. Your community has 1,000 households, each with their own car. Each car is worth $10,000 right now, and each household will be required to purchase this car insurance for their car.

If your car is stolen, the insurance company will pay you the full value of your car, which is $10,000 (in full, with no deductible). The chances of having your car stolen are 1% per year (10 cars per year stolen in your community/1,000 cars total in your community). This probability means the insurance company will expect to pay $100,000 total per year in reimbursements. Averaged among all car owners, that cost would be $100 per year ($100,000 reimbursements per year/1,000 car owners in your community), which is precisely 1% of the car value (excluding other costs, such as administrative costs, personnel costs, and transaction costs). So $100 per year is the insurance premium that would be the "actuarially fair" premium; meaning that the insurance premium is exactly equal to the expected value of the loss. (Insurance companies typically charge a higher premium to cover the additional costs, and these premiums may be regulated by a government agency.)

With insurance, the expected value would be as follows:

$$EV(\text{with insurance}) = (100\%)(\$10,000 - \$100) = \$9,900$$

So with or without theft, the expected value will remain the same. If the $10,000 car is lost, then $10,000 will also be gained in compensation.

The question is: Is insurance a good deal for you? Let's look at the case without insurance:

$$EV(\text{without insurance}) = (99\%)(\$10,000 - 0) + (1\%)(\$10,000 - \$10,000)$$
$$= \$9,900$$

So the expected value with insurance is exactly equal to the expected value without insurance. From your perspective, if you were risk adverse, you would prefer the certainty of paying $100 per year and insuring against the possible $10,000 loss, to the uncertain gamble of a 1% chance of losing $10,000 and a 99% chance of losing nothing, even though the expected value of that outcome would still be $9,900 per year, and the expected value of the loss would be $100 ($10,000 − $9,900). So risk-averse consumers would then be willing to pay more than $100 per year for the insurance.

We just calculated expected values. Now let's look at this decision in terms of utility.

Assume a utility function of wealth, $U(\$x) = \ln(\$x)$. What is the expected utility with insurance?

continued on next page

EU (with insurance) $= U[(100\%)(\$10,000 - \$100)] = \ln(9,900) = 9.20$

EU (without insurance) $= U[(99\%)(\$10,000 - 0)] + U[(1\%)(\$10,000 - \$10,000)] = (0.99)\ln(9,900) = 9.11$

Thus, purchasing insurance would provide you greater expected utility (9.20 vs. 9.11). What is the largest amount that you would pay to remove the risk and obtain an outcome for certain? This is the risk premium.

$RP(\tilde{x}) = \bar{x} - \hat{x} = E(\tilde{x}) - U^{-1}EU(\tilde{x})$

$RP(\tilde{x}) = EV(\text{no insurance}) - U^{-1} EU(\text{no insurance})$

$RP = (\$9,900) - U^{-1}9.11$

$RP = \$9,900 - \$9,045.29 = \$854.71$

Thus, you would be willing to pay up to $854.71 a year in insurance to avoid the risk of loss from car theft.

Let's see how the problem of adverse selection can enter. In this example, the insurance company offers coverage for the same price to all car owners, regardless of their activities or driving history, and all car owners are required to purchase the insurance. Now assume that not all car owners would need to purchase insurance, and further that some car owners would run a higher risk of having their car stolen. Owners with higher risks would find the $100 per year insurance to be more attractive and would be more likely to buy insurance, whereas owners with lower risks would find the $100 per year insurance payment to be excessive and would be less likely to buy insurance.

Consequently, the insurance company gets an adverse selection among the pool of potential car owners who want insurance. As the insurance company finds they have to pay off more on their policies, their average costs rise, they raise their premiums, and lower-risk customers are driven away. The result would be that a greater percentage of higher-risk car owners would have the insurance, which would raise rates for everyone, and which could discourage lower-risk automobile owners from purchasing the insurance because of the higher premiums. Thus, self-selection among car owners would lead to an adverse selection of those purchasing the insurance.

How can the adverse selection problem be reduced in this case? Insurance companies try to distinguish between higher-risk and lower-risk consumers in several ways. One is by obtaining information about car owners, such as their driving record and zip code, before selling them a policy. Another is to charge different rates, depending on the car owners' activities, such as miles driven per day and whether they are a smoker. Insurance companies can analyze what factors influence the probability of an insurable event happening, and they generally have copious statistics on the probabilities of insured events. In reality, high-risk car owners and low-risk car owners are charged different rates.

Now let's see how insurance can create moral hazard. Once car owners obtain insurance, they can act in more risky ways, without the insurance company's knowledge, and can pass the costs onto others. For instance, knowing that a car is covered by insurance, a driver may be more willing to leave the car unlocked, park in higher crime areas of town, or lend the car to friends, because the car owner knows that if the car were stolen, it would be covered by insurance (although the car owner may have to pay a higher insurance premium in the future).

How can the moral hazard problem be reduced? Some auto insurance companies manage this problem by requiring the insured to pay a deductible, such as the first $500, before the rest of the costs are covered. Another way is by increasing the insured's premium after certain events, such as moving violations or a theft of a vehicle. Moral hazard can also be reduced if the insured is concerned that these events could not only raise premiums with the current insurer, but also hinder the chances of getting affordable insurance from another insurer.

DECISION ANALYSIS

Decisions often involve imperfect information. Our expectations and estimates about benefits and costs are not always perfect. In some cases, we may not know all the possible alternatives, outcomes, and their probabilities. In other cases, it may be possible to reasonably specify all possible alternatives, outcomes, and probabilities, even though we don't know what outcome will occur. It is in these latter cases that decision analysis can be used and can be useful.

Decision analysis is a framework for making choices with uncertain outcomes.[24] It uses a decision tree to structure a problem into *alternatives* (possible choices or actions) and *outcomes* (consequences of those choices or actions). These alternatives and outcomes are the branches of the tree, and they stem from *decision nodes* (for making a decisions) and *chance nodes* (uncertain events), where probabilities of the chance nodes add to 100%. Figure 11-7 illustrates this structure for the GPA example given earlier, and we will go through the process of developing a decision tree.

---

[24] For readings on decision analysis, see R. A. Howard and J. Matheson (eds.) (1983), *The Principles and Applications of Decision Analysis* (2 volumes), Palo Alto, CA: Strategic Decisions Group; H. Raiffa (1968), *Decision Analysis*, Reading, MA: Addison-Wesley; D. Kahneman, P. Slovic, and A. Tversky (1982), *Judgment Under Uncertainty: Heuristics and Biases*, Cambridge: Cambridge University Press.

FIGURE 11-7   *Decision Tree for Calculating Expected GPA*

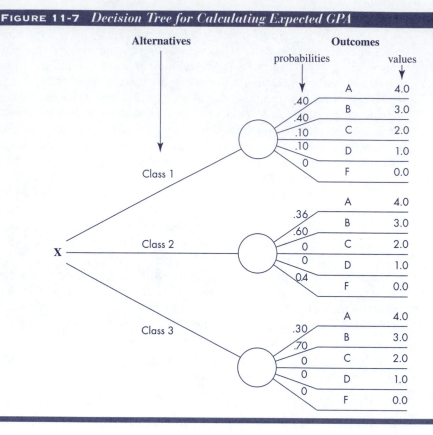

First, think of all the *alternatives* for a given problem. Make each of those as a branch, stemming to the right, from a *decision node* (represented by an *X*). In this case, each alternative is a possible class that you would take.

Next, think of all the possible *outcomes* that could occur as a result of each of those alternatives. Make each of those as a branch, stemming to the right, from a *chance node* (represented by a circle). In this case, the possible outcomes would be the same for each course—a grade of A, B, C, D, or F.

Next, for each outcome, assign both the *probability of occurrence* and the *value*. These outcomes are associated with each branch from a chance node. Make sure that the probabilities stemming from each chance node add up to 100%. Here, the probabilities are based on the grade distributions, and the value is the number of grade points for each letter grade.

Finally, calculate the expected value/utility of each possible alternative by starting at the right-hand ends of the branches and working toward the nodes. The set of outcomes must be exhaustive (all possible outcomes), and mutually exclusive (more than one possible path is not possible), and the probabilities must all add up to 1.0.

We will now develop an example to bring together concepts of expected value, expected utility, value of information, and risk, using a decision tree.

EXAMPLE	**Water Management with Drought Risks**

You are the manager of a water agency in a small town, and you are planning for the next year's water supplies. Your state has been recently hit with severe droughts. You are concerned that next summer will also be unusually dry and that water supplies will be inadequate to meet demands. You have the opportunity to purchase additional water supplies in advance, which would be useful in case of drought and water shortages. But if it's not a drought year, then you may be left with surplus water that can't be stored or sold.

You determine that your alternatives are to (1) buy the additional supplies, or (2) don't buy the additional supplies. The uncertain outcomes are whether (a) it will be a drought year, or (b) it will not be a drought year. In the case of (1)(a), you buy the additional supplies, and it turns out to be a drought year, you will be able to meet the demands and sell the additional water. In (1)(b), you buy the supplies, and it is not a drought year, you may need to dump excess water from the town's reservoir. In (2)(a), you don't buy the supplies, and it is a drought year, your community will suffer losses from the water shortages and water use restrictions. In (2)(b), you don't buy the supplies, and it is not a drought year, conditions are generally good.

What should you do? The decision problem is structured in Figure 11-8. A decision node is represented with an X, and a chance node is represented with a circle. The decision is (1) buy water, or (2) don't buy water. The chance node is (a) drought, or (b) no drought (for next year). The branches of the decision tree represent the number of choices or chances at each node. Note that for a chance node, the sum of the probabilities must be equal to 1.0. This case involves two possible outcomes, but if more outcomes were involved, they still must add up to 100%, or 1.0. This chance node has a 20% chance that it will be a drought year, and 80% not, so you assign the probabilities to those branches of the decision tree.

Next, you assign values, in terms of monetary amounts, for the possible outcomes. These amounts represent the net benefits (benefits minus costs) of each outcome. They are $100, $42, $0, and $80 for outcomes (1)(a), (1)(b), (2)(a), and (2)(b), respectively (see Figure 11-8). These amounts are per capita, and your community has 1,000 people, so $100 represents $100,000 total in this example.

Now you assign utilities to each of these outcomes. Assume a utility scale of 0.0 to 1.0[25], where 0.0 is the least desirable outcome and 1.0 is the most desirable outcome. You assign utilities to outcomes as 1.0, 0.667, 0.0, and 0.91, respectively, which you obtain through the following process.

continued on next page

---

[25] A utility scale of [0.0 to 1.0] or [0 to 100] as previously illustrated, are both common approaches to developing a utility curve.

FIGURE 11-8 *Decision Tree for Water Management Decision*

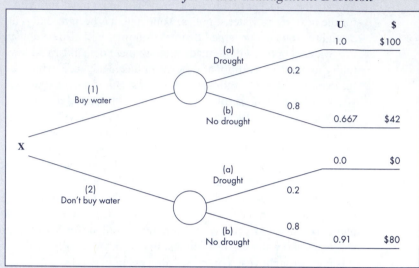

What amount of money (the certainty equivalent) would make you (your water agency) indifferent between that amount of money for certain and a 50-50 probability of $0 or $100? Let's say it's $27.

$$U(\hat{x}) = E[U(\tilde{x})] = 0.5U(\$0) + 0.5U(\$100) = 0.50 = U(\$27)$$

Thus, the utility of $27 is 0.50.

To complete the utility curve, you can go through sequences of lotteries. Find the certainty equivalent of the 50-50 probability of $0 or $27. Let's say it's $17.

$$U(\$17) = 0.5[U(\$0)] + 0.5[U(\$27)] = 0.0 + 0.25 = 0.25$$

Thus, the utility of $17 is 0.25.

Going through the possible combinations of lotteries, you complete the graph of the relationship between money and utility: between the monetary values of $0 and $100, and the utility values of 0 and 1, as in Figure 11-9.

$$U(\$100) = 1$$
$$U(\$42) = 0.667$$
$$U(\$0) = 0$$
$$U(\$80) = 0.91$$

Now you are ready for using the decision tree for calculations. You first calculate the expected monetary value of each alternative. The expected value

FIGURE 11-9   *Utility Curve for Money: $0 to $100*

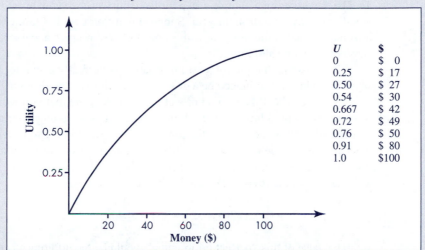

U	$
0	$ 0
0.25	$ 17
0.50	$ 27
0.54	$ 30
0.667	$ 42
0.72	$ 49
0.76	$ 50
0.91	$ 80
1.0	$100

of buying the water would be (0.20)($100) + (0.80)($42) = $53.60, and of not buying the water would be (0.20)(0) + (0.80)($80) = $64. In this approach, you would have a greater expected value from *not buying* the water.

You can also calculate the expected utility of each alternative. The expected utility of buying the water would be (0.20)(1.0) + (0.80)(0.667) = 0.734, and the expected value of not buying the water would be (0.20)(0) + (0.80)(0.91) = 0.728. Based on expected utility, you would have greater expected utility from *buying* the water rather than not buying the water.

Why are the two outcomes different, depending on whether the decision criterion is expected utility or expected monetary value? It goes back to the relationship between utility and money (as depicted in Figure 11-9), which shows that your agency is risk averse, and would prefer a certain outcome to an uncertain outcome (if they had the same expected values), and would view losses as more seriously affecting utility than gains of the same size.

To summarize:

$EV_1 = (0.20)($100) + (0.80)($42) = 53.60
$EV_2 = (0.20)($0) + (0.80)($80) = 64

$EU_1 = (0.20)(1.0) + (0.80)(0.667) = 0.734$
$EU_2 = (0.20)(0) + (0.80)(0.91) = 0.728$

Source: Adapted from D. W. North (1968), "A Tutorial Introduction to Decision Thery," *IEEE Transactions on Systems Science and Cybernetics*, SSC-4(3):200–210.

VALUE OF PERFECT INFORMATION AND IMPERFECT INFORMATION

To take the preceding example a step further, consider the value of information about whether it may be a drought year. Suppose that you could obtain climate forecast information that could tell you, with some degree of relative accuracy, whether next summer would be a drought.

First, assume that the forecast information is perfectly accurate. If the forecast says "drought," it will indeed be a drought, and if it says "no drought," it will not be a drought (i.e., it will be normal or wet instead). Assume that you would follow the forecast: You would buy the water if the forecast says it's going to be a drought, and you would not buy the water if the forecast says it's not going to be a drought. With this new information (see Figure 11-10), note that only two of the eight outcomes are possible because your decision will follow the forecast, and the forecast is always accurate. Thus, the revised expected values are as follows:

$$(0.2)(\$100) + (0.8)(\$80) = \$20 + \$64 = \$84$$

The value of this "perfect information" would be the difference between $84 and the following:

$$EV_1 = (0.20)(\$100) + (0.80)(\$42) = \$53.60$$
$$EV_2 = (0.20)(\$0) + (0.80)(\$80) = \$64.00$$

FIGURE 11-10 *Value of Perfect Information for Water Management Decision*

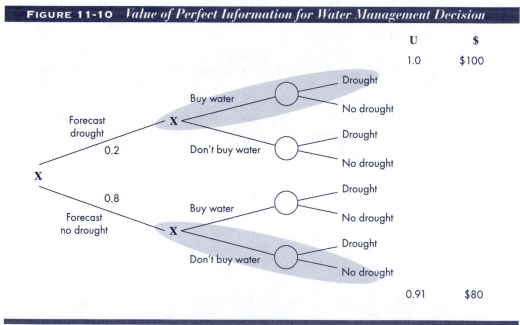

The *expected value of perfect information* is the increase in expected value that would occur from being able to obtain perfectly accurate information. In this case, it would be $30.40 if you buy the water, and $20 if you do not buy the water.

Now let's suppose that the forecasts are not entirely accurate. If a drought will occur, the forecast will correctly say "drought." But if a drought will not occur, the probability is 50% that the forecast will say "drought," and 50% that it will say "no drought." Viewed another way, if the forecast says "no drought," then no drought will occur. But if the forecast says "drought," then the drought may or may not occur.

In this case, obtaining the forecast information will cost $10. This will be subtracted from each of the values of the outcomes ($90, $32, and $70), as shown in Figure 11-11. Note that five of the eight outcomes are not possible, because your decision will follow the forecast, and the forecast is generally accurate, except in the case where the forecast says drought but it is not a drought. Thus, the probabilities of the forecast saying drought/no drought will be changed, because the forecast will no longer be completely accurate. We calculate these probabilities next.

BAYES' THEOREM

What is the probability of the forecast saying drought, in either case of actual drought or no drought? The forecast will say drought when it will be a drought (0.2) and in 50% of the cases when it will not be a drought ($0.5 \times 0.8 = 0.4$). So the probability for the branch of "Forecast drought" is now 0.6 (= 0.2 + 0.4), and the probability for the branch of "Forecast no drought" is now 0.4 (= 0.5×0.8).

FIGURE 11-11   *Value of Imperfect Information for Water Management Decision*

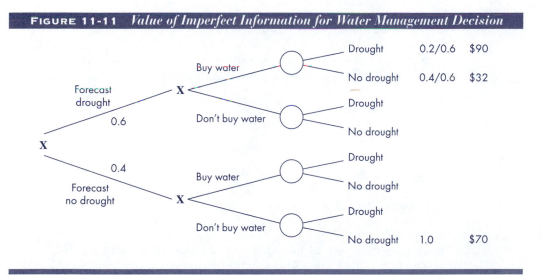

Now, what is the probability of a drought occurring, if the forecast says drought? For this probability, we will use *Bayes' theorem*,[26] which is a mathematical rule for updating existing information in the light of new knowledge or expertise.

The new probability is equal to the existing probability that the forecast will say drought and it really is a drought, divided by the prior estimate that the forecast will say drought regardless of whether it will be a drought.

Let B_1 = drought, B_2 = no drought, A = forecast says drought, $A \cap B$ = joint probability of A and B, $A|B$ = conditional probability of A, given B. Bayes' theorem says

$$P(B_1|A) = P(A \cap B_1)/P(A) = \{P(A \cap B_1)/[P(B_1)P(A|B_1) + \ldots + P(B_n)P(A|B_n)]\}$$

The existing probability that the forecast will say drought and it is really a drought is 0.2. This is $P(A \cap B_1)$. This probability will be divided by the prior estimate that that the forecast will say drought regardless, which is $0.2 + (0.5)(0.8) = 0.6$. This is $P(A)$. So the new probability that a drought will occur if the forecast says drought is $0.2/0.6 = 0.333$. This result is shown as the uppermost branch in Figure 11-11. Similarly, the new probability that a drought will not occur if the forecast says drought is $0.4/0.6 = 0.667$.

Now you can calculate expected values and expected utilities, given this new information. The expected value is as follows:

$$0.6[0.333(\$90) + 0.667(\$32)] + 0.4(1.0)(\$70) = \$58.80$$

which is less than the expected value of $64 of the previous best alternative (don't buy water). Judging by this measure, the information is not worth its $10 cost.

The expected utility is as follows:

$$0.6[0.333U(\$90) + 0.667U(\$32)] + 0.4U(1.0)(\$70) = 0.416 + 0.334 = 0.760$$

which exceeds the expected utility of 0.734 of the previous best alternative (buy water). Judging by this measure, the information is worth (at least) its $10 cost.

$EV_1 = (0.20)(\$100) + (0.80)(\$42) = \$53.60$
$EV_2 = (0.20)(0) + (0.80)(\$80) = \$64$
EV(with information) $= \$58.80$

$EU_1 = (0.20)(1.0) + (0.80)(0.667) = 0.734$
$EU_2 = (0.20)(0) + (0.80)(0.92) = 0.728$
EU(with information) $= 0.760$

---

[26] Rev. T. Bayes (1763), "An Essay Toward Solving a Problem in the Doctrine of Chances," *Philosophical Transactions of the Royal Society of London* 53, 370–418; reprinted (1958) in *Biometrika* 45, 293–315.

DECISION ANALYSIS: STRENGTHS AND LIMITATIONS

Decision analysis has been used in a variety of applications, and has appeal for several reasons: It can clarify the choices and consequences of a decision, it provides a structure and framework for decision making, it explicitly incorporates risk, it permits a quantitative evaluation of alternatives, and it can reveal a "preferred" alternative.

Yet these strengths may have corresponding shortcomings. The problem can involve uncertainty or ignorance and not just risk. Not all outcomes and alternatives are necessarily known, nor can they be structured in a decision tree. Probabilities and values may be uncertain, yet placement in this framework connotes analytic certainty. The focus on quantitative evaluation may drive out crucial qualitative information and issues of context. Multiple criteria collapsed into a single criterion (such a utility or expected monetary value) can also obscure other critical decision factors.

These shortcomings, in turn, highlight the importance of the decision criterion based on the **Precautionary Principle:**[27] "When an activity raises threats of harm to human health or the environment, precautionary measures should be taken even if some cause and effect relationships are not fully established scientifically. In this context the proponent of an activity, rather than the public, should bear the burden of proof."

The Precautionary Principle recognizes that we don't always have perfect information about our decisions, such as about all the possible effects, all the probabilities of those effects, and all the causes of those effects. When consequences of an action involve significant uncertainty, severity, or irreversibility, decision makers should search for alternatives that might have fewer adverse impacts and take precaution before taking action.[28]

In this chapter, we looked at cases in which market participants do not have all the information, because information is uncertain, unknown, inaccurate, hidden, or difficult or costly to obtain. Sellers generally have more information than buyers about the product before they sell it, which illustrates the "lemons" problem and adverse selection. Yet in the case of an insurance policy, buyers often know more about their own condition, and can influence the costs imposed upon sellers (as well as policyholders and the public), which illustrates adverse selection and moral hazard. Often times, the contract between a principal and agent involves imperfect information and differing incentives, so remedies include obtaining more information and providing incentives. Lack of information can cause both inefficiencies and equity concerns, often with no clear answers about the most equitable type of contract. When lack of information concerns risky outcomes, the probabilities and values of possible outcomes can be structured in a decision analysis framework, so values (whether in units of money, utility, or other) can be assigned to different alternatives. Although this

---

[27] Wingspread Statement on the Precautionary Principle, Racine, WI (January 26, 1998).

[28] See J. A. Tickner (ed.) (2003), *Precaution, Environmental Science, and Preventive Public Policy*, Washington, DC: Island Press.

approach offers analytic elegance, it is important that decision makers understand the assumptions underlying these analyses, and view the result as a decision-making assistant, rather than the final decision.

REVIEW QUESTIONS

1. Characterize each of the following as an example of (i) adverse selection, (ii) moral hazard, or (iii) principal-agent problem.
    a) A savings and loan association, with federally insured funds, makes risky investments.
    b) A car owner, with collision insurance, talks on a cell phone while driving.
    c) A physician prescribes drugs that are relatively expensive and ineffective for treating a patient's illness.
    d) An employee signs up for disability insurance, aware of having an illness that is likely to be disabling.
    e) A babysitter, hired to watch a sleeping baby, instead watches TV during the entire evening.
    f) A prospective buyer of a used car obtains a "lemon."
2. Moral hazard can result from many types of insurance policies. Why may some types of policies, such as homeowners' fire insurance or personal life insurance, have an inherent incentive for the policyholder to reduce moral hazard?
3. In any year, 1% of the population suffers from illness X, which costs $10,000 per year to treat. The other 99% of the population does not suffer from this illness, so health care costs for X are $0. Although X strikes at random, people who are going to suffer from X know in advance that they will suffer from X.
    a) Suppose the government currently mandates that all citizens contribute an equal sum to the national health insurance pool. What annual per person contribution is needed to cover the cost of treating X?
    b) The government is considering privatization of health insurance to cover X. Citizens who contribute to the insurance pool will receive treatment for X; those who do not contribute to the pool will not receive treatment for X. For the time being, the government will regulate the per person contribution at the historic average level. What premium would the insurance plan need to charge to break even? Comment on this privatization scheme.[29]
4. The government is offering a new income-contingent option in the federal student loan program. Instead of the fixed term and interest rate in the traditional repayment plan, under the income-contingent option, the repayment plan will depend on the graduate's income. A graduate with a lower income will have a lower repayment burden, and vice versa. How is this program a form of insurance, and how might adverse selection and moral hazard arise?

---

[29] Contributions for Problems 3 and 4 by Michael Ash.

5. You are the head of an environmental agency, are you are developing a policy to regulate X, a potentially dangerous pollutant found in many workplaces. In your jurisdiction, approximately 1 million people are exposed to X at levels that would cause adverse health effects.

    The three policies that you are considering include (1) a complete ban on X, (2) an initiative to reduce exposure to X, and (3) no action (status quo). For policy (1), the implementation cost would be a 50-50 probability of either $6 million or $4 million, and it would reduce 100% of the health risk. For policy (2), the implementation cost would be a 50-50 probability of either $3 million or $2 million, and it would reduce 50% of the health risk. For policy (3), the implementation cost would be $0, and the health risk would remain the same. Based on scientific studies, the probability of developing cancer from exposure to X would be 1/100,000 at the levels found in these workplaces. Assume that the value of life is $500,000 per person (adjusted for age at the time of death). Also assume that your agency and your population is risk neutral.

    Which policy would be chosen, based on expected value? What are some of the assumptions and limitations with this approach?

PART 3

COST-BENEFIT ANALYSIS AND APPLICATIONS

12 INTERTEMPORAL COSTS AND BENEFITS 301

13 COST-BENEFIT ANALYSIS 321

14 COST-BENEFIT APPLICATIONS 349

INTERTEMPORAL COSTS AND BENEFITS

Many decisions, both public and private, generate costs and benefits over time. Consider, for example, a proposed water supply reservoir. Costs would include initial construction costs and then regular operation and maintenance costs. Benefits would include revenues from water sales, recreational amenities, and hydropower. Both costs and benefits occur over many years and can vary each year.

In addition, many decisions require a choice among several competing projects or alternatives. The proposed construction of a reservoir may be only one of several possible options for supplying an area with water, and each option has different costs and benefits over time. In order to assess and finance a project, or to assess the relative merits of several alternatives, decision makers often find it useful to place the monetary amounts of benefits and costs into equivalent terms, such as "net present benefits" or "annual cost."

This chapter details project accounting methods that are common for both public and private sector decisions, such as calculating the annual revenues that would be needed to cover the costs of the reservoir, or determining the annual savings from an investment in new equipment. These methods are also useful for individual decisions, such as comparing monthly payments when purchasing a new car, setting up a fund to pay for college tuition, or deciding how much to invest each year in a retirement plan.

The methods in this chapter are objective because project accounting formulas are objective; they are based on mathematics. Yet the determination of numbers that go into these formulas can involve subjectivity. For instance, how do we place a number on a nonmonetary benefit or cost? What is the appropriate social discount rate? (These issues are treated in more detail in Chapter 13, Cost-Benefit Analysis.)

We will now begin with the fundamental concepts, followed by techniques to analyze decisions over time, including convenient tools such as factors and cash flow diagrams. Throughout this chapter, we illustrate the concepts and techniques with applications.

TIME VALUE OF MONEY

The concept of interest is familiar. When we invest money in a savings account, we plan to have more at the end of a year than originally invested. When we borrow money from a bank to buy a car, we need to pay back more than the amount originally borrowed. **Interest** is the amount of money paid for the use of borrowed money. The **interest rate** is the interest expressed as a percentage of the amount borrowed or invested.

$$\text{Interest rate} = \frac{\text{amount of interest payable at end of period}}{\text{amount of money borrowed or invested at beginning of period}}$$

For instance, if you deposit $1,000 in a bank, and the interest rate is 5% per annum (per year), paid once a year at the end of the year, you would have $1,050 at the end of the first year. The $1,000 investment is the **principal**, the $50 is the interest paid, and 5% is the annual interest rate. In this case, the interest was **compounded** or paid once a year.

Compounding means reinvestment of the interest that was paid. Thus, with compounding, future interest will be paid on both the initial investment and the interest that has already accrued. The total amount of interest, at the end of a time period, will be greater with more frequent compounding.

To demonstrate this concept, suppose that interest were compounded more than once a year, such as semiannually (2.5% every six months) rather than annually (5% every year). Using the same $1,000 investment, you would receive $1,025 after the first six months. Then, that entire amount is reinvested. After the second six months, you would receive an additional 2.5% on the original $1,000, plus 2.5% on the $25 of interest from the first six months. The total amount at the end of the year would be $1,050.625 when compounded semiannually, compared to $1,050.00 when compounded annually.

This example also illustrates an important distinction between the nominal interest rate and the effective interest rate. The **nominal interest rate** is the stated interest rate, excluding the effects of compounding. In each of these cases, the nominal interest rate is still described at 5% per annum, whether it's 5% per year, or 2.5% every six months, or even 1.25% every three months. The **effective interest rate** is the actual interest rate, including the effects of compounding. In each of these cases, the effective interest rate is different, depending on the frequency of compounding. For a nominal rate of 5% per year, compounded annually, the effective rate is 5% per year. That same nominal rate of 5% per year, compounded semiannually, has an effective rate of 5.0625% per year.

$$
\begin{aligned}
\text{Interest rate} &= \frac{\text{amount of interest (at end of period)}}{\text{amount of investment (at beginning of a period)}} \\
&= (\$1,050.625 - \$1,000) / \$1,000 \\
&= .050625 = 5.0625\%
\end{aligned}
$$

The following formulas can be used to determine the effective interest rate:

Nominal interest rate (for a given period, usually a year) = i

Effective interest rate (for a given period, usually a year) = $(1 + i/n)^n - 1$

where i is the nominal interest rate (expressed in decimal form) for a given time period, and n is the number of compounding periods in that time period.

As an example, many lending institutions state the interest rate in terms such as "24% compounded monthly." The number (24%) usually refers to the nominal interest rate per year, which is the **annual percentage rate (APR)**. An APR of 24%, which is a nominal rate, would be equivalent to an effective annual rate of $(1 + 0.24/12)^{12} - 1 = 0.2682 = 26.82\%$ per year, because it would be compounded monthly, and thus $n = 12$ (12 compounding periods per year) for $i = 24\%$ (nominal annual rate). It would also mean an effective monthly rate of $(1 + 0.02/1) - 1 = 0.02 = 2\%$ per month, because $n = 1$ (1 compounding period per month) for $i = 2\%$ (nominal monthly rate).

Interest can also be **compounded continuously**, meaning that interest is reinvested continually. The formula for the effective interest rate for continuous compounding is $e^i - 1$, where e is the base of the natural logarithm ($e = 2.71828...$). To derive this formula, let k equal the value of n/i, so $i = n/k$, and substitute that value into the formula for the effective interest rate to get:

$$(1 + 1/k)^{ki} - 1$$

When n (the number of times of compounding) approaches infinity, k also approaches infinity, the quantity $(1 + 1/k)^k$ approaches the value of e, and the effective rate for continuous compounding becomes $(e)^i - 1$.

Thus, given an initial investment P, the future value F with continuous compounding can be expressed as:

$$F = Pe^i$$

where i is the nominal interest rate for the time period under consideration.

For example, if you invest $1,000 into a bank account with continuous compounding at a 5% nominal interest rate per year, your total savings at the end of one year would be

$$F = (\$1,000)e^{0.05} = (\$1,000)(1.05127) = \$1,051.27$$

Thus, your total savings at the end of one year with continuous compounding ($1,051.27) was greater than that with annual or semiannual compounding (calculated earlier). The amount of $1,051.27 means an effective interest rate of 5.127% per year on your original investment of $1,000, because interest rate = ($1,051.27 − $1,000)/($1,000) = 0.05127 = 5.127% Thus, for a given nominal interest rate, the more frequent the compounding, the greater the interest that accrues.

CALCULATING PRESENT AND FUTURE VALUES

Suppose you have been offered a choice of either $1,000 today, or $1,100 a year from now. Which would you choose? You know from the concept of interest that $1 in the present is worth more than $1 in the future.[1] You can invest the $1 now, at a given interest rate, and have more than $1 in the future. But how much more?

To decide, you need to compare both gifts by equal measures. You can do this one of two ways:

1 Determine the **present value** of the future amount of $1,100, and compare it to the present amount of $1,000.
2 Determine the **future value** of the present amount of $1,000, and compare it to the future amount of $1,100.

Assume that, in both cases, the effective interest rate is 5% per annum.

For the first method of calculation, we determine the present value of the future gift of $1,100. This is the same as determining how much you would have to invest in a savings account today to have an account balance of $1,100 a year from now. The amount invested (P) plus the interest on that amount (Pi) would need to equal the future amount (F) after one year. Stated algebraically, the problem is to solve for a present amount P, given an interest rate i and the future amount F.

$$F = P + Pi = P (1 + i)$$

Plugging in numbers $F = 1,100$ and $i = 0.05$, we get:

$$\$1,100 = P (1.05)$$

which we rearrange as

$$P = \$1,100/1.05$$

Solving for P, the answer is $1,047.62. That amount, if invested today at 5% interest per annum, would grow to $1,100 in one year.

So your decision becomes a comparison between $1,000 (the present gift) and $1,047.62 (the present value of the future gift of $1,100). If you wanted the greatest monetary amount, waiting a year for $1,100 would be preferred, because the present value of $1,100, a year from now, is greater than the $1,000 gift today.

On the other hand, suppose you really need the money now. You may decide to take the $1,000 gift, which is a sure thing now, rather than wait for the equivalent gift of $1,047.62 in a year from now.

---

[1] These analyses of the time value of money do not include the effects of inflation.

For the second method of calculation, we determine the future value of the present gift of $1,000. To do so, we calculate how much you would have one year from now if you invested the $1,000 today. Stated algebraically, as before

$$F = P\,(1 + i)$$
$$F = \$1,000\,(1.05) = \$1,050$$

The $1,000 gift right now would be worth $1,050 a year from now, which is less than $1,100, the amount of the gift one year from now. Again, even though these numbers suggest waiting a year to take the money, other factors may influence your decision. For instance, you may expect the interest rate to rise, which would make $1,000 today worth more in the future.

What interest rate would make the two amounts equivalent?

$$F \quad = \quad P\,(1 + i)$$
$$\$1,100 \quad = \quad \$1,000\,(1 + i)$$

Solve the equation for i:

$$i = (\$1,100/\$1,000) - 1 = 0.10, \text{ or } 10\%$$

DISCOUNTING

The process of taking future amounts and converting them into present values is called **discounting**. The "present" can be any time of reference; it does not need to be this moment. The **discount rate** is similar to the interest rate, except in the reverse time direction: It is the rate at which future benefits or costs are discounted back over time. In the previous examples, the discount rate used was the interest rate. In other situations, as we will examine in Chapter 13, the discount rate may not be the private sector interest rate, and determining the appropriate "social discount rate" can be difficult. (For instance, is the value of a life saved in the future worth less than a full life today, and, if so, how much less?)

Discounting occurs because a dollar in the future is worth less than a dollar received today. So future amounts need to be discounted in order to be meaningful in present value terms. Thus, the present value of a future benefit or cost depends on the discount rate. Using the formula $P = F/(1+i)$ at a discount rate of 5%, the $1,100 payment one year from now has a present value of $1,047.62. At a discount rate of 10%, the present value falls to $1,000, while at 15%, the present value is $956.52. Thus, *the higher the discount rate, the lower the present value of future money.*

To see this relationship, suppose that you were given a third option for a gift: $1,100 in two years. Would that be better than $1,100 in one year, or $1,000 now?

Again, you want to determine the present value P of some future value F ($1,100) two years from now. So the calculations follow this formula:

$$\$1{,}100 = P(1 + i)(1 + i)$$

The expression $(1 + i)$ is repeated because the amount at the end of the first year is reinvested at the same rate of interest for a second year.

Solving for P, and using $i = .05$, we find that the present value of $1,100 two years from today would be $997.73. Note that the present value of a future benefit or cost depends on the time period. When you had the offer of $1,100 in one year, it was worth $1,047.62 in present value dollars. When that same amount was offered after two years, it was worth $997.73. Thus, *the present value of some future amount will decrease as the time into the future increases.*

As an extension of this example, if you were to receive some amount F after n time periods, the present value P could be calculated as follows:

$$P = F / (1 + i)^n$$

Solving for F yields:

$$F = P (1 + i)^n$$

We will see the usefulness of these formulas later in the chapter.

ANNUITY (OR UNIFORM SERIES)

You are probably also familiar with the concept of an **annuity**: a series of equal payments occurring at equal periods of time. Buying a car often means that you pay the same amount every month to pay off the loan. Working a job often means you receive the same amount every pay period until you receive a raise. These payments are types of annuities or uniform series.

It does not matter whether the amount is paid annually or several times a year. Any amount can be converted to an annuity (an equivalent or uniform series) for any time period. The interest rate i must be the effective interest rate, corresponding to the unit of time for n.

We can determine the annuities, given certain present and future values.

The annuity A of a given present amount is

$$A = P\{[i (1 + i)^n]/[(1 + i)^n - 1]\}$$

The annuity for a given future amount is

$$A = F \{i/[(1 + i)^n - 1]\}$$

Rearranging these terms, we can also find present and future amounts, given the annuity:

$$P = A\{[(1 + i)^n - 1]/[i\,(1 + i)^n]\}$$
$$F = A\,\{[(1 + i)^n - 1]/i\}$$

For example, suppose you want to take out a loan to buy a car. The car costs $6,000, and you place a down payment of $2,000. So you need to take out a loan for $4,000. The nominal interest rate is 6% per year, assuming interest is paid monthly. Those terms would mean an effective monthly interest rate of ½%, because (.06/year) / (12 months/year) = .005 (which is ½% per month).

What would be your monthly car payment if you took out a two-year loan for $4,000?

$$A = P\{[i\,(1 + i)^n]/[(1 + i)^n - 1]\}$$
$$A = 4,000\,[(0.005)(1.005^{24})]/[(1.005^{24}) - 1] = \$177.29/\text{month}$$

Note that $n = 24$ refers to 24 monthly payments during the two-year period. The effective monthly interest rate is $i = 0.005$ per month. *Both n and i must refer to the same unit of time.* In this case, the unit of time is months.

What would be your monthly payment if you took out a five-year loan rather than a two-year loan?

$$A = P\{[i\,(1 + i)^n]/[(1 + i)^n - 1]\}$$
$$A = 4,000\,[(0.005)(1.005^{60})]/[(1.005^{60}) - 1] = \$77.34/\text{month}$$

Where $n = 60$ months (5 years) instead of 24, and $i = 0.005$, as before.
What would be the total amount paid under each payment option?

Total amount paid for two-year loan = (24)($177.29) = $4,255
Total amount paid for five-year loan = (60)($77.34) = $4,640

Now we will look at cases where benefits and costs vary over time, but by a uniform amount or rate.

UNIFORM GRADIENTS

A **uniform gradient** is a cash flow series that either increases or decreases by the same amount each period. The gradient method assumes that the end of the first time period is the base payment and that the increase doesn't start until the end of the second time period.

For instance, assume the cost of tuition is $10,000 per year and is expected to increase by $500 each year. The increase will not start until the end of the second year, which is the beginning of the third year. That cash flow series could be represented by an annual payment of $10,000 and a uniform gradient of $500 per year: $10,000 at the end of the first year, $10,500 at the end of the second year, $11,000 at the end of the third year, and so forth.

The present value of a uniform gradient G is

$$P = G \{[(1 + i)^n - (in) - 1]/[i^2 (1 + i)^n]\}$$

From that result, annuities and future values can be determined, using the formulas presented earlier.

$$F = G \{[(1 + i)^n - (in) - 1]/i^2\}$$
$$A = G \{[(1 + i)^n - (in) - 1]/[i (1 + i)^n - 1]\}$$

FACTORS FOR PRESENT VALUES, FUTURE VALUES, ANNUITIES, AND GRADIENTS

These formulas can be represented by **factors**, which can make calculations more convenient. Factors have been calculated for a range of values of n (number of periods) and r (the interest rate or discount rate). The values of these factors, for common interest rates, are presented in Appendix A at the end of the text; a part of it (for $r = 5\%$) is in Table 12.1. In addition, many computer programs include these factors.

We will show the derivation of one factor. The other factors can be derived in a similar way.

As we saw, the present value (P) of a future amount (F) dollars, with n number of payments, and a discount rate of r is equal to:

$$P = F /(1 + r)^n$$

By rearranging, an expression can be derived:

$$P/F = [1/(1 + r)^n]$$

Thus, for any values of r and n, we can calculate the value of the expression P/F. The notation is as follows:

$$[P/F, r\%, n]$$

which is equal to

$$[1/(1 + r)^n]$$

TABLE 12-1 *Compound Interest Table for Discrete Cash Flows (r = 5%)*

	Single Payment		Uniform Series				Uniform Gradients		
	Compound Amount Factor	Present Worth Factor	Compound Amount Factor	Present Worth Factor	Sinking Fund Factor	Capital Recovery Factor	Gradient Present Worth Factor	Gradient Uniform Series Factor	
	To Find F Given P	To Find P Given F	To Find F Given A	To Find P Given A	To Find A Given F	To Find A Given P	To Find P Given G	To Find A Given G	
N	F/P	P/F	F/A	P/A	A/F	A/P	P/G	A/G	N
1	1.0500	0.9524	1.0000	0.9524	1.0000	1.0500	0.0000	0.0000	1
2	1.1025	0.9070	2.0500	1.8594	0.4878	0.5378	0.9070	0.4878	2
3	1.1576	0.8638	3.1525	2.7232	0.3172	0.3672	2.6347	0.9675	3
4	1.2155	0.8227	4.3101	3.5460	0.2320	0.2820	5.1028	1.4391	4
5	1.2763	0.7835	5.5256	4.3295	0.1810	0.2310	8.2369	1.9025	5
6	1.3401	0.7462	6.8019	5.0757	0.1470	0.1970	11.9680	2.3579	6
7	1.4071	0.7107	8.1420	5.7864	0.1228	0.1728	16.2321	2.8052	7
8	1.4775	0.6768	9.5491	6.4632	0.1047	0.1547	20.9700	3.2445	8
9	1.5513	0.6446	11.0266	7.1078	0.0907	0.1407	26.1268	3.6758	9
10	1.6289	0.6139	12.5779	7.7217	0.0795	0.1295	31.6520	4.0991	10
11	1.7103	0.5847	14.2068	8.3064	0.0704	0.1204	37.4988	4.5144	11
12	1.7959	0.5568	15.9171	8.8633	0.0628	0.1128	43.6241	4.9219	12
13	1.8856	0.5303	17.7130	9.3936	0.0565	0.1065	49.9879	5.3215	13
14	1.9799	0.5051	19.5986	9.8986	0.0510	0.1010	56.5538	5.7133	14
15	2.0789	0.4810	21.5786	10.3797	0.0463	0.0963	63.2880	6.0973	15
16	2.1829	0.4581	23.6575	10.8378	0.0423	0.0923	70.1597	6.4736	16
17	2.2920	0.4363	25.8404	11.2741	0.0387	0.0887	77.1405	6.8423	17
18	2.4066	0.4155	28.1324	11.6896	0.0355	0.0855	84.2043	7.2034	18
19	2.5270	0.3957	30.5390	12.0853	0.0327	0.0827	91.3275	7.5569	19
20	2.6533	0.3769	33.0660	12.4622	0.0302	0.0802	98.4884	7.9030	20
21	2.7860	0.3589	35.7193	12.8212	0.0280	0.0780	105.6673	8.2416	21
22	2.9253	0.3418	38.5052	13.1630	0.0260	0.0760	112.8461	8.5730	22
23	3.0715	0.3256	41.4305	13.4886	0.0241	0.0741	120.0087	8.8971	23
24	3.2251	0.3101	44.5020	13.7986	0.0225	0.0725	127.1402	9.2140	24
25	3.3864	0.2953	47.7271	14.0939	0.0210	0.0710	134.2275	9.5238	25
26	3.5557	0.2812	51.1135	14.3752	0.0196	0.0696	141.2585	9.8266	26
27	3.7335	0.2678	54.6691	14.6430	0.0183	0.0683	148.2226	10.1224	27
28	3.9201	0.2551	58.4026	14.8981	0.0171	0.0671	155.1101	10.4114	28
29	4.1161	0.2429	62.3227	15.1411	0.0160	0.0660	161.9126	10.6936	29
30	4.3219	0.2314	66.4388	15.3725	0.0151	0.0651	168.6226	10.9691	30
36	5.7918	0.1727	95.8363	16.5469	0.0104	0.0604	206.6237	12.4872	36
40	7.0400	0.1420	120.7998	17.1591	0.0083	0.0583	229.5452	13.3775	40
48	10.4013	0.0961	188.0254	18.0772	0.0053	0.0553	269.2467	14.8943	48
50	11.4674	0.0872	209.3480	18.2559	0.0048	0.0548	277.9148	15.2233	50
52	12.6428	0.0791	232.8562	18.4181	0.0043	0.0543	286.1013	15.5337	52
60	18.6792	0.0535	353.5837	18.9293	0.0028	0.0528	314.3432	16.6062	60
70	30.4264	0.0329	588.5285	19.3427	0.0017	0.0517	340.8409	17.6212	70
72	33.5451	0.0298	650.9027	19.4038	0.0015	0.0515	345.1485	17.7877	72
80	49.5614	0.0202	971.2288	19.5965	0.0010	0.0510	359.6460	18.3526	80
84	60.2422	0.0166	1184.8448	19.6680	0.0008	0.0508	365.4727	18.5821	84
90	80.7304	0.0124	1594.6073	19.7523	0.0006	0.0506	372.7488	18.8712	90
96	108.1864	0.0092	2143.7282	19.8151	0.0005	0.0505	378.5555	19.1044	96
100	131.5013	0.0076	2610.0252	19.8479	0.0004	0.0504	381.7492	19.2337	100
104	159.8406	0.0063	3176.8120	19.8749	0.0003	0.0503	384.4845	19.3453	104
120	348.9120	0.0029	6958.2397	19.9427	0.0001	0.0501	391.9751	19.6551	120
240	1.217E+05	0.0000	2.435E+06	19.9998	0.0000	0.0500	399.9573	19.9980	240
360	4.248E+07	0.0000	8.495E+08	20.0000	0.0000	0.0500	399.9998	20.0000	360
480	1.482E+10	0.0000	2.964E+11	20.0000	0.0000	0.0500	400.0000	20.0000	480

P/F is called the **present worth factor**. It can be thought of as follows: To determine the present value, multiply this factor times the future value.

$$P \text{ (unknown)} = P/F \text{ (the present worth factor)} \times F \text{ (known)}$$

Using the example presented earlier, suppose you know you will receive a gift of $1,100 in two years ($F = \$1,100$) and the discount rate is 5%. What is the present value?

Using Table 12-1, the value of $[P/F, 5\%, 2] = 0.9070$. So, the present value is

$$P = [P/F, 5\%, 2] * (F) = (0.9070)\,(\$1,100) = \$997.70$$

as we determined earlier.

Appendix A contains the following factors for combinations of *P*, *F*, *A*, and *G*, given values of *r* (discount rate) and *n* (number of interest periods).[2] Also note that these factors can be readily calculated with a spreadsheet or computer program.

F/P Single Payment – Compound Amount Factor
P/F Single Payment – Present Worth Factor
F/A Uniform Series – Compound Amount Factor
P/A Uniform Series – Present Worth Factor
A/F Uniform Series – Sinking Fund Factor
A/P Uniform Series – Capital Recovery Factor
P/G Uniform Gradient – Gradient Present Worth Factor
A/G Uniform Gradient – Gradient Uniform Series Factor

NOTE: The interest rate *i* or discount rate *r* that is used in these formulas *must be an effective rate*, not a nominal rate, and *must correspond to the unit of time used for n*.

For example, if you buy a car and take out a three-year loan for $10,000 at 12% (nominal) interest per year compounded monthly, your equivalent monthly payments would be represented by the following:

$$A = \$10,000\,[A/P, 1\%, 36] = \$10,000(0.0332) = \$332$$

Note that the 12% nominal annual rate is a 1% effective monthly rate, and there are 36 monthly payments.

If you buy that same car and take out a three-year loan for $10,000 at 12% (nominal) interest per year compounded annually, your equivalent annual payments would be represented by

---

[2] If the table does not have a specific rate or time period, the factor can be determined by interpolation between table entries or by calculations using the formulas presented earlier. Note that factors in the tables are rounded and thus may differ slightly from values obtained by using the formulas.

$$A = \$10,000 \, [A/P, 12\%, 3] = \$10,000(0.4163) = \$4,163$$

In this last case, the nominal annual rate is the effective annual rate because interest is compounded once a year, and there are three annual payments.

CASH FLOW DIAGRAMS

Cash flow diagrams are another useful tool to illustrate and calculate benefits and costs over periods of time. Before we apply them to problems, a few conventions are noted:

- The cash flow diagram begins at time $t = 0$, at the beginning of year 1. So the numeral "1" is positioned at the end of "Year 1"; the numeral "2" is positioned at the end of "Year 2"; and so forth (see Figure 12-1).
- A positive cash flow (cash flow in) is shown by an upward arrow. A negative cash flow (cash flow out) is shown by a downward arrow. Refer to Figure 12-2. In this case, an individual deposits an amount of money (P) into a savings account at the beginning of the year, and withdraws an amount (F) at the end of one year.

FIGURE 12-1   *Cash Flow Diagram and Time Positions*

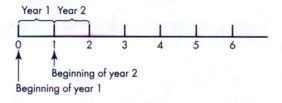

FIGURE 12-2   *Positive and Negative Cash Flows*

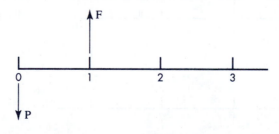

- A present value is represented at the beginning of the time period. A future value is represented at the end of the time period. An annuity is also represented at the end of the time period. A gradient is represented at the end of the second time period.

Suppose you receive a gift of $100 at the end of each year for three years at an effective annual discount rate of 5%. What is (a) the present value of these three gifts? (b) the future value at the end of three years of these three gifts? Then, (c) check the equivalency between the present value and future value. Refer to Figure 12-3 for these cash flow diagrams.

(a) $P = \$100[P/A, 5\%, 3] = \$100(2.7232) = \$272.32$
(b) $F = \$100[F/A, 5\%, 3] = \$100(3.1525) = \$315.25$

To check:

(c) $P = F\,[P/F, 5\%, 3]$

$\$272.32 = \$315.25(0.8638) = \$272.31$

It checks! Now we will work some more problems with factors and cash flow diagrams.

FIGURE 12-3 *Relationships Between Present, Future, and Annual Values*

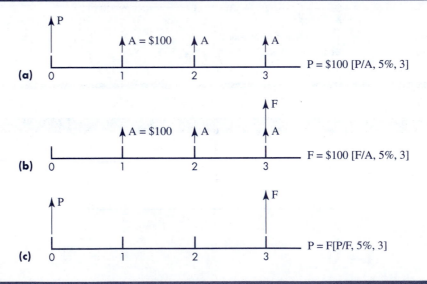

EXAMPLE

Savings and Withdrawals, Project Benefits and Costs

To see the usefulness of these techniques, each of the following problems are solved using factor notations and cash flow diagrams.

(a) If you deposit $1,000 into a bank account at the end of each year, how much can you withdraw at the end of five years, assuming five end-year deposits and an effective rate of 5% per year?

$F = \$1,000\ [F/A, 5\%, 5] = \$1,000\ (5.5256) = \$5,525.60$

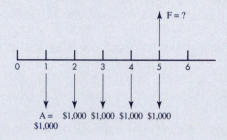

(b) What is the present value of that amount calculated in part (a)?

$P = \$5,525.60\ [P/F, 5\%, 5] = \$5,525.60\ (0.7835) = \$4,329.31$

(c) Instead of making a deposit at the end of each year, you deposit $1,000 at the beginning of each year, starting now. How much can you withdraw at the end of four years, assuming that you will make a deposit at the end of the fourth year?

$F = \$1,000\ [F/A, 5\%, 5] = \$1,000\ (5.5256) = \$5,525.60$

Note that five deposits total are still made, just as before, but here, the time period starts at $t = -1$. The first A occurs at the end of the time period (end of time $t = -1$, which is the beginning of time $t = 0$).

continued on next page

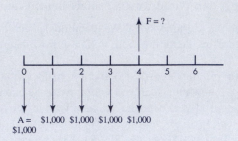

Alternatively, this value calculation could be:

$F = \$1,000\ [F/A,\ 5\%,\ 4] + \$1,000\ [F/P,\ 5\%,\ 4] = \$1,000\ (4.3101 + 1.2155) = \$5,525.60$

The calculation of F from values of A assumes a deposit at the time of withdrawal, but no deposit at the beginning of the first time period. So the deposit at the beginning of the first time period needs to be added.

(d) What is the present value of that future withdrawal in part (c)?

$P = \$5,525.60\ [P/F,\ 5\%,\ 4] = \$5,525.60\ (0.8227) = \$4,546$

Notice the time period is 4, not 5, because F occurs at the end of the fourth time period (time $t = 4$), and P occurs at the beginning of the first time period (time $t = 0$).

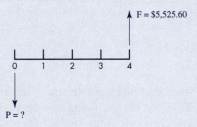

(e) What is the present value of those annual payments in part (c)?

$P = \$1,000\ [P/A,\ 5\%,\ 5][F/P,\ 5\%,\ 1] = \$1,000\ (4.3295)(1.05) = \$4,546$

The first factor translates the five annuities into a present value at $t = -1$. The second factor converts that to time $t = 0$. That conversion factor is $[F/P, 5\%, 1]$.

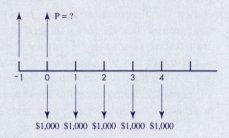

Alternatively, it could be calculated as follows:

$P = \$1,000\ [P/A, 5\%, 4] + \$1,000\ [F/A, 5\%, 1] = \$1,000\ [3.546 + 1] = \$4,546$

The calculation of P assumes that no deposit is made at the beginning of the first year, but a $1,000 deposit was made at the beginning of the first year, so that amount was added. It provides the same answer as in part (d), which shows that the results come out the same, regardless of the method of calculation.

(f) If maintenance on a highway project costs $500,000 each year, and if the costs increase by $50,000 each year (starting at the end of the second year), what will be the present value of all the costs at the end of 10 years? Assume an effective annual rate of 10%.

First find A, the equivalent annual amount, incorporating the gradient:

$A = \$500,000 + 50,000[A/G, 10\%, 10] = \$500,000 + [(\$50,000)(3.7255)]$
$\quad = \$500,000 + \$186,275 = \$686,275$

$P = \$686,275\ [P/A, 10\%, 10] = (\$686,275)(6.1446) = \$4,216,885$

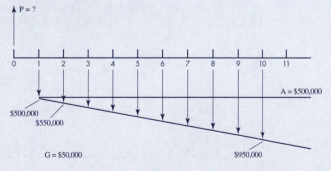

continued on next page

(g) A city is setting up a fund to pay for a bond issue. The bond issue is structured so that the city will need to pay $2,350,000, in 20 years from today. Assume that the city will make its first annual payment at the end of this year, and that its last annual payment will be included in the payment of the bond issue in 20 years. Determine the equal annual payments to the fund that will be needed to pay the bond issue. Assume the effective annual rate is 12%.

A = $2,350,000 [$A/F$, 12%, 20] = $2,350,000 (0.0139) = $32,665

This payment could also be calculated as follows:

P = $2,350,000 [$P/F$, 12%, 20] = $2,350,000 (0.1037) = $243,695
A = $243,695 [$A/P$, 12%, 20] = $2,350,000 (0.1339) = $32,631

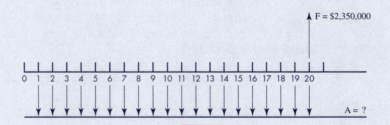

(h) You make an annual payment for which the first payment was due at the end of 2000 and the last payment is due at the end of the year in 2009. The payment is $950 per year. Using a discount rate of 8%, what would the annual payment be if you spread the payments over 20 years instead of 10 years? Assume your first payment would still be at the end of 2000.

P = $950 [$P/A$, 8%, 10] = $950 (6.7101) = $6,374.59
A = $6,374.59 [$A/P$, 8%, 20] = $6,374.59 (0.1019) = $649.57

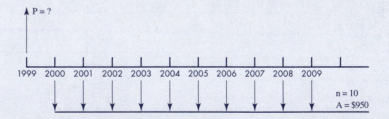

(i)   You are starting a Ph.D. program, which you expect will take four years. The tuition is due at the beginning of each year. Your first year's tuition will be $10,000, and it will increase by $500 each year. In other words, you will pay $10,500 at the beginning of your second year of the Ph.D. program, and then $11,000 at the beginning of your third year, and $11,500 at the beginning of your fourth year. The effective annual rate is 10%. What is the present value of four years of tuition?

The present value of this amount can be calculated in three different ways. First, using a sum of present values of the four future amounts gives you:

$P = 10,000 + 10,500[P/F, 10\%, 1] + 11,000[P/F, 10\%, 2] + 11,500[P/F, 10\%, 3] = \$37,276$

Second, using a sum of future values, brought back to present values gives you:

$P = (10,000[F/P, 10\%, 4] + 10,500[F/P, 10\%, 3] + 11,000[F/P, 10\%, 2] + 11,500[F/P, 10\%, 1])\ [P/F, 10\%, 4] = \$37,276$

Third, using annuities and gradients, brought back to present values gives you:

$P = (10,000 + 500[A/G, 10\%, 4])[P/A, 10\%, 4][F/P, 10\%, 1] = \$37,276$

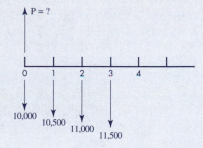

EXAMPLE

Private Investment Decisions

Your neighbor, Patricia, recently won $25,000 on a game show and is looking for ways to invest the money for five years, and then spend it at the end of five years. She needs some help in answering some basic questions about the following investment alternatives. For initial answers to these questions, you can disregard any possible income tax consequences.

Regular Savings Account. One option is a regular savings account. At the local bank, savings earn 5% interest per year, with the interest compounded once a year. With this account, Patricia could have access to her money at any time during the five years.

(A) If Patricia placed all of her money in this regular savings account, how much interest would she earn in the first year?

(B) Assuming Patricia makes no withdrawals, how much money will be in the account at the end of five years?

(C) What is the effective interest rate of this investment?

(D) Another local bank recently began to offer quarterly compounding of interest on regular savings accounts. This bank pays an interest rate of 5% per year, nominally. If Patricia places all of her money in such an account and makes no withdrawals, how much money will be in the account at the end of five years?

(E) What is the percentage increase, over the initial investment, of the final amount from question (D)?

Answers

(A) $F = P(1 + i)^n = (\$25,000)(1.05) = \$26,250$
interest = $\$26,250 - \$25,000 = \$1,250$

(B) $F = \$25,000\ [F/P, 5\%, 5] = \$31,907$

(C) $(\$31,907 - \$25,000)/(\$25,000) = 0.2763$, or 27.63%

(D) The effective interest rate is .05/4 = .0125. For interest compounded quarterly, the nominal annual rate of 5% is an effective quarterly rate of $(.05)/(4) = 1.25\%$. Total number of compounding periods = (5 years)(4 periods/year) = 20 periods.
$P = \$25,000\ [F/P, 1.25\%, 20] = 25,000(1.2820) = \$32,050$

The tables did not provide rates for 1.25%, so the factor was obtained by direct calculation:

$$F/P = (1 + r)^n$$

so

$$[F/P, 1.25\%, 20] = (1 + 0.0125)^{20} = 1.2820$$

This amount after five years ($32,050) due to quarterly compounding is greater than the amount with annual compounding ($31,907).

(E) The effective interest rate is:

$$(\$32,050 - \$25,000)/(\$25,000) = 0.2820, \text{ or } 28.2\%$$

Townhouse Investment. Another option is the purchase of a small income-producing townhouse in an older part of the city for $110,000. This purchase price includes all legal fees and transfer taxes. A bank has offered Patricia a 20-year mortgage for $90,000 at 8% interest with an annual carrying charge of $8,000, which represents a payment on principal and interest due once each year. She makes a down payment of $20,000. In addition to the cost of financing, Patricia estimates the other annual expenses (real estate taxes, utilities, insurance, repairs) to be $12,600 per year.

Patricia anticipates that she will be able to obtain a monthly income from rent of $1,800. If Patricia purchases the property, she would have to sell after five years. Based on a careful study of similar buildings in the area, Patricia believes that she could get $120,000 (after broker fees and other selling costs) for the building after five years. At that time, about $4,700 of the mortgage will have been paid off.

(F) What is the net income during each year of ownership?
(G) What is the net income generated by the sale of the building at the end of year 5?
(H) Because Patricia could invest elsewhere and receive an 8% rate of return, by what factor must the first year's net income be discounted to determine its present value?
(I) What is the total present value of the five-year net cash flow produced by the property?
(J) What is the total future value at the end of year 5, of the five-year net cash flow produced by the property?
(K) Compared with the initial investment, what is the effective interest rate of the amount from question (J)?

Answers
(F) Annual rental income: ($1,800)(12) = $21,600
Annual expenses: ($8,000) + ($12,600) = $20,600
Annual net revenues: $21,600 − $20,600 = $1,000
(G) Remaining mortgage = $90,000 − $4,700 = $85,300

continued on next page

Cash after sale = $120,000 – $85,300 = $34,700

(H) Determining the right discount rate is difficult. An appropriate answer is the rate of the best alternative. In this case, 8% would seem appropriate.

(I) $P = \$1,000[P/A, 8\%, 5] + \$34,700[P/F, 8\%, 5]$
$= 3,993 + 23,617 = \$27,610$

(J) Using the present value calculated in part (I), and converting it to a future value provides
$F = \$27,610[F/P, 8\%, 5] = \$27,610(1.4693) = \$40,567$

(K) ($40,567 – $25,000)/$25,000 = 0.6227, or 62.27%.

Which alternative should Patricia choose? Running the townhouse is more profitable, but it also involves effort and nuisances, and cleaning and fixing the place up. For instance, the opportunity cost of her time for running the townhouse should be included in these calculations, but it was not. The opportunity cost would be the highest value of her time in an alternative activity, such as the wages she could earn if she were not spending time on the townhouse or the value she places on her leisure time. On the other hand, if she enjoys running a townhouse, then those benefits would be considered an opportunity cost of putting the money in a bank and not running the townhouse. Here is another example where, even in private investment decisions, economics can help to inform a decision, but other factors can be important.

REVIEW QUESTIONS

1. You purchased a new car for $15,000, used $5,000 as a down payment, and took out a loan for the remaining $10,000. Your loan is for five years at a 12% interest rate per annum, compounded monthly. What are your monthly payments?

2. You plan to deposit money in a certificate of deposit that pays 8% (nominal) per year, compounded daily. What effective interest rate will you receive (a) annually, and (b) semiannually?

3. How much money would you have, 10 years from now, if you deposited $600 now, $300 two years from now, and $400 five years from now into a savings account with an effective interest rate of 5%?

4. Which would provide a greater present value: an investment that generated $100 a year for five years, or an investment that generated $50 a year for ten years? Answer the problem for two effective annual interest rates: 1% and 10%. How does the interest rate affect the present value of future amounts?

5. What is the difference between the interest rate and the discount rate?

COST-BENEFIT ANALYSIS

Government agencies and private firms regularly make decisions on whether and how to spend resources. These investment decisions often have impacts beyond the present budget year. Benefits and costs can occur for years, if not decades, after initial decisions are implemented.

Cost-benefit analysis (CBA) provides a method for categorizing and quantifying the costs and benefits, that occur over time, of a project, plan, or policy. This method also provides a way to compare alternatives, and to weigh the benefits and the costs. This leads to a basic decision criterion of CBA: If the benefits are greater than the costs, then the action is presumed to be justified on economic principles. Yet this is also a basic criticism of CBA. Cost-benefit analyses should help to inform the decision, not make the decision, especially when costs and benefits are not strictly monetary.

This chapter begins with fundamental concepts and examines the conceptual and analytical differences between CBA in the private and public sectors. It then details the process of conducting a cost-benefit analysis and assessing various costs and benefits. This discussion leads to a section that presents and compares different approaches for project evaluation, weighing the benefits against the costs. This chapter concludes with a look at some of the strengths and limitations of CBA and ways to improve its use in public decision making.

COST-BENEFIT ANALYSIS: PRIVATE VERSUS PUBLIC DECISIONS

In order to evaluate projects, cost-benefit analysis requires placing benefits and costs in monetary terms. Although this approach may be appropriate and straightforward for a private firm, it can be more difficult for public decisions.

Recall that the private sector goal is typically to maximize monetary profits. But public sector goals are often broader, such as to maximize net social benefits.[1] Yet

---

[1] Recall that *net social benefits* are social benefits minus social costs, where benefits and costs are broadly considered.

many social costs and social benefits are difficult to identify and quantify, and may not have clear market prices. Even if all social benefits and costs could be measured in monetary terms, public decisions often require considering more than monetary effects.

Cost-benefit analysis provides a useful framework and systematic approach for evaluating projects. In addition, CBA may be required for a decision. In 1981, President Reagan issued Executive Order 12291, which required federal agencies to conduct cost-benefit analysis for regulations.[2] It also established, within the Office of Management and Budget, a review and clearance policy: Only regulations for which benefits exceeded costs (according to the CBA) could be issued. In 1993, President Clinton issued Executive Order 12866, which continued the requirement for agencies to conduct cost-benefit analysis,[3] but modified the review and clearance policy. For instance, under Executive Order 12866, the benefits need to *justify* the costs, whereas previously, in Executive Order 12291, the benefits needed to *exceed* the costs for the regulation to proceed.

Cost-benefit analysis has also been called *benefit-cost analysis* (BCA). Both refer to essentially the same method. The term *cost effectiveness analysis* (CEA), however, refers to a different approach. In CEA, the objective is to find the most cost-effective or least-cost way to implement a decision.[4] In a sense, CEA focuses on half of a CBA—the cost side. The approach of CEA is commonly used when a decision has already been made, and the goal is to minimize costs of implementation, or when the benefits of alternatives are difficult to determine or alter, and the goal is to find the most cost-effective alternative.

Figure 13-1 provides examples of CBA for both the public sector and private sector. Notice that a "parking deck" appears in both categories. It will be used to illustrate four main differences between private sector and public sector cost-benefit analysis—differences that can make public sector CBA more complex.

1   *The scope of the decision.* The public sector agency would need to include not only the impacts on the agency itself, but also impacts on the broader community. These impacts would include costs and benefits to parking deck users, employers, residents, downtown pedestrians, and businesses, as well as effects on commuting patterns, natural resources, and road congestion, among others. In contrast, the private sector firm would normally include only those costs and benefits directly affecting the firm, such as direct construction costs and revenues from users of the parking deck.

2   *The types of benefits and costs.* For benefits, the public sector agency should include not only revenues from the parking deck, but also consumer surplus, which is the net benefit accruing to consumers that use the parking

---

[2] Executive Order 12291 (February 17, 1981), 46 FR 13193.

[3] Executive Order 12866 (September 30, 1993), 58 FR 51735.

[4] *Cost effectiveness* can be measured in terms of cost per unit of outcome, such as the dollars per life saved or dollars per acre of land preserved.

FIGURE 13-1 *Examples of Private Sector and Public Sector Cost-Benefit Analyses*

	Private Sector	**Public Sector**
Projects	Office buildings Computer systems Manufacturing facilities Parking decks	Airports Dams Highways Parking decks
Policies	Pension plans Training Health care Relocation	Environmental protection Minimum wage Antitrust Health care

deck. Other public benefits would include reduced congestion and parking on neighborhood streets, for instance. The private firm, however, would probably only count revenues and not consumer surplus nor other public benefits. For costs, the public sector agency should include not only construction and maintenance costs, but also costs such as lost revenues from other parking decks in the city, and increased pollution imposed upon neighboring residences. The private sector firm would probably not include those externalized costs, unless they directly affected the firm's profits.

3 *The consideration of transfers.* Transfers are a shift of resources from one group to another within the scope of the defined public. From a public sector perspective, some benefits or costs do not appear in the final analysis because they are simply transfers. Suppose that the city charges $5 per day to park in the deck, and that only city residents may use the deck. From a public sector perspective, the fees would constitute a transfer from the people who use the deck to the rest of the community. The construction of the parking deck, at the outset, represents a transfer from the community (in terms of public funds and resources) to the beneficiaries of the parking deck. Also, the parking deck may operate even if it were not creating a monetary profit to the city, which would also constitute a transfer from the community to the parking deck beneficiaries. From a private sector perspective, the construction and operation of the deck would be considered as costs, and the fees would be considered as benefits. If the deck were not profitable, then the firm might not continue to operate the deck.

4 *The monetization of benefits and costs.* A challenge in public sector CBA is trying to place monetary values on nonmonetary goods, such as adverse

health effects caused by pollution. Another challenge is determining the appropriate discount rate to compare benefits and costs that occur over time. For a private sector decision, the choice of a discount rate is often straightforward, such as what the funds could earn in an alternative investment. For a public sector decision, the choice is not at all clear. Consider, for instance, a decision to allow electric vehicles to use the parking deck for free. That could result in cost savings to nearby residents in terms of reduced pollution, noise, and health effects. How are these cost savings valued over time? That is, what is the appropriate social discount rate? At a 10% discount rate, saving 117 lives, 50 years from now, is worth only one life now. But one might argue that each person, 50 years from now, is at least as important as one life now. (Issues concerning the social discount rate are examined later in this chapter.)

We have just looked at perspectives of private and public sector decisions. We will now look at how costs and benefits are determined and evaluated in order to help make decisions.

COST-BENEFIT ANALYSIS AND EFFICIENCY

In the previous chapters, we focused on a certain type of efficiency: *Pareto efficiency*, also called *Pareto optimality*. According to this standard, everyone is as well off as possible without making someone else worse off.

Cost-benefit analysis employs a different type of efficiency: *Kaldor-Hicks efficiency*, or *potential Pareto efficiency*. According to this standard, some are made better off, some are made worse off, but it is possible (in theory) for the gainers to fully compensate the losers, so that at least one person is better off and no person is worse off. In other words, as long as net benefits are positive, the decision is a potential Pareto improvement.

Some concerns, however, accompany the application of this type of efficiency to public decisions. The first is the distribution of costs and benefits. Even though net (monetary) benefits are positive, the distribution of benefits and costs may not be equitable or socially desirable. Collapsing costs and benefits into a single summary number, as in a cost-benefit analysis, can obscure distributions. The second, and related to the first, is that those who bear the costs are not necessarily those who gain the benefits, and vice versa. This disparity becomes more pronounced in intergenerational decisions, where present consumption often benefits this generation but at the expense of future generations.

Third, compensation occurs in theory. For the Pareto improvement to occur, the beneficiaries of a decision would need to fully compensate the losers. This also would assume that the cost-benefit analysis completely and accurately assessed all social costs and social benefits, and to whom they would accrue, in order for a full compensation to occur. Fourth, a potential Pareto improvement, although it maximizes net benefits in monetary terms, could in some cases reduce net societal utility (as we examined in Chapter 6). Fifth, for public decisions, economic efficiency is often not the only or primary decision criterion. Even after costs and benefits are determined, the final decision requires an explicit consideration of factors such as equity and political feasibility, which may not be answerable by a formula of benefits and costs.

PERFORMING A COST-BENEFIT ANALYSIS

Public expenditures almost always have effects that extend beyond the current year and beyond the target population. The full range of impacts should be evaluated to determine the ways in which a decision will affect a community, both favorably and adversely.

Consider a community government's decision whether to fund a public program. Before the program begins, the community (which includes individuals, firms, and government) possesses a set of resources. These resources include all the community's goods and services that are of value, such as money, property, labor, natural resources, and civic pride. When the government enacts the program, it expends some of these resources and, in return, a new set of resources is created. In addition to the program's effect on the amount of available community resources, specific resources may be redistributed among individuals. Therefore, both total benefits and costs and their distribution are important to program evaluation.

For many programs, a simple "back-of-the-envelope" analysis of costs, benefits, and equity impacts can often provide officials with sufficient information to make a reasoned decision. Thorough investigations of program costs, benefits, and distributional effects take time and money, and public officials must determine which decisions will benefit from extensive CBAs.

In general, the greater the potential impacts of the program, the greater the potential value of a systematic comparison of alternatives. In addition, controversial decisions can benefit from formal analyses. If a consensus exists that a particular spending proposal should be approved, then an elaborate comparison will be of little use. If a debate about a program is expected, however, then the factual base provided by a systematic evaluation can help focus the arguments on the key issues and trade-offs.

The next section provides the framework and methods for conducting a cost-benefit analysis and providing such a factual base. For the sake of simplicity, this section will use the term *program* to refer to the decision, even though the decision can also refer to a project, plan, or policy.

Basic Analytic Procedure for Cost-Benefit Analysis
1   Develop alternatives (including the "no-action" alternative).
2   Determine the scope of the decision (including "the public," temporal scale, and spatial scale).

3 Determine the costs of each alternative.
4 Determine the benefits of each alternative.
5 Quantify the costs and benefits of each alternative.
6 Evaluate the costs versus the benefits.
7 Evaluate the equity impacts.

DEVELOP ALTERNATIVES

Alternatives are the heart of any decision. Developing alternatives for cost-benefit analysis is an important but relatively neglected activity. Historically, attention has focused on analyzing alternatives in a given set, rather than trying to develop new and perhaps superior alternatives for that set. The process of developing alternatives should be an iterative and collaborative process, because improved alternatives can emerge, especially in consultation with the public.

Decision makers need to devote effort to generating all feasible alternatives, including alternative approaches, not just alternative designs. For instance, consider a proposed highway project. An alternative approach to a six-lane highway would be the expansion of a light rail system. An alternative design would be a four-lane highway instead of a six-lane highway. As another example, alternative approaches to constructing a new government building could include sharing or converting existing buildings or leasing a building from the private sector. An alternative design would be a different layout for the new building. One alternative should always be the "no-action" alternative. Here, *no-action* usually means maintaining the status quo, rather than stopping all activity.

Alternatives can be influenced by different biases. Agencies are inclined to focus on alternatives within their purview or mission, which can limit their consideration of alternative approaches (especially if it would involve transferring funds to other agencies). The framing of a problem will also influence the range of alternatives proposed. If the problem of highway congestion is viewed as lack of highway capacity, then proposed solutions will focus on building additional highways. Another framing of the problem may lead to other alternatives to reduce congestion, such as expanding public transit, building sidewalks, and implementing demand management programs.

To be included in the final set of analyses, alternatives often must meet several criteria: economic, environmental, equity, technical, and political, among others. Sometimes the alternative that is best from one criterion may fail to pass other criteria. For instance, even though putting a highway through the middle of an established residential area may be the most cost-effective route, it could fail to meet the criteria of social and environmental acceptability.

DETERMINE THE SCOPE OF THE DECISION

Public programs can affect a community in complex ways, so a complete evaluation of costs, benefits, and distributional aspects of a program may prove difficult. The magnitude and scale of a program's costs and benefits can rarely be predicted with certainty, especially in programs that last many years. Nonetheless, the process of trying to identify the impacts and the affected public is crucial to program evaluation.

Even the most cursory evaluation needs to assess the impact of the decision on the appropriately defined public or community. This assessment requires deciding which costs and benefits are relevant and which community resources would be used and created, with and without the program. It also highlights the importance of determining whether to use a broad or a narrow definition of community. A fundamental issue in cost-benefit analysis, especially in analyses for state or local political jurisdictions, is deciding whether broader community effects should be included in the analysis. For instance, a new airport in a city will have effects on other communities throughout the state, and even on other states.

Determining the relevant "public" can intersect with the issue of who or what has *standing*; that is, which entities have a right, justification, or duty to be considered within the scope of analysis.[5] One approach to determining standing is based on legally defined rights. For instance, in a CBA for a national policy on public education, should undocumented immigrants have standing? If courts determine that children of undocumented immigrants have a right to public education, then those children would reasonably have standing and be included in the CBA. On the other hand, reliance on legally defined rights could lead to unacceptable exclusions. For instance, if a federal CBA were conducted 100 years ago, it might exclude women because, at that time, they did not have the legal right to vote. Therefore, other factors often need to be considered in determining the scope of the public.

Another approach is based on impacts. Here, entities should be considered in the CBA if they accrue benefits or incur costs from the decision. For instance, consider a city that receives federal funds to help build a water treatment plant to reduce river pollution. The city could, in its CBA, consider the effects on downstream cities. The rationales are that federal funds are involved and thus a broader jurisdictional perspective could be adopted; also, downstream cities would be affected by the actions and thus would, in theory, be willing to pay to reduce pollution in the river. On the other hand, the city could argue that it is responsible only for its residents, and that by including other cities, its own benefits and costs could receive less influence in the CBA. The city could also argue that trying to account for all the impacts of its decision could be an infinite task, so the scope needs to be reasonably limited to its own political jurisdiction.

A CBA could also be extended to include effects on future generations. For instance, a CBA concerning hazardous waste disposal should examine the potential effects of human exposure to the waste both now and in the future. A CBA could also consider effects on nonhumans, such as specific plant or animal species, even though CBAs are typically anthropocentric.

---

[5] See, for example, W. N. Trumbull (1990), "Who Has Standing in Cost-Benefit Analysis?" *Journal of Policy Analysis and Management*, 9(2): 201–218.

Once the scope of the decision and the affected public have been defined, a CBA can link program activities to changes in community resources. This process will help to clarify the relative merits of alternative projects. The standard approach of cost-benefit analysis is to translate costs and benefits into monetary amounts. Yet many object to the notion of measuring everything on a single scale: money. Moreover, many public objectives, such as equity, cannot be adequately reduced to that scale. Nonetheless, analysts should assign values to measurable impacts of the project and keep a systematic accounting of impacts that cannot be measured in monetary terms.

Cost-benefit analysis seeks to provide a clear framework for evaluating the relative merits of alternative decisions, even if the measurements of the costs and benefits are often not clear. Thus, it is important for analysts to provide more than just numbers: They need to provide and explain sources of uncertainty and assumptions in the calculations, lest the numbers be perceived as more accurate than they are.

DETERMINE THE COSTS OF EACH ALTERNATIVE

Defining and Assessing Costs

The costs of public decisions can be viewed in three categories: (1) purchases of resources by governments, businesses, households, and individuals, (2) resources already owned, and (3) intangible costs. In principle, a program's costs can be valued according to direct expenditures, opportunity costs of using resources, and indirect measures such as willingness to pay.

The first category of costs is relatively clear, and includes outlays of funds for construction, operation, maintenance, supplies, labor, and other market goods. Standard financial analysis for private firms usually deals with these types of costs. Cost-benefit analysis for public decisions, however, often requires a more complete accounting of resources. Purchases include not only those by the government but also those by others within the scope of analysis. For instance, costs for a new parking deck would include not only the government agency's cost of construction and maintenance, but also the costs to residents who need to relocate because of the deck.

The second category, previously acquired assets, such as land or office space, may represent a real program cost, even though no monetary outlay may be directly related to the program. The extent of the cost depends on opportunity cost: the potential alternative uses of the resources. For example, the use of city-owned land for a parking deck could reduce the amount of land available for other uses, such as a medical facility or recreation. In this instance, using previously owned land generates real costs to the residents of the city—costs that can be measured in terms of the value of the forgone benefits of other uses.

Using this same example, suppose that the city has two options: one is to build and operate a parking deck, and the other is to sell the site to a private firm that would construct a parking deck. Proponents of a municipally built parking deck argue that it would be less expensive for the city to build the structure than for a private operator to purchase, construct, and operate the facility. They claim that, because the city already owns the land, the only costs under this option would be for construction and operations. Because a private firm would have to buy the land, it would need to charge higher fees in order to recover its costs.

From a community-wide perspective, the proponents' argument is not entirely accurate because it neglects the opportunity cost to the city of using the land for the deck. The costs of using scarce publicly owned land, buildings, and equipment can be overlooked or underestimated because they do not entail a current monetary outlay. Yet these resources have many alternative uses, so committing them to one program entails an opportunity cost. Therefore, the cost calculations for each option should contain the land's estimated market value, or the highest value of the land in an alternative use.

The third category of costs recognizes that government programs often require some sacrifice or loss of intangible resources, such as clean air. Although such losses can represent important costs of a program, their monetary value often is impossible to fully measure. At the same time, it is important to try to describe the loss of intangible resources associated with a program.

As a first step, costs can be assessed in terms of changes in physical measurements, even in the absence of monetary equivalents. For instance, changes in air quality can be measured by changes in levels of criteria pollutants. The associated costs (or benefits) would include, among others, the impacts on health and quality of life of citizens. To assess those costs, indirect measures of individuals' willingness to pay could be obtained. For example, houses in areas with clean air or quiet streets may cost more than similar houses in areas lacking these amenities. These cost differences reflect the willingness of individuals to pay for intangible resources. But those types of measures assume perfect markets and perfect information. Even though it may be difficult to assign even an approximate monetary value to costs involving individual and societal welfare, it does not mean that intangible costs should be omitted from decision-making. In fact, these types of costs may be the most significant to a decision. The cost-benefit analysis should try to identify the types of expected impacts, even if they cannot be quantified. If the costs are quantified, any estimates need to be accompanied with explanations of the underlying assumptions, methods of assessment, and sources of uncertainty.

Distinguishing Between Real Costs and Transfers

When resources are neither created nor lost but merely shifted from one entity to another within the defined scope of the decision, the shift is called a **transfer**. Unlike a real cost, a transfer does not decrease a community's total amount of resources. Instead, transfers merely alter the distribution of resources. Most programs involve real costs, real benefits, and transfers.

Consider, for example, a local property tax abatement program that would reduce the property tax payments of elderly people. If the program were implemented, the burden on other taxpayers would increase to compensate for the abatements. Opponents of the program claim that these tax increases would be a cost for the community. But from the perspective of the community as a whole, this program would be a transfer rather than a cost. The program would transfer resources (tax money) from taxpayers to elderly people, but it would not decrease the community's total amount of resources, if the benefits and costs were fully offsetting.

This example, however, assumed that the amount of the tax increase would directly equal the amount of the tax abatement, leaving a zero-sum balance. In many cases of transfers, however, both sides of the ledger (benefits versus costs) do not always equal out. For instance, the implementation of the tax will cause a loss in efficiency (a deadweight loss) that would be considered as a real cost, not a transfer, because social surplus is lost with no offsetting gain. For proper accounting, it is important to itemize all costs and all benefits. In cases of complete or partial transfers, the benefits and costs will completely or partially compensate for each other.

Although transfers are distinct from real program costs, they do represent an important aspect of government programs. By carefully distinguishing transfers from program costs, it is possible to focus attention on distributional aspects of a decision.

DETERMINE THE BENEFITS OF EACH ALTERNATIVE

Defining and Assessing Benefits

Benefits represent additions to the resources of the community that result from a program or project. They include (1) resources that generate revenue, (2) resources that are created, freed, or conserved by a program, and (3) intangible benefits.

The determination of benefits requires determining the relevant community, because many programs generate benefits for nonresidents. Consider, for example, a proposal to build a city park and recreational facilities. Opponents argue that many of the park's potential users will not be residents of the city, and that the city should not build facilities for nonresidents. Proponents argue that the concept of community, for these recreational facilities, should include not only the city's residents but also their close neighbors. There is no simple answer on whether to include the benefits accruing to nonresidents in an analysis. Ultimately, the decision often depends on program characteristics, political factors, and the willingness of city residents to pay for programs benefiting nonresidents.

A program's benefits should be measured by estimating how much new value the program creates for a community. Public programs often produce benefits that are difficult to value in terms of monetary amounts. So, for measurement purposes, benefits can be divided into three groups, just as they were for costs: (1) resources measurable in monetary terms, (2) resources measurable in physical units, but not in monetary terms, and (3) resources valued but not quantifiable.

In the first category, many benefits involve resources sold in the marketplace, and for these goods, the market price reflects the marginal willingness of some individuals to pay for this resource. Consider, for example, the benefits associated with the creation of an electric bus shuttle system. For a nominal fee of 50 cents, residents of a community can ride the shuttle all day and get off and back on the shuttle to shop at local businesses. These revenues (50-cent rider fee, shopping expenditures) represent a benefit to the city, even though they may not capture all of the benefits that citizens and businesses derive from the electric shuttle.

In the second category, even if the monetary value of some benefits cannot be determined, they can be described in discrete units. For instance, this shuttle system reduces vehicular traffic, pollution, and congestion. Although these types of benefits are difficult to measure in monetary terms, the improvements can be measured in physical terms, such as vehicle miles traveled, which may facilitate comparison with other transportation projects.

In the third category, the shuttle also would increase the community's sense of pride and cohesiveness, and increase low-income ridership. In addition, the electric shuttles would replace the diesel-fueled buses that bothered residents. Even though these benefits are intangible and difficult to fully quantify, they are nonetheless important benefits.

Distinguishing Between Real Benefits and Transfers

When a program redistributes resources among groups of individuals, these actions often are mistakenly counted as new benefits instead of transfers. From a recipient group's perspective, the program appears to produce benefits. But the gain to the recipient group may result from a loss to some other group in the community. Unless new resources are created from within or from outside, the program has only resulted in transfers rather than new benefits.

Consider a citizen group's attempt to win support for the construction of a new set of bleachers at the local high school football field. The group urged the school committee to construct the bleachers and to begin charging admission to the school's games. The group claims that within 10 years, the admission fees will have covered the construction costs. So, from the eleventh year onward, the bleachers will create additional revenues for the community.

From a community perspective, the bleachers and the enjoyment they provide can be counted as a new benefit, but not the admission fees—not even during the first 10 years. This is because no new resources will be created when spectators—assuming all are from the community—pay money to sit in the bleachers. The admission fees represent a transfer from spectators to taxpayers. If out-of-state spectators were to attend, then those could be counted as new benefits, but only if the scope of the cost-benefit analysis were limited to the community, in order to count these admission fees as outside resources coming in. Although increased revenue, taxes, sales, and property values are frequently cited as benefits, they are often partial transfers among individuals within a community. They are true benefits only if they make new resources available to the community.

QUANTIFY THE COSTS AND BENEFITS OF EACH ALTERNATIVE

The quantification of costs and benefits over time is one of the most difficult tasks of cost-benefit analysis. Difficulties arise because many public benefits and costs do not have market value equivalents. For instance, methods to compute lost wages do not necessarily incorporate pain and suffering of individuals. Surveys of willingness to pay have been subject to criticism because individuals may be poor judges of the value of the good in question, such as health impacts of environmental changes. Moreover, low-income individuals may have a lower willingness to pay than high-income individuals, even though both groups may suffer similar impacts, because the lower-income group has a lower ability to pay.

To perform a cost-benefit analysis, costs and benefits need to be brought into an equivalent measure, such as present value, which employs the technique of discounting as detailed in Chapter 12. But here arises another challenge. *What is the appropriate discount rate?*

The Influence of Discounting

The choice of the discount rate is critical to cost-benefit analysis. As we have seen, the choice of the discount rate can significantly influence the present value benefits and costs, and the relative desirability of projects. The effect of discounting is the following: Projects with *benefits earlier* and *costs later* look more favorable (have a higher net present value) at *higher discount rates*. Projects with *costs earlier* and *benefits later* look more favorable at *lower discount rates*.

This effect can be illustrated by the following example. A city official must decide whether to spend money to purchase equipment for park maintenance or for street repairs. Table 13-1 presents the costs and benefits of both projects. The net present value (NPV) is defined as the difference between benefits and costs, all placed in present value terms (see Table 13-1, top half).

Using a 5% discount rate, the NPV of both projects is positive, and the NPV of Project A ($2,253) is greater than Project B ($2,079). At a 10% discount rate, the NPV of Project A ($846) is less than Project B ($1,293). At the lower discount rate, Project A is preferred because the benefits come later than for Project B. At the higher discount rate, Project B is preferred because benefits come earlier than for Project A. Indeed, we could calculate that at discount rates over 14%, the NPV of Project A becomes negative (–$89), but the NPV of Project B is still positive ($744). For discount rates over 21%, the NPV of Project B also turns negative (–$80) and the NPV of Project A becomes more negative (– $1,413).

The choice of a discount rate becomes even more difficult when dealing with benefits and costs that are not strictly monetary. Many decisions place a value on human life, either explicitly or implicitly, through the process of cost-benefit analysis. For instance, a CBA may compare the costs of implementing a safety regulation, such as a seat belt law, against the number of lives potentially saved. The value of the life can be determined by comparing the cost of implementation to the number

TABLE 13-1 *Comparison of Alternatives by Different Methods of CBA*		
	Project A Purchase Park Maintenance Equipment	**Project B** Purchase Street Repair Equipment
Initial Investment	-$8,000	-$8,000
Savings		
Year 1	$1,000	$6,000
Year 2	2,000	2,000
Year 3	2,000	2,000
Year 4	7,000	1,000
* * * * * * * * * * * * * * * *		
NPV (5%)	$2,253	$2,079
NPV (10%)	$ 846	$1,293
B/C ratio (5%)	1.28	1.26
B/C ratio (10%)	1.11	1.16
Internal rate of return	13.6%	20.3%
Incremental ROR		
(selected when MARR =)	5%	10%
Payback period	4 years	2 years

of lives saved. But how are lives saved in the future compared to lives saved in the present? That is, if we are willing to spend $1 million to save one life today, how much should we spend today in order to save a life in 15 years?

One answer, using a 10% discount rate, would be approximately $240,000. This 10% discount rate had been prescribed for nearly 20 years (1972–1992) by the Office of Management and Budget, for cost-benefit analyses.[6] After two decades of the 10% rate, the Office of Management and Budget recommended a lower rate, 7%,[7] bringing the present value of one life, 15 years from now, up to approximately $360,000. Still, even this rate has been widely criticized as being too high and inappropriate for public sector decisions.

Thus, we see that the questions of assigning monetary values to nonmonetary goods and selecting an appropriate discount rate become entangled with ethical questions. A discount rate places a lower value on future resources and opportunities, and the higher the discount rate, the lower the valuation of the future. Discounting also diminishes the role of prevention, and assumes that current problems, such as environmental degradation, will not become any worse if we wait to address them. Because

---

[6] OMB Circular A-94, March 27 (1972).

[7] OMB Circular A-94, October 29 (1992).

public sector decisions are not just purely financial decisions, and often involve noneconomic harms, one discount rate may not be appropriate to use for all projects. Many argue that discounting cannot reasonably be used to make trade-offs involving noneconomic harms within this generation nor between this and future generations.[8]

The Choice of a Social Discount Rate

Deciding which discount rate to use for societal decisions has been widely debated, and understandably so, because the rate can significantly influence the outcome of a cost-benefit analysis, and because of the ethical and distributional implications. Despite the quantitative certainty of discounting algorithms, and despite the volume of literature on social discounting, no clear consensus has emerged on the appropriate social discount rate. This section reviews some of the most commonly employed discount rates for public sector decisions and discusses the implications of each.

One commonly recommended rate is the "social rate of time preference." This is the rate at which society is willing to trade off present consumption for future benefits. Many economists argue that this rate should be low, about 1%–2%.[9] This rate would value the well-being of future generations as less but nearly equal to the well-being of the present generation.[10] A second approach is to use the "social opportunity cost of capital." This is what resources could earn in their highest alternative use. These alternative uses include domestic investment, domestic consumption, and foreign borrowing.[11] A third is the rate for relatively risk-free investment, such as government bonds. A fourth is the discount rate used by the private sector. As we have seen, public sector analyses differ philosophically and analytically from private sector decisions, so applying the private sector rate may not be appropriate for public decisions.

---

[8] For an important discussion of the limitations of cost-benefit analysis and discounting, see L. Heinzerling and F. Ackerman (2002), *Pricing the Priceless: Cost-Benefit Analysis of Environmental Protection*, Georgetown Environmental Law and Policy Institute. Available at: http://www.law.georgetown.edu/gelpi/papers/pricefnl.pdf.

[9] The social rate of time preference for intergenerational discounting has been viewed as having two components. The first is a pure time preference that is arguably zero, meaning that the well-being of future generations is equally important as the well-being of the current generation. The second considers the increase or decrease in wealth among generations. Because it is assumed that future generations will likely be wealthier than present generations, a positive discount rate is justified. If growth were to decline, a zero or negative rate could be justified. Taken together, the recommended discount rate is positive but small.

[10] A discount rate of zero would value the well-being of future generations as equal to the well-being of the present generation. A negative discount rate would value the well-being of future generations as greater than the well-being of the present generation.

[11] See R. C. Lind (1982), "A Primer on the Major Issues Relating to the Discount Rate for Evaluating National Energy Projects," in R. C. Lind et al., *Discounting for Time and Risk in Energy Policy*, Washington, DC: Resources for the Future, pp. 21–94.

In practice in the United States, government discount rates vary widely. The U.S. Office of Management and Budget (OMB) directs federal agencies to use a 7% discount rate. The U.S. Congressional Budget Office (CBO) generally favors a 2% discount rate for policies with long-term social implications. And some agencies do not discount at all.[12] Appropriate ranges appear to be between 0% and 7%, and for decisions with uncertain future impacts or high risks, a lower rate is often applied.

EVALUATE THE COSTS VERSUS THE BENEFITS

A cost-benefit analysis requires that benefits and costs be placed in equivalent terms, such as present values, in order to weigh the benefits and the costs. This section covers methods for evaluating benefits and costs, and for ranking alternative projects. These methods are net present value, annual value, benefit-cost ratio, internal rate of return, incremental rate of return, and the payback period.

Net Present Value Method

The **net present value (NPV)** method takes all benefits and costs over the life of the project, discounts them to present value terms, and then subtracts costs from benefits to obtain the net present value (NPV) of the project.

Algebraically, the NPV method can be represented as follows

$$\text{NPV} = \left[\sum_{t=0}^{n} \frac{B_t}{(1 + r)^t} \right] - \left[\sum_{t=0}^{n} \frac{C_t}{(1 + r)^t} \right]$$

where

t = the time period
r = the discount rate
n = the life of the project
B_t = the benefits in time period t
C_t = the costs in time period t

or, in simplified notation:

$$\text{NPV} = \Sigma B_{\text{PV}} - \Sigma C_{\text{PV}}$$

where

ΣB_{PV} = the sum of all benefits in present value terms
ΣC_{PV} = the sum of all costs in present value terms

---

[12] See C. Bazelon and K. Smetters (1999), "Discounting Inside the Washington D.C. Beltway," *Journal of Economic Perspectives* 13(4): 213–228.

The typical decision criterion is that if NPV > 0, then the project is justified. Similarly, if the choice is among projects requiring the same initial investment, all of which have a NPV > 0, select the one with the highest NPV. This method typically employs the methods from Chapter 12 in order to calculate present values.[13]

The strengths of this method are that it is widely used, and it provides a way to compare magnitudes of net benefits among projects. The shortcomings are that it is difficult to accurately and appropriately assess costs, benefits, and discount rates, which are shortcomings inherent to most methods of CBA. Another problem is the time frame for analyses, typically the life of the project. Many benefits and many costs occur even after the end of the project.

Another method, called **annual value** (or **annuity**), is equivalent to the net present value method. Benefits and costs for each project are translated into their equivalent annuities, instead of present values, and then compared. The strengths and shortcomings are the same as with the NPV method, primarily the quantification of benefits and costs and the determination of the appropriate discount rate.

Benefit-Cost Ratio

This method is similar to the net present value method in that both methods place benefits and costs in present value terms. The **benefit-cost ratio (B/C ratio)** divides costs into benefits, whereas the net present value method subtracts costs from benefits.

The B/C ratio is the sum of all discounted benefits divided by the sum of all discounted costs. Algebraically, this method is represented as follows:

$$\text{B/C} = \frac{\left[\sum_{t=0}^{n} \dfrac{B_t}{(1 + r)^t}\right]}{\left[\sum_{t=0}^{n} \dfrac{C_t}{(1 + r)^t}\right]}$$

where

t = the time period
r = the effective discount rate
n = the life of the project
B_t = the benefits in time period t
C_t = the costs in time period t

or, in simplified notation:

---

[13] Recall that the present value (P) of a future amount (F) dollars, with n number of payments (or here, time period), and an effective discount rate of r is equal to: $P = F/(1 + r)^n$.

$$B/C = (\Sigma\,B_{\text{PV}})\,/\,(\Sigma\,C_{\text{PV}})$$

where

$\Sigma\,B_{\text{PV}}$ = the sum of all benefits in present value terms
$\Sigma\,C_{\text{PV}}$ = the sum of all costs in present value terms

The typical decision criterion is that if $B/C > 1$, then the project is justified. Unlike the NPV method, however, comparing magnitudes of B/C ratios for different projects may not be that instructive, because magnitudes of costs and benefits themselves are obscured. For instance, one project may have a higher B/C ratio, but yield a smaller net benefit. In the example below, Project #1 has a higher B/C ratio, but a much smaller NPV.

	Benefits	Costs	B/C	NPV
Project #1	$ 100	$ 25	4	$ 75
Project #2	$100,000	$50,000	2	$50,000

Another issue with the B/C ratio is its sensitivity to definitions of costs or benefits. It matters whether something is counted as a positive benefit or a negative cost, because it determines whether it goes in the numerator or denominator, and thus it will influence the B/C ratio. For instance, in a CBA for a crime prevention program, the reduction of crime could be considered an addition to benefits (increased safety) or a subtraction from costs (decreased crime). This problem with sensitivity to definitions arises with the other methods as well.

Returning to the example in Table 13-1: At a discount rate of 5%, the B/C ratio of Project A would be 1.28 and Project B would be 1.26. At a discount rate of 10%, the B/C ratio of Project A would be 1.11 and Project B would be 1.16. The B/C ratio for all projects is greater than 1.00, so each would be justified according to this criterion.

B/C, 5% (Project A) = ($10,253)/($8,000) = 1.28
B/C, 5% (Project B) = ($10,079)/($8,000) = 1.26

B/C, 10% (Project A) = ($8,846)/($8,000) = 1.11
B/C, 10% (Project B) = ($9,293)/($8,000) = 1.16

Internal Rate of Return

The **internal rate of return (IRR)** is widely used by private sector firms to make capital investment decisions. It has also been used by public sector agencies to evaluate public investments.

The IRR method tries to find the rate r that sets the net present value of cash flows equal to zero. This value of r solves the following equation:

$$\left[\sum_{t=0}^{n} \frac{B_t}{(1+r)^t} \right] = \left[\sum_{t=0}^{n} \frac{C_t}{(1+r)^t} \right]$$

where

t = the time period
r = the internal rate of return
n = the life of the project
B_t = the benefits in time period t
C_t = the costs in time period t

or, in simplified notation:

Find r such that

$$\Sigma B_{PV} = \Sigma C_{PV}$$

where

ΣB_{PV} = the sum of all benefits in present value terms (using r to discount benefits)
ΣC_{PV} = the sum of all costs in present value terms (using r to discount costs)

The decision rule associated with the IRR method is that a decision maker should undertake a project or investment if the internal rate of return (r) on the project is greater than the discount rate. In other words, investment in this project would yield a higher rate of return than an alternative use of resources. An extension of that rule, for several projects, is to select the project that yields the highest IRR.

Shortcomings of this method are that the value of r that solves the equation may not be unique; more than one solution may exist.[14] In addition, the method assumes a single discount rate over the life of the project, and reinvestment at the internal rate of return, not the discount rate. In contrast, the NPV method and B/C ratio assume that net income is reinvested at the discount rate, and both allow different discount rates to be used. Also, like the B/C ratio, the IRR does not convey information about magnitudes of benefits and costs; it is a percentage. Finally, the question again arises about the appropriate discount rate against which to compare the IRR.

The IRR can be readily calculated with the aid of a spreadsheet or computer program. Using the example in Table 13-1, set the net present value of the cash flows for each project equal to zero, and solve for r. This calculation yields the IRR for Project A as 13.6%, and the IRR for Project B as 20.3% (Table 13-1).

Incremental rate of return analysis (ROR) is an approach for comparing multiple and mutually exclusive alternatives. The alternative selected will be the one that

---

[14] Multiple solutions for r can occur when net benefits change more than once between positive and negative values during the time period of discounting.

has the largest initial investment (within budget limits), and that justifies the extra investment over another acceptable alternative, according to a minimum acceptable rate of return (MARR).

In this approach, the IRR is calculated for each incremental investment to determine whether a project satisfies a MARR. The process is as follows:[15]

1   Order the alternatives from the *smallest* to the *largest* initial investment. For each alternative, list the cash flows (benefits minus costs) for each time period. Note that the alternatives need to have equal lives, and they need to be "revenue alternatives" (with positive and negative cash flows, not only negative cash flows).

2   Calculate the IRR for the first alternative (the one with the smallest initial investment). If IRR < MARR, then eliminate the first alternative and move to the second. If IRR ≥ MARR, then that alternative is acceptable and kept. Then call the first alternative the "defender," and the second alternative the "challenger." (If no alternative has IRR ≥ MARR, then the no-action alternative is the only acceptable one.)

3   Calculate the incremental cash flow between the challenger and defender, using the formula:
incremental cash flow = challenger cash flow − defender cash flow.

4   Calculate the IRR for the incremental cash flow series.

5   If IRR < MARR, then the challenger is eliminated, the defender remains, and the next alternative becomes the challenger. If IRR ≥ MARR, then the challenger becomes the defender, the previous defender is eliminated, and the next alternative becomes the challenger.

6   Repeat steps (3) through (5), between pairs of alternatives (challenger and defender), until only one alternative remains, which is then the selected one. Note that a challenger must always be compared with a defender that is an acceptable alternative with IRR ≥ MARR.

Using the example in Table 13-1, we illustrate this process. Assume a MARR of 10%. Also assume a third project is under consideration, Project C, which has an initial investment of $10,000 (Year 0), and annual benefits as follows: Year 1 ($5,000), Year 2 ($3,000), Year 3 ($2,000), Year 4 ($4,000). (See Table 13-2.) The IRR for Project C is 16.2%.

1   Both Project A and Project B have the same initial investment. So either one could be the initial defender. We will order them from Project B (first) to Project A (second), and then Project C (third).

2   The IRR for Project B is 20.3%, which is greater than the MARR of 10%, so it becomes the defender, and Project A becomes the challenger.

---

[15] For details on incremental ROR, see L. Blank and A. Tarquin (2002), *Engineering Economy*, 5th ed., New York: McGraw Hill, pp. 266–301.

TABLE 13-2 *Comparison of Alternatives by Incremental Rate of Return Analysis*

	Project A	Project B	Project C
Initial Investment	−$8,000	−$8,000	−$10,000
Savings			
Year 1	1,000	6,000	5,000
Year 2	2,000	2,000	3,000
Year 3	2,000	2,000	2,000
Year 4	7,000	1,000	4,000
Rate of Return	13.6%	20.3%	16.2%

First Pairwise Comparison	Project A (challenger)	Project B (defender)	Incremental Cash Flow (challenger – defender)
Initial Investment	−$8,000	−$8,000	$0
Savings			
Year 1	1,000	6,000	−5,000
Year 2	2,000	2,000	0
Year 3	2,000	2,000	0
Year 4	7,000	1,000	6,000
Rate of Return	13.6%	20.3%	6.3%

Second Pairwise Comparison	Project C (challenger)	Project B (defender)	Incremental Cash Flow (challenger – defender)
Initial Investment	−$10,000	−$8,000	−$2,000
Savings			
Year 1	5,000	6,000	−1,000
Year 2	3,000	2,000	1,000
Year 3	2,000	2,000	0
Year 4	4,000	1,000	3,000
Rate of Return	16.2%	20.3%	9.6%

First Pairwise Comparison

3 The incremental cash flow, with Project A as challenger and Project B as defender, using data from Table 13-2, is as follows (Project A challenger – Project B defender): Year 0 ($0), Year 1 (–$5,000), Year 2 ($0), Year 3 ($0), Year 4 ($6,000).

4 The IRR for this incremental cash flow is 6.3%, which is less than the MARR of 10%.

5 Thus, the challenger (Project A) is eliminated and the defender (Project B) remains.

6 Repeat steps (3) through (5), for each successive round of pairwise comparisons.

Second Pairwise Comparison

3 Next, Project C is the challenger and Project B is the defender. The incremental cash flow (Project C challenger – Project B defender) is as follows: Year 0 (–$2,000), Year 1 (–$1,000), Year 2 ($1,000), Year 3 ($0), Year 4 ($3,000).

4 The IRR for this incremental cash flow is 9.6%, which is less than the MARR of 10%.

5 Thus, Project B remains the defender, and Project C is eliminated as the challenger. Because all projects have been evaluated in pairs, and Project B remains, it is the one selected.

Repeating the process with a MARR of 5%, it can be shown that Project A would be selected over Project B and over Project C. How could Project A be selected, if it has the lowest internal rate of return (IRR) of all three projects?

This result illustrates an important point with the incremental ROR approach. It assumes that one project will be selected, and that funds not spent on the project will be invested in another way, earning at least the MARR. So even though Project C had a higher internal rate of return than Project A, it also required a larger initial investment (an additional $2,000), which evidently did not yield an incremental ROR that equaled or exceeded the MARR of 5%. And even though Project B had a higher internal rate of return than Project A, and they both had the same initial investment, Project A had benefits later, which makes it more favorable at the lower discount rate of 5%.

Payback Period

The **payback period** method uses, as its decision criterion, the amount of time that it takes for a project to recover its cost. The project that recovers its cost in the shortest period of time is the one chosen. Costs and benefits are *not* discounted in this method.

Although this method is fairly straightforward to apply, it can provide misleading results because it does not consider the time value of money, nor the benefits and costs after the project cost is recovered.

For example, consider two alternative projects with the following cash flows. Using the payback period rule, the decision maker would select Project #1 because it recovers the initial $500 investment within two years, whereas it takes Project #2 three years to recover the investment. However, if full costs and benefits were considered, the decision maker would likely select Project #2 because it generates significant additional benefits after Year 2.

	Year 1	Year 2	Year 3	Year 4
Project #1				
Costs	$500	0	0	0
Benefits	$200	$300	0	0
Project #2				
Costs	$500	0	0	0
Benefits	$200	$200	$1,000	$1,000

Turning again to the example in Table 13-1, the payback period for Project A would be four years, because the sum of (nondiscounted) benefits does not equal or exceed the $8,000 investment until after four years ($1,000 + $2,000 + $2,000 + $7,000 = $12,000), and after three years, the payback is only up to $5,000. The payback period for Project B would be two years, because it pays back the investment of $8,000 and starts to generate benefits after the end of the second year ($6,000 + $2,000 = $8,000).

Comparison of the Methods

To illustrate how different methods can provide different results, consider and compare the two projects in Table 13-1.

Using the NPV method, at a discount rate of 5%, Project A would be chosen, but at a discount rate of 10%, Project B would be chosen.

Using the B/C ratio, all projects would be acceptable, based on the criterion of the B/C ratio greater than one. Using a decision criterion of the highest B/C ratio (which may not be appropriate), at discount rate of 5%, Project A would be chosen, but at a discount rate of 10%, Project B would be chosen.

Using the IRR method, a decision maker would choose Project B, because its IRR (20.3%) is greater than Project A's IRR (13.6%). Using the Incremental ROR method, at 5% MARR, Project A would be selected, and at 10% MARR, Project B would be selected.

Using the payback period, Project B would be chosen because it pays back the initial investment after two years.

Thus, different methods and discount rates for cost-benefit analysis can yield different results with different implications for decisions.

EVALUATE THE EQUITY IMPACTS

Few programs will affect every member of a community equally. Although programs often transfer resources from one group to another, this implies that one group may receive most of the benefits while another group bears most of the costs. These distributional implications can be as important as a program's total benefits or costs. Many programs have been rejected on equity grounds, even if aggregate benefits exceed aggregate costs. This section examines equity impacts, outlines a methodology for evaluating these impacts, and presents examples to illustrate the trade-offs between equity and efficiency.

As we saw in previous chapters, there is no single criterion or method for evaluating and measuring equity impacts. Yet practically every public program has some implications for equity, whether it changes the present distribution of resources or keeps the same distribution. Identifying and evaluating equity impacts can be an enormous task, but the basic objectives can be accomplished by following three steps:

Step 1: Identify which group receives each benefit and which group incurs each cost.
Step 2: Quantify, as far as possible, the program's impact on each group.
Step 3: Determine the distribution of costs and benefits, and how it might affect the program's desirability.

To proceed with the analysis, members of the community can be classified into groups according to characteristics such as income, age, family size, race, and ethnicity. Using a carefully defined set of subgroups, a systematic analysis can help to determine a program's equity or distributional impacts. Merely identifying the types of costs and benefits that each group incurs may sometimes be sufficient because the equity impacts may be so overwhelming or inconsequential that further consideration is unnecessary. If more information is needed, then the costs and benefits to each group should be assessed.

Consider, for example, a proposed program with the benefits and costs within a community consisting of four individuals as shown in Table 13-3.

TABLE 13-3   *Example of Distribution of Benefits and Costs; Net Benefits Positive*

	Susan	Laura	Debra	John
Benefits	$10	$100	$10	$10
Costs	-$20	-$20	-$20	-$20
Benefits – Costs	-$10	+$80	-$10	-$10

Net Benefits = (– 10 + 80 – 10 – 10) = $50

From an economic perspective, the net benefits (+$50) would suggest that the program should be implemented, because the total benefits are greater than the total costs.

Suppose, however, that Laura is a wealthy individual, and that Debra, John, and Susan are poor individuals. In this program, the wealthy individual has a net gain (+$80) and the poor individuals have net losses (–$10 each). Is this equitable? Further, even if a project has net economic benefits, overall social utility could decrease with a transfer from the poor to the wealthy, because the marginal utility of income is typically less for wealthy individuals than for poor individuals (as we studied in Chapter 4).

Consider another example, shown in Table 13-4.

From an economic perspective, the net benefits (–$10) are negative, which would suggest that the program should not be implemented, because the total benefits are less than the total costs. But this program redistributes wealth from the more affluent to the less affluent. So from an equity perspective, this program may be more desirable. Further, overall societal utility could even increase with a transfer from the wealthy to the poor, because the marginal utility of income is typically greater for poor individuals than wealthy individuals.

COST-BENEFIT ANALYSIS: STRENGTHS AND LIMITATIONS

Cost-benefit analysis should be viewed as one tool in a toolbox of methods that can help in decision making. If it is used, its limitations, assumptions, and potential for misuse should be recognized. This section examines the strengths and shortcomings associated with the use of CBA in decision making.

Strengths of cost-benefit analysis are that it provides a straightforward, systematic approach for organizing information and evaluating programs, using a single metric: money. The process of performing a CBA can encourage decision makers to

TABLE 13-4 *Example of Distribution of Benefits and Costs; Net Benefits Negative*

	Susan	Laura	Debra	John
Benefits	$20	$20	$20	$20
Costs	–$10	–$60	–$10	–$10
Benefits – Costs	$10	–$40	$10	$10

Net Benefits = (–40 + 10 + 10 + 10) = –$10

take a hard look at the potential impacts of a program, both positive and negative. The process can also make explicit the basis for a decision and the factors considered, which otherwise may have remained undocumented. Yet the strengths of CBA may have corresponding shortcomings.

First, even though a single metric—money—provides ease of evaluation, all benefits and costs do not necessarily have monetary equivalents. Even for benefits and costs that could be, in some sense, represented by monetary amounts, the process of converting a program impact (such as improved health) into a monetary amount, for a specific time period, can be difficult and subject to inaccuracies. Moreover, impacts that don't have monetary values are often omitted from cost-benefit analyses, even though those impacts may have a large social significance. For instance, many effects are not inherently economic, but concern more fundamental social attributes, such as justice.

Second, uncertainty underlies cost-benefit analysis. It is practically impossible to predict all the future impacts of a program, let alone their magnitudes and their probabilities of occurrence. Analysts generally focus on coming up with numbers to represent costs and benefits, and thus produce a summary number. However, collapsing all benefits and costs into a single number does not reveal the assumptions on which that number is based. Bottom-line myopia sets in, and crucial information about sources of uncertainty is obscured.

Third, analyses can produce varying results. As we saw, even when using the same numbers for costs and benefits, different methods for CBA produced different recommendations. The determination of what is a benefit and what is a cost can influence the result. Also, the costs and benefits of one project may be affected by other projects. The discount rate is highly influential and controversial; it implicitly devalues the future, and the higher the rate, the greater the devaluation.

Fourth, cost-benefit analyses have been criticized for being used to justify or influence a decision, rather than to inform a decision. It can be relatively easy to "construct" a CBA to produce a desired outcome. If the original answer is not as desired, the analyst can go out and find more benefits or more costs. This approach has tended to promote "paralysis by analysis"—a fixation with generating data and analyses rather than using CBA to make informed decisions.

Fifth, CBA has also been criticized for its failure to adequately consider issues of equity, both intragenerational and intergenerational. A potential Pareto improvement is not the same as an actual Pareto improvement unless the redistribution actually takes place. In decisions involving intergenerational impacts, compensation may be practically impossible. A larger concern is that discounting implicitly favors present consumption over future consumption. At most discount rates, benefits and costs in the future can appear relatively insignificant in the present. The result may be a tendency to approve projects that promote short-term consumption at the expense of long-term societal welfare. So at some point, we must ask the question that economics cannot answer: What is the legacy we want to leave for future generations?

REVIEW QUESTIONS

1. Proponents of the construction of a new shipping facility in your city's harbor argue that it is a desirable investment for the state because it will create thousands of jobs. Assume that these jobs will be filled by individuals who are already employed in the state. How would you account for this employment effect in a cost-benefit analysis?

2. A city is planning to construct a swimming pool that would only be open to city residents. In one plan, the city would pay for the facility out of local tax dollars and allow city residents to swim free of charge. In a second plan, the city would charge a $1 admission fee for residents and pay for any remaining deficit out of local taxes. Estimates suggest that, at a price of $1, the pool would attract a daily average of 200 swimmers for each of the 100 days of operation. Reduction of the price to zero would increase the average attendance to 300 swimmers per day. No significant additional costs would be incurred to expand the use from 200 to 300 swimmers per day. The facility would have enough capacity to serve 300 swimmers per day without crowding.

   a) Explain why the admission fees collected under the second plan are a transfer payment.

   b) Which of the two pricing options represents a more efficient use of the proposed facility? Explain.

   c) In order to estimate the benefits of the project under the zero pricing plan, the city estimated the consumer surplus of the pool users and also the potential impact on nearby housing values. Should both estimates be included as benefits to the project? Explain.

3. Suppose your agency faces two possible projects having net benefits shown in the following table. Both projects have initial capital costs of $100 and annual benefits spread over four years. Which project would be best at (a) higher discount rates, and (b) lower discount rates?

Project	0	1	Year 2	3	4
I	-$100	$115	$ 0	$ 0	$ 0
II	-$100	$ 20	$30	$50	$170

4. Your city is evaluating a proposed parking garage. This garage would have a capacity of 600 spaces, and the city would charge $4 per space per day. The city expects the cost of the garage (averaged over the life of the garage) to be $3 per space per day. As part of its evaluation, the city surveyed the five private garages in a neighboring, similar city. This survey obtained the following information, which was used to construct a demand curve for the proposed parking garage.

Garage	Price per Day	Number of Spaces Used per Day
1	$4	600
2	$2	800
3	$5	500
4	$3	700
5	$7	300

On the basis of this information, answer the following questions:

a) What would be the total benefits per day to users of the garage?

b) What would be the net benefits per day to users of the garage?

c) What would be the net benefits per day to the city?

d) What is the consumer surplus to users of the garage?

e) Should the city build a garage with more than 600 spaces? How many more? What price should it charge?

f) Do these calculations include all the benefits and costs or transfers? Explain.

5. Analysts argue that traditional cost-benefit analysis is purely an efficiency test and is free of judgments about equity. Do you agree with this argument? Explain your answer. How would you consider equity in a cost-benefit analysis?

COST-BENEFIT APPLICATIONS

This chapter presents three examples of cost benefit analyses. The first CBA involves a proposed bridge to supplement ferry service to an island. It follows the cost-benefit analysis process that was outlined in the previous chapter. The second CBA concerns recreational facilities on undeveloped parcels of land, and the differential impacts on various groups within the community. The third CBA evaluates a policy that was enacted to reduce air pollutants, and the costs and benefits that accrued during more than two decades. Each of the three examples illustrates a type of cost-benefit analysis, respectively: (1) *ex ante*, which is conducted before the implementation of an activity; (2) *in medias res*, which is conducted for an ongoing activity; and (3) *ex post*, which is conducted after the implementation of an activity, as a retrospective evaluation.[1] Throughout the examples, we investigate and discuss the considerations, techniques, and subtleties of performing a cost-benefit analysis, including both public sector and private sector perspectives.

COST-BENEFIT PROBLEM: SULTAN ISLAND BRIDGE

Sultan Island, a small island off the coast of Maine, can presently be reached only by ferryboat. The ferry service, which is privately owned and operated by a Sultan Island company, makes eight round trips daily and numerous unscheduled trips in response to passenger requests.

The ferry services an annual average of 50,000 one-way vehicle crossings at a fare of $0.50 per vehicle, which provides annual average revenues of $25,000. Vehicle passengers are permitted to ride for free, as are individuals making the crossing without their motor vehicles. The cost of operating the service is $20,000 per year, so owners of the ferry make an annual average profit of $5,000.

Residents of Sultan Island depend heavily on this privately owned ferry service, which is the only way to access the mainland. Consequently, they have become

---

[1] Here the "activity" can refer to a project, plan, program, policy, or other type of decision with benefits and costs.

increasingly concerned about the ferry service raising its fares, decreasing its service, or going out of business.

To address these concerns, the Sultan Island planning board met to explore alternatives to the ferry. A favored alternative is building a bridge that would link the island to the mainland. Engineering data suggest that the least expensive bridge would run from the unpopulated northern end of the island to the mainland and would cost $500,000 to build. (The ferry operates from the relatively populated central part of the island.) Currently, neither state nor federal funds are available for the project. All bridge costs would have to be paid by bridge tolls or local tax revenues.

Although the ferry service is fast and dependable and the bridge project would involve substantial construction costs, the bridge project nonetheless has many supporters. Proponents argue that construction of the bridge would reduce the cost of travel to and from the island. Moreover, construction of the bridge would protect island residents from the uncertainty of an arbitrary fare increase or a discontinuation of ferry services.

For all practical purposes, residents would be indifferent between using a ferry to cross to the island or using a bridge. Both would take approximately the same amount of time for a crossing. The determining factor on which would generate more trips would be the price charged. If the bridge toll were greater than $0.50, more vehicles would use the ferry. At a bridge toll of less than $0.50, more vehicles would be diverted to the bridge, and the ferry might eventually go out of business. The main distinctions between the bridge and the ferry would be the fares and the degree of public control of the services.

Sultan Island planners decided to use a cost-benefit analysis to assist in decision making. Their process follows the basic analytic steps outlined in the previous chapter:

Cost-Benefit Analysis Process
1 Develop alternatives (including the "no-action" alternative).
2 Determine the scope of the decision.
3 Determine the costs of each alternative.
4 Determine the benefits of each alternative.
5 Quantify the costs and benefits of each alternative.
6 Evaluate the costs versus the benefits.
7 Evaluate the equity impacts.

After going through the analysis by the Sultan Island planning board, we provide additional discussion on their use of the cost-benefit analysis, and raise considerations important in this framework.

DEVELOP ALTERNATIVES

As mentioned, the Sultan Island planning board is considering building a bridge that would link the island to the mainland. They considered alternative designs, such as bridge locations and sizes. They also evaluated alternative approaches, such as buying the existing ferry service or establishing a public-run ferry service. The planning board decided that the only viable option would be building a bridge. The other alternative would be "no-action" or the status quo: not building the bridge and continuing to rely on ferry service.

DETERMINE THE SCOPE OF THE DECISION

The Sultan Island planners identified four groups of individuals affected by the project: Sultan Island taxpayers, ferry owners (who are Sultan Island residents), existing travelers, and new travelers. Because the bridge would be constructed and operated using local funds, the planners decided to limit the scope of "the public" to island residents, even though the project would almost certainly have effects on mainland residents. In terms of the temporal scale of the decision, the planners decided to consider costs and benefits over the life of the proposed bridge project. The spatial scale would be Sultan Island, and the travelers to and from the island.

DETERMINE THE COSTS OF EACH ALTERNATIVE

Currently, the ferry provides an average of 50,000 one-way vehicle crossings per year, at a fare of $0.50 per vehicle. This operation generates average total revenues of $25,000 per year. The cost of operating the service is $20,000 per year, resulting in an annual profit of $5,000 to the ferry company.

Figure 14-1 displays the number of crossings that would be made, assuming various bridge tolls. These estimates indicate that if no bridge tolls were charged, the bridge would attract 150,000 one-way vehicle trips per year—an increase of 100,000

FIGURE 14-1   *Demand for Bridge Crossings*

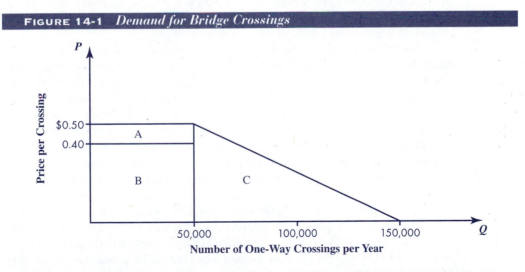

trips per year over the ferry service. At a toll of $0.50, the bridge would service 50,000 one-way vehicle trips per year, the same number of trips serviced by the ferry and at the same price.

If the bridge were operated without charging tolls, then all of the costs of the bridge would be paid by local tax revenues. The costs include the capital costs of borrowing $500,000 at a rate of 5% per year ($25,000 per year), plus annual maintenance and operating costs ($15,000 per year), bringing the cost of the bridge to $40,000 annually.

Building the bridge and operating without a toll could cause the ferry service to shut down. The costs of operating the ferry are $20,000 per year, including ferry boat rental charges, operators' salaries, and fuel. The ferry company can terminate at will its leasing agreement, in which case the boat and the operators would be reassigned to another ferry operation at the same salary. The main effect of service termination on the ferry owners is the loss of profits. With 50,000 vehicles at $0.50 per vehicle, the ferry generated $5,000 profit annually. This profit is displayed as area A in Figure 14-1 and equals the difference between the $0.40 average per vehicle cost and the $0.50 per vehicle fare for each of the 50,000 vehicles.

DETERMINE THE BENEFITS OF EACH ALTERNATIVE

Even though the taxpayers and ferry owners could lose as a result of the bridge project, vehicle owners who had used the ferry crossing could gain. If the bridge were operated without a toll, each of the initial 50,000 ferry crossings could be made at a savings of $0.50 per crossing, for an annual average savings of $25,000. This savings to existing travelers (Figure 14-1) is the sum of area A plus area B. Note that the loss in profit to the ferry owners (area A) is offset by a corresponding gain in consumer surplus to the existing ferry riders (area A plus area B). The net difference between these losses and gains (area B) is equal to the ferryboat operating expenses that would no longer be incurred if the bridge were built.

The potential gains for the new travelers crossing the bridge are more difficult to evaluate. At a fare of $0.50, some potential travelers were almost willing to ride the ferry. For others, the trip would be made only if the crossing were free. The island planners assumed that the demand relationship between fares and the number of vehicle crossings (above 50,000 per year) was linear and they constructed a demand curve as indicated in Figure 14-1. They also assumed that no vehicle owner would be willing to pay more than $0.50 for a bridge crossing, as long as the ferry service was available. As a result, the planners estimated that the average gain for each of the 100,000 new crossings was $0.25, for a total annual gain of $25,000. This is area C in Figure 14-1.

The estimated gain of $25,000 for new travelers is their gain in consumer surplus. It represents the sum of the differences between the maximum each would be willing to pay for the crossing and the amount they actually pay (in this case equal to zero). Even though the planning board defined the public as island residents, they decided to include consumer surplus accruing to travelers who were nonresidents as well. In the case where the demand curve is linear and downward sloping (creating a triangle-shaped area of consumer surplus), the value of generated or additional use will be equal to one-half the change in price times the quantity increase, which is (1/2)($0.50)(100,000) = $25,000. (This formula is frequently employed in project evaluation, especially for small changes in price for which the linearity assumption is a reasonable approximation.)

QUANTIFY THE COSTS AND BENEFITS OF EACH ALTERNATIVE

The preceding determination of costs and benefits involved straightforward calculations, based on monetary revenues and costs. Sultan Island planners realized, however, that many costs and benefits resulting from this project would be nonmonetary and more difficult to quantify. At their meetings, the planners discussed these effects.

For one, the bridge could reduce commuting time, so that benefit could be described in average reduction of commuting time. (Although both the ferry and the bridge take the same amount of time for an actual crossing, the ferry often has long lines of cars waiting to board.) On the other hand, if no toll were charged, the number of trips to the mainland is expected to increase threefold. The added motor vehicle traffic would impose costs on many town residents—costs that would not necessarily be reflected in each individual's willingness to pay for bridge crossings. In addition, the construction of the bridge could damage the scenic beauty of the northern portion of the island, as well as the aquatic ecosystem. Finally, by linking the island to the mainland, the bridge could threaten one of the island's most attractive features: its isolation.

The planning board also raised the following: Although a cost-benefit analysis may correctly exclude benefits or costs going to "outsiders," it would be incorrect to ignore the potential costs and benefits that these "outsiders" could impose on Sultan Islanders. If the bridge generates increased tourist traffic, then the impact of this traffic on the island's environment, economy, and isolated character need to be considered.

Unlike the direct impacts, many of the indirect impacts involve aspects that are difficult, if not impossible, to measure. Nonetheless, some members of the board urged the comparison of both measurable and immeasurable aspects of the bridge proposal. They argued that ignoring the intangible factors could lead to an unwise decision, just as ignoring more easily measured effects would alter the analysis. Even though monetary values could not be obtained for all impacts, it was nonetheless important to describe them in some way, such as "increase in daily vehicle miles traveled."

EVALUATE THE COSTS VERSUS BENEFITS

Table 14-1 summarizes the costs and benefits of the proposed Sultan Island Bridge. Simply adding the gains and losses suggests that the bridge project would generate $50,000 in annual benefits to existing and new travelers, and produce $45,000 in

TABLE 14-1 *Effects of the Sultan Island Bridge*	
Previous ferry riders:	
50,000 crossings at a savings of $0.50 per crossing	+ $25,000
New travelers:	
100,000 new crossings with an average consumer surplus of $0.25 per crossing	+ $25,000
Ferry owners:	
Shut down ferry; lose annual profits	– $ 5,000
Taxpayers:	
Bridge expenses of $25,000 for capital costs ($500,000 × 0.05) plus $15,000 for operating costs	– $40,000
Unadjusted net dollar impact	+ $ 5,000

annual losses to the town's taxpayers and the ferry owners. It would mean that the annual net (monetary) benefit of the bridge service, charging no toll, would be $5,000.

Closer examination of Table 14-1 can help to evaluate the distribution of benefits, costs, and transfers. The benefits accrue to existing riders ($25,000) and new riders ($25,000). The costs go to taxpayers ($40,000) and ferry owners ($5,000). The net loss ($5,000) of the ferry owners can be broken up into revenues lost ($25,000) plus cost savings of not operating the ferry ($20,000). This results in an overall net benefit, for the project, of $5,000 ($50,000 in benefits – $45,000 in costs).

According to Figure 14-1, the net benefit is equal to area A and B ($5,000 + $20,000) plus area C ($25,000) minus the annual cost of the bridge to the taxpayers ($40,000) and minus the loss of profits to the ferry owners of Area A ($5,000). Thus area A is a transfer from the ferry owners to the existing ferry riders.

The problem of comparing gains and losses is made somewhat easier because the planners limited the scope of the decision to Sultan Islanders. They assumed that all affected parties are residents, all bridge costs are paid by island taxpayers, and all owners of the ferry company are local residents.

This assumption enabled the planning board to ignore from their calculations certain types of transfers within the scope of the island community. For instance, the bridge would probably bring more shopping to the north end of the island, but this increase would probably be accompanied by a decrease in shopping from the central part of the island, the location of the ferry terminal. If there were no overall increase or decrease in shopping, this would represent a transfer of revenues from one part of the island to another, between store owners who are island residents. It could also be considered as another type of transfer: from residents (who spend more money) to store owners/residents (who receive more revenue). But new net benefits, not just transfers, could come from nonresidents spending money at stores on Sultan Island (additional revenues). Also, new net costs, not just transfers, could come from residents taking the bridge to shop at mainland stores instead of at island stores (loss of benefits).

The planning board discussed these types of benefits and costs, and eventually decided to retain their focus on the direct monetary impacts. They also decided that, to proceed with the bridge project, it would need to show net monetary benefits, but that nonmonetary factors, such as transportation reliability, would probably influence the final decision.

EVALUATE EQUITY IMPACTS

The issue here is how to evaluate the distribution of gains and losses among different groups in order to make a final determination concerning the project. One approach, raised by the planning board, would be to simply add up gains and losses on a dollar-for-dollar basis, and assume that a dollar's worth of benefits or costs is of equal value to all individuals.

The other approach, discussed by the board, would be to attach differential weights to the benefits or costs flowing to certain income groups or classes of individuals. Here, the planners would attempt to link benefits and costs to specific groups defined by income or other characteristics. These group-specific gains and losses could then be weighted before aggregating to obtain a total net benefit amount. Yet it could be quite difficult to attach meaningful weights to each group. Alternatively, the planners could disaggregate the analyses, with benefits and costs displayed for each group, and leave it to policy makers to apply their own judgments and assess relative weights (if any) to the impacts on each group.

In the end, the planning board decided that an unweighted addition of gains and losses would be reasonable. This decision was made because the Sultan Island population is fairly homogeneous, and the potential beneficiaries are, for the most part, the same individuals who are the local taxpayers.

OTHER CONSIDERATIONS FOR THE SULTAN ISLAND CBA

Based on their analysis so far, the Sultan Island planning board decided that the bridge would be a worthwhile project because the benefits exceed costs by $5,000 per year. Moreover, by building the bridge, the planners felt that Sultan Islanders would no longer face the risk of ferry toll increases or service curtailments. Before deciding to build the bridge, however, the planning board decided to seek public comment on their analysis. Several issues were raised.

Where to Build the Bridge

Throughout their analysis, the Sultan Island planners assumed that the bridge should be built at the north end of the island. Engineering data suggested that alternative locations would substantially increase construction costs. For example, locating the bridge close to the ferry terminal would require construction of several deep-water supports and raise the costs of the bridge to nearly $1 million. This fact alone should not imply that the bridge could not be built there. Locating the bridge closer to the current ferry terminal could substantially reduce the travel time to cross over to the mainland. This location could generate additional users and raise the willingness to pay of existing users. Thus, additional benefits could more than compensate for the additional costs of bridge placement, and that alternative should have been considered more thoroughly.

To Build or to Regulate

Some Sultan Island residents expressed concern over the potential abuse of the monopoly power held by the ferry owners. Although no evidence of this abuse existed, residents were fearful that, in the future, the ferry owners could dramatically raise their fares or curtail services, or in some other way fail to consider the essential public nature of their service. As a public carrier, the ferry service was regulated by a variety of state and federal transportation agencies. If the existing regulation became inadequate, Sultan Island had the option of buying the ferry company. So before deciding to build the bridge, the planning staff needed to evaluate the possibility of public operation of the ferry service. By reducing the fares, public ownership could generate traffic similar to the bridge while at the same time alleviating residents' concerns about the risks of private ownership of the vital ferry service.

Discount Rate

As with many projects, the Sultan Island Bridge project involves benefits and costs that occur over many years. The common approach is to convert all costs and benefits to either present value equivalents or annuities, and examine the net benefits. This approach requires the selection of an "appropriate" discount rate. In this example, the planners used a 5% discount rate, which reflected the town's ability to borrow funds.

However, a small change in the discount rate could considerably influence the relative attractiveness of the project. For instance, if the "correct" discount rate were 8%, then the annual cost would be $55,000 ($40,000 for capital costs plus $15,000 for operating costs). This change would alter the net benefits from positive to negative. A larger question is whether the discount rate should reflect the social rate of time preference, or the social opportunity cost of capital, rather than just the cost of borrowing capital.

Risks

In addition to the discount rate, planners should also consider sources of risks and uncertainty. For Sultan Islanders, the risk of future ferry price increases was a primary factor behind the decision to consider bridge construction. Yet the bridge itself is not without risk. Construction cost figures are only approximate, as are projections of operating expenses and ridership. Moreover, once the bridge is completed, Sultan Island could quickly become an attractive tourist spot, an outcome that could alter both the costs and benefits of the project. Potential errors in estimating one or all of these components should be taken into account.

Before deciding whether to begin construction, the planning staff could consider a "worst possible case" scenario. Such a scenario would consider adverse impacts of increased tourism, cost overruns of construction and operating expenses, and other adjustments to allow for potential underestimates of costs and overestimates of benefits. This worst possible case sets the downside risk of the bridge construction—risks that, in fact, may be greater than the risks associated with the ferry service.

To Charge or Not to Charge

Even if the information employed by the Sultan Island planning board were accurate, project evaluation requires both an analysis of the cost of building the bridge and decisions concerning the financing and use of the bridge. For example, one proposal was to cover bridge expenses directly by toll payments, which would likely alter the number of bridge crossings and the estimates of consumer surplus associated with crossings.

Table 14-2 and Figure 14-2 present estimates of the losses and gains associated with a $0.25 toll, compared with the $0.50 toll. At a toll of $0.25, 100,000 one-way crossings would be made: 50,000 existing trips and 50,000 new trips.

TABLE 14-2 *Impacts of Sultan Island Bridge Assuming $0.25 Toll*	
Previous ferry riders:	
50,000 crossings at a savings of $0.25 per crossing	+$12,500
New travelers:	
50,000 new crossings with an average consumer surplus	
of $0.25 per crossing	+$ 6,250
Ferry owners:	
Shut down ferry; lose annual profits	–$ 5,000
Taxpayers:	
Bridge expenses in excess of tolls—tolls equal	
$25,000; bridge expenses equal $40,000	–$15,000
Unadjusted net dollar impact	–$ 1,250

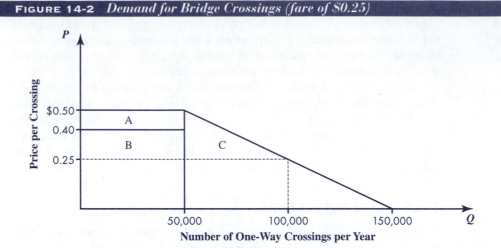

FIGURE 14-2 *Demand for Bridge Crossings (fare of $0.25)*

For existing riders, the change in net benefits (consumer surplus) is $12,500, which is equal to the change in price ($0.25) times existing ridership (50,000). This amount is represented by area A and area B in Figure 14-2.

For new riders, the change in net benefits is $6,250, which is equal to one-half times the change in price ($0.25) times the change in ridership (50,000). This amount is represented by area C in Figure 14-2.

For ferry owners, the losses are the same as in the previous case, but for taxpayers, some of the $40,000 bridge costs are offset by tolls. At a fare of $0.25, the 100,000 crossings would generate $25,000 in revenue. The net loss to the taxpayers would, therefore, be only $15,000.

The plan outlined in Table 14-2 substantially reduces the taxpayers' burden, yet, at the same time, charging a fare reduces the net impact of the bridge project to –$1,250 because of the loss of consumer surplus. If unweighted addition were performed, then building the bridge and charging a fare would not appear to be desirable. The amount of the fare would depend on how decision makers weigh taxpayers' interests against the travelers' interests.

The No-Action Alternative

The planning board's CBA considered only one alternative: the bridge. The point was raised that, at a minimum, the bridge alternative should be compared to the costs and benefits of the no-action alternative. Otherwise, the CBA appeared to serve only the purpose of justifying the bridge project, rather than comparing the proposed bridge project to other reasonable alternatives (including the status quo).

Under the no-action alternative, if the bridge were not built and the ferry service continued to operate, it would generate net annual benefits of $5,000 in annual profit to the ferry company—the same as net benefits from the bridge project. In other words, because the ferry company is considered to be part of "the public," then the net benefits between the two alternatives would be the same, in terms of monetary measures.

Another point was raised: This analysis of the no-action alternative focused on ferry owner profits, and excluded consumer surplus of ferry riders, which would increase the total net benefits of the ferry service. A different demand curve would need to be generated—demand for ferry rides—to account for consumer surplus of ferry riders. Demand for bridge crossings with an existing alternative in place (ferry service), as in Figure 14-1, cannot be assumed to be the same as demand for ferry crossings with no alternative in place (the bridge).

The planners conducted some additional analyses and derived the demand curve as shown in Figure 14-3. As they expected, if no alternative existed, individuals would be willing to pay more than $0.50 to make the crossing. So at a price of $0.50, the consumer surplus would be equal to the willingness to pay minus price, or $12,500 (area D). According to this analysis, the net benefits of the no-action alternative would be $17,500 per year ($12,500 in consumer surplus + $5,000 in ferry owner profits).

Yet another point was raised: Although this analysis for the ferry may suggest that the ferry service provides greater net benefits than the bridge, the analysis for the bridge assumed that the ferry would already be in place. If no ferry were in place, then the demand for bridge crossings would resemble demand for ferry crossings, as in Figure 14-3, assuming that consumers are indifferent between a ferry and a bridge. This situation would also result in consumer surplus equal to $12,500. So the net

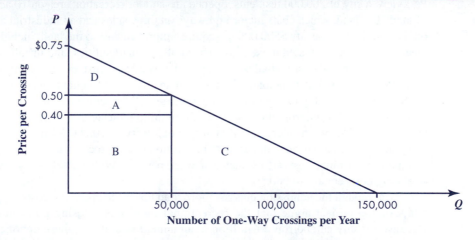

FIGURE 14-3   *Demand for Ferry Crossings (assuming no alternative, such as the bridge)*

monetary benefits for a bridge, with no ferry in place, would also be equal to $17,500 per year.

Other Project Effects

The Sultan Island planning board limited their evaluation to the direct effect of the changes in the number of crossings. It is also important to recognize and trace indirect effects, or feedback effects. For example, bridge construction could cause ferry service to go out of business. This linkage between the availability of bridge service and ferry service is an important part of the Sultan Island analysis. Other potentially important feedback includes the congestion resulting from additional bridge traffic. The congestion effect may be partially offset by the improved accessibility to the mainland, but the added traffic may reduce the value of properties in the northern portion of the island. In addition, the construction of the bridge will almost certainly cause adverse environmental impacts in the surrounding area. Bonding of the bridge may also affect the island's ability to borrow funds in the future. Moreover, tax collections to pay for the bridge may force some low-income residents to leave the island. In short, the effect in one market (such as transportation) often triggers effects in other markets (such as real estate). Although a strictly correct way to perform a cost-benefit analysis is to develop a model of the economy and then forecast the effects "with" and "without" the project, this analysis can be exceedingly difficult. Therefore, analysts often must rely on reasonable approximations of the effects of the proposed project, and then decide which effects will be the most significant for the analysis.

COST-BENEFIT PROBLEM: RECREATIONAL FACILITY

Parkview, a city of 200,000 residents, opened an outdoor recreation area on 10 acres of land. The land, which abuts major highways on three sides and an industrial area on the fourth, cost the city $500,000 to acquire. Improvements to the land, including clearing away accumulated junk, construction of parking facilities, and installation of baseball diamonds, basketball courts, and bike pathways, cost another $500,000. Following the initial plan, prepared by a land management consultant, the city limits the use of the facility to city residents, but charges $0.50 per person for a one-day admission ticket. Data from the first year of operation indicate that with an admission charge of $0.50, the recreational facility would service 70,000 people per year and generate $35,000 in annual revenues. In addition to construction and land acquisition costs, operating costs are estimated at $0.20 per user. With 70,000 users, yearly operating costs equal $14,000.

Even though the admission charges more than cover the operating costs, opponents of the project argue that the recreational facility is a losing proposition. Because the city can borrow $1 million at an annual rate of 5%, these opponents claim that each year of operation is costing the city $50,000 per year ($1,000,000 × 0.05) to cover the costs of construction and land acquisition. Moreover, the city loses the tax revenues on the parcel on an annual basis. Prior to purchasing the land, the city collected $10,500 on the parcel from the owners, a group of land speculators from another state. According to this accounting, the true annual costs of the project are $74,500. These costs are summarized in Table 14-3.

Based on their assessment of the costs, the opponents argue that the facility should be sold at once. In fact, the previous owners offered to purchase the property back for $600,000, assuming that the land will be rezoned for commercial use, the zoning designation prior to the city's acquisition. Reassessment of the property reflecting the higher market value would raise the annual tax revenues to $12,600. Although the merits of selling the parcel are disputed, all available information suggests that the sales price estimate presented by the project opponents is reliable, as is the estimate of the impact of returning the parcel to the tax roles.

Proponents of the project reject selling the land and argue that the city would make the best use possible of the land by providing recreational facilities. Their estimates indicate that the reduction of the admission fee from $0.50 to $0.20 would increase the number of users to 100,000 per year. A further reduction in the admission fee to $0.10 would expand its use to 110,000 people per year. Table 14-4 and Figure 14-4 present estimates of the relationship between the annual use and admission fees. Based on this evidence, the proponents argue that the admission fee should be cut to $0.20, a charge exactly equal to the estimated per-person operating expenses. At this fee, both operating costs and revenues would equal $20,000 ($0.20 × 100,000).

As a recreational facilities planner, you have been asked to answer several questions concerning the Parkview facility described in preceding text. In preparing your responses, you may assume that the demand relationship presented in Table 14-4 (and illustrated in Figure 14-4) is reasonably correct. Moreover, you may assume that no significant impacts will result from the price change other than the direct impacts on the number of users, the cost of the operation, and the revenues collected. In addition,

---

TABLE 14-3 *Parkview Recreational Facility Annual Costs*

Construction and land aquisition costs ($1,000,000 × 0.05)	$50,000/year
Forgone tax revenue ($500,000 × effective tax rate of 2.1%)	10,500/year
Annual operating expenses ($0.20 × 70,000 users)	14,000/year
	$74,500/year

because the facility is well served by existing roadways and public transit, and because recreational trips tend to be "off peak," the expanded use is not expected to add significantly to congestion or pollution in the area. Furthermore, in making your calculations, you may assume that Parkview is a fairly homogeneous community and that cost and demand estimates are fairly reliable.

TABLE 14-4 *Demand for Parkview Recreational Facility*

Admission Fee	Annual Number of Users
$1.20	0
1.10	10,000
1.00	20,000
0.90	30,000
0.80	40,000
0.70	50,000
0.60	60,000
0.50	70,000
0.40	80,000
0.30	90,000
0.20	100,000
0.10	110,000
0	120,000

FIGURE 14-4 *Demand for Parkview Recreational Facility*

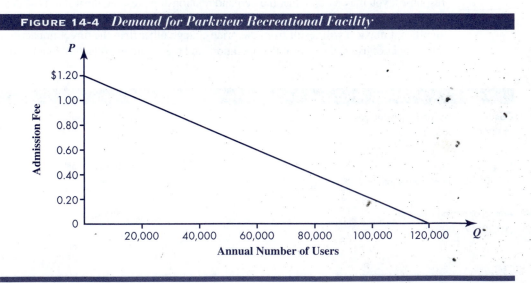

Questions:

a) Calculate the change in net benefits for all park users that would result from a reduction in the admission fee from $0.50 to $0.20.

b) Calculate the change in net operating costs (to taxpayers) resulting from the reduction of the admission fee.

c) What is the annual net cost to the taxpayers of the project, including the opportunity cost of the land and improvement, assuming the entry fee is set at $0.50? What is the annual net cost to taxpayers, including opportunity costs, at $0.20?

d) Based on these estimates of benefits and costs, do you recommend that the city sell the facility? If so, why? If not, should the city operate the facility at a fee of $0.50, $0.20, or some other rate? Why?

Another city in the state, Newland, is considering a similar project. It could purchase land for $500,000, improve the land for $500,000, and operate the recreational facility for the same per-user cost of $0.20. At present, a site similar to the Parkview site is available for purchase from a group of investors from another state. As in the case of the Parkview site, the Newland site consists of 10 acres, is bounded by highways and an industrial zone, and currently generates $10,500 in tax revenues. Moreover, reliable evidence suggests that at each entry fee, the Newland recreational facility would generate the same number of users displayed in Figure 14-4 and Table 14-4. Note, however, that Parkview and Newland would probably not be competing facilities because Newland is located about five hours away from Parkview.

e) Assuming that no significant impacts would result from the project other than the direct impacts of additional recreational use and added taxpayer costs, and assuming again that no equity or risk adjustments are needed, what are the total costs, total benefits, net costs to taxpayers, and net benefits to recreational users that would result if the project were built and admission fees were set at $0.20?

f) Based on an assessment of total benefits and total costs to city residents, should Newland build a recreational facility? Explain why this answer is the same or different from the answer to whether Parkview should operate a recreational facility.

Some people in Newland are concerned that children of low-income households have insufficient recreational opportunities. Yet they argue that providing low-income children with free recreational passes would be demeaning. Instead, they propose that the facility should be made available to all residents free of charge, which would expand users to 120,000. This group argues that the total demand estimates presented

FIGURE 14-5 *Low-Income and Total Demand for Recreational Facilities*

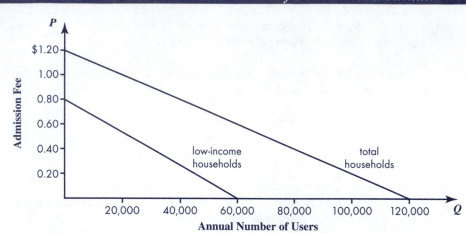

earlier are reliable, but note that at a fee of $0.80, no low-income children use the facility. Figure 14-5 displays the demand relationship for recreational facility use and admission fee. As indicated by the figure, at a zero admission fee, 60,000 of the total demand of 120,000 users would be low-income children, while the remaining users of the facility would be other town residents. Finally, in terms of tax impacts, 20% of the tax dollars are collected from low-income households, with 80% coming from other households in the city.

g) Assuming that no fee will be charged, calculate the benefits and costs of the Newland recreational facility construction project, highlighting the differential impacts of the project on low-income households and other households in the city.

h) How many times would you have to "weight" the net benefits to low-income households to justify the construction of the recreational facility and its operation with no admission fees?

i) What types of costs and benefits were omitted in the analyses for both Parkview and Newland? What does this imply about the use of cost-benefit analysis for decision making?

Answers:

a) Use the area under the demand curve to measure total benefits to consumers, and then subtract the admission fee to measure net benefits:

	Total Benefits	Total Admission Fees	Net Benefits
At $0.50 admission fee	$59,500	$35,000	$24,500
At $0.20 admission fee	70,000	20,000	50,000
Change	10,500	-15,000	25,500

Net benefits for users increase at the lower fee of $0.20.

b) Change in net operating costs to local taxpayers. Net operating costs are equal to total operating costs minus total admission fees. A negative number for "net costs" implies a gain to taxpayers.

	Total Operating Costs	Total Admission Fees	Net Costs (to taxpayers)
At $0.50 admission fee	$14,000	$35,000	-$21,000
At $0.20 admission fee	20,000	20,000	0
Change	6,000	-15,000	21,000

Net costs to taxpayers increase at the lower fee of $0.20, by an amount of $21,000.

c) Annual net costs to taxpayers, including opportunity costs.

	Fee $0.50	Fee $0.20
Operating cost	$14,000	$20,000
Forgone return on sale of land (600,000 × 0.05)	30,000	30,000
Forgone tax revenue	12,600	12,600
Total costs	$56,600	$62,600
Revenues	35,000	20,000
Net costs	$21,600	$42,600

d) Recommend that the city keep the facility because benefits are greater than costs. The fee of $0.20 generates greater net benefits.

	Fee $0.50	Fee $0.20
Benefits (to users)	$59,500	$70,000
Costs (to taxpayers)	56,600	62,600
Benefits – Costs	$ 2,900	$ 7,400

or

	Fee $0.50	Fee $0.20
Net benefits (to users)	$24,500	$50,000
Net costs (to taxpayers)	21,600	42,600
Net benefits – Net costs	$ 2,900	$ 7,400

Note that the admission fees represent a transfer from the users to the taxpayers.

e) Cost and benefits for Newland.

	Fee $0.50	Fee $0.20
Operating costs	$14,000	$20,000
Interest payment	50,000	50,000
(1,000,000 × 0.05)		
Forgone tax revenue	10,500	10,500
Total costs (to taxpayers)	$74,500	$80,500
Total benefits (to users)	$59,500	$70,000
Total costs to taxpayers	$74,500	$80,500
Revenues from admission fees	35,000	20,000
Net costs to taxpayers	$39,500	$60,500
Total benefits (to users)	$59,500	$70,000
Admission fees	35,000	20,000
Net benefits to users	$24,500	$50,000

f) Based on just this analysis, Newland should not build the facility because benefits are smaller than costs (for both fees). The difference in the recommendations is based on differences in the opportunity costs. In the Parkview case, the facility has already been built, so the interest payments on the $1 million are not included, but the forgone return on the sale is included. In the Newland case, the facility has yet to be built, so the interest payments are included.

g) Costs and benefits to Newland with no fee. With no charge, low-income households would receive a net benefit of $7,100 and other households (taxpayers) a net loss of $19,600. Overall, the project produces a net loss of $12,500.

	No fee
Operating costs	$24,000
Interest payment	50,000
Forgone tax revenue	10,500
Total Costs	$84,500
Cost to low-income households (20%)	16,900
Cost to others (80%)	67,600
Total benefits to all users (1/2)($1.20)(120,000)	$72,000
Total benefits to low-income (1/2)($0.80)(60,000)	24,000
Total benefits to others (by subtraction)	$48,000

	Low-Income	Others	Total
Benefits to users	$24,000	$48,000	$72,000
Cost to taxpayers	16,900	67,600	84,500
Benefits − Costs	$ 7,100	−$19,600	−$12,500

h) The net benefits to low-income households would need to be weighted (by approximately three times) to offset the net costs to other households.

$7,100 x weight = $19,600
weight = 2.77

i) This cost-benefit analysis exemplifies the approach taken by many communities to evaluate a proposed project. It focuses primarily on the monetary revenues and costs to the community and to the users of the project. This approach, however, overlooks other sources of benefits and costs that may be important, if not decisive, in the evaluation of the project.

For example, in terms of benefits, analysts for the park facilities did not explicitly consider the following: the benefits of green space and leaving the parcel essentially undeveloped; the increased sales to local businesses in the area; the increased property values around the park; the aesthetic value of the cleaned up property to the community; and the new jobs created by the facility, among other benefits.

In terms of costs, the following were not considered: the opportunity cost of the land in terms of other uses, not just forgone return on a sale or tax revenues; the lost revenue incurred by other recreational sites or businesses in town because of the new park facilities; the health costs to park users (relative to other possible locations), because the facility is located by major highways; and the additional traffic generated by the facility, among other costs.

In the analysis, some of these benefits and costs will cancel each other out, either partially or wholly, and thus they would be considered as transfers (if within the scope of the defined public). For instance, the increased sales to businesses around the park (a benefit) may be offset by the decreased sales to other businesses in town (a cost). Only the net effect, either a gain or a loss, should influence the final analysis.

Finally, what does this example show about cost-benefit analysis? CBA is a useful and systematic approach for considering the impacts of a proposed decision on the public. Yet many impacts are difficult to quantify and include. Thus, a CBA can be a part of decision making, but not the only part. The analysis can help to frame some of the effects and trade-offs of a decision, but it does not substitute for the larger social discussions that are normally a part of public sector decision making.

COST-BENEFIT PROBLEM: AIR POLLUTION CONTROL[2]

In the early 1970s, Tokyo, Japan, sought to curb NO_2 emissions by imposing strict regulations by the national and municipal governments. To assess the effectiveness of this policy, a team of researchers performed an ex post cost-benefit analysis of

[2] Based on A. S. Voorhees, S. Araki, R. Sakai, and H. Sato (2000), "An Ex Post Cost-Benefit Analysis of the Nitrogen Dioxide Air Pollution Control Program in Tokyo," *Journal of the Air & Waste Management Association* 50: 391–410.

Tokyo's NO_2 air pollution control strategies. This study was cited as the first published systematic cost-benefit analysis of Japan's environmental policies.

Nitrogen dioxide (NO_2), a noxious pollutant emitted from motor vehicles and soot-and-smoke-emitting facilities, causes a range of adverse health effects in humans, such as lower respiratory illness, pneumonia, and bronchitis, leading to increased medical costs, reduced productivity, and lost wages in workers. In addition to health effects, NO_2 also causes damage to crops, livestock, buildings, and amenities such as visibility.

The costs and benefits of NO_2 control policies were calculated using environmental, economic, political, demographic, and medical data from 1973 to 1994. Benefits of NO_2 control examined effects on health, productivity, and amenities. Costs of NO_2 control included the implementation of regulations and control technologies.

To estimate benefits, researchers calculated the benefits of past control policies for each city and ward (borough) in Tokyo, using a model of environmental and resource valuation.[3] The air concentrations of NO_2 that would have occurred without pollution control were estimated and compared to the actual post-control concentrations. The Tokyo Metropolitan Government (TMG), the Japan Environment Agency (JEA), and the Environmental Protection Agency (EPA) furnished the data and information required for the research.

Researchers identified three types of air pollution effects: health, productivity, and amenity. Health effects concerned humans, animals, and plants. Productivity effects included lost work time by human workers due to illness, and damage to crops, livestock, and buildings. Amenity effects included both the pleasure derived by visiting a park or natural area for recreational purposes, and the effects of odor, noise, and impaired visibility. Market valuation techniques were used to value health and productivity effects, and contingent valuation, while not applied in this study, was identified as appropriate for amenity effects valuation.

Researchers calculated the increases in NO_2 concentrations that would have occurred in 1994 in the absence of controls, compared to the prepollution control baseline year of 1972. The year of 1994 was chosen because it was the most recent year for which complete data on NO_2 concentrations were available, and because regulations were not changing then. The year of 1972 was selected because it was the last year before governmental NO_2 controls were first required in Tokyo. Measurements used in the calculations included actual reported nitrogen oxides (NO_x) emissions, hypothetical calculated no-control NO_x emissions, the NO_x emission rate, the number of registered motor vehicles in Tokyo, the number of NO_x sources, the number of motor vehicle trips into and within Tokyo per working day, and stationary sources.

Researchers then estimated and valued excess incidences of respiratory illness and lost productivity. Incidences of phlegm and sputum in adults and workers, and

---

[3] Model based on A.M. Freeman, III (1993), *The Measurement of Environmental and Resource Values: Theory and Methods*, Washington, DC: Resources for the Future.

incidences of lower respiratory illness in children (defined as colds going to the chest, chronic wheeze and cough, bronchitis, chest cough with phlegm, and episodes of respiratory illness) were estimated. Human productivity impact in Tokyo due to exposure to NO_2 was calculated using the change in incidence of lower respiratory illness, the change in incidence of phlegm and sputum, the duration of outpatient illness due to pollution, and the percentage of working mothers who stayed at home with sick children aged 5 to 12. Valuation of human health productivity impact was calculated using measures of productivity, the medical expense of illness due to pollution in Tokyo, the value of NO_2 exposure, and the average wage in Tokyo.

To estimate costs, researchers identified both direct and indirect costs of implementing environmental regulations, using a cost control model used by the U.S. Environmental Protection Agency,[4] and procedures used by the Asian Development Bank and the World Bank.[5] Direct costs of past control policies were estimated using data from Tokyo NO_x sources and governmental agencies.

Costs associated with implementing environmental policies were examined in three economic sectors: private, government, and society. Direct costs incurred by the private sector include both capital and operating costs. In addition, regulated industries and the private sector as a whole incurred indirect costs from pollution control requirements. In the case of indirect costs for the private sector as a whole, shifts in economic activity between industries were also examined, including changes in distributions of labor, capital, and other production factors within the economy, and changes in the distribution of goods and services. Government costs consisted of the portion of national and local regulatory agency budgets devoted to implementing and overseeing environmental programs, including personnel, contracts, and financial assistance to regulated businesses. The costs borne by society, here considered as societal opportunity costs, were defined as the forgone income from other uses of a resource, which could not be realized because the resource was used for these environmental regulations.

Researchers estimated direct pollution control costs for soot-and-smoke-emitting facilities, motor vehicles, and national and local governmental costs. The impact of societal opportunity costs was estimated in a sensitivity analysis. To assess the costs of control equipment for the 13,611 stationary sources (baien hassei shisetsu, or soot-and-smoke-emitting facilities) in Tokyo, data were collected from the TMG on the aggregate numbers of each type of NO_x control used by Tokyo boilers and incinerators, 2 of the 15 source categories which together comprised 70% of the sources and 90% of the NO_x emissions in Tokyo. Cost estimates were obtained, for instance, for low-NO_x combustion control techniques and flue gas denitrification techniques by identifying flue gas volumes released by soot-and-smoke-emitting

[4] U.S. Environmental Protection Agency (1990), *Environmental Investments: The Cost of a Clean Environment*, EPA-230-12-90-084, Washington, DC.

[5] J. A. Dixon, L. Fallon Scura, R. A. Carpenter, P. B. Sherman, (1994), *Economic Analysis of Environmental Impacts*. London: Earthscan, in association with the Asian Development Bank and the World Bank.

facilities, and determining the number of facilities in Tokyo within each range of flue gas volumes.

Motor vehicle pollution control costs were estimated using measurements of the number of buses, automobiles, and trucks, in addition to the percent contribution of vehicle type to motor vehicle NO_x emissions, the total cost of NO_x control, and the reduction in NO_x emissions due to pollution control. Government cost data were collected for personnel and financial expenses from the JEA, the TMG, and the national government.

The major findings of the cost-benefit analysis (annualized amounts for 1994) were the following:

1 The estimate of the avoided medical costs in adults was 730 billion yen ($6.08 billion); upper limit 770, lower limit 680.

2 The estimate of the avoided medical costs in children was 93 billion yen ($775 million); upper limit 100, lower limit 86.

3 The estimate of the avoided costs of lost wages in workers was 760 billion yen ($6.33 billion); upper limit 810, lower limit 720.

4 The estimate of the avoided costs of lost wages in mothers caring for sick children was 100 billion yen ($833 million); upper limit 110, lower limit 95.

5 The estimate of the total mean costs for soot-and-smoke-emitting facilities, motor vehicles, and government agencies was 280 billion yen ($2.17 billion); upper limit 300 billion, lower limit 260 billion.

The benefit-cost ratio, using the human health and productivity benefits and annualized capital and operating costs, was 6:1 (1,683 billion yen/280 billion yen). Alternatively, using the highest and lowest values from the sensitivity analyses, the benefit-cost ratio ranged from an upper limit of 44:1 to a lower limit of 0.3:1. Thus, researchers concluded that the benefits of control of NO_2 in Tokyo exceeded the costs for all but a few low-benefit–high-cost scenarios. Moreover, researchers noted that the inclusion of other benefits, such as reduced incidence of other human health effects or reduced ecological impacts, would have increased benefits by 50% to 100% or more. The study recommended that future cost-benefit analyses develop procedures for assigning value to additional human health benefits as well as ecosystem health and productivity benefits.

EPILOGUE

Now that we have studied these theories and tools of economics, let us reflect on what we have learned and look ahead to where economics can go from here. Throughout this text, we have emphasized that economics is designed to help decision makers, not replace them. Economics can be used to clarify benefits and costs, to compare alternatives, and to evaluate effects of decisions. Yet economic analyses need to be tempered by human judgment and, for public decisions, viewed within the context of larger societal goals. Economists often say that any decision can be evaluated using economics—that it is just a matter of doing the economics "right"—whether it means placing a monetary value on something inherently nonmonetary or attempting to compare projected future amounts with present amounts. Yet economic tools are often imprecise, and analyses can be performed and interpreted in different ways. Subjectivity and uncertainty often underlie seemingly objective and convincing economic analyses. Therefore, it is important to understand the assumptions and values underlying these analyses, and to keep in mind the strengths and limitations of what economics can do.

Based on what we have learned, what might be useful directions for economics in the future? As we have seen, public sector decisions frequently involve effects, both positive and negative, and trade-offs that are not easy to quantify or compare. Yet economics typically tries to monetize and combine these effects into a single number, using cost-benefit analysis, for instance, in order to make decisions. Perhaps economics can move beyond a strict cost-benefit analysis, recognizing that this framework may be inadequate for decisions whose effects are not purely monetary. Further, this framework can obscure distributional effects—that is, who benefits and who bears the costs. Because individuals have differing marginal utilities of income, even a decision with positive net monetary benefits could decrease net societal utility. Plus, willingness to pay depends on ability to pay, so those with less wealth may have less influence in the analyses, raising equity concerns.

Rather than relying upon a summary number to represent all benefits and costs, think about creating better alternatives, looking for actual Pareto improvements, practicing precaution in decisions with significant uncertainty and irreversibility, and promoting multiple societal goals such as economic efficiency, environmental quality, and equity. Even Adam Smith, while writing on the efficiency of the Invisible Hand, also spoke of the need for equity: "No society can surely be flourishing and happy, of which the far greater part of the members are poor and miserable." Economics can develop new ways to "manage the house," to meet basic needs of food, clothing, and shelter for as many as possible, rather than to measure economic progress solely by aggregate and quantitative increases in consumption and production. Further, people's "unlimited wants" are not just for material goods, but also for nonmaterial aspects of life. Economics can try to consider such noneconomic goods, or at least recognize limitations in its ability to quantify all that is important in public life.

APPENDIX A: COMPOUND INTEREST TABLES FOR DISCRETE CASH FLOWS

0.25%

	Single Payment		Uniform Series				Uniform Gradients		
	Compound Amount Factor	Present Worth Factor	Compound Amount Factor	Present Worth Factor	Sinking Fund Factor	Capital Recovery Factor	Gradient Present Worth Factor	Gradient Uniform Series Factor	
N	To Find F Given P F/P	To Find P Given F P/F	To Find F Given A F/A	To Find P Given A P/A	To Find A Given F A/F	To Find A Given P A/P	To Find P Given G P/G	To Find A Given G A/G	N
1	1.0025	0.9975	1.0000	0.9975	1.0000	1.0025	0.0000	0.0000	1
2	1.0050	0.9950	2.0025	1.9925	0.4994	0.5019	0.9950	0.4994	2
3	1.0075	0.9925	3.0075	2.9851	0.3325	0.3350	2.9801	0.9983	3
4	1.0100	0.9901	4.0150	3.9751	0.2491	0.2516	5.9503	1.4969	4
5	1.0126	0.9876	5.0251	4.9627	0.1990	0.2015	9.9007	1.9950	5
6	1.0151	0.9851	6.0376	5.9478	0.1656	0.1681	14.8263	2.4927	6
7	1.0176	0.9827	7.0527	6.9305	0.1418	0.1443	20.7223	2.9900	7
8	1.0202	0.9802	8.0704	7.9107	0.1239	0.1264	27.5839	3.4869	8
9	1.0227	0.9778	9.0905	8.8885	0.1100	0.1125	35.4061	3.9834	9
10	1.0253	0.9753	10.1133	9.8639	0.0989	0.1014	44.1842	4.4794	10
11	1.0278	0.9729	11.1385	10.8368	0.0898	0.0923	53.9133	4.9750	11
12	1.0304	0.9705	12.1664	11.8073	0.0822	0.0847	64.5886	5.4702	12
13	1.0330	0.9681	13.1968	12.7753	0.0758	0.0783	76.2053	5.9650	13
14	1.0356	0.9656	14.2298	13.7410	0.0703	0.0728	88.7587	6.4594	14
15	1.0382	0.9632	15.2654	14.7042	0.0655	0.0680	102.2441	6.9534	15
16	1.0408	0.9608	16.3035	15.6650	0.0613	0.0638	116.6567	7.4469	16
17	1.0434	0.9584	17.3443	16.6235	0.0577	0.0602	131.9917	7.9401	17
18	1.0460	0.9561	18.3876	17.5795	0.0544	0.0569	148.2446	8.4328	18
19	1.0486	0.9537	19.4336	18.5332	0.0515	0.0540	165.4106	8.9251	19
20	1.0512	0.9513	20.4822	19.4845	0.0488	0.0513	183.4851	9.4170	20
21	1.0538	0.9489	21.5334	20.4334	0.0464	0.0489	202.4634	9.9085	21
22	1.0565	0.9466	22.5872	21.3800	0.0443	0.0468	222.3410	10.3995	22
23	1.0591	0.9442	23.6437	22.3241	0.0423	0.0448	243.1131	10.8901	23
24	1.0618	0.9418	24.7028	23.2660	0.0405	0.0430	264.7753	11.3804	24
25	1.0644	0.9395	25.7646	24.2055	0.0388	0.0413	287.3230	11.8702	25
26	1.0671	0.9371	26.8290	25.1426	0.0373	0.0398	310.7516	12.3596	26
27	1.0697	0.9348	27.8961	26.0774	0.0358	0.0383	335.0566	12.8485	27
28	1.0724	0.9325	28.9658	27.0099	0.0345	0.0370	360.2334	13.3371	28
29	1.0751	0.9301	30.0382	27.9400	0.0333	0.0358	386.2776	13.8252	29
30	1.0778	0.9278	31.1133	28.8679	0.0321	0.0346	413.1847	14.3130	30
36	1.0941	0.9140	37.6206	34.3865	0.0266	0.0291	592.4988	17.2306	36
40	1.1050	0.9050	42.0132	38.0199	0.0238	0.0263	728.7399	19.1673	40
48	1.1273	0.8871	50.9312	45.1787	0.0196	0.0221	1040.0552	23.0209	48
50	1.1330	0.8826	53.1887	46.9462	0.0188	0.0213	1125.7767	23.9802	50
52	1.1386	0.8782	55.4575	48.7048	0.0180	0.0205	1214.5885	24.9377	52
60	1.1616	0.8609	64.6467	55.6524	0.0155	0.0180	1600.0845	28.7514	60
70	1.1910	0.8396	76.3944	64.1439	0.0131	0.0156	2147.6111	33.4812	70
72	1.1969	0.8355	78.7794	65.8169	0.0127	0.0152	2265.5569	34.4221	72
80	1.2211	0.8189	88.4392	72.4260	0.0113	0.0138	2764.4568	38.1694	80
84	1.2334	0.8108	93.3419	75.6813	0.0107	0.0132	3029.7592	40.0331	84
90	1.2520	0.7987	100.7885	80.5038	0.0099	0.0124	3446.8700	42.8162	90
96	1.2709	0.7869	108.3474	85.2546	0.0092	0.0117	3886.2832	45.5844	96
100	1.2836	0.7790	113.4500	88.3825	0.0088	0.0113	4191.2417	47.4216	100
104	1.2965	0.7713	118.6037	91.4793	0.0084	0.0109	4505.5569	49.2522	104
120	1.3494	0.7411	139.7414	103.5618	0.0072	0.0097	5852.1116	56.5084	120
240	1.8208	0.5492	328.3020	180.3109	0.0030	0.0055	19398.9852	107.5863	240
360	2.4568	0.4070	582.7369	237.1894	0.0017	0.0042	36263.9299	152.8902	360
480	3.3151	0.3016	926.0595	279.3418	0.0011	0.0036	53820.7525	192.6699	480

0.50%

N	Single Payment		Uniform Series				Uniform Gradients		N
	Compound Amount Factor	Present Worth Factor	Compound Amount Factor	Present Worth Factor	Sinking Fund Factor	Capital Recovery Factor	Gradient Present Worth Factor	Gradient Uniform Series Factor	
	To Find F Given P F/P	To Find P Given F P/F	To Find F Given A F/A	To Find P Given A P/A	To Find A Given F A/F	To Find A Given P A/P	To Find P Given G P/G	To Find A Given G A/G	
1	1.0050	0.9950	1.0000	0.9950	1.0000	1.0050	0.0000	0.0000	1
2	1.0100	0.9901	2.0050	1.9851	0.4988	0.5038	0.9901	0.4988	2
3	1.0151	0.9851	3.0150	2.9702	0.3317	0.3367	2.9604	0.9967	3
4	1.0202	0.9802	4.0301	3.9505	0.2481	0.2531	5.9011	1.4938	4
5	1.0253	0.9754	5.0503	4.9259	0.1980	0.2030	9.8026	1.9900	5
6	1.0304	0.9705	6.0755	5.8964	0.1646	0.1696	14.6552	2.4855	6
7	1.0355	0.9657	7.1059	6.8621	0.1407	0.1457	20.4493	2.9801	7
8	1.0407	0.9609	8.1414	7.8230	0.1228	0.1278	27.1755	3.4738	8
9	1.0459	0.9561	9.1821	8.7791	0.1089	0.1139	34.8244	3.9668	9
10	1.0511	0.9513	10.2280	9.7304	0.0978	0.1028	43.3865	4.4589	10
11	1.0564	0.9466	11.2792	10.6770	0.0887	0.0937	52.8526	4.9501	11
12	1.0617	0.9419	12.3356	11.6189	0.0811	0.0861	63.2136	5.4406	12
13	1.0670	0.9372	13.3972	12.5562	0.0746	0.0796	74.4602	5.9302	13
14	1.0723	0.9326	14.4642	13.4887	0.0691	0.0741	86.5835	6.4190	14
15	1.0777	0.9279	15.5365	14.4166	0.0644	0.0694	99.5743	6.9069	15
16	1.0831	0.9233	16.6142	15.3399	0.0602	0.0652	113.4238	7.3940	16
17	1.0885	0.9187	17.6973	16.2586	0.0565	0.0615	128.1231	7.8803	17
18	1.0939	0.9141	18.7858	17.1728	0.0532	0.0582	143.6634	8.3658	18
19	1.0994	0.9096	19.8797	18.0824	0.0503	0.0553	160.0360	8.8504	19
20	1.1049	0.9051	20.9791	18.9874	0.0477	0.0527	177.2322	9.3342	20
21	1.1104	0.9006	22.0840	19.8880	0.0453	0.0503	195.2434	9.8172	21
22	1.1160	0.8961	23.1944	20.7841	0.0431	0.0481	214.0611	10.2993	22
23	1.1216	0.8916	24.3104	21.6757	0.0411	0.0461	233.6768	10.7806	23
24	1.1272	0.8872	25.4320	22.5629	0.0393	0.0443	254.0820	11.2611	24
25	1.1328	0.8828	26.5591	23.4456	0.0377	0.0427	275.2686	11.7407	25
26	1.1385	0.8784	27.6919	24.3240	0.0361	0.0411	297.2281	12.2195	26
27	1.1442	0.8740	28.8304	25.1980	0.0347	0.0397	319.9523	12.6975	27
28	1.1499	0.8697	29.9745	26.0677	0.0334	0.0384	343.4332	13.1747	28
29	1.1556	0.8653	31.1244	26.9330	0.0321	0.0371	367.6625	13.6510	29
30	1.1614	0.8610	32.2800	27.7941	0.0310	0.0360	392.6324	14.1265	30
36	1.1967	0.8356	39.3361	32.8710	0.0254	0.0304	557.5598	16.9621	36
40	1.2208	0.8191	44.1588	36.1722	0.0226	0.0276	681.3347	18.8359	40
48	1.2705	0.7871	54.0978	42.5803	0.0185	0.0235	959.9188	22.5437	48
50	1.2832	0.7793	56.6452	44.1428	0.0177	0.0227	1035.6966	23.4624	50
52	1.2961	0.7716	59.2180	45.6897	0.0169	0.0219	1113.8162	24.3778	52
60	1.3489	0.7414	69.7700	51.7256	0.0143	0.0193	1448.6458	28.0064	60
70	1.4178	0.7053	83.5661	58.9394	0.0120	0.0170	1913.6427	32.4680	70
72	1.4320	0.6983	86.4089	60.3395	0.0116	0.0166	2012.3478	33.3504	72
80	1.4903	0.6710	98.0677	65.8023	0.0102	0.0152	2424.6455	36.8474	80
84	1.5204	0.6577	104.0739	68.4530	0.0096	0.0146	2640.6641	38.5763	84
90	1.5666	0.6383	113.3109	72.3313	0.0088	0.0138	2976.0769	41.1451	90
96	1.6141	0.6195	122.8285	76.0952	0.0081	0.0131	3324.1846	43.6845	96
100	1.6467	0.6073	129.3337	78.5426	0.0077	0.0127	3562.7934	45.3613	100
104	1.6798	0.5953	135.9699	80.9417	0.0074	0.0124	3806.2855	47.0250	104
120	1.8194	0.5496	163.8793	90.0735	0.0061	0.0111	4823.5051	53.5508	120
240	3.3102	0.3021	462.0409	139.5808	0.0022	0.0072	13415.5395	96.1131	240
360	6.0226	0.1660	1004.5150	166.7916	0.0010	0.0060	21403.3041	128.3236	360
480	10.9575	0.0913	1991.4907	181.7476	0.0005	0.0055	27588.3573	151.7949	480

0.75%

	Single Payment		Uniform Series				Uniform Gradients		
	Compound Amount Factor	Present Worth Factor	Compound Amount Factor	Present Worth Factor	Sinking Fund Factor	Capital Recovery Factor	Gradient Present Worth Factor	Gradient Uniform Series Factor	
	To Find F Given P	To Find P Given F	To Find F Given A	To Find P Given A	To Find A Given F	To Find A Given P	To Find P Given G	To Find A Given G	
N	F/P	P/F	F/A	P/A	A/F	A/P	P/G	A/G	N
1	1.0075	0.9926	1.0000	0.9926	1.0000	1.0075	0.0000	0.0000	1
2	1.0151	0.9852	2.0075	1.9777	0.4981	0.5056	0.9852	0.4981	2
3	1.0227	0.9778	3.0226	2.9556	0.3308	0.3383	2.9408	0.9950	3
4	1.0303	0.9706	4.0452	3.9261	0.2472	0.2547	5.8525	1.4907	4
5	1.0381	0.9633	5.0756	4.8894	0.1970	0.2045	9.7058	1.9851	5
6	1.0459	0.9562	6.1136	5.8456	0.1636	0.1711	14.4866	2.4782	6
7	1.0537	0.9490	7.1595	6.7946	0.1397	0.1472	20.1808	2.9701	7
8	1.0616	0.9420	8.2132	7.7366	0.1218	0.1293	26.7747	3.4608	8
9	1.0696	0.9350	9.2748	8.6716	0.1078	0.1153	34.2544	3.9502	9
10	1.0776	0.9280	10.3443	9.5996	0.0967	0.1042	42.6064	4.4384	10
11	1.0857	0.9211	11.4219	10.5207	0.0876	0.0951	51.8174	4.9253	11
12	1.0938	0.9142	12.5076	11.4349	0.0800	0.0875	61.8740	5.4110	12
13	1.1020	0.9074	13.6014	12.3423	0.0735	0.0810	72.7632	5.8954	13
14	1.1103	0.9007	14.7034	13.2430	0.0680	0.0755	84.4720	6.3786	14
15	1.1186	0.8940	15.8137	14.1370	0.0632	0.0707	96.9876	6.8606	15
16	1.1270	0.8873	16.9323	15.0243	0.0591	0.0666	110.2973	7.3413	16
17	1.1354	0.8807	18.0593	15.9050	0.0554	0.0629	124.3887	7.8207	17
18	1.1440	0.8742	19.1947	16.7792	0.0521	0.0596	139.2494	8.2989	18
19	1.1525	0.8676	20.3387	17.6468	0.0492	0.0567	154.8671	8.7759	19
20	1.1612	0.8612	21.4912	18.5080	0.0465	0.0540	171.2297	9.2516	20
21	1.1699	0.8548	22.6524	19.3628	0.0441	0.0516	188.3253	9.7261	21
22	1.1787	0.8484	23.8223	20.2112	0.0420	0.0495	206.1420	10.1994	22
23	1.1875	0.8421	25.0010	21.0533	0.0400	0.0475	224.6682	10.6714	23
24	1.1964	0.8358	26.1885	21.8891	0.0382	0.0457	243.8923	11.1422	24
25	1.2054	0.8296	27.3849	22.7188	0.0365	0.0440	263.8029	11.6117	25
26	1.2144	0.8234	28.5903	23.5422	0.0350	0.0425	284.3888	12.0800	26
27	1.2235	0.8173	29.8047	24.3595	0.0336	0.0411	305.6387	12.5470	27
28	1.2327	0.8112	31.0282	25.1707	0.0322	0.0397	327.5416	13.0128	28
29	1.2420	0.8052	32.2609	25.9759	0.0310	0.0385	350.0867	13.4774	29
30	1.2513	0.7992	33.5029	26.7751	0.0298	0.0373	373.2631	13.9407	30
36	1.3086	0.7641	41.1527	31.4468	0.0243	0.0318	524.9924	16.6946	36
40	1.3483	0.7416	46.4465	34.4469	0.0215	0.0290	637.4693	18.5058	40
48	1.4314	0.6986	57.5207	40.1848	0.0174	0.0249	886.8404	22.0691	48
50	1.4530	0.6883	60.3943	41.5664	0.0166	0.0241	953.8486	22.9476	50
52	1.4748	0.6780	63.3111	42.9276	0.0158	0.0233	1022.5852	23.8211	52
60	1.5657	0.6387	75.4241	48.1734	0.0133	0.0208	1313.5189	27.2665	60
70	1.6872	0.5927	91.6201	54.3046	0.0109	0.0184	1708.6065	31.4634	70
72	1.7126	0.5839	95.0070	55.4768	0.0105	0.0180	1791.2463	32.2882	72
80	1.8180	0.5500	109.0725	59.9944	0.0092	0.0167	2132.1472	35.5391	80
84	1.8732	0.5338	116.4269	62.1540	0.0086	0.0161	2308.1283	37.1357	84
90	1.9591	0.5104	127.8790	65.2746	0.0078	0.0153	2577.9961	39.4946	90
96	2.0489	0.4881	139.8562	68.2584	0.0072	0.0147	2853.9352	41.8107	96
100	2.1111	0.4737	148.1445	70.1746	0.0068	0.0143	3040.7453	43.3311	100
104	2.1751	0.4597	156.6843	72.0344	0.0064	0.0139	3229.4936	44.8327	104
120	2.4514	0.4079	193.5143	78.9417	0.0052	0.0127	3998.5621	50.6521	120
240	6.0092	0.1664	667.8869	111.1450	0.0015	0.0090	9494.1162	85.4210	240
360	14.7306	0.0679	1830.7435	124.2819	0.0005	0.0080	13312.3871	107.1145	360
480	36.1099	0.0277	4681.3203	129.6409	0.0002	0.0077	15513.0866	119.6620	480

1.00%

	Single Payment		Uniform Series				Uniform Gradients		
	Compound Amount Factor	Present Worth Factor	Compound Amount Factor	Present Worth Factor	Sinking Fund Factor	Capital Recovery Factor	Gradient Present Worth Factor	Gradient Uniform Series Factor	
N	To Find F Given P F/P	To Find P Given F P/F	To Find F Given A F/A	To Find P Given A P/A	To Find A Given F A/F	To Find A Given P A/P	To Find P Given G P/G	To Find A Given G A/G	N
1	1.0100	0.9901	1.0000	0.9901	1.0000	1.0100	0.0000	0.0000	1
2	1.0201	0.9803	2.0100	1.9704	0.4975	0.5075	0.9803	0.4975	2
3	1.0303	0.9706	3.0301	2.9410	0.3300	0.3400	2.9215	0.9934	3
4	1.0406	0.9610	4.0604	3.9020	0.2463	0.2563	5.8044	1.4876	4
5	1.0510	0.9515	5.1010	4.8534	0.1960	0.2060	9.6103	1.9801	5
6	1.0615	0.9420	6.1520	5.7955	0.1625	0.1725	14.3205	2.4710	6
7	1.0721	0.9327	7.2135	6.7282	0.1386	0.1486	19.9168	2.9602	7
8	1.0829	0.9235	8.2857	7.6517	0.1207	0.1307	26.3812	3.4478	8
9	1.0937	0.9143	9.3685	8.5660	0.1067	0.1167	33.6959	3.9337	9
10	1.1046	0.9053	10.4622	9.4713	0.0956	0.1056	41.8435	4.4179	10
11	1.1157	0.8963	11.5668	10.3676	0.0865	0.0965	50.8067	4.9005	11
12	1.1268	0.8874	12.6825	11.2551	0.0788	0.0888	60.5687	5.3815	12
13	1.1381	0.8787	13.8093	12.1337	0.0724	0.0824	71.1126	5.8607	13
14	1.1495	0.8700	14.9474	13.0037	0.0669	0.0769	82.4221	6.3384	14
15	1.1610	0.8613	16.0969	13.8651	0.0621	0.0721	94.4810	6.8143	15
16	1.1726	0.8528	17.2579	14.7179	0.0579	0.0679	107.2734	7.2886	16
17	1.1843	0.8444	18.4304	15.5623	0.0543	0.0643	120.7834	7.7613	17
18	1.1961	0.8360	19.6147	16.3983	0.0510	0.0610	134.9957	8.2323	18
19	1.2081	0.8277	20.8109	17.2260	0.0481	0.0581	149.8950	8.7017	19
20	1.2202	0.8195	22.0190	18.0456	0.0454	0.0554	165.4664	9.1694	20
21	1.2324	0.8114	23.2392	18.8570	0.0430	0.0530	181.6950	9.6354	21
22	1.2447	0.8034	24.4716	19.6604	0.0409	0.0509	198.5663	10.0998	22
23	1.2572	0.7954	25.7163	20.4558	0.0389	0.0489	216.0660	10.5626	23
24	1.2697	0.7876	26.9735	21.2434	0.0371	0.0471	234.1800	11.0237	24
25	1.2824	0.7798	28.2432	22.0232	0.0354	0.0454	252.8945	11.4831	25
26	1.2953	0.7720	29.5256	22.7952	0.0339	0.0439	272.1957	11.9409	26
27	1.3082	0.7644	30.8209	23.5596	0.0324	0.0424	292.0702	12.3971	27
28	1.3213	0.7568	32.1291	24.3164	0.0311	0.0411	312.5047	12.8516	28
29	1.3345	0.7493	33.4504	25.0658	0.0299	0.0399	333.4863	13.3044	29
30	1.3478	0.7419	34.7849	25.8077	0.0287	0.0387	355.0021	13.7557	30
36	1.4308	0.6989	43.0769	30.1075	0.0232	0.0332	494.6207	16.4285	36
40	1.4889	0.6717	48.8864	32.8347	0.0205	0.0305	596.8561	18.1776	40
48	1.6122	0.6203	61.2226	37.9740	0.0163	0.0263	820.1460	21.5976	48
50	1.6446	0.6080	64.4632	39.1961	0.0155	0.0255	879.4176	22.4363	50
52	1.6777	0.5961	67.7689	40.3942	0.0148	0.0248	939.9175	23.2686	52
60	1.8167	0.5504	81.6697	44.9550	0.0122	0.0222	1192.8061	26.5333	60
70	2.0068	0.4983	100.6763	50.1685	0.0099	0.0199	1528.6474	30.4703	70
72	2.0471	0.4885	104.7099	51.1504	0.0096	0.0196	1597.8673	31.2386	72
80	2.2167	0.4511	121.6715	54.8882	0.0082	0.0182	1879.8771	34.2492	80
84	2.3067	0.4335	130.6723	56.6485	0.0077	0.0177	2023.3153	35.7170	84
90	2.4486	0.4084	144.8633	59.1609	0.0069	0.0169	2240.5675	37.8724	90
96	2.5993	0.3847	159.9273	61.5277	0.0063	0.0163	2459.4298	39.9727	96
100	2.7048	0.3697	170.4814	63.0289	0.0059	0.0159	2605.7758	41.3426	100
104	2.8146	0.3553	181.4640	64.4715	0.0055	0.0155	2752.1818	42.6884	104
120	3.3004	0.3030	230.0387	69.7005	0.0043	0.0143	3334.1148	47.8349	120
240	10.8926	0.0918	989.2554	90.8194	0.0010	0.0110	6878.6016	75.7393	240
360	35.9496	0.0278	3494.9641	97.2183	0.0003	0.0103	8720.4323	89.6995	360
480	118.6477	0.0084	11764.7725	99.1572	0.0001	0.0101	9511.1579	95.9200	480

2.00%

N	Single Payment		Uniform Series				Uniform Gradients		N
	Compound Amount Factor	Present Worth Factor	Compound Amount Factor	Present Worth Factor	Sinking Fund Factor	Capital Recovery Factor	Gradient Present Worth Factor	Gradient Uniform Series Factor	
	To Find F Given P	To Find P Given F	To Find F Given A	To Find P Given A	To Find A Given F	To Find A Given P	To Find P Given G	To Find A Given G	
N	F/P	P/F	F/A	P/A	A/F	A/P	P/G	A/G	N
1	1.0200	0.9804	1.0000	0.9804	1.0000	1.0200	0.0000	0.0000	1
2	1.0404	0.9612	2.0200	1.9416	0.4950	0.5150	0.9612	0.4950	2
3	1.0612	0.9423	3.0604	2.8839	0.3268	0.3468	2.8458	0.9868	3
4	1.0824	0.9238	4.1216	3.8077	0.2426	0.2626	5.6173	1.4752	4
5	1.1041	0.9057	5.2040	4.7135	0.1922	0.2122	9.2403	1.9604	5
6	1.1262	0.8880	6.3081	5.6014	0.1585	0.1785	13.6801	2.4423	6
7	1.1487	0.8706	7.4343	6.4720	0.1345	0.1545	18.9035	2.9208	7
8	1.1717	0.8535	8.5830	7.3255	0.1165	0.1365	24.8779	3.3961	8
9	1.1951	0.8368	9.7546	8.1622	0.1025	0.1225	31.5720	3.8681	9
10	1.2190	0.8203	10.9497	8.9826	0.0913	0.1113	38.9551	4.3367	10
11	1.2434	0.8043	12.1687	9.7868	0.0822	0.1022	46.9977	4.8021	11
12	1.2682	0.7885	13.4121	10.5753	0.0746	0.0946	55.6712	5.2642	12
13	1.2936	0.7730	14.6803	11.3484	0.0681	0.0881	64.9475	5.7231	13
14	1.3195	0.7579	15.9739	12.1062	0.0626	0.0826	74.7999	6.1786	14
15	1.3459	0.7430	17.2934	12.8493	0.0578	0.0778	85.2021	6.6309	15
16	1.3728	0.7284	18.6393	13.5777	0.0537	0.0737	96.1288	7.0799	16
17	1.4002	0.7142	20.0121	14.2919	0.0500	0.0700	107.5554	7.5256	17
18	1.4282	0.7002	21.4123	14.9920	0.0467	0.0667	119.4581	7.9681	18
19	1.4568	0.6864	22.8406	15.6785	0.0438	0.0638	131.8139	8.4073	19
20	1.4859	0.6730	24.2974	16.3514	0.0412	0.0612	144.6003	8.8433	20
21	1.5157	0.6598	25.7833	17.0112	0.0388	0.0588	157.7959	9.2760	21
22	1.5460	0.6468	27.2990	17.6580	0.0366	0.0566	171.3795	9.7055	22
23	1.5769	0.6342	28.8450	18.2922	0.0347	0.0547	185.3309	10.1317	23
24	1.6084	0.6217	30.4219	18.9139	0.0329	0.0529	199.6305	10.5547	24
25	1.6406	0.6095	32.0303	19.5235	0.0312	0.0512	214.2592	10.9745	25
26	1.6734	0.5976	33.6709	20.1210	0.0297	0.0497	229.1987	11.3910	26
27	1.7069	0.5859	35.3443	20.7069	0.0283	0.0483	244.4311	11.8043	27
28	1.7410	0.5744	37.0512	21.2813	0.0270	0.0470	259.9392	12.2145	28
29	1.7758	0.5631	38.7922	21.8444	0.0258	0.0458	275.7064	12.6214	29
30	1.8114	0.5521	40.5681	22.3965	0.0246	0.0446	291.7164	13.0251	30
36	2.0399	0.4902	51.9944	25.4888	0.0192	0.0392	392.0405	15.3809	36
40	2.2080	0.4529	60.4020	27.3555	0.0166	0.0366	461.9931	16.8885	40
48	2.5871	0.3865	79.3535	30.6731	0.0126	0.0326	605.9657	19.7556	48
50	2.6916	0.3715	84.5794	31.4236	0.0118	0.0318	642.3606	20.4420	50
52	2.8003	0.3571	90.0164	32.1449	0.0111	0.0311	678.7849	21.1164	52
60	3.2810	0.3048	114.0515	34.7609	0.0088	0.0288	823.6975	23.6961	60
70	3.9996	0.2500	149.9779	37.4986	0.0067	0.0267	999.8343	26.6632	70
72	4.1611	0.2403	158.0570	37.9841	0.0063	0.0263	1034.0557	27.2234	72
80	4.8754	0.2051	193.7720	39.7445	0.0052	0.0252	1166.7868	29.3572	80
84	5.2773	0.1895	213.8666	40.5255	0.0047	0.0247	1230.4191	30.3616	84
90	5.9431	0.1683	247.1567	41.5869	0.0040	0.0240	1322.1701	31.7929	90
96	6.6929	0.1494	284.6467	42.5294	0.0035	0.0235	1409.2973	33.1370	96
100	7.2446	0.1380	312.2323	43.0984	0.0032	0.0232	1464.7527	33.9863	100
104	7.8418	0.1275	342.0919	43.6239	0.0029	0.0229	1518.0873	34.7994	104
120	10.7652	0.0929	488.2582	45.3554	0.0020	0.0220	1710.4160	37.7114	120
240	115.8887	0.0086	5744.4368	49.5686	0.0002	0.0202	2374.8800	47.9110	240
360	1247.5611	0.0008	6.233E+04	49.9599	0.0000	0.0200	2483.5679	49.7112	360
480	1.343E+04	0.0001	6.715E+05	49.9963	0.0000	0.0200	2498.0268	49.9643	480

3.00%

	Single Payment		Uniform Series				Uniform Gradients		
	Compound Amount Factor	Present Worth Factor	Compound Amount Factor	Present Worth Factor	Sinking Fund Factor	Capital Recovery Factor	Gradient Present Worth Factor	Gradient Uniform Series Factor	
	To Find F Given P	To Find P Given F	To Find F Given A	To Find P Given A	To Find A Given F	To Find A Given P	To Find P Given G	To Find A Given G	
N	F/P	P/F	F/A	P/A	A/F	A/P	P/G	A/G	N
1	1.0300	0.9709	1.0000	0.9709	1.0000	1.0300	0.0000	0.0000	1
2	1.0609	0.9426	2.0300	1.9135	0.4926	0.5226	0.9426	0.4926	2
3	1.0927	0.9151	3.0909	2.8286	0.3235	0.3535	2.7729	0.9803	3
4	1.1255	0.8885	4.1836	3.7171	0.2390	0.2690	5.4383	1.4631	4
5	1.1593	0.8626	5.3091	4.5797	0.1884	0.2184	8.8888	1.9409	5
6	1.1941	0.8375	6.4684	5.4172	0.1546	0.1846	13.0762	2.4138	6
7	1.2299	0.8131	7.6625	6.2303	0.1305	0.1605	17.9547	2.8819	7
8	1.2668	0.7894	8.8923	7.0197	0.1125	0.1425	23.4806	3.3450	8
9	1.3048	0.7664	10.1591	7.7861	0.0984	0.1284	29.6119	3.8032	9
10	1.3439	0.7441	11.4639	8.5302	0.0872	0.1172	36.3088	4.2565	10
11	1.3842	0.7224	12.8078	9.2526	0.0781	0.1081	43.5330	4.7049	11
12	1.4258	0.7014	14.1920	9.9540	0.0705	0.1005	51.2482	5.1485	12
13	1.4685	0.6810	15.6178	10.6350	0.0640	0.0940	59.4196	5.5872	13
14	1.5126	0.6611	17.0863	11.2961	0.0585	0.0885	68.0141	6.0210	14
15	1.5580	0.6419	18.5989	11.9379	0.0538	0.0838	77.0002	6.4500	15
16	1.6047	0.6232	20.1569	12.5611	0.0496	0.0796	86.3477	6.8742	16
17	1.6528	0.6050	21.7616	13.1661	0.0460	0.0760	96.0280	7.2936	17
18	1.7024	0.5874	23.4144	13.7535	0.0427	0.0727	106.0137	7.7081	18
19	1.7535	0.5703	25.1169	14.3238	0.0398	0.0698	116.2788	8.1179	19
20	1.8061	0.5537	26.8704	14.8775	0.0372	0.0672	126.7987	8.5229	20
21	1.8603	0.5375	28.6765	15.4150	0.0349	0.0649	137.5496	8.9231	21
22	1.9161	0.5219	30.5368	15.9369	0.0327	0.0627	148.5094	9.3186	22
23	1.9736	0.5067	32.4529	16.4436	0.0308	0.0608	159.6566	9.7093	23
24	2.0328	0.4919	34.4265	16.9355	0.0290	0.0590	170.9711	10.0954	24
25	2.0938	0.4776	36.4593	17.4131	0.0274	0.0574	182.4336	10.4768	25
26	2.1566	0.4637	38.5530	17.8768	0.0259	0.0559	194.0260	10.8535	26
27	2.2213	0.4502	40.7096	18.3270	0.0246	0.0546	205.7309	11.2255	27
28	2.2879	0.4371	42.9309	18.7641	0.0233	0.0533	217.5320	11.5930	28
29	2.3566	0.4243	45.2189	19.1885	0.0221	0.0521	229.4137	11.9558	29
30	2.4273	0.4120	47.5754	19.6004	0.0210	0.0510	241.3613	12.3141	30
36	2.8983	0.3450	63.2759	21.8323	0.0158	0.0458	313.7028	14.3688	36
40	3.2620	0.3066	75.4013	23.1148	0.0133	0.0433	361.7499	15.6502	40
48	4.1323	0.2420	104.4084	25.2667	0.0096	0.0396	455.0255	18.0089	48
50	4.3839	0.2281	112.7969	25.7298	0.0089	0.0389	477.4803	18.5575	50
52	4.6509	0.2150	121.6962	26.1662	0.0082	0.0382	499.5191	19.0902	52
60	5.8916	0.1697	163.0534	27.6756	0.0061	0.0361	583.0526	21.0674	60
70	7.9178	0.1263	230.5941	29.1234	0.0043	0.0343	676.0869	23.2145	70
72	8.4000	0.1190	246.6672	29.3651	0.0041	0.0341	693.1226	23.6036	72
80	10.6409	0.0940	321.3630	30.2008	0.0031	0.0331	756.0865	25.0353	80
84	11.9764	0.0835	365.8805	30.5501	0.0027	0.0327	784.5434	25.6806	84
90	14.3005	0.0699	443.3489	31.0024	0.0023	0.0323	823.6302	26.5667	90
96	17.0755	0.0586	535.8502	31.3812	0.0019	0.0319	858.6377	27.3615	96
100	19.2186	0.0520	607.2877	31.5989	0.0016	0.0316	879.8540	27.8444	100
104	21.6307	0.0462	687.6913	31.7923	0.0015	0.0315	899.4781	28.2923	104
120	34.7110	0.0288	1123.6996	32.3730	0.0009	0.0309	963.8635	29.7737	120
240	1204.8526	0.0008	40128.4209	33.3057	0.0000	0.0300	1103.5491	33.1340	240
360	41821.6241	0.0000	1394020.8023	33.3325	0.0000	0.0300	1110.7976	33.3247	360
480	1451669.8550	0.0000	48388961.8342	33.3333	0.0000	0.0300	1111.0993	33.3330	480

4.00%

N	Single Payment		Uniform Series				Uniform Gradients		N
	Compound Amount Factor	Present Worth Factor	Compound Amount Factor	Present Worth Factor	Sinking Fund Factor	Capital Recovery Factor	Gradient Present Worth Factor	Gradient Uniform Series Factor	
	To Find F Given P F/P	To Find P Given F P/F	To Find F Given A F/A	To Find P Given A P/A	To Find A Given F A/F	To Find A Given P A/P	To Find P Given G P/G	To Find A Given G A/G	
1	1.0400	0.9615	1.0000	0.9615	1.0000	1.0400	0.0000	0.0000	1
2	1.0816	0.9246	2.0400	1.8861	0.4902	0.5302	0.9246	0.4902	2
3	1.1249	0.8890	3.1216	2.7751	0.3203	0.3603	2.7025	0.9739	3
4	1.1699	0.8548	4.2465	3.6299	0.2355	0.2755	5.2670	1.4510	4
5	1.2167	0.8219	5.4163	4.4518	0.1846	0.2246	8.5547	1.9216	5
6	1.2653	0.7903	6.6330	5.2421	0.1508	0.1908	12.5062	2.3857	6
7	1.3159	0.7599	7.8983	6.0021	0.1266	0.1666	17.0657	2.8433	7
8	1.3686	0.7307	9.2142	6.7327	0.1085	0.1485	22.1806	3.2944	8
9	1.4233	0.7026	10.5828	7.4353	0.0945	0.1345	27.8013	3.7391	9
10	1.4802	0.6756	12.0061	8.1109	0.0833	0.1233	33.8814	4.1773	10
11	1.5395	0.6496	13.4864	8.7605	0.0741	0.1141	40.3772	4.6090	11
12	1.6010	0.6246	15.0258	9.3851	0.0666	0.1066	47.2477	5.0343	12
13	1.6651	0.6006	16.6268	9.9856	0.0601	0.1001	54.4546	5.4533	13
14	1.7317	0.5775	18.2919	10.5631	0.0547	0.0947	61.9618	5.8659	14
15	1.8009	0.5553	20.0236	11.1184	0.0499	0.0899	69.7355	6.2721	15
16	1.8730	0.5339	21.8245	11.6523	0.0458	0.0858	77.7441	6.6720	16
17	1.9479	0.5134	23.6975	12.1657	0.0422	0.0822	85.9581	7.0656	17
18	2.0258	0.4936	25.6454	12.6593	0.0390	0.0790	94.3498	7.4530	18
19	2.1068	0.4746	27.6712	13.1339	0.0361	0.0761	102.8933	7.8342	19
20	2.1911	0.4564	29.7781	13.5903	0.0336	0.0736	111.5647	8.2091	20
21	2.2788	0.4388	31.9692	14.0292	0.0313	0.0713	120.3414	8.5779	21
22	2.3699	0.4220	34.2480	14.4511	0.0292	0.0692	129.2024	8.9407	22
23	2.4647	0.4057	36.6179	14.8568	0.0273	0.0673	138.1284	9.2973	23
24	2.5633	0.3901	39.0826	15.2470	0.0256	0.0656	147.1012	9.6479	24
25	2.6658	0.3751	41.6459	15.6221	0.0240	0.0640	156.1040	9.9925	25
26	2.7725	0.3607	44.3117	15.9828	0.0226	0.0626	165.1212	10.3312	26
27	2.8834	0.3468	47.0842	16.3296	0.0212	0.0612	174.1385	10.6640	27
28	2.9987	0.3335	49.9676	16.6631	0.0200	0.0600	183.1424	10.9909	28
29	3.1187	0.3207	52.9663	16.9837	0.0189	0.0589	192.1206	11.3120	29
30	3.2434	0.3083	56.0849	17.2920	0.0178	0.0578	201.0618	11.6274	30
36	4.1039	0.2437	77.5983	18.9083	0.0129	0.0529	253.4052	13.4018	36
40	4.8010	0.2083	95.0255	19.7928	0.0105	0.0505	286.5303	14.4765	40
48	6.5705	0.1522	139.2632	21.1951	0.0072	0.0472	347.2446	16.3832	48
50	7.1067	0.1407	152.6671	21.4822	0.0066	0.0466	361.1638	16.8122	50
52	7.6866	0.1301	167.1647	21.7476	0.0060	0.0460	374.5638	17.2232	52
60	10.5196	0.0951	237.9907	22.6235	0.0042	0.0442	422.9966	18.6972	60
70	15.5716	0.0642	364.2905	23.3945	0.0027	0.0427	472.4789	20.1961	70
72	16.8423	0.0594	396.0566	23.5156	0.0025	0.0425	481.0170	20.4552	72
80	23.0498	0.0434	551.2450	23.9154	0.0018	0.0418	511.1161	21.3718	80
84	26.9650	0.0371	649.1251	24.0729	0.0015	0.0415	523.9431	21.7649	84
90	34.1193	0.0293	827.9833	24.2673	0.0012	0.0412	540.7369	22.2826	90
96	43.1718	0.0232	1054.2960	24.4209	0.0009	0.0409	554.9312	22.7236	96
100	50.5049	0.0198	1237.6237	24.5050	0.0008	0.0408	563.1249	22.9800	100
104	59.0836	0.0169	1452.0911	24.5769	0.0007	0.0407	570.4164	23.2095	104
120	110.6626	0.0090	2741.5640	24.7741	0.0004	0.0404	592.2428	23.9057	120
240	12246.2024	0.0001	306130.0591	24.9980	0.0000	0.0400	624.4590	24.9804	240
360	1355196.1137	0.0000	33879877.8425	25.0000	0.0000	0.0400	624.9929	24.9997	360
480	149969472.3341	0.0000	3749236783.3515	25.0000	0.0000	0.0400	624.9999	25.0000	480

5.00%

	Single Payment		Uniform Series				Uniform Gradients		
	Compound Amount Factor	Present Worth Factor	Compound Amount Factor	Present Worth Factor	Sinking Fund Factor	Capital Recovery Factor	Gradient Present Worth Factor	Gradient Uniform Series Factor	
N	To Find F Given P F/P	To Find P Given F P/F	To Find F Given A F/A	To Find P Given A P/A	To Find A Given F A/F	To Find A Given P A/P	To Find P Given G P/G	To Find A Given G A/G	N
1	1.0500	0.9524	1.0000	0.9524	1.0000	1.0500	0.0000	0.0000	1
2	1.1025	0.9070	2.0500	1.8594	0.4878	0.5378	0.9070	0.4878	2
3	1.1576	0.8638	3.1525	2.7232	0.3172	0.3672	2.6347	0.9675	3
4	1.2155	0.8227	4.3101	3.5460	0.2320	0.2820	5.1028	1.4391	4
5	1.2763	0.7835	5.5256	4.3295	0.1810	0.2310	8.2369	1.9025	5
6	1.3401	0.7462	6.8019	5.0757	0.1470	0.1970	11.9680	2.3579	6
7	1.4071	0.7107	8.1420	5.7864	0.1228	0.1728	16.2321	2.8052	7
8	1.4775	0.6768	9.5491	6.4632	0.1047	0.1547	20.9700	3.2445	8
9	1.5513	0.6446	11.0266	7.1078	0.0907	0.1407	26.1268	3.6758	9
10	1.6289	0.6139	12.5779	7.7217	0.0795	0.1295	31.6520	4.0991	10
11	1.7103	0.5847	14.2068	8.3064	0.0704	0.1204	37.4988	4.5144	11
12	1.7959	0.5568	15.9171	8.8633	0.0628	0.1128	43.6241	4.9219	12
13	1.8856	0.5303	17.7130	9.3936	0.0565	0.1065	49.9879	5.3215	13
14	1.9799	0.5051	19.5986	9.8986	0.0510	0.1010	56.5538	5.7133	14
15	2.0789	0.4810	21.5786	10.3797	0.0463	0.0963	63.2880	6.0973	15
16	2.1829	0.4581	23.6575	10.8378	0.0423	0.0923	70.1597	6.4736	16
17	2.2920	0.4363	25.8404	11.2741	0.0387	0.0887	77.1405	6.8423	17
18	2.4066	0.4155	28.1324	11.6896	0.0355	0.0855	84.2043	7.2034	18
19	2.5270	0.3957	30.5390	12.0853	0.0327	0.0827	91.3275	7.5569	19
20	2.6533	0.3769	33.0660	12.4622	0.0302	0.0802	98.4884	7.9030	20
21	2.7860	0.3589	35.7193	12.8212	0.0280	0.0780	105.6673	8.2416	21
22	2.9253	0.3418	38.5052	13.1630	0.0260	0.0760	112.8461	8.5730	22
23	3.0715	0.3256	41.4305	13.4886	0.0241	0.0741	120.0087	8.8971	23
24	3.2251	0.3101	44.5020	13.7986	0.0225	0.0725	127.1402	9.2140	24
25	3.3864	0.2953	47.7271	14.0939	0.0210	0.0710	134.2275	9.5238	25
26	3.5557	0.2812	51.1135	14.3752	0.0196	0.0696	141.2585	9.8266	26
27	3.7335	0.2678	54.6691	14.6430	0.0183	0.0683	148.2226	10.1224	27
28	3.9201	0.2551	58.4026	14.8981	0.0171	0.0671	155.1101	10.4114	28
29	4.1161	0.2429	62.3227	15.1411	0.0160	0.0660	161.9126	10.6936	29
30	4.3219	0.2314	66.4388	15.3725	0.0151	0.0651	168.6226	10.9691	30
36	5.7918	0.1727	95.8363	16.5469	0.0104	0.0604	206.6237	12.4872	36
40	7.0400	0.1420	120.7998	17.1591	0.0083	0.0583	229.5452	13.3775	40
48	10.4013	0.0961	188.0254	18.0772	0.0053	0.0553	269.2467	14.8943	48
50	11.4674	0.0872	209.3480	18.2559	0.0048	0.0548	277.9148	15.2233	50
52	12.6428	0.0791	232.8562	18.4181	0.0043	0.0543	286.1013	15.5337	52
60	18.6792	0.0535	353.5837	18.9293	0.0028	0.0528	314.3432	16.6062	60
70	30.4264	0.0329	588.5285	19.3427	0.0017	0.0517	340.8409	17.6212	70
72	33.5451	0.0298	650.9027	19.4038	0.0015	0.0515	345.1485	17.7877	72
80	49.5614	0.0202	971.2288	19.5965	0.0010	0.0510	359.6460	18.3526	80
84	60.2422	0.0166	1184.8448	19.6680	0.0008	0.0508	365.4727	18.5821	84
90	80.7304	0.0124	1594.6073	19.7523	0.0006	0.0506	372.7488	18.8712	90
96	108.1864	0.0092	2143.7282	19.8151	0.0005	0.0505	378.5555	19.1044	96
100	131.5013	0.0076	2610.0252	19.8479	0.0004	0.0504	381.7492	19.2337	100
104	159.8406	0.0063	3176.8120	19.8749	0.0003	0.0503	384.4845	19.3453	104
120	348.9120	0.0029	6958.2397	19.9427	0.0001	0.0501	391.9751	19.6551	120
240	1.217E+05	0.0000	2.435E+06	19.9998	0.0000	0.0500	399.9573	19.9980	240
360	4.248E+07	0.0000	8.495E+08	20.0000	0.0000	0.0500	399.9998	20.0000	360
480	1.482E+10	0.0000	2.964E+11	20.0000	0.0000	0.0500	400.0000	20.0000	480

6.00%

	Single Payment		Uniform Series				Uniform Gradients		
	Compound Amount Factor	Present Worth Factor	Compound Amount Factor	Present Worth Factor	Sinking Fund Factor	Capital Recovery Factor	Gradient Present Worth Factor	Gradient Uniform Series Factor	
	To Find F Given P	To Find P Given F	To Find F Given A	To Find P Given A	To Find A Given F	To Find A Given P	To Find P Given G	To Find A Given G	
N	F/P	P/F	F/A	P/A	A/F	A/P	P/G	A/G	N
1	1.0600	0.9434	1.0000	0.9434	1.0000	1.0600	0.0000	0.0000	1
2	1.1236	0.8900	2.0600	1.8334	0.4854	0.5454	0.8900	0.4854	2
3	1.1910	0.8396	3.1836	2.6730	0.3141	0.3741	2.5692	0.9612	3
4	1.2625	0.7921	4.3746	3.4651	0.2286	0.2886	4.9455	1.4272	4
5	1.3382	0.7473	5.6371	4.2124	0.1774	0.2374	7.9345	1.8836	5
6	1.4185	0.7050	6.9753	4.9173	0.1434	0.2034	11.4594	2.3304	6
7	1.5036	0.6651	8.3938	5.5824	0.1191	0.1791	15.4497	2.7676	7
8	1.5938	0.6274	9.8975	6.2098	0.1010	0.1610	19.8416	3.1952	8
9	1.6895	0.5919	11.4913	6.8017	0.0870	0.1470	24.5768	3.6133	9
10	1.7908	0.5584	13.1808	7.3601	0.0759	0.1359	29.6023	4.0220	10
11	1.8983	0.5268	14.9716	7.8869	0.0668	0.1268	34.8702	4.4213	11
12	2.0122	0.4970	16.8699	8.3838	0.0593	0.1193	40.3369	4.8113	12
13	2.1329	0.4688	18.8821	8.8527	0.0530	0.1130	45.9629	5.1920	13
14	2.2609	0.4423	21.0151	9.2950	0.0476	0.1076	51.7128	5.5635	14
15	2.3966	0.4173	23.2760	9.7122	0.0430	0.1030	57.5546	5.9260	15
16	2.5404	0.3936	25.6725	10.1059	0.0390	0.0990	63.4592	6.2794	16
17	2.6928	0.3714	28.2129	10.4773	0.0354	0.0954	69.4011	6.6240	17
18	2.8543	0.3503	30.9057	10.8276	0.0324	0.0924	75.3569	6.9597	18
19	3.0256	0.3305	33.7600	11.1581	0.0296	0.0896	81.3062	7.2867	19
20	3.2071	0.3118	36.7856	11.4699	0.0272	0.0872	87.2304	7.6051	20
21	3.3996	0.2942	39.9927	11.7641	0.0250	0.0850	93.1136	7.9151	21
22	3.6035	0.2775	43.3923	12.0416	0.0230	0.0830	98.9412	8.2166	22
23	3.8197	0.2618	46.9958	12.3034	0.0213	0.0813	104.7007	8.5099	23
24	4.0489	0.2470	50.8156	12.5504	0.0197	0.0797	110.3812	8.7951	24
25	4.2919	0.2330	54.8645	12.7834	0.0182	0.0782	115.9732	9.0722	25
26	4.5494	0.2198	59.1564	13.0032	0.0169	0.0769	121.4684	9.3414	26
27	4.8223	0.2074	63.7058	13.2105	0.0157	0.0757	126.8600	9.6029	27
28	5.1117	0.1956	68.5281	13.4062	0.0146	0.0746	132.1420	9.8568	28
29	5.4184	0.1846	73.6398	13.5907	0.0136	0.0736	137.3096	10.1032	29
30	5.7435	0.1741	79.0582	13.7648	0.0126	0.0726	142.3588	10.3422	30
36	8.1473	0.1227	119.1209	14.6210	0.0084	0.0684	170.0387	11.6298	36
40	10.2857	0.0972	154.7620	15.0463	0.0065	0.0665	185.9568	12.3590	40
48	16.3939	0.0610	256.5645	15.6500	0.0039	0.0639	212.0351	13.5485	48
50	18.4202	0.0543	290.3359	15.7619	0.0034	0.0634	217.4574	13.7964	50
52	20.6969	0.0483	328.2814	15.8614	0.0030	0.0630	222.4823	14.0267	52
60	32.9877	0.0303	533.1282	16.1614	0.0019	0.0619	239.0428	14.7909	60
70	59.0759	0.0169	967.9322	16.3845	0.0010	0.0610	253.3271	15.4613	70
72	66.3777	0.0151	1089.6286	16.4156	0.0009	0.0609	255.5146	15.5654	72
80	105.7960	0.0095	1746.5999	16.5091	0.0006	0.0606	262.5493	15.9033	80
84	133.5650	0.0075	2209.4167	16.5419	0.0005	0.0605	265.2163	16.0330	84
90	189.4645	0.0053	3141.0752	16.5787	0.0003	0.0603	268.3946	16.1891	90
96	268.7590	0.0037	4462.6505	16.6047	0.0002	0.0602	270.7909	16.3081	96
100	339.3021	0.0029	5638.3681	16.6175	0.0002	0.0602	272.0471	16.3711	100
104	428.3611	0.0023	7122.6844	16.6278	0.0001	0.0601	273.0829	16.4233	104
120	1088.1877	0.0009	18119.7958	16.6514	0.0001	0.0601	275.6846	16.5563	120
240	1.184E+06	0.0000	1.974E+07	16.6667	0.0000	0.0600	277.7742	16.6665	240
360	1.289E+09	0.0000	2.148E+10	16.6667	0.0000	0.0600	277.7778	16.6667	360
480	1.402E+12	0.0000	2.337E+13	16.6667	0.0000	0.0600	277.7778	16.6667	480

7.00%

	Single Payment		Uniform Series				Uniform Gradients		
	Compound Amount Factor	Present Worth Factor	Compound Amount Factor	Present Worth Factor	Sinking Fund Factor	Capital Recovery Factor	Gradient Present Worth Factor	Gradient Uniform Series Factor	
	To Find F Given P	To Find P Given F	To Find F Given A	To Find P Given A	To Find A Given F	To Find A Given P	To Find P Given G	To Find A Given G	
N	F/P	P/F	F/A	P/A	A/F	A/P	P/G	A/G	N
1	1.0700	0.9346	1.0000	0.9346	1.0000	1.0700	0.0000	0.0000	1
2	1.1449	0.8734	2.0700	1.8080	0.4831	0.5531	0.8734	0.4831	2
3	1.2250	0.8163	3.2149	2.6243	0.3111	0.3811	2.5060	0.9549	3
4	1.3108	0.7629	4.4399	3.3872	0.2252	0.2952	4.7947	1.4155	4
5	1.4026	0.7130	5.7507	4.1002	0.1739	0.2439	7.6467	1.8650	5
6	1.5007	0.6663	7.1533	4.7665	0.1398	0.2098	10.9784	2.3032	6
7	1.6058	0.6227	8.6540	5.3893	0.1156	0.1856	14.7149	2.7304	7
8	1.7182	0.5820	10.2598	5.9713	0.0975	0.1675	18.7889	3.1465	8
9	1.8385	0.5439	11.9780	6.5152	0.0835	0.1535	23.1404	3.5517	9
10	1.9672	0.5083	13.8164	7.0236	0.0724	0.1424	27.7156	3.9461	10
11	2.1049	0.4751	15.7836	7.4987	0.0634	0.1334	32.4665	4.3296	11
12	2.2522	0.4440	17.8885	7.9427	0.0559	0.1259	37.3506	4.7025	12
13	2.4098	0.4150	20.1406	8.3577	0.0497	0.1197	42.3302	5.0648	13
14	2.5785	0.3878	22.5505	8.7455	0.0443	0.1143	47.3718	5.4167	14
15	2.7590	0.3624	25.1290	9.1079	0.0398	0.1098	52.4461	5.7583	15
16	2.9522	0.3387	27.8881	9.4466	0.0359	0.1059	57.5271	6.0897	16
17	3.1588	0.3166	30.8402	9.7632	0.0324	0.1024	62.5923	6.4110	17
18	3.3799	0.2959	33.9990	10.0591	0.0294	0.0994	67.6219	6.7225	18
19	3.6165	0.2765	37.3790	10.3356	0.0268	0.0968	72.5991	7.0242	19
20	3.8697	0.2584	40.9955	10.5940	0.0244	0.0944	77.5091	7.3163	20
21	4.1406	0.2415	44.8652	10.8355	0.0223	0.0923	82.3393	7.5990	21
22	4.4304	0.2257	49.0057	11.0612	0.0204	0.0904	87.0793	7.8725	22
23	4.7405	0.2109	53.4361	11.2722	0.0187	0.0887	91.7201	8.1369	23
24	5.0724	0.1971	58.1767	11.4693	0.0172	0.0872	96.2545	8.3923	24
25	5.4274	0.1842	63.2490	11.6536	0.0158	0.0858	100.6765	8.6391	25
26	5.8074	0.1722	68.6765	11.8258	0.0146	0.0846	104.9814	8.8773	26
27	6.2139	0.1609	74.4838	11.9867	0.0134	0.0834	109.1656	9.1072	27
28	6.6488	0.1504	80.6977	12.1371	0.0124	0.0824	113.2264	9.3289	28
29	7.1143	0.1406	87.3465	12.2777	0.0114	0.0814	117.1622	9.5427	29
30	7.6123	0.1314	94.4608	12.4090	0.0106	0.0806	120.9718	9.7487	30
36	11.4239	0.0875	148.9135	13.0352	0.0067	0.0767	141.1990	10.8321	36
40	14.9745	0.0668	199.6351	13.3317	0.0050	0.0750	152.2928	11.4233	40
48	25.7289	0.0389	353.2701	13.7305	0.0028	0.0728	169.4981	12.3447	48
50	29.4570	0.0339	406.5289	13.8007	0.0025	0.0725	172.9051	12.5287	50
52	33.7253	0.0297	467.5050	13.8621	0.0021	0.0721	176.0037	12.6967	52
60	57.9464	0.0173	813.5204	14.0392	0.0012	0.0712	185.7677	13.2321	60
70	113.9894	0.0088	1614.1342	14.1604	0.0006	0.0706	193.5185	13.6662	70
72	130.5065	0.0077	1850.0922	14.1763	0.0005	0.0705	194.6365	13.7298	72
80	224.2344	0.0045	3189.0627	14.2220	0.0003	0.0703	198.0748	13.9273	80
84	293.9255	0.0034	4184.6506	14.2371	0.0002	0.0702	199.3046	13.9990	84
90	441.1030	0.0023	6287.1854	14.2533	0.0002	0.0702	200.7042	14.0812	90
96	661.9766	0.0015	9442.5233	14.2641	0.0001	0.0701	201.7016	14.1405	96
100	867.7163	0.0012	1.238E+04	14.2693	0.0001	0.0701	202.2001	14.1703	100
104	1137.3991	0.0009	1.623E+04	14.2732	0.0001	0.0701	202.5960	14.1942	104
120	3357.7884	0.0003	4.795E+04	14.2815	0.0000	0.0700	203.5103	14.2500	120
240	1.127E+07	0.0000	1.611E+08	14.2857	0.0000	0.0700	204.0813	14.2857	240
360	3.786E+10	0.0000	5.408E+11	14.2857	0.0000	0.0700	204.0816	14.2857	360
480	1.271E+14	0.0000	1.816E+15	14.2857	0.0000	0.0700	204.0816	14.2857	480

8.00%

	Single Payment		Uniform Series				Uniform Gradients		
	Compound Amount Factor	Present Worth Factor	Compound Amount Factor	Present Worth Factor	Sinking Fund Factor	Capital Recovery Factor	Gradient Present Worth Factor	Gradient Uniform Series Factor	
	To Find F Given P	To Find P Given F	To Find F Given A	To Find P Given A	To Find A Given F	To Find A Given P	To Find P Given G	To Find A Given G	
N	F/P	P/F	F/A	P/A	A/F	A/P	P/G	A/G	N
1	1.0800	0.9259	1.0000	0.9259	1.0000	1.0800	0.0000	0.0000	1
2	1.1664	0.8573	2.0800	1.7833	0.4808	0.5608	0.8573	0.4808	2
3	1.2597	0.7938	3.2464	2.5771	0.3080	0.3880	2.4450	0.9487	3
4	1.3605	0.7350	4.5061	3.3121	0.2219	0.3019	4.6501	1.4040	4
5	1.4693	0.6806	5.8666	3.9927	0.1705	0.2505	7.3724	1.8465	5
6	1.5869	0.6302	7.3359	4.6229	0.1363	0.2163	10.5233	2.2763	6
7	1.7138	0.5835	8.9228	5.2064	0.1121	0.1921	14.0242	2.6937	7
8	1.8509	0.5403	10.6366	5.7466	0.0940	0.1740	17.8061	3.0985	8
9	1.9990	0.5002	12.4876	6.2469	0.0801	0.1601	21.8081	3.4910	9
10	2.1589	0.4632	14.4866	6.7101	0.0690	0.1490	25.9768	3.8713	10
11	2.3316	0.4289	16.6455	7.1390	0.0601	0.1401	30.2657	4.2395	11
12	2.5182	0.3971	18.9771	7.5361	0.0527	0.1327	34.6339	4.5957	12
13	2.7196	0.3677	21.4953	7.9038	0.0465	0.1265	39.0463	4.9402	13
14	2.9372	0.3405	24.2149	8.2442	0.0413	0.1213	43.4723	5.2731	14
15	3.1722	0.3152	27.1521	8.5595	0.0368	0.1168	47.8857	5.5945	15
16	3.4259	0.2919	30.3243	8.8514	0.0330	0.1130	52.2640	5.9046	16
17	3.7000	0.2703	33.7502	9.1216	0.0296	0.1096	56.5883	6.2037	17
18	3.9960	0.2502	37.4502	9.3719	0.0267	0.1067	60.8426	6.4920	18
19	4.3157	0.2317	41.4463	9.6036	0.0241	0.1041	65.0134	6.7697	19
20	4.6610	0.2145	45.7620	9.8181	0.0219	0.1019	69.0898	7.0369	20
21	5.0338	0.1987	50.4229	10.0168	0.0198	0.0998	73.0629	7.2940	21
22	5.4365	0.1839	55.4568	10.2007	0.0180	0.0980	76.9257	7.5412	22
23	5.8715	0.1703	60.8933	10.3711	0.0164	0.0964	80.6726	7.7786	23
24	6.3412	0.1577	66.7648	10.5288	0.0150	0.0950	84.2997	8.0066	24
25	6.8485	0.1460	73.1059	10.6748	0.0137	0.0937	87.8041	8.2254	25
26	7.3964	0.1352	79.9544	10.8100	0.0125	0.0925	91.1842	8.4352	26
27	7.9881	0.1252	87.3508	10.9352	0.0114	0.0914	94.4390	8.6363	27
28	8.6271	0.1159	95.3388	11.0511	0.0105	0.0905	97.5687	8.8289	28
29	9.3173	0.1073	103.9659	11.1584	0.0096	0.0896	100.5738	9.0133	29
30	10.0627	0.0994	113.2832	11.2578	0.0088	0.0888	103.4558	9.1897	30
36	15.9682	0.0626	187.1021	11.7172	0.0053	0.0853	118.2839	10.0949	36
40	21.7245	0.0460	259.0565	11.9246	0.0039	0.0839	126.0422	10.5699	40
48	40.2106	0.0249	490.1322	12.1891	0.0020	0.0820	137.4428	11.2758	48
50	46.9016	0.0213	573.7702	12.2335	0.0017	0.0817	139.5928	11.4107	50
52	54.7060	0.0183	671.3255	12.2715	0.0015	0.0815	141.5121	11.5318	52
60	101.2571	0.0099	1253.2133	12.3766	0.0008	0.0808	147.3000	11.9015	60
70	218.6064	0.0046	2720.0801	12.4428	0.0004	0.0804	151.5326	12.1783	70
72	254.9825	0.0039	3174.7814	12.4510	0.0003	0.0803	152.1076	12.2165	72
80	471.9548	0.0021	5886.9354	12.4735	0.0002	0.0802	153.8001	12.3301	80
84	642.0893	0.0016	8013.6168	12.4805	0.0001	0.0801	154.3714	12.3690	84
90	1018.9151	0.0010	1.272E+04	12.4877	0.0001	0.0801	154.9925	12.4116	90
96	1616.8902	0.0006	2.020E+04	12.4923	0.0000	0.0800	155.4112	12.4406	96
100	2199.7613	0.0005	2.748E+04	12.4943	0.0000	0.0800	155.6107	12.4545	100
104	2992.7509	0.0003	3.740E+04	12.4958	0.0000	0.0800	155.7634	12.4652	104
120	1.025E+04	0.0001	1.281E+05	12.4988	0.0000	0.0800	156.0885	12.4883	120
240	1.051E+08	0.0000	1.314E+09	12.5000	0.0000	0.0800	156.2500	12.5000	240
360	1.078E+12	0.0000	1.347E+13	12.5000	0.0000	0.0800	156.2500	12.5000	360
480	1.105E+16	0.0000	1.381E+17	12.5000	0.0000	0.0800	156.2500	12.5000	480

9.00%

	Single Payment		Uniform Series				Uniform Gradients		
	Compound Amount Factor	Present Worth Factor	Compound Amount Factor	Present Worth Factor	Sinking Fund Factor	Capital Recovery Factor	Gradient Present Worth Factor	Gradient Uniform Series Factor	
	To Find F Given P	To Find P Given F	To Find F Given A	To Find P Given A	To Find A Given F	To Find A Given P	To Find P Given G	To Find A Given G	
N	F/P	P/F	F/A	P/A	A/F	A/P	P/G	A/G	N
1	1.0900	0.9174	1.0000	0.9174	1.0000	1.0900	0.0000	0.0000	1
2	1.1881	0.8417	2.0900	1.7591	0.4785	0.5685	0.8417	0.4785	2
3	1.2950	0.7722	3.2781	2.5313	0.3051	0.3951	2.3860	0.9426	3
4	1.4116	0.7084	4.5731	3.2397	0.2187	0.3087	4.5113	1.3925	4
5	1.5386	0.6499	5.9847	3.8897	0.1671	0.2571	7.1110	1.8282	5
6	1.6771	0.5963	7.5233	4.4859	0.1329	0.2229	10.0924	2.2498	6
7	1.8280	0.5470	9.2004	5.0330	0.1087	0.1987	13.3746	2.6574	7
8	1.9926	0.5019	11.0285	5.5348	0.0907	0.1807	16.8877	3.0512	8
9	2.1719	0.4604	13.0210	5.9952	0.0768	0.1668	20.5711	3.4312	9
10	2.3674	0.4224	15.1929	6.4177	0.0658	0.1558	24.3728	3.7978	10
11	2.5804	0.3875	17.5603	6.8052	0.0569	0.1469	28.2481	4.1510	11
12	2.8127	0.3555	20.1407	7.1607	0.0497	0.1397	32.1590	4.4910	12
13	3.0658	0.3262	22.9534	7.4869	0.0436	0.1336	36.0731	4.8182	13
14	3.3417	0.2992	26.0192	7.7862	0.0384	0.1284	39.9633	5.1326	14
15	3.6425	0.2745	29.3609	8.0607	0.0341	0.1241	43.8069	5.4346	15
16	3.9703	0.2519	33.0034	8.3126	0.0303	0.1203	47.5849	5.7245	16
17	4.3276	0.2311	36.9737	8.5436	0.0270	0.1170	51.2821	6.0024	17
18	4.7171	0.2120	41.3013	8.7556	0.0242	0.1142	54.8860	6.2687	18
19	5.1417	0.1945	46.0185	8.9501	0.0217	0.1117	58.3868	6.5236	19
20	5.6044	0.1784	51.1601	9.1285	0.0195	0.1095	61.7770	6.7674	20
21	6.1088	0.1637	56.7645	9.2922	0.0176	0.1076	65.0509	7.0006	21
22	6.6586	0.1502	62.8733	9.4424	0.0159	0.1059	68.2048	7.2232	22
23	7.2579	0.1378	69.5319	9.5802	0.0144	0.1044	71.2359	7.4357	23
24	7.9111	0.1264	76.7898	9.7066	0.0130	0.1030	74.1433	7.6384	24
25	8.6231	0.1160	84.7009	9.8226	0.0118	0.1018	76.9265	7.8316	25
26	9.3992	0.1064	93.3240	9.9290	0.0107	0.1007	79.5863	8.0156	26
27	10.2451	0.0976	102.7231	10.0266	0.0097	0.0997	82.1241	8.1906	27
28	11.1671	0.0895	112.9682	10.1161	0.0089	0.0989	84.5419	8.3571	28
29	12.1722	0.0822	124.1354	10.1983	0.0081	0.0981	86.8422	8.5154	29
30	13.2677	0.0754	136.3075	10.2737	0.0073	0.0973	89.0280	8.6657	30
36	22.2512	0.0449	236.1247	10.6118	0.0042	0.0942	99.9319	9.4171	36
40	31.4094	0.0318	337.8824	10.7574	0.0030	0.0930	105.3762	9.7957	40
48	62.5852	0.0160	684.2804	10.9336	0.0015	0.0915	112.9625	10.3317	48
50	74.3575	0.0134	815.0836	10.9617	0.0012	0.0912	114.3251	10.4295	50
52	88.3442	0.0113	970.4908	10.9853	0.0010	0.0910	115.5193	10.5158	52
60	176.0313	0.0057	1944.7921	11.0480	0.0005	0.0905	118.9683	10.7683	60
70	416.7301	0.0024	4619.2232	11.0844	0.0002	0.0902	121.2942	10.9427	70
72	495.1170	0.0020	5490.1891	11.0887	0.0002	0.0902	121.5917	10.9654	72
80	986.5517	0.0010	1.095E+04	11.0998	0.0001	0.0901	122.4306	11.0299	80
84	1392.5982	0.0007	1.546E+04	11.1031	0.0001	0.0901	122.6979	11.0507	84
90	2335.5266	0.0004	2.594E+04	11.1064	0.0000	0.0900	122.9758	11.0726	90
96	3916.9119	0.0003	4.351E+04	11.1083	0.0000	0.0900	123.1529	11.0866	96
100	5529.0408	0.0002	6.142E+04	11.1091	0.0000	0.0900	123.2335	11.0930	100
104	7804.6923	0.0001	8.671E+04	11.1097	0.0000	0.0900	123.2929	11.0978	104
120	3.099E+04	0.0000	3.443E+05	11.1108	0.0000	0.0900	123.4098	11.1072	120
240	9.602E+08	0.0000	1.067E+10	11.1111	0.0000	0.0900	123.4568	11.1111	240
360	2.975E+13	0.0000	3.306E+14	11.1111	0.0000	0.0900	123.4568	11.1111	360
480	9.220E+17	0.0000	1.024E+19	11.1111	0.0000	0.0900	123.4568	11.1111	480

10.00%

N	Single Payment		Uniform Series				Uniform Gradients		N
	Compound Amount Factor	Present Worth Factor	Compound Amount Factor	Present Worth Factor	Sinking Fund Factor	Capital Recovery Factor	Gradient Present Worth Factor	Gradient Uniform Series Factor	
	To Find F Given P F/P	To Find P Given F P/F	To Find F Given A F/A	To Find P Given A P/A	To Find A Given F A/F	To Find A Given P A/P	To Find P Given G P/G	To Find A Given G A/G	
1	1.1000	0.9091	1.0000	0.9091	1.0000	1.1000	0.0000	0.0000	1
2	1.2100	0.8264	2.1000	1.7355	0.4762	0.5762	0.8264	0.4762	2
3	1.3310	0.7513	3.3100	2.4869	0.3021	0.4021	2.3291	0.9366	3
4	1.4641	0.6830	4.6410	3.1699	0.2155	0.3155	4.3781	1.3812	4
5	1.6105	0.6209	6.1051	3.7908	0.1638	0.2638	6.8618	1.8101	5
6	1.7716	0.5645	7.7156	4.3553	0.1296	0.2296	9.6842	2.2236	6
7	1.9487	0.5132	9.4872	4.8684	0.1054	0.2054	12.7631	2.6216	7
8	2.1436	0.4665	11.4359	5.3349	0.0874	0.1874	16.0287	3.0045	8
9	2.3579	0.4241	13.5795	5.7590	0.0736	0.1736	19.4215	3.3724	9
10	2.5937	0.3855	15.9374	6.1446	0.0627	0.1627	22.8913	3.7255	10
11	2.8531	0.3505	18.5312	6.4951	0.0540	0.1540	26.3963	4.0641	11
12	3.1384	0.3186	21.3843	6.8137	0.0468	0.1468	29.9012	4.3884	12
13	3.4523	0.2897	24.5227	7.1034	0.0408	0.1408	33.3772	4.6988	13
14	3.7975	0.2633	27.9750	7.3667	0.0357	0.1357	36.8005	4.9955	14
15	4.1772	0.2394	31.7725	7.6061	0.0315	0.1315	40.1520	5.2789	15
16	4.5950	0.2176	35.9497	7.8237	0.0278	0.1278	43.4164	5.5493	16
17	5.0545	0.1978	40.5447	8.0216	0.0247	0.1247	46.5819	5.8071	17
18	5.5599	0.1799	45.5992	8.2014	0.0219	0.1219	49.6395	6.0526	18
19	6.1159	0.1635	51.1591	8.3649	0.0195	0.1195	52.5827	6.2861	19
20	6.7275	0.1486	57.2750	8.5136	0.0175	0.1175	55.4069	6.5081	20
21	7.4002	0.1351	64.0025	8.6487	0.0156	0.1156	58.1095	6.7189	21
22	8.1403	0.1228	71.4027	8.7715	0.0140	0.1140	60.6893	6.9189	22
23	8.9543	0.1117	79.5430	8.8832	0.0126	0.1126	63.1462	7.1085	23
24	9.8497	0.1015	88.4973	8.9847	0.0113	0.1113	65.4813	7.2881	24
25	10.8347	0.0923	98.3471	9.0770	0.0102	0.1102	67.6964	7.4580	25
26	11.9182	0.0839	109.1818	9.1609	0.0092	0.1092	69.7940	7.6186	26
27	13.1100	0.0763	121.0999	9.2372	0.0083	0.1083	71.7773	7.7704	27
28	14.4210	0.0693	134.2099	9.3066	0.0075	0.1075	73.6495	7.9137	28
29	15.8631	0.0630	148.6309	9.3696	0.0067	0.1067	75.4146	8.0489	29
30	17.4494	0.0573	164.4940	9.4269	0.0061	0.1061	77.0766	8.1762	30
36	30.9127	0.0323	299.1268	9.6765	0.0033	0.1033	85.1194	8.7965	36
40	45.2593	0.0221	442.5926	9.7791	0.0023	0.1023	88.9525	9.0962	40
48	97.0172	0.0103	960.1723	9.8969	0.0010	0.1010	94.0217	9.5001	48
50	117.3909	0.0085	1163.9085	9.9148	0.0009	0.1009	94.8889	9.5704	50
52	142.0429	0.0070	1410.4293	9.9296	0.0007	0.1007	95.6351	9.6313	52
60	304.4816	0.0033	3034.8164	9.9672	0.0003	0.1003	97.7010	9.8023	60
70	789.7470	0.0013	7887.4696	9.9873	0.0001	0.1001	98.9870	9.9113	70
72	955.5938	0.0010	9545.9382	9.9895	0.0001	0.1001	99.1419	9.9246	72
80	2048.4002	0.0005	2.047E+04	9.9951	0.0000	0.1000	99.5606	9.9609	80
84	2999.0628	0.0003	2.998E+04	9.9967	0.0000	0.1000	99.6866	9.9720	84
90	5313.0226	0.0002	5.312E+04	9.9981	0.0000	0.1000	99.8118	9.9831	90
96	9412.3437	0.0001	9.411E+04	9.9989	0.0000	0.1000	99.8874	9.9898	96
100	1.378E+04	0.0001	1.378E+05	9.9993	0.0000	0.1000	99.9202	9.9927	100
104	2.018E+04	0.0000	2.018E+05	9.9995	0.0000	0.1000	99.9435	9.9948	104
120	9.271E+04	0.0000	9.271E+05	9.9999	0.0000	0.1000	99.9860	9.9987	120
240	8.595E+09	0.0000	8.595E+10	10.0000	0.0000	0.1000	100.0000	10.0000	240
360	7.968E+14	0.0000	7.968E+15	10.0000	0.0000	0.1000	100.0000	10.0000	360
480	7.387E+19	0.0000	7.387E+20	10.0000	0.0000	0.1000	100.0000	10.0000	480

12.00%

	Single Payment		Uniform Series				Uniform Gradients		
	Compound Amount Factor	Present Worth Factor	Compound Amount Factor	Present Worth Factor	Sinking Fund Factor	Capital Recovery Factor	Gradient Present Worth Factor	Gradient Uniform Series Factor	
	To Find F Given P	To Find P Given F	To Find F Given A	To Find P Given A	To Find A Given F	To Find A Given P	To Find P Given G	To Find A Given G	
N	F/P	P/F	F/A	P/A	A/F	A/P	P/G	A/G	N
1	1.1200	0.8929	1.0000	0.8929	1.0000	1.1200	0.0000	0.0000	1
2	1.2544	0.7972	2.1200	1.6901	0.4717	0.5917	0.7972	0.4717	2
3	1.4049	0.7118	3.3744	2.4018	0.2963	0.4163	2.2208	0.9246	3
4	1.5735	0.6355	4.7793	3.0373	0.2092	0.3292	4.1273	1.3589	4
5	1.7623	0.5674	6.3528	3.6048	0.1574	0.2774	6.3970	1.7746	5
6	1.9738	0.5066	8.1152	4.1114	0.1232	0.2432	8.9302	2.1720	6
7	2.2107	0.4523	10.0890	4.5638	0.0991	0.2191	11.6443	2.5515	7
8	2.4760	0.4039	12.2997	4.9676	0.0813	0.2013	14.4714	2.9131	8
9	2.7731	0.3606	14.7757	5.3282	0.0677	0.1877	17.3563	3.2574	9
10	3.1058	0.3220	17.5487	5.6502	0.0570	0.1770	20.2541	3.5847	10
11	3.4785	0.2875	20.6546	5.9377	0.0484	0.1684	23.1288	3.8953	11
12	3.8960	0.2567	24.1331	6.1944	0.0414	0.1614	25.9523	4.1897	12
13	4.3635	0.2292	28.0291	6.4235	0.0357	0.1557	28.7024	4.4683	13
14	4.8871	0.2046	32.3926	6.6282	0.0309	0.1509	31.3624	4.7317	14
15	5.4736	0.1827	37.2797	6.8109	0.0268	0.1468	33.9202	4.9803	15
16	6.1304	0.1631	42.7533	6.9740	0.0234	0.1434	36.3670	5.2147	16
17	6.8660	0.1456	48.8837	7.1196	0.0205	0.1405	38.6973	5.4353	17
18	7.6900	0.1300	55.7497	7.2497	0.0179	0.1379	40.9080	5.6427	18
19	8.6128	0.1161	63.4397	7.3658	0.0158	0.1358	42.9979	5.8375	19
20	9.6463	0.1037	72.0524	7.4694	0.0139	0.1339	44.9676	6.0202	20
21	10.8038	0.0926	81.6987	7.5620	0.0122	0.1322	46.8188	6.1913	21
22	12.1003	0.0826	92.5026	7.6446	0.0108	0.1308	48.5543	6.3514	22
23	13.5523	0.0738	104.6029	7.7184	0.0096	0.1296	50.1776	6.5010	23
24	15.1786	0.0659	118.1552	7.7843	0.0085	0.1285	51.6929	6.6406	24
25	17.0001	0.0588	133.3339	7.8431	0.0075	0.1275	53.1046	6.7708	25
26	19.0401	0.0525	150.3339	7.8957	0.0067	0.1267	54.4177	6.8921	26
27	21.3249	0.0469	169.3740	7.9426	0.0059	0.1259	55.6369	7.0049	27
28	23.8839	0.0419	190.6989	7.9844	0.0052	0.1252	56.7674	7.1098	28
29	26.7499	0.0374	214.5828	8.0218	0.0047	0.1247	57.8141	7.2071	29
30	29.9599	0.0334	241.3327	8.0552	0.0041	0.1241	58.7821	7.2974	30
36	59.1356	0.0169	484.4631	8.1924	0.0021	0.1221	63.1970	7.7141	36
40	93.0510	0.0107	767.0914	8.2438	0.0013	0.1213	65.1159	7.8988	40
48	230.3908	0.0043	1911.5898	8.2972	0.0005	0.1205	67.4068	8.1241	48
50	289.0022	0.0035	2400.0182	8.3045	0.0004	0.1204	67.7624	8.1597	50
52	362.5243	0.0028	3012.7029	8.3103	0.0003	0.1203	68.0576	8.1895	52
60	897.5969	0.0011	7471.6411	8.3240	0.0001	0.1201	68.8100	8.2664	60
70	2787.7998	0.0004	23223.3319	8.3303	0.0000	0.1200	69.2103	8.3082	70
72	3497.0161	0.0003	29133.4675	8.3310	0.0000	0.1200	69.2530	8.3127	72
80	8658.4831	0.0001	72145.6925	8.3324	0.0000	0.1200	69.3594	8.3241	80
84	13624.2908	0.0001	1.135E+05	8.3327	0.0000	0.1200	69.3880	8.3272	84
90	26891.9342	0.0000	2.241E+05	8.3330	0.0000	0.1200	69.4140	8.3300	90
96	53079.9098	0.0000	4.423E+05	8.3332	0.0000	0.1200	69.4281	8.3315	96
100	83522.2657	0.0000	6.960E+05	8.3332	0.0000	0.1200	69.4336	8.3321	100
104	1.314E+05	0.0000	1.095E+06	8.3333	0.0000	0.1200	69.4373	8.3325	104
120	8.057E+05	0.0000	6.714E+06	8.3333	0.0000	0.1200	69.4431	8.3332	120
240	6.491E+11	0.0000	5.409E+12	8.3333	0.0000	0.1200	69.4444	8.3333	240
360	5.230E+17	0.0000	4.358E+18	8.3333	0.0000	0.1200	69.4444	8.3333	360
480	4.214E+23	0.0000	3.511E+24	8.3333	0.0000	0.1200	69.4444	8.3333	480

15.00%

	Single Payment		Uniform Series				Uniform Gradients		
	Compound Amount Factor	Present Worth Factor	Compound Amount Factor	Present Worth Factor	Sinking Fund Factor	Capital Recovery Factor	Gradient Present Worth Factor	Gradient Uniform Series Factor	
	To Find F Given P	To Find P Given F	To Find F Given A	To Find P Given A	To Find A Given F	To Find A Given P	To Find P Given G	To Find A Given G	
N	F/P	P/F	F/A	P/A	A/F	A/P	P/G	A/G	N
1	1.1500	0.8696	1.0000	0.8696	1.0000	1.1500	0.0000	0.0000	1
2	1.3225	0.7561	2.1500	1.6257	0.4651	0.6151	0.7561	0.4651	2
3	1.5209	0.6575	3.4725	2.2832	0.2880	0.4380	2.0712	0.9071	3
4	1.7490	0.5718	4.9934	2.8550	0.2003	0.3503	3.7864	1.3263	4
5	2.0114	0.4972	6.7424	3.3522	0.1483	0.2983	5.7751	1.7228	5
6	2.3131	0.4323	8.7537	3.7845	0.1142	0.2642	7.9368	2.0972	6
7	2.6600	0.3759	11.0668	4.1604	0.0904	0.2404	10.1924	2.4498	7
8	3.0590	0.3269	13.7268	4.4873	0.0729	0.2229	12.4807	2.7813	8
9	3.5179	0.2843	16.7858	4.7716	0.0596	0.2096	14.7548	3.0922	9
10	4.0456	0.2472	20.3037	5.0188	0.0493	0.1993	16.9795	3.3832	10
11	4.6524	0.2149	24.3493	5.2337	0.0411	0.1911	19.1289	3.6549	11
12	5.3503	0.1869	29.0017	5.4206	0.0345	0.1845	21.1849	3.9082	12
13	6.1528	0.1625	34.3519	5.5831	0.0291	0.1791	23.1352	4.1438	13
14	7.0757	0.1413	40.5047	5.7245	0.0247	0.1747	24.9725	4.3624	14
15	8.1371	0.1229	47.5804	5.8474	0.0210	0.1710	26.6930	4.5650	15
16	9.3576	0.1069	55.7175	5.9542	0.0179	0.1679	28.2960	4.7522	16
17	10.7613	0.0929	65.0751	6.0472	0.0154	0.1654	29.7828	4.9251	17
18	12.3755	0.0808	75.8364	6.1280	0.0132	0.1632	31.1565	5.0843	18
19	14.2318	0.0703	88.2118	6.1982	0.0113	0.1613	32.4213	5.2307	19
20	16.3665	0.0611	102.4436	6.2593	0.0098	0.1598	33.5822	5.3651	20
21	18.8215	0.0531	118.8101	6.3125	0.0084	0.1584	34.6448	5.4883	21
22	21.6447	0.0462	137.6316	6.3587	0.0073	0.1573	35.6150	5.6010	22
23	24.8915	0.0402	159.2764	6.3988	0.0063	0.1563	36.4988	5.7040	23
24	28.6252	0.0349	184.1678	6.4338	0.0054	0.1554	37.3023	5.7979	24
25	32.9190	0.0304	212.7930	6.4641	0.0047	0.1547	38.0314	5.8834	25
26	37.8568	0.0264	245.7120	6.4906	0.0041	0.1541	38.6918	5.9612	26
27	43.5353	0.0230	283.5688	6.5135	0.0035	0.1535	39.2890	6.0319	27
28	50.0656	0.0200	327.1041	6.5335	0.0031	0.1531	39.8283	6.0960	28
29	57.5755	0.0174	377.1697	6.5509	0.0027	0.1527	40.3146	6.1541	29
30	66.2118	0.0151	434.7451	6.5660	0.0023	0.1523	40.7526	6.2066	30
36	153.1519	0.0065	1014.3457	6.6231	0.0010	0.1510	42.5872	6.4301	36
40	267.8635	0.0037	1779.0903	6.6418	0.0006	0.1506	43.2830	6.5168	40
48	819.4007	0.0012	5456.0047	6.6585	0.0002	0.1502	43.9997	6.6080	48
50	1083.6574	0.0009	7217.7163	6.6605	0.0001	0.1501	44.0958	6.6205	50
52	1433.1370	0.0007	9547.5798	6.6620	0.0001	0.1501	44.1715	6.6304	52
60	4383.9987	0.0002	2.922E+04	6.6651	0.0000	0.1500	44.3431	6.6530	60
70	1.774E+04	0.0001	1.182E+05	6.6663	0.0000	0.1500	44.4156	6.6627	70
72	2.346E+04	0.0000	1.564E+05	6.6664	0.0000	0.1500	44.4221	6.6636	72
80	7.175E+04	0.0000	4.783E+05	6.6666	0.0000	0.1500	44.4364	6.6656	80
84	1.255E+05	0.0000	8.366E+05	6.6666	0.0000	0.1500	44.4396	6.6660	84
90	2.903E+05	0.0000	1.935E+06	6.6666	0.0000	0.1500	44.4422	6.6664	90
96	6.714E+05	0.0000	4.476E+06	6.6667	0.0000	0.1500	44.4434	6.6665	96
100	1.174E+06	0.0000	7.829E+06	6.6667	0.0000	0.1500	44.4438	6.6666	100
104	2.054E+06	0.0000	1.369E+07	6.6667	0.0000	0.1500	44.4441	6.6666	104
120	1.922E+07	0.0000	1.281E+08	6.6667	0.0000	0.1500	44.4444	6.6667	120
240	3.694E+14	0.0000	2.463E+15	6.6667	0.0000	0.1500	44.4444	6.6667	240
360	7.099E+21	0.0000	4.733E+22	6.6667	0.0000	0.1500	44.4444	6.6667	360
480	1.364E+29	0.0000	9.096E+29	6.6667	0.0000	0.1500	44.4444	6.6667	480

18.00%

	Single Payment		Uniform Series				Uniform Gradients		
	Compound Amount Factor	Present Worth Factor	Compound Amount Factor	Present Worth Factor	Sinking Fund Factor	Capital Recovery Factor	Gradient Present Worth Factor	Gradient Uniform Series Factor	
	To Find F Given P	To Find P Given F	To Find F Given A	To Find P Given A	To Find A Given F	To Find A Given P	To Find P Given G	To Find A Given G	
N	F/P	P/F	F/A	P/A	A/F	A/P	P/G	A/G	N
1	1.1800	0.8475	1.0000	0.8475	1.0000	1.1800	0.0000	0.0000	1
2	1.3924	0.7182	2.1800	1.5656	0.4587	0.6387	0.7182	0.4587	2
3	1.6430	0.6086	3.5724	2.1743	0.2799	0.4599	1.9354	0.8902	3
4	1.9388	0.5158	5.2154	2.6901	0.1917	0.3717	3.4828	1.2947	4
5	2.2878	0.4371	7.1542	3.1272	0.1398	0.3198	5.2312	1.6728	5
6	2.6996	0.3704	9.4420	3.4976	0.1059	0.2859	7.0834	2.0252	6
7	3.1855	0.3139	12.1415	3.8115	0.0824	0.2624	8.9670	2.3526	7
8	3.7589	0.2660	15.3270	4.0776	0.0652	0.2452	10.8292	2.6558	8
9	4.4355	0.2255	19.0859	4.3030	0.0524	0.2324	12.6329	2.9358	9
10	5.2338	0.1911	23.5213	4.4941	0.0425	0.2225	14.3525	3.1936	10
11	6.1759	0.1619	28.7551	4.6560	0.0348	0.2148	15.9716	3.4303	11
12	7.2876	0.1372	34.9311	4.7932	0.0286	0.2086	17.4811	3.6470	12
13	8.5994	0.1163	42.2187	4.9095	0.0237	0.2037	18.8765	3.8449	13
14	10.1472	0.0985	50.8180	5.0081	0.0197	0.1997	20.1576	4.0250	14
15	11.9737	0.0835	60.9653	5.0916	0.0164	0.1964	21.3269	4.1887	15
16	14.1290	0.0708	72.9390	5.1624	0.0137	0.1937	22.3885	4.3369	16
17	16.6722	0.0600	87.0680	5.2223	0.0115	0.1915	23.3482	4.4708	17
18	19.6733	0.0508	103.7403	5.2732	0.0096	0.1896	24.2123	4.5916	18
19	23.2144	0.0431	123.4135	5.3162	0.0081	0.1881	24.9877	4.7003	19
20	27.3930	0.0365	146.6280	5.3527	0.0068	0.1868	25.6813	4.7978	20
21	32.3238	0.0309	174.0210	5.3837	0.0057	0.1857	26.3000	4.8851	21
22	38.1421	0.0262	206.3448	5.4099	0.0048	0.1848	26.8506	4.9632	22
23	45.0076	0.0222	244.4868	5.4321	0.0041	0.1841	27.3394	5.0329	23
24	53.1090	0.0188	289.4945	5.4509	0.0035	0.1835	27.7725	5.0950	24
25	62.6686	0.0160	342.6035	5.4669	0.0029	0.1829	28.1555	5.1502	25
26	73.9490	0.0135	405.2721	5.4804	0.0025	0.1825	28.4935	5.1991	26
27	87.2598	0.0115	479.2211	5.4919	0.0021	0.1821	28.7915	5.2425	27
28	102.9666	0.0097	566.4809	5.5016	0.0018	0.1818	29.0537	5.2810	28
29	121.5005	0.0082	669.4475	5.5098	0.0015	0.1815	29.2842	5.3149	29
30	143.3706	0.0070	790.9480	5.5168	0.0013	0.1813	29.4864	5.3448	30
36	387.0368	0.0026	2144.6489	5.5412	0.0005	0.1805	30.2677	5.4623	36
40	750.3783	0.0013	4163.2130	5.5482	0.0002	0.1802	30.5269	5.5022	40
48	2820.5665	0.0004	1.566E+04	5.5536	0.0001	0.1801	30.7587	5.5385	48
50	3927.3569	0.0003	2.181E+04	5.5541	0.0000	0.1800	30.7856	5.5428	50
52	5468.4517	0.0002	3.037E+04	5.5545	0.0000	0.1800	30.8057	5.5460	52
60	2.056E+04	0.0000	1.142E+05	5.5553	0.0000	0.1800	30.8465	5.5526	60
70	1.076E+05	0.0000	5.977E+05	5.5555	0.0000	0.1800	30.8603	5.5549	70
72	1.498E+05	0.0000	8.322E+05	5.5555	0.0000	0.1800	30.8613	5.5551	72
80	5.631E+05	0.0000	3.128E+06	5.5555	0.0000	0.1800	30.8634	5.5554	80
84	1.092E+06	0.0000	6.065E+06	5.5556	0.0000	0.1800	30.8637	5.5555	84
90	2.947E+06	0.0000	1.637E+07	5.5556	0.0000	0.1800	30.8640	5.5555	90
96	7.956E+06	0.0000	4.420E+07	5.5556	0.0000	0.1800	30.8641	5.5555	96
100	1.542E+07	0.0000	8.569E+07	5.5556	0.0000	0.1800	30.8642	5.5555	100
104	2.990E+07	0.0000	1.661E+08	5.5556	0.0000	0.1800	30.8642	5.5556	104
120	4.225E+08	0.0000	2.347E+09	5.5556	0.0000	0.1800	30.8642	5.5556	120
240	1.785E+17	0.0000	9.918E+17	5.5556	0.0000	0.1800	30.8642	5.5556	240
360	7.543E+25	0.0000	4.190E+26	5.5556	0.0000	0.1800	30.8642	5.5556	360
480	3.187E+34	0.0000	1.770E+35	5.5556	0.0000	0.1800	30.8642	5.5556	480

20.00%

N	Single Payment		Uniform Series				Uniform Gradients		N
	Compound Amount Factor	Present Worth Factor	Compound Amount Factor	Present Worth Factor	Sinking Fund Factor	Capital Recovery Factor	Gradient Present Worth Factor	Gradient Uniform Series Factor	
	To Find F Given P	To Find P Given F	To Find F Given A	To Find P Given A	To Find A Given F	To Find A Given P	To Find P Given G	To Find A Given G	
N	F/P	P/F	F/A	P/A	A/F	A/P	P/G	A/G	N
1	1.200	0.833	1.000	0.833	1.000	1.200	0.000	0.000	1
2	1.440	0.694	2.200	1.528	0.455	0.655	0.694	0.455	2
3	1.728	0.579	3.640	2.107	0.275	0.475	1.852	0.879	3
4	2.074	0.482	5.368	2.589	0.186	0.386	3.299	1.274	4
5	2.488	0.402	7.442	2.991	0.134	0.334	4.906	1.641	5
6	2.986	0.335	9.930	3.326	0.101	0.301	6.581	1.979	6
7	3.583	0.279	12.916	3.605	0.077	0.277	8.255	2.290	7
8	4.300	0.233	16.499	3.837	0.061	0.261	9.883	2.576	8
9	5.160	0.194	20.799	4.031	0.048	0.248	11.434	2.836	9
10	6.192	0.162	25.959	4.193	0.039	0.239	12.887	3.074	10
11	7.430	0.135	32.150	4.327	0.031	0.231	14.233	3.289	11
12	8.916	0.112	39.581	4.439	0.025	0.225	15.467	3.484	12
13	10.699	0.094	48.497	4.533	0.021	0.221	16.588	3.660	13
14	12.839	0.078	59.196	4.611	0.017	0.217	17.601	3.818	14
15	15.407	0.065	72.035	4.676	0.014	0.214	18.510	3.959	15
16	18.488	0.054	87.442	4.730	0.011	0.211	19.321	4.085	16
17	22.186	0.045	105.931	4.775	0.009	0.209	20.042	4.198	17
18	26.623	0.038	128.117	4.812	0.008	0.208	20.681	4.298	18
19	31.948	0.031	154.740	4.844	0.007	0.207	21.244	4.386	19
20	38.338	0.026	186.688	4.870	0.005	0.205	21.740	4.464	20
21	46.005	0.022	225.026	4.891	0.004	0.204	22.174	4.533	21
22	55.206	0.018	271.031	4.909	0.004	0.204	22.555	4.594	22
23	66.247	0.015	326.237	4.925	0.003	0.203	22.887	4.648	23
24	79.497	0.013	392.484	4.937	0.003	0.203	23.176	4.694	24
25	95.396	0.011	471.981	4.948	0.002	0.202	23.428	4.735	25
26	114.476	0.009	567.377	4.956	0.002	0.202	23.646	4.771	26
27	137.371	0.007	681.853	4.964	0.002	0.202	23.835	4.802	27
28	164.845	0.006	819.223	4.970	0.001	0.201	23.999	4.829	28
29	197.814	0.005	984.068	4.975	0.001	0.201	24.141	4.853	29
30	237.376	0.004	1181.882	4.979	0.001	0.201	24.263	4.873	30
36	708.802	0.001	3539.009	4.993	0.000	0.200	24.711	4.949	36
40	1469.772	0.001	7343.858	4.997	0.000	0.200	24.847	4.973	40
48	6319.749	0.000	31593.744	4.999	0.000	0.200	24.958	4.992	48
50	9100.438	0.000	45497.191	5.000	0.000	0.200	24.970	4.995	50
52	13104.631	0.000	65518.155	5.000	0.000	0.200	24.978	4.996	52
60	56347.514	0.000	2.817E+05	5.000	0.000	0.200	24.994	4.999	60
70	3.489E+05	0.000	1.744E+06	5.000	0.000	0.200	24.999	5.000	70
72	5.024E+05	0.000	2.512E+06	5.000	0.000	0.200	24.999	5.000	72
80	2.160E+06	0.000	1.080E+07	5.000	0.000	0.200	25.000	5.000	80
84	4.479E+06	0.000	2.240E+07	5.000	0.000	0.200	25.000	5.000	84
90	1.338E+07	0.000	6.688E+07	5.000	0.000	0.200	25.000	5.000	90
96	3.994E+07	0.000	1.997E+08	5.000	0.000	0.200	25.000	5.000	96
100	8.282E+07	0.000	4.141E+08	5.000	0.000	0.200	25.000	5.000	100
104	1.717E+08	0.000	8.587E+08	5.000	0.000	0.200	25.000	5.000	104
120	3.175E+09	0.000	1.588E+10	5.000	0.000	0.200	25.000	5.000	120
240	1.008E+19	0.000	5.040E+19	5.000	0.000	0.200	25.000	5.000	240
360	3.201E+28	0.000	1.600E+29	5.000	0.000	0.200	25.000	5.000	360
480	1.016E+38	0.000	5.081E+38	5.000	0.000	0.200	25.000	5.000	480

25.00%

N	Single Payment		Uniform Series				Uniform Gradients		N
	Compound Amount Factor	Present Worth Factor	Compound Amount Factor	Present Worth Factor	Sinking Fund Factor	Capital Recovery Factor	Gradient Present Worth Factor	Gradient Uniform Series Factor	
	To Find F Given P F/P	To Find P Given F P/F	To Find F Given A F/A	To Find P Given A P/A	To Find A Given F A/F	To Find A Given P A/P	To Find P Given G P/G	To Find A Given G A/G	
1	1.2500	0.8000	1.0000	0.8000	1.0000	1.2500	0.0000	0.0000	1
2	1.5625	0.6400	2.2500	1.4400	0.4444	0.6944	0.6400	0.4444	2
3	1.9531	0.5120	3.8125	1.9520	0.2623	0.5123	1.6640	0.8525	3
4	2.4414	0.4096	5.7656	2.3616	0.1734	0.4234	2.8928	1.2249	4
5	3.0518	0.3277	8.2070	2.6893	0.1218	0.3718	4.2035	1.5631	5
6	3.8147	0.2621	11.2588	2.9514	0.0888	0.3388	5.5142	1.8683	6
7	4.7684	0.2097	15.0735	3.1611	0.0663	0.3163	6.7725	2.1424	7
8	5.9605	0.1678	19.8419	3.3289	0.0504	0.3004	7.9469	2.3872	8
9	7.4506	0.1342	25.8023	3.4631	0.0388	0.2888	9.0207	2.6048	9
10	9.3132	0.1074	33.2529	3.5705	0.0301	0.2801	9.9870	2.7971	10
11	11.6415	0.0859	42.5661	3.6564	0.0235	0.2735	10.8460	2.9663	11
12	14.5519	0.0687	54.2077	3.7251	0.0184	0.2684	11.6020	3.1145	12
13	18.1899	0.0550	68.7596	3.7801	0.0145	0.2645	12.2617	3.2437	13
14	22.7374	0.0440	86.9495	3.8241	0.0115	0.2615	12.8334	3.3559	14
15	28.4217	0.0352	109.6868	3.8593	0.0091	0.2591	13.3260	3.4530	15
16	35.5271	0.0281	138.1085	3.8874	0.0072	0.2572	13.7482	3.5366	16
17	44.4089	0.0225	173.6357	3.9099	0.0058	0.2558	14.1085	3.6084	17
18	55.5112	0.0180	218.0446	3.9279	0.0046	0.2546	14.4147	3.6698	18
19	69.3889	0.0144	273.5558	3.9424	0.0037	0.2537	14.6741	3.7222	19
20	86.7362	0.0115	342.9447	3.9539	0.0029	0.2529	14.8932	3.7667	20
21	108.4202	0.0092	429.6809	3.9631	0.0023	0.2523	15.0777	3.8045	21
22	135.5253	0.0074	538.1011	3.9705	0.0019	0.2519	15.2326	3.8365	22
23	169.4066	0.0059	673.6264	3.9764	0.0015	0.2515	15.3625	3.8634	23
24	211.7582	0.0047	843.0329	3.9811	0.0012	0.2512	15.4711	3.8861	24
25	264.6978	0.0038	1054.7912	3.9849	0.0009	0.2509	15.5618	3.9052	25
26	330.8722	0.0030	1319.4890	3.9879	0.0008	0.2508	15.6373	3.9212	26
27	413.5903	0.0024	1650.3612	3.9903	0.0006	0.2506	15.7002	3.9346	27
28	516.9879	0.0019	2063.9515	3.9923	0.0005	0.2505	15.7524	3.9457	28
29	646.2349	0.0015	2580.9394	3.9938	0.0004	0.2504	15.7957	3.9551	29
30	807.7936	0.0012	3227.1743	3.9950	0.0003	0.2503	15.8316	3.9628	30
36	3081.4879	0.0003	12321.9516	3.9987	0.0001	0.2501	15.9481	3.9883	36
40	7523.1638	0.0001	30088.6554	3.9995	0.0000	0.2500	15.9766	3.9947	40
48	4.484E+04	0.0000	1.794E+05	3.9999	0.0000	0.2500	15.9954	3.9989	48
50	7.006E+04	0.0000	2.803E+05	3.9999	0.0000	0.2500	15.9969	3.9993	50
52	1.095E+05	0.0000	4.379E+05	4.0000	0.0000	0.2500	15.9980	3.9995	52
60	6.525E+05	0.0000	2.610E+06	4.0000	0.0000	0.2500	15.9996	3.9999	60
70	6.077E+06	0.0000	2.431E+07	4.0000	0.0000	0.2500	16.0000	4.0000	70
72	9.496E+06	0.0000	3.798E+07	4.0000	0.0000	0.2500	16.0000	4.0000	72
80	5.660E+07	0.0000	2.264E+08	4.0000	0.0000	0.2500	16.0000	4.0000	80
84	1.382E+08	0.0000	5.527E+08	4.0000	0.0000	0.2500	16.0000	4.0000	84
90	5.271E+08	0.0000	2.108E+09	4.0000	0.0000	0.2500	16.0000	4.0000	90
96	2.011E+09	0.0000	8.043E+09	4.0000	0.0000	0.2500	16.0000	4.0000	96
100	4.909E+09	0.0000	1.964E+10	4.0000	0.0000	0.2500	16.0000	4.0000	100
104	1.199E+10	0.0000	4.794E+10	4.0000	0.0000	0.2500	16.0000	4.0000	104
120	4.258E+11	0.0000	1.703E+12	4.0000	0.0000	0.2500	16.0000	4.0000	120
240	1.813E+23	0.0000	7.252E+23	4.0000	0.0000	0.2500	16.0000	4.0000	240
360	7.720E+34	0.0000	3.088E+35	4.0000	0.0000	0.2500	16.0000	4.0000	360
480	3.287E+46	0.0000	1.315E+47	4.0000	0.0000	0.2500	16.0000	4.0000	480

30.00%

N	Single Payment		Uniform Series				Uniform Gradients		N
	Compound Amount Factor	Present Worth Factor	Compound Amount Factor	Present Worth Factor	Sinking Fund Factor	Capital Recovery Factor	Gradient Present Worth Factor	Gradient Uniform Series Factor	
	To Find F Given P F/P	To Find P Given F P/F	To Find F Given A F/A	To Find P Given A P/A	To Find A Given F A/F	To Find A Given P A/P	To Find P Given G P/G	To Find A Given G A/G	
1	1.3000	0.7692	1.0000	0.7692	1.0000	1.3000	0.0000	0.0000	1
2	1.6900	0.5917	2.3000	1.3609	0.4348	0.7348	0.5917	0.4348	2
3	2.1970	0.4552	3.9900	1.8161	0.2506	0.5506	1.5020	0.8271	3
4	2.8561	0.3501	6.1870	2.1662	0.1616	0.4616	2.5524	1.1783	4
5	3.7129	0.2693	9.0431	2.4356	0.1106	0.4106	3.6297	1.4903	5
6	4.8268	0.2072	12.7560	2.6427	0.0784	0.3784	4.6656	1.7654	6
7	6.2749	0.1594	17.5828	2.8021	0.0569	0.3569	5.6218	2.0063	7
8	8.1573	0.1226	23.8577	2.9247	0.0419	0.3419	6.4800	2.2156	8
9	10.6045	0.0943	32.0150	3.0190	0.0312	0.3312	7.2343	2.3963	9
10	13.7858	0.0725	42.6195	3.0915	0.0235	0.3235	7.8872	2.5512	10
11	17.9216	0.0558	56.4053	3.1473	0.0177	0.3177	8.4452	2.6833	11
12	23.2981	0.0429	74.3270	3.1903	0.0135	0.3135	8.9173	2.7952	12
13	30.2875	0.0330	97.6250	3.2233	0.0102	0.3102	9.3135	2.8895	13
14	39.3738	0.0254	127.9125	3.2487	0.0078	0.3078	9.6437	2.9685	14
15	51.1859	0.0195	167.2863	3.2682	0.0060	0.3060	9.9172	3.0344	15
16	66.5417	0.0150	218.4722	3.2832	0.0046	0.3046	10.1426	3.0892	16
17	86.5042	0.0116	285.0139	3.2948	0.0035	0.3035	10.3276	3.1345	17
18	112.4554	0.0089	371.5180	3.3037	0.0027	0.3027	10.4788	3.1718	18
19	146.1920	0.0068	483.9734	3.3105	0.0021	0.3021	10.6019	3.2025	19
20	190.0496	0.0053	630.1655	3.3158	0.0016	0.3016	10.7019	3.2275	20
21	247.0645	0.0040	820.2151	3.3198	0.0012	0.3012	10.7828	3.2480	21
22	321.1839	0.0031	1067.2796	3.3230	0.0009	0.3009	10.8482	3.2646	22
23	417.5391	0.0024	1388.4635	3.3254	0.0007	0.3007	10.9009	3.2781	23
24	542.8008	0.0018	1806.0026	3.3272	0.0006	0.3006	10.9433	3.2890	24
25	705.6410	0.0014	2348.8033	3.3286	0.0004	0.3004	10.9773	3.2979	25
26	917.3333	0.0011	3054.4443	3.3297	0.0003	0.3003	11.0045	3.3050	26
27	1192.5333	0.0008	3971.7776	3.3305	0.0003	0.3003	11.0263	3.3107	27
28	1550.2933	0.0006	5164.3109	3.3312	0.0002	0.3002	11.0437	3.3153	28
29	2015.3813	0.0005	6714.6042	3.3317	0.0001	0.3001	11.0576	3.3189	29
30	2619.9956	0.0004	8729.9855	3.3321	0.0001	0.3001	11.0687	3.3219	30
36	1.265E+04	0.0001	4.215E+04	3.3331	0.0000	0.3000	11.1007	3.3305	36
40	3.612E+04	0.0000	1.204E+05	3.3332	0.0000	0.3000	11.1071	3.3322	40
48	2.946E+05	0.0000	9.821E+05	3.3333	0.0000	0.3000	11.1105	3.3332	48
50	4.979E+05	0.0000	1.660E+06	3.3333	0.0000	0.3000	11.1108	3.3332	50
52	8.415E+05	0.0000	2.805E+06	3.3333	0.0000	0.3000	11.1109	3.3333	52
60	6.864E+06	0.0000	2.288E+07	3.3333	0.0000	0.3000	11.1111	3.3333	60
70	9.463E+07	0.0000	3.154E+08	3.3333	0.0000	0.3000	11.1111	3.3333	70
72	1.599E+08	0.0000	5.331E+08	3.3333	0.0000	0.3000	11.1111	3.3333	72
80	1.305E+09	0.0000	4.349E+09	3.3333	0.0000	0.3000	11.1111	3.3333	80
84	3.726E+09	0.0000	1.242E+10	3.3333	0.0000	0.3000	11.1111	3.3333	84
90	1.798E+10	0.0000	5.995E+10	3.3333	0.0000	0.3000	11.1111	3.3333	90
96	8.681E+10	0.0000	2.894E+11	3.3333	0.0000	0.3000	11.1111	3.3333	96
100	2.479E+11	0.0000	8.264E+11	3.3333	0.0000	0.3000	11.1111	3.3333	100
104	7.081E+11	0.0000	2.360E+12	3.3333	0.0000	0.3000	11.1111	3.3333	104
120	4.712E+13	0.0000	1.571E+14	3.3333	0.0000	0.3000	11.1111	3.3333	120
240	2.220E+27	0.0000	7.401E+27	3.3333	0.0000	0.3000	11.1111	3.3333	240
360	1.046E+41	0.0000	3.487E+41	3.3333	0.0000	0.3000	11.1111	3.3333	360
480	4.930E+54	0.0000	1.643E+55	3.3333	0.0000	0.3000	11.1111	3.3333	480

35.00%

	Single Payment		Uniform Series				Uniform Gradients		
	Compound Amount Factor	Present Worth Factor	Compound Amount Factor	Present Worth Factor	Sinking Fund Factor	Capital Recovery Factor	Gradient Present Worth Factor	Gradient Uniform Series Factor	
	To Find F Given P	To Find P Given F	To Find F Given A	To Find P Given A	To Find A Given F	To Find A Given P	To Find P Given G	To Find A Given G	
N	F/P	P/F	F/A	P/A	A/F	A/P	P/G	A/G	N
1	1.3500	0.7407	1.0000	0.7407	1.0000	1.3500	0.0000	0.0000	1
2	1.8225	0.5487	2.3500	1.2894	0.4255	0.7755	0.5487	0.4255	2
3	2.4604	0.4064	4.1725	1.6959	0.2397	0.5897	1.3616	0.8029	3
4	3.3215	0.3011	6.6329	1.9969	0.1508	0.5008	2.2648	1.1341	4
5	4.4840	0.2230	9.9544	2.2200	0.1005	0.4505	3.1568	1.4220	5
6	6.0534	0.1652	14.4384	2.3852	0.0693	0.4193	3.9828	1.6698	6
7	8.1722	0.1224	20.4919	2.5075	0.0488	0.3988	4.7170	1.8811	7
8	11.0324	0.0906	28.6640	2.5982	0.0349	0.3849	5.3515	2.0597	8
9	14.8937	0.0671	39.6964	2.6653	0.0252	0.3752	5.8886	2.2094	9
10	20.1066	0.0497	54.5902	2.7150	0.0183	0.3683	6.3363	2.3338	10
11	27.1439	0.0368	74.6967	2.7519	0.0134	0.3634	6.7047	2.4364	11
12	36.6442	0.0273	101.8406	2.7792	0.0098	0.3598	7.0049	2.5205	12
13	49.4697	0.0202	138.4848	2.7994	0.0072	0.3572	7.2474	2.5889	13
14	66.7841	0.0150	187.9544	2.8144	0.0053	0.3553	7.4421	2.6443	14
15	90.1585	0.0111	254.7385	2.8255	0.0039	0.3539	7.5974	2.6889	15
16	121.7139	0.0082	344.8970	2.8337	0.0029	0.3529	7.7206	2.7246	16
17	164.3138	0.0061	466.6109	2.8398	0.0021	0.3521	7.8180	2.7530	17
18	221.8236	0.0045	630.9247	2.8443	0.0016	0.3516	7.8946	2.7756	18
19	299.4619	0.0033	852.7483	2.8476	0.0012	0.3512	7.9547	2.7935	19
20	404.2736	0.0025	1152.2103	2.8501	0.0009	0.3509	8.0017	2.8075	20
21	545.7693	0.0018	1556.4838	2.8519	0.0006	0.3506	8.0384	2.8186	21
22	736.7886	0.0014	2102.2532	2.8533	0.0005	0.3505	8.0669	2.8272	22
23	994.6646	0.0010	2839.0418	2.8543	0.0004	0.3504	8.0890	2.8340	23
24	1342.7973	0.0007	3833.7064	2.8550	0.0003	0.3503	8.1061	2.8393	24
25	1812.7763	0.0006	5176.5037	2.8556	0.0002	0.3502	8.1194	2.8433	25
26	2447.2480	0.0004	6989.2800	2.8560	0.0001	0.3501	8.1296	2.8465	26
27	3303.7848	0.0003	9436.5280	2.8563	0.0001	0.3501	8.1374	2.8490	27
28	4460.1095	0.0002	12740.3128	2.8565	0.0001	0.3501	8.1435	2.8509	28
29	6021.1478	0.0002	17200.4222	2.8567	0.0001	0.3501	8.1481	2.8523	29
30	8128.5495	0.0001	23221.5700	2.8568	0.0000	0.3500	8.1517	2.8535	30
36	4.921E+04	0.0000	1.406E+05	2.8571	0.0000	0.3500	8.1610	2.8564	36
40	1.634E+05	0.0000	4.670E+05	2.8571	0.0000	0.3500	8.1625	2.8569	40
48	1.803E+06	0.0000	5.152E+06	2.8571	0.0000	0.3500	8.1632	2.8571	48
50	3.286E+06	0.0000	9.389E+06	2.8571	0.0000	0.3500	8.1632	2.8571	50
52	5.989E+06	0.0000	1.711E+07	2.8571	0.0000	0.3500	8.1632	2.8571	52
60	6.607E+07	0.0000	1.888E+08	2.8571	0.0000	0.3500	8.1633	2.8571	60
70	1.329E+09	0.0000	3.796E+09	2.8571	0.0000	0.3500	8.1633	2.8571	70
72	2.421E+09	0.0000	6.918E+09	2.8571	0.0000	0.3500	8.1633	2.8571	72
80	2.671E+10	0.0000	7.632E+10	2.8571	0.0000	0.3500	8.1633	2.8571	80
84	8.872E+10	0.0000	2.535E+11	2.8571	0.0000	0.3500	8.1633	2.8571	84
90	5.371E+11	0.0000	1.535E+12	2.8571	0.0000	0.3500	8.1633	2.8571	90
96	3.251E+12	0.0000	9.289E+12	2.8571	0.0000	0.3500	8.1633	2.8571	96
100	1.080E+13	0.0000	3.085E+13	2.8571	0.0000	0.3500	8.1633	2.8571	100
104	3.587E+13	0.0000	1.025E+14	2.8571	0.0000	0.3500	8.1633	2.8571	104
120	4.366E+15	0.0000	1.247E+16	2.8571	0.0000	0.3500	8.1633	2.8571	120
240	1.906E+31	0.0000	5.445E+31	2.8571	0.0000	0.3500	8.1633	2.8571	240
360	8.321E+46	0.0000	2.377E+47	2.8571	0.0000	0.3500	8.1633	2.8571	360
480	3.633E+62	0.0000	1.038E+63	2.8571	0.0000	0.3500	8.1633	2.8571	480

APPENDIX B: ANSWERS TO REVIEW QUESTIONS

CHAPTER 1 ANSWERS

1. Because it overlooks other types of costs, such as nonmonetary costs, externalized costs to society, and opportunity costs.

2. Economics is a social science. It studies human systems, and often must make assumptions and abstractions about economic behavior. The same data may produce different results, depending on the analyses. Even the same results may be interpreted in different ways, leading to different policy recommendations.

3. Yes, because the first is often a positive statement, involving facts, and the second is a normative statement, involving value judgments. But a seemingly positive statement may actually be normative, because methods for gathering and analyzing data often involve subjectivity and value judgments. Thus "facts" may be subjective rather than objective.

4. Because ecosystem services are often nonmarket goods, and provided for free or below their true social value or cost, producers and consumers may not recognize or fully account for them in their decisions. The implications are that producers and consumers may use more resources and generate more waste than they would if ecosystem goods were strict market goods.

5. Using money makes it possible to place benefits and costs into a single quantitative measure, and it permits ease of comparison among decision alternatives. For public sector decisions, other factors should normally be considered. Because society has multiple goals, often difficult to quantify, no single metric would probably be appropriate for all decisions.

CHAPTER 2 ANSWERS

1. I = increase; D = decrease

	Supply	Demand	Price	Quantity
a)	D		I	D
b)		I	I	I
c)		D	D	D
d)	I		D	I
e)		I	I	I
f)	D		I	D
g)	D		I	D

2. a) Decrease, b) Decrease, c) Decrease, d) Increase, e) Increase, f) Decrease, g) Increase

3. a) Increase, b) Decrease, c) Decrease, d) Increase, e) Decrease, f) Increase, g) Increase

4. Both an increase in supply and an increase in demand will increase quantity. But an increase in supply will decrease price, whereas an increase in demand will increase price. It's not clear which will outweigh the other on price effects.

   Both an increase in supply and a decrease in demand will decrease price. But an increase in supply will increase quantity, whereas a decrease in demand will decrease quantity. So it's not clear which will outweigh the other on quantity effects.

5. Cutting the employer's share from 90% to 80% doubles the effective price to workers, from 10% to 20%. So %ΔP = +1, or a 100% increase in price. Recall that E_D = %ΔQ/%ΔP, and E_D= –0.2. Thus, %ΔQ = –0.2(1) = –0.2, or a 20% decrease in quantity demanded of health care. With the decrease in amount covered, workers' demand for health care falls to 80% of its original level.

   Let X = the original, total expenditure by workers on health care. Let Y = the new, total expenditure by workers on health care. Thus Y = 0.8X, because demand falls to 80% of its original level.

   The employer used to pay 0.9X, now it pays 0.8Y. So the employer now pays 0.8(0.8X) = 0.64X. The change from 0.9X to 0.64X represents a 29% decrease in expenditures, because (0.64 – 0.9)(0.9) = –0.29.

CHAPTER 3 ANSWERS

1. I = increase; D = decrease; ? = indeterminate

	Price	Quantity
a)	D	D
b)	I	D
c)	D	D
d)	I	I
e)	?	I
f)	D	?
g)	?	D
h)	I	?

2. There is no inconsistency. Refer to Figure Q3-1 and assume a competitive equilibrium price = P^* and equilibrium quantity = Q^*.

A price floor P_F (e.g., minimum wage) occurs above P^*. A surplus of labor occurs because quantity supplied is greater than quantity demanded at the price P_F as shown in Figure Q3-1(a).

A price ceiling P_C (e.g., rent control) occurs below P^*. A shortage of housing occurs because quantity demanded is greater than quantity supplied at P_C as shown in Figure Q3-1(b).

With free exchange, the quantity actually exchanged at a given price, the equilibrium quantity Q_E, is whichever is lower: quantity supplied or quantity demanded.

FIGURE Q3-1 *(a) Price Floor and (b) Price Ceiling*

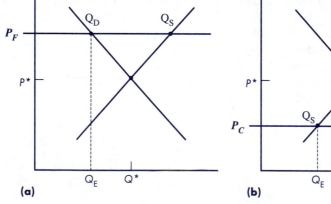

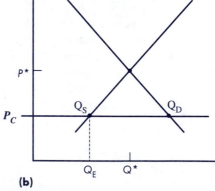

(a) (b)

3. a) The ordinance would place a limit on the supply of apartments and retail outlets. If demand for these structures exceeds current supply, then limiting the supply could increase the price of those already existing.

b) It depends. If the area were not rezoned, the price of single-family houses could either fall or rise. On one hand, the price could fall because of reduced demand. Removing the single-family character of the community could reduce its appeal to potential homeowners. On the other hand, price might increase because of increased demand. Potential single-family home-owners might prefer to live in a mixed community with apartments and retail shops. Demand could also increase because of the ability to convert these homes to other uses. The price could also rise because of reduced supply. By allowing other types of development, existing single-family homes could become more valuable if demand exceeds supply.

4. Because milk has relatively inelastic demand, compared to supply, consumers will probably bear the largest proportion of the tax burden. In addition, the tax is regressive, meaning that it will disproportionately burden low-income consumers, who spend relatively more of their income on milk. There could be induced impacts, such as increased prices on dairy products and school lunches. Other forms of direct assistance to dairy farmers, such as subsidies to reduce and stabilize the costs of production, might be more efficient and equitable.

5. The price to consumers will rise by the full amount of the tax under either of two conditions: (1) demand is perfectly inelastic (vertical demand curve), or (2) supply is perfectly elastic (horizontal supply curve). See Figure Q3-2(a). Producers will bear the full amount of the tax under two conditions: (1) supply is perfectly inelastic (vertical supply curve), or (2) demand is perfectly elastic (horizontal demand curve). See Figure Q3-2(b).

CHAPTER 4 ANSWERS

1. Senator Tobin: income grant
   Senator Eckmann: tied grant
   Senator Kronen: subsidy

2. a) Additional highway capacity could increase demand for auto trips by reducing the apparent price to a consumer of making an automobile trip (because of decreased time costs, decreased annoyances of congestion, etc.). It could also reduce the price of auto trips relative to the price of a mass transit trip, thus shifting trips from mass transit to auto. The new highway could also increase demand for highway trips by encouraging individuals to take trips they wouldn't have taken before. The appeal of additional capacity can induce demand that leads to even worse congestion, because increased capacity can support increased number of cars.

FIGURE Q3-2   *(a) Consumers Bear Full Amount of Tax and (b) Producers Bear Full Amount of Tax*

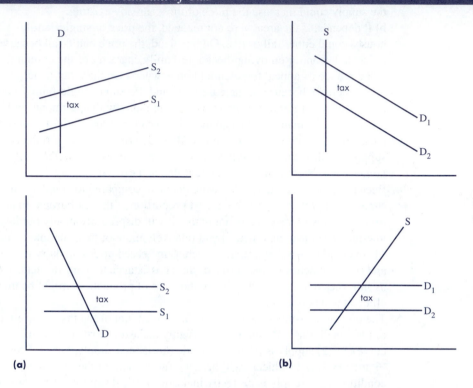

(a)   **(b)**

b) The economist's view of demand relates consumption to price. Consumers will choose to drive the highway as long as they are willing to pay the price, which includes costs of operating the auto, travel time, and congestion. This price, however, does not necessarily cover the full social costs of highways. Thus, consumers may appear to "need" (demand) auto trips more than they would if they were required to pay the full social costs of highways. It is also difficult to assess the true demand for highways when they are offered at virtually no direct cost to individual drivers. Further, as discussed in the previous answer, a new highway can induce "need" for the highway by attracting more automobile trips.

3. The reduction in the price of transportation to the park should increase the gain consumer surplus already reaped by the decrease in admission fees, because transportation to the park and admission to the park are complementary goods. Consider the demand curve in Figure Q4-1, which is based on the total costs of going to the park. Assume the initial cost of attending

FIGURE Q4-1 *Change in Consumer Surplus*

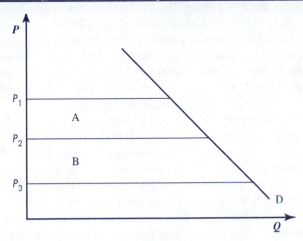

the park is P_1. The drop in admission fees decreased the total cost from P_1 to P_2, and resulted in a gain of consumer surplus of A. Then, the drop in transportation costs reduced the total costs from P_2 to P_3, and resulted in an additional gain in consumer surplus of B.

4. The noncash gift can provide additional value to both the gift giver and the recipient. For instance, the gift giver may enjoy spending time to pick out a special gift, rather than just giving a generic gift of money. The gift recipient may value and appreciate all the time and thought that the gift giver devoted to shopping, selecting, and wrapping a personal gift, rather than just giving money.

5. There are several reasons. Utility cannot be measured directly or in absolute terms. One person's utility cannot be validly compared to another person's utility. Isoutils lack a real-world equivalent. Utility curves cannot be validly combined through algebraic operations to derive an aggregate (social) utility function.

CHAPTER 5 ANSWERS

1. a) At the margin, additional workers cost $7 per hour because no additional federal subsidies are available, and existing workers are currently employed on other jobs. The fact that the new workers may not work on the mayor's project directly is irrelevant; the project has "caused" their hiring. In other words, the newly hired workers would either work on the mayor's project,

or replace existing workers on other projects who would then be transferred to the mayor's project. Thus, if 100 additional labor-hours are needed, the cost of the mayor's project is $700, not $400.

b) If workers must be pulled off other projects, the costs are the opportunity costs of not being able to do those projects. If the commissioner has to do the mayor's project, workers should be pulled off jobs where their marginal productivity is lowest. The opportunity cost of these workers then may be more (or less) than their wage of $7 per hour.

2. The employees' union is likely referring to the average total costs of operating a car. A large number of costs (such as insurance, monthly loan payments, and annual parking fees) are essentially fixed with respect to the number of miles driven. Those fixed costs are part of average total costs. The marginal costs, however, just consider the costs of driving an additional mile, such as the cost of gasoline. Hence, the marginal cost of driving a mile is probably less than the average cost ($0.45). Apparently, given the workers' eagerness to drive their cars, the marginal cost is probably below $0.25 per mile.

3. The fact that he had already paid for the trip and cannot get a refund *is* relevant to the current decision, because it affects the marginal cost of travel. His choice now is (1) stay home, or (2) go skiing and risk back pain. If he had not paid, or could get a refund, his choice would be (1) stay home, or (2) go skiing and risk back pain and pay several hundred dollars for the ski trip. His decision to take the prepaid trip would show "irrational" attention to sunk costs only if he would have refused a free skiing trip in equivalent circumstances.

4. Breakeven point is where MR = ATC

$$MR = ATC = AFC + AVC = TFC/X + TVC/X$$
$$\$200 = \$100,000/X + \$100/1$$

multiply through by X

$200X = \$100,000 + \$100X$
$100X = \$100,000$
$\qquad X = 1,000$ (producing 1,000 copies) is the breakeven point

5. All of these costs, to some extent, include some fixed and some variable costs. For instance, to start up the service, the cafe needed to buy some paper plates, stock the refrigerator with food, and fill up the van with gas, even if they never sold any meals. But in general, the costs can be characterized as follows:

a) Variable; b) Variable; c) Fixed; d) Fixed; e) Fixed, but if employees work overtime delivering meals, then that would also count as variable costs; f) Fixed and variable, because some electricity is needed to keep the cafe open (fixed), and to cook each meal (variable).

CHAPTER 6 ANSWERS

1. One critique is that if societal welfare depends only on the well-being of the worst-off individual, then that overlooks the well-being of other individuals and possible trade-offs among individuals' welfare. Another argument is that even if individuals were not aware of their relative wealth, some might take a risk in order to benefit at the expense of others.

2. While few markets are perfectly competitive, it does not follow that government intervention is always warranted. Government action to eliminate inefficiencies and inequities might improve the prospects for a more competitive and equitable market. Yet government involvement could also contribute to market inefficiencies and inequities.

3. Even though the receiving community is compensated, residents who bear the costs of the landfill (such as increased exposure to hazards and decreased property values) may not receive equivalent benefits (such as improved public services paid for by money given to the community for accepting the LULU). Also, those who bear these costs of the LULU may have little information and little influence in the decision-making process.

4. The requirements are perfectly competitive conditions (many buyers and sellers, homogenous product, no entry or exit barriers), and no market failures (e.g., monopolies, externalities, public goods, imperfect information). To some extent, virtually all markets exhibit characteristics of market failures.

5. Many challenges exist, and here are a few. One is determining the needs of future generations. What will those needs be, and what should we leave them? Some economists argue that monetary wealth is all that we are obligated to leave the future. Yet others point out that all resources are not "fungible" (exchangeable); that is, money is not a perfect substitute for natural resources. Therefore, we also need to ensure a nondeclining stock of natural capital. Another challenge is the temporal scale: How far into the future do we need to look? Then, how do we determine the future impacts of our current decisions, and, in turn, the present value equivalents of future benefits and costs? Economics tends to focus on present consumption, and discounts future benefits and costs. Yet the process of discounting may not be appropriate for goods such as human lives and irreplaceable natural resources. Finally, questions of definition and measurement pose challenges: What is an "equitable distribution," and how do we measure it across generations?

CHAPTER 7 ANSWERS

1. Yes, it is possible. The tax revenue is the tax rate times the quantity sold. (Here, labor is "sold.") A higher tax rate generally reduces quantity sold. Eventually, the increase in the tax rate may not be enough to compensate for the decrease in quantity sold, and thus revenues decline. So lowering the tax rate could then increase tax revenues. In general, as the tax rate increases (from zero on up), tax revenues rise and then decline.

2. Social surplus is consumer surplus plus producer surplus, which becomes consumers' willingness to pay minus producers' costs. (Social surplus also includes revenues or costs to government.) This calculation can overlook, for instance, benefits to individuals who would derive utility from the good but are unable to obtain the good, and benefits that are not adequately represented by markets. In terms of costs, it would exclude social costs that are not represented in producers' supply curves, such as costs resulting from externalities or other market failures. Other types of social costs include those of implementing and administering a government intervention (such as a tax) and a transfer program (such as the distribution of tax revenues).

3. From an efficiency perspective, a tax on milk would have a relatively small deadweight loss because the demand for milk is typically price inelastic. From an equity perspective, the tax is likely regressive, meaning it would disproportionately burden low-income individuals, because they spend a higher proportion of their income on milk products than high-income individuals.

4. Refer to Figure Q7-1.
   a) Changes in Domestic Surplus

	Before Tariff	After Tariff	Change
Consumer surplus	I + II + III + IV + V + VI + VII	I + II + III	–IV – V – VI – VII
Producer surplus	VIII	IV + VIII	IV
Government			VI
Social surplus	I + II + III + IV + V + VI + VII + VIII	I + II + III + IV + VIII	– V – VII

b) Many arguments can be made on both sides; the following are only a few. Tariffs can support and protect domestic industries and reduce reliance on imports. On the other hand, tariffs can lead to decreased domestic consumption and higher domestic prices than in world markets. Although the preceding analysis indicates that domestic producers and the government both gain surplus from tariffs, these gains are offset by losses in consumer surplus.

FIGURE Q7-1 *Effect of a Tariff on Social Surplus*

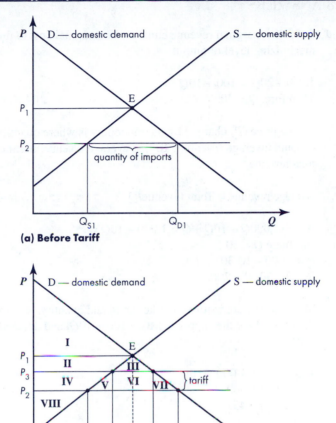

(a) Before Tariff

(b) After Tariff

5. Economic welfare, as measured by social surplus, is in turn based on measures of efficiency. Efficiency is but one aspect of what might be "desirable" in a society. In addition, the accurate measurement of efficiency depends on perfectly competitive markets with no market failures. The policy under analysis may deviate from these ideal conditions.

CHAPTER 8 ANSWERS

1. a) Set the marginal revenue equal to the marginal cost to find the profit-maximizing level of output.

   $1,000 - 20Q = 100 + 10Q$
   Therefore, $Q = 30$.

      The price (P) charged by the monopoly is where quantity intersects with demand (average revenue). To find average revenue, use the formula for total revenue.

   Average revenue = Total revenue/Q

   $AR = (1,000Q - 10Q^2)/Q = 1,000 - 10Q = P$
   substitute $Q = 30$
   $P = 1,000 - 10(30) = 700$
   So, $Q = 30$, $P = 700$.

   b) To find the competitive market price and quantity, let supply equal demand, where the supply is MC = $100 + 10Q$, and demand is AR = $1,000 - 10Q$.

   $100 + 10Q = 1,000 - 10Q$
   $\qquad 20Q = 900$
   $\qquad\quad Q = 45$

   Now AR = $1,000 - 10Q = P$

   $P = 1,000 - 10Q$
   $P = 1,000 - 10(45)$
   $P = 550$

   So, $Q = 45$, $P = 550$. Output is higher and price is lower under competitive conditions.

2. A perfectly competitive firm is a price-taker, and faces a horizontal demand curve. The monopolist is a price-maker, and faces a downward-sloping demand curve. In other words, the perfectly competitive firm is not able to influence price. The monopolist, however, can determine the price.

3. Regulation seeks to ensure a fair price and appropriate level of output. A monopolist can set a higher price and lower output than what would occur in a competitive market, resulting in a loss of consumer surplus and excess profits for the monopolist. Historically, these profits have been viewed as

unjust, causing inequalities and inefficiencies. On the other hand, some argue that monopoly regulation can cause greater inefficiencies (losses of social surplus) than without. Also, when economies of scale have created the monopoly, the monopoly could provide the service at a lower cost than a competitive industry. If regulated at the socially efficient price ($P = MC$), the monopoly can suffer losses because $MC < ATC$. If regulated at the fair return price ($P = ATC$), the monopoly can cover costs, but price is still higher and output still lower than socially efficient. Deregulation has sought to promote competition and lower prices, but if regulatory controls are removed before competition is effective, the monopolist can use its market power without restrictions on price.

4. Here are a few of the reasons. Because the monopoly does not face competitive pressure, it may become lax. It may innovate, but at its own pace. On the other hand, free from those competitive pressures, the monopoly may engage in research, development, and experimentation, and thus can be the source of innovations.

5. Not necessarily. Taxing profits would address the monopoly effect of increased price but would not directly address the effect of decreased output. Setting a price equal to average total cost could result in more output, a reduced price, and still allow the monopolist to earn a normal profit.

CHAPTER 9 ANSWERS

1. Because premiums are based on average safety records for all firms in the industry, rather than individual safety records, an individual firm does not bear the full cost of its accidents. Those costs are spread out over all other firms in the rating class, thus creating a negative externality from one firm to others. On the other hand, an individual firm with relatively fewer accidents could create a positive externality for the other firms by reducing the average number of accidents and thus the premiums.

2. The benefits should be distributed to those who bear the costs of the negative externality. In theory, the revenues from the tax could be used to offset some of the damages. Yet in practice, that can be difficult, because some externalized costs, such as CO_2 emissions, affect all individuals in society to some extent. Determining who bears what portion of the costs, now and in the future, can be difficult if not impossible.

3. The plan is inefficient because the marginal costs and marginal benefits of pollution reduction will differ across cars. The same benefits of reduction could be achieved at a lower cost by (a) making greater reductions where marginal costs are low or where marginal benefits are high, and (b) making lesser reductions where marginal costs are high or where marginal benefits are low.

4. In many ways, yes, from both efficiency and equity perspectives. Recall that externalities cause inefficiencies because producers and consumers do not recognize the full social costs of their production and consumption activities. The artificially low price (not incorporating all social costs) of gasoline to consumers leads to an overconsumption of the good. A tax would raise the price to consumers and provide incentives to decrease driving. From an equity perspective, those who impose external costs upon society would bear more of the costs. The tax revenues could help to offset the negative externalities. But the gasoline tax would likely be regressive: It could disproportionately burden poor people more than wealthy people. In addition, a uniform excise tax may not be the most efficient approach because the marginal costs of gasoline consumption (and marginal benefits of pollution reduction) would likely vary across gasoline users.

5. This case contains many examples of externalities, and here are a few. The producers of the toxic materials externalized costs to the university (which bears costs such as lost worker days and reduced productivity due to people's illnesses) and to people in the building (who bear costs such as pain and suffering, medical expenses, and longer term health problems). The university externalized costs of using the toxic materials to people in the building as well as to their families, friends, and coworkers (who bear costs such as financial hardships, lost leisure time, and increased workloads). The producers and users of the toxic materials also externalized costs to health insurers (which cover a percentage of the costs of medical care for the illnesses), and to the university and its health plan members (who may face higher insurance premiums because of the costs of the illnesses).

CHAPTER 10 ANSWERS

1. The free market would be unlikely to provide a pure public good because a producer could not collect payment for each use of the good, nor exclude people from receiving full benefits of the good. With a governmental solution, it is difficult to get people to pay for a good when they can receive the good without paying (the free rider problem). In addition, it is difficult to determine the appropriate level of production, which requires assessing the total social benefits from providing that good.

2. Any individual family would have little incentive to pay for the plant because it could receive treated water regardless of payment. To be profitable, the firm would have to be able to extract payment from all those who received treated water.

3. Conceptually, a market demand curve for a private good indicates the total quantity demanded at each price. An aggregate demand curve for a public

good indicates the total benefits, or social willingness to pay, at each quantity provided. Graphically, the market demand curve for a private good is found by summing all individual demand curves horizontally. For a public good, the aggregate demand curve is found by summing all individual demand curves vertically.

4. The preservation of natural areas provides a benefit to many people who do not actually visit the park. In this sense, the park is nonrival and nonexclusive, even if an entrance fee were charged. (Friedman recognizes this argument, but argues that the benefits to people who are not actually visiting the park are trivial.) One could also argue that national parks should be provided to the entire public to enjoy and that no attempt should be made to exclude.

5. Possible considerations include the following: Is exclusion possible? If so, is it relatively easy and inexpensive to collect the fee? Is the fee efficient? At the efficient level, what portion of costs would the fee cover? Is it equitable? Who might not be able to afford the service if the fee were imposed?

CHAPTER 11 ANSWERS

1. a) Moral hazard; b) Moral hazard; c) Principal-agent problem; d) Adverse selection; e) Principal-agent problem (and moral hazard); f) Adverse selection

2. Fire is an event that homeowners may want to avoid, regardless of potential compensation. The loss of belongings (such as family photos and irreplaceable heirlooms), the inconvenience of having to move, the risks to health, among other factors, are incentives to avoid the insured-against event. Similarly, with life insurance, people still have incentives not to take their own lives. (Nonetheless, arson is considered an example of the moral hazard problem of fire insurance, and murder an example of the moral hazard problem of life insurance.)

3. a) The average health care cost for treating X is

$$0.01(\$10,000) + 0.99(\$0) = \$100$$

Under the government scheme, each person must contribute this average cost to cover the total cost of treating X. Therefore, each person contributes $100 (the average cost per person, spread among the population, assumed to include transaction costs, etc.).

b) Under the privatization scheme, participation becomes optional. Only citizens who suffer from X will probably contribute to the pool for receiving treatment for X. If only citizens with X contributed, then each would need to pay $10,000 for the pool to break even (or more than $10,000, to include a normal profit for the private insurer). But each pays only $100, which was the historic level. Thus, each participant generates $9,900 in excess costs for the private insurer. Each participant would need to pay $10,000 or more for the insurance plan to break even; consequently, participants may choose to pay out of pocket.

Thus, this example illustrates an aspect of adverse selection. Because an insurance pool must charge the average cost to break even, participants with lower costs may leave the pool. (Some lower-cost participants may still remain, in order to insure against the risk of getting X.) When the lower-cost participants leave, then costs for everyone remaining rise, and so forth, until participants with the greatest costs are those who remain in the pool.

4. A student may worry about a low salary after graduation, and an inability to repay a college loan. Thus, the student may decide not to attend college, or once in college, to pursue majors for higher-income careers rather than, for instance, lower-paying but publicly oriented careers. Under the income-contingent option, the loan program functions as insurance against low wages and inability to repay the loan. Assuming that students are risk averse, this insurance may encourage more students to attend college, and to pursue majors that can generate benefits in a broader sense.

For adverse selection: If students expect their income will be high, they may not enroll in the plan. If students expect their income will be low, they may likely enroll in the plan, which would raise the cost of the plan by including a higher percentage of low-earning graduates. For moral hazard: Once students sign up for this plan, they may be less concerned with academic performance, getting good grades, and obtaining a well-paying job after graduation, because they have insurance against a low-paying job.

5. The expected value of risk reduction policies:

Policy 1: $(1/100,000)(1,000,000)(\$500,000) - [(0.50)(\$6,000,000) + (0.50)(\$4,000,000)] = \$5$ million $- \$5$ million $= \$0$

Policy 2: $(0.50)(1/100,000)(1,000,000)(\$5000,000) - [(0.50)(\$3,000,000) + (0.50)(\$2,000,000)] = \$2.5$ million $- \$2.5$ million $= \$0$

Policy 3: $0

According to this analysis, each of the policies has an expected value of zero. But does that expected value mean a policy to regulate X should not be implemented? Not necessarily. It is important to look at the assumptions and limitations, and how additional information could change the expected values.

For instance, cancer is the only health risk considered here, and pollutants can cause a range of other mortality and morbidity risks. The value of life is arbitrarily set at $500,000, and many argue that such a value cannot be placed and indeed would be too low. The risk imposed is largely involuntary rather than voluntary. The direct comparison of administrative costs and human health costs may not be appropriate. The assessment does not address equity issues, such as who suffers and who benefits. Further, the agency should also consider the value of taking precautionary action when faced with uncertain but potentially harmful outcomes.

CHAPTER 12 ANSWERS

1. $A = \$10,000 \ [A/P, 60, 1\%] = \$10,000 \ [0.0222] = \$222$
2. a) $i = (1 + 0.08/365)^{365} - 1 = 0.08328$, or 8.328%
   b) $i = (1 + 0.04/182.5)^{182.5} - 1 = 0.04081$, or 4.081%
3. $F = 600[F/P, 5\%, 10] + 300[F/P, 5\%, 8] + 400[F/P, 5\%, 5]$
   $= 600[1.6289] + 300[1.4775] + 400[1.2763]$
   $= \$1,931.11$
4. $P = \$100[P/A, 10\%, 5] = \$100[3.7908] = \$379.08$
   $P = \$50[P/A, 10\%, 10] = \$50[6.1446] = \$307.23$
   $P = \$100 \ [P/A, 1\%, 5] = \$100[4.8534] = \$485.34$
   $P = \$50 \ [P/A, 1\%, 10] = \$50[9.4713] = \$473.56$

   At higher discount rates, the present value of the cash flow stream is lower because higher discount rates make future benefits less valuable in the present. At both higher and lower discount rates, the present value of $100 for 5 years is greater than the present value of $50 for 10 years; although the two sums are closest at the lower discount rate. At lower discount rates, the time value of money is less influential.

5. The discount rate implies taking future amounts of money and discounting them into an earlier time period. The interest rate implies taking a sum of money and letting interest accrue into a future time period.

CHAPTER 13 ANSWERS

1. From the state's perspective, the new jobs could be considered as transfers from one part of the state to another part, and should not be included in the CBA if no new resources were created or lost. Even if workers received higher (or lower) wages than in their previous jobs, these wage differentials would still be counted as transfer payments from the state to the workers (or from the workers to the state). Yet workers who were more valuable and productive at the new site than at the previous site would create new benefits for the state that should be included in the CBA. Workers who were less valuable and productive at the new site would create new costs that should also be included.
2. a) The community will build the pool and finance its costs. Charging admission fees would mean that a larger portion of the cost burden for the

pool would be on pool users instead of on the community. Those fees would represent a transfer payment from pool users to the rest of the community.

b) An efficient use of the proposed facility would set the price of admission equal to the marginal cost of admitting each additional pool user. In this case, the marginal cost is nearly equal to zero, because additional swimmers would not significantly increase the operating cost and would not significantly limit the benefits of the facility for others. To let residents swim free of charge would then be the more efficient pricing option.

c) Only the estimated consumer surplus of the pool users should be included as benefits generated by the pool. An increase in property values would not represent new resources if the value increased solely because of proximity to the pool. Those property values would only indicate the benefits that nearby residents would derive from being able to use the pool conveniently. New benefits would be generated if an aspect of the pool facility (other than pool use), such as a large grass lawn around the facility, increased the value of homes in the neighborhood. Also, new costs would be generated if the pool resulted in additional traffic and noise, and thus decreased the property values for nearby residents.

3. The projects would be best under the following changes in the discount rate:

Project I: Best at high discount rates (here, more than 8%)
Project II: Best at low discount rates (here, less than 8%)

4. The information in the problem describes the following demand curve in Figure Q13-1.

FIGURE Q13-1   *Demand for Parking Spaces*

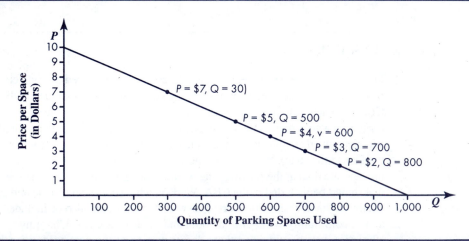

a) At a price of $4, all 600 spaces will be used. The total (gross) benefits to users equal the total willingness to pay shown by the area under the demand curve up to 600 spaces.

$$[(1/2)(6)(600)] + [(4)(600)] = \$4,200$$

b) The users' willingness to pay is $4,200; they actually pay $4 per space:
$4 \times 600 = \$2,400$

Their net benefits are total benefits minus total costs:
$4,200 - \$2,400 = \$1,800$

c) The net benefits to the city are revenues from the parking garage minus the costs of the parking garage, plus net benefits to the users, assuming they are city residents or otherwise considered in the CBA.

Net benefits to city = (parking garage revenues to city − parking garage costs to city) + net user benefits
$$= (2,400 - 1,800) + \$1,800 = \$2,400$$

Note, however, that this definition of benefits and costs is narrow and focuses on monetary equivalents. It also excludes benefits and costs to other members of society that may be affected by the garage.

d) Consumer surplus is the net benefits to users, or the area between the demand curve and the price. It provides the same answer as in part (b): $1,800.

e) In terms of scale, 600 spaces is not the efficient size. If additional spaces cost $3 per day, then the city should build a 700-space garage and charge $3, or $P = MC$. If additional spaces cost less than $3, the city should build until $P = MC$.

f) No, they do not. They exclude nonmonetary costs, such as the disruption to neighborhood residents and the incentive for garage users to drive their car instead of walk or take public transit. Further, the entire facility could be considered as a transfer if no new benefits or costs were created and if all those who gained benefits or bore costs were within the scope of the "public" as defined for this project.

5. Cost-benefit analysis makes implicit equity judgments about who benefits and who bears the costs. It also presumes that the existing distribution of wealth is appropriate, and that a potential Pareto improvement would constitute an actual Pareto improvement. Further, even if aggregate benefits were to exceed aggregate costs for the community as a whole, net societal utility could still decrease. Thus, for CBA, the distributional effects of proposed decisions need to be considered. The following steps could be taken in order to consider equity in a cost-benefit analysis:

Step 1: Identify which group receives each benefit and which group incurs each cost.

Step 2: Quantify, as far as possible, the program's impact on each group.

Step 3: Determine the distribution of costs and benefits, and how it might affect the program's desirability.

GLOSSARY

A

adverse selection When lower quality products are self-selected or attracted to a market, driving out higher quality products. (Chapter 11)

annual percentage rate (APR) The nominal annual interest rate, which includes the effects of compounding. (Chapter 12)

annuity A series of equal payments occurring at equal periods of time. (Chapter 12)

average fixed cost (AFC) Total fixed cost divided by the level of output. (Chapter 5)

average total cost (ATC) The sum of average fixed cost and average variable cost. (Chapter 5)

average variable cost (AVC) Total variable cost divided by the level of output. (Chapter 5)

B

benefit-cost ratio The sum of all benefits divided by the sum of all costs, where benefits and costs are in present value terms. (Chapter 13)

breakeven point The economic point at which marginal revenue (price) equals average total cost; MR = ATC. (Chapter 5)

C

capital Category of economic resources that includes non-human resources, such as buildings, machines, and inventory, used to produce and deliver other goods and services. (Chapter 1)

certainty equivalent An amount, for certain, that would make a decision maker indifferent between an uncertain outcome and that certain amount. (Chapter 11)

change in demand A shift in the entire demand curve that occurs when some factor other than price changes. (Chapter 2)

change in quantity demanded A movement along the demand curve that occurs when the price of that good changes. (Chapter 2)

change in quantity supplied A movement along the supply curve that occurs when the price of that good changes. (Chapter 2)

change in supply A shift in the entire supply curve that occurs when some factor other than price changes. (Chapter 2)

competitive market A market in which no individual producer or consumer can significantly influence the price of a good. (Chapter 3)

complements Two goods that go together; the consumer who purchases one will need to purchase the other. (Chapter 2)

compounded The reinvestment of the interest paid. (Chapter 12)

constant returns to scale Long-run average total costs that remain constant, regardless of level of output. (Chapter 5)

consumer surplus The difference between the amount a consumer is willing to pay and the price the consumer actually paid; the total value to the consumer minus the total cost to the consumer. (Chapter 4)

consumption The process of using or deriving benefits from an economic good or service. (Chapter 1)

cost-benefit analysis (CBA) A method for categorizing, quantifying, and comparing the costs and benefits of one or more alternatives, and for determining whether benefits outweigh costs. (Chapter 13)

cross-price elasticity of demand A measure of how a change in the price of one good affects the quantity demanded of another good; the percentage of change in the quantity of demanded good *a* divided by the percentage change in the price of good *b*. (Chapter 2)

D

deadweight loss The reduction in social surplus resulting from deviations in efficiency. Also known as welfare cost. (Chapter 7)

decision analysis A framework for making choices with uncertain outcomes, where outcomes are represented by their values and their probabilities of occurrence. (Chapter 11)

demand The quantity of a good that consumers would buy at each price, for a particular period of time, all other factors held constant; the consumers' side of a market. (Chapter 2)

demand curve The relationship between the price of the good and the quantity demanded of that good during a specific time period. (Chapter 2)

diminishing marginal returns A principle stating that increasing increments of one input will result in decreasing increments of output, even though total output can increase. (Chapter 2)

diminishing marginal utility A principle stating that additional satisfaction derived from each additional unit of a good consumed will decrease. (Chapter 2)

discount rate The rate at which future benefits or costs are discounted back over time. (Chapter 12)

discounting The process of taking future amounts and converting them into present amounts, where "present" is an earlier time of reference (Chapter 12)

diseconomies of scale The increase in long-run average total costs as output increases. (Chapter 5)

E

economic regulation Government rules, laws, or incentives to control the price or production of goods. (Chapter 8)

economics The study of how society allocates its scarce resources to produce and distribute goods to satisfy society's material wants. (Chapter 1)

economies of scale The decrease in long-run average total costs as output increases. (Chapter 5)

effective interest rate The actual interest rate, including the effects of compounding. (Chapter 12)

efficiency The absence of waste in which an economy's resources are used to produce goods and services that provide the greatest benefit at the least cost. (Chapters 1, 6)

elasticity The measure of the responsiveness of one variable to changes in another variable. (Chapter 2)

equilibrium A balance between quantity supplied and quantity demanded. (Chapter 3)

equilibrium point The intersection of supply and demand that represents the equilibrium price and equilibrium quantity; known as the point at which the market clears. (Chapter 3)

equilibrium price The price that equates quantity supplied by producers and quantity demanded by consumers. (Chapter 3)

equilibrium quantity The quantity both supplied and demanded at the equilibrium price. (Chapter 3)

equity A distribution of benefits and costs among individuals or groups based on some concept of fairness, equality, or need, among others. (Chapters 1, 6)

expected utility (EU) The probability-weighted average of all outcomes in terms of utility. (Chapter 11)

expected value (EV) The probability-weighted average of all outcomes. (Chapter 11)

expected value of imperfect information The increase in expected value that would occur from being able to obtain information with some degree of accuracy. (Chapter 11)

expected value of perfect information The increase in expected value that would occur from being able to obtain perfectly accurate information. (Chapter 11)

externality A market failure that occurs when the actions of a producer or consumer causes additional costs or benefits for others, without providing to or receiving compensation from those others; when private costs or benefits do not equal social costs or benefits. (Chapter 9)

F

firm A basic unit of production (and consumption)—corporation, partnership, or sole proprietorship—that converts inputs into outputs (goods and services). (Chapter 1)

fixed cost Cost that does not vary with the level of output. (Chapter 5)

future value Value of an amount in the future, considering time the value of money. (Chapter 12)

G

government intervention Government actions in an economy to affect price, quantity, methods of production, resource distribution, and other aspects of efficiency, equity, and societal welfare. (Chapter 6)

H

household A basic unit of consumption (and production), consisting of one or more individuals. (Chapter 1)

I

imperfect information A lack of all the information needed for a market participant to make an efficient decision, which can lead to market failures. (Chapter 11)

incidence The ultimate economic effect of a tax or subsidy on a producer or consumer. (Chapter 3)

income effect The change in quantity demanded of a good due to the change in a consumer's overall purchasing power as the price of a good changes, with relative prices held constant. (Chapter 2)

income elasticity of demand A measure of the responsiveness of quantity demanded to changes in income; the percentage change in quantity demanded of a given commodity divided by the percentage change in consumer income. (Chapter 2)

independent goods Goods for which a price change in one has no direct effect on the quantity demanded of the other. (Chapter 2)

indifference curve The graphical representation of different combinations of two goods that would provide equal utility to a consumer. (Chapter 4)

inferior good A good with a negative income elasticity of demand. (Chapter 2)

interest The amount of money paid for the use of borrowed money. (Chapter 12)

interest rate The interest expressed as a percentage of the amount borrowed or invested. (Chapter 12)

internal rate of return (IRR) method The rate that sets the net present value of cash flows equal to zero. (Chapter 13)

isoquant A curve of constant quantity showing all possible combinations of inputs that produce a certain output. (Chapter 5A)

K

Kaldor-Hicks efficiency A resource allocation that makes some better off and some worse off, but results in positive net benefits such that the gainers could, in theory, fully compensate the losers. (Chapters 1, 6)

L

labor Category of economic resources that refers broadly to all the physical and mental talents of people used to produce goods and services. (Chapter 1)

land Category of economic resources that consists of natural resources such as forests, mineral deposits, water, and air. (Chapter 1)

law of demand The inverse relationship between price and quantity demanded: when the price of a good increases, the quantity demanded typically decreases, and vice versa. (Chapter 2)

law of supply The direct relationship between price and quantity: when the price of a good increases, the quantity supplied typically increases, and vice versa. (Chapter 2)

long run Period of time during which a producer can fully adjust all factors; all costs become variable costs. (Chapter 5)

M

macroeconomics The study of the behavior of the economic system as a whole, using aggregate measures such as interest rates and unemployment. (Chapter 1)

marginal cost (MC) The change in total cost for one more or one less unit of output. (Chapter 5)

marginal product The change in the level of output that results from a one-unit change in one factor of production, holding all other factors or inputs constant. (Chapter 5A)

marginal rate of substitution The amount of one good that would be given up to obtain one additional unit of another good while maintaining the same level of utility. (Chapter 4)

marginal rate of technical substitution (MRTS) The rate at which one input can be substituted for another input while maintaining a constant output. (Chapter 5A)

marginal utility of income The utility of an additional unit of income to a given individual. (Chapter 4)

marginal utility The additional amount of utility that an individual derives from consuming an additional unit of a good, holding the consumption levels of all other goods constant. (Chapter 4)

market An organization or structure that brings together consumers (buyers) and producers (sellers) of particular goods and services. (Chapter 1)

market demand curve The horizontal sum of the individual demand curves for all consumers participating in a market, showing the relationship between price and quantity demanded of a particular good or service. (Chapter 3)

market failure A condition under which a market economy may not achieve an efficient allocation of resources. (Chapters 1, 6)

market supply curve The horizontal sum of the individual supply curves for all producers participating in a market, showing the relationship between price and quantity supplied of a particular good or service. (Chapter 3)

microeconomics The study of the behavior of individual economic units, such as households, business, organizations, and governments. (Chapter 1)

monopoly A market with a single producer. (Chapter 8)

moral hazard When an insured individual has a reduced incentive to avoid the insured-against event, and thus can influence the probability and magnitude of payment. (Chapter 11)

N

natural monopoly A monopoly that arises naturally because of economies of scale; a single producer can supply the entire market at lower total average cost than more than one producer. (Chapter 8)

negative externality Actions of producers or consumers that imposes costs on others without providing compensation to those others. (Chapter 9)

net benefits Total benefits minus total costs. (Chapter 4)

net present value (NPV) The sum of all benefits minus the sum of all costs, where benefits and costs are in present value terms. (Chapter 12)

nominal interest rate The stated interest rate, excluding the effects of compounding. (Chapter 12)

nonexclusive One cannot be excluded from deriving the benefits of the good; a characteristic of a public good. (Chapter 10)

nonrival One's consumption of a good does not reduce its benefits to others; a characteristic of a public good. (Chapter 10)

normal good A good with a positive income elasticity of demand. (Chapter 2)

normative statements Value judgments or opinions about "what should be." (Chapter 1)

O

opportunity cost The highest value of the resource in an alternative use. (Chapter 5)

output quota A restriction on the quantity supplied of a good. (Chapter 3)

P

Pareto efficiency A resource allocation in which no one could be made better off without making someone else worse off. (Chapters 1, 6)

payback period The amount of time it takes for a project to recover its costs, where benefits and costs are not discounted. (Chapter 13)

perfectly competitive market A competitive market in which three conditions hold: many consumers and producers, homogeneous or indistinguishable products, easy entrance into and exit from the market. (Chapter 3)

positive externality Actions of producers or consumers that creates benefits for others without receiving compensation from those others. (Chapter 9)

positive statements Facts or objective analyses about "what is." (Chapter 1)

present value Value today (or a time designated as the present) of an amount in the future. (Chapter 12)

price The amount of one thing that is exchanged for another; the amount of money needed to purchase a good or service. (Chapter 2)

price ceiling An established maximum price for a good. (Chapter 3)

price elasticity of demand A measure of the responsiveness of quantity demanded to changes in price of a good; the percentage change in the quantity demanded of a good relative to the percentage change in price of that good. (Chapter 2)

price elasticity of supply A measure of the responsiveness of quantity supplied to changes in price of a good; the percentage change in the quantity supplied of a good divided by the percentage change in the price of the good. (Chapter 2)

price floor An established minimum price for a good. (Chapter 3)

principal The actual amount of money borrowed or invested. (Chapter 12)

principal-agent problem Differing incentives between a principal (one who employs an agent) and the agent who is employed to achieve objectives for the principal. (Chapter 11)

private sector The part of the economy that includes private consumers and producers, such as firms. (Chapter 1)

producer surplus The net gain to producers in a given market that results when the price that producers receive is greater than the minimum needed to supply a certain quantity of a good. (Chapter 5)

production The process of creating or making available an economic good or service. (Chapter 1)

production function A relationship showing the maximum output that can be attained from given inputs to production. (Chapter 5A)

profits Total revenues minus total costs. (Chapters 1, 5)

public Constituents within a defined scope, including individuals, households, public agencies, and private firms. (Chapter 1)

public goods Goods that are nonrival and nonexclusive; thus, they are often provided by the public sector. (Chapters 1, 6, 10)

public provision When the public sector provides a good or service. (Chapter 6)

public sector The part of the economy that includes governmental bodies, public authorities, and not-for-profit organizations. (Chapter 1)

Q

quantity demanded The quantity that consumers would demand at a particular price. (Chapter 2)

quantity supplied The quantity that producers would supply at a particular price. (Chapter 2)

R

rational A characteristic of consumers that assumes they will use their money to buy the collection of goods and services that will lead them to the highest possible level of utility. (Chapter 4)

risk averse Preferring a certain outcome to a risky outcome if both have the same expected value. (Chapter 11)

risk neutral Being indifferent between a certain outcome and a risky outcome if both have the same expected value. (Chapter 11)

risk premium The maximum amount that a risk-averse person would pay to avoid a risk and get an amount for certain; the difference between the expected value of an uncertain outcome and its certainty equivalent. (Chapter 11)

risk prone Preferring a risky outcome to a certain outcome if both have the same expected value. (Chapter 11)

S

short run Period of time during which a producer cannot fully adjust all factors. (Chapter 5)

shortage Occurs when the quantity supplied by producers is less than the quantity demanded by consumers. (Chapter 3)

shutdown point The economic point at which marginal revenue (price) is less than or equal to average variable cost; $MR \leq AVC$. (Chapter 5)

social regulation Government rules, laws, or other actions to promote public health, safety, and societal welfare. (Chapter 8)

social surplus The sum of consumer surplus (willingness to pay minus amount paid), producer surplus (payments received minus costs), and third-party surplus (revenues and costs to government). (Chapter 7)

subsidy A payment by the government for the production or consumption of a good or service. (Chapter 3)

substitutes Two goods that can be used in place of each other; the consumer is relatively indifferent between the two. (Chapter 2)

substitution effect The change in quantity demanded of a good due to a price change that affects quantity demanded for substitute goods, with utility held constant. (Chapter 2)

sunk cost Previously incurred cost that cannot be recovered. (Chapter 5)

supply The quantity of a good that producers would sell at each price, for a particular period of time, all other factors held constant; the producers' side of a market. (Chapter 2)

supply curve The relationship between the price of the good and the quantity supplied of that good during a specific period of time. (Chapter 2)

surplus Occurs when the quantity supplied by producers is greater than the quantity demanded by consumers. (Chapter 3)

T

tax A payment to the government on the production or consumption of a good or service. (Chapter 3)

total cost (TC) The sum of total fixed cost and total variable cost. (Chapter 5)

total fixed cost (TFC) The sum of all fixed costs. (Chapter 5)

total revenue (TR) The price of the good (P) multiplied by the quantity sold of the good (Q), or the total sales. (Chapter 2)

total utility The total amount of satisfaction derived from the consumption of goods or services. (Chapter 4)

total variable cost (TVC) The sum of all variable costs. (Chapter 5)

transfer When resources are neither created nor lost, but merely shifted from one entity to another within the defined scope of the decision. (Chapter 13)

U

uniform gradient A cash flow series that either increases or decreases by the same amount each period. (Chapter 12)

utility The satisfaction or pleasure derived from consumption. (Chapter 4)

V

value of information The difference between the expected value of a choice with information and the expected value of that choice without that information. (Chapter 11)

variable cost Cost that does vary with the level of output. (Chapter 5)

W

welfare cost The reduction in social surplus resulting from deviations in efficiency. Also known as deadweight loss. (Chapter 7)

welfare economics The study of how decisions affect the allocation of resources, and thus the well-being among members of society. (Chapter 7)

willingness to pay (WTP) The monetary amount a consumer is willing and able to pay for a certain quantity of a good or service. (Chapter 4)

INDEX

A

Accounting profit, 115–116
Adverse selection, 255–257
    overview, 14
AFC (average fixed costs), 108
Aggregate demand curves, 225–227
Agricultural subsidies as price floor,
    69–70
Air pollution control
    cost-benefit applications and,
    367–370
Akerlof, George, 263–264
Alternatives, 285–286. *See also*
    Cost-benefit analysis
Annual percentage rate, 301
Annual value, 336
Annuities, 304–305
    compound interest tables for,
    373–393
    factors, 306–309
    net present value method and,
    336
Answers to review questions,
    395–413
Antitrust policies, 184–185
    Federal Trade Commission and,
    184
APR (annual percentage rate), 301
Asymmetric information, 251–254
    market responses, 254–255
    nonmarket responses, 254–255
ATC (average total costs), 108
Automobile insurance and risk,
    283–285

AVC (average variable costs), 108
Average cost pricing, 239–240
Average fixed costs, 108
Average total costs, 108
Average variable costs, 108
Averting behavior, 205–206

B

B/C ratio (benefit-cost ratio),
    336–337
Barriers to entry, 173–175
Bayes' Theorem, 291–292
Benefit-cost analysis. *See* Cost-
    benefit analysis
Benefit-cost ratio, 336–337
Bentham, Jeremy, 75–76
Breakeven point, 114–115
Budget constraints, 87–89
    budget lines, 87–88
    point of maximum utility, 89

C

California electricity crisis, 70–73
Capital, 6
Cardinal measure, 76
Cardinal utility, 271
Cash flow diagrams, 309–318
    savings and, 311–315
    withdrawals and, 311–315
CBA. *See* Cost-benefit analysis

CE (certainty equivalents), 272–276
CEA (cost-effectiveness analysis),
    322
Ceilings. *See* Price ceilings
Certainty equivalents, 272–276
Chance nodes, 285–286
Change in demand, 21–24
Change in quantity
    demanded, 22–24
    supplied, 26–28
Change in supply, 26
"Cherry picking," 257–258
Children's Health Insurance Program
    imperfect information and, 249
    public provision, 263
Choice and demand, 75–100
Coase Theorem, 142, 198
Cobb-Douglas functions, 132
Collective decision making, 230–232
Community development activities
    and costs, 123–125
Competition
    market equilibrium and, 51–52
    social surplus and, 158–160
Competitive markets
    conditions, 51
    efficiency and, 140
Complements
    defined for goods, 44
Compound interest
    continuously compounded, 301
    defined, 300
    tables, 373–393
Congressional Budget Office dis-
    count rate, 335

Constant returns to scale, 118
Consumer surplus
    distribution of benefits and,
        82–83
    willingness to pay and, 80–82
Consumers, 7–9
Consumption, 7
Contingent valuation, 203–204
Corporations, 8
Cost-benefit analysis, 297–370
    benefits of alternatives, 330–331
    cost-benefit applications,
        349–370. *See also* Cost-
        benefit applications
    cost-effectiveness analysis, 322
    costs of alternatives, 328–330
    developing alternatives, 326
    discounting, influence of,
        332–334
    efficiency and, 324–325
    equity impacts, evaluating,
        342–344
    evaluating costs versus benefits,
        335–342
        annual value, 336
        benefit-cost ratio, 336–337
        comparison of methods, 342
        incremental rate of return
            analysis, 338–339
        internal rate of return,
            337–341
        net present value method,
            335–336
        payback period, 341–342
    intertemporal costs and benefits,
        299–318. *See also* Inter-
        temporal costs and benefits
    Kaldor-Hicks efficiency and, 324
    limitations, 344–345
    Pareto efficiency and, 324
    performing analysis, 325–344
    private versus public decisions,
        321–324
        consideration of transfers,
            323
        monetization of benefits and
            costs, 323–324
        scope of decisions, 322
        types of benefits and costs,
            322–323
    scope of decision, determining,
        326–328
    social discount rate, 334–335
    strengths, 344–345
    transfers, 329–331

Cost-benefit applications, 349–370
    air pollution control and,
        367–370
    bridges and, 349–360
    equity impacts, evaluating, 355
    ex ante analysis, 349–360
    ex post analysis, 367–370
    in medias res analysis, 360–367
    no-action alternative, 358–360
    recreational facilities and,
        360–367
Cost-effectiveness analysis, 322
Cost recovery, 236–237
Costs, 105–135
    community development activi-
        ties and, 123–125
    marginal analysis, 109–114
        private sector production
            decisions, 113–114
        public sector production
            decisions, 113–114
        Meals-on-Wheels programs
            and, 110–113
    nonmonetary costs, 106
    opportunity costs, 106–107
    production costs, 108–109
    production decisions, factors in,
        114–125. *See also* Production
        decisions, factors in
    sunk costs, 107–108
    types of costs, 105–109
"Cream skimming," 257–258
Cross-price elasticity of demand,
    43–44
CV (contingent valuation), 203–204

D

Deadweight loss, 160
Decision analysis, 285–294
    Bayes' theorem, 291–292
    decision trees, 285–286
    precautionary principle, 293
    valuation of imperfect informa-
        tion, 290–291
    valuation of perfect information,
        290–291
    water management and, 287–289
Decision nodes, 285–286
Demand, 19–24
    change in demand, 21–24
    change in quantity demanded,
        22–24

choice and, 75–100
cross-price elasticity of demand,
    43–44
curves. *See* Demand curves
defined, 9, 19
diminishing marginal utility,
    20–21
income effect, 20
income elasticity of demand,
    42–43
law of demand, 19–20
market demand, 47–50
    market demand curves, 47–49
monopolies and, 175–178
price, effect of, 19–20
price elasticity of demand,
    29–31. *See also* Price elastic-
    ity of demand
public goods, 224–228
quantity demanded, 19
substitution effect, 20
Demand curves, 19–20
    aggregate demand curves,
        225–227
    derivation, 89–99
    elasticity and, 37
    market demand curves, 47–49,
        225–227
    monopolies, 175–176
    public goods, 224–228
Deregulation, 186–187
Development impact fees, 242–248
Diminishing marginal returns, 24–25
Diminishing marginal utility, 20–21
Discount rate, 303
    choice of, 334–335
    government rate, 334–335
Discounting, 303–304
    cost-benefit analysis, influence
        on, 332–334
    overview, 16
Diseconomies of scale, 118
Distribution of benefits
    consumer surplus and, 82–83
Dynamics. *See* Market dynamics

E

Economic profit, 115–116
Economic regulation, 182
Economic rent, 232
Economics
    defined, 5

ecosystem and, 9–10
public sector economics,
    137–295. *See also* Public sec-
    tor economics
systems of economics, 7–9
welfare economics, 157–172. *See
    also* Welfare economics
Economies of scale, 118
Ecosystem and economics, 9–10
Effective interest rate, 300
Efficiency, 139–143
    competitive markets and, 140
    cost-benefit analysis and,
        324–325
    criteria, 143
    defined, 11, 140
    equity, balancing, 143, 155–156
    government interventions, effect
        of, 142, 148–155
    "invisible hand" doctrine,
        139–140
    Kaldor-Hicks efficiency, 11, 141
        cost-benefit analysis and, 324
    market failures and, 146–148
    monopolies, effect of, 173
    Pareto efficiency, 11, 141
        cost-benefit analysis and,
            324
        welfare economics and,
            157–158
    perfectly competitive markets
        and, 140
    public pricing and, 234–236
    public provision, effect of,
        148–155
    subsidies, effect of, 149
    taxes, effect of, 149
    types of efficiency, 140–142
Elastic goods, 29
Elasticities, 28–44
    cross-price elasticity of demand,
        43–44
    income elasticity of demand,
        42–43
    price elasticity of demand,
        29–31. *See also* Price elastic-
        ity of demand
    price elasticity of supply, 41–42.
        See also Price elasticity of
        supply
    total revenue and, 31–35
Endowments, equity of, 144–145
Equilibrium. *See* Market equilibrium
Equilibrium point, 51
Equilibrium price, 51

Equilibrium quantity, 51
Equity, 143–146
    defined, 15–16
    efficiency, balancing, 143,
        155–156
    endowments, equity of, 144–145
    government interventions, effect
        of, 148–155
    health insurance and, 153–155
    individual equity, 262
    monopolies, effect of, 173
    outcomes, equity of, 145–146
    process, equity of, 145
    public pricing and, 237–238
    public provision, effect of,
        148–155
    subsidies, effect of, 149
    taxes, effect of, 149
    types of equity, 143–144
EU. *See* Expected utility
EV. *See* Expected value
Expected utility, 271–272
Expected value, 266–271
    calculation, 268–269
    lotteries and, 269–271
    probability of outcome, 267
    risk and, 269–271
    value of outcome, 267–268
Externalities, 191–221
    benefits, determining, 202–203
    challenges in resolving, 199–203
        cumulative impacts, 200
        free riders, 199
        inequities, 200
        lack of information, 200–201
        multiple jurisdictions, 200
        multiple parties, 199
        opportunism, 199
        resource protection, 200
        transaction costs, 199
        unclear property rights, 199
    Coase Theorem and, 198
    costs, determining, 202–203
    defined, 13, 147, 191
    as market failures, 147
    methods for nonmarket valuation,
        203–208
        averting behavior, 205–206
        contingent valuation,
            203–204
        hedonic pricing, 205
        travel cost method, 204
    negative externalities, 192–194
        defined, 13, 191
    optimal level of production,

determining, 201–202
    positive externalities, 194–195
        defined, 13, 191
    strategies for dealing with,
        209–220
        directives, 212–213
        marketable permits, 218–
            220
        prohibitions, 210–211
        regulation, 213–214
        separation, 211–212
        subsidies, 216–218
        taxes, 214–216
        voluntarism, 210

F

Factors, compound interest, 306–
    309
    present worth factors, 308
Failures. *See* Market failures
Firms, 7–8
Fixed costs, 108
Floors. *See* Price floors
Foundations of economics, 5–9
Free riders, 199, 261
    public goods and, 230
Friedman, Milton, 248
Future values, 302–303
    compound interest tables for,
        373–393
    factors, 306–309

G

GDP. *See* Gross domestic product
General equilibrium analysis, 58–
    59
Goods
    complementary goods, 44
    durability of, 36
    elastic goods, 29
    independent goods, 44
    inelastic goods, 29
    inferior goods, 43
    normal goods, 43
    public goods, 221–248. *See also*
        Public goods
    substitute goods, 44
    unitary elastic goods, 29
Government bonds and discount
    rates, 334

Government interventions, 148–155
Government services. *See* Public services
Gradients. *See* Uniform gradients
Grants
  Community Development Block Grant Program, 94
    costs and, 123–125
  housing grants, 91–93
  income grants, 91
  intergovernmental grants, 91–93
  tied grants, 93
  water supply infrastructure grants, 91–93
Greenways and contingent valuation, 206–208
Gross domestic product (GDP), 5, 7, 10
Growth, relationship to ecosystem, 10

H

Health insurance
  Children's Health Insurance Program, 263
  defined contribution health plans, 261
  equity and, 153–155
  market imperfection and, 153–155
  Medicaid, 150–153
  Medicare, 150–153
  public provision, 262
  subsidies and, 150–153
Hedonic pricing, 205
Households, 7

I

Imperfect information, 249–295
  adverse selection and, 255–257
  asymmetric information, 251–254
  automobile insurance and, 283–285
  Bayes' Theorem and, 291–292
  certainty equivalents and, 272–276
  "cherry picking," 257–258
  Children's Health Insurance Program and, 249

"cream skimming," 257–258
decision analysis, 285–294. *See also* Decision analysis
defined, 14, 147, 251
expected utility and, 271–272
expected value, 266–271. *See also* Expected value
insurance premiums and, 272–276
as market failures, 147, 250–265
Medicare and, 249
moral hazard and, 258–259
Nobel Prize, 263–265
principal-agent problem and, 259–261
public provision and, 262–263
risk, 279–281
risk premiums and, 272–276
Social Security and, 249
utility function of money and, 281–282
variability and risk, 280–281
Incidence of subsidy, 63–65
Incidence of tax, 60–63
Income
  elasticity of demand, 42–43
  expenditures relative to, 35–36
Income effect, 20
  indifference curves and, 85–87
Income expansion paths, 89–90
Income grants, 91
Incremental rate of return analysis, 338–339
Independent goods, 44
Indifference curves, 84–87
  income effect and, 85–87
  substitution effect and, 85–87
Individual equity, 262
Inelastic goods, 29
Inferior goods, 43
Insurance premiums, 272–276
Interest, 300–301
Interest rate, 300
Internal rate of return and cost-benefit analysis, 337–341
Intertemporal costs and benefits, 299–318
  annuities, 304–305
  cash flow diagrams, 309–318
  discounting, 303–304
  future value, 302–303
  interest, 300–301
  present value, 302–303
  time value of money, 300–301
  uniform gradients, 305–306

Intervention. *See* Market intervention
"Invisible hand" doctrine, 139–140, 372
IRR (internal rate of return) and cost-benefit analysis, 337–341
Isoquants, 130
Isoutils, 84

J

Jevons, William Stanley, 76

K

Kaldor-Hicks efficiency, 11, 141, 142
  cost-benefit analysis and, 324

L

Labor, 6
Land, 6
Law of demand, 19–20
Law of supply, 24–25
Long-run average total cost curves, 118–121
Long-run equilibrium, 120–121
Long-run production, 117–120
LRATC (long-run average total cost) curves, 118–121

M

Macroeconomics, 5
Marginal, defined, 20
Marginal analysis, 109–114
  Meals-on-Wheels programs and, 110–113
  private sector production decisions, 113–114
  public sector production decisions, 113–114
Marginal cost pricing, 238–239
Marginal costs, 109
Marginal product, 129
Marginal rate of substitution, 101–104
Marginal rate of technical substitution, 131

Marginal revenue, 114, 117
Marginal utility, 76
    of income, 77
Market demand, 47–50
Market demand curves, 47–49
    public goods, 225–227
Market dynamics, 54–59
    equilibrium point, 54–56
    equilibrium price, 54–56
    equilibrium quantity, 54–56
    general equilibrium analysis,
        58–59
    partial equilibrium analysis, 59
    supply and demand, changes in,
        54–56
Market economics framework, 10–17
    public decisions and, 11–12
    public sector involvement, 12–16
Market equilibrium, 51–54
    competition and, 51–52
    equilibrium point, 51
        social surplus and, 158–160
    equilibrium price, 51
    equilibrium quantity, 51
    shortages, 52–53
    surplus, 53–54
Market failures, 137–295
    defined, 12–13, 146
    efficiency and, 146–148
    externalities, 191–221. See also
        Externalities
    imperfect information, 249–295.
        See also Imperfect informa-
        tion
    monopolies, 173–189. See also
        Monopolies
    public goods, 221–248. See also
        Public goods
    transaction costs and, 147–148
    welfare economics, 157–172. See
        also Welfare economics
Market intervention, 60–73
    agricultural subsidies as, 69–70
    electricity, California crisis, 70–73
    output controls, 66–73. See also
        Output controls
    price controls, 66–73. See also
        Price controls
    rent control as, 68–69
    social surplus and, 160–168
    subsidies, 60–66. See also
        Subsidies
    taxes, 60–66. See also Taxes
Market supply, 47–50
Market supply curves, 48–50

Marketable permits, 218–220
Markets, 8–9
Maximum utility, point of, 89
MC (marginal costs), 109
Meals-on-Wheels and marginal anal-
    ysis, 110–112
Medicaid, 150–153
Medicare
    imperfect information and, 249
    public provision, 262
    subsidies and, 150–153
Menger, Carl, 76
Microeconomics, 1–135
    defined, 5
    demand, 19–24. See also
        Demand
    market dynamics, 54–59.
        See also Market dynamics
    market intervention, 60–73. See
        also Market intervention
    supply, 24–28. See also Supply
    utility, 75–77. See also Utility
Minimum acceptable rate of return,
    339
Minimum wage violations, 279–
    280
Mirrlees, James, 263, 265
Monopolies, 173–189
    antitrust policies, 184–185
    barriers to entry, 173–175
    defined, 13, 146
    demand and, 175–178
    economies of scale, 174
    effect, 180–181
    efficiency, effect on, 173
    equity, effect on, 173
    higher prices, 179–180
    inefficient allocation of
        resources, 180
    as market failures, 146, 173
    natural monopolies, 13, 174
    output determinations and,
        178–179
    price determinations and,
        178–179
    price regulation, 182–183
    professional sports leagues and,
        187–188
    public ownership of, 183–184
    public policy implications,
        185–188
    rate-of-return regulation, 183
    redistribution of resources,
        180–181
    regulation of, 182–183, 185–186

    supply and, 175–178
    welfare cost and, 181
Monopsonies, 181
Moral hazard
    imperfect information and,
        258–259
    overview, 14
MR (marginal revenue), 114, 117

N

Natural monopolies, 13, 174
Negative externalities, 192–194
    defined, 13, 191
Net benefits, 11
Net present value method, 332
    annuities and, 336
    cost-benefit analysis and,
        335–336
No-action alternative, 358–360
Nobel Prize, 263–265
Nominal interest rate, 300
Nonexclusivity, 14, 221
Nonmonetary costs, 106
Nonrivalry, 14, 221
Normal goods, 43
Normative statements, 5
NPV. See Net present value method

O

Office of Management and Budget
    discount rate, 335
Oligopolies, 181
Opportunity costs, 106–107
Optimal level of production,
    201–202
    public goods, determining,
        227–228
Ordinal measure, 76
Ordinal utility, 271
Organically grown produce and mar-
    ket dynamics, 56–59
Outcomes
    defined, 285–286
    equity of, 145–146
Output and monopolies, 178–179
Output controls
    efficiency, effect on, 150
    equity, effect on, 150
    as market intervention, 66–73
Output quotas

overview, 66–67
social surplus and, 163–164
Overview, 3–18

P

Pareto efficiency, 11, 141
cost-benefit analysis and, 324
welfare economics and, 157–158
Pareto improvements, 141, 155–156, 169
Partial equilibrium analysis, 59
Partnerships, 8
Payback period and cost-benefit analysis, 341–342
Peak pricing, 241–242
Perfectly competitive markets
conditions, 51–52
efficiency and, 140
Point of maximum utility, 89
Positive externalities, 194–195
defined, 13, 191
Positive statements, 5
Precautionary principle, 293
Premises, 6–7
Premiums, insurance, 272–276
Present values, 302–303
compound interest tables for, 373–393
factors, 306–309
Present worth factors, 308
Price
demand, effect on, 19–20
future prices, expectations about, 36
monopolies and, 178–179
public facilities, 233
public pricing, 233–248. See also Public pricing
public services, 233
public utilities, 233
Price ceilings
overview, 66
rent control as, 68–69
social surplus and, 162–163
Price controls
ceilings
overview, 66
rent control as, 68–69
social surplus and, 162–163
efficiency, effect on, 149–150
equity, effect on, 149–150

floors
agricultural subsidies as, 69–70
overview, 66
social surplus and, 160–162
as market intervention, 66–73
Price discrimination, 240–241
Price elasticity of demand, 29–31
factors influencing, 35–40
public transit and, 38–39
Price elasticity of supply, 41
factors influencing, 42
Price floors
agricultural subsidies as, 69–70
overview, 66
social surplus and, 160–162
Price regulation, 183
Principal
investment money, 300
in principal-agent relationship, 14
Principal-agent problem
imperfect information and, 259–261
overview, 14
Private benefits, 194
Private costs, 192
Private sector
defined, 8
discount rate, 334
perspectives, 3–4
Probability of outcome and expected value, 267
Process, equity of, 145
Producer surplus
production decisions, factors in, 121–122
profit, distinguished, 122–123
Production. See also Supply
defined, 7
market economics framework, in, 11–12
Production costs, 108–109
Production decisions, factors in, 114–125
accounting profit, 115–116
breakeven point, 114–115
economic profit, 115–116
long-run equilibrium, 120–121
long-run production, 117–120
producer surplus, 121–122
profit, distinguished, 122–123
short-run production, 116–117
shutdown point, 114–115
supply curves, deriving, 117

Production functions, 127–135
Cobb-Douglas functions, 132
constrained maximization or minimization, 135
diminishing marginal productivity, 133–135
factor substitution, 130–131
mathematics, 131–133
Professional sports leagues and monopolies, 187–188
Profit. See also Accounting profit; Economic profit
defined, 179
distinguished from producer surplus, 122–123
as goal of firms, 7
Public, definition of, 4
Public facilities
development impact fees, 242–248
price, 233
Public goods, 221–248
classification, 221–224
collective decision making and, 230–232
defined, 13–14, 221
demand, 224–228
free riders and, 230
as market failures, 147
nonexclusivity, 221–224
nonrivalry, 221–224
optimal level of production, determining, 227–228
public pricing, 233–248. See also Public pricing
public provision, 228–232
rent-seeking behavior and, 232
taxes and, 230
theory, 221–224
valuation, 224–228
Public pricing, 233–248
administrative considerations, 238
average cost pricing, 239–240
cost recovery and, 236–237
development impact fees, 242–248
efficiency and, 234–236
equity and, 237–238
evaluation criteria, 234–238
functions, 234
institutional considerations, 238
marginal cost pricing, 238–239
peak pricing, 241–242
price discrimination, 240–241

revenue generation and, 236–237
two-part tariffs, 240
Public provision, 148–155
    health insurance, 262–263
    imperfect information and,
        262–263
    monopolies and, 183–184
    public goods, 228–232
    Social Security, 262
    unemployment compensation,
        262
Public regulation by federal agen-
    cies, 182, 186
Public sector
    defined, 8
    discount rate, 334
    perspectives, 3–4
Public sector economics, 137–295
    efficiency, 139–143. *See also*
        Efficiency
    equity, 143–146. *See also*
        Equity
    externalities, 191–221. *See also*
        Externalities
    imperfect information, 249–295.
        See also Imperfect information
    monopolies, 173–189. *See also*
        Monopolies
    public goods, 221–248. *See also*
        Public goods
    welfare economics, 157–172. *See
        also* Welfare economics
Public services
    development impact fees,
        242–248
    government provision of, 12
    loss, provided at, 99
    pricing, 233, 234
Public transit
    fare changes and demand curves,
        94–97
    price elasticity of demand and,
        38–39
Public utilities
    pricing, 233
    regulation of, 182

Q

Quantity demanded, 19
Quantity supplied, 24
Quotas
    overview, 66–67
    social surplus and, 163–164

R

Rate-of-return regulation, 183
Rawls, John, 156
Recreational facilities and cost-
    benefit applications, 360–367
Regulation, 213–214
    deregulation, 186–187
    economic regulation, 182
    federal agencies and, 182, 186
    of monopolies, 182–183,
        185–186
        price regulation, 182–183
        rate-of-return regulation, 183
    of public utilities, 182
    social regulation, 186
Rent control as price ceiling, 68–69
Rent-seeking behavior and public
    goods, 232
Revenue generation, 3, 5, 236–237
Revenue-sharing programs, 94
Review question answers, 395–413
Risk
    automobile insurance and,
        283–285
    aversion, 276–280
    defined, 266
    expected value and, 269–271
    minimum wage violations and,
        279–280
    neutrality, 276–280
    proneness, 276–280
    variability and, 280–281
ROR (incremental rate of return)
    analysis, 338–339
RP (risk premiums), 272–276

S

Savings and cash flow diagrams,
    311–315
Short-run average total cost curves,
    118–121
Short-run production, 116–117
Shortages, 52–53
Shutdown point, 114–115, 117
Smith, Adam, 139–140, 372
Social adequacy, 262
Social benefits, 194
Social costs, 192
Social discount rate and cost-benefit
    analysis, 334–335
Social opportunity cost of capital,
    334

Social rate of time preference, 334
Social regulation, 186
Social Security
    imperfect information and, 249
    public provision, 262
Social surplus, 158–168
    competition and, 158–160
    equilibrium point and, 158–160
    market intervention and, 160–168
    output quotas and, 163–164
    price ceilings and, 162–163
    price floors and, 160–162
    subsidies and, 166–167
    taxes and, 164–166
Sole proprietorships, 8
Spence, Michael, 263, 264
SRATC (short-run average total cost)
    curves, 118–121
Standard deviation, 281
Stiglitz, Joseph, 263, 264–265
Subsidies, 216–218
    agricultural subsidies, 69–70
    defined, 60, 92
    efficiency, effect on, 149
    equity, effect on, 149
    health insurance and, 150–153
    housing, 65
    incidence of subsidy, 63–65
    as market intervention, 60–66
    as negative taxes, 63
    social surplus and, 166–167
Substitutes
    defined for goods, 44
Substitution effect, 20
    indifference curves and, 85–87
Sunk costs, 107–108
Supply, 24–28
    change in quantity supplied,
        26–28
    change in supply, 26
    curves. *See* Supply curves
    defined, 9, 24
    diminishing marginal returns,
        24–25
    law of supply, 24–25
    market supply, 47–50
        market supply curves, 48–50
    monopolies and, 175–178
    price elasticity of supply, 41
        ease in changing production,
            42
        factors influencing, 42
        time period, 42
    quantity supplied, 24
Supply curves, 24–26
    deriving, 117

market supply curves, 48–50
monopolies, 175–176
Surplus, 53–54
consumer surplus
distribution of benefits and, 82–83
willingness to pay and, 80–82
producer surplus
production decisions, factors in, 121–122
profit, distinguished, 122–123
total social surplus, 158–168
Systems of economics, 7–9

T

Taxes, 214–216
defined, 60
efficiency, effect on, 149
equity, effect on, 149
incidence of tax, 60–63
as market intervention, 60–66
progressive, 66
proportional, 66
public goods and, 230
regressive, 66
social surplus and, 164–166
TC (total costs), 108
TFC (total fixed costs), 108
Tied grants, 93
Time value of money, 300–301
Total costs, 108
Total fixed costs, 108
Total revenue, 31–35
Total utility, 76
Total variable costs, 108
TR (total revenue), 31–35
Transaction costs, 199
market failures and, 147–148
Transfers, 329–331
defined, 323, 329

Travel cost method, 204
TVC (total variable costs), 108
Two-part tariffs and public pricing, 240

U

Uncertainty, 266
Unemployment compensation, 262
Uniform gradients, 305–306
compound interest tables for, 373–393
factors, 306–309
Uniform series. *See* Annuities
Unitary elastic goods, 29
Utility, 75–77
cardinal utility, 271
defined, 20
diminishing marginal utility, 20–21
expected utility and imperfect information, 271–272
marginal rate of substitution, 101–104
marginal utility, 76
of income, 77
maximization, 103–104
point of maximum utility, 89
total utility, 76
utility function, 101–104
of money, 281–282
von Neumann-Morgenstern utility functions, 271

V

Valuation
expected value, 266–271. *See also* Expected value

imperfect information, 290–291
perfect information, 290–291
public goods, 224–228
Value of information, 276
Value of outcome and expected value, 267–268
Variability and risk, 280–281
Variable costs, 108
Vickrey, William, 263, 265
von Neumann-Morgenstern utility functions, 271

W

Walras, Léon, 76
Water management and decision analysis, 287–289
Welfare, defined, 157
Welfare costs
defined, 160
Welfare economics, 157–172
distributional effects, 168–170
fundamental theorems, 157–158
Pareto efficiency and, 157–158
social surplus, 158–168. *See also* Social surplus
Willingness to pay, 77–83
consumer surplus and, 80–82
contingent valuation and, 203–204
greenways and, 206–208
Withdrawals and cash flow diagrams, 311–315
WTP. *See* Willingness to pay

X

X-inefficiency, 181